Communicating through
letters and reports

*[You learn more by thinking about what you're
doing than by simply thinking or simply doing.]*

Communicating through letters and reports

C. W. WILKINSON
Professor of English and Chairman (emeritus)
Business and Technical Communication Courses
University of Florida

PETER B. CLARKE
President, Arcus Company

DOROTHY COLBY MENNING WILKINSON
Assistant Professor of Business Communication
College of Commerce and Business Administration
University of Alabama

SEVENTH EDITION   1980

RICHARD D. IRWIN, INC.   Homewood, Illinois   60430
IRWIN-DORSEY LIMITED   Georgetown, Ontario   L7G 4B3

ISBN 0-256-02270-4
Library of Congress Catalog Card No. 79–88786

Printed in the United States of America

1 2 3 4 5 6 7 8 9 0 MP 7 6 5 4 3 2 1 0

Preface

Note to teachers and students (in and out of school):

This Seventh Edition of a popular and respected book retains the basic content, spirit, and special teaching and learning aids which met with wide approval in the first six editions. Yet it brings you many improvements beyond those necessary for updating.

As before, the central purpose is to help you improve your business communications. We have retained the original philosophy that the emphasis should be on the effective presentation of messages; so we stress how to use our remarkably flexible language effectively.

Though this edition is considerably changed from the previous one, the changes are evolutionary, not revolutionary. Briefly, we have:

1. Not only interwoven the application of principles to oral communication throughout the book but have added a new Part Four treating the main kinds of business speaking situations.
2. Increased emphasis on some areas (memos, short reports, and job applications) and reduced emphasis (and pages) on some kinds of business communications where specialists or changing techniques are taking over (orders and acknowledgements, sales letters, credit and collection letters, and library research and long reports).
3. Made more frequent use of always appreciated and effective parallel-column presentations.
4. Tightened up the style—removing passives, expletives, sexually biased expressions, and long sentences and paragraphs—to make it more modern, readable, and concise.
5. Provided full illustrations of both complete and short analytical reports.
6. Rearranged and reworded the thorough reports checklist to make it more concise and usable for both students and teachers.
7. Helped both teachers and students through a new *Teacher's Guide* with special emphasis on grading procedures, grading spreads, and the transparency masters provided for class discussion of various kinds of business writing.

v

8. Increased, clarified, and updated brief treatments of relevant legal cautions (especially on libel, product liability, credit, and employment).
9. Brought up to date and extended treatment of the matters of letter preparation, formats, and postal handling for economy and efficiency.
10. Made more use of case series—for better student insight into business operations and for conciseness.

Students and teachers of college courses in communicating through letters, through reports, and through combinations of the two will find the book easily adaptable to varying standards and student abilities. By attention to only the major principles and the easier problems, freshmen and sophomores of average ability can use the book effectively. By attention to all the refinements and the more difficult cases, upperclassmen in our best universities will find it among their most challenging texts.

Note to students

In learning anything as complex as preparing superior letters, reports, and oral presentations, you need instruction in *principles,* then *illustrations,* and finally *practice* in applying the principles. Accordingly, the first four chapters (Part One) present what we consider to be the basic principles applicable to all business letters. If you go no further, you will have a sound fundamental concept of the appearance, language, style, and psychology of tone and persuasiveness for effective business letters and memos.

For more detailed analysis and application, the next eight chapters (Part Two) show you how to handle your letters and short memos functionally according to three basic plans: good-news, disappointing, and persuasive messages. Though the book presents analyses and examples of inquiries, replies, orders and acknowledgments, claims, adjustments, credits, sales, job applications, requests, and collections, the presentation is not in that order nor is the emphasis on such specific types. As you read through the book, you will see the fundamentals applied in the many illustrations.

Four chapters (Part Three) cover all important aspects of writing reports, including their importance, nature, definition and classification, preparation, and appropriate style.

Part Four (new) presents the basic principles of effective oral business communication in the main kinds of situations (reports, interviews, conferences, and dictation).

All of the illustrations are from actual business letters, memos and reports, or based on actual situations. But because even comparatively good business letters that go through the mail may not serve well as textbook illustrations, we have sometimes edited them beyond merely changing the names of companies, products, and individuals. And in some instances, we have written our own illustrations. We are fully aware, however, that the perfect letter never has been and never will be written.

Having studied the principles and seen them illustrated, you can then make the principles stick in your mind (and thus make their application habitual) by putting them to use in working out selected cases from the many given at the ends of chapters. The ample number and variety of cases (many of them in a new, more succinct style) allow selection to fit your interests, abilities, and desired emphasis.

The situations and problems embodied in the cases are drawn from our collective experiences in business and industry, from our reading, and from other sources. We have endeavored to make them as realistic and up-to-date as possible. Indeed, many of them are problems actually faced by real people recently. In a few instances we have the letters these people wrote, and they are included in the *Teacher's Guide*.

Preparing and presenting *perfect* business letters, reports, or oral communications is next to impossible for all of us. Doing even *good* ones does not just come naturally to most. If you are content to do them as many *are* done, instead of as they *should* be, you will gain little or nothing from studying this book. But with a concentrated effort to improve, you can learn to present superior ones.

Please remember, however, that this book is not a dictionary, formula book, or cookbook to be followed blindly. Your aim should be thoughtful consideration of principles for use in creating your own original work rather than slavish imitation of textbook models. You should learn and follow the *principles* illustrated, *not the wording* of the illustrations.

Likewise, the checklists (a special feature of this book) are thought starters rather than thought-stopping rules to be followed blindly. They are summary reminders of points about the particular kind of communication under discussion, not formulas for or straitjackets on it. They do *not* mean that all the points discussed earlier about a kind of message and summarized in a checklist are applicable to every one of that general class. Thoughtful consideration of a point in a checklist will quickly tell you whether the point is applicable to your particular problem, but ignoring the lists will frequently lead to omission of important points; and slavish following of a list will often lead to inappropriate contents. Hence, when used properly, the checklists can help you produce better messages, help teachers to mark student shortcomings quickly, and thus help you to see where you went wrong.

From our own business experience, from the many people in business and industry we have talked and worked with, from thousands of articles in business magazines, from associating with many other teachers on the job, through long and active membership in the American Business Communication Association (including a charter membership, three terms as president, and at least one in amost every job in the association), from widely varied consulting work, and from college students and business people we have taught, we have learned much about business communications and effective ways for teaching people to improve theirs. We have brought together and modified what we have learned through many years of experience. And we have contributed our own ideas.

In studying this book, then, you learn what we think is the best that has been thought and said about communicating in business through the years. By learning its suggestions, you can improve your own effectiveness as a business communicator.

December 1979

C. W. Wilkinson
Peter B. Clarke
Dorothy C. Wilkinson

Contents

PART FOUR.   ORAL BUSINESS COMMUNICATION

APPENDIXES

CHECKLISTS

The cases in this book are disguised and sometimes slightly modified real situations. Mostly they are from among the more difficult communication situations of business. Most names of firms and individuals, however, are fictitious for obvious reasons.

We have tried to give you the basic information needed without complicating details. You are expected to fill in details from your own imagination. But you are not to go contrary to the statements or implications in the cases, and your imaginary details must be reasonably likely.

The writing in the cases is intentionally not good—nor is the order of points the best—because you would learn nothing from copying from us. So beware of copying our sentences and clauses. Put your ideas in your own words.

Why study letter and memo writing?

THE MAIN REASONS you should study letter writing are:

1. You are almost certain to write many business letters and memos during the rest of your life, regardless of the kind of work you do. Letters and memos are the most common forms of written communication for managing business affairs, and everybody has business affairs to manage.
2. Your degree of failure or success in managing many of those affairs will depend on whether you write ordinary letters and memos or really good ones.
3. All too often the untrained, unthinking business writer writes bad letters and memos. Usually the procedure is to follow the bad writing style, the bad tone, the ineffective psychology, and even the messy or old-hat appearance of bad ones that have been received or read in the files.
4. Through systematic study and practice you can learn to write good letters and memos and thus greatly increase your chances of success in handling your personal business or business affairs on a job.

The importance of effective business writing is increasing, too. Continuing rapid changes since the mid-1960s in the technology of word processing are speeding up and making cheaper the processing of information. Word processing machines have incorporated microcomputers to gain text-editing capabilities, and then joined with minicomputers to produce complete word processing/data processing systems that are within reach of even the smallest offices and businesses.

What, then, does the spread of word processing mean to business communication and, more important, to teachers and students of business communication? Contrary to some popular expectation, the business letter and memo are not dead.

Letters will still be the preferred means of communication between organizations for a good many years to come. Their format may change slightly: letters produced by computer printers may become acceptable (though we doubt this), and letters transmitted through the sender's telephone to the receiver's CRT screen (a TV-like screen) will become more popular. But whether a letter or memo is on a computer print-out, an electronic screen, or whatever else comes along, it will still be a letter or memo. The devices of style and interesting, clear, inconspicuous writing will still be important. Positional emphasis will work on a CRT screen as well as on a letterhead; and whether a reader reads from an electronic display or a piece of paper, deadwood phrases and incorrect spelling and grammar can still defeat the purpose of a message.

Perhaps the biggest change effected by the new computerized data/ word processing systems will be an increase in the flow of information. We already have evidence of the trend; and as the amount of information communicated by words increases, the more necessary it becomes that people write clearly, concisely, and correctly. Employers already put a premium on people who can capably communicate in English.

In the next several years, as computerized data/word processing becomes a common part of the American office, we can look forward to an increased emphasis on writing that quickly and effectively communicates the message—exactly what *Communicating Through Letters and Reports* teaches.

The need is already so great that American business is concerned—and acting. A few excerpts from "Why Business Takes Education into Own Hands" (*U.S. News & World Report*, 87:70, July 16, 1979) reveal the problem:

—American business is moving into the field of education with a multibillion-dollar drive to improve the performance of its employees. Courses from basic English and math to sophisticated instruction in . . . human relations. . . .

—Laments a company official in a recent study on education in industry by the Conference Board in New York: "We're doing what the educators ought to be doing. College graduates can't write reports; . . . can't read, spell or write; . . . ."

—Robert Craig of the American Society for Training and Development adds: "Engineers and managers need to be taught how to write and speak and how to hold meetings."

—The Conference Board Study made these findings . . . companies with 500 or more employees: Seventy-five percent . . . offer some in-house courses. . . . Seventy-four percent . . . outside courses. . . .

—General Motors operates its own . . . engineering and business college . . . the curriculum includes social science, the humanities and oral and written com-communication skills.

Other things you learn

In learning to write better letters and memos, you will also learn some principles of practical psychology that will enable you to get along better professionally and socially with other people.

When you improve your ability to write clear, concise, persuasive, and natural English (which *is* the desirable language of business), you gain accuracy and naturalness in phrasing anything else you have to write or speak.

Through your study of letters you will get further insight into the ways of the business world: practices used in getting people to buy; handling orders; gaining and refusing credit; making collections; adjusting claims; and selecting employees.

You will learn how to save time and money on business writing. As a good business writer, you can often write one letter to settle a business transaction that would require two or three from an untrained writer. By using form letters and form paragraphs, you can cut down on costs when the form message will do the job. When, however, you have situations requiring individual letters, you will recognize them and know better than to waste money on forms.

You will also be able to dictate or write the necessary individual letters and memos more rapidly because you will have gained the self-confidence that comes from knowing how to tackle a job. You will write freely and effectively the letters and memos you *have* to write and the many others you *should* write.

Perhaps most important of all, you will realize that every letter and memo you write is an item in your overall public relations—and you will try to make each one win, instead of lose, friends.

Letter volume and costs

According to its latest available annual report, the U.S. Postal Service handled 56 billion pieces of first-class mail and 26.3 billion pieces of third-class (business) mail. Since about 86 percent of first-class mail (or 48.2 billion pieces) also is business, that is a total of 74.5 billion pieces of business mail the Postal Service handled in one year. If we accept the Dartnell Corporation's latest figure of $4.77 as the estimated cost of preparing a business letter (materials, time, equipment), and take 50 cents as the average cost of preparing each direct mail piece, we come up with a total year's expenditure for business letters and direct mail of *$243 billion* (48.2 billion pieces × $4.77 plus 26.3 billion pieces × $0.50). That's BIG business—big enough to justify considerable attention to its efficiency!

Letter advantages

When you consider the advantages of letters, you see why people in business write so many letters and spend so much money on them. Despite the cost of a letter, it is often the most economical way to transact business. You can't go far (not even across town, if you figure your time and traveling expense) or talk much by long distance during business hours or say much in a Telex for the cost of a letter. But for that money you can put your message in a letter and send it anywhere in the country and almost anywhere in the world.

Even if you do talk to another person, you do not have a written record, as you do if you follow the almost universal business practice of making a copy of your letter. Because a letter and its answer can make a written contract, letters often replace personal calls and telephone calls even when the two parties are in the same city.

Telex, Teletype, and facsimile transmission provide written records of communications and have the added advantage of being virtually immediate, though only people with access to the systems can receive messages. But their cost makes them impractical unless a company can make heavy use of them. This fact generally restricts their use to large organizations with numerous locations.

Still another advantage of letters is that both the writer and reader can handle a letter at their most convenient times. Therefore, it can get by receptionists and secretaries many times when a telephone call or a personal call cannot. Moreover, the reader usually gives it full attention without raising partially considered objections and without interruption, a decided psychological advantage.

Emphasis in business

When executives began to realize how much letters cost, how important letters and reports are to the smooth operation of their firms, and how few of their employees were capable writers, many of them started training and correspondence control programs. At General Electric, Westinghouse, Southern Pacific, Marshall Field's, the New York Life Insurance Company, and the big mail-order houses (Montgomery Ward, Spiegel's, and Sears, Roebuck), to mention only a few of the leaders, such programs have demonstrated the economy and efficiency resulting from improved correspondence. Even these firms, however, prefer to hire people who can already write rather than train them on company time.

A frequent question in employment interviews and inquiry letters to professors, therefore, concerns the ability of college graduates to do such writing. An applicant who presents evidence of ability to write good letters, memos, and reports becomes a favored applicant for nearly any job.

Emphasis in schools

Many of the executives who are aware of the importance of good letters and memos are graduates of the few schools that have taught business writing since early in the 1900s. These business leaders are the main reason why today in the majority of respectable colleges and universities literally thousands of students are studying and practicing how to write more effectively for business. Without exception, surveys by such organizations as Delta Sigma Pi, the American Assembly of Collegiate Schools of Business, and the American Business Communication Association have confirmed the high regard of former students for the work.

Business writing instructors frequently hear student comments such as "I learned more English in letter writing than in any other course I ever had!" or "*Everybody* should be required to take a course in letter writing!" or "This course is good preparation for living in general."

Common misconceptions

Yet some people—mostly for lack of information—do not respect even university work in business writing. They sometimes think courses in letter writing are merely about letter forms. Although this is a part of the course, it is only a small part (less than 2 percent of this book).

You may even hear the mistaken idea that students of letter writing learn the trite, wordy, and nearly meaningless expressions so common at the beginnings and endings of letters written by some untrained writers. Actually, you learn to write naturally, concisely, and clearly, to take care of business without beating about the bush, and to end letters when you are through—without wasting first and last sentences saying nothing.

Still others think that in the study of letter writing the emphasis is on high-pressure techniques and tricks and gadgets. Just the opposite is true. In drawing on the findings of psychologists, we are *not* advocating that you attempt to *manipulate* or outsmart your reader in sly, unethical fashion. The intent of the writer toward a reader should always be morally and ethically proper. Our intent is to help you write acceptable things in an acceptable way more likely to convince your reader of the legitimacy and the attractiveness (or soundness) of your proposal or position.

You may hear that letter writing is "just a practical study." It certainly is practical, for the ability to write good business letters is useful. But it is also a cultural study because its primary purposes are the development of (1) your ability to maintain pleasant relations with others and (2) your language effectiveness.

Why the high regard for business writing?

One of the reasons why courses in business writing have found increasing favor with students, executives, and college administrators is that they are blends of the cultural and the practical.

The business correspondent writes to an individual for a definite, practical purpose—and must write with the same exactness as other good writers. The purpose is not, however, entertainment (or self-expression in purple passages and deathless prose). *Action* is usually the goal. Letter and memo writing is partially a study of probable or estimated human *reaction* as a basis for securing the desired *action*. Since the quality of persuasion is more important to the business writer than to most writers, a good knowledge of practical psychology is essential.

The good business writer must learn to do more than just sell goods and services. Successful handling of claim, adjustment, credit, and collection letters requires learning tact, patience, consideration of the other person, a necessarily optimistic attitude, and the value of saying things pleasantly and positively instead of negatively. These are the reasons why you can expect more successful social and business relations with other people after a thorough, conscientious, and repeated analysis and application of the principles of good letter and memo writing.

Furthermore, the good business writer must learn to be concise, interesting, and easy to follow—to hold a reader's attention. For reasons of courtesy a listener will bear with a long-winded, dull, or unclear conversation— maybe even ask for explanations. But the reader of a letter or memo feels no such obligation toward it. The good writer therefore edits carefully to phrase ideas more effectively in writing than in talking.

In conversation one can cushion the effect or shade the meaning with the twinkle of an eye, inflection of the voice, or gesture of a hand and can adjust and adapt the presentation according to the listener's reaction. With far less chance of failure a speaker can get along by "doin' what comes naturally." The letter or memo writer has no such chance to observe the effects of the first part of a presentation and adapt the last part accordingly —and therefore must learn to *foresee* the reader's reaction all the way through. This situation requires more thorough knowledge of practical psychology, more preliminary reader analysis, and more careful planning of messages and phrasing of thoughts than in oral communication.

Such reader analysis, planning, and editing establish good habits of expression—habits which carry over to the spoken message. This fact is the reason we say that you will learn to talk better if you learn to write better. It is also the reason we say that, in learning to write effective letters and memos, you will learn to do a better job of writing anything else you have to write.

Art, science, or skill?

The use of the language—in clear, concise adaptation to one's readers so that they can absorb the message with the least amount of effort and the greatest amount of pleasant reaction—is an art. Several generations of business writers have shown that the proper language for business in general and for letters and memos in particular is just plain good English. Though it is more concise and more precise, it is neither more nor less formal than the conversational language of people for whom letters and memos are intended.

Good business letters and memos are also the result of a conscious use of principles which have evolved since the turn of the century. No one would claim that business writing is an exact and thoroughly developed science, but prominent business writers who have experimented with letters and memos for over 70 years have given us a near-scientific framework of principles as a starting point. Though many of these principles have not been demonstrated with scientific exactness, they have taken a great deal of the speculative out of letter and memo writing. We can therefore approach business writing with considerable knowledge of what good writing principles are and *when, where,* and *how* to apply them.

Writing good business letters and memos, then, is neither exclusively an art nor exclusively a science. Yet it is certainly more than what we frequently call a skill. It involves thinking of a very complex kind: analyzing both a situation and a reader, and then using good judgment in applying knowledge of English, business, and psychology.

Summary

In studying letter and memo writing, you not only learn how to get the desired results from the many you will have to write. You will also get a greater understanding of people and how to influence them, an increased facility in the use of language (both oral and written), a more thorough knowledge of business practices and ethics, and a resultant confidence in yourself.

You may want to make a career of business writing. Correspondence supervisors, business writing consultants, and direct-mail specialists have found it highly rewarding. But in *any* business, industry, or profession—as well as in your private life—your ability to write effectively will be a vital tool and a powerful factor in your eventual success.

PART ONE

How a reader reacts to a letter or memo

*[Through your letters you quickly reveal the kind
of polite person or stinker you are.]*

chapter 1 | # Appearance: What the reader sees

[Appropriate dress is usually the first indication of competence.]

Stationery
Letterhead
Placement on the page
    Standard-line plan
    Picture-frame plan
Position and spacing of letter parts
    Standard parts
    Special parts
Forms of indention and punctuation
Addressing the envelope; folding and inserting the letter
Interoffice memorandums

JUST ABOUT EVERYBODY has to write business letters and memos. Most people consider themselves "pretty fair" writers, too. Actually, however, the statement "Anything done by everybody is seldom done well" is as true of business writing as it is of any other activity.

If you do write good business letters and memos, you can answer yes to these questions:

1. Is their appearance pleasant and unobtrusive?
2. Is your writing style interesting, clear, and inconspicuous?
3. Do your letters and memos reflect basic goodwill?
4. Does your writing follow good persuasion principles?

You and any other business writer should apply these four tests because

—A pleasant and unobtrusive (undistracting) appearance, giving the first impression the reader gets, is important. If the appearance is bad, you start off with one strike against you.

—Your letter or memo may establish a favorable first impression **yet fail** completely because its language is dull, vague, inaccurate, difficult to follow, unnatural, or full of errors.

—Even with good appearance and style, your message can fail if it reflects poor tone and/or fails to reflect a desire to be of service to the reader.

—Your letter or memo may be appropriate in appearance, easily readable because of its clear and natural style, and pleasant because of its good tone and service attitude, yet fail because it does not follow good psychology or does not stress benefits to the reader.

With all four desirable qualities—good looks, good style, goodwill, and appropriate persuasion—your letters and memos will accomplish their purposes in most instances.

To explain and illustrate these four essentials of any good letter or memo is the function of Part One of this book. To show how the principles apply in all kinds of letters and memos is the main function of Part Two.

We do not believe you can write the good business messages you are capable of without understanding each of these four essentials. For that reason we ask you to read extensively before you start writing; and for the same reason no letter or memo cases appear until the end of Part One.

✻ ✻ ✻ ✻ ✻

The appearance of an individualized letter or memo is like a person's appearance: Since it is not the most important thing, the less it attracts attention to itself, the better. The wording, a desirable tone reflecting goodwill, and the persuasive qualities are more influential than the looks of a letter in determining its success or failure. Just as some listeners will reject the messages of speakers who do not come up to expected standards of appearance, however, so will many readers reject a written message that calls attention to its format and thereby distracts from the content.

A personalized (individualized) letter sent by first-class mail will nearly always get a reading. Flashy designs and lavish colors are like yelling at a person whose attention you already have. Even worse, if it is either too messy or too gaudy, or if it violates the conventions of letter form, the appearance distracts the reader's attention from the important feature —your message.

Direct mail/marketing (sales) letters are sometimes justifiable exceptions. Because they are often unpersonalized mass mailings, they often must struggle to get read at all. In striving to capture attention, their writers may use cartoons, gadgets, bright colors, important-seeming messages on the envelopes, and other gimmicks. Except for such direct mail, however, the physical letter should serve only as a vehicle for your message. The reader should not notice it since it would distract attention from the message and thus weaken it.

STATIONERY

The first thing noticed if it is inapproprate is your stationery. The most common business stationery—and therefore the least noticed—is 20-pound white bond with some rag content in 8½- by 11-inch sheets. Variations acceptable under appropriate circumstances include heavier and lighter paper, different sizes, and various colors and shades.

Paper heavier than 20-pound is more expensive, too stiff for easy folding, and too thick for clear carbons; and lighter than 16-pound (especially onionskin) is too flimsy and transparent for letters. (If used, carbon copies are usually on light paper, both because it is cheaper and because you can make a greater number of clear copies with it.)

The main off-standard sizes are Executive or Monarch letterheads (7½ by 10½ or 11 inches, used mainly by top executives) and half sheets (8½ by 5½ inches, used most frequently in intracompany memos or notes).

Though white is the standard, only the rainbow and your sense of appropriateness to your kind of business set the limits for color variations. Some tests have shown that colored papers sometimes produce better results in sales mailings. If you are sending out large mailings, however, you may be wise to run your own test on a small sample to see what color works best for that particular situation.

Paper with some rag content is more expensive than all-pulp paper, but it gives the advantages of pleasant feel, durability, and resistance to yellowing. The plasticized papers on the market usually claim to be easily erasable; but they have a "hard" feel, may be somewhat transparent, and typing on them tends to smudge even after some time. With the generally accepted use of liquid and paper white-out products to facilitate typing corrections, the erasable papers have found only a limited market in business and industry.

Whatever your choice of paper for the letter and memo sheets, you should use the same quality and color for envelopes and second pages.

The acceptable variations in stationery allow you to reflect the personality of your business, just as you select clothes appropriate to your personality. The big points are appropriateness and inconspicuousness. In selecting the paper for your letterheads, then, you should have a good reason before choosing something other than 20-pound white bond, 8½ by 11 inches. Anything else may distract the reader's attention from the message.

LETTERHEAD

The main trend in letterheads for many years has been toward simplicity. Letterheads once took up a good part of the sheet with slogans, names of officers, and pictures of the firm's plant and product. Good modern letterheads usually take no more than two inches at the top, and may occupy just a corner. They use wording, design, color, and graphic techniques to convey the necessary information and communicate an atmosphere symbolic of the firm represented.

The minimum content is the name, address, and telephone number of the firm, including area and ZIP codes. Sometimes an added trademark or slogan indicates the nature of the business. Firms doing much nationwide or international business frequently give a toll-free telephone number and/or a code address for cablegrams.

The past ten years have shown a marked movement toward the use of color in stationery. This trend is partly the result of increased acceptance of colored paper and color printing and partly from heightened awareness of the role of letterheads as representatives of a company. Firms wishing to present a modern image are turning to carefully designed graphics, such as the imaginative use of special colors and blind embossing. Good designers, however, are careful to avoid garish combinations and tasteless designs.

PLACEMENT ON THE PAGE

Even with appropriate paper and a well-designed letterhead, you can still spoil the appearance (and thus distract from the message) unless you place the letter on the page properly. Two methods are in common use: the standard-line plan and the increasingly less-popular picture-frame plan.

Standard-line plan

The standard-line plan of placing a letter on the page saves time and money because the typist does not have to reset marginal stops for letters of varied length. Typewriters set to the company's standard line (usually six inches, 60 spaces of pica type or 72 of elite) give all letters the same side margins. The top margin is about the same as the side margins, and the bottom margin is about one and a half times as wide. By varying from the standard spacing between letter parts (more or less between the date and inside address, for example, or three spaces instead of two between paragraphs), the typist can adjust letters of differing lengths for proper height (illustrated on p. 23) or just float the letter in the middle of the page.

Picture-frame plan

Typing a letter so that it looks like a picture framed by the white space around it takes a little more time than the standard-line method because you have to set the typewriter's marginal stops according to your estimate of each letter's length. With patience, however, it enables you to fit long and short letters to the page in more conventional fashion.

The idea is that a rectangle drawn around the typed letter (not including a printed letterhead) should look like a picture framed in the marginal white space. You determine the width of side margins according to your letter length and make the top margin about the same. The bottom marginal white space. You determine the width of side margins according half times as long (deep) as the other margins. (See p. 22 for an illustration.)

In gaining experience, a typist soon learns where to set a typewriter's marginal stops for letters of varied lengths. If you're just starting to gain the experience, however, you might well try this general plan. For short letters (100 words or less) leave about 2-inch margins at the top and sides. For long letters (over 250 words) leave at least 1-inch margins. Split the difference for middle-length letters.

POSITION AND SPACING OF LETTER PARTS

Standard parts

The usual business letter has six standard parts. *As a general rule, single space within parts and double space between parts*. But note exceptions as they come up in the following explanation.

The conventional *heading* or first part of a letter on paper with no letterhead (p. 24) usually includes the sender's address (but not name) and date. It establishes both top and side margins because it is the first thing on the page, and the end of the line going farthest to the right sets the margin. It may appear on the left, too, in a pure block form. Such a heading is usually three lines but often more. Thus it affects the number of words you can fit into a given typewriter setting.

Increasingly, writers are moving the sender's address to below the signature or title. This is a logical place for it and leads the reader to begin reading with the important part of the message, the content.

On printed stationery you can write the dateline as a unit with the letterhead or as a separate part (pp. 22 and 23). As a unit with the letterhead, place the typed-in date for best appearance according to the design of the printed part. Usually it retains the balance by appearing directly under the center of a symmetrical letterhead; often it rounds out one that is off balance. As a separate part, it fixes the upper right or left corner of the letter. Thus it is the *first exception* to the general rule of double spacing between letter parts.

The *inside address* includes the title, name, and address of the person to receive the letter, including the ZIP code. The beginning of the address establishes the upper left corner of the letter if the date is a unit with a printed letterhead. Otherwise, it begins at the left margin, two to six spaces lower than the dateline. So it is the *second exception* to double spacing between letter parts. (*Warning:* Be careful to spell names right and to use the proper title; people do not like to have their names misspelled or to be given the wrong title. And *always* put some form of title—professional, honorary, or courtesy—in *front* of *other* people's names, even when a professional or position title follows and though the point gives trouble these days on courtesy titles for women. See next section.)

The *salutation* or friendly greeting, the third standard part, begins at the left margin a double space below the inside address and ends with a colon (:) or no punctuation whatsoever. The wording must match the first line of the address, disregarding any attention line. If you address an individual, the salutation must fit (usually *Dear* plus title and name); if you address a firm or other group, you must choose an appropriate salutation.

Since a salutation is the first indication of the formality of a letter, you should give some thought to the implications of how you greet your reader and how you match the tone of your salutation in the complimentary close. Until recent years that obligation gave letter and memo writers little problem more than knowing whether to address a woman as Miss or Mrs. The main forms for letters addressed to persons *were* (in descending order of formality, with appropriate complimentary closes):

My dear Sir (or Madam)	Respectfully yours (or) Yours truly
My dear Mr. (or Mrs. or Miss) White	Yours truly (or) Sincerely yours
Dear (appropriate title plus surname)	Sincerely yours (or) Yours truly
Dear (surname or given name)	Sincerely yours (or) Cordially yours
Dear (given name, nickname, or such more familiar term as originality produced and good taste allowed)	Cordially (or) Regards (or some more familiar phrasing, as long as in good taste)

"Gentleman" *was* the proper salutation for letters addressed to a company, regardless of formality and regardless of an attention line (even when some of the "gentlemen" were ladies). In line with the trend toward informal friendliness of business letters, most business writers used the person's name in the salutation when they could and matched the friendly tone with some form of *sincerely* or *cordially.*

More recently, however, new developments have made more difficult the problems of (1) addresses and salutations to women and (2) salutations to mixed-sex groups and business firms. Many business firms and individuals avoid the difficulties by continuing to use the long-time conventional forms. Since the new abbreviation "Ms." came into our language to solve the earlier problem of how to address a woman of unknown marital status, many women have come to dislike it. But—many other women dislike the old forms of "Miss" and "Mrs." (even when right, according to past practice); and most resent the use of "Gentlemen" for a firm or group involving even one woman. Consequently, as of now no generally acceptable solutions have come.

Of course if a woman has given you her preference (as she should—see "signature block" later), you would use it. Beyond that (and until the present storm ends and the dust settles a bit), we can give you only some not-completely-satisfactory guidelines to choices for handling the two problems.

1. For addressing women whose preference of courtesy title you don't know, you can (*a*) continue the standard forms of a few years ago (Miss or Mrs. when you know and Ms. when you don't), though you will thereby antagonize some women; (*b*) skip the title and explain why (thus in a way asking the lady's preference—particularly desirable if the correspondence seems likely to continue); (*c*) use the AMS (Administrative Management Society) Simplified form (a reincarnation of the old NOMA Simplified form which developed in the forties and essentially died in the fifties), which omits both salutations and complimentary closes (illustrated on p. 23) but does not help you on inside or outside addresses; (*d*) skip the title and in the salutation use only the first name—all right if you're properly on a comfortable first-name basis.

2. For salutations to mixed-sex groups and business firms, you can (*a*) do as in 1*a* (but here you will probably misfire worse and with more women); (*b*) use the AMS Simplified form (probably your best choice); or (*c*) use "Ladies and Gentlemen" when addressing a mixed group (though we don't like it except when making a speech). We do not subscribe to "Dear Sir or Madam" (old hat and too formal; and many women do not like to be thought of as madams). Dodging with "Dear Business Executive" or ". . . Owner" is like running into a river to dodge a pothole.

The *body* or message of the letter begins a double space below the salutation. Usually you single-space within paragraphs and double-space between, though for the standard-line layout in very short letters you may use double spacing within and triple spacing between paragraphs. Since the body is all one part, regardless of the number of paragraphs, the standard double spacing between paragraphs is a *third exception* to the general rule of spacing. In any case, the number of paragraphs affects the fit of a letter to a given typewriter setting. A letter of 250 words in seven paragraphs, for example, will take at least four more lines than the same number of words in three paragraphs. Yet you should not overlook the chance to improve readability by such means as keeping paragraphs short and itemizing points when helpful.

The *complimentary close* (worded appropriately according to the descending scale of formality illustrated above) goes a double space below the last line of the body. It may begin at the center of the page, in line with the beginning of a typed heading, in line with the dateline used as a separate part, at a point to space it evenly between the center and right margin of the letter, or (in full block) flush at the left margin. As you've seen, the most common forms employ one of four key words—*cordially, sincerely, truly,* and *respectfully*—each ordinarily used with *yours.* Juggling the order of the key word and *yours* or adding *very*—as *Yours truly, Yours very truly, Very truly yours*—makes little difference. The key word is the main consideration.

Proper form for the *signature block* depends on whether the letter is about your private affairs or company business where you are an employee. In writing about your own business, you space four times below the complimentary close and type your name. The typed name is important for legibility—and consideration for your reader. You then pen your signature above it.

If you're writing about company business and the company is to be legally responsible for the letter, however, the company name should appear above the signature. The fact that the letter is on company stationery makes no difference. So if you want to protect yourself against legal involvement, type the company name *in solid capitals* a double space below the complimentary close; then make the quadruple space for your signature before your typed name. You also give your title on the next line below the typed name or, if there is room, put a comma and your title on the same line with your name. Thus you indicate that you are an agent of the company legally authorized to transact business.

Very truly yours,	Sincerely yours,
ACME PRODUCTS, INC.	LOVEJOY AND LOEB
John Y. Bowen	*Phyllis Bentley*
John Y. Bowen	(Miss) Phyllis Bentley, Treasurer
Comptroller	

Because the possibility of legal involvement is usually remote, many writers prefer to omit the company name from the signature block in the hope of gaining a more personal effect through a letter from an individual instead of from a company. If you feel that way and are willing to take the legal risk, you can set up the signature block as follows:

Cordially yours,	Sincerely yours,
H. P. Worthington	*Phyllis B. Hudson*
H. P. Worthington	(Mrs.) Phyllis B. Hudson
Assistant Public Relations	Treasurer
Manager	

Before you do, however, we suggest that you (1) get official agreement to bail you out of any legal involvement and (2) remember that some readers feel greater security in dealing with a company instead of an individual.

Women's signatures bring up a special problem. Note that in all the men's signatures illustrated, no title precedes the names. Without some indication, however, the person who answers a woman's letter does not know what courtesy title to give her. (For help on how to solve this problem, see our discussion of salutations.) As a matter of consideration, a woman should indicate how she wants to be addressed—the way Miss Bentley, who became Mrs. Hudson, did in the preceding examples.

Special parts

Besides the six standard parts of a business letter, you will often find good use for one or more of seven widely used special parts.

You can use an *attention line* in a letter addressed to a company if you want a certain individual to read it. If you don't know the person's name, you may just use the job title. It's equally good form to write "Attention of Mrs. Bevers," "Attention: Purchasing Agent," or "Attention, Purchasing Agent." In either position, flush at the left margin or centered, put it between the inside address and salutation with a double space above and below. Remember, however, that *an attention line has no effect on the salutation, which relates to the inside address instead.*

A *subject line* may save words by telling your reader quickly what the letter is about or referring to former correspondence for necessary background. It usually appears at the left margin a double space below the salutation; but when space is at a premium, it may appear centered on the same line as the salutation. To make it stand out, either underscore it or use solid capitals. The old forms "Re" and "In re" have all but disappeared. The informal "About" is increasing in use. And more and more correspondents omit the word *Subject* or its equivalent. The position and wording make clear what the subject line is.

Initials of the dictator and the typist often appear at the left margin a double space below the last line of the signature block. The trend is toward omitting the dictator's initials because of repetition from the signature block; but if used, they come first (usually in unspaced capitals), separated from the typist's by a colon, a diagonal, a dash, or an asterisk. A good method that saves time is to lock the shift and type CRA:MF or just write all in lower case as cra/mf. Some writers place the typed name here and omit it from the signature block.

An *enclosure notation,* a single or double space below the identifying initials (or in their place), is a reminder to the person putting up the mail to actually make the enclosure. Sometimes offices use an asterisk in the left margin at the line in the body referring to the enclosure. The word *Enclosure* may be spelled out or abbreviated *Encl.* or *Enc.,* followed by a number indicating how many enclosures or by a colon and words indicating what the enclosures are.

Copy designations (carbon- or photo-) are useful when persons other than the addressee should be informed of the contents of the letter. The names of people to receive copies are usually listed after *CC* (or *Cc* or *cc* or just *Copy to*) at the left margin, a single or double space below either the initials or the enclosure notation if it is used. If you don't want the addressee to know others are receiving copies of the letter or memo, you can type *Bc* and the names on the copies only, to indicate "blind copies."

Postscripts are rare in business today in the original sense of afterthoughts. Rather than arouse a reader's resentment by poor planning, the modern business writer would have the letter typed over, or in informal correspondence might add a handwritten note. (Incidentally, some research evidence suggests that such notes actually increase pulling power —probably because they give a letter or memo a more personal touch.)

The main use of postscripts now is as punch lines. Since they have the advantage of the emphatic end position, writers often plan them from the beginning to emphasize an important point. The well-planned postscript that ties in with the development of the whole message and stresses an important point is effective, especially if handwritten.

When you do decide to use a postscript, it should be the last thing on the page, a double space below the last of the preceding parts. The "P.S." is optional; position and wording clearly indicate what it is.

Second-page headings are essential for filing and for reassembling multipage letters that become separated. Since pages after the first should be on plain paper, even when the first page has a printed letterhead, for identification they should carry at least the addressee's name, the date, and the page number, typed down from the top the distance of the side margin something like one of the following:

```
Mr. C. R. Jeans              -2-              March 21, 19—
```

or

```
Mr. C. R. Jeans
March 21, 19—
Page 2
```

or (for speed and equal acceptability)

```
Mr. C. R. Jeans, March 21, 19—, page 2
```

The body of the letter continues a quadruple space below this.

FORMS OF INDENTION AND PUNCTUATION

The main letter forms in use today are semiblock and block with mixed or open punctuation. The example letters (Figures 1–1, 1–2, and 1–3) ex-

FIGURE 1–4

1445 Essex
San Diego, CA 92103

> Ms. Gail Motola, Secretary
> Editorial Department
> Richard D. Irwin, Inc.
> 1818 Ridge Road
> Homewood, IL 60430

Alabama	AL	Montana	MT
Alaska	AK	Nebraska	NE
Arizona	AZ	Nevada	NV
Arkansas	AR	New Hampshire	NH
California	CA	New Jersey	NJ
Colorado	CO	New Mexico	NM
Connecticut	CT	New York	NY
Delaware	DE	North Carolina	NC
District of Columbia	DC	North Dakota	ND
Florida	FL	Ohio	OH
Georgia	GA	Oklahoma	OK
Guam	GU	Oregon	OR
Hawaii	HI	Pennsylvania	PA
Idaho	ID	Puerto Rico	PR
Illinois	IL	Rhode Island	RI
Indiana	IN	South Carolina	SC
Iowa	IA	South Dakota	SD
Kansas	KS	Tennessee	TN
Kentucky	KY	Texas	TX
Louisiana	LA	Utah	UT
Maine	ME	Vermont	VT
Maryland	MD	Virginia	VA
Massachusetts	MA	Virgin Islands	VI
Michigan	MI	Washington	WA
Minnesota	MN	West Virginia	WV
Mississippi	MS	Wisconsin	WI
Missouri	MO	Wyoming	WY

3. For the speedy OCR handling, you must follow additional specific requirements for the main address, as explained below and illustrated in Figure 1–5 on a No. 10 envelope (4⅛ by 9½ inches):

—Single space, capitalize everything, omit all punctuation, use no more than four lines.

—Put nothing to the left, right, or below the address, which must begin at least an inch from the left edge, end at least an inch short of the right edge, and be more than one and a half inches from the bottom.

—Use both the ZIP code number and the two-letter state abbreviations (see list above), along with other abbreviations in the "Address Abbreviations" section of the *National ZIP Code Directory*, to keep the last line to no more than 22 positions (spaces and characters): a maximum of 13 for the city, plus 1 space; plus 2 for the state, plus 1 space; plus 5 for the ZIP number.

Enjoying the economies of window envelopes (largely through only one typing of the address) requires only folding the letter so that the inside address shows through the window without showing any other part.

When you're not using window envelopes, for the No. 6¾ envelope you fold the bottom of a letter up to ¼ inch of the top; fold from right to left about one third the width; then fold from left to right about one third, so that the last fold just fails to meet the other edge. For the No. 10 envelope, fold up from the bottom about one third the distance, then down from the top about one third, so that the last fold just fails to meet the other edge.

In either case, you then insert the letter in the envelope with the last fold to the back and the open edge up. Thus, and only thus, the letter will avoid annoying and distracting the reader because it will unfold easily,

FIGURE 1–5

quickly, and naturally—in the expected way—with the typed side forward and right side up!

INTEROFFICE MEMORANDUMS

The business letter is the main conventional form of written communication *between* companies and individuals or other companies. But interoffice memorandums (commonly called memos) now replace many letters as message carriers, especially *within* companies.

Memos first came into widespread use largely to combat the high costs of producing formal business letters. Since the major cost of a letter or memo is the time spent in composing and dictating, however, about the only cost savings in memos today come from not using expensive letterheads, envelopes, and postage and from the easier job of typing them (despite the simplified letter forms discussed above).

The usual reasons now for using memos are:

1. The situation does not justify the expense of a formal letter.
2. Face-to-face communication is not possible or not desirable.
3. The information to be communicated is too complex for oral comunication.
4. One or both parties desire a written record.
5. The receiver asks for a written comunication as a way of providing time to think about the problem or obtain additional information before responding.

For anyone in a medium or large company, memos will be the most common form of written communication with other people in the firm, especially those in other locations. What they know about you and how they think of you will depend on how you communicate with them—in short, by your memos.

The same is true, too, for upper management. Early in your career, especially, your only contacts with higher echelons in your organization will likely be the reports and memos you send up. Further, as you progress in your career, you will have to demonstrate your abilities as a manager—often by the memos you send down to your subordinates directing their activities. And finally, in dealing with your peers, you will find memos are important tools in establishing and maintaining your position.

Memos vary widely in format, from simple handwritten "From the desk of . . ." notes (Figure 1–6) to carefully designed forms with interleaved carbon copies and provisions for assuring an answer and proper filing. But since they usually go from one person to another in the same organization, memo messages are less formal than letters. Whether handwritten or typed, they share with letters the single purpose of communicating information in writing so as to effect an action.

FIGURE 1–6

June 00, 19--

From the Desk of
PETER B. CLARKE

Clyde —

You wanted to know how informal a memo can be.

It can be as simple as this — just a written note to quickly and economically convey information, a request, or a directive.

And it would be perfectly suitable for you to jot your answer below and send this back to me.

Memos have conventional, stylized headings (Figure 1–7). The universal elements are a date line, a "To" line (addressee's name with courtesy title—and job title unless known to all who get copies, or in a very informal message), a "From" line (writer's name—and identifying position title unless known), and a "Subject" line. (Leaving plenty of room to make the subject clear and precise is a good idea. The more comprehensively you describe the subject here, the less you will have to say in the body to introduce it and identify it before you can say anything of significance.)

The body begins right under the "Subject" line and continues until you've said what you need to, which may take three lines or three pages. No salutation or complimentary close appears, though when needed three other items may. When the memo needs authentication, the writer signs or initials it next to the "From" line, or underneath the body, following personal or company preference. Also, a typist's initials may appear at the bottom as on a letter. If copies are to go to other people, the typist may also type a copy designation and the names of receivers.

Because memos are usually less formal than letters in both format and language, some writers give them inadequate attention. That is a mistake, and it can be a very bad one. *Just about everything we say in this book about letters also applies to memos.* Whether your memos will accomplish their purpose depends on the writing style, their organization, the principles of successful business communication we discuss in the first two parts of the book, and even their appearance. Memos deserve care in preparation just as letters do, for they are important to your company's success, and yours.

Though the interoffice memos we discuss here are not exactly the same as the memo reports discussed in Chapter 16, the similarities may make it worth your while to look there. You will find more details on form, some illustrations, and a checklist.

(All the cases for the first four chapters are at the end of Part One because we think you should cover all four basic tests of a good business message before trying to write one. We urge you to read the first four chapters quickly but thoroughly so that you can put all the basic principles to use even in your first letter or memo.)

30

LETTERHEAD
Street Address
City & State

DATE: April 20, 19—

TO: Mrs. Margaret Maywald

FROM: John Cullerton

SUBJECT: NEW COMPANY MEMO FORM

I'm sure your people in the Word Processing Department are going to be happy to see this new standard company memo form. It should simplify and ease their work considerably.

As you can see, it carries our corporate letterhead and printed "Date," "To," "From" and "Subject." If your people follow our regular standard-line format, they can type on this form without changing a thing on their typewriters and printers, and with just one tab stop.

You will probably want to follow the common conventions for memos, such as using courtesy titles (Mr., Miss, Mrs., Ms.) for the addressees, but none for the writer. You should not supply addressees' and senders' job titles unless the occasion demands them, they are not on informal terms with each other, or job titles or departments are necessary to specify people's locations. Type the subject in capitals; this form will make it stand out and help divide the prefatory matter from the body of the memo.

Since the writer will sign or initial the memo next to the typed name (at "From"), we will not use signature blocks on our memos. However, you may wish to include the typist's initials (probably desirable since the writer will not otherwise know who typed the memo if your department rather than one of the administrative assistants does the typing), and an "Enc." if suitable. Please use our standard letter copy-distribution designations and lists with "cc" or "bcc" for multiple addressees. We can then simply check the name each copy will go to.

I know you have only a small stock of the old memo forms left; so we should quickly be able to get this new form into the works as soon as you use up the old ones. If you have any immediate reaction to the new form, I'd appreciate hearing it; and I'll certainly want to know how it's working after your people have had some experience with it.

chapter 2

Style:
What the reader reads

[Transmission of ideas and enthusiasm is essential to great accomplishment.]

How to think about your writing
How to write interestingly
   Depend mainly on content
   Put the emphasis where it belongs
   Write concisely but completely
      Ideas which don't deserve to be put into words
      Deadwood phrases
   Write vividly: Avoid indefiniteness
      People in action
      Active rather than passive voice
      Concrete rather than abstract language
      Specific rather than general words
      Enough details to make the picture clear
   Write naturally to avoid triteness and pomposity
   Vary sentence pattern, type, and length to
      avoid monotony
How to make your writing clear
   Make it easy to read
      Words your reader understands
      Reasonably short and direct sentences
      Adjustment of paragraph pattern and length
      Frequent personal references
      Itemizations and tabulations
      Proper pace
   Plan for unity, coherence, progress, and proper
      emphasis
   Use accurate wording, punctuation, grammar, and
      sentence structure
How to keep your style inconspicuous
   Choose the right level of usage for the situation
      Informal English
      Formal English
      The illiterate level of usage
   Follow the conventions
      Spelling
      Word choice
      Standard punctuation
      Grammar and sentence structure
Exercises

HOW TO THINK ABOUT YOUR WRITING

For its second test, if your letter or memo is to be considered good, ask yourself: *Is it written in interesting, clear, and inconspicuous style?*

If it is so uninteresting that it isn't read, you've obviously wasted your time.

If your letter or memo is interesting enough to be read but is not clear, you've probably confused and annoyed your reader. You may therefore get no response—or have to write again to answer your reader's inquiry.

And if your style is conspicuous because of something unexpected, inappropriate, or incorrect, it distracts your reader from *what* you've said (by calling attention to *how* you've said it) and causes doubt that your facts and reasoning are any more reliable than your writing. Both weaken your message's impact, and your message is what is important in any communication.

To be effective, then, your style should be—to your reader—interesting enough to be read, clear when read, and inconspicuous. Its *total effect on your reader* is what you should test—not just whether you get some immediate result you want.

Your first step toward assuring that your style is interesting, clear, and inconspicuous is to think about it. Most people take style for granted, rarely thinking much about how they say things. When you realize that how you say it vitally affects how your reader gets your message and its effect, you are starting to take your first step in thinking properly about your writing. Remember our title fly slogan: "You learn more by thinking about what you're doing than by simply thinking or simply doing."

Thinking about your style means not taking anything about it for granted. For example, consider articles. We generally throw them into whatever we're saying without any thought at all; yet they have considerable effect on what words mean. In fact, most people use too many articles (*a, an,* and *the*) and so rob their writing of readability. Too many definite articles make writing complicated and confusing. By making everything specific, they obscure what should be specific and thus turn strong phrases and sentences into weak, generalizing ones.

Next time you write something, go over it and mark every article. Then see how many of them you can omit. If any of your words or phrases can stand alone without articles supporting them, consider omitting those articles.

Please don't misunderstand us. We are not against using articles. Without them, English would be rough and awkward; and it would not adequately communicate specificness. We have made them our example because *we want you to think about your writing, to consider whether everything you put on paper is really necessary to your message.*

Many things in English that most writers take for granted as being essential are not. If you think, you can even write fairly well without using articles at all, as we have done so far in this chapter.

A very important part of thinking about your writing is thinking about it *in context*. A word, phrase, clause, or whole sentence that would be all right in one situation may be laughably wrong under different circumstances. For instance, the ending of a letter acknowledging an order you're filling might well read "We appreciate your business and hope to continue serving you, soon and often." Because of context (a different *milieu*), however, it was not good when an unthinking tombstone manufacturer used it.

Even perfectly good words, phrases, clauses, or sentences may misfire if you don't think about what they mean in the sentence—*their context*, including their sequence. We've given you many examples in the exercises at the end of this chapter; but here's one more for now (the heading on a statistical table): "Population in the U.S. Broken Down by Age and Sex."

HOW TO WRITE INTERESTINGLY

Depend mainly on content

In writing for business and industry, you should depend on content, not style, to arouse and hold your reader's interest. After all, the purpose is *not* to entertain. Usually you have an inquiry or other indication that your reader is interested in your general subject. A memo or individually typed and addressed letter will therefore nearly always get a reading. Tricks of style are unnecessary and even distracting.

If bare facts have insufficient appeal to get your reader's attention, you can make them both interesting and persuasive if you *show how those facts point to benefits for the reader* (**YA** in Appendix B). In writing about a product, for example, merely giving the physical facts (size, shape, color, and/or material) may be pretty dull. But if you interpret the facts as providing reader benefits (**PD** in Appendix B), the content is much more interesting: "Made of aluminum, the Gizmo is light and rust-free—you don't need to paint." And if you write so that the reader imagines successfully using the product and enjoying its benefits (dramatized copy; **DC** in Appendix B), the content is even more interesting.

If you have no indication of interest, you may have to work for temporary attention by means of gadgets, tricks of style, and other artificial means at the beginning of your letter. Even then, however, you will have accomplished nothing unless your stunt leads into the message naturally and promptly.

A perfectly good message can become dull, however, if poorly presented. Wordiness, indefiniteness, triteness and pompousness, monotony, and difficult reading are the most common offenders. By replacing these with their opposites, you will speed up your message rather than slow it down or lose it completely—and that's all you can expect style to contribute to making your letters interesting.

Put the emphasis where it belongs (Emp and Sub in Appendix B)

Since content is the greatest means of gaining interest, the big ideas of your message deserve the major emphasis.

Though you may use minor mechanical means of emphasis (underscoring, capitalizing, itemizing, using two colors), your four primary means of emphasizing an idea are (1) position, (2) space, (3) phrasing, and (4) sentence structure.

The most significant ideas need to appear in the emphatic beginning and ending *positions* of the letter, of your paragraphs—even of your sentences.

In addition, you write more about points you think need stressing. If you write ten lines about the efficiency of a dishwasher and two lines about its convenience, by *space* you emphasize efficiency more than convenience.

As a third major means of emphasis, you should select concrete, specific words and *phrasing* to etch welcome or important ideas in your reader's mind. When an idea is unwelcome or insignificant, choose general words that merely identify, not stress. *General:* "The typewriter needs several new parts and. . . ." *Specific:* "Your versatile IBM Memory Typewriter will. . . ."

Because an independent clause carries more emphasis than a dependent one, you can also stress or subordinate ideas through your choice of *sentence structure.* An important idea calls for statement in one independent clause (a simple sentence). Sometimes, however, you have two equally important and closely related ideas; so you should put two independent clauses together in a compound sentence. If you have two related ideas of different importance, a complex sentence of one independent and one dependent clause divides the emphasis properly. You may have noticed, for example, that we merely named (parenthetically in a dependent clause) the minor mechanical means of stressing ideas. The four primary means, however, we first itemized; then we gave each a separate paragraph of discussion and thereby emphasized them by independent-clause statement and by means of space.

In messages carrying ideas which the reader will welcome, then, use those ideas to begin and end the messages. They usually should begin and end paragraphs. They should take up most of the space of the letter or memo. Their phrasing should be specific. And they should enjoy the benefits of independent instead of dependent construction. Conversely, you should embed unwelcome or unimportant ideas in a middle paragraph, cover them just enough to establish their true meaning, and strip them of the emphasis of concrete, specific words.

Controlling emphasis in your writing is a technique you can put into immediate successful use—in the next piece of writing you do. We recommend that you work first on emphasis by position, since that technique is easy to use, as well as extremely effective. At first you will have to think about getting important ideas at the beginnings and ends of your letters and paragraphs, but you will be surprised how quickly this procedure becomes almost automatic . . . and how it will improve the effectiveness of all your writing.

The letter and memo samples throughout this book use the principles for appropriate emphasis and its opposite—subordination. Two special points, however, deserve your attention right here:

1. You may be inclined to write something the reader already knows. If it serves no purpose, think about your writing and omit it. But if you need to say it (for emphasis or as a basis for something else you want to say), put it subordinately. That is, do *not* put it in an independent clause: *not* "Summer will soon be here . . ." but "Since summer will soon be here, ..."

2. When you need to refer the reader to an enclosure for more information, word your reference to emphasize what to look for or get from it. *Don't* emphasize that it is enclosed: *not* "Enclosed is (or worse, "please find") . . ." but something like "You'll find further details of construction and users' satisfaction in the enclosed pamphlet."

    Here's a simple test of whether you're on the right track: To *de*-emphasize a word like *enclosed*, be sure you use it as an adjective before the thing enclosed (the pamphlet) and not as the verb of the sentence. (See **Emp** 2 in Appendix B.)

Write concisely but completely (**Conc** and **Dev** in Appendix B)

Every word you can spare without reducing the effectiveness of your writing is wasteful if it remains. Too many words for ideas stretch interest to the breaking point. But if you leave out necessary information and vivid details in trying to achieve brevity, you frequently fail to develop enough interesting ideas to hold or persuade your reader. You therefore face the dilemma of length.

A first step in the solution of that dilemma is a clear distinction between brevity and conciseness. Brevity is mere shortness—which is often overstressed. Sacrificing completeness because of a mistaken notion about the importance of brevity is a common mistake. Writing a letter or memo lacking necessary information (and therefore lacking interest and persuasion) is poor economy. Either it is pure waste because it produces no result, or both you and your reader have to write again to fill in the missing information. Even people who say a letter or memo should be brief do not want to make decisions without all the pertinent information.

What these people who are overly conscious of brevity really want—

what you want—is conciseness, making every word contribute to your purpose. A 50-word letter is brief; but if you can write the message in 25 words, the 50-word letter is not concise. A 400-word letter is not short; but if all the words contribute to the purpose, it is concise. So if you need three pages to cover all your points adequately and make your letter do what you want it to do, use that much space. Conciseness, then, comes not from omitting details that contribute to clearness, persuasiveness, or interest but from writing all you should say in as few words as possible.

Experience may teach you to compose first drafts that are both complete and concise; but while you are gaining that experience, you need to

1. Avoid expressing ideas that don't deserve to be put into words.
2. Revise first drafts to eliminate deadwood.

Besides obviously irrelevant material, *ideas which don't deserve to be put into words* are

Things the reader already knows which you do not wish to emphasize.
Ideas you can imply with sufficient emphasis.

Because it is often insulting as well as wasteful and dull, avoid using an emphatic independent clause for things the reader already knows. For example, a heating engineer's letter to an office manager about the discomfort of workers is flat, wordy, and dull because it emphasizes things known:

Poor	*Improved*
Three days ago you asked us to investigate the problem of discomfort among your office workers. (Assumes that the reader has a short memory.) We have made our study. (Obviously, since you're reporting results.) Too low humidity is apparently the main cause of your trouble. Your building is steam-heated. (Doesn't the reader know?) Therefore our solution is to. . . .	Too low humidity is apparently the main cause of your workers' discomfort. Since your building is steam-heated, your solution is to. . . .

To show the reasoning behind your suggestion, you do need to mention the steam heat; but the subordinating *since* implies "Of course you and I know this, but it has to go in for the record and for completeness of logic." When you *have* to establish something the reader knows, or when the reader probably knows it but you can't be sure, give the information subordinately—as the "Since . . ." does.

As a general principle, in answering a recent letter or memo from an individual, don't waste words to say "I have your letter of . . ." or to tell what it said. Obviously, you got the message or you wouldn't be answering it; and starting to discuss the same subject will remind your reader adequately. Instead of

> You asked us to let you know when the new model of the Clarion radio came on the market. It is obtainable now.

you can say the same thing with

> The new Clarion radio is now available.

That clearly implies that you got the letter and the idea of "You asked us to let you know."

Of course, if the inquiry is not recent, or if somebody other than the original inquirer may read the answer (as often happens in big organizations), you may need to make specific reference (by topic and date) to the communication you are answering. But even then you can use a subject line to save words and allow the emphatic first sentence to say something important.

Rather than this	*You might better write*
On February 20 you inquired about our experience with Mr. James H. Johnson. We are glad to tell you about his work for us. Johnson was a steady, conscientious worker during the 18 months he kept books for us.	Mr. James H. Johnson, about whom you inquired on February 20, was a steady, conscientious bookkeeper here for 18 months.

Under no circumstances do you need to waste words as in the following:

> Permit me to take this opportunity to thank you for your letter which I have just received. In reply, I wish to state that we shall be very glad to exchange the electric water heater in question for a similar one in a larger size in accordance with your request.

Through implication you can reduce that wordy beginning to

> We'll be glad to exchange your water heater for a similar one in a larger size.

In most refusals you can save words and your reader's feelings by eliminating the negative statement of what you won't do and concentrating on what you will do. You thus *imply* the negative idea, for economy as well as interest. For illustrations, see "Positive Statement" (p. 88).

If your first draft contains any wasteful expressions, revision should eliminate them as well as *deadwood phrases* (those which take the long way around or contribute nothing to the ideas expressed).

Consider the following far from complete list of offenders, in which a line blocks out the deadwood or the concise statement follows in parentheses:

long ~~period of~~ time
is ~~at this time~~
at ~~a price of~~ $50
~~important~~ essentials
enclosed ~~herewith~~
remember ~~the fact~~ that
held a meeting (met)
main problem is ~~a matter of~~ cost
your ~~order for a~~ cultivator was shipped
~~in the opinion of~~ Mr. Johnson (thinks)
that is the situation ~~at this time~~ (now)
the X plow is quite different ~~in character~~
made the announcement that
    (announced)
for the purpose of providing
    (to provide)
all the people who are interested in
    (interested people)
at an early date (soon) [if you have to
    be indefinite]
decide at a meeting ~~which will be held~~ Monday
eliminate needless words ~~that may be present~~
~~there is~~ only one point ~~that~~ is clear, ~~and that is~~
the price was higher than I expected ~~it to be~~
the workers ~~are in a position to~~ (can)
    accept or reject

during ~~the course of~~ the evening
~~engaged in~~ making a survey
~~the color of~~ the X is blue
until ~~such time as~~ you can
in regard to (about, regarding)
in the development of (developing)
in this day and age (today, now)
the soldering process proved ~~to be of an~~ unsatisfactory ~~nature~~
the general ~~consensus of opinion~~
    among most students is that
    (most students think that)
~~the trouble with~~ the light was ~~that it was~~ too dim
in ~~the state of~~ Texas
neat in ~~appearance~~
at ~~the hour of~~ 4:00
eight ~~in number~~
circular ~~in shape~~
throughout the ~~entire~~ week
~~at a~~ later ~~date~~
during ~~the year of~~ 1980
costs ~~the sum of~~ $10
came ~~at a time~~ when
at all times (always)
in the event that (if)
put in an appearance (came)
during the time that (while)
these facts ~~serve to~~ give an idea
made stronger ~~with a view~~ to
if ~~it is~~ possible, let me have
~~according to~~ Mr. Johnson (says)
arrived at the conclusion (concluded)

Sometimes you can save several words by changing a whole clause to one word. For example:

buying new machines which are expensive (buying expensive new machines)
using processes that are outmoded (using outmoded processes)
saving work that does not need to be done (saving unnecessary work)

Write vividly: Avoid indefiniteness

Even good content concisely stated can be uninteresting if your reader gets only an inactive or fuzzy mental picture. The sharper you can make that picture, the better it will be. You will write vividly if you apply these five techniques:

1. Write about people in action, Make people the subject or object of many sentences.
2. Use active rather than passive voice most of the time.
3. Use concrete rather than abstract language.
4. Use specific rather than general words.
5. Give enough details to make the picture clear.

The most interesting thing in the world is *people in action*. Most things happen because people make them happen. The most interesting, the most natural, and the clearest way to write about those happenings, therefore, is to talk about those people who are the principal actors. That is why we suggest that you make people the subject or object of your sentences.

And since each reader is most interested in personally related things, interest in your letter will depend on how you put that person into the picture as the main actor. "You can save 30 minutes at dinner time with a Pronto pressure cooker" is more vivid than "A Pronto pressure cooker saves 30 minutes at dinner time." (For psychological reasons, if a point is a criticism and hence unpleasant, however, make your actor a third person or your message impersonal, rather than accuse. See **Accus** in Appendix B.)

Consistent use of people as subjects will help you to write in *active* rather than passive voice. The passive "30 minutes at dinner time can be saved" lacks the vividness of the original illustration because it omits the all-important *who*. Besides, passive constructions are usually longer, weaker, and fuzzier than active ones (**Pas**). Excessive use of "to be" verbs, (*be, is, am, are, was, were, been, being*) usually produces flat writing, partly because it leads to a passive style. If the basic verb in more than half your sentences derives from "to be," your style will seem flat instead of lively.

"There are" and "It is" beginnings (**Expletives**) delay the real idea of the sentence and frequently force a writer to use the unemphatic passive voice. The sentence "There are 1 million people in Cincinnati" is not so vivid as "One million people live in Cincinnati." "It was felt that . . ." becomes more vivid when the writer rephrases with "We felt. . . ."

You can eliminate most passives and expletives if you will *think*—that is, conscientiously try to use action verbs. People live, run, eat, buy—in short, act. They do not just exist, as indicated by *is, was, were, have been*. The price of a stock *creeps up, rises, jumps, zooms*—or *plummets*. For vividness (and for economy) good writers make their verbs do a big share of the work. Far be it from us to encourage you to coin needless and frivolous words; but *dip, curve, skyrocket, phone, wire*, and many other original nouns are now verbs because people recognized their vividness as verbs. The more action you can pack into your verbs, the more specific and concrete you can make your writing.

When you *use concrete rather than abstract language*, you give your reader sharper mental pictures. When you write *superiority, efficiency,* and *durability* in telling about a product, your words are abstract; they give your reader only hazy ideas. To make the picture sharp and lively, give the evidence back of the abstraction (though requiring more words) rather than naming the abstraction itself. If you think your product is of highest quality, you must have reasons for thinking so. To establish the idea of superiority in cloth, for instance: Thread count? Number of washings before fraying? Tensile strength? Resistance to shrinkage and fading?

In job applications you need to put across the ideas of your sociability, initiative, and dependability. But just claiming that you have those abstract qualities will make you look more conceited than competent. You can demonstrate them, however, by citing activities and organization memberships, ideas and plans you originated, attendance records, and completed projects. Thus you give evidence of these qualities and let your reader draw the abstract conclusions.

You further eliminate haziness and dullness when you use *specific rather than general words*. An investment, for instance, may be a stock, a bond, or a piece of real estate. To illustrate further, stock may be common or preferred. The closer you can come to making your reader visualize the special type of thing named rather than just its general class, the more specific and hence the more vivid your writing is.

Take the verb *walk* as another example. Does a person amble, trudge, skip, or one of the 50 or more other possible ways of walking? When you are inclined to write *contact*, do you mean write, go see, telephone? You present a sharper picture if you name the specific action.

Comparisons help you explain the unknown or variable in vivid terms of the known. *Slowly* becomes sharper if you say "about as fast as you normally walk." "A saving of 2 percent when paid within 10 days" becomes more vivid if you add "$2.80, or a free box of Lane's choice chocolates, on your present invoice of $140."

Even when you are specific and concrete in the kind of information you give, however, unless you *give enough details to make the picture clear*, you will fail to be vivid. Specifications for a house may call for painting it, for example; but unless they tell the kind of paint, how many coats, and what colors, the painter does not have a clear enough picture to know what to do. You need to flesh out skeletons to bring them to life, even if it sacrifices some brevity.

Write naturally to avoid triteness and pomposity (Nat in Appendix B)

All kinds of trite expressions and jargon—usually the result of hazy thinking, or not thinking, by the writer—dull interest and put the reader to sleep. They are even called "bromides" ("flat, commonplace statements," Webster says) because of the use of bromides as sleep-inducing medicines.

One person meeting another on the street would not say, "I am glad to say that we have received your letter of March 14th, and in response we wish to state that. . . ." A good business writer would not write it either, but more likely, "Those tonnage figures for April were just what I needed," or "Your suggestions about the committee memberships helped a lot in my decision. Thanks." The first is slow, vague, roundabout, and stilted; the others are clear, direct, and natural.

Bromidic style goes back to the times when people in business first began to have social status enough to write to kings, princes, and others at court. Feeling inferior, they developed a slavish, stilted, and elaborately polite style to flatter the nobility. They "begged to advise" the nobleman that his "kind favor of recent date" was "at hand" and "wished to state" that "this matter" would "receive our prompt attention" and "begged to remain your humble, obedient servant." Today people in business need not be so meek. Unfortunately, however, too many do sheepishly follow somebody else, learn all they know about writing from the frequently bad letters and memos they receive, and thus continue an outmoded, inappropriate, and unnatural style. Like parrots, they use expressions unthinkingly.

Pompous writing (puffed-up, roundabout, and using big words) is as dull and confusing as the use of bromides. Why many people write "We will ascertain the facts and advise accordingly," when in conversation they would say quite naturally, "We'll find out and let you know" is a mystery. A Washington blackout order during wartime originally read: "Obscure the fenestration with opaque coverings or terminate the illumination." A high official who wanted the message understood revised it to read: "Pull down the shades or turn out the lights."

A young lawyer was certainly pompous in writing as follows about a husband being sued for divorce:

```
The defendant is renowned as a person of intemperate habits.
He is known to partake heavily of intoxicating beverages.
Further, he cultivates the company of others of the distaff
side, and wholly, regularly, and consistently refuses, demurs,
and abstains from earnest endeavor to gain remuneration.
```

The judge summed up that "Mrs. Rigoni's husband drinks, chases other women, and refuses to work."

Stuffed-shirt writers frequently use a phrase or a whole clause when a well-chosen verb would express the idea better. For example: "Smith raises the objection that . . ." instead of "Smith objects that (or objects to). . . ." One writer stretched a simple "Thank you" to "I wish to assure you that it has been a genuine pleasure to have been the recipient of your gracious generosity."

Good writers avoid both bromides and pompous wording to make letters natural. Common advice is to write as you talk. That advice, however, can be taken too literally. You would have an extremely hard job trying to write just as you talk; and even if you could, the informal style appropriate to letters and memos is more precise and concise than good conversation. What the advisers really mean is that you should not stiffen up, use big words and trite expressions, or get involved in complicated and formal sentences when you write letters. Rather, let the words flow out naturally and informally in phrases and sentences with the general tone and rhythm of the language actually used by people rather than stuffed shirts.

Write like this	Not like this
Many people	A substantial segment of the population
Know well	Are fully cognizant of
Object	Interpose an objection
Wait	Hold in abeyance
Carry out the policy	Effectuate (or implement) the policy
As you requested	Pursuant to your request
Before, after	Prior to, subsequent to
Get the facts	Ascertain (secure) the data
Ask the defendant	Interrogate the defendant
Find it hard to	Encounter difficulty in
Big difference	Marked discrepancy
Begin (or start)	Initiate (or institute)
Complete (or finish)	Consummate
In the first place	In the initial instance
Haste makes waste	Precipitation entails negation of economy
Make unnecessary	Obviate the necessity of
Think of	Conceptualize
Here is	Enclosed please find

Vary sentence pattern, type, and length to avoid monotony

Unvaried sentence pattern, type, length, or rhythm causes many a reader's mind to wander. Though much necessary variety will come naturally from writing well, revision can often enliven your style by removing a dull sameness.

The normal English sentence pattern is subject-verb-complement. Most of your sentences should follow that sequence; but if all of them do, they produce monotony. Particularly noticeable are series of sentences all beginning the same way, especially with "I" or "We." (One critical lecturer stressed the point by laughing at such "we-we" letters.) The following list suggests possible variations of sentence beginnings:

With a subject:

```
A simple way to key returns is to use different return
envelopes with the several different letters being tested.
```

With a clause:

> Because human beings are unpredictable, the sales process cannot be riveted to a formula.

With a phrase:

> For this reason, no large mailing should be made until tests have proved which letter is best.

With a verb:

> Should you find that all pull about the same, you have the usual dilemma!

With correlative conjunctions:

> Not only the lack of funds but also the results of continual overcrowding and busing in secondary schools will continue to lower the caliber of work in American colleges.

With an adverb:

> Ordinarily, students like courses in business letter writing.

With a verbal:

> Allowing plenty of time, the student started the report early in the semester.

With an infinitive:

> To be a successful business letter writer, a student must be able to lose selfishness in contemplation of the reader's problem.

With adjectives:

> Congenial and cooperative, Dorothy worked many nights until midnight when we faced a deadline.

Proper emphasis of ideas is the main reason for varying sentence type, but the variation also avoids monotony and retains interest. Choosing sentence patterns in terms of needed emphasis (as explained on p. 34) will nearly always result in enough variety to prevent monotony.

Sameness of sentence length (and to some extent, paragraph length) can be just as monotonous as unvarying sentence pattern and type. Together they produce an interest-killing rhythm characteristic of a childish style. Children's books often put both listener and reader to sleep—but business writing should not.

Although readability specialists have done much good by inducing some people to keep their sentences down to reasonable length, they have done some harm by leading others who have misunderstood them to write too mechanically in trying to average about 17–20 words a sentence. That is a recommended *average*, remember. Nothing could be more monotonous than a series of 14-word sentences—or of 4-word sentences or of 24-word sentences. Even interesting sentences are useless in business, however, unless they are clear.

HOW TO MAKE YOUR WRITING CLEAR

The strongest rebuke a reader can give a writer is "I don't understand; what do you mean?" Conciseness helps clarity as well as interest because your reader avoids the job of separating the important from the unessential, and vividness helps by giving a sharp picture. But other more important aids to clearness are

1. Making your writing easy to read.
2. Planning for unity, coherence, progress, and proper emphasis.
3. Using accurate wording, punctuation, grammar, and sentence structure.

Make it easy to read

Your responsibility as a writer is to present ideas so that your reader understands with the least possible effort. As the difficulty of understanding an idea increases, people are more inclined to skip it. Any time your reader has to back up and reread or has to slow down to understand you thoroughly, you are risking the chance of arousing disgust and being ignored or of being misunderstood. So readability affects interest, but it relates more intimately to clarity.

Using only those words your reader understands immediately and sharply is a first step in making letters easy to read. You will usually be wise to choose the more commonly known of two words; an uneducated person will understand you, and an educated reader will appreciate your making the reading job easy.

Short words add force to what we say, for we all know what they mean. Big words can trip us up, for what they mean may be hard to pin down. Small words can say all the things you want to say. Finding the small words you need may take time, but it will be time well spent. Your letters will be easier to read if you use one-syllable words most of the time. If you have 50 percent more syllables than words, your writing requires more reader effort than it should. And the greater number of polysyllabic profundities you use, the greater the likelihood that you'll strike your reader as pompous.

A man well known for his way with words, Arthur Kudner, once said, "Big, long words name little things. All big things have little names, such as life and death, peace and war, or dawn, day, night, hope, love, home. Learn to use little words in a big way; they say what you mean. When you don't know what you mean, use BIG words. . . . That often fools little people."

Keeping your sentences reasonably short and direct will also help to make your letters easy to read and hence clear. An average of 17–20 words is a healthy one for readability. But you need not avoid sentences of 4 or 5 words—or 40, if necessary for presenting an idea exactly. If the average length is not too much above 20, smooth sequence of thought and directness are more important than the word count. To avoid involved, indirect sentences, look at the punctuation. It cannot make a basically bad sentence into a good one. If you have to punctuate a sentence heavily, you will be wise to rephrase it more directly. Sometimes the best solution is to break it up into two or three sentences.

Paragraph pattern and length influence readability, too. The usual pattern of letter and memo paragraphs is a topic sentence followed by supporting or developing details. But if you write one sentence which says all you need to on the topic, start the next topic—in another paragraph. Padding one with needless stuff or covering two topics in it because some composition books ban single-sentence paragraphs is *baaad* writing.

Frequently a single-sentence paragraph is highly desirable to give an idea the emphasis you want!

Especially in letters, long paragraphs are uninviting and hard to read. First and last paragraphs of more than four lines and others of more than eight are likely candidates for breaking up.

Frequent personal references (names of people and pronouns referring to them) also make your writing more interesting and readable. Since you and your reader are the two persons most directly involved in the actions, desires, and benefits you write about in letters, most of your pronouns will be "you"—or "you" understood—and "I" or "we." (If you're ever tempted to use *we* without clear meaning, however, remember what Mark Twain once said: "The only people entitled to use the indefinite *we* are kings, editors, and people with tapeworms.")

Itemizations and tabulations may help to make your whole letter or memo or a paragraph clear and easy to read. For instance, if your topic sentence mentions three big advantages in using XYZ Wafers, the three will stand out more clearly and emphatically if you number them and list them on separate lines.

Proper pace also affects the readability of what you write; so you will also want to pay some attention to it. Pace is simply the frequency with which you present ideas. The physical actions of our eyes in reading have little relation to our mental actions or comprehension. The speed of reading is unlikely to vary much; but if ideas come too fast or too slow, comprehension will drop. A reader will be unable to assimilate ideas that come too quickly or will become bored and inattentive if they come too slowly. New writers often make the mistake of presenting snippets of undeveloped ideas too rapidly, one ofter the other, in an effort to be brief. What they achieve is a loss of comprehension by their readers because of too many hazy ideas too fast for the reader to figure them out. Further, too fast a pace often leads to curtness and a brusque, unfeeling tone.

Plan for unity, coherence, progress, and proper emphasis

Later you will study planning for psychological effect as a principle of persuasion, but planning also affects clarity. If you are answering a letter or memo, underscore points in it to be covered. In any case think your answer through before you start to write or dictate; you can't plan anything more than a simple message by just thinking as you write. Clear writing is usually the product of a three-step process which stresses organization and coherence.

1. The preliminary planning step requires specific answers to four questions:

   a.   What effect do I want the letter or memo to produce? Decide specifically what you want to happen as a result of your message. Without keeping this central purpose in mind, you cannot achieve one of the main objectives of organizing—unity. Good organization should result in a oneness by showing how every part relates to the general theme or idea.

   b.   Who is the reader? Until you make a clear estimate of what your reader is like, you cannot hope to apply the principles of adaptation (p. 85).

   c.   What facts and ideas must I present to produce the desired effect on this kind of reader? List not only points of positive interest but probable reader objections to be overcome.

   d.   What is the best order of presenting the items listed in answer to Question c? Later you will be prepared to answer generally as plan A, B, or C (from your study of "Planned Presentation," p. 78 ff). But those are only general plans. Organization includes much more.

   You can organize well only by answering specifically all four of the questions in preliminary planning. In preparing a nonroutine message, usually you need to spend about 40 percent of your total preparation time on preliminary planning.

2. The second step of writing well-organized messages is continuous fast writing. You merely follow your preliminary plan and *keep going.* Write the entire piece without stopping. Only that way will you be efficient (using only about 20 percent of the time) and get the natural coherence that comes from following a chain of thought straight through.

3. In the third step—revising for tone (see p. 60 ff.), conciseness (p. 35 ff.), coherence, and correctness (p. 52 ff.) and using about 40 percent of your time—you may need to reorganize a bit by shifting words, sentences, or whole paragraphs into better position. But usually the main work on organization through revision will be a few changes in wording for better coherence. You may find that all you need to strengthen coherence is some transitional words like *and, but, for,* and the variants of each (see **Coh 3** in Appendix B).

Although you should not leave out any necessary bridges between parts, the fewer you can use and still make the sequence of thought clear, the better. Try especially to avoid overformal and slowing references like *the latter, the above-mentioned*, and *namely*.

Use accurate wording, punctuation, grammar, and sentence structure

Conventions, not rules, establish proper usage of words, punctuation, and grammar. The important thing is to use them with the exact significance the reader attaches to them. Words, for example, are mere labels we apply to actions, things, and ideas.

Moreover, words and sentences sometimes change meanings according to what precedes and succeeds them. For instance, a would-be secretary brought laughs when the last two sentences of her ad for a job read "No bad habits. Willing to learn." Similarly, the following last two sentences in an ad of a big dog for sale brought more laughs than prospective buyers: "Will eat anything. Loves children." (For proper word relations, guard particularly against the errors discussed in **Mod** 1 and 2 in Appendix B.)

The difficulties of accurate expression stem partly from the way words pick up related meanings and personal significance from everyday use (connotations, in addition to their denotations or dictionary meanings). Consider the difference between *cheap* and *inexpensive* or between *house* and *home*. And note that *hope, trust* and *if* can suggest doubt. "You claim" or "you say" even suggests doubt of the reader's truthfulness. The accurate user of words will be alert to connotations and implications—if not to avoid confusion, at least to produce effectiveness.

Exceptional cases of failure to follow the conventions have led to readers' getting a completely wrong idea. But rarely does such failure *leave* a reader confused. Much more frequently, unconventional usage of words confuses a reader temporarily. Usually at least the approximate meaning will come—after study. Of course, if you say *profit* for what we generally call the selling price, however, you will mislead your reader.

The words you use should give not only the general idea but the precise idea quickly. If you say *soon* or *later*, your reader doesn't know just when you mean. If you say *checks, notes, stocks, etc.*, nobody can tell whether you mean to include bonds. (*Etc.* is clear only in such statements as "I am particularly interested in the odd-numbered questions, 1, 3, 5, etc." But it then becomes unnecessary, as it usually does when what it refers to is clear.)

A large vocabulary enables you to choose the precise word to give the exact idea. But if you don't use judgment with a big vocabulary, you sometimes use words that leave the reader in the dark or slow up the pace. For example, you may be inclined to write *actuarially*, but most readers will get the meaning more quickly if you write *statistically*.

Punctuation marks, like words, mean only what a reader takes them to mean. They can be helpful by breaking your sentences into thought groups if you follow the conventions and use them in standard ways (**P1–P13** in Appendix B). But if you use a system of your own which your reader does not understand, you mislead just as if you used words in unfamiliar ways. For instance, if you put up a sign on a parking lot to mean

> No Parking: Reserved for Our Customers

you will certainly mislead people if you write:

> No Parking Reserved for Our Customers

Like faulty wording, faulty punctuation often not only confuses but distracts the reader's mind from the key idea. You've surely seen the laughable highway sign "Slow Men Working."

Fortunately, the system of English punctuation is pretty well established (by convention, not by rules), and most readers know at least the main parts of the conventions. Unfortunately many people who know how to *read* most simple punctuation marks correctly do not know the conventions well enough to use the marks precisely *in writing*. If you have any doubts about the following main troublesome areas of punctuation, see the symbol **P** in Appendix B for explanation and illustration:

Semicolon between independent clauses except with strong conjunction (**P2**).

Comma after all dependent clauses at the beginnings of sentences and with nonessential ones elsewhere (**P3**).

Comma to separate coordinate adjectives (**P5**).

Pair of commas around a parenthetical expression unless you want to de-emphasize by parentheses, emphasize by dashes, or avoid confusion with other commas by using parentheses or dashes (**P4, 7**).

Hyphen between words used as a single modifier of a following noun (**P8**).

So-called "errors" in grammar and sentence structure also mislead readers just as unconventional uses of words and punctuation do. They also slow up reading and produce indefiniteness, disrespect, and distrust. The statement "You should not plant strawberries where tomatoes have been grown for several years" will mislead readers if you mean "Wait several years before planting strawberries where tomatoes have grown." And the dangling participle in "Smelling of liquor, the officer arrested the reckless driver" (**Mod.** 1) did lead to a policeman's being asked why he was drinking on duty.

Faulty pronoun references, shifts in number, and wrong verb forms can confuse too—though often only temporarily. Most readers will understand despite shifts in number like "The Acme Company is located in Chicago. They manufacture . . . ," wrong verb forms like "He come to my house at 10 P.M.," or the wrong choice between *lie* and *lay*. Those same understanding readers will, however, notice the bad English, become amused and/or sympathetic, and lose respect for and confidence in the obviously ignorant or careless writer. All these reactions are *distractions from the message* because the style calls attention to itself—becomes conspicuous.

HOW TO KEEP YOUR STYLE INCONSPICUOUS

When a reader starts reading, the point of interest is what you say, not how you say it. In reading a well-ordered sentence, a reader will receive no jolt. Your style, therefore, becomes noticeable and distracting only if you do something unexpected with it. But consciously noticing an expression as an artificiality is distracting—as the writer you lose attention to your message. Simplicity and naturalness are good guides on the right road.

If you make your style too flowery, formal, or stiff for the situation, or if you make it too flippant and familiar, it will distract the reader from your message and arouse doubts about your sense of appropriateness. (An obvious striving for such "style" is a sign of immaturity.) If you violate any of the conventions of word choice, spelling, punctuation, sentence structure, or grammar, your unconventional practice will both distract and cause your reader to doubt your general knowledge and ability. For instance, if you cause the reader to say, "Why, that writer can't even spell," the *even* strongly implies "So of course I can't depend on the correspondent to know anything else either."

The two main ways a writer does something unexpected with style and thus draws undue attention to it, then, are

1. Choosing the wrong level of usage for the situation.
2. Violating any of the more common conventions of word choice, spelling, punctuation, grammar, or sentence structure.

Both weaken the impact of the important thing—your message.

Choose the right level of usage for the situation

The appropriate level of language, like proper dress, is a highly variable thing. What is effective in one situation may not be suitable in another. A tuxedo is no better for a day in the office or a weiner roast than blue jeans are for a formal party, or a bathing suit for church.

The first step in choosing the right level of usage is to analyze the situation in the light of the five communication factors (sometimes called the communication formula):

1. A writer (or speaker) who has
2. A particular message to communicate through
3. A medium (letter, memo, report) to
4. A definite readership (or audience) for
5. A definite purpose (in business, a *practical* purpose—not entertainment).

If any of the factors of communication change, the situation shifts so that a formerly good sentence may become bad, or vice versa. Still, many thoughtless writers almost ignore the last two factors—readership and purpose. Only in view of all of them can you classify the situation and choose the appropriate level of usage.

Having classified the communication situation, you can take the second step in choosing the appropriate level of usage by considering the nature of the different levels. Several whole books name and describe them. More concise treatments also appear in some modern college composition books. Some linguists/philologists have distinguished as many as seven levels, but a more usual and functional modern classification names three: formal, informal, and illiterate.

Informal English is much the most useful level for letters and memos and for most other kinds of functional speaking and writing today. In it, the writer's interest is more on content than on style. The emphasis is more on being functional than on being elegant. Its general tone is that of the natural speech of educated people in their usual business and social affairs. In its written form it is more concise and more precise than normal conversation; but its vocabulary, phrasing, sentence structure, and grammar, and hence its natural rhythm and tone, are essentially the same as in good conversation among educated people. That—rather than a literal interpretation of the words—is the meaning of the often-heard advice that you should write as you talk.

But informal English is a broad category, ranging all the way from a style which verges on formal English to that which verges on the illiterate. When informal English approaches the formal, it does not allow slang, shoptalk, contractions, or omission of relative pronouns and other connecting words. It may use generally understood allusions, figures of speech a little more complex than similes, and words and sentences that are somewhat long. Some writers insist on the highly questionable requirement of impersonal style (no pronouns referring to writer or reader) for reports and research papers at this dignified-informal level of usage.

Near the deep end of the informal level of usage is what we call "familiar-informal." Its whole attention is on content and to heck with style. It's OK if you're writing to somebody you know pretty well or if the two of you have lots in common. In using it you have to assume that you don't need to show your reader that you know English. As in this paragraph, it uses contractions, a light touch, and rather simple sentence structure and words. If you want to use some slang and shoptalk, you just let go. Its value is its freshness, vividness, emphasis, and naturalness. The danger point, which this paragraph flirts with, is that it will be abused in an attempt to be clever and thus will call attention to itself.

Formal English is characterized by precision and elegance of diction, sentence structure, and grammar. Like the person dressed in formal clothes, it often appears stiff and unnatural, more to be admired for its appearance than for any function it may perform. It admits of no contractions, ellipses, or indignities of any kind. Of necessity, it uses many everyday words, but by design it includes many in the *précieuse* category. Like the person of high society, it sometimes chooses its associates with more attention to their paternity than to their practicality. As a consequence, its words are frequently somewhat rare and long, with histories traceable back to the first word families of Old French or Latin. It is often fraught with abstruse literary and historical allusions, perhaps to impress the reader with the writer's erudition or skill with *bons mots*. Rather than concerning itself with facilitating the reader's comprehension, it employs lengthy and labyrinthine sentences more fanciful than functional, more rhythmical than reasoned, more literary than literate, more artificial than accurate, and more absurd than acceptable. Following an unsound belief that they are thereby being more objective, its writers often strive for an impersonal style and bring forth a mountain of words from a molehill of an idea, or a diarrhea of words and a constipation of ideas. Its worst misguided practitioners—some lawyers, sociologists, engineers, and politicians, apparently hoping to achieve dignity (and defending their practices by claiming that they achieve precision)—frequently abuse acceptable formal English by carrying it to the ridiculous extremes of the too technical, the pompous, and the flatulent (commonly called "gobbledygook" or "bafflegab").

Abused formal English has no reason for being. Even in its best sense, formal English is nearly always unsuitable for business writing. It would be noticed as inappropriate in all but the most formal occasions.

The illiterate level of usage is the third one of them three we dun named. It ain't got no bizness in bizness. Ya see, folks who reads letters spects you ta right right. If'n ya writes wrong, he shore sees ya errors and knows ya ain't eddicated so he thinks ya don't know nuthin else neither if ya cain't get yer rightin right.

An easy way to choose the appropriate level of usage for a situation you have analyzed is to ask yourself which type of dress would be most suitable if you were going to see your reader and talk your message. If the answer is formal dress, choose formal English or dignified–informal. If the answer is an everyday business suit, use the broad middle ground of informal English. If the answer is sport clothes, use familiar-informal.

Follow the conventions

You have already seen how following the conventions of wording, punctuation, sentence structure, and grammar affects clarity. But violations of those and other conventions have an even more important bearing on keeping your style inconspicuous. If you go contrary to the conventions, you do something your reader doesn't expect of an educated writer. You therefore distract attention from your message *and* lose the reader's respect and confidence in you.

After all, if a writer has not even mastered the fundamentals of the native language, knowing anything else of importance or value seems unlikely. This idea is what enters most readers' minds when they come across letters marred with misspellings and grammatical errors.

Even the following first paragraph in a letter from a hotel manager to an association president is clear. You know what the writer means, despite poor sentence structure, but you are distracted and you can't hold much respect for the manager or the hotel.

```
Your recent convention over with and successful, we are
wondering if since then you have decided on the next year's
meeting city, and you jotting down on the margin of this
letter the city and dates selected, this will be indeed
appreciated.
```

From this, don't you get the impression that the sloppy language probably means the hotel might not be a very well run, clean place to stay?

Spelling is probably the most exactly established convention in the English language. Even the dictionary spells a few words two ways, but it lists most of them in only one way. Because of this definiteness, spelling has acquired much more importance in the minds of most people than it deserves in terms of any confusion bad spelling causes. A misspelled word almost never leads to confusion and therefore makes little difference in terms of what is in the words. But total communication is more than that. Most readers (even relatively uneducated ones) will notice your errors and look down on you for them. And that is a big part of total communication. So unless you prefer to write in other languages (nearly all of which have more systematic and easier-to-learn spelling), you had better accept your fate and learn English spelling.

Because it is so unsystematic, you'll find no easy way. Consider yourself fortunate if you have learned to spell by observing the words you read and by listening closely to their pronunciation. If you have not used these methods, you should start now; but don't assume that pronunciation is always a safe guide. (You will find some helpful guidelines, however, under **Sp** in Appendix B.)

Poor *word choice* that is close enough to meet the basic requirement of clarity is usually not so noticeable as misspelling, but it may be distracting and even degrading. Among the thousands of possible bad choices, the pairs listed under Diction in Appendix B give the most trouble. If you are unsure of any of the distinctions, look up the words; any educated reader will notice if you confuse them.

Variations from *standard punctuation* may lead to misunderstanding, but more frequently they distract and retard the reader. If you have trouble with punctuation, study the material under **P** in Appendix B.

Grammar and sentence structure are so closely related that you should consider them together. They have a definite bearing on clarity (see discussion on p. 47), but they have more significance in terms of making your style inconspicuous. Most of the troubles come from

—A writer's having heard uneducated people speak unconventionally, particularly family and fellow workers. (Solution: Observe the skill of other writers and speakers, study writing, practice.)

—Simple carelessness (Solution: Proofread and revise.)

—Trying to use big words and complicated sentence structures before mastering them. (Solution: Remember that they are unnecessary to dignity or effectiveness; write simply, at least until you can use more involved structures precisely and clearly.)

In trying to keep your style unnoticed by avoiding violations of the conventions of good English, you would have an easier job if all your readers were modern philologists. Language scholars know that many of the so-called rules of English are

—Latin rules foisted off on English by early writers who knew Latin and thought English should follow the same system (but it doesn't).

—Rules concocted to systematize English by people who ignored the true nature and history of the language.

Here is a realistic interpretation of some points that language scholars make in contradiction to statements of some less well-informed people:

—A split infinitive is undesirable only if it is awkward or unclear.

—*And, but,* and *so* are good sentence beginnings if they deserve the emphasis they get there. The same applies to *however* and other transitional words, but some people object only to *and, but,* and *so*.

—Prepositions are perfectly good at the ends of sentences if you want them to have the emphasis they would get there.

—One-sentence paragraphs are perfectly good. The ban on them is nonsense. Often a one-sentence paragraph, especially the first or last in a letter, is just what you need.

—Passive voice is usually undesirable because it is weak, wordy, and awkward; but it still exists in the language because it is useful in some situations (to avoid direct accusations, for example). To ban it completely is high-handed.

—What some people still call colloquial expressions and slang are important and useful parts of the language; when the situation calls for the informal level of usage, they can improve language effectiveness.

—Many words have varied meanings when used alone; but if the context makes the interpretation readily clear and definite, to ban use of these words or to limit them (*while* or *since*, for example) to one use is unrealistic and lordly.

—The distinctions between *shall* and *will* are almost completely gone except in formal English; *will* is much more widely used.

Unfortunately, not all your readers will have studied courses on the history of the language and modern English usage or have read books on those subjects. Many of them will have been misled by linguistically unsound books and teachers. But they will *think* they know what is right and wrong. If you don't do what they *think* is right, you will distract them and lose their respect.

If you are writing to someone likely to be linguistically misinformed, we advise you to adhere to the widespread, though unsound, "rules" when you can do so easily. Otherwise, we suggest that you forget unjustifiable restrictions on the language and give your attention to the more important aspects of good style—interest, clarity, and inconspicuousness.

Appendix B covers some common violations of the conventions and gives suggestions for avoiding criticism.

(*All the cases for the first four chapters are at the end of Part One because we think you should cover all four basic tests of a good business message before trying to write one. We urge you to read the first four chapters quickly but thoroughly so that you can put all the basic principles to use even in your first letter or memo.*)

(*Since you will remember the principles of good style better if you practice them while concentrating on them alone, however, you may profit by working through at least some of the following exercises.*)

EXERCISES

A. Determine what is not good about the following "sentences" and rewrite them or be prepared to discuss them, as your teacher directs. Some of them have more than one thing wrong. You may also benefit from finding (in Appendix B) the appropriate symbol(s) for criticism of each and reading the discussion of the symbol(s).

1. Having rotted in the damp cellar, my brother was unable to sell any of the potatoes.

2. Since our regular instructor had to meet with the dean that afternoon we attended Mr. Andersons class.

3. We had to finish the work however on a hot, humid, muggy, day.

4. On February 7 1981 his term of office will end, however, the new director will not come until March 1.

5. Neither the coaches nor the captain have had much experience with the wishbone offense.

6. She is not certain who's dog she hit, but she thinks it was your's.

7. Although many of Jason's friends are fishermen, he does not enjoy it.

8. He said that a good sales representative should know how to dress and approach a customer.

9. The parole board said that Jones was found to be mentally ill after listening to three psychologists.

10. (*From an ad.*) Solid oak posture chairs for secretaries with built-in padding.

11. When I had more time, I use to lay down for an hour or two in the afternoon.

12. The catcher, who was usually accurate threw the ball over the short-stops head.

13. The dinner is to honor residents and interns who are leaving the hospital and their wives.

14. The roommates decided that the simplest solution to the problem was for each girl to have their own key.

15. Walter likes engineering, but he is not sure he would like to be one.

16. Schubert wrote much of his music while sitting in a restaurant on the back of a menu.

17. The income of a western farmer is often higher than an eastern manufacturer.

18. She said Riggs is a forester and has five children, and I know he went to college to learn how to do that.

19. Remember that as the dictator you are responsible for errors, not the typist.

20. Our M–798 carries a lifetime guarantee against damage under normal use, the National Luggage Dealers Association approval, and come in four beautiful colors.

21. Approximately 66 percent had made their most recent hardware purchase in Denver. This is an increase over previous findings of 42 percent.

22. Our cutbacks and layoffs are mostly results of production prices, we are experiencing maximum work loads on our staff and our presses.

23. Had we expected a reprint response such as we have received we would have made preparations to accomodate them.

24. The copy contained in your library now should remain as a reference and perhaps utilize the enclosed reprint for photocopying important selections.

25. Only having two parts, the screen will give your customers the protection they need for their cars while being light weight.

26. Living only four miles from a paper manufacturer, the odor controller seem ideal for my situation.

27. I would like to refer you to Dr. John Smith my college advisor Professor Raymond my instructor in chemistry and the Reverend Bill Dudley the pastor of my church.

28. The workers who had been with the company ten years were given a bonus by the president and thus their morale was increased.

29. By mailing the enclosed card promptly we will enter a subscription in your name.

30. My own evaluation of Honeywells is the same as that of the engineers and should be installed in our plant.

31. Originally a means of entertainment only, the Church was quite late in accepting the organ (long considered a pagan device).

32. It was found that there are 12 main reasons why goods are returned. The most significant of these being entirely or almost entirely customer faults. The 12 reasons are: . . . .

33. While I worked with the fire crew I was only involved in one run.

34. Included in the shipment are three one ounce packages and one sixteen ounce package.

35. In conformance with our conversation on March 30, the report of the uranium corporation has been reviewed, to determine wherein the operations of the corporation may have been presented inadequately; further, suggested changes in format, illustrations, and treatment of text have been developed, for consideration in the preparation of subsequent reports.

B. As an exercise in the proper handling of passives, study the subject (look it up in the Index and under **Pas** in Appendix B), then rewrite the following passage from a company's management report. In rewriting, change all passive sentences to active and all active ones to passive.

The entire firm was investigated, one department at a time. It was decided that a complete explanation of the exercise would be given to employees prior to the investigation. Fourteen employees were selected to administer the program. Training by a consultant agency was given over a period of one month. Flow charts were compiled showing what was done by whom on every task performed. Workers were given time spans in which certain tasks were to be performed and asked for suggestions for improvement and time saving techniques. Time was recorded for every action. A report was drawn up and reviewed when a change was needed. Rearrangements were made. Even the largest division was rearranged so that each employee was given knowledge of all the tasks involved. Throughout the four-year program, a running account of the costs and savings in each department was kept by the company to determine net gains. Workers found their work to be more challenging and much more interesting after the change.

C. Without looking at the following ten words (printed upside down), get somebody to pronounce them for you to spell (in writing). Then check them against the "spelling tips" (under **Sp** in Appendix B) to understand why the spelling of each is as it is.

(Most) ladies' preferences, forfeit
deceive, referred, owing, tallies, forty-four, donkeys, noticeable,

D. Rewrite in modern language.
1. Your remittance should be forwarded to this office by return mail.
2. Your order of recent date for a catalog will be sent under separate cover.
3. Your correspondence of the 3rd inst. has been referred to the writer for reply.
4. Enclosed herewith is a draft in the amount of twenty-three dollars ($23).
5. Please find enclosed a stamped self-addressed envelope for convenience in replying.
6. In reference to your request for an instruction booklet, please find same attached hereto.
7. Hoping to hear from you in the near future and trusting you will be able to fill our order promptly, we remain.
8. We trust you will send check in full payment at your earliest convenience.
9. We are in receipt of your letter and wish to thank you for your promptness in sending the information we requested.
10. We beg to advise that there is a balance due of $23 in the above-captioned account in your name.

E. Rewrite more vividly and specifically.
1. Long-distance telephoning is economical.
2. Chicago has many advantages as a convention site.
3. An XX TV set gives you a better picture.
4. We have a large stock of paperback books.
5. Telephones are now available in color.

F. Rewrite for you-attitude, positive aspect, and goodwill.

1. It will be necessary that you complete the enclosed request for exchange before we can make this adjustment.

2. We cannot quote you a price on the installation of air conditioning until our engineers have submitted an estimate.

3. If you sent the beneficiary change form to our agent, as you state, he failed to forward it to us.

4. We regret that we neglected to answer your letter sooner. Unfortunately, we did not have all the necessary information.

5. Unfortunately, I am afraid that we will not be able to make this change until the 15th of the next month.

6. We do not send receipts of payment because of the extra work involved and because your canceled check serves as a receipt.

7. You neglected to sign the enclosed check.

8. If your correct name is Lou V. Harwood, you may complete the enclosed Request for Correction of Name, and return it with your contract for endorsement.

9. We cannot process this claim until we receive additional information.

10. You cannot join our Mutual Fund until you contribute a minimum of $300.

chapter 3

Goodwill:
How the reader feels

[Disagreements come from lost accord.]

Tone
    Acceptable balance of personalities
        Undue humility
        Flattery
        Condescension
        Preachiness
        Bragging
    Courtesy
        Anger
        Accusations
        Unflattering implications
        Sarcasm
        Curtness
        Stereotyped language
        Untidy physical appearance
    Sincerity
        Effusiveness
        Exaggeration
        Undue familiarity
    Gratitude
Service attitude
    Resale material
    Sales promotion material
    Special goodwill messages

MOST BUSINESS PEOPLE define goodwill as the disposition of customers to return to a place where they have been treated well. A good business communication helps to produce that positive disposition in the reader or listener by developing a friendly, confident feeling toward the writer or speaker.

No business firm or individual intentionally drives away present or potential customers or friends by creating ill will or by seeming indifferent.

For lack of conscious effort and know-how to build goodwill, however, many people do drive customers away. Proper *tone* and *service attitude* are the methods of winning customers' friendliness and confidence—that is, goodwill or disposition to return to you because you treat people well.

TONE

[Beware of those who fall at your feet; they may be reaching for the rug.]

No doubt you have heard someone complain, "It isn't *what* he said—it's the *way* he said it!" Inflections and modulations of voice, facial expressions, hand gestures—all affect the tone or overall impression of a spoken remark almost as much as the words do, sometimes even more. The point applies in writing too—especially in writing letters and memos, the most personal, me-to-you kind of writing. If you want your writing to build goodwill, you *will make a conscious effort to control the tone.*

Basic to a desirable tone is a balance of personalities (writer's and reader's) acceptable to both. Without an attitude of mutual respect, you will have difficulty achieving the other qualities necessary for good tone—courtesy, sincerity, and proper gratitude.

Acceptable balance of personalities

As a good business writer you will need to subordinate your own wishes, reactions, and opinions; the suggestion "Make it **big you** and little me" can be overdone, however. Anything you say that looks up to or down on the reader will throw the relationship off balance.

Undue humility usually backfires. Such a tone as in the following is unwise because it is obviously insincere-sounding; no reader expects a writer to be so humble.

```
I'm sorry to ask a busy person like you to take valuable time
to help me, but without your help I do not know how to
proceed.  Since you are a world authority on . . . , and I
know nothing about it. . . .
```

Flattery is another reason why readers question the sincerity of some writers, especially when it is obvious flattery in an attempt to get the reader to do something. The reader, sure that the writer has an ax to grind, discounts such passages as the following:

```
Your keen discrimination in footwear shows in your order of
the ninth.
```

--

```
Your eminent position in commercial aviation, Mr. Pogue, is the
subject of much admiration.
```

--

When an Atlanta girl marries, she immediately thinks of Rich's,
the merchandising cynosure of the South!

Instead of gaining favor, the writer loses face and the reader's faith.

Passing deserved compliments or giving credit where credit is due, however, is something else; it is expected of anybody except a boor. So when
you want to indicate your sincere awareness of the reader's position or
accomplishment, avoid the smell of flattery by making the compliment
subordinately. For example:

Obvious flattery	*Better*
You are receiving this questionnaire because you are an authority in retailing.	As an authority in retailing, how do you think the passage of HR–818 will affect co-ops?

Now the compliment is so short and touched so lightly that it may give a
faint glow of satisfaction, and consideration of the question precludes
unfavorable reaction.

As you see, handling a compliment subtly is frequently a question of inserting a complimentary phrase in a statement intended primarily to accomplish something else like this:

How, in your opinion, will passage of HR–818 affect co-ops?

‐‐

After successful experience in the field, would you say that
any single area of preparation is more important than others
for effective public relations work?

More frequent than undue humility and flattery, however, is a writer's
implication of too much self-respect and too little for the reader. Lack of
respect usually reflects itself in (1) condescension ("talking down" to the
other person), (2) preachiness (*didacticism* is another word for it), and
(3) bragging.

Condescension is quick evidence that the writer feels superior to the
reader and shows little respect. Almost everybody has a good share of self-
respect. No one wants to be considered a nobody and looked down on or
talked down to.

Yet, in attempting to be bighearted, a business executive insulted a
reader with "It is unlikely that the machine is defective, but a firm of our
size and standing can afford to take it back and give you a new one." In
the same category go sentences like "I am surprised that you would question the adjustment procedure of a firm like Blank's" and "You are apparently unaware of the long history of satisfactory customer relations at
Blank's." Even the statement "We shall allow you to" has condescending
connotations not present in "We shall be glad to" or "Certainly you may."

A particular danger lies in writing to children, who are not lacking in
respect for their own ways of looking at things. When the secretary of a

boys' club requested that a department store manager contribute some boxing gloves to the club, the manager answered: "When you grow up to have the heavy business responsibilities I have, and you're asked for contributions by all kinds of charitable organizations, you'll understand why I cannot make a donation to your club." And to make matters worse, the manager began the next sentence with "You are probably unaware. . . ." The boy's vocabulary failed him, but what he tried to express was "That pompous ass!"

A slightly different form of condescending attitude crops up in job application letters in statements like "You may call me at 743–4601." The implication is that the writer is permitting the reader a privilege when just the opposite is true. An applicant is in no position to appear so aloof.

Repeated use of such phrases as "we think," "we believe," and "we suggest" often appears to be condescension. The writer who reflects such a sense of superiority is almost certain to erect a barrier of incompatibility. Far from attracting a reader, such egocentric talk more likely causes a sputter like "Well Bigshot, I can think for myself!" When this happens, it can virtually destroy goodwill.

Preachiness (didacticism), which is an extension of condescension, is undesirable because, when you tell your reader what ought to be done, you imply reader ignorance or incapability and thus suggest your superiority, which will be resented. The juvenile-sounding marketing lecture some sales writers put into letters to retailers is one of the most frequent offenders:

```
The only way for you to make money is by offering your
customers merchandise that has utility, good quality, and an
attractive price.
                         --
It's time for all dealers to get in their Christmas stock!
```

A retailer's reaction to such preachy statements will likely be an emphatically negative one like "Don't tell me how to run my business!"

When a statement is flat and obvious (see **Obv** in Appendix B), it is frequently irritating because it implies stupidity, even though the writer's intent is good:

```
Satisfaction of your customers means turnover and profits
to you.
                         --
You need something new and different to show your customers.
```

You, as a business writer, will do well to examine such expressions as "you want," "you need," and "'you should"—and to eliminate them whenever you can without altering the meaning. The following illustrations from sales and application letters are flat (known) and preachy:

Flat and preachy	*Better*
Spring will soon be here . . . rain in the morning, cold and clear in the afternoon. To be safe, you should carry both a topcoat and a raincoat with you every day. But that's a bother.	For these early spring days when it's raining in the morning but clearer and colder in the afternoon, a topcoat which is also a raincoat will give you protection to and from work —and without your having to worry each morning over "Which shall I take today?"
The business cycle is changing from a seller's market to a buyer's market. You are going to need a strong force of good salespeople.	Now that business is shifting from a seller's market to a buyer's market, you're probably thinking about the strong force of good salespeople with which you'll meet competition.
Do you want Davison's to keep growing and keep getting better?	Good merchandise at the right prices is not the only reason Davison's has grown as it has in the last five years. The team of Davison men and women has been equally influential.
Of course you do!	
Then you should employ only those who want to move steadily forward and push Davison's on to greater heights.	

As you see, careful phrasing can eliminate most of the irritation due to preachiness—and the psychological browbeating in the third example (**BB** in Appendix B). Often the key is to subordinate information that is obvious or known to the reader but must, for a reason, be included. Put it in the middle of a paragraph, preferably in a phrase or dependent clause.

Bragging is another undesirable extension of the writer's ego. It brings to the minds of readers the sometimes comical, sometimes pitiful, sometimes disgusting, chest-pounding would-be caveman. Conscious use of superlative wording ("newest," "latest and greatest," "outstandingly superior," "final word") is a flagrant and obvious way to make your reader react unfavorably—and not believe you. Even experienced writers sometimes annoy readers with undesirable—and almost always unsupported—references to size of company, efficiency of operations, or quality of product, like:

In a business as large as ours—with literally thousands of retailers selling our products— . . .

--

Even in a firm as large and as well run as Bowen and Bowen, such incidents are bound to happen occasionally.

--

You are unfortunately a victim of routine made necessary by the vastness of an institution so well operated as the White Sands Hotel.

64

The desirable balance of personalities between reader and writer (through elimination of undue humility, flattery, condescension, preachiness, and bragging) will help to improve the tone of your writing; but it will not assure courtesy, the second element in desirable tone.

Courtesy

[Kindness is the oil that reduces friction between people.]

Being courteous is being considerate of the other person's feelings through exercising patience and tact. But often one's immediate, emotional, or unthinking reaction is an impatient or tactless expression. For that reason, one famous lecturer regularly suggests the use of a "soaking drawer"— a special drawer in the desk to put nasty-toned letters and memos overnight, for revision the next day.

The idea is good. Courtesy often requires a conscious effort to be understanding and forgiving, to anticipate another's likely reaction, and to avoid offense. "Sleeping on" a nasty message can provide the better conditions. Besides that, correspondents need to keep in mind the major causes of discourtesy and to respect an old French proverb which says "To speak kindly does not hurt the tongue."

Anger displayed is almost certain to cause loss of friendliness toward you and confidence in you. Most business people have a good deal of self-respect and confidence in the wisdom of their decisions. An attack on them produces a wave of anger and a consequent necessity for self-defense. The result is two people seriously estranged. Such sentences as the following are almost sure to produce that result:

```
We cannot understand why you are so negligent about paying
bills.
```

--

```
What's going on in the office at your place?
```

--

```
We certainly have no intention of letting you get away with
that!
```

Crude slang or profanity, especially if used in connection with a display of heightened feeling, is likely to be interpreted as anger, whether or not it is intended as such. Don't use either. (And don't try to be coy and cute with quotation marks for questionable slang—or dashes in words that are obviously profanity.)

Petulance (peevishness or fretfulness) is simply anger in a modified degree. It is comparable to the scoldings children often must receive from parents (and unfortunately from teachers too!). Here is how a woman scolded an interior decorator: "When do you expect to return my furniture? You've had it now for more than two weeks. That ought to be long enough to do a little upholstering job." A calm request that the work be finished as soon as possible because of the need for the furniture would probably bring just as quick action, and it would leave the upholsterer in a better mood to do a good job.

Business people have usually graduated from sandbox psychology too. When they read "We have played fair with you; why don't you play fair with us?" they are likely to regard the writer's whining as unnecessarily and undesirably juvenile.

Both anger and petulance are the result of impatience and unwillingness to accept the responsibilities of successful human relations.

Accusations, on the other hand, are usually the result of insensitivity to how another person will react to a remark. One cannot cultivate tact (skill in dealing with others without giving offense) without a deep and almost constant concern for the feelings of others. The sensitive, thoughtful person knows that people do not like to be reminded of their carelessness or ignorance—*and* that they will be unfriendly to the person who insists upon reminding them of their errors.

The customer may not always be right; but if you are going to keep the greatest friendliness (goodwill), you will remember not to call attention to errors if you can avoid doing so—or when necessary, to do it with the least likely offense (in impersonal style or by implication). The writer of the letter at left below displayed an almost completely insensitive attitude:

Accusing	*Revised, better*
Much as we dislike doing so, we shall have to delay your order of May 12.	Since we want you to be entirely satisfied with the blue sweater you ordered on May 12, will you please let us know which shade you prefer?
<u>You neglected </u>to specify which shade of sweater you desire.	
Kindly check your catalog and <u>this time</u> let us know whether you want navy, midnight, or powder blue.	You may obtain the cardigan style in navy, midnight, or powder blue. All are popular this spring.
We have enclosed an envelope for your convenience.	Just check the appropriate blank on the enclosed reply card. As soon as we receive it, we will mail your sweater.

The revised version has far better tone and is thus more likely to retain the goodwill of the reader. It eliminates the accusation and the unfavorable reminder in the underlined words of the original, the sarcasm the reader would probably read into *kindly,* and the pompous-sounding reference to the enclosure. In the revision the reader would no doubt put the blame for carelessness where it belongs but would feel more friendly toward the writer and the firm for the courteous way of asking for additional information without accusing. You could practice the same technique if speaking with the customer.

The contrast between the two versions of that letter points to an important principle in business communication: *When you have sincere compliments to give, personalize them for full effect; on the contrary, when you are inclined to point the accusing finger, shift to impersonal, passive, or other unaccusing phraseology.*

Unflattering implications are usually the result of tactlessness combined with suspicion or distrust. The collection correspondent who wrote, "When we sold you these goods, we thought you were honest," implied an unfavorable idea of much greater impact than the literal statement.

The adjustment correspondent who says, "We are investigating shipment of the goods *you claim* you did not receive," need not be surprised to receive a sharp reply. Similarly, "*We are surprised* to receive your report" and "*We cannot understand* why you have had trouble with the Kold-Hold when other people like it so well" establish by implication semiaccusing doubts of the other person's reasonableness, honesty, or intelligence.

And the sales writer who begins a message by implying doubts about a reader's alertness can expect few returns from the letter:

```
Alert hardware dealers everywhere are stocking No-Flame, the
fire-resistant. . . . Are you prepared to meet the demands of
your home-building customers?
```

In similar vein the phrases "Do you realize . . . ?" and "Surely you are . . ." immediately suggest doubts that the reader or listener measures up on either score.

Such lack of tact is usually unintentional. Most people, however, do not question whether it is intentional; the result is ill will.

Sarcasm, on the other hand, is generally deliberate. And it is extremely dangerous in business correspondence. The smile which accompanies friendly sarcastic banter cannot find its way onto paper; unfriendly sarcasm is sheer malice. It is the direct opposite of the attitude necessary for a tone of goodwill because it shows a lack of respect for the other person and a deliberate attempt to belittle. The sales manager sending the following memo to a group of employees falling short of their quotas would build no goodwill:

```
Congratulations on your magnificent showing!
We're only $50,000 short this week.
How do you do it?
```

The United Way leader who included the following in a public report could hardly expect future cooperation from the people indicated:

```
The ABC employees, with an assigned goal of $800, magnificently
responded with $452.  Such generosity should not go
unmentioned.
```

Sarcasm should never be used in business writing. It's too risky. The moment of triumph is short-lived; the loss of friendship may be permanent.

Curtness, born of impatience and a false sense of what constitutes desirable business brevity, reflects indifference and thus seems discourteous. The woman who received the following letter promptly labeled the manufacturer sending it as a boor:

> We have your request for our booklet and are enclosing same.
> Thanking you for your interest, we are. . . .

A poor letter like this, reflecting such lack of interest, destroys much of the favorable impression made by even a good booklet.

This writer might very well have helped to convert a casual inquiry into a sale by taking the time to show interest in serving the customer with a letter like the following, with its good service attitude, positive and specific resale material, and action ending (all of which we discuss later):

> Here is your copy of Siesta's booklet <u>Color at Mealtime</u>.
> When you read it, you'll understand why we say that in Siesta you can now have handsome dinnerware that is sturdy enough for everyday use, yet surprisingly inexpensive.
> No photography, however, can do justice to the delicacy of some Siesta shades or to the brilliance of others.
> Your friendly local dealer will be glad to show you a selection of Siesta. Unless the stock is complete, the dealer will be glad to order additional colors for your examination.
> See your dealer soon and start enjoying Siesta's color at mealtime.
> You can find Siesta in Omaha at (name and address of dealer).

This letter adapts easily as a form letter with only the last line and the inside address and salutation individually typed.

Stereotyped language is another mark of discourtesy because it suggests indifference. And nobody likes to be treated in an indifferent, routine way. Writers of messages like the following jargonistic disgrace can expect little feeling of friendliness from their readers:

> We have your letter of the 19th and in reply wish to state that the interest on your mortgage is now $361.66.
> We trust this is the information you desired, and if there is any other way we can oblige, please do not hesitate to call upon us.

Since stereotyped language is primarily a question of style, see page 40 for fuller discussion and more examples.

Untidy physical appearance is another factor affecting the apparent courtesy of letters and memos, in the eyes of most readers. Sleazy paper, poor placement, strikeovers, messy erasures, dim or clogged type, poorly matched type and processed material, and penciled signatures are like trying to gain an audience's respect when you're dressed in an old tweed suit and they are in formal wear . . . and your socks don't match!

In putting your best foot forward through courtesy, however, you must be careful not to trip up; overdone attempts to be courteous may seem insincere and thus destroy the third element in desirable tone.

Sincerity
[Don't stretch the truth; it snaps back.]

When a reader or listener feels the first flashes of doubt, with an unexpressed reaction of "Well, I'll take that with a grain of salt," confidence in the writer or speaker wanes—because of apparent insincerity.

Sincere cordiality is entirely free of hypocrisy. It is unwillingness to exaggerate or fictionalize upon the true state of a situation. Inappropriate cordiality (usually unbelievable and sometimes distasteful) is commonly the result of effusiveness, exaggeration, or undue familiarity. (Flattery and undue humility, it is true, often sound insincere. But in our opinion they relate more closely to the balance of personalities discussed in a preceding section.)

Effusiveness means gushiness. It is excessive politeness, which often *is* insincere and always *sounds* insincere. "Overdone" means the same thing. You can sound effusive simply because you've used too many and/or too strong adjectives and adverbs, as in the following examples:

```
We are extremely happy to place your name on our list of
highly valued charge customers, and we sincerely want you to
know that we have hundreds of loyal employees all very eager
and anxious to serve.
                        --
Your excellent choice of our fine store for the opening of a
charge account we consider a distinct compliment to the superb
quality of our merchandise and outstanding service.  And we're
genuinely happy about it.
                        --
I was exceptionally pleased to note your name on this
morning's list of much-appreciated new charge customers.
```

The plain fact is that in a business relationship such highly charged personal reactions as those suggested in the foregoing examples do not exist—and business people know it. Phrases like "do all we can" and simply "happy" or "pleased" are appropriate because they are believable.

Furthermore, the coy quality of the following endings is unrealistic in a business situation—and therefore unbelievable:

```
We do hope you'll come in soon.  We can hardly wait!
                        --
Don't forget to come in soon.  We'll be looking for you!
                        --
Simply note your color choice on the enclosed card, mail it to
us—and then sit back with an air of expectancy.
```

In avoiding effusiveness, you'll do well to watch especially overused words like *very, indeed, genuinely, extremely, really,* and *truly*—which begin to gush in a very short time.

Exaggeration is stronger, and therefore more destructive of sincerity, than effusiveness. The person who wrote, "Work is a pleasure when you use these precision-made tools," appears to be overstating the case to a carpenter-reader. And the writer of the following, if around to overhear, should be prepared for an unrestrained, emphatic *"Bull!"* when a retailer-customer opens the letter and reads:

```
New customers, happy and eager to buy, will surely applaud
your recent selection of 4 dozen Tropical Holiday shorts
for women.
```

```
Especially made for the humidity of Macon, these garments will
lead girls and women for miles around to tell their friends
that "Thompson's has them!"
```

Superlatives and other forms of strong wording are among the most frequent reasons why so many letters sound exaggerated, unbelievable, and therefore insincere. The trite "more than glad" is nearly always an insincere attempt to exaggerate a simple "glad." And "more than happy," if translated literally, could mean only slaphappy. The classic illustration is the misguided "What could be finer than . . . ?" Any reader can and usually does supply at least one quick answer of something which seems finer than the product or service mentioned.

Exaggerated wording is nearly always challenging. Few things are actually *amazing, sensational, revolutionary, ideal, best, finest,* or *perfect.* Simple, accurate, specific statements of quality and value not only avoid the impression of insincerity; they are often more forceful than the general superlatives made nearly meaningless by years of misuse. If you describe products or services in terms like the following, you are inviting negative responses toward yourself and your firm:

```
Want Amazing Protection
That Can Never Be Canceled?
```

```
Here is a really magnificent opportunity.  Imagine a health
and accident policy that can never be canceled.
```

```
--
```

```
This new mower is revolutionary in build, style, performance,
and customer appeal.  Amazing, of course!  Here is your golden
opportunity!  A sensational solution to your spring sales
problems!
```

Whether the reader or hearer of such statements feels irritation or disgust is relatively immaterial. What counts is the disbelief aroused. Confidence in the writer or speaker and the house, and therefore goodwill, take a sharp downturn.

Undue familiarity also causes people to lose favor. Sometimes it crops out merely because the writer or speaker is uncouth. The reader or hearer may feel sympathy for the person who does not know how to act with people—but will not likely have the disposition to return for more uncouthness.

Undue familiarity results from (1) calling the reader by name too frequently or writing or speaking in too informal language to a stranger and (2) making references to subjects which are entirely too personal for business discussions. For an obvious purpose the writer or speaker pretends a closeness of friendship or an overweening interest which does not exist. It is characteristic of the high-pressure (and maybe not-quite-honest) salesperson. Like other forms of pretense, it brings resentment. In the following letter giving information on home insulation to a college professor, the jocularity doesn't just fall flat; it boomerangs!

> Just set the thermostat and relax. That's all you have to do, Professor Eckberg. Pick up your book and settle down in a cozy chair. The Mrs. won't be continually warning you to get your old sweater, or nagging you to keep turning up the thermostat, or to put another blanket on the cherubs.
>
> Yes, Professor Eckberg, Isotemp will guard over your household. Take a gander at the statistical table in the folder, <u>Modern Insulation for Older Homes.</u> This table shows that out of every 8,000 cases of respiratory diseases, 6,536 occurred in uninsulated homes—over 75 percent from the very type of home you're now living in!
>
> Didn't you say you spent over $600 for fuel last year, Professor Eckberg? That's a lot of money out of a professor's salary; and as you said, "Even then the place wasn't always warm."
>
> If you fill in and return the enclosed card, we will send Mr. Don Diller, our Milwaukee representative, to answer any of your questions. Incidentally, Professor Eckberg, Mr. Diller is a graduate of the University of Wisconsin with a degree in heating engineering. He may be the guy who slept through half your classes six years ago, but somewhere he learned how to make your home more comfortable and reduce those high fuel bills. Then the Mrs. can buy that fur coat she's been nagging you about for when she goes outside, where it <u>is</u> cold!

Such diction as *cherubs, gander,* and *nagging* might be all right in breezy conversation with an old friend and perhaps in a letter to the old friend, but certainly not in a letter to someone the writer does not know. Using the reader's name four times in such short space furthers the impression of fawning. And the assumptions and references to family relations and activities are typical of familiarity that breeds contempt. These spring from insincerity, but they are discourteous in the truest sense and thus destructive of goodwill.

Gratitude

In business communication as in social relations with others, proper handling of deserved gratitude is a significant point in the tone of relationships. When people extend favors, they expect to receive some recognition; and everybody except the self-centered, boorish, or inept gives it. Probably because of early training, most of us have little trouble showing gratitude properly in face-to-face relations; but in business writing the what, when, and how seem to be problems for many.

To help, we offer the following suggestions:

1. When the reader has already done you a favor—
   a. Don't begin with "Thank you . . ." unless that is your most important or most likely acceptable point. Instead, go ahead with your message and
      (1) Let the overall pleasant spirit show your good feeling without wasting words saying "Thanks . . ." explicitly, or
      (2) Tuck the expression in a subordinate position and word it to give due (not overdue) emphasis.
   b. If you feel that you must begin with gratitude, be sincere (don't gush or exaggerate) and word your expression to relate naturally to what follows—perhaps as a "buffer" (explained in the next chapter).
2. When you want to show gratitude for future favors (asked for or hoped for)
   a. Don't express it in the present tense ("I appreciate") or in unqualified future indicative mood ("I will appreciate . . ."). Either way presumes that the reader will do as you ask, and you have no right to be so presumptuous.
   b. Either
      (1) Qualify the future indicative with an "iffy" or questioning request ("I shall appreciate it if you will . . ." or "Will you please . . . ?"), or
      (2) Use the future conditional ("I would appreciate your . . .").

See the Index for help on handling gratitude in special situations.

SERVICE ATTITUDE

In addition to a desirable tone as a means of maintaining goodwill, good business communicators show that their concern extends beyond making a profit or other purely selfish interests. They're like the very successful business executive who said that the difference between the average person and the exceptional person usually lies in three words—"and then some."

The top people, he said, "did what was expected of them—and then some. They met their obligations and responsibilities—and then some. They were good friends to their friends—and then some. They could be depended upon in an emergency—and then some. . . ."

A business organization obviously must make profits if it is to exist; both reader and writer accept that premise. To deny it is to fly under false colors. The answer is neither to deny nor to affirm; just don't talk about it! Instead, let your messages remind others of your thoughtfulness and genuine desire to be of service—to meet your obligations, and then some— through:

1. Resale material on the goods and/or the house.
2. Sales promotional material on other goods (in some cases).
3. Special-occasion messages.

Resale material

Often you need to assure a customer of the wisdom of an earlier choice of goods and services—or of the house (business firm) chosen to do business with—and thus stress satisfaction. In *keeping the goods sold*, resale material helps keep unfilled orders on the books, fosters repeat orders, and forestalls complaints. It is an effective device in meeting competition.

As the phrase is most frequently applied in business to goods and services, *resale* means favorable talk about something the customer has already "bought"—that is by purchase, practice, or approval, although it may not yet be delivered. Most buyers would feel better about the product upon reading the following resale idea woven into an acknowledgment of an order:

> The Henshaw electric boudoir clocks you ordered on March 1 (eight at $22) are our fastest-selling models in this price range. Because they are accurate as well as beautiful, they make excellent gifts.

One of the most prestigious restaurants in Austin, Texas, helps promote its fine dinners by sticking this little sign into the skin of each baked potato served:

> For goodness sake <u>Don't skin me</u>! I've been rubbed, tubbed, and scrubbed. I'm clean as a whistle . . . and a lot tastier. You may eat me skin and all—for I'm an Idaho Potato—baked and served the XXX way.

The woman receiving the following would most likely feel much more secure in her choice of a dress—and thus happier with the dress as well as the company that sold it to her:

> You'll stay fresh, neat, and comfortable in your 100 percent Visa polyester blue separates from Meredith Palmer.

A prosperous TV dealer promotes the main line by delivering, with each set sold, a bouquet and this note:

```
A red, red rose and congratulations . . .on your selection of
a new XXX.  Be assured it will provide the finest in beauty
and entertainment for years.  Enjoy it with pride.
```

Such material is *most effective when it is relatively short and when it is specific.* Tell a customer buying a shirt, for instance, that

```
It will launder rapidly and easily because of the no-iron
finish.
```

or

```
The seams are double-lockstitched for long life.
```

or

```
Made from long-staple California cotton, your Pallcraft shirt
will give you the wear you expect from a shirt of this quality.
```

But don't try to tell your reader *all* these points in a resale passage. And for your own greatest effectiveness as a writer, don't try just to get by with a lame generality like "Pallcraft shirts are a good buy."

Used most frequently in acknowledgments, resale material on the goods may also appear in certain credit, collection, and adjustment messages, as you'll see later.

Resale material on the house consists of pointing out customer-oriented policies, procedures, guarantees, and special services sometimes called "the little extras" (the "and then some's") a good firm (the "house") provides its customers. Resale is especially helpful in the beginning of a business relationship. But any time you add a new service, improve an old one, or expand a line is an appropriate occasion to tell customers about the firm's continued attempt to give satisfaction. You want to tell your dealers about services you render—sales assistance, advertising aids, and the like. The following excerpt from a message to a dealer is typical:

```
Along with your shipment of Lane candies are some display
cards and window stickers which you'll find valuable aids in
bringing these delicious candies to the attention of your
customers.  Our Advertising Department will regularly furnish
you with seasonal displays and will be glad to help you on any
special display problem in connection with the sale of Lane's.
```

Retail stores often write their customers about lounges, lunchrooms, and personal shoppers, to mention only a few such services. Good samples of resale on the house, from retail stores to new customers, are:

```
You are welcome to use Rosen's air-conditioned lounging and
rest rooms on the mezzanine, the fountain luncheonette on the
first floor, or the spacious parking lot right behind the
store.  It is absolutely free to customers shopping at
Rosen's, whatever the size of your purchase.
```

--

> When you cannot come to the store, call or write Lola Lane,
> our personal shopper, who will gladly do your shopping for
> you. Most of the time she can have your merchandise on the
> delivery truck or in the mail the same day she receives your
> order.

Resale passages are the writer's (or speaker's) attempts to confirm or increase the buyer's faith in goods, services, or the firm in which committed interest already exists. Sales promotion material (on new and different goods or services) seeks to promote interest in something *else* the firm can supply.

Sales promotion material

For a number of reasons, sales material about related products is desirable in some acknowledgment, credit, collection, and even adjustment messages. The most obvious business reason is that regardless of what you try to market, you must constantly seek to sell more of it to more customers all the time. In terms of communication, however, *the most significant reason is the concrete demonstration that the firm desires to be of further service.* A third function of sales promotion material is that it can end a message naturally and easily, with emphasis on further service. The following example illustrates the point:

> We shipped your carpenter's tools, as itemized on the enclosed
> invoice, by parcel post this morning; they should reach you by
> October 15. Thank you for your check, which covers all
> charges.

Resale

> The Crossman level with aluminum frame is stronger and weighs
> less than wooden ones, and it will remain bright and true.
> The tempered steel used in the Flex-Line tape is permanently
> oiled; so you can be sure it will easily and rapidly unwind
> and rewind every time you use it.

Sales promotion

> When you receive the fall and winter catalog we're sending
> separately, turn to page 126 and read the description of the
> Bradford 6½-inch electric handsaw. This is the lowest price
> at which it has ever been offered. To enjoy the savings in
> time and energy this efficient piece of equipment offers, use
> the handy order blank at the back of the catalog.

You'll need to observe three precautions in the use of sales promotion material:

1. Above all, it should reflect *the desire to be of service* rather than the desire to sell more goods. It is low-pressure sales effort, comparable to the way a salesclerk, after selling a woman a pair of shoes, may casually pick up a matching or complementary purse and say, "Perhaps you'd like to examine this purse, which goes with your shoes so well." Only after the customer displays an interest in the suggested item does the salesclerk be-

gin a real sales talk. If another sale results, that's good. But if not, it's still good: most customers are pleased because of the demonstrated interest in their welfare or happiness.

If, however, the insatiable sales appetite of "I want to sell you more" shows through selfish, greedy terminology, you neither promote sales nor please the customer. When emphasis is on *what we want* rather than *what you get*, the effect is unfavorable, maybe even repellent. When emphasis is on *order* instead of *service*, Greedy Gus overtones are almost inevitable:

Greedy Gus original

```
We also sell attractive summer
purses, silk and nylon hosiery,
and costume jewelry to complete
your excellent line of goods.
We are sending you our catalog.
And we hope to fill many more
orders for you.
```

Service-minded revision

```
The summer purses and costume
jewelry shown on pages 29 to 32
of the accompanying catalog
have also sold well for many of
our other customers—and we
think would for you.  We'll be
glad to handle your order for
these items on the same terms
as this one.  Use the handy
order blank and reply envelope
in the back of the catalog.
```

2.   *Appropriateness* is also a factor. When a woman buys a suit, a natural item to call to her attention is a blouse; a man buying a suit may be interested in matching or blending shirts, ties, or shoes. But to tell a purchaser of heavy-duty truck tires about the good buy you now have in refrigerators or the buyer of a washing machine about your special on tires would be questionable most of the time. Such suggestions appear to be dictated by the greedy desire for further sales rather than by an eagerness to render service. Almost always, *sales promotion material should be on items related to those under consideration.*

3.   Before using sales promotion material, consider also *the kind of message* you are writing and what it is supposed to do. A message requiring further action on the reader's part needs final emphasis on that action, not on sales material. In acknowledgments, for example, you can use sales promotion material endings to good purpose when you are sending the goods as requested, but not when additional action by the customer is necessary.

Also, although you might use such material in an early collection mailing to a good customer, it is decidedly inappropriate as soon as your message shows concern over the account. And in adjustments you may safely use sales promotion material to end a full-reparation message, because you can be fairly sure the customer is going to be pleased with the results; but its use in a compromise or a refusal is usually questionable.

Both resale and sales promotion material help to sell more merchandise, but they are even more effective as goodwill builders because they imply positively and emphatically the general statement "We are eager to serve you well."

Special goodwill messages

Also, to demonstrate continuing interest in the customer and the desire to serve, special goodwill letters subtly use resale material on the goods and the house, and sales promotion material. They have often been called the "letters you don't have to write—but should." Since the customer does not expect them, since they usually bring something pleasant, and since your reader knows you do not have to write them, they are doubly welcome and thus greater builders of goodwill than some other types.

Because they are of great variety in function and occasion, and because you can write them with greater understanding and skill after studying some other kinds of business messages, however, we treat them in greater detail in Chapter 6. Suffice it to say here—before we take up some other kinds of business communications—that your study of special goodwill messages will reinforce the central theme of the preceding chapters: consideration for the other person.

(All the cases for the first four chapters are at the end of Part One because we think you should cover all four basic tests of a good business message before trying to write any kind. We urge you to read the first four chapters quickly but thoroughly so that you can put all the basic principles to use from the start.)

| # Persuasion: What the reader does

[Knowledge or skill without justice is cunning, not wisdom.]

Planned presentation
    Good-news or neutral messages
    Disappointing messages
    Persuasive messages
You-viewpoint
Adaptation
    Adapting talking points
    Adapting language and style
    Referring to common experiences
    Personalizing
Positive statement
Success consciousness

SINCE MOST business messages, unless just reporting information, try to produce an action or a reaction which may lead presently to an action, many business communicators maintain that every communication situation is a sales situation. In the broad sense that you are usually trying to persuade someone that your suggestion (whether it's a product, a service, or an idea) is a good one and/or that yours is a good firm to deal with, that's right. In other words, you're always "selling" something.

If you are going to be successful in that mission, you'll want to make conscious use of five principles of persuasion which have proved helpful in getting the desired positive response:

1. Planned presentation in the light of your objective.
2. You-viewpoint interpretation.
3. Adaptation—even personalization when possible.
4. Positive statement.
5. Success consciousness.

PLANNED PRESENTATION

You can make your job of beginning a letter, memo, or talk fairly simple if you will classify it according to one of the following three probable reactions of your readers or listeners:

1. Will they welcome it? That is, does it report information or ask action they will be glad to hear or at least not unhappy to hear? Does it take action they have requested? Does it request action they are prepared to take? (A–plan)
2. Will they be displeased with the basic message? Does it contain bad news? (B–plan)
3. Or does it request action they are probably not already willing to take? (C–plan)

According to subject matter, you can list hundreds of different kinds of business letters, memos, and talks; but for predetermining your beginning and subsequent development of points, all you need to decide upon is whether your message contains good news or neutral information (A–plan), disappointing information (B–plan), or persuasion intended to motivate the reader to action (C–plan).

Good-news or neutral messages

Most A–plan letters and memos say or imply yes, as in favorable replies to requests, acknowledgments in which you can ship goods as ordered, adjustments fully complying with the reader's request, credit approvals, and the like. Since you are doing what the reader wants you to do, *the first sentence should contain the big idea.* That is what the reader most wants to know. Then you follow up with necessary details in order of relative importance or natural sequence. Frequently messages of this kind (including oral ones) end with a short punch line recalling the benefits of the good news in the beginning, as suggested by Figure 4–1.

FIGURE 4–1   A–plan (good-news
and neutral) messages

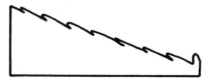

Letters, memos, and talks which merely seek or transmit business information follow the same basic order: inquiries and replies about job or credit applicants and explanations or identifications of something about an organization, its personnel, or its products. All these are neutral situations (neither very pleasing nor displeasing), readily taken for granted. The messages should therefore have the same directness and dispatch as the following "yes" letter (replacing a clock ordered for a birthday gift and damaged in transit):

> Your new Admiral desk clock, mailed by insured parcel post this morning, should be at your door about January 23.
>
> The same kind of heavy padding carefully protecting your new Admiral in the large corrugated box will be standard for all our future shipments of fragile articles so that they will arrive in the same perfect condition in which they leave the store.
>
> And now will you take a moment to assist us in recovering for the clock from the Postal Service? Just sign the enclosed notification forms and return them with the original clock. Of course we will reimburse you for returning it.
>
> The recipient of the new Admiral on January 26 will no doubt be pleased with its beauty and practicality. It is an appropriate birthday surprise.

Disappointing messages

B–plan letters, memos, and talks—those that say no or "yes, but . . ." (that is, modified refusals)—should not be direct. If you have to tell someone that you can't give the booklet requested, that you can't fill an order as specified, that you can't extend credit, or that you can't make the adjustment desired, you have a situation which is potentially goodwill-killing—especially if you blurt out the disappointing information immediately. But you can do better.

We assume throughout this book that you are a fair-minded person who does not act high-handedly or arbitrarily and that you therefore have good reasons when you refuse anything. We know, too, that in most cases you can show that some of your reasons are beneficial to the other person—as when a mother refuses her child something for the child's good as well as (sometimes even *rather than*) her own. The following psychology of refusing therefore depends on your having good reasons, as does any satisfactory refusal.

You know that when you refuse anybody anything considered due, disappointment and frustration develop unless you give justifying reasons (not just excuses or no explanation at all). You know further that if you begin with the refusal, you will at least disappoint (maybe even anger) that person. You also know that an angry person is not a logical one. So even if you did give good reasons *after* the refusal, they would fall on an illogical mind, where they would not take effect.

But if you start pleasantly and give justifying reasons *before* a refusal, your logical reasons fall on a logical mind; and the reasons which caused you to feel justified in refusing can convince the other person that you *are* justified. Thus your reader or listener is much more likely to accept your refusal without irritation because you show the justice of it. This psychology directs you to a rather specific plan for all refusals.

To soften the effect, you try to catch favorable interest in your opening remarks with *something from the situation on which both of you can agree.* Effective business communicators use this kind of pleasant beginning (commonly called a "buffer") for two reasons: (1) to suggest that they are reasonable persons who can see two sides of the question, and (2) to set the stage for a review of the facts in the case. A good buffer will therefore be

—Pleasant, usually agreeing with something the other person has said.

—Relevant, thus quickly showing the subject.

—Equivocal, avoiding any implication that the answer is yes or no.

—Transitional, carefully worded for a natural movement into the explanation.

This word of caution about buffers is due, we feel: In being pleasant and agreeable, be careful about the third point and do *not* say something that misleads the reader into feeling that something you say later is contradictory. Research done by Dr. Kitty Locker shows that a buffer inconsistent with later statements loses its effectiveness.

After you establish compatibility, you analyze the circumstances sympathetically and understandingly, giving the reasons why you can't do what the other person wants you to do. Not until you have tactfully prepared the way with these justifying reasons do you want to reveal the disappointing news. You further attempt to soften the blow by such subordinating means as embedding the refusal, giving it minimum space or time, and positive statement when you have to state it; but better, when possible, you may be able to make the refusal clear by implication. Certainly you do not want to stress it.

Nor do you want to end on a note of disappointment. To close, select some point of favorable interest which demonstrates your desire to retain the friend and/or customer relationship.

Graphically, your procedure looks like the line in Figure 4–2. The following positive refusal illustrates the strategy:

```
Your comments, Professor McGinnis, on the effectiveness of the
"More Business" series are helpful to those of us at Read's
who worked on these practical guides for users of direct mail.

When we first planned the booklets for our customers, we had
in mind a checklist for a business using direct mail
extensively rather than a thoroughgoing treatment suitable for
a textbook.  Accordingly, we set our quota for noncommercial
users at a low figure—partly because we did not expect
many requests.
```

FIGURE 4–2   B–plan (disappointing) messages

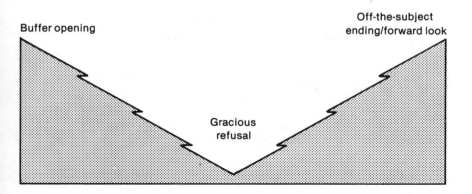

Since the series has proved so popular with our customers, we
have for over a month been distributing copies only to
commercial users, although we are glad to make available what
we can to training institutions.

Perhaps you may be able to use the extra copy—sent to you
this morning by parcel post—as a circulating library for your
students. Two or three days' use should be ample for most of
them, and they're perfectly welcome to copy anything they
care to.

Will you give us the benefit of your suggestions for making
the series more extensive after you have had an opportunity to
test its teachability more thoroughly?

Persuasive messages

For the third basic kind of situation, the C–plan, starting need not be
difficult if you will make your most honest and concrete attempt to figure
out something you can offer that the reader or listener wants, needs, or
at least is interested in. Preferably it will be a promised or implied benefit,
thus catching attentive interest from the start. You then develop your
message in concrete pictures of that benefit.

When you have developed the benefits available for complying with
your suggestion and have supplied enough evidence for conviction, you are
in a psychological position to ask for the action you want. If you can start
off in interested agreement and maintain this agreement as you explain the
worth (and benefits) of your proposition, you can wind up getting the
action you want. Figure 4–3 illustrates the plan.

Prospecting (cold-turkey) sales and application letters, executive memos
calling for improved operations, persuasive requests, and some collections
follow this pattern, as in the following persuasive request for a confidential
manual:

FIGURE 4–3 C–plan (persuasive) messages

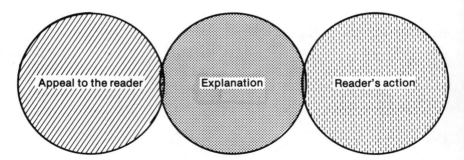

How often have you received—even from well-educated people—
letters that are not worth your attention?

As a public relations director and an employer, you are of
course interested in this problem. And I, as a teacher of
business communication, am too. Here at Harwood we're turning
out a thousand students each year who are better trained in
writing effective letters and memos than the usual college
graduate. We'd like to be sure that we're giving them what
business wants.

It's quite likely, you know, that some of these students will
some day be writing for companies like yours. Wouldn't they
be better prepared if we instructors could stress the ideas
that you have emphasized in your recent correspondence manual?
Both the students and business firms would benefit from your
letting us have a copy for our teaching files. Of course,
we'd handle the material with whatever confidence you specify.
And we'd be most grateful for this practical teaching aid.

But the ones especially benefiting from your sending a copy
would be the students and business firms like GE.

Will you send us a copy today?

The planned steps in all selling are here. Whether you want to call them
four steps (Attention, Interest, Conviction, and Action; or Promise, Picture, Prove, and Push) or three steps (Attentive Interest, Conviction or
Evidence, and Action) or more doesn't matter. But it does matter that you
get attentive interest quickly by promising a benefit, give evidence backing up that promised benefit, forestall or minimize any objections you can
foresee, and confidently ask for the action you want.

YOU-VIEWPOINT

[People wrapped up in themselves are usually small packages.]

The you-viewpoint or you-attitude is a state of mind: always ferreting
out and emphasizing the benefits to the other person resulting from your
suggestion or decision and subordinating or eliminating (***but not denying***)
your own.

Of course, it isn't pure unselfishness. When you try to sell something,
obviously you are trying to make some money; but you don't need to put

that idea into words. When you attempt to collect, obviously you want—maybe even need—the money; you don't need to put that idea into words. When you apply for a job, obviously you either want or need work to earn some money; you don't need to put that idea into words. Both parties involved *assume* all these ideas. Putting them into words merely sounds selfish, wastes words, and helps your cause not one bit.

Nor is the you-attitude a question merely of politeness, courtesy, or good manners. The hard business reason for you-viewpoint presentation is that when you show you are aware of and are doing something about another person's needs or problems, your suggestion will get a more favorable reaction. In other words, you can get the action you want if—and only if—you show benefits worth the cost and trouble.

So in C–plan messages (asking for action the other person is not already motivated to take) you show by central theme and wording that you are thinking of what you can offer in return.

The you-viewpoint requires imagination, certainly. The old story of the village half-wit's answer to how he found the mule is apt ("Why, I just thought, 'If I was a mule, where would I go?' "). The ability to visualize someone else's desires, circumstances, and probable reactions and write or speak in those terms is the answer. It requires that you be able to play many roles. When you communicate to secretaries, you *are* a secretary; to doctors, you *are* a doctor; to merchants, you *are* a merchant—and you try to see things through *their* eyes. Without this basic outlook and attitude, you-viewpoint presentation will be superficial.

Phrasing helps, it is true. You are more likely to communicate in terms of another person if you use more *you's* and *your's* than the first-person pronouns *I, me, mine, we, us, our.* But if you apply that test alone, the sentence "We want your check" has more you-viewpoint than "We want our check," when obviously neither has any. The other-dominated sentence might well read, "To keep your account in the preferred-customer class, please send your check for $142.63 today," or "Get your account in shape for the heavy Christmas buying coming up by sending your check for $142.63 today." Whether you say "sending *us* your check" or not is immaterial, except that it wastes a word; the *us* is clearly understood. But what is a much more significant point is that the *you*-viewpoint is there.

We-viewpoint	*You-viewpoint*
We are shipping your order of June 2 this afternoon.	You should receive the Jurgin crosscut saw you ordered June 2 no later than Saturday, June 7.
We have spent 27 years making the Jurgin a fast-selling saw.	Back of your Jurgin blade are 27 years of successful testing and remodeling. Because it is taper-ground alloy steel, it slides through the wood more freely than other models.

Making your reader or listener the subject or object of most sentences will help you keep you-viewpoint interpretation too. As you've already seen in the discussion of writing interestingly (p. 133), psychological description and dramatized copy are effective because they keep the reader involved and show that you have the you-viewpoint. The only way to get it in the first place, however, is to subordinate your own reactions to those you estimate are the other person's and then to show that attitude clearly by your wording.

An example of well-intentioned writing that is fundamentally writer-dominated is the conventional thank-you beginning: "Thank you for your order of June 2 for one Jurgin crosscut saw blade" and "We are grateful for. . . ." Even worse is the selfish "We are glad to have your order for. . . ." All three variations have this strike against them: They emphasize the personal reaction of the writer rather than something the reader is interested in knowing. The same is true of the common, and weak, speech openings "I'm glad to be here . . ." and "Thank you for. . . ."

If you can (or will) make shipment, an opening like the following has more you-viewpoint than any of the foregoing because it is something your reader wants to know:

> Your Jurgin crosscut saw blade should arrive by prepaid
> UPS no later than Friday, June 7.

If you can't make shipment, a resale comment is a better example of you-viewpoint than the selfish statement of pleasure upon the receipt of another order or a disappointing statement about not now getting the ordered goods. If you have to delay shipment only a few days, this is a possibility for retaining positiveness and you-viewpoint:

> The Jurgin crosscut saw blade you ordered will give you long
> and faithful service.

When the reader has done you a favor and your main message is appreciation, some form of thank you may be one of the best beginnings you could use. In other situations, in place of the conventional "Dear Mr. Miller," the salutation "Thank you, Mr. Miller!" has directness and enthusiasm which are heartwarming. The first paragraph may then concentrate on a more significant point:

> Those articles about palletization which you suggested contain
> some of the best information I've been able to uncover.

But doesn't the statement of the significance you attach to your reader's contribution adequately establish your appreciation, without wasting words with "Thank you"?

We do not mean to imply that an expression of gratitude is out of place (see p. 71). No one ever offended with a genuine, appropriate thank you. But we do want to stress that you can accomplish the same function with some statement which will place more emphasis on your reader—where it should be!

The preceding remarks concerning planned presentation and you-viewpoint apply whether you're writing a memorandum, a speech, or a special or form letter—a sales, credit, collection, application, or simple reply. The closer you can come to making your reader or listener nod in agreement and think "That's what I want to hear," the greater your possibilities for a favorable reception.

ADAPTATION

When you can make the other person also think "That sure fits me," you have an additional advantage. Successful adaptation gives the feeling that you had the one person specifically in mind.

Even in addressing a large number of people, you will have identifiable common characteristics (of geography, age, educational level, vocation, or income status, for example) that will enable you to adapt your persuasion points, language, and style and to make references to circumstances and events recognized as common to each member of the group.

Adapting talking points

In adapting talking points (or theme), you simply seek out and emphasize those reasons you believe will be most influential in causing the action or reaction you want. Specifically, you would try to sell a typewriter to a secretary on the basis of ease of operation, to an office manager on ease of maintenance and durability, but to a purchasing agent on the basis of long-range cost. The lawn mower which you would sell to a homeowner because of its ease of handling and maintenance, you would sell to a hardware dealer because of its salability and profit margin. A car may appeal to one person on the basis of economy, power, or dependability of operation; to another the appeals of appearance and comfort may be stronger.

Accordingly, you adapt your talking points for increased persuasiveness. This is a fairly simple procedure when you are dealing with one person and is entirely possible in a group if you study the characteristics common to all people involved.

Adapting language and style

You adapt language and style, in general, in the light of the other person's age, educational level, and vocation (which influence social and economic position). As years, education, professional and social prestige, and financial status increase, you are safer in using longer sentences, uncommon words, and more formal language. Sometimes you will want to use the specialized terms of vocational classes such as doctors, lawyers, and insurance people. Although some of these terms are more technical than you would use for a general audience, to specialists they convey the impression that you understand their special problems. The application of this suggestion means that when you write or talk to doctors, references to patients, laboratories, diagnoses, and the like help; to a person in insurance, prospects, premiums, and expirations are likely referents.

Referring to common experiences

Better adaptation than language and style, however, are references to common experiences. A reference to vocation, to a geographical factor, to some home and family status—in fact, to any activity or reaction you can be reasonably sure your readers or listeners have experienced—rings the bell of recognition and makes them feel that very definitely you are talking to them and about their conditions.

In a letter to college students, for instance, the following reference would almost universally bring positive (and in most cases humorous) recognition:

```
When your teacher talks on . . . and on . . . and on . . .
(even when it's two minutes past the bell!). . . .
```

To parents:

```
When your child yawns, turns over, and finally goes to sleep.
```

To school superintendents:

```
. . . to reduce the necessary and healthy noise of active
adolescents when they're changing classes.
```

To anyone who is or has been a secretary:

```
An hour's transcription to get in the night's mail—and at
five minutes to 5:00!
```

Any of the preceding phrases could go into a mass form or an individualized message. The more specifically you can phrase these references to make them pinpoint one person, however, the more effective your adaptation will be.

Personalizing

To further the impression that the message has been prepared for the individual and to heighten the feeling of friendliness, business communicators sometimes use names or other references so specific as to be individualizing in a few of the sentences. At about the middle, much as you use a friend's name in conversation—or near the end in the same way you frequently use a person's name in ending a conversation—such references as the following help to give the impression that your message is for one person rather than a group:

```
You'll also appreciate the lightness of the Multimower,
Mr. Bowen.

              --

Your Atlanta Luminall dealer will be glad to call on you and
answer any other questions you may have, Mr. Bowen.
```

In individually typed messages the placement of the name presents no problem; in forms, try to put the name at the end of a line (as in the preceding examples) so that typing in the reader's name is easy, regardless of length.

Lest we overemphasize the effectiveness of this name-calling, we point out these shortcomings and dangers:

1. It is a somewhat mechanical process and probably the least effective means of adapting.
2. In typing in names on forms, you may do more harm than good unless you match type perfectly. Of course if you can afford a word-processing machine, it can do the job.
3. And, as you saw on p. 70, using a person's name too frequently (as many computerized letters do) may do more harm than good by seeming unctuous and fawning.

You can also increase the feeling of friendliness in letters by the wording of your salutation and complimentary close. *Dear Sir* and *Very truly yours*, although appropriate many times, are somewhat formal (if not obsolescent) and do not reflect the warmth of *Dear Mr. Bowen* and *Sincerely yours* or some other less formal phrasing. The main forms and their order of formality appear in detail on page 16.

Of far greater significance are adaptation of talking points and lifelike references to the reader's activities. The following letter answers the lady's questions in a sound sales presentation and enhances the persuasiveness of the message with special references (such as to the housekeeper and the power failure mentioned in her inquiry) that could apply to no one but the reader:

```
Dear Mrs. Jackson:

The Stair-Traveler you saw in the June Home and Yard will
certainly make daily living easier for you and your faithful
old housekeeper.  You can make as many trips upstairs and
downstairs as you care to every day and still follow your
doctor's advice.

Simply sit down on the bench (about the same size as a
dressing-table stool) and press the button.  Gently and
smoothly your Stair-Traveler takes you upstairs at a rate just
a little faster than ordinary walking.  Should the electricity
fail in Greenbriar while you're using your Stair-Traveler,
```

automatic brakes bring it to a gentle stop and hold it in
place until the current comes on. Then you just press the
button to start it again.
Folded back against the wall when not in use, the Stair-
Traveler's simple, straight lines of mahogany will blend in
well with your antiques. Your Stair-Traveler will be right at
home on your front straight stairway, Mrs. Jackson. It will
be more convenient for you there, and the installation is
simple and economical. Notice the folded Stair-Traveler on
page 3 of the booklet I'm sending; it looks somewhat like a
console table.
To explain how simple and economical installing your Stair-
Traveler can be, Mr. J. B. Nickle, our Memphis representative,
will be glad to call at a time convenient for you. Will you
use the enclosed postcard to let him know when that will be?

Such specialized references do increase costs when they mean writing
an individualized message rather than using a form. But many times you
must if you are to get the job done. Even in form paragraphs and entire
form letters, however, you usually can make some adaptation to the reader's
situation.

You can find out a great deal about your reader through letters to you,
your credit records (including credit reports), sales representatives' reports, and the like. Even a bought or rented mailing list contains the names
of people with some common characteristics of vocation, location, age,
sex, finances, and buying and living habits. You won't make your message
do all it could do if you don't use your knowledge of these common characteristics to adapt it according to talking points and endow it with the
marginal pulling power of known references to familiar events, activities,
places, or persons.

POSITIVE STATEMENT

Your letters, memos, and oral communications have greater prospects
for success if you focus on positive ideas because people—most of them,
at any rate—respond more favorably to a positive prospect than to a negative one.

Saying the cheerful, positive thing that people want to hear rather than
the unpleasant or unhappy, negative thing they do not want to hear is
really just an extension of you-viewpoint presentation and tact. It comes
from staying optimistic yourself and superimposing a positive picture on a
negative one, thus completely eliminating, or at least subordinating, the
negative idea. Translated into business communication procedures, it is the
result of stressing what something is rather than what it is not, emphasizing
what the firm or product can and will do rather than what it cannot, leading
with action rather than apology or explanation, and avoiding words that
convey basically unpleasant ideas.

Test after test of both advertising copy and letter copy has demonstrated the wisdom of positive statement. That is why nearly 60 years ago successful copywriters warned against the denied negative (and today's writers still issue the same warning). That is why the effective writer or speaker will make the following positive statements rather than their negative counterparts:

Negative	*Positive*
Penquot sheets are not the skimpy, loosely woven sheets ordinarily in this price class.	Penquot sheets are woven 186 threads to the square inch for durability and, even after 3-inch hems, measure a generous 84 by 108 inches.
We are sorry that we cannot furnish the club chairs by August 16.	After checking with the Production Department, we can definitely assure you your club chairs by August 29.
We cannot ship in lots of less than 12.	To keep down packaging costs and to help customers save on shipping costs, we ship in lots of 12 or more.
I have no experience other than clerking in my father's grocery store.	Clerking in my father's grocery store for three summers taught me the value of serving people courteously and promptly.

A special form of negativism is the challenging question which invites a negative answer. Although it contains no negative wording, "What could be finer than an XYZ dishwasher?" will elicit, among other answers, "A full-time maid!" Such questions, along with the apparently harmless "Why not try a Blank product?" get people out of step with you and, because they invite a negative response, are deterrents to the success of your suggestion.

Keeping your messages positive also means deliberately excluding negative words. You can't be "sorry" about something without recalling the initial unhappy experience. You can't say "unfortunately" without restating some gloomy aspect of a situation. Nor can you mention "delay," "broken," "damages," "unable to," "cannot," "inconvenience," "difficulty," "disappointment," and other negatives without stressing some element of the situation which makes people react against you rather than with you. Even a *however*, after you've been talking pleasant things, will surely give a kind of sinking feeling.

For all these reasons the effective advertiser will say "ABC Dog Biscuits will help keep your dog healthy" instead of "ABC Dog Biscuits will help keep your dog from getting sick." It's just a question of accentuating the positive, eliminating the negative where possible, and otherwise subordinating it (see **Emp** and **Neg** in Appendix B).

SUCCESS CONSCIOUSNESS

Success consciousness is the confident attitude that your reader or listener will do what you ask or accept the decision you present. To reflect this attitude, guard against any phrasing which suggests that you may not get the action you want.

Success consciousness is your own conviction that your explanation is adequate, your suggestion legitimate and valuable, and your decision the result of adequate evidence and logical, businesslike reasoning. Thus assured yourself, you are not likely to say something which suggests or even implies that you are unsure of your ground. The sales writer who says

```
If you'd like to take advantage of this timesaving piece of
equipment, put your check and completed order blank in the
enclosed envelope and drop it in the mail today. . . .
```

would be better off not to remind the reader of the option to reject the proposal. Simply omitting the phrase *if you'd like* establishes a tone of greater confidence. The one word *if* is the most frequent destroyer of success consciousness.

Likewise, when tempted to say

```
Why not try a sample order?
```

you should remember that the suggestion is stronger with the elimination of *why not*. It has not only the disadvantage of suggesting that you are not sure but also the distinct disadvantage of inviting consideration of reasons for not doing what you want. A little mental effort will probably produce several reasons.

Hope and its synonym *trust* are second only to *if* as destroyers of success consciousness. In proposing an adjustment, the sentence

```
We hope you'll approve of our decision.
```

gains success consciousness (and thus better response) when reworded:

```
With this extension of your subscription to Vacation you can
continue to read each month about the world's most interesting
places.
```

By assumption (implication)—by definitely omitting the doubtful-sounding expression—the adjuster seems to say, "Of course, you and I realize that this is what you want."

In refusals something like the following sentence sometimes appears in an otherwise well-written message:

```
We trust you will understand our position.
```

Usually, however, it appears in a poor one. And it is most frequently the result of inadequate explanation. The writer seems to despair of giving an adequate explanation and to hope that the reader will figure out one. If you find yourself feeling that way, go back and see whether your explanation is ample. If it is, omit such a sentence; if it is not, revise your explanation so that it is convincing—and substitute some positive, confident statement for the weak-kneed expression.

Even in simple replies the problem arises with such a sentence as

`We hope this is the information you wanted.`

The implications of doubt disappear quickly and easily with

`We're glad to send you this information.`

This principle of success consciousness applies in all types of business writing and speaking, but it is most significant in sales situations—and especially in the action ending.

A word of caution against high-pressure presumptuousness is in order here, however. To omit a reference to an alternative is one thing; to imply that no alternative exists is quite another! The job applicant who so boldly and confidently asks

<u>`When`</u>` may I come in to see you?`

gives the impression that the prospective employer has no alternative but to set up an interview. Such presumptuousness may irritate—at a critical time. Rephrased like the following, a request for an interview would strike most people favorably:

`Will you give me a convenient time when I may come in and tell`
`you more about why I believe I am the aggressive sales`
`representative you're looking for?`

The proper degree of success consciousness requires careful wording, particularly at the end. Basically, you need to consider what your purpose is.

Sometimes you want someone to take no overt action on the topic—as in most B–plan messages and some A–plans. In that case you may end with a pleasant comment or further support for something said earlier (thanks or resale, for example), with an off-the-subject comment (usually a pleasant look to the future, perhaps sales promotion material), or with something else pleasant. Certainly you want to avoid suggesting inadequacy of treatment and such jargon as "Please do not hesitate . . ." or "Feel free to. . . ." And in B–plan messages guard particularly against referring back to the trouble you've supposedly cleared up.

At other times you are asking for action that is simple, éasy, and likely —as in most A–plan messages (no strong reader resistance). Here a subtle reference to or suggestion of that action is most appropriate:

`I shall appreciate your answers to. . . .`
`You are cordially invited to. . . .`
`When you send in your check for the $27.50 now due,`
`please. . . .`

In C–plan letters, memos, and talks you are asking for action the reader or listener may be at first reluctant to take. The force of your push for action —to overcome resistance—must therefore continue to the end. Here particularly, such words as *if*, *trust*, and *hope* will show a lack of success consciousness that will be self-defeating.

As you see, each of the three situations requires an ending quite different from what is appropriate for the others. You will do well, therefore, to keep in mind the principle of success consciousness as you study the discussions, illustrations, and checklists for different classes of business messages throughout this book.

One important general point deserves your attention here, however: Even though the earlier part of the letter, memo, or talk may have indicated a desired action, you need to refer to, suggest, ask for, or push for that action *at the end*.

Applications of
Part One principles

1. As an *Appearance Practice Exercise*, set up one of the following letters in acceptable format as directed by your instructor:

a. *Letterhead: Tempo,* 1234 Rockefeller Center, New York, N.Y. 10032. *Inside address:* Marion Baker, 874 Walnut Grove, Grand Rapids, MI 49507. *Signature block:* David J. Cook, Circulation Credit Manager. *Body:* If the attached bill for your past year's reading of *Tempo,* the magazine that makes news clear and exciting at the same time, were just a little individual matter betwen the two of us, I certainly wouldn't mention it, any more than I'd make an issue of who would take the check if you and I were eating together.

But if 5,000 people and I happened to fall in together for a meal, I couldn't very well take all the checks . . . any more than you could.

Tempo's subscriptions are like that. Somebody has to take the numerous checks. Since it was, after all, a dutch-treat arrangement, I know you won't mind my reminding you of the original agreement: we furnish the magazine—each person at the feast picks up a check. Here's yours.

Use the handy return envelope today, please.

b. *Letterhead:* Lyon's Building Supplies, Berry Road, Olathe, Kansas 66061. *Inside address:* George P. White, Chattahoochee Brick Company, Atlanta, GA 30305. *Signature block:* Sincerely yours, Joseph Morrison Young, President. *Subject:* Requested confidential information about Paul Rhodes. *Body:* Since Rhodes came here as an accountant and assistant business manager 18 months ago, he has advanced until he is now plant manager. Paul is a hard worker and very eager to succeed in everything he attempts. Sometimes he drives himself into a tense condition, but he always seems to thrive on the challenge his job offers him, and I am sure that in a larger plant like Chattahoochee he would be confronted with enough challenge to satisfy him. Also Paul and his wife want to live in a larger city where they can enjoy all the cultural opportunities a city has to offer. Although at Lyon's Paul has no opportunity to sell, saleswork probably wouldn't be hard for him because he does enjoy people, is impressive looking, and is persistent. All of our employees like Paul—even our truck drivers, for whom he has to plan very strict budgets. In many ways I would hate to lose Paul, but I know he wants larger horizons.

    c. No letterhead, but instead use a *heading* that includes the sender's address (606 Queens Road, Indianapolis, IN 46220) and the current date. *Inside address:* Mr. Andrew Blackweld, Teacher of Vocational Agriculture, Newberry High School, Newberry, Indiana 44714. *Signature block:* Sincerely, Joseph M. Knight. *Body:* Are you finding it is hard to get enough money to operate your land laboratories effectively? Even with the high cost of agricultural products and the country's constant requests for explanations, many agricultural teachers feel that their school boards do not allocate enough funds to operate their labs. I feel that most board members simply do not know very accurately either the costs of operating a good school lab for vocational agriculture or the educational values that can come from one. By answering the enclosed short questionnaire, and having your students do the same, you may help me relieve this problem. The questionnaires will help me to write a better report to the county school board concerning the value of land laboratories relative to their cost. Only I will see the returned questionnaires. You can be certain that what you say will be held in the strictest of confidence. But, if you have no objections, I would like to be able to quote you. Please answer the questionnaire and add any other thoughts you may have. When finished, just put them in the enclosed stamped envelope and drop it in the mailbox. You will be doing yourself, your fellow teachers, and your students a great service. Since the final report is due the last week of May, the information would be most helpful if you would return it by May 12.

    d. Letterhead: Florida Farm Bureau Insurance Companies, Post Office Box 730, Gainesville, FL 32601. Use current date. *Inside address:* Dr. Paul R. Gregory, 1125 Northwest 61st Place, Gainesville, FL 32603. *Signature block:* Sincerely yours, Harold McCallister, Vice President. *Body:* Your Better Letters course was excellent. Just how much practical application is being used by our graduates remains to be seen. At your convenience, please review the enclosed letters. We would appreciate your evaluation of them, and your comments on improvement, or the lack of it.

    e. Letterhead: University of Washington, Seattle, WA 98195. August 18, 19—. *Inside address:* Dr. Paul R. Gregory, 1125 Northwest 61st Place, Gainesville, FL 32603. *Signature block:* Cordially yours, Bertha P. Mullins. *Body:* Probably you're wondering why you're hearing from me today during your summer vacation. The main reason is that I respect your good judgment—and will appreciate a bit of information from you. Do you recall that in our brief chat at the American Business Communication Association Convention in Philadelphia you mentioned that your graduate students, in comparing business communications textbooks, had narrowed the field down to two—yours and ours? You added that they had some likes and dislikes about both books. Ever since then my curiosity has been tormenting me. The questionnaire responses I have received so far are gentle and mainly complimentary, though they do reveal some helpful suggestions. Above them all, I'd value *your* comments. Will you be good enough to jot down—*in general*—what your students (and you too if you wish) consider the strong and weak parts of our book? Because I'll make a major decision about the second edition in a few days, I'll be most grateful for your reply this week. The enclosed airmail envelope will help speed your reply. I look forward to seeing you in Houston in December, and hope to find a way to show you how much I appreciate your good deed. In the meantime, have a happy summer and autumn.

2. Correct the obvious violations of good usage and form. *Letterhead:* Green Light Hospital Service, 301 Troy Drive, Madison, WI 53701. *Inside address:* Mr. and Mrs. Troy Adams, Rt. 4, Box 241, Madison 53704. *Signature block:* Sincerely yours, Herman Alston, Executive Director. *Body:* Congradulations! Green Light Hospital Service are glad to share in the program of welcomeing the new air. So that you will know the exact hospital service benifits that were provided we are furnishing a copy of the hospitals bill.

Naturally youll want your baby to have Green Light insurance service too, so please dont overlook the necessity of filling in the supplimental application and sending it to us right away. As soon as the application is recorded in this office benefits will be available to your baby as explained in the notation at the bottom of the application.

Constructive criticism and helpful suggestions from our members has been an invaluable aide in the constant advancement of our program. Your Green LIGHT is eager for your comments on the services and charges which may be made on the enclosed form and returned with the supplimental application for including the baby in insurance. Use the convient return self addressed envelop.

3. Select the better in each pair and tell why:

(1)   *a.*   I only wish we could send your entire order to you right now, but we are out of stock of C8245 curtains. They should be here in a few days.

       b.   You should have your C8245 curtains in about ten days since our supplier just promised us a new shipment by then.

(2)   *a.*   Because the top-rated Penncrest iron has the self-cleaning feature, we are now stocking it exclusively.

    b. We regret that we do not carry the Beach Hamilton iron. We do have the Penncrest which has a true self-cleaning feature.

(3) *a.* Your casters for your bed are on their way by UPS.

    b. We are indeed sorry that we failed to send the casters for your bed with your shipment. They were mailed UPS this morning.

(4) *a.* Your order mentioned below could not be shipped because we did not have sufficient or correct information.

    b. So that we can make immediate shipment, please fill in the enclosed card telling us where you wish your gift of Waynecross stationery sent.

(5) *a.* For trays measuring 12″ × 18″, we suggest you write Montgomery Speciality Shop, 1190 Greenview Road, Canoga Park, California 91503, and ask for extra-strong hangers.

    b. We regret to advise the fact that we do not make the large tray holders anymore. Try Montgomery Speciality Shop in Canoga Park, California.

(6) *a.* Please be good enough to fill in the information requested on the enclosed forms. We can't help you recover for damages you claim you received as a result of an accident dated June 10 because you failed to give the necessary information.

    b. Please fill in the information requested on the enclosed forms, so that we can help you recover on your insurance for the accident June 10.

(7) *a.* Robinson's Department Store, 900 Congress, Austin, Texas 78781, is your nearest retail outlet for SWISSEWN BEDSPREADS.

    b. Thank you for your recent inquiry about Swissewn Bedspreads. We do not sell directly at retail, so would like to refer you to the store in your city, or nearest you, listed below.

4. Rewrite.

    a. I am disturbed by the prolonged delay in receiving the special equipment ordered from your fine, big firm five months ago. Since costly penalties will be assessed against us if construction is not completed on time, I should like to have you investigate the details surrounding our urgently needed order and let me have your personal determination of its status.

    b. Thank you for your order of September 16. As you may know, our production workers have been on strike for the past five weeks and we only resumed production yesterday. For this reason, we anticipate a delay of approximately three weeks in filling your order. We regret that we are not able to provide our customary prompt service at this time and hope that the delay will not inconvenience you.

c. Upon receipt of our order October the tenth via Blue and Gray Line, there was no external evidence of any damage. However, when the box was opened, it was found that a number of pieces were broken. It is our opinion that the breakage was caused by improper packing by the manufacturer. By cannibalizing the sets in which breakage occurred, we were able to assemble 19 complete sets. Enclosed you will find a list of the pieces necessary to complete the remaining sets. Ship the pieces necessary to complete our order as soon as possible. We will hold the broken pieces until we receive further instructions from you.

5. Rewrite.

a. Ref. the return of the Rustrak recorder and motors.

The error of the motors was ours. Credit will be issued for the incorrect motor. We will ship the correct 12VDC motors shortly.

We will also issue credit for the material portion of the recorder proper. However, we cannot issue credit for the labor to calibrate this recorder. Mainly credit for $100.00 will be issued. You will be billed for $35.00.

When we ship the correct recorder, you will be billed for that recorder in total.

b. I am in receipt of your check No. 17638, in the amount of $674.00, which was presented to me today, to be used by our clients here at Sunland Training Center.

We plan to use these funds for Summertime Fun, such as camping, picnics, etc. Things that cannot be reasonably asked for in our budget. This is a welcomed donation, without it a good many clients would go without any summer fun.

We hope that you will pass the word that this generous donation is appreciated by all here at Sunland and we trust it will be possible to do the same for another year.

Thanking you with kindest regards.

c. Your delay in shipping 500 theater-type chairs promised six weeks ago under Order #9805-J has seriously impaired our performance schedule for the Civic Assembly Hall Project. Please indicate immediately when we may expect the balance of our order.

6. A week ago Dr. and Mrs. Wayne Beaver of 1008 NE 14th Avenue, Gainesville, Florida 32601, were in your interior-decorating shop (Atrium, 764 May Street, Jacksonville, Florida 32607) trying to replace some aging lamp shades. They brought along a sample. You have now received samples from the lamp manufacturers and have decided that the Beavers' was the

Toyo; and so you have ordered the two shades in that material sent directly to the Beavers from the manufacturer.

The same day, you sent in the order for the Herman Miller MAX chair the Beavers wanted. It should arrive in about four weeks. Write the Beavers for Atrium.

7. Rewrite.

a. MEMORANDUM   October 14, 197–
TO: English Faculty Members
FROM: Bankhead Kelly
English Department Faculty Members

Attached is a copy of a letter sent to the three public high schools, T. M. Sullivan Laboratory School, and the two private high schools. I am writing to ask your assistance in carrying out the program described in paragraph three. Many of you, I am sure, could and would put together a 45 minutes to an hour talk that would stimulate and challenge these bright high school English students. All I ask at this point is your tentative agreement, subject to your availability, to present one lecture-discussion as a part of the program.

Thank you,
Bankhead Kelly

b. I am in receipt of your recent letter in which you claim that you had not received a check for dividends due June 1.

We immediately asked our records division to check into this. Today we received their reply.

Attached is a photostat of the check issued June 1 showing your endorsement on the back. Please examine this photo and return it to our office with your reply.

I am enclosing a stamped, self-addressed envelope for your convenience.

8. Rewrite.

a. We are in receipt of your Proxy Card, but you failed to sign it.

In order for your Proxy to be voted, it is necessary that it be signed. Therefore, we are returning your Proxy and would appreciate if you would sign and date it and return it in the enclosed self-addressed and stamped envelope.

Thank you for your cooperation in this matter.

b. *Letterhead:* Saint John's Episcopal Church, 41 Crockett Avenue, Roanoke, Virginia 24012: *Inside Address:* Jerry Sands, Sand's Real Estate, 409 Brunswick, Roanoke 24015. *Signature Block:* Loyally, Father Raymond Bowers. *Body:* I want to take this opportunity to thank you for heading up our Every-Member Canvas this year. It was great the way you got the teams organized and furthered the spirit of working together. I feel we are off to a good start for Saint John's Episcopal Church. Our dreams of having a daycare center are now reality. I wish I could shake the hand of each person who gave his time and money to our drive.

c. We regret very much that your order No. B–42987 for special components has been delayed. A strike at the plant of one of our major suppliers halted our production for a period of three days and forced us to seek another source of supply. Your order is now in process and will be shipped to you within the next few days. We shall pay the additional costs involved in shipping your order by air express. We hope that the delay in filling your order will not seriously inconvenience you.

9. As your teacher, assume that the chairman of the nominating committee (referred to in the letter below) asked for your suggestions on revising the letter. The letter goes to all faculty members of the college. Rewrite the letter.

Dear Colleague:

As you are aware, Dean X is retiring at the end of June, having served the University as Dean of the College since 1955.

You have elected a faculty committee to serve in an advisory capacity and consult with Vice-President Y regarding the nomination of Dean X's replacement. Your committee held its first meeting with Vice-President Y on (date). It is now undertaking the task of securing nominees for this position.

You are invited to submit your suggestions to any of the members of the advisory committee whose names and campus addresses are listed below. Such suggestions should be in writing. It would be a great help to the committee if, at the time you submit names, you would also furnish any information you may have about your nominees. Additional details may be requested at a later date. Those responsible for bringing about the appointment of a new Dean are faced with a very critical question of timing. There are only a few months available. The committee, therefore, needs to have your nomination in hand by no later than the first of next month.

All concerned thank you for your cooperation in this matter.

10. Assume that you are the editor of a widely distributed free-subscription magazine put out by some branch of your state or school and that you suspect that many copies are going to people who do not really want them. Write a letter to clean up your mailing list.

Unless you provide some motivation and make the action easy, many of them will simply ignore you. You may include benefits to yourself, but emphasize benefits to your readers.

Make clear that you are not interested in cutting off anybody who really wants the magazine. Also, invite them to send you the names and addresses of people who might be interested in receiving it. Check to be sure that you have the correct names and addresses of those who do want to continue on the mailing list.

PART TWO

How to win the reader's approval and motivate action

chapter 5 | # Neutral and good-news messages

As YOU LEARNED back in Chapter 4, messages that give what the receiver wants should do so in the opening phrases. The emphasis should be on speed, specificness, completeness, and conciseness. Inquiries, favorable replies, credit approvals, and adjustment approvals are typical of A–plan, direct-style messages.

Routine claims also should be direct, since they are reports most firms welcome as means for improving service.

Similarly, in courtesy exchanges of information about job and credit applicants (where regardless of whether the information is favorable or unfavorable to the *applicant*, it *is* what the inquirer wants to know), the message should begin directly with a key point.

DIRECT INQUIRIES

Any firm that wants to stay in business welcomes inquiries about products, services, operations, and personnel. The possibility of making a sale will motivate a reply to an inquiry concerning the products or services the firm sells. An inquiry about routine operations will get a reply out of simple business friendship. Requests for information about job and credit applicants get ready answers because giving such information for business purposes is established business courtesy based on the principle of reciprocity.

In no case would the attitude toward such inquiries be negative; if it is not one of eagerness to comply, at least it is willingness. You therefore have no problem of motivating a response; your problem is making clear exactly what you want, so that the willing responder can give you the necessary information with as little expenditure of time and energy as possible. Resolve this problem by beginning directly and by being specific and concise.

About products.   Requests for catalogs, price lists, descriptive folders, and other information about products and services should be direct, specific, and brief:

```
What day in October have you decided on for the annual
R & D Plans board meeting?  I want to be sure both my
department heads will be free to attend.
Will we meet in the main conference room at headquarters as
we did last year?
```

Notice the direct question and the specific phrases "What day in October" and "in the main conference room."

The following letter to a resort hotel is another good example of desirable directness and specificness:

```
Please send me descriptive material about your accommodations,
recreational facilities, and rates.
My wife, 16-year-old daughter, and I are planning a two- or
three-weeks' stay in the South this fall and are considering
the Edgewater Gulf.
```

Without the second paragraph, the writer would get much more information than needed, and that only in general terms. With the second paragraph, however, the hotel can give the necessary basic information *and* only the special information that would be of interest to this family group.

A specific paragraph indicating special interest would help even more:

My wife and I are primarily interested in the golf facilities and in dinner dancing; our daughter insists that she be able to ride horseback every day.

Out-of-the-ordinary questions involving special conditions require detailed answers for satisfaction. Because they also require explanation before the reader can get a clear picture, they are better set out in expository paragraph form, as in the following:

SUBJECT: INQUIRY ABOUT THE $149.50 DISHWHISK

How complex—and expensive—is installation of the Dishwhisk you advertised on page 69 of the September Better Homes and Gardens?

I am attracted by your price, but can your unit be installed without carpentering or plumbing changes where the present unit is? The under-the-counter place for my dishwasher measures 25" × 27" × 34". What are the outside dimensions of the Dishwhisk? Will it fit in my space or would I have to have a carpenter make changes?

Will low water pressure reduce the cleansing effectiveness of the Dishwhisk? Because low water pressure is the rule rather than the exception in my community, this is an important consideration.

I would appreciate your answers to these questions, the name and address of a local owner of a Dishwhisk, and the name of a local dealer.

An inquiry should start with a direct question or identification of the subject *before* explanations of why you ask. A question commands more attention than a statement; the reader sees the reason for the explanation; and such an arrangement nearly always saves words.

About people. Similarly, *personnel inquiries* should begin with the key question to be answered and follow with necessary explanations and specific questions:

SUBJECT: REQUEST FOR INFORMATION ABOUT JAMES R. SULLIVAN

While Mr. Sullivan worked under you as a part-time instructor in marketing, did he show an aptitude for selling? Was he naturally friendly and able to get along with faculty and students alike?

We are considering him for the job of sales manager in the North Ohio territory. Since he listed you as a former supervisor, we would welcome your comments.

As sales manager he would have to supervise the work of two junior salesmen in this territory. We are particularly interested, therefore, in your evaluation of his leadership ability.

The job will take much time and energy and will also require
that he be away from his family a great deal. Do you think he
will do his best work under these conditions? And has he
demonstrated physical stamina and willingness, suggesting that
he can stand up under the strain of much traveling for long
periods?

We would appreciate your giving us this and any other
confidential information that will help us come to a decision
and shall be glad to help you in the same way when we can.

Direct credit applications—those where no question exists about the
desirability of the account—are just as simple and concise as other direct
inquiries. A telephone call or a direct-style letter immediately phrasing the
request and giving the necessary information is appropriate:

Will you please open a charge account in the name of

> Mr. or Mrs. J. T. Tolloway
> 76 Idlewild Drive
> Dallas, Texas 75221

We have just moved here from 27 Crescent Drive, Denver 80202.

Stores with which we have had accounts for about five years in
Denver are the White House, Foleys, J. P. Price & Co., and
the Town and Country Shop.

I am employed as a supervisor at the L. B. Price Distributing
Company where I earn $22,500 annually; Mrs. Holloway is
not employed.

The Merchants National Bank handled our checking account in
Denver. Our local bank is the First National.

Despite having given enough information of the kind usually required
as a basis for the extension or refusal of credit, the writer of the foregoing
letter need not be surprised to receive an application form. Most stores
have standard forms which they require all charge customers to fill in to
complete a contractual agreement. In fact, a telephone call or visit to the
credit department giving the same information or asking for the form might
serve the purpose just as well.

Requests from business firms of national reputation, with solid capitalization and unquestioned ratings, are also perfunctory. Information about
such firms is readily available from any number of credit sources. They
can assume acceptability of their credit; so the application for it is only by
implication. Signed by an authorized agent (usually a purchasing agent),
an order might contain no more than the following:

Please ship subject to your usual terms 6 dozen Samson 10-inch
locking plier wrenches.

If the company name might not be recognized at once, adding a note like
"We are listed in Dun & Bradstreet" or "We have done credit business
with . . ." would be proper.

Credit inquiries from one business house to another are as routine as those about products. Both should be direct, concise, and specific. And because they ask for the same kind of information over and over again (explained under "Credit Approvals," p. 135), in most instances they should be forms. The following form inquiry is typical, with a time-saving provision for putting the answer(s) on the inquiry:

```
Gentlemen:

Will you please give us the confidential information requested
below?

In applying for credit with us, the applicant gave us your
name as a reference.

We would appreciate the courtesy.  Any time we can return the
favor, please call on us.

                                        Very truly yours,




                                        Credit Manager

Applicant:  John Y. Bowen
Length of time sold on credit _____
Credit limit (if any) _____Credit terms _____
Current amount due_____Past due_____
Highest credit extended _____Most recent credit_____
Paying habits  _____
Remarks  _____
```

When, however, special circumstances arise which the form does not cover, you'll need to write a special letter. Like any direct request, it should get right down to business:

```
SUBJECT:  CREDIT INQUIRY ABOUT MR. H. F. GREEN,
          GROCER, VINITA, OKLAHOMA

Will you please send us a confidential summary of your credit
experience with Mr. Green?

Naturally we'd like to have the usual items which reveal his
buying and paying habits.

But since we learned from one of the companies here in
McAlester that Mr. Green buys a large amount of his supplies
from you and that he has given your name as a credit reference
very recently, we'd like to have your explanation of why he
did not list your firm when he applied for credit with us.

We shall appreciate your help and shall be glad to assist you
in the same way any time we can.
```

When you ask your reader to give information about people, as in inquiries about job and credit applicants, both of you face a special problem —*compliance with the libel and other laws.* You have a duty to help protect your information source as far as possible. Of course, truth is the most important protection, but truth alone is not complete protection in some states.

You can help by making the reply what lawyers call a privileged communication. You show that you have an interest to protect, and you promise to keep the information confidential.[1] As a matter of courtesy but with no legal significance, you say that the inquiry was authorized (if true). Otherwise, inquiries and replies about people are the same as those about other things.

Perhaps you noticed that the preceding examples expressed appreciation and offered to return the favor. Especially when asking people to do things without any obvious benefit to themselves, courtesy demands just that. Usually the best way is in connection with your request for specific reader action (generally the last paragraph). But don't be presumptuous or jargonistic about it by using the lazy "Thank you in advance." Instead, express it in first person, future tense—as those writers did. And if *shall* or *will* sounds too presumptuous or imperious, change to *should* or *would*. To be sure you do it properly, see "Gratitude," p. 71.

You can increase your chances of getting an answer, or a faster answer, if you can justifiably ask for it by a certain date. (People are inclined to put things off—especially if the benefit is not obvious and immediate.) Therefore you should consider justifying and end-dating:

    Because Mr. Sullivan wants our decision by the end of the
    month, we would especially appreciate your answer by the 25th.

The most important considerations to keep in mind about direct inquiries, however, are to get started in a hurry, to be as specific in your questions as you can, and to explain enough (but only enough) for your reader to answer well and easily. The accompanying Direct Inquiry Checklist of suggestions (p. 109) will help you with most of your inquiry problems, although it is not a prescription, a cover-all, or a cure-all.

None of the checklists in this book are. And they are especially *not* outlines. If you try to use the appropriate checklist as an outline, you will simply not be able to come up with a good message to handle the particular situation. Instead, use the checklists for what we designed them for. First, draft your message. *Then* use the checklist to make sure you have not neglected anything you should have done, or said something inappropriately, though we realize that not all points apply to every case.

---

[1] You go ahead and promise confidentiality despite the fact that you can't keep the information confidential under certain conditions. The Fair Credit Reporting Act (effective April, 1971) empowers the subject of such a report to see what was said to whom and by whom if the information bears on a turndown for credit, insurance, or employment.

Direct Inquiry Checklist

1. Get this message under way quickly.
   a. A subject line may help by showing the nature of the inquiry.
   b. Start the key question in the first line.
   c. Make your question(s) specific (not just "some information" but "what colors . . .").
   d. For a fast opening, imply ideas or refer to them subordinately.
      Slow, plodding:
      > Will you please give us some information about Travis Brannon? He reports that. . . .

      Fast-moving:
      > What would be your reaction if Travis Brannon, your former assistant, walked into your office trying to sell you . . . ?
   e. When you use a subject line, don't depend on it for coherence in the letter or as the antecedent for any pronoun.
2. Cover at least all the basic questions to which you want answers.
   a. Ask the minimum number of questions to get the information.
   b. Arrange questions in the most appropriate order.
   c. Provide explanations the reader needs for pointed answers.
3. Be careful about the form and wording of the questions.
   a. Ask directly for information; don't hint. "I should like to know if . . ." is wordy and slow. "What does the . . ." is faster.
   b. Word questions to get what you want—not just "yes" or "no" when you need explanation. Avoid questions phrased to suggest a certain answer, too broad questions (". . . any information you have"), and double-barreled questions (". . . whether . . . and, if so, . . . ?").
   c. If you want to run a series of questions, itemize (tabulate); but see 2c.
4. Express gratitude cordially in first person, future tense: "I would be grateful (or appreciate)" eliminates the awkwardness and wordiness of "It will be appreciated if . . ." and the presumptuousness of "Thank you in advance." If appropriate, offer to reciprocate.
5. At the end, confident and positive references to the reader's next action makes a coherent summary to the entire message, leaves your reader clear as to what you want done, and stimulates action. For a surer, faster response, justify and ask for an answer by a certain date.
6. In inquiries about people, establish the privileged aspects.
   a. Be sure your explanation shows you have an interest to protect.
   b. Promise confidential treatment of the information.
   c. If the inquiry is authorized, say so (for courtesy, not legal reasons).

FAVORABLE REPLIES

Any company or person desiring the goodwill of others replies to all reasonable inquiries—and does so promptly. If a delay is necessary, some explanation should go quickly to the inquirer indicating the reason and approximately when to expect a complete answer:

> Your request for information about palletization is one for
> Mr. J. S. McConnough, our materials-handling specialist, who
> will be in California for another 10 days.
>
> Shortly after he returns to the office, he will write you.

The situation appears to contain no possibilities of sales but, as in the case of any inquiry, represents at least a good opportunity to make a friend. Proper handling might well lead to a sale.

Because some inquiries ask only for assistance, whereas others readily indicate a potential customer (and a quite different reply), we divide this discussion into (1) replies to inquiries without apparent sales possibilities (including reports dealing with personnel and credit applicants) and (2) replies to inquiries with sales possibilities (often called invited sales messages).

Replies without sales possibilities

When someone asks you something, you say either yes or no—in an A–plan or a B–plan reply. For all practical purposes an undecided, noncommittal response like "Well, I'll think it over" is a refusal and needs to be handled in the B–plan inductive style (reasons before conclusion). Since this section is concerned only with good-news (A–plan) replies complying with the request, however, refusals and modified refusals come later.

In favorable replies without sales possibilities, particular points to watch are the direct beginning, completeness of coverage, and (when appropriate) resale.

Direct beginning. The fundamental principle in all A–plan replies is to say yes immediately and thus gain increased goodwill, as well as save time and words. When you can do what somebody has asked you to do, begin by doing it or with a statement indicating that you will do it. Your compliance is the point of greatest interest—of far greater interest than any expressions of your gratitude. And from the standpoint of economical wording, the direct beginning establishes many ideas by implication, thus shortening your message considerably. Often it need contain no more than the notification of compliance:

> We are glad to send you these last three annual reports of
> National Reaper, Inc. and to add your name to our mailing list

to receive future copies as they come out, around March 1 each year.

The direct beginning also establishes a cheerful, ungrudging tone and eliminates pompousness. Observe the difference between the following slow, grudging, jargonistic original and the revision:

Indirect, wordy, grudging	*Direct, compact, cheerful*
We have your request for our <u>HOW</u> book.	Here is your copy of the <u>HOW</u> book.
It was prepared primarily for material-handling engineers, and so we were not prepared for the numerous requests we have received from schools. We are sending you one, however, and hope you will find it helpful.	We prepared it after extensive research by our material-handling engineers with the help of consultants and plant men who specialize in material-handling methods. We're sure you'll find it useful in the classroom.
If there is any other way we can be of assistance, please do not hesitate to call on us.	Call on us again when you think we can help you.

Note that the revised version not only begins directly but makes comments on the book showing it is something special. In such situations, where you send helpful information, you have every reason to enhance the desirability of what you've done and to offer to do more (unless you specifically do not want to). You will also note that the revision wasted no words referring to receipt of the inquiry. The direct beginning makes such references unnecessary and saves space better used for worthwhile information.

Completeness of coverage. Obviously, you need to take up every question in an inquiry; when you fail to do so, extra correspondence results (or your reader marks you as careless, indifferent, or ignorant). At times, of course, you can't answer—because you don't know, or because you can't reveal the information. In either case simply tell your reader so, but don't ignore the question.

When questions call for strictly factual answers, when the request tabulates questions and leaves space for answering, your job is easy. When the necessary answers must be evaluative and expository, your job is sometimes not so easy.

The following personnel report answers a typical inquiry about the subject's selling ability, personality, cultural background, character, and integrity. Note the effect of embedding the necessary negative in the middle and interpreting it along with a positive characteristic of the applicant. Note, too, that the reply is *not* a "recommendation" but a *personnel report* of the writer's experience with and evaluation of the applicant—as it should be.

SUBJECT: CONFIDENTIAL REPORT BY REQUEST ON TRAVIS BRANNON

Mr. Brannon is a careful, accurate worker with lots of
initiative.   And he makes friends readily.

I got to know Travis quite well while he made two A's in my
courses, Sales Management and Public Relations, and later
when he graded papers, had conferences with students, and did
clerical jobs as a student assistant.   His questions in class
and in conferences showed a keen understanding of business
problems and a calm, practical approach to their solution.
And his term reports showed solid, serious, yet original
business thinking.

Impressed with his scholastic performance, his friendliness and
ability to get along with people, and his obvious wide range
of interests, I asked Travis to be my assistant.   Then I
particularly liked the quickness with which he caught on to
assigned jobs and the willingness and accuracy with which he
did a job every time it came up after I had explained it to
him only once.   On many small jobs and some not so small he
went ahead and did what was necessary without being told.

As he demonstrated ability, I let him do more and more.   And
he accepted the added responsibility and authority with
obvious delight.   As a result of such unbridled enthusiasm, I
occasionally had to change a grade or contradict what he had
told a student in conference.   When that happened, he was
noticeably silent for a few days; then he apparently forgot
the incident and became his cheerfully helpful self again.

I must say, Mr. Parks, that I never had to lower a grade
Travis gave a student.   I never had one single reason to
suspect that any student had an inside track with him.   He was
completely trustworthy with examinations, grade records, and
the like.

Perhaps the most noticeable things about Travis were his
eagerness, his efficiency in making use of all his time, and
his general alertness.   These qualities, though they sometimes
led him to interrupt conferences with students and colleagues,
stood him in good stead with students and faculty alike.

I feel sure that if Travis walked into the office of a college
professor on almost any campus, the reaction toward him and
your company would be favorable.

In most cases giving information about an applicant for credit, all
you'll need to do is look at your customer's record and fill in the blanks
provided on the inquiry. But when some atypical factor presents itself (or
when the inquiring firm does not provide blanks), you'll need to write a
special message.

In addition to the standard information (listed on p. 107) you may need
to incorporate explanations of the effects of local conditions on the size and
timing of purchases or on paying habits. And of course, any unusual question—like the one about Mr. Green (p. 107)—requires special attention.
Since it is usually the reason for the special letter, it often merits the beginning position, like this:

SUBJECT: CREDIT REPORT ON MR. H. F. GREEN, VINITA, OKLAHOMA

I suspect that Mr. Green did not list us as a reference for
fear we would retaliate. About a month ago he was a little
miffed when we guessed wrong on one of his vague orders—and
he told us so.

Our relations have always been satisfactory, however, from our
point of view. Since we started doing business with Mr. Green
in August, 1967, we've been safe in allowing him credit up to
$700 several times. He has a yearly account of about
$4,000; his monthly purchases vary from $30 in the summer to
$700 in the fall. When crop money in the fall spurs payments,
Mr. Green generally takes advantage of our 2/10 EOM discount.
With only a few exceptions, he has paid his net bill by the
30th. On the two occasions that we had to press him for
collection, he paid up promptly.

Right now is the slack season in the farming regions; so Mr.
Green has let ride his May and June accounts totaling $700.30.
Of this amount, only the May bill of $382.40 is now overdue.
Since, on June 16, he sent in his $366.60 check in payment of
his April account, we know that Mr. Green pays his bills as
soon as he gets his money. A retired farmer who still owns
three farms, he is the sole owner of his modest store.

I am glad to send you, at your request, this confidential
letter about Mr. Green.

Completeness of coverage does *not*, however, mean recommendation.
Note that neither the preceding personnel report nor the credit report
recommends the applicant—and hence such letters should *not* be mis-
named "letters of recommendation."

But in replying about people, completeness *does* require covering the
legal aspects. You could get into a peck of trouble by sending damaging
information without meeting the obligations of doing so. Conversely, if
you play it straight you need have no fear.

Legally and morally you are on safe ground only if your report meets
the requirements of a *privileged* communication (see p. 108). First, *don't
volunteer information; send it only if requested by somebody with an interest to protect,* and incidentally make that clear. Beyond that you owe
the inquirer, the person reported on, and the state *the truth as you see it
(including your evaluations and opinions), good faith to avoid misleading
or malice, and reasonable care to be right about facts.*

The accompanying reminder checklist on page 114 summarizes the most
important points to keep in mind as you write replies complying with a
request which has no sales possibilities.

Replies with sales possibilities

Failure to answer inquiries and requests of the types we have been
discussing will mark you as uncooperative and probably lose you lots of

Favorable Reply Checklist

1. Make your opening show that you are doing as asked.
   a. When you are saying yes, sending something, or giving information, do so immediately!
   b. The most effective way to show that you're glad to do something is to do it immediately: not "I am very glad to tell you . . ." but "Henry Benton, about whom you inquired, has served us well as. . . ."
   c. Don't emphasize the obvious: "This is an answer to . . ."; "Concerning your inquiry . . ."; "We have received. . . ."
   d. Consider using a subject line to get you off to a fast start.

2. Completeness, specificness, and correctness are essential.
   a. Answer every question—direct or implied—of the inquiry. Scant, skimpy treatment implies that you are unwilling to extend an ordinary courtesy or that you are dubious.
   b. You want to evaluate when evaluation will be helpful. But do more than editorialize with "fine," "splendid," "excellent." Give specific evidence. In a personnel report, for instance, tell things the applicant did, work habits, personality.
   c. Be careful of the facts; avoid malice or carelessness.

3. Tone is all-important.
   a. In a personnel report:
      (1) Remember that you are reporting, not recommending.
      (2) Beware of superlatives, for accuracy and believability.
   b. Don't do anything grudgingly or parade your generosity.

4. You often have negative material to handle.
   a. Be honest; don't ignore the shortcomings and mislead.
   b. Watch space, word choice, and position to avoid overemphasis on either favorable or unfavorable points.
   c. When you must restrict the use of what you give, be definite —but place the negative in the middle.

5. Remember the libel laws (p. 107) when writing about a person.
   a. Label the information confidential.
   b. Indicate that it has been requested.
   c. Subordinate these ideas in the beginning or ending statements.

6. When sending something tangible, add a few enhancing words.
   a. Make them short.
   b. Make them as specific as you can.

7. End graciously and confidently.
   a. Your expression of willingness—more appropriate here than in the beginning—nullifies any possible curt impression.
   b. Don't suggest inadequacy: "I hope" or "If this is not. . . ."
   c. Omit bromides: "Please do not hesitate" or "Feel free to."

goodwill and a good many sales in the long run. But failure to answer inquiries with direct sales possibilities is business suicide.

When someone inquires about your goods or services, clearly an unsatisfied need or desire exists and the inquiry implies that you might satisfy it. Whether the request is for manufacturing data, a price list, a catalog or descriptive folder, or the name of your nearest dealer, you have an *interested*, potential customer—in other words, a prospect. *If* you give satisfactory information and treatment, you'll probably have a real customer.

Your selling job here is certainly much easier than making a sale through the usual sales letter that has to start from scratch with a "cold" prospect (as discussed in Chapter 8) because the inquirer is already interested and has practically invited you to send a sales letter. You probably spend a lot on advertising to get people into this mood. So don't just sit there!

Although you will be able to write better invited sales letters after studying special sales techniques, we take them up here because they are the most significant kind of reply any business firm sends. They are more than goodwill builders; they are sales builders. Accordingly, they draw heavily on the principles discussed in Chapter 4.

In answering an inquiry with sales possibilities, you have no problem securing attentive interest; your problem is to tell enough to overcome reluctance, to tell it interestingly and convincingly, and to get the reader to take the appropriate steps that lead to a sale. Your effort, then, must go toward starting favorably, answering all questions, subordinating unfavorable information, handling price positively, and stimulating action.

Getting started positively. When a prospective customer writes you the equivalent of "Tell me more," an indifferent reply like this is going to feel like a dash of cold water in the face:

    Two Endurtone outlets operate in your locality. Kindly contact
    them with your problem.

Such unconcern will send most readers to other sources for their needs. This, of course, is an extreme example, but it happens often enough to merit special warning.

The thing the reader most wants to know is the information requested —as specifically as you can give it. That is far more interesting than any of your expressions of pleasure or gratitude.

But in most cases involving a detailed inquiry, you will want to check the importance and nature of the questions before framing your reply. Some you can answer with more positiveness than others. The most important one you can answer favorably is what you should start with:

    With your Pow-R-Pac you will feel safe even when traveling
    alone at night on the country roads you spoke of.

--

> The Rover bicycle you saw advertised in <u>U.S. Youth</u> is made of
> lightweight, high grade steel of the same quality used in
> motor bikes.

Such positiveness stimulates enthusiasm and increases the desire to read further.

Answering all questions. In some instances you cannot give the requested information. For example, the letter about the Stair-Traveler (p. 87) could not give cost details because installation varies according to the placement of the machine in a particular home. The visit of the representative (clearly referred to) would have to clear up that point. But *if you cannot supply an answer, do not ignore it.* Such action only leads to suspicion, irritation, or disgust. Indicate that you are supplying the information some other way or that you are getting it.

Most of the time you can give all the requested information, even though it runs to considerable length. The following reply to a request for more information about reconditioned Lektrasweeps is good. It has you-viewpoint and positiveness, and it answers every question (though answers about the motor, repairs in the home, and a trial period had to be partly unfavorable).

> The reconditioned Lektrasweep you asked about has the following
> attachments: a 6-inch upholstery brush, a 6-inch lampshade
> brush, a 12-inch prober, and a plastic blower attachment, in
> addition to the standard 12-inch rug brush.
>
> These are the same attachments that come with vacuum cleaners
> costing $40 to $80 more. Were we to include a 1-hp. motor
> (necessary only for spraying attachments), the price would
> have to be considerably increased. Since most users want their
> Lektrasweeps for cleaning purposes only, we eliminate the
> spray attachments and thus are able to give you a good
> low-cost cleaner operating efficiently on a ½-hp motor.
>
> I believe we have the machine you'll find convenient for your
> cleaning. The quiet operation of the motor is especially
> desirable in small living quarters, and the brown crackle
> finish will resist nicks and scratches and clean easily.
> Another convenience is the 20-foot cord, which enables you to
> clean an entire room from one wall plug.
>
> The Lektrasweep guarantee protects you against mechanical
> failures of the vacuum cleaner for a full two years. If any
> parts fail because of defective materials or workmanship,
> specially trained servicemen at the central plant in Cleveland
> will put your Lektrasweep in service again and return it to you
> within a week. Although we consider all sales final (another
> of the economies resulting in the low price of your
> Lektrasweep), as long as the machine shows evidence of proper
> care, as explained on the written guarantee, we absorb the
> charges for servicing and new parts, and return your Lektrasweep
> charges prepaid. The few returns to the central plant have
> been handled to the customers' satisfaction.
>
> Next time you're in Madison, come in and let us demonstrate
> a Lektrasweep. After a thorough test of its effectiveness in

```
picking up dust, lint, and other particles from rugs,
upholstery, and walls, you'll see why we are so confident
of the Lektrasweep.

To get your Lektrasweep before you can come to Madison, use
the enclosed order blank and reply envelope to send us your
payment and instructions.  You can be enjoying easy
Lektrasweeping the day after we hear from you.
```

This was a particularly difficult reply to write because so many of the questions had to be answered with limitations, reservations, or an implied no.

To get full value out of the replies about Lektrasweeps and Roanoke lamps (next example), you need to look at each a second time. Both effectively illustrate two aspects of you-viewpoint especially important in all sales writing—including the answers to the questions of a product inquiry:

1. *Psychological description.* Except in the first paragraph about the Lektrasweep, every time the writers give a physical fact about the product, they *tell* and *emphasize* a resultant benefit. As you look again, see how many more pieces of psychological description you can find like the italicized part of ". . . 20-foot cord *which enables you to clean an entire room from one wall plug.*"

2. *Dramatization.* The most effective kind of sales writing gets the reader to imagine actually using and enjoying the benefits of the product. Where else in the two letters can you find dramatized copy like "You and Mrs. Baines will agree that the Roanoke is a handsome, efficient lamp when you place a pair in your own living room"?

For further help on answering all questions, see the second group of form enclosures, pages 123–24.

Subordinating unfavorable information. Only a very poor sales writer would have started the Lektrasweep reply with

```
No, the Lektrasweep does not have a 1-hp motor.
```

or even with

```
The Lektrasweep is equipped with a ½-hp motor.
```

Another case will more firmly implant the reasons for positive handling of unfavorable information in invited sales. The inquiry asked whether

1. The Roanoke lamp was three-way.
2. The shade was of parchment or paper.
3. The shade was available in a design.
4. The lamp was weighted to prevent tipping.
5. The base was real brass or an alloy.
6. A pair could be returned for full refund if they didn't fit in with the 18th-century living room.

Answers to all but question 5 contained negative information. Here is one way of handling this inquiry to turn it into a sale despite the unfavorable circumstances:

> Yes, the base and standard of the Roanoke lamp you saw in
> Home and Yard are of solid brass, which will blend in
> tastefully with almost any style of 18th-century furnishings.
> For durability and ease in cleaning, the 10-inch shade is
> lightweight metal. Either the forest green or the royal red
> shade will contrast effectively with your drapes, and the
> quarter-inch gold bands around the top and bottom give the
> Roanoke lamp a distinction which most of our customers prefer
> to a design.
>
> The white lining of the shade and the milk-white bone china
> reflector enable the single 150-watt bulb to give you good
> reading light—10 foot-candles within a radius of 8 feet,
> which is more than the minimum recommended by the American
> Institute of Lighting. Then, too, the indirect lighting
> reflected from the ceiling is pleasant for conversational
> groups.
>
> To make the Roanoke more stable than other lamps of this size
> and shape, our designers put six claw feet instead of the
> usual four on the base and thus eliminated the necessity for
> weighting. Claw feet, as you know, are characteristic of
> much 18th-century design.
>
> You and Mrs. Baines will agree that the Roanoke is a handsome,
> efficient lamp when you place a pair in your own living room.
> Should you decide to return them within 10 days of our
> shipping date, we will refund your money less shipping charges.
>
> Use the enclosed order blank and envelope to tell us your
> choice of color. Include with the order blank your check or
> money order for $80 (including shipping charges). Within five
> days after we hear from you, you will be enjoying your
> Roanoke lamps, which will give you good lighting at a moderate
> price and will make appropriately decorative additions to your
> living room.

The letter wisely begins and ends with positive ideas and, as positively as circumstances permit, establishes the negative answers of "No, the Roanoke is not three-way; no, it is not weighted; no, the shade is not available in a design; no, the shade is not parchment or paper; no, we won't refund *all* your money if you return the lamps." It does so through the usual means available to any writer: embedded position and positive statement (see p. 34, 88 and **Emp** in Appendix B).

Handling price. When you have a genuine bargain, a real price reduction—one which the reader will recognize as such—that information may be the best lead you can choose for your message.

Most of the time, however, you are trying to sell at an established price. And most of the time you are writing to someone who wishes the price were less! For these reasons, good sales writers attempt to minimize the effect of price by one or more of several methods:

—Introducing price after presenting most of the sales points.

—Stating price in terms of a unit ("$1.67 a wrench" rather than "$20 a dozen").

—Identifying the daily, monthly, or even yearly cost based on an estimated life of the product ("10 cents a night" for a good mattress sounds much easier to pay than "$182.50").

—Suggesting a series of payments rather than the total (an alumnus is more likely to contribute "$10 a month for the next year" than to contribute "$120 next year").

—Comparing the present price with the cost of some product or activity the reader accepts readily. ("For the price of six cigarettes a day your child can have better schools" was the punch line of an ad promoting a school-bond drive. Likewise, a sales writer sold air-conditioned sleep for the price of a daily Coke.)

—Associating the price with a reminder of the benefits to be gained.

The first and the last of the suggestions you can always apply. You may want to use the others as indicated by the following varying factors.

In general, the higher the income bracket of your readers, the less desirability for applying the techniques.

The higher the price of your product or service, the greater the desirability for minimizing price in one or more of these ways. The less familiar your readers are with your product or service, the greater the desirability of justifying price. Minimizing price has more effect on consumers than on dealers or corporate customers.

Often you will be able to omit direct price talk because a sales representative will handle it in a face-to-face interview or because you need more information before determining price. Sometimes you can shift the burden of price discussion to an enclosure. But *when you are trying to close a sale, you must identify what it is going to cost and help your reader justify the expenditure.*

Securing action.   Having convinced your reader that your product or service is worth the price, you want to get action before a change of mind, before forgetfulness defeats you, before the money goes for something else —before any of the things that could happen do happen.

A word of caution here, however: The bromidic, high-pressure, general expressions like "Act today!" "Do it now!" "Don't delay!" are more likely to produce reactions ranging from indifference to disgust than the favorable reaction you seek.

Instead, in all persuasive messages, your good action ending:

—Makes clear the specific action you want your reader to take.

—Clears up any question about how to take the action.

—Makes the action easy (and makes it sound as easy as possible).

—Supplies a stimulus to action, preferably immediate action.

On finishing your letter, your reader should know just exactly what you want done. In invited sales it's to send in an order or take some step in furthering the order, such as to invite the visit of a sales representative, make a visit to a demonstration or salesroom, or try out the product. The psychological urge is stronger if you *name the explicit action* rather than resort to the vague "Let us hear from you soon" or any of its equivalents.

At times you may have to name two actions and ask the reader to take one or the other. If you possibly can, avoid doing so. Some folks faced with a choice resolve their dilemma by doing nothing.

Facilitating devices—order blanks, order cards, and postcards or envelopes already addressed and requiring no postage—remove some of the work in taking action. References to them—*preferably directing the reader to use them* (see "Enclosures," pp. 123–24)—reassure your reader that what you are asking is simple, requiring little time or effort.

Moreover, through careful wording, you can further this impression. "Write us your choice" suggests more work than "Check your choice of colors on the enclosed card." "Jot down," "just check," "simply initial" are examples of wording that suggests ease and rapidity in doing something. Wording like this will help to reduce some of your reader's reluctance to take action.

The final suggestion for a good action ending—that of supplying a stimulus to action—is a matter of either threatening your reader or promising something. Remember a stimulus is motivation—a reader benefit! Talk of limited supply, price rises after a certain date, introductory offers for a limited time, premiums, and the like is all very well *provided it is true* and *provided it is specific*, so that the reader is likely to accept your statement as accurately depicting the conditions. Otherwise, readers of average intelligence and experience read such statements skeptically.

In many circumstances you have nothing you can use as a stimulus but the desirability of your product or service. You *always* have that, however. In the final analysis your reader buys for what the product contributes to life; when you ask for money, mention *again what benefits will result.*

Such a stimulus comes appropriately as the ending idea. This placement has decided psychological value too, for it emphasizes the service attitude—rather than the greed stressed if you end with dollars and cents talk or the mechanics of ordering.

Desirably, the stimulus is short—often only a phrase, at most a short sentence, restating the theme. The Stair-Traveler letter, for example, could have ended effectively with

```
Mr. J. B. Nickle, our Kansas City representative, will be glad
to call at a time convenient for you.  Fill out and mail the
enclosed postcard, and he will come to your home and explain
```

how simply and economically your Stair-Traveler can make your daily living more pleasurable.

For other examples, reread the endings about the Roanoke lamp and the Lektrasweep.

Invited sales are persuasive (C–plan) presentations. You should therefore apply all the points discussed in Chapter 4. The accompanying checklist on page 122 summarizes the most significant points from it and the discussion here.

ROUTINE TRANSMITTAL MESSAGES

A frequent written communication is the routine transmittal letter or memo. Often people in a firm send information or material to other people either in their company or with other companies. This information or material usually has a short cover letter or memo which carries the address, announces what is enclosed, and identifies the sender.

These short notes do not strictly fall into the category of favorable replies, since generally no question arises about your compliance with the request, if there is one. The reason we talk about this routine type of writing is that for most young people early in their careers, such messages are their primary (and maybe only) contact with upper management. Such writing deserves some care.

The routine transmittal message should be short. Though you may sometimes need to explain what you are sending, you do not need to spout eloquence over simply sending information. In any case, do not be trapped into using the old-fashioned "Enclosed you will find" or "Attached is" beginnings. Much more natural and direct beginnings are "Here is the information on . . ." or "This is the material you asked for. . . ." Custom within your firm will dictate whether you need to mention the date of your reader's request, but any file number or other formal identification should appear in the first sentence or a subject line.

After announcing that the material is here (which should be pretty evident), quit unless you have something else relevant to say. Simply sign off, assuming that your transmittal letter or memo has done its job.

What your note can go on to say after the initial announcement is interpretation of data you've dug up, or suggestions or questions on what to do with the information, that you're sending more information than your reader expected, or that the information is dated, perhaps, or not yet complete, or whatever the situation calls for. Keep this second part of your message short and direct; and resist the temptation to add an ending offering further assistance. If your reader does need more information, you'll hear about it! And anyhow, you should have sent all the information in the first place.

Invited Sales Checklist

1. Get started in a hurry!
   - *a.* The direct, specific, favorable answer to one of your reader's main questions is the surest way of maintaining interest.
   - *b.* At least give a good sales point if no answer can be affirmative.
   - *c.* "Thank you for"—while perfectly nice—is slow.
   - *d.* Keep out the selfish sounds like "We're glad to have...."
   - *e.* Do not begin with an answer containing negative information.
   - *f.* You don't need to work for attention: you already have it.

2. Arrange points for natural coherence and favorable information at the beginning and end (even of paragraphs as well as the whole). Embed touchy points.

3. Answer every question, stated or implied, or explain why.
   - *a.* You need specific statements for conviction.
   - *b.* Avoid denied negatives. If a product isn't something, what is it?

4. Psychological description (you-viewpoint) is good selling.
   - *a.* Put the product to work in the life of the reader right from the start, and let reader-use sentences (dramatization) predominate throughout to give a visual image of benefits. (See pp. 117, 265–66.)
   - *b.* Depict reader possession and/or participation instead of mere mechanical you-beginnings.

5. Consider using an enclosure for details, economy, and pictures.
   - *a.* Don't mention it too early. (See pp. 123–24.)
   - *b.* Don't emphasize that you have enclosed it; what the reader is to do with it or get from it is what counts: not "Enclosed you will find a folder," but "Read on page 2 of the enclosed folder...."

6. Adaptation is easy here; the inquiry gives you cues.
   - *a.* Maybe use the name a time or two beyond the salutation.
   - *b.* Work in a reference to home town, firm, or organization.
   - *c.* Refer casually to a commonplace action or event characteristic of the reader's job, community, area, or economic status.
   - *d.* Fit your style to the person's way of life.

7. Try to cushion the shock of price when you have to state it.
   - *a.* Use the appropriate method(s) of minimizing price.
   - *b.* Make price and payment method clear, or give a reason.

8. In a full-fledged four-point action ending (what to do, how, aids to easy action, stimulus to promptness) confidently ask the reader to take the action you want (preferably order, if fitting).

FORM ENCLOSURES AND LETTERS

Invited sales messages (and various other kinds) do take time and therefore money. Unless a firm has practically unlimited money and trained personnel, it will have to use form messages some of the time for speed and economy in handling inquiries with sales possibilities.

Form enclosures and letters can decrease the cost of correspondence by cutting time needed for dictation, transcription, handling, and filing. The closer you can come to completely eliminating one or more of these steps, the more you can save. The big problem is to determine when you can save enough in costs to justify the loss in effectiveness.

Before you can decide, however, you need to know the potentials of forms.

Enclosures

Three classes of *form enclosures* deserve your attention:

1. Forms which are the basic reason for the mailing.
2. Forms which give supplementary information.
3. Forms which aid the reader in responding.

Since the *first group* are the key things in the envelopes (checks, requested pamphlets, brochures, and the like), they deserve to come to the reader's attention immediately. In some cases they may properly be the only thing necessary. In most situations, however, you should *make something of them* by saying something about them—if for no reason than goodwill. You've already seen earlier in this chapter the reasons and approaches for comment when transmitting requested booklets. Similarly, simple and typical covering letters (often forms themselves) beginning something like the following could hardly help making their readers feel better:

> Here is your current quarterly dividend check (our 200th
> without interruption, raised to 50¢ a share this time) and
> our thanks for your continued confidence in Rushman.
>
> --
>
> The enclosed check paying for your services as consultant
> carries with it our thanks for the good advice you gave us.
>
> --
>
> This check will tell you more clearly than words that when we
> guarantee satisfaction with Acme products or your money back,
> we mean it.

Unlike the first group of form enclosures, the enclosures in the *second group* are *not* the basic reason for writing but are *helpful to give additional details* and thus avoid cluttering and lengthening the main message unduly.

Most frequently useful in sales letters as brochures and detailed price lists, they also help in job application letters (as résumés or data sheets) and in answering various inquiries about products (as installation, operating, and repair guides). As supplements, these informative enclosures do not deserve mention until late in the message—usually the next-to-last paragraph, *after* the key points and *near enough to the end* that the reader will finish before turning to the enclosure (perhaps never to return). As with the first group, the important thing to say about these enclosures is *not* their mere existence—NOT "We have enclosed . . . ," and certainly NOT "Enclosed please find . . ." (the reader has probably already found)—but what the reader should get from them.

```
As you'll see from the enclosed brochure, . . .
                            --
The illustrations and explanations on pages 3 and 4 of the
enclosed installation guide will answer, better than I can,
your questions about wiring the two thermostats in
combination.
```

The *third useful group* of form enclosures (reader aids in replying) naturally deserve mention only in the ending—where you ask for action. Order blanks and reply or return cards and envelopes (usually stamped and addressed—but *not* properly called "self-addressed," unless you insist on being jargonistic, illogical, and wordy) can often help you get an answer when the reader might not go to the trouble necessary without them. As in referring to other form enclosures, the point to stress is *not* the idea that they are enclosed but the suggestion that the reader use them.

If you'll use the word *enclosed* as an adjective instead of a verb, you'll probably put the emphasis where it belongs in referring to all three classes of form enclosures, like this:

```
By filling out and mailing the enclosed reply card
promptly, . . . .
                            --
Sending in your order today on the enclosed form will bring
you. . . .
```

Form letters

Although most readers like the implied extra consideration of the individual letter, few business people will object to a form letter *because* it is a form but only if it seems to give them less attention than they desire. New customers and those writing you about important affairs are most likely to feel that way. Anybody, however, will rightly object to a sloppy form or a form message which does not contain the necessary information. And many people will object to a form which tries to masquerade as an individualized message but fails because of discrepancies in type, faulty alignment, or inept wording. The undisguised form, however, can success-fully carry its message in many situations, especially those involving numer-ous similar inquiries to which you will give similar replies, somewhat like the following:

```
Here's Your Copy of
The Buying Guide
to Fine Furniture.
You will be delighted with the wealth of information condensed
into this conveniently indexed booklet.

Here, in a comparatively few pages, are guideposts experts with
a lifetime of experience use in weighing true furniture
values.  And here are features illustrated and described to
guide you in your purchases of furniture so that the pieces
you select to furnish your home will give you utmost pleasure
as the years roll by.

Even though every piece of furniture bearing the Langston seal
is handcrafted to certified standards of quality, nationwide
popularity makes possible budget prices.  For a pleasant
surprise, see your dealer, whose name you'll find imprinted
on the back page of the booklet.
```

Even the signature of this letter is printed. When an inquiry comes in, addressing the envelope is the only time-consuming step. Thus a reply which could cost $3 or more if individually handled runs to no more than a quarter. And the firm gains extra goodwill by a prompt answer.

You can print *strict form* messages by the thousands at very low cost. The only additional expense is for addressing. And you can adapt them in talking points and references even to a large mailing list. They can answer an inquiry (or order), express gratitude, convey some evidence of service attitude, and look forward to future business relations, as in the following postcard acknowledgment:

```
We will give your recent order our immediate careful attention
and follow your shipping instructions exactly.

You may be sure we appreciate this opportunity to serve you
and shall be happy to do so when you again decide to order
Wolf's fine confections for yourself or as a gift.
```

But completely printed letters have limitations. Personalizing is impos-sible. And if you print the body and then insert individual inside addresses and salutations, you will have greatly increased costs and likely discrep-ancies between the two types. Unless you sell only one product or have a different form for each product, you can't include resale talk on the goods, although you can for the firm.

Fill-ins enable you to be more specific than you can be in a strict form. For example, the strict form above could read like this as a fill-in (the filled-in parts are in parentheses):

```
We sent a carefully packed (2-pound box of Wolf's famous Texas
Chewie Pecan Pralines) today, as you requested, by (parcel
```

post) addressed to (Mr. and Mrs. E. F. Blanton, 2443 Hathaway
Road, Syracuse, New York 13247).

When it arrives within the next few days, we know (they)
will enjoy the rich, nutty flavor of this fine candy.

Many thanks for your order. When you want more of Wolf's
fine candies for yourself or for pleasing a friend with an
inexpensive gift distinctly different, we shall be glad to
serve you again.

But even if you do a good job of matching print and type in a fill-in
like this by using word processing equipment, in most instances the irregular spacing calls attention to the fact that the message is a form fill-in.
That is one of the reasons why so many users fill in these forms by hand,
with no attempt to disguise.

With proper planning, equipment, and patience, however, fill-ins can
appear to be individual letters. The following is a good example, where
the necessary insertions are the name of the city (at the end of a line),
name of the dealer (displayed attractively with additional spacing all
around), and the reader's name (again, at the end of the line and with
enough space to allow for a "Mr. Abbott" or a "Miss Getzendannerich"):

Dear (Mr. Abbott:)

Mallard sample cases enjoy tremendous popularity because they
come in a wide range of sizes, offer virtually infinite
interior arrangements, and maintain their good looks.

The rugged aluminum frame protects the case's contents
without adding unnecessary weight—your people will appreciate
that! And you can compartment the inside by permanent or
movable partitions, cut-out foam rubber, or shaped rigid
foam, whatever best meets your needs. You'll like the tough,
positive latches, too, as well as the optional key or
combination locks for security.

But best of all, you'll like the way the smart, durable
exteriors help your representatives maintain their quality
image. Mallard cases are scuff-proof, scratch-resistant, and
washable. And note on page 4 of the enclosed brochure the
full range of exterior options and colors available,
(Mr. Abbott.)

But nothing beats seeing the real thing. That's why your
Mallard distributor has so many different cases on display.
Your distributor in (Las Vegas is:)

    (Desert Case Company
    1438 Mountain Road
    Las Vegas, Nevada 89101
    Phone: 702/555-1700)

The people there will be happy to work with you to see that
your salespeople have sample cases that are "Active Partners
in Selling . . . by Mallard."

But because type is hard to match and exact alignment is difficult, many
firms now use word processing equipment for multiple correspondence
like this.

What we have said can apply to form paragraphs as well as to whole letters or memos. The procedure is to write an excellent paragraph covering each frequently recurring point in the firm's correspondence. Usually half a dozen ending paragraphs and a dozen beginnings will cover most situations. Other paragraphs will be about the various products of the company. Each company correspondent and each typist then gets a book of the coded paragraphs, which may be typed manually or recorded for use in word processing equipment.

A letter may be designated simply 13, 27, 16, 42. That would mean a four-paragraph letter made up of those standard paragraphs in that order. If no ready-made paragraph covers what should be in the second paragraph, dictation would be "13, special, 16, 42," followed by the wording for the special second paragraph. If the same point comes up frequently enough, the firm should prepare a good paragraph for it and put it into the correspondent's book.

Because such paragraphs get frequent use, they should get careful preparation so they are better than most people would write quickly under the pressure of dictation. Obviously, the same advantage applies to an entire form message.

Simple arithmetic shows that even if you spend 30 to 50 hours on one message, when you send it to a thousand people, dictation time and transcription time are only a fraction of the time individual messages would require. In a nutshell, this is the whole theory back of forms. They have to be used to cut correspondence costs, to reduce the burdensome human aspects of the ever-increasing correspondence problems of management, and to expedite replies to people who want information as quickly as they can get it.

Certain *dangers* exist, however. *The greatest is the tendency to use a form when it simply does not apply.* When a person asks if Sure-Clip tee-nuts can withstand temperatures up to 2,400° F, answering that "Sure-Clip tee-nuts are specially finished to resist corrosion and be compatible with a wide range of ferrous and nonferrous metals" is nice but doesn't answer the question.

One good solution, if a form does not answer one of the specific questions, is to add a postscript. If you cannot answer all questions by adding a little to an existing form, you need to write an individual message.

Another danger is in broadcasting that the message is a form with such references as

    To all our customers:
    Whether you live in Maine or California. . . .

In a broadside (circular) such mass impersonality may be necessary and accepted. But in a letter or memo the personal touch pays off. The wording of even a form letter, then, should *give each reader the feeling that it fits.*

And remember that in every test ever made, the form letter that makes no pretense of being anything else (like the earlier furniture letter on p. 125) results in more returns than the imperfectly disguised form, whether the slipup is due to poor mechanics or inept wording.

The suggestions made about forms in this chapter should help with *any repetitive writing situation, whether it is one involving replies to inquiries, acknowledgments of orders, sales, credit, collections, or adjustments.* So except for occasional incidental references pointing out the ease or wisdom of form treatment in a particular situation, the remainder of this book deals with individualized, personalized messages because:

1. You can learn more about communication principles and their application that way.
2. As a result of such specific study and practice, you will write much better forms when you need to.
3. In most circumstances calling for a letter or memo, an individualized copy will do a more effective job for you than a form.

SHORT NOTE REPLY

In an effort to expedite many day-to-day answers to inquiries (and reduce correspondence costs), many executives turn to the short note reply (SNR). One leading copying-machine manufacturer in its advertising explains this way:

1. Just jot a personal note on the margin of the letter you received—no wasted time in dictation.
2. Insert the letter and a sheet of copy paper into a copying machine.
3. In just four seconds you have the letter ready to mail back to the sender —plus the copy for your files.

Certainly most readers will appreciate the thoughtfully fast answer. The practice seems to be gaining favor—rightly so, in our opinion.

One of the big mailers of the United States—Book-of-the-Month Club —uses a slightly different method combining a form and short notes to reduce costs and speed up parts of its correspondence. The front of a neat little 3½- by 6½-inch folder contains the printed name and address of the club and the typed name, address, and membership number of the reader, followed by

QUICK REPLY FOLDER   SEE WITHIN

Inside, the first page contains this form note, signed by the Membership Director:

Dear Member:

    You will find enclosed in this folder the answer—or answers
—to the questions you raised in your recent letter. We have
developed this system of "Quick-Reply-Notes" because we have
found it results in much better and more satisfactory service
to our members. We receive literally tens of thousands of
letters every day, and to dictate and type individual replies
would inevitably mean considerable delay in every case. We
have found that this is a much faster and more efficient way of
answering inquiries than separate individual letters.

The third and fourth pages of the folder are blank. But stapled over the
third page is a slip of paper carrying the brief typed message (and, if
needed—say to return merchandise—a small envelope containing postage
and an addressed sticker).

ORDERS

Buying and selling by mail has long involved much more than just the
big mail-order houses. It includes mail sales through large department
stores; national marketing of seasonal and regional produce like fruit, game,
syrup, and candy; farmers' orders for various supplies, machinery, and replacement parts; office equipment and supplies from manufacturers and
distributors; and even industrial tools and materials.

To overcome the disadvantage of buying without seeing, feeling, and
trying the product, sellers by mail usually provide pictures and full information, and they offer guarantees and return privileges and provide necessary installation, operation, and service manuals.

Since sellers by mail usually supply well-designed order blanks and
addressed envelopes with their catalogs, the only problems connected with
writing an order appear when you do not have the blanks and must write
a letter.

But an order is probably the easiest kind of letter to write. The reader
is in business to sell goods, and if you clearly specify what you want and
make satisfactory plans to pay for it, you'll get an answer. A poor order
letter may, however, bring results different from what you really want.

The basic requirements for an order letter, as you can see from almost
any order blank, are five (which will serve as a checklist for order letters):

1. Make them orders, not just hints. The *acceptance of a definite offer to
    sell* or *an offer to buy* is contractural. The usual beginning for an order
    is therefore "Please send me. . . ."
2. Describe the goods adequately. Although the catalog number alone
    usually identifies except for color and size, give four or five clean-cut
    columns of information:

a. Quantity desired.

b. Catalog item number, if any, and catalog page number.

c. Name of product and as many details as are appropriate, such as model, color, size, material, grade or quality, pattern, finish, monogram initials.

d. Unit price.

e. Total price for the designated quantity of the item (column *a* times *d*).

In the absence of a catalog, to supplement the inexact information you may need to explain more fully by telling how the product is to be used, and in some cases by sending drawings.

In ordering replacement parts for machines, be sure to give the name and model number of the machine and the name and number of the part. Frequently, you can find the number on the part itself if you have no parts list.

3. Write a separate, single-spaced paragraph for each item, with double spacing between paragraphs.

4. Make clear how you expect to pay. If you have not established credit but want goods charged, you should provide credit information with the order (see pp. 106 and 135).

If you want neither credit nor c.o.d. shipment (which costs you more), several methods of remitting are open to you: check, money order, certified or cashier's check, or bank draft.

Regardless of how you remit, refer to the remittance in the order and tell its form, amount, and intended application.

5. Be sure the *where* of shipment is clear—especially for a shipment to an address different from yours—and also the *when* and *how* unless you want to leave them to the seller.

The following typical order illustrates the five points:

```
Please send me the following items listed in your current
spring and summer catalog:
   1   60 C 6587L   Glass casting rod, Model 162, extra
                    light action, 5 ft. 8 in. ............ $18.95
   1   60 CP 6302   Pflueger Summit reel, Model 1993L ....   33.75
   2   60 C 6846    Cortland "Cam-o-flage" nylon
                    casting line, 10-lb. test, 100-yd.
                    lengths @ $4.30 ......................    8.60
          Total ........................................... $61.30
The enclosed check for $69.63 covers the price, sales tax, and
parcel post charges.

As I plan to go fishing a week from next Saturday (June 26),
I will want the equipment by that time.
```

The following letter covers a more difficult job of ordering. Test it against the five requirements set up for a good order. Note how the writer made the specifications very clear without benefit of a catalog or parts list to give code numbers and prices of the items.

```
Please send me the following parts for Little Giant Shallow
Well Water System P4/12818.  Since I have no catalog, I am
describing each part carefully.

1 Valve rubber, 1¼ inches in diameter with 5/16-inch hole.  It
  is one of four that work under springs on the valve plate.

1 Crank pin.  Apparently this is a steel pin of a highly
  special design.  Its threaded end, 7/16 inch in diameter and
  11/16 inch long, screws into the eccentric arm on the end of
  the drive shaft so that the rest of the pin forms the
  crankshaft.  That is, the big end of the connecting rod fits
  around it.  (See drawings on the attached sheet.)  The
  crankshaft part of this pin is an eccentric ½ inch in
  diameter and 11/16 inch long.

1 Connecting rod, as shown on the attached sheet.  Apparently
  it is brass or bronze.  Please note the specifications as to
  size of hole.  For other models, I know that the sizes are a
  little different.

I estimate that these parts will cost approximately $16.  I am
enclosing my check for $20 to cover all charges, including tax
and shipping.  You can send me a refund check if the charges
are less or I'll send the difference if they are more.

I'll appreciate your trying to fill the order promptly.  My
pump, much needed these days, is about to quit on me.
```

STANDARD ACKNOWLEDGMENTS

Acknowledgments should be an effective means of increasing goodwill and promoting business. A person who orders from you evidently has a favorable attitude toward your firm and its goods. Your job in acknowledging the order is to keep it that way by giving satisfaction.

A buyer expects to get the product quickly, and to be appreciated—or to get a prompt and reasonable explanation. To give less is to make a customer for somebody else. (According to a U.S. Department of Commerce survey, indifference is responsible for at least 67 percent of lost customers.)

Frequently a correspondent who handles a large volume of orders, however, comes to look upon them as routine matters and answers accordingly. Doing so overlooks two things: (1) The individual customer usually sends comparatively few orders and does *not* look on them as routine at all; (2) a routine acknowledgment seems like indifference.

Justifying reasons (strikes, impossibility of always estimating demand accurately, as well as incomplete orders from buyers) may prevent a seller from filling some orders promptly, or at all. But no reason justifies not acknowledging orders promptly and appreciatively. The following fill-in forms let a large department store acknowledge quickly (fill-ins underscored here):

```
Thank you for your letter ordering a ladder.
We're processing your order now, and you should receive the
shipment promptly.
                        --
As you requested, we have sent the pocket calculator to
Mrs. M. W. Colby.
Thank you for calling on us.  We try to make our service
convenient.  Order from us again when we can serve you.
```

Neither does the seller have much excuse for not doing more than the minimum the customer ordinarily expects. A large order—or even a small first order from a new customer—is an opportunity to cement a lasting business relationship through a well-written acknowledgment.

Clearly *the standard acknowledgment* of an order you can fill immediately is a good-news letter. The beginning should be a direct answer to the reader's biggest question—what you are doing about the order. Tell immediately the *when* and *how* of shipment, preferably timed and worded to indicate that it's on the way, and identify what it includes, the charges, and (here or later) the financial arrangements if necessary. (But remember that you are sending goods, not an order, which is what you received.) The approximate arrival date is also desirable, not only as a convenience to the customer but also for the psychologically favorable effect of helping the reader imagine actually receiving and using the goods.

Give the date and one or more of order number, relisting, or a general naming of the class of goods, or list them on an attached invoice or shipping list and refer to it in the letter.

To a new customer, a hearty welcome, resale, and a forward look are even more important than to an old customer; and service attitude and appreciation are important to every customer.

The middle section of a standard acknowledgment is the place for financial details, resale talk of more than phrase length, and explicit evidence of your service attitude. For instance, in acknowledging dealers' orders, you might talk about having your sales representative set up window and counter displays, offer free envelope stuffers (small promotional pamphlets about your products for the dealer to send to customers), or describe your radio, TV, and magazine ads that call customers' attention to your products and help the dealer sell more.

Encouragement to future ordering (just preceded by any appropriate sales promotion material) is almost invariably the best ending for the standard acknowledgment.

Here's an example of how the parts go together for an effective personalized acknowledgment covering all points specifically:

```
You should receive your eight cases of Tuff Paper towels in
time for Friday afternoon shoppers; we sent them by prepaid
express this morning.
```

The $3.27 voucher attached to this letter is your change after
we deducted $76.80 charges and $4.93 express from your $85
check.

Thank you for your order. We're glad to serve you with this
first shipment of paper products to you.

You'll find these Tuff Paper Towels have a fast turnover,
Mr. Ford, because homemakers like the way they soak up grease,
dust off spots, and save cloth towels from many dirty jobs.
And you'll like their attractive small packaging that takes
up a minimum of display and shelf space. Your markup figures
out at exactly 29 percent.

For more information about Tuff Paper dishrags and window
washers, colorful shelf paper your customers will like for
their pantries, and other paper products every household
needs, look in the enclosed booklet. Notice that each article
carries the usual Tuff Paper margin of profit.

Perhaps you'd like to take advantage of our regular terms of
2/10, n/60 on future orders. If so, we'll be glad to consider
your credit application when you fill in and return the
enclosed form.

And when you order, if you want window and shelf displays to
help you sell, just say so. Then watch Tuff kitchen paper
products bring Altoona customers into your store for frequent
repeat sales.

The trouble with this kind of acknowledgment is that it is costly. To be
specific on all points, to adapt the message to an individual, and to make
it persuasive require an average-length, individually dictated letter. But
when the prospect of numerous future orders depends on the letter, to do
less is foolish.

In many cases, however, a form can serve as an acknowledgment, as we
illustrated in the discussion of forms (p. 124). The Tuff Paper situation
could be handled in a form message like this one (which, incidentally,
could serve for acknowledging a repeat order):

You should receive the Tuff Paper products you ordered in just
a few days; they are already on the way.

Thank you for your order. We are glad to serve you in
this way.

You'll find that Tuff Paper products have a fast turnover;
homemakers like them for many messy household cleaning jobs.

You will like their attractive packaging that takes up a
minimum of shelf and display space. And the sizable markup!

Read the enclosed booklet for more information about Tuff
Paper dishrags, window washers, colorful shelf paper, and
other paper products every household needs.

Use the handy order blank and business reply envelope in the
back of the booklet when you want to order the additional Tuff
Paper products your customers will be asking for.

Checklist for Standard Acknowledgment

1. Of greatest interest to the customer is complete, accurate shipment.
   a. Emphasize the good news (sending the goods—not an order) in the first sentence, preferably also indicating method, arrival time, and use.
   b. Clearly identify the order by one or more of date, number, reference to the goods by name—perhaps a complete listing.
   c. If you list, tabulate—in the letter if short; on a referred-to invoice or shipping list if long.
   d. Clear up any uncertainty about payment details.
   e. Appreciation (and a welcome to a new customer) may come early in the letter but probably will fit better near the end— if not adequately implied.

2. Resale is part of acknowledgments to reassure the reader.
   a. Make it specific and short.
   b. Adapt it to your product and reader (consumer versus dealer).

3. Service attitude, especially important to new customers, may help with others.
   a. For a consumer: personal shopping, delivery schedules, free installation, and credit possibilities.
   b. For an industrial customer: full stock, quick shipment, custom or special capabilities, maybe credit.
   c. For a dealer: sales and service representatives, manuals, displays, and advertising aids and programs (mats, envelope stuffers, etc.) If you talk credit, invite application without promising approval.
   d. If you talk advertising, give publications and radio or TV stations, amount of space or time, schedules; and emphasize how the advertising promotes sales: "Your customers will be asking for . . . because of the full-page ads running. . . ."

4. Sales promotion material can indicate service attitude and build sales.
   a. Keep it appropriate—usually on seasonal or allied goods.
   b. You-attitude and specificness are essential in sales promotion.
   c. Emphasize your service to the customer—how the suggested product might help—not your selfish desire to sell more, as implied by "Our product . . . ," "We also make . . . ," or "We'd also like to sell you. . . ."
   d. Emphasize reader action when referring to enclosures.

5. Look forward to future orders.
   a. If sales promotion is the basis, suggest specific, easy action.
   b. If resale talk is the basis, continue in terms of reader satisfaction rather than suggest that something will go wrong.
   c. Guard against bromides and greedy wording as you close.

If the situation is one in which specificness would add to the effectiveness of an acknowledgment, a fill-in rather than a strict form could serve. For instance, you could add a postscript of special material to the preceding.

Forms of any kind, however, can go sour from overuse. If, for instance, the buyer above orders Tuff products weekly, blindly sending the same letter week after week would not only overuse the letter, it would shortly have the undesired opposite effect of convincing the buyer that you take such business for granted. If you have a situation where someone may repeatedly get the same form letter from you, you would be wise to revise it periodically to keep it fresh and effective.

The situation will govern whether to use forms and, if so which kind. Pinching pennies by dashing off personalized letters that are just a little too short to be adequate, or resorting to forms that don't do the job, is poor economy. The result is comparable to throwing out *almost* enough rope to reach a drowning person. If you are going to write a personalized letter, make it a good one. Its cost does not increase in proportion to length. A question you should always answer before cheapening your correspondence is whether you lose more in results, including goodwill, than you save on costs.

CREDIT APPROVALS

In naming what they commonly call the four *C*'s of credit—the bases for evaluating individual as well as corporate credit applicants—credit specialists name character first, followed by capacity, capital, and conditions.

Character is honesty. It is one's good word. In business it is living up to the spirit as well as the letter of the contract. In credit, it is meeting obligations as one promises to do.

Capacity is the ability to earn the means for payment.

Capital is the already available money behind the debtor. It may be cash, land, buildings, machinery, securities, patents, and copyrights, to mention the most common forms. It could as a last resort furnish the money for payment in the event of reversals.

Conditions (plural) has two parts. One is general business trends. The other is special or local conditions or the trends of the debtor's business as shown in its comparative financial statements.

Because these four *C*'s—especially the first two—are reflections of "personal" qualities of an individual or business, credit communications are surcharged with negative possibilities. When you question honesty, earning ability, or judgment, you are treading on potentially dangerous ground. With tact, patience, and a positive attitude, however, communications about credit can be goodwill builders.

One of the fundamental concepts that will help you to write successfully about credit is this: The credit privilege is *earned;* it is not handed out indiscriminately, given away—or sold. For that reason you should not talk about *granting* credit; more appropriate terminology is *approval* or *extension* of credit.

On the basis of one or more of the four *C's* an individual or firm merits credit. For many, character is the primary reason. They earn little, and they have little or no capital, but they pay their bills and thus earn the right to credit. And this is the bedrock of credit extension. Firms or individuals may enjoy high earnings but will not continue to enjoy ordinary credit privileges with a record of not taking care of obligations as promised.

Anticipating those who may be unable or unwilling to pay is one of the primary functions of the credit manager. To hold down losses from bad debts, the credit officer evaluates applicants' credit records and estimates their financial stability in the light of general business ups and downs.

But approving only gilt-edged applications will seriously curtail sales. Accordingly, a credit manager must be sales-minded, and well informed about the firm's goods, to help build customer confidence and increase sales.

Since marginal risks are vital for profitable operations, evaluating and encouraging borderline cases must get careful attention. For both the firm and its customers the credit manager is part counselor, part sales promoter, and part detective.

When the information you receive about an applicant is favorable, you will of course approve the application and set up the account. Because of the sheer weight of numbers, most credit approvals are form messages, especially when they involve no purchase (and shipment) of goods. Many stores do no more than send a printed announcement card like the following:

THE J. P. BOWEN COMPANY

Is pleased to open a charge
account for you and welcome you to
our family of regular patrons

We hope you will make regular use
of your charge account

Such a notification sent promptly is certainly better than nothing. Yet it falls far short of what a good credit message can do to strengthen the credit relationship, promote goodwill, forestall collection problems, and stimulate sales.

Establishing the basis for credit

In credit approvals you may take advantage of the simple, obvious psychology of praise or approval. If you place a customer on the credit list because of a prompt-pay rating, you should say so. Hearing about the good rating encourages the customer to maintain that rating. The same is true for some reflections of favorable capacity or capital positions.

The reference should not be lengthy; in fact, it is preferably absorbed subordinately in the extension of credit or the explanation of terms. It is a significant reminder to the customer that credit is an earned privilege which requires care, thought, and effort to maintain. Too, thus established, it may serve as an effective collection appeal to the customer if the account begins to get slow.

So forceful is this device in the opinion of one experienced credit manager that approval notices to credit applicants with prompt-pay records were often only one sentence:

> We have received from your references the reports of your fine
> pay habits and shall be very happy to have a regular monthly
> charge account with you.

Obviously, this should accomplish more than it does, even if no more than a little resale or sales promotion, as you'll see later.

Explanation of terms

Unless a firm wants to encourage delayed payments, the initial extension of credit should make unmistakably clear how payments are expected, with the confident assumption that the customer will comply with the terms. Even a form can easily incorporate a simple statement like one of the following:

> On the first of each month you will receive an itemized
> statement of your purchases made through the 25th day of the
> preceding month; purchases made after the 25th appear on the
> following month's bill. Your payment is due by the 10th.
>
> --
>
> Under our system of cycle billing your statement of a month's
> purchases will go to you on the 17th of each month; we
> expect settlement within 10 days.

Clear, specific explanations of terms can not only prevent misunderstanding and delay but also serve as a stimulus to prompt pay.

How far to go with the explanation depends on the reader's credit knowledge and reputation. To those you think know and respect credit practices, you would tell only what the terms are; explaining that 2/10, n/30 means a deduction of 2 percent if paid in 10 days or pay the whole in 30 days would insult such a reader. To a reader who is new to credit business or barely passes your credit evaluation, however, you had better make the terms not only clear and emphatic but concrete (i.e., show the prompt-pay benefits as savings in money, what it will buy, and the continued credit privilege):

Under our regular credit terms of 2/10, n/30, you can save
$1.36 on this order alone if your check is in the mail by
July 10—which will almost pay for another enamel display
tray. Your check for the net of $68 by July 30, however, will
keep you in the preferred-customer class.

Such specificness is not possible, of course, except in an individualized message. But the credit extension, whenever possible, should be individualized; it is worth the extra money in its favorable effect on the customer.

To stop with the approval, the basis, and the terms would be foolish, however; a good credit writer can also help to further sales—through the goodwill elements of resale material on goods, resale on the house, or sales-promotion material on other allied goods. All should focus on repeat sales.

Stimulating sales

In credit approvals, sales-building passages should definitely be low pressure; if the service attitude does not dominate, the greedy overtones can repel the reader. But the writer of the following, you will note, is careful to tie in a service-to-you reference to all sales-building passages and thus make the customer feel welcome rather than pounced upon:

Your company's fine record of promptly paying invoices,
confirmed by the references you supplied, certainly qualifies
you for an open account with Rutherford Chemicals. Now your
company is only a telephone call away from one of the country's
largest stocks of laboratory chemicals, and we promise "same
day" shipment for almost every order.

We will invoice your purchases to you as they are shipped,
and date the invoices two days after the date of shipment.
Terms are 2/10, net 45,up to $4,000, and we are sure you will
want to take advantage of the discount for prompt payment.

Since we regularly stock every item in our catalog, you will
experience a minimum of back orders with Rutherford, and
rarely an "out of stock." In fact, over the last two years
we have achieved a 98.5% rate of "same day" shipments, a
record our people are pretty proud of.

A new service to our customers is our Small Order Department.
We set this unit up specifically to handle your needs for
small or sample quantities of many chemicals. Our Small Order
Department allows us to do something unequalled in our
industry—do away with minimum order requirements. This
means you can order most chemicals in any quantity, from
an ounce to a tank load, from one source. That's Rutherford
convenience!

Few credit approvals to consumers identify a limit (although one may go on the office record), whereas most business credit arrangements and consumer bank credit cards like Visa and Master Charge include limits as parts of the explanation of terms.

To prevent the limit from appearing to be a penalty, with consequent negative reactions, a good writer phrases it in positive language:

```
The No-Flame you ordered

        20 gallons @ $6 ................ $120
```
should arrive in Jackson by the weekend. It went out freight prepaid this morning by the L & M Railroad. The amount of this shipment has been debited to your newly opened account, which we are glad to open on the basis of your strong personal capital.

Under our regular terms of 2/10, n/60, your No-Flame will cost you only $117.60 if you send your check by May 2; the full $120 is due on June 21. At any one time you may carry as much as $250 worth of No-Flame or other Bronson products on account.

With the increasing demand for No-Flame you will find it a rapid seller—and a good profit item at the usual markup of $3 a can. With your shipment you will receive attractive window displays which our other dealers have found helpful.

Silentol, a flame-resistant, sound-decreasing wall coating, is another item your home-building customers will like. The cost is only a fraction more than for conventional paint. For a trial shipment, just fill out the enclosed order blank and drop it in the mail; we'll send your Silentol to you—along with display material—within a few days.

Making the customer feel welcome and appreciated

Credit-approval writers nearly all seem to know that making new credit customers feel welcome and appreciated helps to promote frequent and continued use of the account (increasing sales and profits). Indeed they so often begin by welcoming the customer to "our growing number of satisfied customers" that it is not only bad writing but is stereotyped. *The customer is more interested in finding out the decision on the application. So that decision should get the emphatic beginning position.*

Besides, do you really need to waste words on welcomes and thankyous? If you approve the credit (implied by sending the goods immediately when the application accompanies an order), establish the basis, explain the terms positively, and then follow with resale and sales promotion material concretely implying the desire to be of service, your reader will not doubt whether you appreciate business. By implication you adequately establish such welcomes and thank-yous (See "Gratitude," p. 71.)

If, despite these suggestions and illustrations, you feel the necessity for either of these expressions, place it near the end of your letter.

The relevant checklist (p. 140) summarizes our major suggestions about credit approvals, although, as always, you should apply them with discretion. We *know* they don't all apply in all cases.

Credit Approval Checklist

1. The direct opening should approve credit quickly.
   a. If you have no order, approve credit immediately in a cheerful, welcoming, ungrudging tone.
   b. When you are shipping goods, say so in the first line. Shipping the goods first also implies credit approval.
   c. Name the goods specifically (don't call them an "order"!); state the amount (of goods and dollars) or send an invoice.
   d. In general, you'd better identify the method of shipment.
   e. Choose words that get the goods to the reader and in use; don't stop with just getting them onto a freight car.
   f. A touch of resale (say a favorable adjective) is desirable early, but don't slow up your opening with much resale/goodwill.
   g. Use figures and symbols in orders and acknowledgments.
   h. Take care of all legal details: item prices, freight charges, total. You may assume an invoice or tabulate here.

2. The credit agreement/relation:
   a. For restraint, explain how the customer earned credit.
   b. Although you might identify terms incidentally in the opening, later (for people who might not understand or respect them properly) explain by
      (1) Attaching your interpretation of the terms to a purchase (present or future).
      (2) Concretizing the discount with specific savings figures (maybe a free unit of a purchase, a month's phone bill . . .).
      (3) Bringing in prompt-pay education, in a tone that implies your confidence that the reader will comply.
   c. With its negative potentialities, any credit-limit talk needs a you-viewpoint introduction and positive statement. You might want to label it temporary.
   d. But don't imply "If you don't like these terms, we'll change them."

3. Your resale or sales promotion material in closing the letter:
   a. Include reassuring comments about the reader's good choice.
   b. Mention your services and selling aids concretely.
   c. Consider selling the reader some seasonal or allied goods.
   d. Regardless of how you close, let it point to future orders.
   e. Be specific, not wooden and dull, as in "We have enjoyed serving you and look forward to supplying your future needs."

4. Your appreciation is best worked in incidentally, subordinately.

5. Transitions are easier with a logical order of points.

6. Watch the tone throughout.
   a. Avoid FBI implications about the credit investigation and condescending, mandatory, or selfish explanation of terms.
   b. Proportion affects your tone too; don't talk terms too much.

SIMPLE CLAIMS AND ADJUSTMENT APPROVALS
[When things go wrong, see that you don't go with them.]

Claims offer you as a buyer the opportunity to get adjustments on unsatisfactory goods and services. If you are a seller and therefore receive claims, welcome them! They offer you an opportunity to discover and correct defects in your goods and services. And your adjustment letters are excellent opportunities for you to build or destroy goodwill. Whether you make the most of your opportunities in either claims or adjustments depends heavily on your attitude.

Any claim and adjustment situation necessarily involves negatives. Somebody is dissatisfied and unhappy. One of the major jobs in writing either claim or adjustment messages, therefore, is to keep these emotionally based negatives from stealing the show and making the situation worse. What you have learned about goodwill, resale, and handling negative material is especially important in adjustments.

In three kinds of situations you may have reason to write a persuasive claim: (1) you've tried a simple (direct) one and been turned down; (2) you know you're dealing with a tight-fisted firm; or (3) the claim is unusual or the facts leave at least some doubt about the justice of the claim. We treat such persuasive claims in Chapter 11.

Here we are talking about direct (A–plan) claims—situations where you have facts justifying the claim and you are supposedly dealing with an open-minded and fair person or firm.

Direct claims

You will probably write good direct claims if you remember these five often-forgotten points (which serve as a checklist for direct claims):

1. *If you think you have a just claim, go ahead.* Progressive firms like claims because they suggest ways of improvement. Many firms even advertise the request: "If you like our products, tell others; if you don't, tell us." Often they encourage claims by "double-your-money-back" guarantees and the like.

2. *Keep your shirt on! When things go wrong, the firm surely did not intend to mistreat you. Almost certainly the person handling your claim had nothing to do with the dissatisfaction. So restrain your anger or sarcasm!*

Very few manufacturers expect every item they manufacture to be perfect. Most know that ZD (zero-defect) production is an ideal rarely achieved even by the best quality controls. So nearly always they expect to replace or repair defective merchandise. This is more efficient than to insist on perfection in manufacturing—and consequently higher prices. The consumer who gets defective merchandise and takes the attitude that the seller tried to cheat, then, is usually wrong.

Furthermore, in most cases all that's necessary to get satisfaction is to make a simple claim and calmly give the justifying facts.

> Your last shipment to us (our order No. A–1753, your invoice No. 45602, dated May 6, 1980), was incorrect. Instead of the socket-head set screws with cup points we ordered, you sent screws with flat points. We were able to hold this shipment of screws intact, having opened only one box.
>
> Will you please rush us 5,000 5–40 × 1/4-inch socket-head set screws, black finish, with cup points. Our plant manager says we have enough of the proper screws on hand to last us through June 12, so we must have the replacement screws by then.
>
> How shall we ship the screws with flat points back to you? Do you want to cancel your invoice No. 45602 or let it cover the replacement order? We want to take advantage of your 2% cash discount.

To be nasty to the almost certainly innocent person who handles your claim is to be unfair and unreasonable, even foolish. Instead of creating a favorable mood that will help you get satisfaction, you turn this possible ally against you if you write in a nasty mood.

3. *Give the facts—calmly, specifically, thoroughly.* Usually a firm will grant an adjustment merely on the strength of a customer's adequate explanation of what is wrong and suggestions for a fair settlement. In that case you would be ridiculous to misjudge the situation and write a too-strong claim. Unless you have good reason to believe otherwise, assume that the firm will be cooperative. Little or no persuasion seems necessary; hence you use no appeal beyond a possible brief reference to the guarantee, reputation for fair dealing, and the like.

This kind of direct claim (A–plan) may start with the requested action, or it may start with the history of the case—date and conditions of purchase, conditions of use, development of troubles, and on to present condition. Beginning with the history of the case is a little less antagonizing and a little more persuasive.

The middle part is a carefully planned, complete, and specific explanation of the facts. A test of the adequacy of the explanation is to ask whether it is all you would want to know if you had to decide on the claim—and whether it is convincing. Since claims adjusters aren't stupid, they know that some people lie. Hence you may need to use other evidence to back up your word. The ending, then, is a request for action. It should be as specific as the conditions will permit.

4. *When you know just what is wrong and what is necessary to set things right, you should make a definite claim; otherwise, explain and ask for an inspection.*

Sometimes you can be sure that the only fair adjustment is a refund of your money or a complete replacement of the product. On other occasions you can see that replacement of a part or proper adjustment of a machine will correct the trouble. You therefore ask definitely for what is necessary to make things right, as in the preceding claim.

Sometimes, however, the product just isn't right, but you don't know exactly what is wrong. Your claim then should be an explanation of how the product is failing to satisfy you and a request for the necessary action. You can make your own estimate and request that action, call in third parties to estimate (as on automobile insurance claims), or ask the firm to investigate and take the indicated action.

> The Dexter fluorescent desk lamp I purchased at your store October 5 has been satisfactory in every way but one.
>
> When in use, the lamp operates coolly and soundlessly; but as soon as the lamp is switched off, something inside produces a humming sound. Not only is the hum annoying, but I fear that it suggests a fire hazard.
>
> I'm returning the lamp to you for repair or replacement, whichever you find necessary.
>
> Since I've lots of reading to do, will you please rush it back to me?

5. *Sometimes a touch of humor can relieve the pressure in small claims.* Somewhat like the nasty tone (Point 2), another common error in writing claims is that many writers become deadly serious about small matters. A claim for replacement of a defective $3 item makes the writer look silly when written as if it were a matter of life and death. If the situation is really serious, of course, you would not want to treat it lightly. But to avoid the too-serious tone in small matters and make the reader an ally instead of a critic, you can often use humor effectively. You may inject only a touch or two, or the whole thing may be humorous.

Several dangers confront you, however, if you decide to be humorous:

1. A failing attempt to be funny is worse than no attempt.
2. Humor may make you write a longer letter than necessary.
3. Humor making the reader the butt will nearly always arouse resentment.
4. Humor which verges on the vulgar or sacrilegious may offend.

The following successful letter avoids at least the last two dangers:

> We all need air to live, I admit, but don't you think 89¢ a tube is a little high for atmosphere?
>
> In San Antonio, Texas, a few days ago, I bought a tube of Dento toothpaste. At least, that's what I thought I bought. But when I started to brush my teeth at home that night in Dallas, I found a little gob of toothpaste in the top of the tube, a little gob of toothpaste in the bottom, and air in between.
>
> I thought maybe you had a new type of toothpaste, so I tried it out. I'm sorry to have to tell you that air is pretty tasteless. And it doesn't do much of a job cleaning teeth, either.

I could go back to the drug store in San Antonio and demand another tube, but I don't see much profit in making a 540-mile round trip to replace an 89¢ tube of toothpaste—even when it's Dento.

Now, would you prefer to send me a round-trip airplane ticket to San Antonio so I can make a claim to the dealer, or a new tube—one with toothpaste in it?

I have instructed my attorneys not to bring suit until your Board of Directors has had a chance to meet and settle this important question of policy. Meanwhile, my breath is getting steadily worse—my wife and children won't kiss me, and my dog avoids me. I'm in an awful fix!

Adjustment approvals

Adjustment policies. Invariably a claim represents loss of goodwill and of confidence in the goods or in the firm. The adjustment writer's key job is to minimize those losses by satisfying customers as far as possible at a reasonable cost to the company.

Some companies try to dodge the basic problem by almost literally adopting the policy that the customer is always right. They figure that the few unfair claims cost less in adjustment losses than the liberal policy pays in goodwill.

Other firms take the opposite view and make all sales final. Usually they depend on low prices rather than goodwill to attract a type of customer to whom price is the strongest possible appeal.

The great majority take the middle ground between those two extremes: *Treat each claim on its merits and lean a bit toward giving the customer the benefit of the doubt for the sake of unquestioned fairness and the resulting goodwill.*

Generally a customer will not leave a firm or product after only one disappointment if the firm applies this honest and reasonable policy with finesse. Usually a reasonable person will allow at least a second chance, unless the adjuster loses further goodwill by a poor attitude toward the claim or by bungling techniques in handling it.

Carrying out the recommended policy therefore requires

1. Careful analysis and classification of each claim according to the cause of dissatisfaction and consequently what adjustment is fair.
2. Retaining a reasonable attitude even with angry claimants.
3. Skill in the use of the tools and techniques of adjustment.

Analysis and classification of adjustments. If the evidence in a claim (and from inspection when deemed necessary) shows clearly that the company or the product was at fault, you may replace the article free with a perfect one, repair it free, or take it back and refund the money.

The last is the least desirable for both buyer and seller. The purchaser bought the article to get the service it would render. If you take it back, you give the purchaser a problem—to make other arrangements or do without that service. If you replace or repair it, you give the service, regain goodwill, and make a satisfied customer who will perhaps buy from you again and pass on the good word about you and your products to other prospects. Indeed, about the only occasion when you would refund the money is when you see that a perfect specimen of the article will not do the job. And even then, if you have another (perhaps larger or of better quality) which you think will satisfy, you should try to give the service wanted and justify any higher price in terms of advantages.

If the dissatisfaction is clearly the buyer's fault, you will ordinarily refuse the claim. In rare cases you may decide that a compromise or even a full-reparation adjustment will be the wise thing because of the amount of goodwill you can regain at small cost. The weakness in this decision is that it implies your acceptance of responsibility and increases your difficulty in regaining confidence in your goods and service.

Whatever your action when the buyer is at fault, your major job is justifying your decision and (usually) educating the customer. By educating the buyer in the proper use and care of the product, you may establish the responsibility by implication, avoid irritating the claimant, and prevent future trouble.

If responsibility for the dissatisfaction is uncertain or divided between buyer and product, you will suggest a compromise or make a full adjustment. Again the educational function is usually important.

When you decide to approve the adjustment, our earlier discussion of favorable replies to inquiries and requests prepares you rather well to write full-reparation adjustments, which are in fact answers to requests (claims). They are essentially the same in organization and psychology, but with some basic differences. In answering other requests you have no legal or moral obligation to do anything against your will; in answering claims, you have a legal and ethical obligation to be fair.

Attitude of the adjuster. If a firm's adjuster thinks most claims are dishonest or from chronic gripers, this attitude will eventually reduce the number of claims—and probably the firm's sales too. People won't continue to trade where they are considered dishonest or unreasonable.

But most claimants are honest. Out of 5 million customers, only 2,712 tried to take advantage of one firm in five years. So an adjuster who thinks every claim is an attempt to defraud the firm is wrong in both fact and attitude.

Claims are an invaluable clue to weaknesses in a company's products, methods, services, or personnel. But the weaknesses won't be corrected if the adjuster considers most claims dishonest.

On the other hand, if you start with the attitude that a claimant may be misinformed but is honest and reasonable, you will be right most of the time, and you will do much better. You will use claims as pointers to improve your firm's goods and operations, and your adjustment letters will thank customers for the help they have given. (Even claims where the buyer seems completely at fault may point to a need for better instructions to users.) But more important, you create a pleasant climate in which people will buy more freely because they know they can get reasonable adjustments if anything goes wrong.

In addition to this sound attitude, you need a thick skin to be an adjuster. Many claimants are not calm. As a wise adjuster, therefore, you will ignore personal taunts. Remember the old saying, "You can't win an argument with a customer; even when you win you lose." So defend your firm, your products, and yourself insofar as you can by explanations; otherwise accept the claims made. Thus you create a climate of goodwill and good business.

A claim represents customer dissatisfaction all right, but it does not necessarily involve really strong negatives which you cannot almost completely overcome with your fair-minded attitude and skillful use of the adjuster's tools and techniques.

Adjustment tools and techniques. *Using resale.* Since the adjustment writer's main job is to regain goodwill and confidence, you will find resale a highly useful tool. Probably nowhere else is it more important. Indeed, the main job of an adjuster is essentially the same as the purpose of resale—to recover or strengthen goodwill and confidence in the integrity and efficiency of a firm and/or the quality of its goods. Naturally, then, resale is the main tool for doing that job.

Making positive explanations. Effective resale is impossible, however, unless you avoid the following special pitfalls which frequently trap the untrained adjuster:

1. Inadequate or inept explanation that leaves the customer thinking slipshod methods of manufacturing or marketing caused the trouble. Explain how careful you really are.
2. Dwelling on the reader's dissatisfaction or likelihood of being a lost customer.
3. Passing the buck by attributing the difficulty to a new clerk or an act of God.
4. Trying to hide in the bigness of your firm. About the only way you can use bigness as an acceptable explanation is to sell it in terms of customer benefits along with its weaknesses.
5. Stressing your openhandedness. The customer does not want to be considered a beggar.
6. Suggesting future trouble. You only put undesirable ideas into the customer's head if you say, "If you have any more difficulty, let us know," or even "I don't believe you'll have any more difficulty." In fact, a big problem in adjustments is what to do about the inherent negatives in them.

Handling inherent negatives.   As an adjustment writer, you therefore need to be a master of the techniques for dealing with negatives. They will be one of your stumbling blocks, for every adjustment situation is full of them. You'll do well to remember the definition of *negative* as anything unpleasant to the reader. Moreover, you should remember that *a good business communicator avoids negative material when possible and otherwise subordinates it.* You'll find that you can usually avoid most of the goodwill killers like the following, which creep into the work of untrained adjusters:

you claim	policy	damaged	delay
you say	amazed	broken	inconvenience
you state	fault	defective	regret
you (plus any accusing verb)	surprised	unable	sorry

Such wording need not appear. Prune out the negative wording (and implications). Substitute positive phrasing.

Adjustment-approval messages.   Since an adjustment approval is good news (A–plan), you answer the big question in the first sentence as fast as you can. Not only should this sentence tell that you are approving the adjustment, but it should avoid any grudging tone and refrain from recalling the dissatisfaction any more than necessary.

The fact that you have approved the adjustment gives you a natural basis for some resale talk on the house. You should use it by interpreting the approval as evidence that you stand behind guarantees and treat the customer right, or something similar.

Somewhere, but not necessarily right after the good news and its interpretation, you should express appreciation for the claimant's report (because the information helps the firm to keep goods and services up to par). This "thank you" does several important things quickly:

1.   It shows that you are fair-minded and do not take a distrusting or bitter attitude toward claims.
2.   It is basically resale in showing that you are interested in retaining (if not improving) your standards for goods and services.
3.   It makes the customer feel good because a claim seems welcome and appears to get careful consideration.

Of course, if you are taking any steps to prevent recurrence of claims such as you are answering, you should explain them (to rebuild confidence) and give the customer as much credit as the facts allow. Anybody likes to hear that "On the basis of helpful suggestions like yours, we have decided. . . ."

Your explanation of the situation will be important. If the product was obviously defective or the firm was at fault and no explanation will put either in a better light, you'd better accept the fact and frankly admit the error or defect rather than make excuses. If you explain specifically how your firm tries to see that everything goes well, most people will accept it as due precaution and will understand that mistakes do occasionally creep in, despite reasonable care—ZD production is an unattainable ideal.

If you have statistics to show how effective your system is in avoiding mistakes and defective goods, they may be effective in rebuilding the customer's confidence and goodwill. Be careful, though, not to present such data in a way that seems to say the reader must be odd to have trouble when nearly all your other customers don't.

Although you can't honestly or safely promise that a similar situation will never happen again, you can end pleasantly. Having covered the good news, the explanation, the thanks, and any necessary action of the reader, you can end looking forward, not backward. (Apologies or other reminders of past dissatisfaction merely leave a bad taste in the mouth.) A light touch of resale—or even sales promotion material, if you have a related article you think would serve well—can provide you with a sincere, success-conscious look forward to future business. Customers so well treated will probably return.

Although the following letter does not actually send the check in the first sentence, as is usually desirable, it does emphatically approve the adjustment. Moreover, it gives a clear explanation and strong resale (in answer to the claim on p. 387):

> You most certainly will get a refund on the XXX suit you purchased, for we support our salespeople in whatever they promise a customer.
>
> The person who told you that we would have no sale on XXX suits was sincere. The XXX manufacturers have never before allowed their suits to be sold at reduced prices. We were notified one week before our summer clothing sale this year that they were permitting a reduction for the first time.
>
> We thank you for calling our attention to this situation, and we are glad to enclose our check for $21.87.
>
> When you again need clothing, see our salespeople. You can rely on what they tell you, with full confidence that we will back them up.

Sometimes you will need the customer's help on a few details such as filling out blanks for recovery of damages from a transportation company or returning defective articles. Be sure to cover such points in the one letter to avoid unnecessary correspondence. And in doing so, make the reader's action as easy as possible.

> Your Old South cream and sugar set is going out prepaid today so that it will arrive two or three days before the wedding.
>
> Since the Old South set is in keeping with southern traditions, it will attract favorable glances and comments as guests look over the gifts.

The set is being carefully wrapped with plenty of foam and
shipped in a corrugated box of 3/16-inch thickness. This box
is thicker than required by freight carriers, but it will be
standard packing for all Old South china from now on. Your
report has helped us to improve our service. Thank you.

To simplify getting the insurance due from the Postal Service
on the first shipment, we are sending a form completely
filled out except for your signature. Will you please sign it
and use the reply envelope to mail it back?

The bride and groom will like the antebellum motif of the Old
South set and will attach many pleasant memories to it as the
years go by.

The related checklist for approving adjustments (p. 150) is comprehensive enough to cover most situations, but not all points are likely to apply to
any one situation.

CASES

Direct inquiries

1. As the representative for Imports from Hong Kong, 303 Bellevue
Avenue, Tucson, AZ 85715, you have to travel a great deal throughout the
Southwest selling your custom-made suits and dresses to men and women.
You have been robbed once (over $700 stolen); so today when you read
the ad in *Car and Driver* by Aerodata, Inc., Jefferson County Airport Executive Building, Broomfield, CO 80020, for an Auto Alert, you took down
some questions in preparation for writing an inquiry. The ad read—Low-
Cost Pocket Pager & Theft Warning System by Coded Radio Signal. Calls
you—only you—the moment a thief or vandal tries to enter your car, home,
boat, or plane. Guard your valuables 24 hours a day at low, low cost!
Your own, private, HF radio signal in your pocket; one full watt power,
one-mile range, transmitter will fit any car or truck, one-year warranty, 10-
day money-back guarantee, $149.95 retail.

There's no mention of installation. You have put in auto tape decks
and would like to install the Auto Alert if the job is not too difficult. If it
were too difficult, who would you get to finish the job? Does the receiver
work effectively indoors? What type of warning sound does it make? Is
the page signal different from the alarm tone? Will CB radio or lightning
set off false alarms? What power sources operate the transmitter and receiver? Is the transmitter a sound-sensitive device, a motion detector, or
is it switch activated?

2. In *Playboy* magazine you see a small ad picturing an automobile
radio with a built-in TV ($200) by JVD Americana, Inc., 798 Stratford
Midtown Expressway, Maspeth, NY 11259 (phone 212/555–3890). You
would like to install the radio-television in your 1980 Cutlass and use it

Checklist for Approving Adjustments

1. Make the beginning fast, informative, pleasant, and reassuring.
   a. Open with the full reparation—a specific statement of what you are doing.
   b. Avoid any grudging tone.
   c. Build up the favorable reaction with a few resale words.
   d. Too much resale on defective products before explanation may bring an "Oh yeah?"

2. Avoid emphasis on disappointing aspects and negative words.

3. Explain fully, honestly, and reassuringly any favorable facts.
   a. Include a goodwill-building sentence—either that you're glad to make the adjustment or that you welcome the report as a way of improving quality and service.
   b. Whichever you choose, be sure your facts relate logically to your wording of the adjustment you've made.
   c. Judicially, impartially—and preferably impersonally—establish the reason for the mishap in the minimum number of words. Often you can effectively imply the reason in your explanation of corrective measures taken or your ordinary care.
   d. Whether you name or imply the source of error, give concrete evidence of normally correct, safe shipments of high-quality goods, or—if applicable—explain changes you are making to prevent recurrence of the difficulty.
   e. Be quick to admit error; don't appear to be buck-passing.
   f. Avoid suggesting frequency of error.

4. Ask for any necessary cooperation from the customer. For example:
   a. Be tactful in asking the customer to sign necessary forms.
   b. What about the original article if you're replacing it? Make any customer action as easy as possible ("When the driver calls to pick up the original shipment, just have . . .").

5. Close pleasantly with a forward look.
   a. Don't ruin your good positive efforts with a backward look apologizing or otherwise recalling the disappointing aspects.
   b. Do leave the customer with a pleasant reminder of the pleasurable use of the perfect article now in hand, if applicable.
   c. You may end with resale talk, but sales promotional material on an allied or seasonal article may well suggest your additional thoughtfulness—and just may pick up an extra sale.

while dove hunting during football season. Since you also will use it while driving over bumpy roads to your cabin in the woods, you wonder if the equipment is built to withstand rough and bumpy treatment. You also need to know how complex is the installation, the name of a local dealer, kind of guarantee, and if there are any antennae available that would add to the reception and range capabilities. Write the inquiry.

3. This past summer you did not get the job you had hoped to—the job which would have paid enough to provide the extra money you need to attend school this fall. In June, an inquiry to the Financial Aids Office brought the bad news that all aid for the coming year has been used up. Thus, you decided to write the dean's office of the school you attend to find out if any scholarships are available to persons with your qualifications and need, and how and when you have to apply if any scholarships are available. Use an attention line (Scholarship Committee) and a subject line. Use your own qualifications (class, grade average, and major or career interests).

4. Write a letter that can go to any of three western U.S. hotels selected by your committee (site committee for the annual management conference of ICM, Inc., Greenbrier at Centennial, Muncie, IN 47304). As chairperson you must have the information soon, so that you can firm up the plans for the meeting three months from now. You have been examining brochures from three hotels which were selected because of their accessibility to all ICM divisions and which listed "convention facilities" as one of their attractions. You need to know, however, the sizes of the auditoriums and conference rooms, whether these rooms are in the hotel or some adjoining area, and what kind of PA systems they have. Since the conference will be a week long—Monday through Sunday—(use exact dates) and last over a weekend (the main banquet will be scheduled in each of the three areas for that week), what shows, exhibits, concerts, etc. are available? You would like more information about each hotel's tennis courts, golf course, and swimming pool, especially the tennis courts since the ICM Interdivision Doubles Tennis Tournament is always one of the conference highlights.

5. Clip (or copy) from the pages of any newspaper or magazine an ad featuring a product or service in which you are interested. Write an inquiry to the manufacturer or distributor asking for details not furnished by the ad. Price and local availability are possibilities. Servicing is another. Ask four significant questions, *at least one of which requires explanation on your part*. Attach the ad or copy to your letter.

6. *Letterhead:* Leslie and Meade, 6922 N. Meridian, Puyallup, WA

98371. *Signature block:* Sincerely yours, you, Director, Customer-Auditor Relations. This is a form letter to Wilhelm customers about bills they received from P. J. Wilhelm & Sons Company. *Information:* As a part of an extensive audit, Leslie and Meade has to check the invoices which Wilhelm has sent its customers. Because of the volume of transactions involved, it is customary to examine accounts for selected, rather than continuous, periods during the year. You are interested in the amount of the invoice recorded as $331.18 which was mailed to this customer (you make up the name and address) on (a specific date about six weeks before you're writing). If the customer received this invoice and found it to be correct, the customer may simply disregard this letter. If, however, the customer either did not receive the invoice or received an invoice listing an incorrect amount, inform Leslie and Meade of the circumstances. Enclose a franked envelope for easy replying. Explain that any audit involving customer transactions must have the cooperation of the customers contacted in order to be successful. Your clients as well as your team of auditors are counting on the customer to help them to keep the audited company honest and correct.

7. Write Fair Havens Home for Senior Citizens, 500 Owyhee, Paradise Valley, NV 89426, and ask for details about making arrangements for an 86-year-old relative of yours. Find out what the monthly charges are for basic, intermediate, and skilled care. Ask about facilities (private room, semiprivate). Ask what down payment is necessary and what the charges cover. Your relative insists on not living with you but wants to live near the old hometown, and that is why you considered this home. Your relative has circulatory problems and has to have a shot for pernicious anemia every ten days to two weeks. You want your relative to have a comfortable place to live, but the cost of comfort is a real consideration. You and the relative have limited funds.

8. Assume you are a hospital administrator (Mercy Hospital, New Orleans, LA 70122) who is considering granting an internship to C. W. Brown, health care management student at Tulane University. Brown talked with you and filled out an application form. Before you talk with the applicant again, you want some information from references. Compose a letter to one of them, Melvin Hinkley, professor of health care management, Tulane University, Tulane Avenue, New Orleans, LA 70118. Ask some specific questions.

9. As the person with responsibility for in-service training at Americana Life Insurance Company, 10099 Choctaw, Independence, MO 64554, you want your trainees to see the film *Charisma* from Lynfield Industries, 150 Meyer Avenue, Jamaica, NY 11412. Lynfield provides the film free to

firms requesting it—if it can be scheduled on a date when others are not using it. You have in mind three specific dates (about two months from now) on which you could show the film to 600 employees. Write a letter asking that the film be sent to you for showing on any of the dates designated. If those dates are taken, you want to know when the film would be available.

10.   Getting up several times a night to let your three-foot, 95-pound German Shepherd out has become a pain in the neck. "Why Be a Doorman for Your Pet?" says a headline in this month's *Esquire*. The copy reads "Flex Port ends scratched doors and whining. Keeps out flies, wind, rain. Gives you and your dog or cat complete freedom. Turen, Inc., Dept. E–92, Cottage Ave., Danvers, MA 01923." But would the door be large enough for your Shepherd (and if so, why not a burglar?)—and what about the cost of the door as well as installation cost? Where you live you have heavy rainfall, especially during February, March, and April. Ask the company if this door will protect the inside of the house against severe weather. Durability? Colors?

11.   In *Tennis World* you saw a full-page ad from King Manufacturing, Inc., P.O. Box 4598, Princeton, NJ 08540 (609/555-8686), picturing three tennis ball machines—Little King, King, and King Professional. The ad said (as you'll see in Case 1, p. 289), "Tennis has become one of the world's most popular pastimes. To help players of all ages and abilities improve their game, King has perfected the impersonal practice partner. You can sharpen your game with practice, anytime, anywhere with a King machine. Moderate in price, the King machine can make the best personal coaching show greater results. Top professionals vote King their favorite ball machine. Write or phone for full information and nearest dealer's name." You want to know prices, sizes, operation procedures, guarantee. Assume that you are going to give this as a gift to a business associate who has just taken up tennis at the ripe age of 30. Which machine would be best for your avid tennis player?

12.   Write the Stars Motel, 1840 Chandler Avenue, St. Paul, MN 55113, to reserve a room, one bed (preferably queen or king), two people, one night, July 9. Your AAA book lists widely varying prices and says part of the Stars has been renovated and part not. Ask for a room in the new part. You want to guarantee your reservation, so include your Visa number 4367–090–078–876 and date of expiration, and your AAA membership number 09–07–009243. If the Stars cannot accommodate you, ask the clerk to make reservations at some comparable place nearby. You will be leaving your city before you can get confirmation.

13. In your Sunday newspaper you noticed an ad from Orbit Products, 2126 Coopers Lane, Jeffersonville, IN 47130, on inflatable boats. The ad said that these boats could be stored in a closet, transported in a car's trunk, set up quickly at a beach, riverbank, or pier. Since you are a roving fisherman, the idea of an inflatable boat appeals to you, but you have some questions. What size outboard motor would be best? Since your wife and son often like to fish with you, would the boat be big enough to hold the three of you? Also, you often like to use a boat for water skiing fun; so you'd want to know if an inflatable Orbit could be used in this way. Cost, too, is a consideration as well as safety. Write the letter.

14. With the Fourth of July weekend coming up, you and your family decide you would like to go camping at Gulf State Park, Gulf Shores, Alabama; so you will write to Travel Department, State Capitol, Montgomery, AL 36130, inquiring about trailer hookups. What is the difference in cost between a trailer hookup and a tent campsite? Do they both have electric and water hookups? What activities are provided? Since you enjoy motorcycling, you want to know if you can rent motorcycles from the park. Are pets permitted? (You have two you want to bring along.)

15. From your home address write Holstein and Meyer, Real Estate Agents, P.O. Box 1415, Hot Springs, AR 71901, inquiring about land on a fishing lake. You and your spouse can make a trip to Hot Springs next month, but before you go you want to know if there are any houses for sale on any fishing lakes. You need a two- or three-bedroom house, preferably one story. You want a sunny area near the house or lake where you can have a garden. You insist on having heat and air conditioning; and you would like to buy in the range of $50,000 to $60,000, depending on what you get. Also, you would hope that any property you buy now will go up in value when the heirs to your estate decide to sell (on your death). You are now in your late sixties and want this home for your retirement years.

16. Your 86-year-old aunt, Dorothy Shade Rose, is moving to Fair Havens Home for Senior Citizens (Case 7, p. 152), where she needs basic care. She walks with a cane, is alert, and is an ardent supporter of the Episcopal church. Write the rector at Christ Episcopal Church, 406 Main Street, Paradise Valley, NV 89426, and ask if the church has any program for the elderly. Your church has provisions for taking the senior citizens from the nursing homes to the church. Also inquire if the church has a system of calling the elderly, of taking them presents, of visitation. Explain that your Aunt Dorothy was a member of the Altar Guild for 50 years and a member of Saint Martha's Guild for 40. She also taught church school for 15 years.

17.   While traveling through Amarillo, Texas, last summer, you and your friend stopped at the Patio Motel, I–40 at Ross, for lunch. What really impressed you was the tasty pepper relish served at the salad bar. Once home you write the Patio Motel and ask what kind of relish that was and where you could buy it. Naturally you are interested in the price. Also find out what size jars it comes in.

18.   As the person in charge of personnel placement with a big chain of discount stores, Buy-Mart, 3440 La Grande Boulevard, Sacramento, CA 95813, you interview and place in stores (after a management training program of one year) able people first as assistant managers and then as managers. This morning you talked with a volatile but nervous 24-year-old, John Ruff. As he is soon to graduate from the University of California, Ruff applied for work in your training program. He seemed to be ambitious, energetic, and determined to please. While working on his business administration degree (majoring in marketing), he clerked 22 hours a week for four years at Golden's Menswear, 1851 S. Orange Avenue, Monterey Park, CA 91754. Besides waiting on customers, he sometimes helped decorate the windows, move merchandise, and mark goods. The only other work experience he had was checking stock, sweeping out, and carrying out packages in Palmer's Supermarket the summer after he was a junior in high school. As you talked with him, you noticed how much he interrupted you—was this just a nervous habit? Apparently he has plenty of determination. In some ways you felt that he was so busy thinking about his own ambition that he didn't follow what you were saying. To answer your questions about him, write Albert Golden, owner of Golden's Menswear. Also find out if Golden thinks Ruff would irritate customers. As a manager, would he be able to direct salespeople?

19.   In *Professional Builder,* page 202, this month, you read about the original Sun Garden Window that brings light, air, and sunshine into a home. The window expands the room visually and provides a perfect setting for decorative plants. Ad said the miniature greenhouse is available single glazed or with insulating Spaceglass. It's made in nine popular sizes and three finishes. It's easy to install, extremely well built and competitively priced. To find out price and to see if one would fit your west window casing, 38 inches horizontally and 48 inches vertically, write General Aluminum Corporation, P.O. Box 34221, Dallas, TX 75234. Your walls are veneered with tan brick; so you want to know which Sun Garden Window finish the company would recommend. Once installed, you wonder how far the window protrudes. Because of the extreme west sun in the summer, you also are concerned about the loss of air conditioning through the Spaceglass insulated window.

20. In the "What's New" section of the Sunday supplement to your paper you see a small ad for "Power-Now Converter, an inexpensive, quickly installed plant that delivers 110 volts AC from your car to your camper or other place needing electric power." This sounds like a good possibility for your new fleet of pizza delivery vehicles, each of which carries a 275-watt warming oven. Write Converter Products Company, 915 N. Ann Street, Lancaster, PA 17602, and ask about guarantees, installation, costs, wattage, capacity, operation. Since you will be wanting 12 units, can you get a discount?

21. For other memo cases, see GS 22, 24, 26 (p. 305).

Favorable replies (no sales possibilities)

1. *Charisma* is available (see Case 9, preceding series). It will be sent for showing on the requester's first choice of dates. Return postage and insurance must be paid by the user, but there's no charge for the film. Write a short letter, and enclose a newly printed folder of related films available from Lynfield. Address: Ms. Temo Callahan, Training Director, Americana Life Insurance Company. As an alternative (if your instructor directs), set your letter up as a fill-in form letter.

2. Professor Treavor Bean, head of a faculty-promotion committee, is trying to gather information to decide whether Professor Anton Young should be promoted from associate professor to full professor. As one of Professor Young's students two years ago, you were randomly selected to write a reference letter. The committee did not send a questionnaire or ask specific questions; it did not want to influence your thinking. The committee wants an objective appraisal. Would you recommend Professor Young? Why or why not? Assume that you had an excellent relationship with Professor Young (good thinker, dynamic teacher, refreshing, warm hearted, clever, hard working, dedicated, but unconventional). You earned two A's through a great deal of hard work under Professor Young.

3. As a broker for Senna & Smith, Inc., 2099 Tomahawk Avenue, Topeka, KS 66607, answer the inquiry from one of your good customers, Ellen Schuster, 79 Mirror Lake, Olathe, KS 66061. Mrs. Schuster, a wealthy widow, is concerned about the 500 shares of common stock she has in Northern Company, an electric utility holding company in Kansas, Missouri, Oklahoma, and North and South Dakota. She read in *The Wall Street Journal* that Northern is having financial difficulty and will have to raise utility rates in order to meet its growth needs. In checking her portfolio, she notes that she bought for 12 and the stock is selling for 16. Should she sell Northern? Answer Mrs. Schuster with these facts: Stronger earnings last year reflect higher sales and a rate increase. Recent rate increase in Oklahoma and Missouri may be insufficient to maintain earnings levels. Rate relief needed. In October two years ago Missouri Power filed for $173.9 million rate increase; on January 10 the next year $37.7 million of emergency relief was granted through April of that year. On March 18 a year ago Kansas Power filed for a $197.6 million rate hike, and was allowed a $50 million rate hike. Because of rising fuel costs and lower earnings, suggest Mrs. Schuster sell.

4.   Combined with or separate from Case 3, above, do some research and tell Mrs. Schuster what she should do with the proceeds of her sale of the Northern stock. Name two stocks she should invest in and why.

5.   As the rector of Christ Episcopal Church (Case 16, p. 154), answer the inquiry with this information: You do not have a program that picks up the elderly and brings them to church. Perhaps Aunt Dorothy can share a cab with someone at Fair Havens. The women in Saint Ann's Guild do call on fellow Episcopalians and do take presents at Christmas and on birthdays. You'll ask Ms. Jennie Richardson to call on Aunt Dorothy next week and welcome her to Paradise Valley and Christ Episcopal Church. Saint Ann's Guild meets on Monday mornings from 9:00 to 12:00, and the ladies do a great deal of sewing (slippers and aprons) for the yearly bazaar always held in November. Church services are held each Sunday at three times: 7:30 morning communion, 10:00 A.M. church school, and 11:00 A.M. family worship, with communion always the first Sunday of the month. As rector you will also call on Aunt Dorothy and welcome her. Address: Ms. Jean Morr, 47 Pavilion Street, Winnemucca, NV 89445.

6.   As a young executive trainee in Fayetteville, Arkansas (101 Lansbrook Drive, 72701), you have frequently attended alumni meetings of your college professional business organization, Iota Theta Lambda. It's a good group; you enjoy the programs and contacts. At a recent meeting you met the national president and the two of you talked enthusiastically about the worthwhile activities of the organization for college students and business people. You knew you made a favorable impression on the president, but you're surprised to receive a letter this morning asking you to become the state supervisor for Arkansas. A quick look in your directory shows you that there are only six chapters, no one of them more than 160 miles from you. And, you reason, all meetings are in the evening—you wouldn't have to miss many working hours; Iota Theta Lambda pays traveling expenses; it means only about three trips a month (none in the summer). Write C. R. Reeves, 3411 34th Place N.W., Washington, DC 20016, saying you'll accept the appointment and asking for further necessary instructions and materials.

7. One of your bright students last year, Jean B. Staley, asks you (a professor in your school) to write a letter to go along with a form you filled out to Farmer, Jameson, and Menoy Accounting, 345 White Horse Pike, Hammonton, NJ 08037. Staley wants an accounting internship for next summer. You can report favorably on Staley's 100 percent attendance, A— overall grade-point average, and good performance in your business communication class. This attractive, bright-eyed woman not only is a good accounting student, but she can write well, an asset most accounting firms like to see.

8. As manager of the Patio Motel (Case 17, p. 155), answer the inquiry from Jerry Garner, 56 Woodacres, Portland, OR 97202. The relish is bought by Patio in 112-ounce or 7-pound cans at a cost of $36 a case, or $6 a can. The relish, made from red peppers, water, sugar, vinegar, onions, tomato paste, modified food starch, salt, spices, and flavoring, is made by LeGout Foods Division, 9680 Belmont Avenue, Franklin Park, IL 60131. You cannot sell the relish direct, but suggest Garner write the manufacturer.

9. Answer the inquiry (Case 8, p. 152) of T. P. Shumaker, Mercy Hospital in New Orleans, about C. W. Brown, your former student in health care management at Tulane University. You remembered Brown as a hard-working, soft-spoken, gentle-mannered student. In kindness to a fellow student, Brown gave him a copy of a long report which Brown thought was just to help guide the student. But the student copied the report and turned it in to a fellow professor. Brown was not punished but was called in and warned not to be so generous again. In your course Brown earned a B. From your observation Brown got along well with the other class members, was serious about class work, and had a drive to want to get ahead.

10. As Jackie M. Vincent, 904 W. Lincoln Street, Urbana, IL 61801, you receive an inquiry on one of your former tenants, Tom Gregory, 49 Redwing Drive, Peoria, IL 61607, from Fenner, Snow, Colby and Adams, Inc., 350 Bethel Drive, St. Paul, MN 55104. Last year Gregory rented one of your two-bedroom apartments for $250 a month. His mother came with him in her Cadillac when he moved in, and she paid the first month's rent. Gregory seemed quiet, shy, and dominated by his mother at that time. When the rent came due the second month, you had to call Gregory and remind him. But from that time on he paid faithfully. Right before school was out he wrote you a note saying that he wanted the apartment in the summer because he had to finish one accounting course in order to graduate. Between the end of school and summer, you checked on the apartment in order to do the necessary cleaning and you found two torn

mattresses, a torn screen, and fleas everywhere. To get the screen fixed and the mattresses replaced and to have the apartment treated for the fleas cost $129.95. You wrote Gregory and asked him to pay the cost. His mother quickly sent back a check. You had an oral agreement of no pets which Gregory had not lived by. When he returned in summer, you had a newly worded contract with the "no pets" in it. Gregory sulked when confronted with this news, but he moved in anyway and continued to live in semifilth.

11.   As an assistant professor, marketing department, Michigan State University, East Lansing, MI 48823, you have a letter from Marion Palmer, owner of Palmer Skating Rink, Grand Rapids, MI 49508, asking you to do an analysis and write a report on whether or not Palmer should build a skating rink at Traverse City, Michigan. You have formerly talked on the phone with Palmer about the success of his Grand Rapids skating rink and he felt you out on your thinking about the growth and future of Traverse City. But Palmer did not come out and ask you on the phone if you would do a study, and no price was mentioned. Agree to do the study if Palmer meets your price of $1,500 plus expenses. Explain that you'll have to make several trips to Traverse City; you'll have to do a great deal of primary and secondary research.

12.   For additional cases, see SY 5, 7, 11 (p. 200) and GS 5 (p. 301).

Favorable replies (with sales possibilities)

1.   Sit in for the director of sales, Aerodata, Inc. (Case 1, p. 149), and answer the Imports from Hong Kong representative with the following information: $149.95 is cost (less than $10 a year). Takes three weeks or less to be enjoying this low-cost pocket pager and theft warning system. To lower or increase the loudness of the pager or alarm to match your surrounding, simply adjust the volume control. Can distinctly hear the intermittent beeping alarm and the continuous page tone of the Auto Alert over the usual office and household noises, as well as over such outdoor sounds as low-flying jets or football games. To prevent false alarms, Aerodata engineers designed a tone-activated squelch circuit for the receiver and a shielding circuit for the transmitter, thereby virtually eliminating the possibility of CB radio wave or lightning interference. The Auto Alert transmitter comes with complete, detailed installation instructions. Having installed tape decks before, should be familiar with polarity and wiring in cars, and will find installation of your alarm comparatively simple. Will need a volt-ohmmeter to complete installation and to test the operation of your personal, coded alarm signal. If problem arises with installation of transmitter, Service Consultants, 4020 Dunedin Avenue, Phoenix, AZ

85004 will help. They also do any repairs under the one-year warranty. Send a folder picturing the Auto Alert and drive for the order with an enclosed order blank.

2. As sales director, JVD Americana, Inc. (Case 2, p. 149), answer Steve McCamy with these facts: The three-step instruction booklet makes installation easy. JVD is designed for normal highway driving and not built for off-the-road driving. Because of the multiple-head jack, any type of VHF portable antenna will fit. The JVD Roundabout X–4 (an antenna decades ahead of its time in long-range reception, estimated on flat terrain 450 miles) is recommended. Company equips each set with its own powerful speaker (150 watts), but McCamy can easily hook up his own vehicle speakers if he so desires. Nearest dealer is The Radio Shack, Brookwood Village, Nashville (35 miles). You do not sell direct; you recommend The Radio Shack (to sell, install, be responsible). One-year guarantee on labor and parts. JVD operates with standard D batteries, and with AC adapter, or with car and boat adapter (included). McCamy can keep in touch with news, weather, music, and public-service band radio and see favorite TV programs.

3. Answer the inquiry (Case 13, p. 154), of Vernon and Anne Timme, 2872 S. Santa Fe Avenue, Vista, CA 92083, under the signature of Sales Manager, Orbit Products. For a 25-hp motor an Orbit Master Runabout for $875 will work, and can take up to a 40-hp motor. Has rigid hull, handles and maintains course well, has two self-bailing transom plugs, handles on outer sides, comes with inflation gauge. Pump can also deflate. Internal one-way valves allow inflation from a single point (separate valves provide for deflation). Length is 12 feet, weighs 146 pounds. Comes with floorboards and foot pump, inflatable keelson, lifelines on outer sides, oarlocks, two oars, generous repair kit, dull gray finish. Can set up in 20–25 minutes. Can accommodate four passengers, but three more comfortably.

4. As manager of industrial sales, Converter Products Company (Case 20, p. 156), answer R. N. Zeier, Pop's Perfect Pizza Parlours, 10801 Ridgecrest Drive, St. Anne, MO 63074, about the Power-Now Converter (5 inches long, 3 inches wide, and 3½ inches deep), delivered price $29.95. It delivers 110 volts AC electrical power from car's or truck's alternator. Operates heavy-duty impact wrenches, pipe threaders, drills, cement mixers, and many more types of heavy equipment. Easy to install. No belts or pulleys. No moving parts. Does not shorten life of alternator. Power-Now will operate any 110-volt brush-type motor and/or heating element up to 300 watts. Power-Now quickly starts cars with dead batteries, thereby eliminating need for jumper cables. Provides fast, ten-minute or less battery charging (any voltage, 6, 12, 24, 32). Power-Now Converter can be

removed and installed into a new car or truck in 20 minutes. All converters sold with warranty against parts and workmanship defects. The units will be repaired or replaced for five years for any unit that fails to perform properly (except unauthorized alterations or repairs damage) for a maximum charge of $5, regardless of condition of unit. Order will be processed and Power-Nows sent within 72 hours after receipt of enclosed order form.

5.   As director of sales, King Manufacturing, Inc., answer the inquiry (Case 11, p. 153), from Francis Ambrose, president of General Dynamics, 987 Elm Street, Tempe, AZ 85282, recommending the Little King (holds up to 60 balls and can be set at rate of 60 miles per hour, costs $332, has plastic hopper and aluminum tube with plastic ends, operates easily). Fill machine with balls, turn knob to set speed, timing, and travel direction of the ball. All parts guaranteed for five years. Can order direct from company. Machine can be sent UPS at a cost of $11.98. Can't gift wrap but can enclose a card with appropriate message for sender. Drive for the order.

6.   As director of Fair Havens Home for Senior Citizens (Case 7, p. 152), answer the inquiry with the following information: Prices are subject to change, but at present in semiprivate room basic care runs $610 monthly (or $23.00 daily), intermediate care $745 ($26.00 daily), skilled care $920 ($32.00 daily). Private rooms cost $100 per month in addition to the monthly care charge. Drugs, visits from doctors, beauty shop or barber shop service, cable TV, phone, cost of handcraft supplies not included. Charges are payable monthly in advance. No down payment needed. Each resident's condition is evaluated periodically and if the resident needs to be moved to another unit, then the resident will be moved when there's a vacancy. Basic care includes minimal assistance in activities of daily living (brushing teeth, combing hair, bathing, dressing, moving self). Intermediate care includes moderate help with the activities of daily living, assistance with general grooming, observation due to mild confusion. Skilled care includes moderate to total assistance with activities of daily living. Residents in the skilled care category must see their physician every 30 days, others every two months. Semiprivate room means sharing a room with someone else, and the two share a bath with one other room; so four people share one bath. Barber or beauty shop service costs $4. Residents may bring small TV and a chair.

7.   As area sales representative for General Aluminum Corporation (Case 19, p. 155), convince the writer that Sun Garden Window insulated with Spaceglass will add beauty to the living room and keep out the cold and hot air, too—thoroughly tested by company engineers to ensure customer satisfaction. You have a Model 10512 to fit the 38 by 48-inch casing without any alterations. Each window comes with installation instructions

that help make the job easy. Only tools required to install the window are a hammer and a screwdriver. Lightweight aluminum frame beautifully coated—three coats of chateau brown paint (will blend with decor and protect the window from corrosion for years). The window protrudes 12 inches—a nice display area for potted plants. Price, including tax and shipping, would run $254.69. Enclose a colored brochure with color chart and order blank.

8. For the same case (Case 7, above), answer an inquiry from a housing contractor who is considering the Sun Garden Window (one each for the 16 homes he presently has under construction). Window openings are 51 inches wide by 47 inches, not a standard size. You can supply Sun Garden Window units with adapter frames for contractor's price, $175 each, plus shipping. Color white, as specified. Emphasize ease of installation, and especially attractive appearance which will help sell houses. Ask for the order. Address: Koch Builders, Route 2, Box 165, Holmen, WI 54636, Sidney Koch, Owner.

9. Reply to the direct inquiry (Case 4, p. 151) of ICM, Inc., answering the most important questions first and sending along a brochure showing your golf course, swimming pool, and hotel. You cannot give anyone preference in seating in the dining room but will of course honor reservations. Also, tennis courts cannot be closed for a private tournament, but your tennis pro will try to schedule starting times to accommodate guests' wishes. You can and should answer all questions, subordinating weak or unpleasant items.

10. Do your job for PPG Industries, Inc., One Gateway Center, Pittsburgh, PA 15222, by answering an inquiry from Margaret Cohen, 85 Scotland Road, Pueblo, CO 81001. Notes: Solarcool glass cuts air-conditioning energy costs approximately 20 percent (based on a normal proportion of glazed area) a year. For the small amount of about $10 per square foot, glass can be professionally installed. Should stand heavy dust storms (tested successfully in El Paso, Texas; Bismarck, North Dakota). Nearest dealer Harry Haring, PPG, Colorado Springs, CO 80910. If Cohen will authorize by filling out enclosed card, representative will call, discuss window area in her new house plans. Better to have professional glass employees install windows, but trained, skilled builder can follow PPG directions, do the installation. Enclose folder with pictures/descriptions of attractive Solarcool glass homes. Other sales points: Until now, PPG Solarcool Bronze reflective glass used mainly for commercial buildings and institutions. Now available in ⅛-inch thickness, practical for homes. In daytime, mirrored Solarcool sharply reduces visibility from outside. When resident is inside, has comparative privacy. Nice to look out because

glare is cut down. Ultraviolet light, major cause of interior fading, greatly reduced. Any builder will appreciate fact that it's in ⅛-inch thickness (standard for residences) so is practical to work with—can be cut, fitted into insulating units right in construction area.

11.   Answer Case 15, p. 154, with the following facts: You have 40 acres of land with a spring-fed lake that sells for $66,000, and price includes a 20-year-old one-story, two-bedroom brick home on the land with no air conditioning. Central air could be added to the heat system for a reasonable price. The six-acre lake has several sunny spots nearby where a garden could be planted. A paved road leads three-quarters mile to the property off feeder to Interstate 30. Although the area around this land is not built up now, the future looks bright (new home area just five blocks west). The rolling land could be developed into building lots with the right developer behind the scenes. Assure Mr. and Mrs. Rudnick that you will be glad to take care of the loan at going rate at the time. Suggest that you make an appointment to show the land next month. Add logical details that you think appropriate. Address: Mr. & Mrs. Sam Rudnick, 11510 Natural Bridge Road, Bridgeton, MO 63044

12.   For another case, see GS 6 (p. 301).

Orders

1.   As your teacher directs, assume the conditions of one of the acknowledgments cases (next section of cases). Write the order letter in the situation. (Federal law prohibits collection of sales tax on mail sales unless delivery is in the same state as the seller.)

2.   As a professor, author, and coordinator of a program in business communication, you want to order from the publisher of your textbook, Richard D. Irwin, Inc., 1818 Ridge Road, Homewood, IL 60430, ten desk copies of the seventh edition of *Communicating Through Letters and Reports*, 1980, with *Teacher's Guide* for each (free), and ten sets of 25-count computerized tests (80 cents for each set). Five more copies of the text should be mailed to you and charged against your royalties, plus one examination copy of the second edition of *Communications in Business* by Mary Fish Rogers and Martin Mayer, 1979, and one examination copy of *Clear Technical Reports*, Hamilton Jordan, 1980.

3.   Move the clock up many years and assume that you are now 65 and are a member of AARP (American Association of Retired Persons). As members you and your spouse can order your drugs at greatly reduced rates. In this order you are enclosing three doctor's prescriptions for blood pressure medicine, thyroid, diabetes. Besides the medicine, you want a yellow queen-size electric blanket with dual controls, one blood pressure monitor, two bars of Neutrogena dry-skin soap unscented, a bottle of 100 Geritol tablets, one tube (5 ounces) greaseless Bengay, and one red mercury fever thermometer (oral). Send this order to Pharmacy Department, P.O. Box 1444, 3823 Broadway, Kansas City, MO 64141, and charge to your Visa account 3314–090–064–456.

4. Using your charge account at Horchow Collectors, International Drive, Norwich, VT 05055, write to the personal shopping department and order a two-ounce bottle of L'Envoi perfume E31976 ($150) sent to Ms. Rennie Champion, 1200 Jorgenson Street, Toronto, Ontario, Canada M5B 1E8 (gift wrapped for a birthday present); M49865 crested brandy sniffers, set of six, $60 (gift wrapped for a new-house present and sent to Dr. and Mrs. Mark Clevenger, 11620 Cumberland Road, Kirkland, WA 98033); one P65895 Lalique cat, $400; X08542 Advanced Childcraft Unit Building Blocks (104 pieces, $70.65) to be sent to Master David J. Schaffer, 7306 Oliver Smith Drive, Denver, CO 80204. The blocks are to be a birthday present to David.

5. For Steck's Office Supply Company, 42 North Street, Cobleskill, NY 12043, write a proposal letter telling Underwind Manufacturing Company, 9876 Hanover Drive, Detroit, MI 48103, the machines you plan to sell and propose to order this season: one dozen Underwind Praxis compact electric office typewriters, $595 each; one Scriptor electric typewriter with 13-inch carriage, $710; one T. A. Slick Model 52 electric folder, $553; one Underwind Audit 402 numerical accounting machine, $1,555. You are a customer of good standing who usually takes advantage of the 2/10, n/60 discount. Ask for confirmation of prices, approval of credit for the order, and shipping dates.

6. As a person who enjoys fishing, order the following from Hector's, Inc., large sporting goods supplier on Route 3, Ann Arbor, MI 48190. Since you've used or lost all the order blanks that came with your catalog, you'll need to set the information up in columns: 100 each of sizes 5/0 and 7/0 Kirby Hooks (Cat. No. 31854M), at 8¢ and 6¢, respectively, weighing 40 oz. per hundred; 300-yd. spool of No. LC2D nylon monofilament line in natural color, 30-lb. test, $8.49, wt. 9 oz.; a No. 25–6000 Pylon Minnow Bucket, $12.95, 64 oz.; a dozen each of sizes 1 and 2, No. BJ4B Ball Bearing Snap Swivels, 8 oz./dozen, prices 12¢ and 15¢ respectively; a RB6U Heavy-Duty Rod Kit (with red thread), $24.50, 96 oz.; and four Plastic Shell Boxes, Style II, SP1E, $4.25 each, 32 oz. Since you can't figure charges exactly for the total weight, send your check for the goods.

7.   Priester's Pecans, 227 Old Fort Drive, Fort Deposit, AL 36032, specializes in nationwide selling by mail of shelled pecans and pecan-filled candies and fruitcakes. As an old customer, you have Priester's brochure picturing, describing, and pricing 25 items. The price list gives the identifying numbers, the name, and the net weight of each item. But you have no order form—you used it a few months ago. For the next holiday season (Christmas, Mother's Day, or the like) or special occasion (birthday, wedding, anniversary) you want to send gifts to two friends in different cities: No. 35 Pecan Logs, net weight 1½ lbs., $7.50; and Fiddle Sticks, No. 37, 1¾ lbs., $8.90. In the same letter, you want to order (for your own cooking) some Small Pecan Pieces (No. 190, 4¼-lb. bag, $14.50) and some Mammoth Pecan Halves (No. 85, 2-lb. tin, $10.25). Prices include postage, but you have to add sales tax (4 percent) for the items to be delivered within Alabama (Small Pecan Pieces and Mammoth Pecan Halves). Send your check for the proper amount, quoting it in your letter. Be sure to make clear where and when to send the gifts.

8.   From the Lakeland Nurseries, Hanover, PA 17331, order four A–105049E Manchurian apricot trees @ $14.25 for yourself. For Mr. and Mrs. Morton P. Mergal, 112 Cedar Drive, Sun City, AZ 85351, order a No. A–105114E all-season hanging strawberry kit for $8.50, and for Professor Kermit G. Poole, Department of Business Education, Eastern Washington State College, Cheney, WA 99004, two indoor chocolate pudding trees @ $8.50, No. A–007435E. Use your Master Charge card number 5211–0003–8685, bank number 1361, expires next June.

9.   From Kyle Office Supply Company, 987 Main Street, Bowling Green, KY 42101, ask for a credit application form and a new catalog of office equipment. Since you're in a hurry, order (from your last year's catalog) four paper shredders (one Model PNT–765, $42.95, one Model TNP–987, $101.95, two Model RPT @ $59.95); and one dozen clear textured floor mats, 36 by 48 inches, $34.99 each. According to a sales letter you have from Kyle, the goods are to be sent freight prepaid. Your address: General Service Corporation, 876 West 54th Street, New York, NY 10022.

10.   From Meier & Taylor Sports Distributors, 26422 Groesbeck Highway, Warren, MI 48089, order for your university athletic department: three King tennis ball machines—Little King, $332; King, $595; and King Professional, $695; one gross of King tennis balls (three to a can) for $143.63; one gross Black Eagle golf balls at $7.50 a can; one gross Par Straight golf balls at $7.50 a can (both come packed three in a vacuum can); one gross Red Lion golf balls, $5.50 (cardboard and cellophane boxes, three to a box). Charge to the university athletic department the total plus $8.97 shipping costs.

11. As you, 14 Vester Gade, St. Thomas, VI 00820, you order from an old familiar establishment, L. L. Ream, Inc., Freeport, ME 04033. For Christmas you want to send one pair of Ream's Sure Grip fur-lined gloves, 1154C, size 9½, $27, to Charles Dodson, 6845 Juniper Avenue, Omaha, NE 68147. Gift wrap with card saying "Happy holidays, Grandpa." To granddaughter Mary Courtney, you want to have gift wrapped one 4235 Eskimo Parka, red, size 8, $120. Address 49 Epson Court, Jamaica, NY 11413, and have card read "To my favorite grandchild, happy holidays, D. C." For Mary's mother, Hazel Courtney, ask for a shetland pullover 4356C in powder blue, yoke pattern, size 36, $28.50. In this gift-wrapped box ask for a card saying "To my only and best daughter." Ream is to charge this order on your Bank of Life card, ML 321–29–3418.

Standard acknowledgments

1. As your instructor directs, write the appropriate acknowledgment for any of the order cases detailed in the preceding section.

2. Reply to an order you received from J. P. Foster, owner of the House of Lights, 987 Bedford Way, Eugene, OR 97401, for the following: six No. 2489765 music-stand style lamps for plants (design permits straddling large plants; plastic head with high-low switch; chrome-plated fold-up stand adjusts from 40½ to 55½ inches high, wholesale $8, suggested retail $16.95); and one dozen 15-watt fluorescent Plant-Grow bulbs @ $2.00, one dozen 20-watt size @ $2.25, one dozen 40-watt size @ $2.50. Foster sent a check for the correct amount but also included three credit references who rated Foster a good customer when you called them (because Foster asked for credit later). Ship the goods and ask Foster to fill out and return the enclosed credit application. Your firm is Westinghome Manufacturing Company, Industrial Park, Pittsburgh, PA 15289. Your best ending will probably be resale on the firm.

3. As director of sales, Meier & Taylor Sports Distributors, acknowledge the order of Harry Clifton, purchasing agent for (your) university athletic department (Case 10, p. 165). For resale points on the King tennis ball machines see Case 11, page 153. For allied sales on the golf balls, see the Golf Sales, page 298.

4. As a pharmacist in the Pharmacy Department, American Association of Retired Persons, acknowledge the drug order from Mr. and Mrs. C. M. Newton, 904 Sumner Street, Wausau, WI 54401 (Case 3, p. 163). Since this is the first time the Newtons have ordered, welcome them by telling them about your low prices and fast service. Enclose a card for other new-member recommendations. Separately you'll send a 30-page catalog with order blanks.

5.   Victory Shirt Company, 345 Madison Avenue, New York, NY 10017 (212/555–9543), manufactures pure cotton shirts, which none of the commercial shirt makers do. The average commercially made shirt is sewn with approximately 12 stitches to the inch; Victory has 30. Victory has a split-yoke back which is made by setting the back of the shirt in four pieces so that it conforms to the natural curvature of a man's shoulder. Seven buttons are sewn on the shirt's front so that it stays tucked in. A Victory shirt can be purchased through the mail for between $20 and $32.50, depending on the fabric, cut, and cuffs. In the stores, the shirts are offered in the $42.50, $45, and $47.50 price range. Three basic styles are offered—short sleeve, long sleeve, and French cuff. To get your mailing list you ran daily and Sunday ads in *The Wall Street Journal* and *The New York Times* with a clip-out coupon that is sent in and redeemable for a brochure showing new shirts. You also bought a list of attorneys. Acknowledge the order from Hugh Sprague, attorney, for three shirts, 14½–32, white: No. 125, The Carlton Classic, $28; No. 20, Traveler's Broadcloth, $23; and No. 75, French Pongee, $25.50. Besides resale add appropriate sales promotional material on the new, fine tailored shirts for women in sizes 32–40, priced from $20 to $32.50. Women would pay in stores $42.50, $45, and $47.50 for such shirts.

6.   As a correspondent in the sales office of Estelle Laudel, Inc., a cosmetic company, 1090 Bainbridge Blvd., Kansas City, MO 64109, you have to acknowledge an order from D. W. Maughn, Maughn's Drug Store, 916 Broadway, Wichita, KS 67203:

2 doz. 8-oz. bottles sunscreen	$1.50 each	$ 36.00
1 doz. 6-oz. jars cleansing cream	3.00 each	36.00
1 doz. 8-oz. tubes hand cream	2.00 each	24.00
1 doz. 2-oz. jars moisturizing cream	10.00 each	120.00
		$216.00

You are sending these cosmetics UPS, charges collect to Maughn, a long-established credit customer. Tell Maughn about Estelle Laudel national advertisements in *Vogue* and *Seventeen* and about the spot commercials on CBS–TV by the well-known Molly Paully. Spot TV commercials are at prime time (around the 5:30 P.M. news) Monday through Saturday. Suggest that if Maughn would like to increase sales by tying in local advertising with this national campaign, you can send mats (from which a local newspaper can make a printing plate and incorporate Maughn's name and address). Also tell Maughn about an allied product such as bath oil, lipstick, or eye shadow.

7. As your instructor directs, assume that the trouble element(s) do not exist in one of the cases in a group beginning on page 252, 255, 258, or 260 and write the standard acknowledgment accordingly.

8. For an additional case, see GS 7 (p. 301).

Credit approvals

1. *To:* M. Latif Javed, Auto-Rite Service Station, 1711 Royale Drive, Muncie, IN 47304. *From:* T & M Automotive Parts Company, 1400 East Hanna Avenue, Indianapolis, IN 46227. *Credit:* 3/10, n/60. Javed has built up a good gasoline service station business (much of it monthly credit sales) during the last five years. Credit Bureau reports he is slow in paying his personal bills fully. Because the battery-selling season is near, you approve credit but remind him of due dates and the advantages of cash discount. *Send:* three dozen auto batteries (called Cat-Bat, because of nine lives) totaling $1,440. They went out today.

2. As credit manager for Walker Wholesalers, Atlanta, GA 30356, you are going to approve Albert Baernstein's request for credit. He operates the small Toggery Shop, 465 Prince Avenue, Athens, GA 30601. Send him the following men's robes on terms of 2/10, n/30:

6 navy nylon and acetate robes, S, M, L @ $15	$ 90.00
6 wine triacetate robes, S, M, L @ $12.50	75.00
	$165.00

They are lightweight, easy to pack, two roomy pockets, notched collar and cuffs, self-belt. Two references stated that on several occasions Baernstein had to be reminded of his overdue account, another said he had always paid on time, and still another said only once in five years had he been reminded. As far as you can determine, his store is not in a busy district of Athens. He just relocated it, and his capital investment in the business doesn't make you feel it is a thriving business. Until you determine whether or not he is keeping his account up to date, you are limiting his credit to $250. Explain your credit terms and educate him on taking advantage of the discount. Tell him about your special on tan leather, soft-soled slippers by Aristo, usually $7.50 but now reduced to $6.25 (sizes 6 to 14 in medium and wide widths—pictured in catalog you're sending).

3. As credit manager for the Hickory Manufacturing Company, 190 North State Street, Chicago, IL 60601, write a credit-granting letter to Scott Moran, Moran's Hardware Company, 8181 Airline Highway, Baton Rouge, LA 70805, which will prevent collection problems and build future sales. You checked three references. The Chicago house, St. Louis house,

and Memphis house all reported the same story: they've been doing business with the Moran store since its beginning (five years ago); Moran's payments are usually approximately 75 days after date of invoice (terms are n/60) or discounted about 15 days after date of invoice (and the terms are 2/10). He owns lots of real estate and a couple of farms, and the store statements show profitable operations since the beginning. So you're going to grant him credit on his first order for 20 gallons of No-Fire (flame-resistant paint) under your credit terms of 2/10, n/60 and on all subsequent purchases up to $500. You do want him observing your terms, however. As a close, tell him that he may have window and counter-display sales aids for No-Fire.

4.   Mark Landers, who was your sales representative for the North Florida territory of Warner Electric, 968 Main Street, Orlando, FL 32709, your small appliance distributorship, and now is the Jacksonville director for the federal government's aid-to-small-business program, has written on behalf of James Porter, who has recently opened The Appliance Mart, 421 Center Street, Jacksonville, FL 32814. Porter's location, you realize, is in the part of the city that was burned and looted during the riots six years ago. The neighborhood, which is on the edge of the ghetto, is predominantly black and has a high insurance risk. Porter, himself a black, has had some difficulty getting financial backing and credit from Jacksonville banks and businesses; and although there is a strong movement in the city to establish a black financial basis from which to finance black-owned businesses, Porter cannot afford to wait for black financial backing. The same afternoon you have received Porter's order for six table-model TV sets @ $71.70 and 12 small radios @ $11.97. Porter sent a $300 check and asked you to extend credit for 90 days for the $273.84 balance. He also included several credit references which you checked out and found satisfactory. Ship his merchandise UPS and extend credit (explain your terms—after the 90 days, 2/10, n/60, with limit of $500).

5.   As credit manager, Charles Knopf Publishers, 597 Fifth Avenue, New York, NY 10017, write a credit-granting letter to Ellen Weaver, The Book Mall, 642 Poplar Street, Denver, CO 80220, and send the books she ordered totaling $375.56. Your terms are 2/10, n/30. Even though Weaver has not had retail experience, she chose an excellent location for her store, has inherited money, has a husband with a good job, and is bright. Your sales representative, T. F. Pail, reports that she graduated with honors from Smith College 30 years ago. She got into the book business because she was bored with country club life and because she had always wanted a book store. In checking Weaver's accounts, you found she lived in a paid-for $100,000 home, had an excellent credit rating, and was well thought of as a leader in the community, as was her husband. By complimentary com-

ment on the high intellectual level of her book selections, related to her personal background (including lack of business training or experience), try to hint that some Babbitry might be good business. In other words, as an analogy, a wise fisherman (though he loves steak) will use worms (not steak) for bait—because fish prefer worms. So push some lower-brow, more popular books.

6. John Oldham, one of your salesmen, has just written you, the credit manager of The Wisconsin Cheeseman, Stevens Point, WI 54481, about Eldon McKay, formerly a general manager for a large grocery store, who has opened a cheese business of his own, The Rat Hole, North Point Shopping Center, Cedar Falls, IA 50617. As general manager, he bought about $4,000 worth of your merchandise a year; and now he would like to stock the same lines of cheeses. According to Oldham, McKay will place a first order of $500, but he needs 90-day terms while he is getting started. You also learn from Oldham that McKay has borrowed on his life insurance and home and has used all his savings. He is a good businessman and knows the cheese business; so you write him allowing him the 90-day terms he wants, but with a top limit of $500 and a subtle caution about cutting his capital cheese too close to the rind.

7. As the credit manager of King's Imports, 13–69 Satsukigaoka, Chiyoda-ku, Tokyo 100, Japan, acknowledge the first order and credit application of Mary Goodson, owner of The Odd-Ball Shop, 900 Tijeras, N.W., Albuquerque, NM 87101. She operates a new, exclusive, expensive gift shop. According to reports from the Albuquerque National Bank, her store is making progress and meets obligations in satisfactory fashion despite questionably high accounts receivable. On terms of 2/10, n/30 send the dozen Japanese ceramic hand-painted pots for plants (No. TMT–987 at $18 each) and enclose a folder showing other Chinese and Japanese import ceramics. The usual markup is 50 percent.

8. You are credit director, Paige Office Supply Company, 8400 North Barry, Kansas City, MO 64109. *Send to:* Mott Office Supply Company, 8675 Morehead Street, Stillwater, OK 74074, the following: Executive swivel chair, PYTR–89 at $50; desk, PYTT–90 at $80; file cabinet, PYTM–91 at $50. *Terms:* 2/10, n/60. Shipment will go by freight collect. *Allied sales:* Secretarial swivel chairs with Naugahyde vinyl upholstery with seat measuring 18 by 17 inches for $40. Send catalog that gives valuable information on other office furniture.

9. Sara M. Shannon, who owns and manages a large jewelry store in Belmont, MA 02178 (2100 Moorpark), has sent a first order to the Taos

Jewelry Company, Tierra Amarilla, Taos, NM 87571. Your sales representative who visited Shannon's store reports that she seems to have a good turnover, an orderly store, and a good rating in Dan & Broadstreet (which you verify). There are only four jewelry stores in Belmont, and hers is the largest and one of the oldest (in business 30 years). Grant terms of 2/10, n/30 and send the ordered turquoise and silver Indian-made rings, bracelets, squash necklaces, and earrings, $300. Tell her about your half-page ads in *Vogue*. Encourage other orders—say, the Taxco silver necklace by Lucio Batalla which consists of handcrafted silver beads and inlays of crushed turquoise ($60).

10.   For another case, see GS 16 (p. 303).

Claims

1.   One of your apartment dwellers, Tom Gregory (Case 10, p. 158), left school at the end of spring semester and left two torn mattresses, a torn screen, and lots of fleas. Even though you had an oral agreement of *no pets*, Tom took in two stray dogs. Replacing the two torn mattresses and torn screen and hiring professional exterminators cost $129.95. Sit in for Jackie Vincent and write Tom a letter asking for payment for the damage his dogs did. He will return to the university next fall, and you will be glad to have him back on your terms (no pets).

2.   From the Revolving Credit Department, P.O. Box 10105, Louisville, KY 40505, you get a bill from United Charge for $578.55 which includes a $16.55 charge for not paying your bill last month. You never received a bill for last month or the month before. Three months ago you charged an 18-karat gold necklace that you purchased from Ilias Lalanounis (Athens, Greece) for $541, and two months ago you charged $21 for a single room at Holiday House, Mishawaka, Iowa. Write a letter from your Box 64, Williamsburg, KY 40770, explaining the situation and asking that the finance charge be removed. Your account number is 52446–01–18–12184.

3.   Today your long-overdue shipment from Ispanky, 7543 Stickman Avenue, Englewood, NJ 07204, arrived—and what a mess! One side of the box was badly smashed. Of the five dozen assorted Ispanky figurines, only five were not broken. What makes the situation even worse is that you are having a sale celebrating your 20th anniversary in ten days. The dozen figurines you have in stock plus the five good ones just received will not be adequate. Perhaps a hurried effort on the part of Ispanky will get a replacement shipment to you before it is too late. Write a special-delivery letter to Ispanky (listing the five unbroken pieces) from your gift shop, The Gift Emporium, 999 Carver Road, Durham, NC 27701.

4. Assume that you are Procurement Services Officer, Office of Business Services, Arizona State University, Tempe, AZ 85281. Today you get a report from the chief maintenance worker, Clark Benson, that 20 chairs were broken last week out of the new shipment from Stanley Seating Company, 1399 Pleasant Avenue, Des Moines, IA 50322. Reports of broken furniture are nothing new in your line of work, but 20 chairs in one week —*Whew!* Especially is it unusual since the Stanley representatives described these chairs as ones that can hold up and withstand the most rugged treatment from college students for years and years. On the basis of the representatives' report, you bought 600 ($15 each); and now, one week since you received them, 20 have been broken. Write Stanley about your unsatisfactory experiences. You want immediate replacement of the 20 chairs that have been broken, and you will expect replacement for others that break within the next year. If this is not OK, you want to return the 600 chairs and get your money back. Supply any necessary details with your logical imagination.

5. After studying the Hopkins and Perkins catalog, you ordered one dozen specially priced and assorted tree roses from Keywood Nurseries, Rutherford, NJ 07073. Though you planted the roses immediately on their arrival (and when the directions said you should), in specially prepared soil, only seven of them have grown. Even though Keywood Nurseries didn't guarantee that they would grow, you feel that some adjustment is due you, especially in view of the fact that some of the roses had poor-looking roots. Keywood had advertised "healthy, fast-growing roses." Also, your shipment reached you ten days later than promised, and it was poorly packed. None of the rose bushes was labeled. Write the letter requesting replacement of the five that died.

6. United Van Lines of Chicago moved your household belongings from one city to another (assume the specific cities and dates). Upon unpacking you noticed severe and disfiguring scratches on the tops of a mahogany chest and a cherry table. Report the circumstances to the company and ask for necessary damage forms for making claim. You are fairly certain the tops of both pieces will have to be refinished. You paid $10 extra for an additional $2,000 of insurance beyond the carrier's liability during shipment.

7. Now, three weeks after returning from a trip to Florida, you receive your statement and billing invoices for gasoline purchases on your oil company credit card. All seem to check with your copies except one— where your copy shows no amount of gasoline and a charge of $8.30 but the duplicate from the company has been filled in to show 22.3 gallons and $20.09. You've never spent that much for gasoline at once, partly because your small car's tank holds only 15 gallons. Your first inclination is to write the oil company; but as a member of AAA, you decide AAA should know about such shenanigans. So you mail copies of both the purchase tickets (which show the name and address of the particular station on the Florida Turnpike) to AAA with a letter asking it to look into the matter for you and get your bill corrected.

8. Parson's, Inc., 568 Arch Street, Philadelphia, PA 19107, wholesale distributor of trophies, will replace all merchandise that is defective in workmanship or material if claims are made within ten days after purchase. The Aquatic Club (for swimmers aged 5–18) ordered one trophy from Parson's three weeks ago, invoice No. 6540, 25-inch classic walnut trophy, No. R625, $45.50 plus $6 engraving cost for "Midwestern Swimming Meet." The handsome trophy with the gleaming metal figure of a swimmer arrived at The Aquatic Club yesterday, but the engraving said "Mideastern Swimming Meet." As the swimming coach of The Aquatic Club, 801 Grove Street, Urbana, IL 60801, ask Parson's to replace the trophy with one that has the correct engraving. Urge immediate action. You certainly do not expect to pay $6 more for correct engraving.

9. William P. Cade, selling for Snow & Johns Company, 8076 Commerce Street, Houston, TX 77012, took a first order for four dozen pairs of Stride-Built all-leather children's shoes, style MP5439, in assorted sizes, from you, the owner of the Children's Bootery, Palestine, TX 75801. When Cade sold you the shoes, the price entered on the order was $8 a pair. When the invoice from Snow & Johns came today, you were billed for $8.95 a pair. Ask for a correction—and extension of the 2/10 discount period.

10. As a secretary, 987 Burlington Street, Aberdeen, WA 98520, you want to give your employer a nice, practical, but inexpensive wedding present. In a gift catalog of the exclusive Little Travelers Gift Shop, 11 Fairweather Drive, Sacramento, CA 95833, you saw a good-looking glazed casserole dish for $18.95. You ordered it to be sent right away. But when it comes, the stand is bent and the dish is broken into many pieces—the only thing that is left is the lid. Ask Little Travelers for a new casserole dish right away so that it will get to Aberdeen in time.

11. Because you are moving, you scheduled two ads to run a week beginning Sunday, June 8; and you paid $23.76 the Friday before, June 6. Sunday, one ad for the house ran under 86A, p. 11C, column 3, under the Garage Sales section, and the ad about your garage sale ran under 53, p. 6C, column 3, under House Sales. You were not able to call the paper Sunday (recorder answering service); so the ads ran the same way Monday (and more sales were lost). When you called early Monday, you were told that

you would not be charged for ads run incorrectly. Later in the week you called to cancel the garage sale ad. Since you paid in advance for two ads for a week (and the check for $23.76 has cleared), you ask the classified department to figure and send the refund due. You will address Classified Department, Kansas City Star, Kansas City, MO 64132, from your present address.

12. Thinking you were going to save money on Christmas cards this year, you ordered 200 cards and envelopes (and sent a colored negative along so that the cards would have a family picture printed on them) from Gift House, P.O. Box 21102, Minneapolis, MN 55421. Today the cards and bill arrive and you are charged $36 for the cards plus 6 percent sales tax and $1.05 handling charge. The ad said nothing about the handling charge or 6 percent sales tax. In checking further you realize that you never have to pay sales tax on goods mailed from another state. To complicate matters more, your name was spelled incorrectly on the cards. Write a letter refusing to pay the sales tax and refusing to accept the cards. Ask if you may send the cards back for correct printing and the bill back for correct billing.

13. From The Collector's Shop, 908 Broadview Street, Petosky, MI 49770, you found a most unusual gift for the man who has everything —a "plantern" (a planter about ten inches square containing five different live plants and a two-foot high lamp). You turn the lamp on and off by simply clamping forefinger and thumb together on any leaf. The electronic planter has a foam rubber padding in the bottom that must be kept moist. You bought jade, aluminum, tiger, and sword plants for the plantern and left them in their original pots. Two weeks after buying the gift in Petosky, you got ready to wrap it at home (1008 West Healy, Champaign, IL 61820), and you discovered that the plants when squeezed will not turn the light on. Before writing the gift shop, however, you took the "plantern" to several electric repair shops in Champaign-Urbana and found no one who knew how to fix it. Write The Collector's Shop and explain your problem and ask for help (or approval to return).

14. For an additional case, see GS 18 (p. 304).

Adjustment approvals

1. As adjustment manager for Ispanky (Case 3, p. 171), write S. D. Jackson, The Gift Emporium, that you are replacing (already have) the figurines that were broken (55). The UPS truck that carried the figurines from New Jersey to Durham, NC, was in a serious wreck and the truck driver was killed. Ask Jackson to sign some enclosed forms from UPS (to

recover on insurance) and wish The Gift Emporium well on its 20th anniversary sale. Add allied sales promotion on your imported wine glasses from Germany. These 5½-ounce glasses are now on special for $8 a stem (usual retail price $20).

2.   As director of sales, Victory Shirt Company (Case 5, p. 167), write a full-reparation adjustment letter to Paul Brooks. Brooks ordered and charged on Visa one $75 French Pongee white shirt, size 15, for $22.50 plus $1.69 shipping charges. A week after he received the shirt he mails it back to you with a note saying that it does not fit—send size 16. Upon examination you find evidence of collar grease and pulled threads around the bottom button. Because you would like to keep Brooks as a customer, you are going to absorb the loss of this worn shirt and send him size 16. But because you don't want him to do this again, you'll write a letter that will have some education about the care of fine French Pongee. Include not only resale talk, but some sales promotional talk on the fine tailored shirts you have for women.

3.   As adjustment manager, Hudson's Department Store, 1509 22nd Street, Montreal, Quebec, Canada, write Mrs. Victor G. Baker, 76 Woodland Lakes, Timmins, Ontario, that she can send the doubleknit boy's polyester suit back to you and you'll credit her account for $99.95. The only suits that you have like the one she ordered are made in Taiwan instead of (as you erroneously advertised) Quebec. Point out to her, however, that she has an excellent, durable, stylish suit and try to get her to keep it.

4.   As sales director for Grandma Mary's fruitcakes (bakers of fine white and dark cakes, thousands of which are sold by mail), 7101 Corsica Drive, Germantown, TN 38138, answer the letter from one of your unhappy customers, Mary Battle, Apartment 707, 2200 South Ocean Blvd., Delray Beach, FL 33444. She reports that over a month ago she sent her order and check for one five-pound Grandma Mary's White Fruitcake, along with her card to be sent to her hostess of several days, Mrs. Ward Burtram, Sun Trap, West Pages, Scarrington, Bermuda. In Bermuda again last weekend, she called the Burtrams and discreetly found out that the gift had never been received. "Unless you have gone out of business—in which case you'd surely return my check for $18.95—will you please trace this or send at once and write a note to Mrs. Burtram confirming that I did order this gift very shortly after I was a guest in her home?" she ended. The facts are (a) you were caught short on the special raisins from Turkey and currants from California, without which Grandma Mary's White Fruitcakes would not be the distinctive culinary treats they are, and (b) someone slipped in not notifying the buyer or the recipient of the atypical delay in shipment. You've resumed baking and shipping, filling orders in the order received;

the cake in question is en route and may already have arrived. Write the necessary letters (to one or both Mary Battle and Mrs. Burtram, as your teacher directs). (You should send Battle a carbon of your letter to the lady in Bermuda.) Certainly you'll want to try to convince both that a Grandma Mary's White Fruitcake is an appropriate gift any time and is well worth waiting for.

5. At the manager's desk in the Carriage House, a gift shop selling artistic, unusual items (1003 Westaway Boulevard, Nashville, TN 39612), answer the letter from Tolliver Lee, 792 Spring Mill Road, Cincinnati, OH 45239. When Lee and his wife were in Nashville visiting, they bought from you a handsome parchment lampshade with color photographs of Nashville landmarks (the Parthenon, the Hermitage, etc.) and asked that you ship it to their home address, since they had little space in their car and did not want to run the risk of soiling or crushing it. But apparently in shipment the lampshade got smashed up. Lee wants another one right away. He offers to return this one (which is not necessary, but you will have to ask him to sign a statement-of-damage form you are enclosing so that you can collect from the insurance company under the blanket policy covering your shipments). To be sure that his new 15-inch shade gets to him safely, you are packing it in one of your stronger ⅛-inch corrugated boxes (the original box was ¹⁄₁₆-inch), to which you'll attach the letter you are going to write.

6. Mrs. Henry Thoreau, 1400 Fruitvale Avenue, Lincoln, NE 68508, ordered from Katz American Company, 21 East 40th Street, New York, NY 10016, a mother-of-pearl Wesam Carryall with the initials MWC on the front. The Carryall is practical, for it has a lipstick case, mirror, and cigarette case all in one. The price, as advertised in last month's *Glamour*, $18.95, includes the charges for initials and shipping. This morning she writes you (the adjustment manager) that she got her Wesam Carryall (which she paid for by check) with the initials TWC and that she is sending it back; she wants it either fixed right or her money back. When you check her order, you see she is correct and the only explanation you can find is that Wesam has added new help in preparation for the Christmas rush. From now on, you will have one worker be responsible for checking the initials before the Carryalls are mailed. In two days the correct initials MWC can be put on the case, and it can be mailed to her by the first of next week. Make the full adjustment, and keep Mrs. Thoreau pleased with the Carryall.

7. As adjustment manager for Parson's, Inc. (Case 8, p. 173), write Coach J. R. Foster (The Aquatic Club) that you will be happy to have the trophy sent back to you right away. Tell the coach there is a way the expert engravers can change the wording to say what is preferred: "Midwestern

Swimming Meet." Urge Foster to order less expensive sport "Oscars" (durable plastic bases with gleaming metal figures). These come in three sizes: 10-inch, $6; 11-inch, $6.60; and 12-inch, $7. Suggest these Oscars for the next big swimming meet.

8. As manager of the claim department for United Van Lines of Chicago (Case 6, p. 172), you promptly sent loss and damage forms to John Burnham, 5490 Jefferson Avenue, Janesville, WI 53545, who reported a damaged chest and table upon his recent move from Baton Rouge. You asked him to submit an estimate from a local furniture repair shop along with the completed forms. These you now have before you. The papers are in good order; the estimate—$100—you consider reasonable and have therefore approved. You're sending him his check. Write the letter to accompany it.

9. In the office of the Little Travelers Gift Shop (Case 10, p. 173) is a letter from Phoebe Rowan who is quite upset over the ceramic casserole dish she ordered two weeks ago as a wedding gift for her employer. The sparkling glazed casserole dish was in many little pieces, and the brass stand that holds the candle (which goes underneath the dish to keep it warm) was bent. The only thing left of the shipment was the smart contrasting black metal cover for the dish—and what good is that? So that you, the manager, will see how broken up the dish is, she sent it back. With the wedding just eight days from now, you have to rush another casserole dish to her. This time you're going to pack it in ³⁄₁₆-inch corrugated boxes (two of them), and you're going to wrap each piece with plenty of paper. The original mailing box was only ⅛-inch. Ask her to sign a statement-of-damage form, which you're enclosing. Emphasize by diction, space, and position the *restoration* of the casserole dish. Make her feel that this beautiful dish will come in handy for many informal dinners—the kind that most people have these days.

10. As owner of The Collector's Shop, 908 Broadview Street, Petosky, MI 49770, answer the claim from Mrs. Francis Andrews, 1008 West Healy, Champaign, IL 61820, about the plantern (Case 13, p. 174). Suggest that she try several different approaches to the plantern: (*a*) be sure that the metal disc in the center touches all of the pots; (*b*) the disc should not be sitting in water; and (*c*) the pots should be of about equal weight.

Resale on this product could be that Peggy Cederberg just bought one of these unusual planterns for the President of the United States for his birthday.

11. For another case, see GS 21 (p. 305).

WHERE PEOPLE TRADE—retail, wholesale, or industrial—depends not just on quality, price, and convenience. These are usually comparable in several different outlets. We trade where we do partly because we like the people, trust them and their products, and like their special attention, appreciation of our business, and extra-service considerations—the personal and friendly aspects.

All too often, however, the only times a customer receives word from a firm are when it wants to make a sale or to collect for something or when it has to handle a claim. This apparent lack of interest shows up in practically all reliable surveys of why firms lose customers. About seven out of ten lost customers just drift away. Yet eight out of ten are reclaimable if given some attention. Only 1 percent of lost customers have real grievances that need adjusting. And a large part of the 70 percent who do drift away would undoubtedly not do so *if they were reminded that the business firm appreciates their patronage and has a continuing interest in their welfare.*

You see why, therefore, in the preceding chapters we made clear that all business communications should retain and even try to increase the reader's favorable attitude toward the writer, even when working primarily on something else.

Certain situations, however, call for messages that have no other immediate purpose than cementing friendly relations between writer and reader. Although they may not ask for any immediate action, indirectly these special goodwill messages pave the way for continued business from old customers and new business from prospects.

Because your readers know you do not have to send them, these unexpected special goodwill messages are especially effective in overcoming the impression of indifference—indifference to business given and to serving new customers.

In theory, goodwill messages sell only friendship. Some do no more than that—ostensibly. But we should admit to ourselves that a letter on a firm's letterhead, signed by a representative of the firm, is promotional, regardless of its personal nature. The cultivation of business is inherent in the circumstance itself. No business writer need be reluctant to establish the virtues of a firm's services and goods and to place them at the disposal of the reader. *The main thing to guard against is appearing to be offering only friendship in the first part and then shifting to an obvious, immediate sales pitch.*

Some of these "unnecessary" special goodwill messages are of such highly personal nature that to use an obvious form would be insulting, to include sales or even resale talk on either the firm or its merchandise would be ludicrous, and to write very much would likely result in gushiness. Notes giving deserved praise or extending sympathy certainly fall into this category. Those expressing appreciation, extending seasonal greetings, issuing invitations, accompanying favors (or services), or offering helpful information also do if they are strictly for purposes of goodwill; but most of these are forms including sales-building talk and thus are promotional.

GIVING DESERVED PRAISE

Although letters and notes praising people do not have to contain the word *congratulations* in them, you are recognizing a significant event or accomplishment in the life of your reader: a job promotion, election to an office, receiving an honor, winning a contest, graduation, marriage, birth of a child, or completion of a new plant, office, project, or report. All these and many more are instances when you can show not only customers but also friends and acquaintances that you are interested in what happens to them. Some of the better ones are just a few lines:

```
When I saw that you've been named plant manager of Tri-States,
I was delighted!
It's a well-earned recognition.
And it couldn't happen to a more deserving person!
```

Any good effects of the foregoing passages would disappear if the writer followed with such an idea as "Now that you're earning more, surely you'd like to consider more insurance" or ". . . buy more clothes."

```
I have just completed your article about credit control in the
recent issue of Credit World.
Heartiest congratulations on a job well done!
```
--

```
We share your pride and happiness in the completion of the new
Henderson plant.

It is a criterion of business, as well as civic,
accomplishment.

Good wishes from all of us.  (Or Sincere wishes for your
continued success.)
```

As illustrated here, timeliness and conciseness are important in these congratulations. The friendly thought behind the message counts most.

A note like the following from any boss would certainly engender good feeling (and probably stimulate the reader to do even better work):

```
Your analysis of production difficulties at the Saginaw plant
was one of the clearest, most easily read reports I've ever
been privileged to study.

We're carrying out some of your recommendations immediately.

Several of us look forward to discussing the report with you
when you return to the home office.

In the meantime, thanks for a job well done.
```

Many people in both their business and their private lives have discovered the gratifying responses of associates, customers, and personal friends to the receipt of a newspaper or magazine clipping of interest to the reader. A simple greeting (it may be no more than "Good morning") and a line or two like "This clipping made me think of you" or "I thought you might be interested in this clipping" are enough, followed by a note like:

```
Let me add my commendation to those you've undoubtedly already
received as a result of the enclosed clipping.
```

Still another variation on deservedly praising someone goes to a third person. The person who wrote the following letter to an airline official made at least two friends:

```
On your Flight 127 from Chicago to San Francisco last Tuesday,
I was pleased with every phase of the service.  But I was
especially pleased with the conduct of Captain A. L. Lutz.

While at the controls he kept us well informed on flight
conditions and frequently pointed out places of interest en
route.  When he walked through the cabin, he was the soul of
hospitality and courtesy to every passenger—particularly to a
six-year-old boy making his first flight!

As we came in over San Francisco in bright moonlight and
crossed the Bay, Captain Lutz pointed out sights of interest.
It was a thoughtful gesture that all of us appreciated.

My thanks and commendations to the line and to him.
```

Any time someone renders outstanding service is an appropriate occasion to relay your understanding and appreciation of its significance. Such a gesture not only impresses the reader with the writer's "humanness"; but it also can and often does earn preferential treatment on subsequent occasions.

> We appreciated the promptness with which your representative,
> Mr. John Wade, answered our call for help last Friday when
> one of our motors failed at a crucial time. But we appreciated
> even more his efficiency in getting it running again. He was
> even considerate and thoughtful enough not to leave a mess for
> us to clean up.
>
> Our thanks to you and to Mr. Wade; we shall remember on other
> occasions.

Obviously, under such circumstances you could also write directly to the
person whose performance you praise, as in the following instance:

> If an award were given by the U.S. Chamber Workshop, you'd
> certainly get the "E" for excellence, John.
>
> Your Thursday afternoon clinic met with more enthusiastic
> reactions than I've observed in a long time.
>
> It is a rewarding experience to work with people like you.

EXPRESSING APPRECIATION

You have observed that most congratulatory messages also involve an
element of thanks. Likewise, most thank-you letters contain some com-
mendatory passages. It's really just a question of where you want your
emphasis to go.

Strictly goodwill thank-you messages—in response to a favor extended,
for work on a project (member of a fund-raising team, for example), or for
a contribution—often have their origins in civic, educational, and religious
surroundings rather than in business.

> Many thanks for the untiring, cheerful way you worked on the
> recent United Way drive.
>
> Through effort like yours we exceeded our goal.
>
> Possibly the knowledge that you have helped materially to
> provide clothing, food, and medical care during the coming
> year for underprivileged children will be more gratifying with
> this expression of appreciation.
>
> --
>
> For the 32,000 youths of Athens . . .
>
> Thanks a million!
>
> Your generous gift to the new "Y" building is another evidence
> of your concern for the boys and girls of our city and county.
>
> We appreciate your cooperation in this project. As citizens
> and parents, we'll all be happy about our share in it for
> years to come.

Though these brief thank-you notes do not sell directly, the resale phrases
help to convince the reader of the worth of the projects and thus encourage
a repeat performance the next time a request comes along. When written
by business firms, they are even more definitely promotional.

Any time is a good time to express appreciation to good customers for their patronage or for handling accounts satisfactorily. Even the notation on a current bill, "One of the pleasures of being in business is serving a good customer like you," has a heartening effect. But many firms wisely do more. Upon the first use of the account—or later in the first year—many send a thank-you note like the following:

Thank you for using your newly opened account. Surely you found it a quick, convenient way to shop at Tilford's.

To make sure our merchandise and service are just the way you want them, we'll always welcome any comments you may have about improvements you would like us to make.

We want to continue to serve you well, and we pledge our efforts to keep your trust.

Because of the rush of business, such messages too often go out only around holiday and special-event times. In many such cases they don't do the effective job they might because too many other people and business firms are doing the same thing on those special occasions. By arriving unexpectedly and without apparent reason at some other time, something like the following note is probably a more effective pleasant reminder of the firm's appreciation:

Believe us—

—we appreciate your continued patronage and friendship.

And to hold your friendship and patronage, we certainly intend to continue giving you the sort of service and honest values you deserve. See us again when we can serve.

When an account goes unused for some time and then an entry appears, many credit managers wisely send a thank-you note:

Thank you for the purchase you made recently.

It's good to hear you say "Charge it" again, for we've really missed you. We try to serve you well.

Messages thanking customers for paying promptly are simply a more specialized version of the ones we've been examining. They also help to discourage or reduce collection problems. Such a simple note as the following not only pleases the customer; it reinforces determination to maintain the good habit:

Your check this morning in prompt payment of your last purchase made me think, "I wish all our accounts were handled so efficiently."

It's a real pleasure to service an account like yours, and we thank you sincerely for your cooperation.

You can also easily tie in the expression of appreciation with a concrete reminder of the benefits the customer gains from taking care of obligations as promised:

```
Thank you for the splendid manner in which you paid up your
recent account.
Your record of prompt payments firmly establishes your credit
at Blacks.  You will find it handy in purchasing the many
things this large, complete store can offer you.
```

If you keep your eyes and ears open, you'll find many other occasions for saying thank you to your customers. When a customer recommends you or your firm to another person, you'll certainly benefit in the long run by sending a cheerful, personalized note like the following:

```
Thank you for telling Wexell Associates about us.  On the
strength of your recommendation one of the Associates came in
to see us yesterday and we were able to contract to blister
package many of Wexell's small parts.
We appreciate your thinking of us, and we pledge to continue
our efforts to supply you with the best packaging service we
possibly can.
We have to live up to our reputation!
```

When a firm expresses appreciation to an individual, it expects no reply. And when an individual takes the time to pay a business firm a compliment or express appreciation for good service, no answer is *required*. But you establish yourself as courteous and polite if you do reply.

When a company receives suggestions for improved service, some of which will be outright complaints requiring adjustments, an acknowledgment *is* required, particularly if it has invited the suggestion.

```
You are quite right, Mr. Von Bergen.  The exhaust on your
new Servaire portable air compressor should point away from
the air intake, not toward it.  That is how we originally
designed the compressor.  But apparently we did not make
clear to our dealer how to install the pipe when assembling
the unit for sale to you.  We're glad you were able to
reinstall it correctly.
As a result of your experience, we are altering the exhaust
flange mounting to make it impossible to install the exhaust
improperly.  Thank you for telling us about the problem.
You have helped us to make an important modification that will
result in improved and safer service for all our customers.
```

SENDING SEASONAL GREETINGS

A modified form of thank-you is the seasonal greeting. By far the most common times are around Christmas and New Year, although some retail stores send such messages shortly before Easter, Valentine's Day, or Thanksgiving, when they have less competition from other mailings. Since they must be mass mailings in most firms (to keep down costs), they are rarely personalized.

The United Way and the "Y" thank-yous (p. 181) were printed forms, thus conserving the funds of the organizations. Business firms, too, must save time and money by using some modifications of form treatment for their many thank-yous and seasonal greetings. The undisguised form can be successful, however:

> Business firms, too, pause at this season to count their blessings.
> Good friends and customers like you are one of our greatest.
> So we want to tell you how much we appreciate your business at the same time we send heartiest wishes for
> A VERY MERRY CHRISTMAS AND A HAPPY, SUCCESSFUL, NEW YEAR!

With the references to customers and business, that is promotional in effect. Most emphatically, however, *you would not want sales material in it after such an opening theme*. Still, the following holiday greeting, an overt attempt to cultivate business, is perhaps justifiably so in the light of how a savings and loan association functions and the kinds of service it provides:

> GREETINGS AT THE NEW YEAR!
> Hearts are never as full of peace and happiness as when friends and loved ones gather in the home at this season of good cheer and fellowship.
> Through the years your Association has played a part in providing homes for its members through sound home-financing plans that lead to real debt-free home ownership. Won't you please tell your friends about your Association and recommend its services to them? They will appreciate knowing of the easy, convenient terms upon which they may repay a loan.
> Our officers and directors join in thanking you for your friendship in the past year and in wishing you happiness and health in 19— and for years to come.

Most of the time, however, you will be on safer ground if you exclude such promotional passages (like cutting out that middle paragraph) and concentrate on a simple wish for the customer's well-being, along with an expression of gratitude.

Unlike seasonal greetings, congratulatory and thank-you messages are practically always individualized. Expressions of sympathy—the most personal of special goodwill messages—must be.

CONVEYING SYMPATHY

Most of us are accustomed to lending a helping hand and extending expressions of encouragement when friends and family suffer some adversity. The same sympathetic attitude should prevail when a business friend experiences misfortune.

Admittedly, condolences are some of the most difficult special goodwill messages to write because of the melancholy circumstances (which you can reduce by avoiding specifics). But certainly everyone appreciates them. When a report of a retailer's illness reaches a wholesaler or a manufacturer, a short, human, and essentially positive note like the following can gain goodwill.

```
Sorry, Sam—
—to hear that you're in the hospital again.
But with rest and good care you'll be back at work soon.
I've always valued you as a friend and appreciated you as a
business associate; so for two reasons I hope all goes well
with you.
```

Most of us sooner or later find ourselves having to write letters concerning the death of someone we've known. To the surviving partner of a business, for example, the following would be a comfort and goodwill builder by showing the writer's friendly interest and concern:

```
We were genuinely distressed to learn of the death of Mr.
Guin, your partner and our good friend for many years.

Although the firm of Guin and Beatty will feel the effects of
his absence, the greater loss is to the community and the Guin
family.  The good judgment, vision, and integrity Mr. Guin
displayed as a business leader in your city undoubtedly carried
over into his private life.

In extending these words of sympathy, we also want to add
a few of encouragement and confidence in the future; we feel
sure that would have been Mr. Guin's attitude.
```

Even though the writer of the preceding might not have met the widow, certainly she would not take offense at a message such as the following:

```
For many years we enjoyed a business friendship with Mr. Guin.

We respected him as a good businessman who insisted on high
standards in serving the public and was always just, fair, and
cooperative in his relations with us.  We admired the good
judgment, vision, and integrity he showed as a business leader
in your community.

To you who saw these and other fine qualities in greater
detail and frequency  than we were privileged to, we offer our
sympathy.
```

Such a letter will necessarily have an emotional impact. But that effect can be less if writers will refrain from quoting Scripture or poetry. And sepulchral overtones will not be so powerful if you accept death as the inevitability it is and use the word itself rather than euphemisms like "passed away," "passed to his reward," and "departed." For greater comfort, emphasize the good characteristics and the outstanding contributions of the dead individual rather than the sorrow and anguish of the survivor. Accept the thought that good, worthwhile people continue to exert their influence in the hearts and minds of those who knew them.

Adversity also strikes in other forms—fires, floods, accidents and law-suits, labor unrest, and work stoppage. When it does, the victim(s) will appreciate a message that says, "We're your friends; we understand the significance of this to you; we hope everything will work out well." If you really mean the offer and are in a position to extend it, you can add the equivalent of "Call on us if we can help."

> All of us were sorry to hear of the fire that destroyed your warehouse last night.
>
> It's a tough break.
>
> We're sure, however, that the same determination and ingenuity that helped you to build your business so successfully will also see you through this temporary setback.

Now, if you had some unused storage space and wanted to offer it, you might very well close with

> We have a 30 × 40 room that we won't need for another 90 days; if that will help tide you over in any way, give me a ring.

But to propose to rent the space would change the complexion of the message and destroy any goodwill built up.

EXTENDING WELCOMES AND INVITATIONS

One of the most popular forms of goodwill message greets newcomers to a community and offers to be of assistance, particularly during the orientation period. Almost always it is an invitation to come in and get acquainted; it also emphasizes the services of the inviting firm. One un-usual and unexpected example is the following from a public library:

> Welcome to Evansville!
>
> We're glad to have you as new members of our progressive city.
>
> Your library card is ready for your use. We hope you'll be down soon to pick it up and to become acquainted with the staff and the services. For your reading pleasure and research over 100,000 volumes are available. Staff members will gladly assist you in finding what you seek. All of the leading magazines and newspapers are available in the lounge.
>
> The children's room is also well supplied with both fiction and nonfiction books on a wide variety of topics of interest to youngsters 6 to 15.
>
> If you enjoy musical recordings, you may want to check out some of the thousand-odd albums, ranging from the most recent popular music to the classics.
>
> We shall be glad to give you maps of the city, to supply directions—in short, to help you in any way we can to know Evansville better.
>
> The library is open from 9 a.m. until 10 p.m. every weekday. We are glad to answer telephone inquiries during that time.
>
> Please come in soon.

Such a welcome—with no sales ax to grind—is the essence of goodwill in its spirit. The library has nothing to sell except service—free. A bank or other firm with commercial/profit aspirations would have to be subtle to have its welcome accepted at face value—not such as the following:

> As a new resident of our friendly city, you are cordially
> invited to visit the Federal Bank. We should like to get to
> know you. Even though you may already have selected a bank,
> it would be a pleasure to welcome you to Blankville personally
> and to explain the many services the Federal offers its
> customers.
>
> The Federal has given prompt, courteous, and efficient banking
> services to the people of Blankville for over 75 years, and we
> would appreciate the opportunity of serving you.
>
> Among the conveniences in Federal's modern banking quarters are
> the four drive-in teller windows that enable you to bank
> without alighting from your car. And in the parking garage
> right in our own building you may have 30 minutes of free
> parking while taking care of your banking business.
>
> You may also bank around the clock at the Federal; a complete
> mail deposit service and a 24-hour depository are located in
> our parking garage.
>
> Won't you come in for a friendly visit soon?

That letter is an obvious attempt to get a new account, and the attempts to establish friendly feeling are thin and transparent, revealing the wolf in sheep's clothing it is. Better to discard the talk of "get to know you" and "friendly visit" and get right down to brass tacks with an opening like "Since you are a newcomer to Blankville and will need a conveniently located bank with complete facilities, may we tell you what we can offer you at the Federal?"

Someone connected with credit control also can easily maintain a list of newcomers to the community and mail a welcoming form (which does not promise credit, please note, but only invites the application):

> Welcome to this community.
>
> Our Credit Department will be glad to handle your credit
> application at your request.
>
> We invite you to use our lounging and rest rooms on the
> mezzanine, or the fountain luncheonette where you can get a
> deliciously prepared, well-balanced luncheon at a reasonable
> price. Rollins's spacious parking lot, 15 feet from the rear
> entrance, is free to you when you shop here.
>
> On Rollins's remodeled third floor you'll find home
> furnishings. The advice of our interior decorators is
> available to you with no obligation. And in the remodeled
> downstairs section you'll find an entirely new and complete
> food mart and new housewares department.
>
> We are here to serve you. And we hope that you too will soon
> feel as one of our customers recently was kind enough to say,
> "The longer people live in this community, the more they trade
> at Rollins."

When you verify credit reliability (usually an easy thing to do), you may elect to set up the account and so inform the reader:

We know that stores, too, make a difference to a person establishing a home in a new community.

To serve you in the best way possible is one of our aims.

As an assurance of our desire to establish a permanent and happy business friendship, we have opened a convenient charge account in your name.

The next time you are in the store, simply say "Charge it" to the person waiting on you.

On the other hand, the invitation to a special event extended in the following letter would probably be read with interest; it builds goodwill because it expresses a desire to render service; no sales promotion (except that inherent in the action itself) distracts:

Will you come to our free seminar on industrial fire prevention?

Between OSHA regulations and the advent of new industrial chemicals and manufacturing processes, upgrading plant fire protection has become a necessity, not an option. That's why we have scheduled a free three-hour seminar on new fire prevention technology for Tuesday, February 22. We promise no sales pitches, just information. We'll even show you some of our competitors' products!

You'll hear about and see the latest in extinguishers, wireless remote alarms, foam systems, smoke detectors, and much more. We won't promise to make you an expert, but after our seminar you'll have a far better idea of what is available in fire prevention to meet your company's needs.

For your convenience we're scheduling two sessions, one from 8:30 to 11:30 in the morning, the other from 7:00 to 10:00 in the evening. Use the enclosed reply card to tell us which session you want to attend and how many of your people will come. Since the hall we've rented at Frederick and Eighth Streets will hold only 160 people, we'll have to accept registrations on a first-come, first-served basis, so send in the card today. We're looking forward to seeing you!

The following to a new shareholder is typical of what many corporations do to cement goodwill (and possibly forestall some gripes when things don't go too well for the corporation):

On behalf of the Board of Directors and employees of Pushman, I welcome you as a Pushman stockholder.

Through your shares in Pushman, you participate in ownership of one of America's leading corporations . . . one with a bright and promising future.

Your company has operations in virtually every part of the world, activities that reach into a broad range of products and services that help to make human life better.

As your company progresses, you will receive regular reports.

Besides our annual and quarterly reports, we will send you
special reports when circumstances warrant them.

I've enclosed your company's latest annual report to give you
an in-depth view of our achievements and status last year.
If you would like more information on some aspect of our
activities, please write me.

Again, welcome to Pushman. We look forward to sharing with
you in the future.

Attempts to revive an account are but modified versions of invitations.
When an account remains unused for three months or six months, depending on management's choice—it may be a signal that the customer is
drifting away because of the firm's indifference, or it may be the result
of a real grievance. Form notes inviting the customer back, reselling your
products or services, stressing "How can we serve you better?" and finally
asking forthrightly, "May we continue to serve you?" can go out individually or in a series:

Spring fever?

Here's a sure cure—a Beachstone suit, coat, or dress,
spiced with the right accessories.

Easy to choose, easy to buy too. Simply use your charge
account at Wilson's. It's just waiting for your "charge it"
to be as useful as ever.

So come on in soon! See and try on the beautiful new spring
apparel, hats, shoes, and other accessories we have assembled
for your Easter pleasure.

You can easily build your messages around special events, such as
Christmas (although you may lose some effect by competition with many
others):

A welcome warm as Santa's smile awaits you at Bowen's!

We're all decked out with our Christmas best; so you can easily
find the right gift for everyone on your Christmas list.

Practical gifts, starry-eyed gifts . . . all conveniently in
one store . . . where you can just say "Charge it" for ALL
your Christmas giving.

Warmest holiday greetings!

Accompanying a new credit card, one letter solicited the renewal of the
customer's business with:

Ordinarily we'd send you this enclosure with our monthly
statement. Since your account hasn't been used recently,
we're sending it along with some back-to-school suggestions.

Whether you're thinking of complete outfits for your child or
a back-to-school gift for a favorite niece, nephew, or friend,
you'll find complete selections of dependable, quality Bowen
merchandise in every department.

Your charge account is just as good as ever—whether you come
to the store, phone, or shop by mail.

Some writers studiously avoid asking whether anything is wrong (see p. 411). Others send a series of mailings before asking. A favorite form is the letter written on only one half of the page (usually the left side) with the caption "Here's Our Side of the Story." At the top of the right-side blank space appears another caption, "Won't You Tell Us Your Side of the Story?" (The message/reply duplicate memo form, p. 27, serves particularly well.)

TRANSMITTING PREMIUMS

Often as a goodwill reminder an alert executive finds some item to mail inexpensively along with a note stressing the desire to be of service, such as the following from a jewelry and optical shop:

```
The special pocket-size Rausch & Lomb Star Ban spray
accompanying this note is for your use in keeping your
handsome Everett glasses spotless.

Accept it with our compliments and the assurance that we want
you to be completely happy with your recent selection from
Everett's collection of fine frames for the discriminating
woman.
```

In a somewhat humorous vein one firm recently mailed a pocket-size calorie counter to customers and prospects with this short note:

```
"Everything's expanding—especially my waistline," grumbled a
friend recently.

Just in case you (or someone you know) may need to fight this
perennial battle, we're sending you this handy calorie counter
that you can use at home, at a banquet, or at a lunch counter.

Accept it with our compliments—and the hope that we'll be
seeing you soon.
```

Small gadgets galore come into play in this manner. Like tricks in sales presentations, however, they work only if directly related to the product or service of the firm. A real estate agency might appropriately send a pocket-size map of the city to which a person has just moved, along with the following:

```
Welcome to Jacksonville.

To help you get places faster and to know your new city
better, this map shows the principal thoroughfares and
locations of the principal landmarks and facilities.

Note that the Coleman Agency is located in an accessible area
with adequate parking facilities nearby.

We would welcome the opportunity to help you in any way we can.
```

OFFERING HELPFUL INFORMATION

Large companies sponsoring radio and TV programs, as well as research projects and publications, rapidly accumulate names and addresses of people who want to be kept informed. As part of their public relations programs, many of these companies periodically send letters like the following to them:

> Perhaps you will be interested in a program, "Life under the Sea," scheduled for Sunday, January 22, at 8 p.m. over NBS-TV.
>
> "Life under the Sea" was directed by Emile Ravage, with the assistance of the marine biologist Albert Gaudin. It is the third in a series of such productions sponored by the Rawlston System.
>
> We hope these programs will help to broaden public understanding of science and to encourage some young people at least to consider scientific careers.
>
> We shall welcome your comments after you have seen the program.
>
> --
>
> The exciting events in Detroit leading up to the introduction of the new models last month made a story too detailed to print completely in <u>Tempo</u>.
>
> If you read the condensed version in the issue of two weeks ago, you'll agree that the accompanying report-analysis we're sending to selected educators and business executives is a worthwhile supplement. If you didn't . . . well, we think you'll want to now.

ANTICIPATING RESISTANCE

In business as in medicine, prevention is much better than a cure. In the interest of forestalling complaints and minimizing dissatisfaction, many business executives therefore give advance notice when they foresee something like an interruption of service, a curtailment of service, or a necessary price increase. In almost all instances these notices (often only postcards) must be obvious forms. They need to stress service—improved service, if possible; at least, maintaining superior service or quality of goods—as an antidote for the inherently negative material the message has to establish. This message from a power company is typical (dates and times varied according to areas and so were stamped in):

> To provide better service for you and our other customers in your area, we have installed new equipment, which we plan to place in service
>
> April 15, 19—
> between 1 and 2 p.m.
>
> To safeguard the men who do this work, we shall have to shut off power during this time. Service will resume as promptly as possible. We appreciate your cooperation in making this improved service possible.

A notification of a coming price increase is even more unwelcome. Admittedly, it is never easy to write. But with specific details supporting the increase, it may be successful in retaining the goodwill of some otherwise-lost complaining or rumor-mongering customers. The following notice went to all customers:

> It's been a tough year, hasn't it? Wages have gone up, costs
> of materials and supplies have gone up, utility bills have gone
> up, insurance has gone up, transportation costs have gone up.
>
> Of course this isn't news to you. Everybody's in the same
> boat. Including us.
>
> Our highly trained operators need more money, our costs for
> machines and supplies are rising, electricity is more expensive
> . . . everything is more expensive.
>
> To continue to give you the same prompt, efficient polygraph
> service we have in the past, and to add new technological
> advances as they become available, we have to increase our
> charges for preemployment screening, personnel evaluations, and
> theft investigations. The rates on the attached rate sheet
> will go into effect July 1.
>
> Thus we can and do continue to guarantee, as always, absolute
> confidentiality and strictly professional lie detection.

Such a notice as the preceding can be even more convincing (and hence effective) if you can give the specifics of your cost increases for the past few months or years. Power companies, magazine publishers, and TV cable companies (to name a few) can and do make such specific explanations. In fact, we have some of their notices. We have not used one of them here only because their figures are changing so rapidly.

✿   ✿   ✿   ✿   ✿

We could classify and illustrate hundreds of situations in which a special goodwill message would be appropriate and would cement a friendship for you and your firm. If you are alert to conditions, if you keep informed about what is happening to your clientele, if you honestly like people and enjoy pleasing them, however, you'll see plenty of opportunities. In this short treatment, therefore, we have tried to concentrate on the most common instances; it is intended as a springboard for your thinking and practice rather than an extensive catalog.

In fact, opportunities for helpful goodwill messages are so numerous and varied that we cannot give you a checklist for them. We encourage you, however, to

1. Write all you can of these "letters you don't have to write but should." The subheads in this chapter provide you some starting points for thinking of appropriate situations.

2. Make them specific enough to fit and be meaningful even when forms (*not* as one big company began, "If you are one of the many motorists enjoying the benefits of an XX credit card. . .").

3. In these most personal of business messages, be especially careful to get names, addresses, and facts right (if you write Mr. Wilkinson, he does NOT like to be addressed as Mr. Wilkerson; nor does Clarke like to be called Clark).

4. Avoid gushing in tone or length.

Special goodwill messages can do a big *extra* job for you, but remember that *all* your business communications should build goodwill through courteous, sincere tone and the service attitude (Chapter 3). That is sometimes hard to do in the basically bad-news situations discussed in the next chapter.

GOODWILL CASES

1.   As dean of your school write a form letter to students congratulating them on being on the Dean's List for the term recently ended. Remind them that only 7 percent of the student body makes this special list.

2.   As your teacher, write a thank-you note to Dee Morris, Morris and Fuller Direct Marketing, 9987 University Avenue, Columbus, OH 43261, direct marketing wizard, lawyer, rancher, father of four children. Morris spoke to all your classes two days ago. He had been a former student of yours and had learned the principles of good writing. While in school he began selling birthday cakes by writing parents of students. His first year he made $10,000 from his direct marketing business just selling cakes. By the time he was 32 he had made over $6 million selling various things through direct marketing. When you next met your classes, your students yearned to learn how to make at least $1 million by good sales letters— and almost to drool for one of those birthday cakes.

3.   As senior vice president, American Bank, 21 West Fayette Street, Baltimore, MD 21201, write a thank-you for the new checking account to Mr. and Mrs. Malcolm B. Simons, 104 The Highlands 21203. Enclose a folder showing pictures and addresses of your seven branches and giving the banking hours. Invite Mr. and Mrs. Simons to use your other services (savings accounts, safety deposit boxes, loans, credit cards. . .). Invite these new customers to ask questions regarding any of your services.

4.   As B. Mason Allen, Trust Department, First National Bank, 625 West Broadway, Sarasota, FL 33578, set up a form letter to be sent to well-to-do customers acquainting them with your monthly bulletin, *Taxes and Estates*. This bulletin briefly presents facts and ideas which deal with the conservation of property and the protection for beneficiaries through modern estate planning. You hope that your bulletin will raise questions and generate comments so that your staff can assist in reviewing the overall estate plan.

5.   From Mutual Savings, 1005 Congress, Austin, TX 78767, send a form letter to your customers from the president, James O. Gant, telling them how much you appreciate their business. The enclosure of the 1099

form shows the earnings on the customer's savings last year (which is more money than customers could have earned at a bank in a similar type of account). Enclose a booklet that compares income rates from various types of investments (stock market, Treasury notes or bills, money market mutual funds, floating-rate notes, etc.). If, after reading the booklet, customers feel that funds now invested in maturing instruments elsewhere, or funds from other sources, will best serve invested in one of Mutual's high-return, no-risk savings accounts, they should come in for gladly given professional discussion/help.

6. For Wutzlers, 212 North Howard, Baltimore, MD 21201, Baltimore's oldest and largest department store, write to newcomers Mr. and Mrs. R. Lee Christy, 2510 5th Avenue East, Atlanta, GA 30310, welcoming them. Your local newspaper ran a story about the important new jobs they have taken in Baltimore. All your stores—the downtown one on Howard Street near Saratoga, the suburban stores at Towson, Westview, Eastpoint, and Southdale, and the Salisbury, Maryland, store on the famous Eastern Shore—carry complete stock of quality merchandise, and all have convenient parking facilities. Sales Associates in each store are prepared to provide assistance in decorating and furnishing a new home. Enclose an application form for a Wutzler charge account.

7. For Preston State Bank, 900 Greenmere Road, Dallas, TX 78142, write a letter to all depositors whose personal checking accounts often run over $1,000 telling them about your new CD program. Under the new program, customers can get their interest payments each month instead of quarterly. The bank will deposit an interest payment into the customer's checking or savings account automatically; or, if the customer desires, mail out a check. Interest on these CDs is compounded daily, which provides a higher effective annual yield. Prior to the new program customers had to buy at least three staggered 90–day CDs, one each month, to get monthly payments.

8. Select a current article from *U.S. News & World Report* that impressed you. Write a letter praising the article and send it to the Letters Editor, 2300 N Street N.W., Washington, DC 20037. Be very specific (answer the *why*).

9. After seeing the television program "60 Minutes" (or a similar program on topics of concern), write CBS (or another appropriate broadcaster) a letter of appreciation/congratulations. Be specific (saying not just *good* or *interesting*, but why, and possibly including comment on the on-screen performers).

10. Write your alums giving a progress report on your fraternity/sorority, Alpha Mu Omega, and thanking them for their help/support of all kinds. At the national convention in St. Louis a month ago your chapter received the national trophy for outstanding achievement and the scholarship trophy. First semester the chapter took 35 new members. Two were invited to Alpha Lambda Delta, freshman honorary. Two seniors made Phi Beta Kappa. Call attention to the names and honors on an enclosed sheet. You may add other appropriate details. You have three of the eight officers of the Student Government Association. The new president of the Marketing Society is an Alpha Mu. Two were taken into Mortar Board and one was selected for *Collegiate Who's Who.*

11. Four nights ago you had the pleasure of staying at the Phoenix Inn, 379 Wagon Wheel Drive, Phoenix, AZ 85021. Because you were so impressed by the friendly atmosphere, cleanliness, and good food, you were writing a deserved complimentary letter from your home when your mail came bringing your author-autographed copy of this book. The inn manager found the book in your room (214) (give specific date) and sent it to you.

12. For William Davis, Vice President—Public Affairs, Carolina Power and Light, Charlotte, NC 28212, set up a form letter to go along with a refund which is due some customers because, on testing, their meters were shown to be running fast. You have a regular program of testing meters. Stress the idea that your meters are the best you can buy, but they occasionally get out of adjustment. What you're doing is approved by the Public Service Commission. Any questions? They're welcome.

13. Assume that you are William Dowse, Route 6, Box 290, Fargo, ND 58431. When you received your promotional letter from Intergalactic Airlines, you were persuaded to fill out the questionnaire in order to get a personalized vacation plan. The computer really did a good job for you, your wife, ten-year-old son, and eight-year-old daughter. It recommended that you take a vacation at Christmas time and fly to four Caribbean islands (Cap-Haiten, Haiti; San Juan, Puerto Rico; Charlotte Amalie, San Thomas; Puerto Plata, Dominican Republic). You and your family were glad to get away from the snow and barren wheat fields and go to the warm climate, buy distinctive trinkets and useful things, sit on beautiful sandy beaches, and swim in the bright blue Caribbean waters. Add any specific details to your goodwill letter to Intergalactic's computer and the people who feed it, and the rest of the staff (one of whom you single out for specific praise/thanks).

14. As executive director of the American Business Communication Association, an organization for people teaching or practicing business communication, you have (as one of your pleasant duties) to acknowledge members' advancement to the rank of Senior Member. Draft a form letter that will be individually typed (and personalized) and sent to each new Senior Member when elected. Be congratulatory, say something about what this professional recognition means to the members in terms of advancement in both career and the association, including the privilege of sitting at the speaker's table at the annual president's luncheon. The Senior Member certificate accompanies the letter; the Senior Member tie tack or pin, as appropriate, is sent separately.

15. For the Southland Corporation, 2828 North Haskell Avenue, Box 719, Dallas, TX 75221 (owner of 7-eleven Stores), draft a form letter to go to stockholders who return their proxies for the next-month Annual Shareholders Meeting. Refer naturally to your recent Annual Report, which you sent them and which reflects the greatest year in Southland's 47-year history. You expect the next to be another successful year as new merchandising and marketing programs are being initiated and efforts toward reduction and control of expenses are being intensified.

16. Guaranty Savings and Loan, 1700 West 13th, Little Rock, AR 72201, established in 1932, plans to open a branch office in a newly developed residential area. Prior to the formal opening of the branch, help James Thompson, head of the branch, write to customers who have been doing business with the company in its main (and only) office and suggest to these customers that they transfer their accounts to the branch office for their own convenience (free, easy parking; five full-time experienced employees; convenient location). The branch at 10500 Dreher Road (at the intersection of Doyle Springs Road) opens a week from today.

17. Using the information in the preceding case, assist Thompson in drafting another letter to newcomers to the community telling them of the services of your branch office. (Thompson gets names at a nickel each from registration employees at the school, realty, telephone, and other utilities offices. Banks would not cooperate.)

18. Industrial Heating Co., 9770 N. Avers, Skokie, IL 60076, a long-established company installing and servicing gas and oil heating plants in large buildings, plans to open a branch on Chicago's south side, completely across Chicagoland from the Skokie headquarters. Prior to the formal opening of the branch, help Marvin Jacobson, head of the branch, write a letter to south-side companies who have contracts with Industrial

Heating for maintenance and repairs to their heating plants, telling them you are transferring their contracts to the new branch. Pluses: office will be in their area and familiar with the area and the various codes of the many small municipalities; quick service—within minutes in an emergency; experienced installers and servicemen; traditional Industrial Heating service; no change in their contracts or billing arrangements. The branch at Western Avenue and Hammond Highway opens in two weeks.

19. Using the information in the preceding case, assist Jacobson in drafting another letter to companies coming into the area, telling them of the services your branch office offers. (Jacobson gets the names from real estate offices, city halls, utilities, and the like.)

20. Use the current date and write Ms. Jane Simpson, Institute of Botany, 678 Boone Street, Boulder, CO 80229, from Scientific Publications, Inc., 171 Newberry Road, Philadelphia, PA 19104. As Marcus Janes, Executive Vice President, you are delighted to have her new manuscript and welcome her to your family of authors. Compliment her on a good job in making the changes reviewers of the first draft suggested. Send a publication schedule which will give her some idea of the time required for processing the manuscript and time needed for publication. As a little bug for her in this ice cream—and a little paving your road for a smooth-running publication schedule—tell this first-book author about a few weeks of hard work reading galley proof about six weeks hence and again reading page proof about four months hence.

21. As T. J. Real Estate Company, your city, write a letter to Tom Slade, Slade and Bennet Insurance Company, also of your city, congratulating him on his two years of service to the YMCA. During Tom's term of office the YMCA opened a new cafeteria, new swimming pool lighting was installed, a new large gymnasium ceiling and improved lighting became realities, dues were not raised despite increasing costs, and membership was the highest it has ever been since the Y was founded in 1915.

22. Triton College is a private school in River Grove, Illinois. One of the main supports for this school is through gifts from individuals. Today, you (assume you are Jarvis Moore, president of the National Citizens Bank, River Grove, IL 60171) write a note of congratulations to Joseph Belisle (Belisle, Pierce, and Smith Accountants, 908 South Water Street, Decatur, IL 62522). Belisle has been named chairman of Triton College's River Grove community campaign this year. Belisle will head an effort by approximately 100 business people who will call on friends of the college to seek their continued support. Belisle is past chairman of the Triton Associates and was special-gifts chairman in Triton College's building campaign. He happens to be a graduate of the Wharton School at the University of Pennsylvania.

23.   After 37 years of selling Metagas, you have sold out to Howe Gas Incorporated, a company you felt would give your customers the same type of treatment you have always given. You are sad to leave a business, people you love, and employees who have been part of the family, but you are glad to find a company with a hundred years of service. In a form letter, thank your customers for their past loyalty and tell them about the new company (same phone number, 376-5392). Howe Gas serves hundreds of thousands of residential, commercial, and industrial customers in ten states. The showroom at 12 S.W. First Avenue, Tulsa, OK 74112, remains open eight hours a day. Sam Samuelson is the district manager.

24.   For five additional cases, see GS 12 (sympathy), 17 (praise), 25 (appreciation), 27 (apology), and 30 (anticipating resistance), beginning on page 303.

THE AL YOUMIN SERIES (SY, FOR SERIES YOUMIN)

Here in a compact package you find an interesting story and a varied series of *18 possible writing assignments* involving the same few people and only two companies. We put it here, rather than somewhere else, merely because a goodwill letter started the whole thing.

Before writing any one of the assignments, you almost have to read all of the preceding and the appropriate text chapter (as indicated along with the kind of letter right after the case number).

On first looking at the series, you might be inclined to draw some moral —like "Don't write goodwill letters; they get you into trouble." But that misinterpretation of the facts is comparable to Mark Twain's intentionally humorous conclusion that being in bed is the most dangerous thing you can do because more people die in bed than anywhere else.

If you analyze the facts thoroughly, you should conclude, instead, that you should write all the goodwill letters you can find time for. The series shows how a simple goodwill letter led to one minor inconvenience for Al Youmin (writing seven letters) but brought him two big benefits—lots of favorable publicity and a good advertising manager for his business.

The series involves two goodwill situations (SY 1 and 13, related to Chapter 6), five requests and one persuasive complaint (2, 4, 6, 8, 10, and 14; Chapter 11), three refusals (3, 9, 15; Chapter 7), three favorable replies (5, 7, 11; Chapter 5), one sales (12; Chapter 8), and (for Chapter 10) one personnel selector letter (inquiry; 16), one letter "fielding" a loose job offer (17), and one job-resignation letter (18). That's six out of the eight chapters on specific kinds of letters treated in this book (skipping only Chapter 9 on self- and job-analysis preparatory to writing applications and Chapter 12 on collections).

SY 1 (Goodwill—Chapter 6). You, Al Youmin, are owner of a machine shop specializing in high-precision metal working, Youmin Company, 3838 West Douglas Avenue, Peoria, IL 60445. With your high investment in machines, tool life and downtime for resetting and retooling are primary concerns. Recently a customer sent you a job involving close-tolerance machining of some aluminum, one step of which involved difficult threading. Problems arose: Part was to specifications, but appearance was unacceptable, and micro-particle buildup on the cutting edge of the tool required resetting or retooling after every 40 parts were done. Tried kerosene as a coolant: Got better finish, but vaporizing created hazardous condition. Switched to Slick-Flo 1000, mixed 15 to 1 with water. Great results: Beautiful satin finish and no micro-particle buildup. Completed 600-part job with one tool, no resetting or retooling necessary, and tool was still capable of close-tolerance work. Saved $150 in tool costs, eliminated expensive downtime, did away with hazardous vaporizing. Customer so pleased he has given you additional work. Write your experience to the manufacturer of Slick-Flo 1000, Levi Gate Specialties, Industrial Park, IN 68556.

SY 2 (Request—Chapter 11). As the advertising manager of Levi Gate Specialties, reply to the unexpected but welcome letter from Al Youmin. You are so impressed with how well Slick-Flo 1000 worked for him, you would like to feature him and his letter in your advertising and direct mail efforts. Ask his permission—a persuasive request selling him on the idea.

SY 3 (Refusal—Chapter 7). When you wrote to Levi Gate Specialties about Slick-Flo 1000, you had no intention of publicly endorsing the product, and you do not want your company to be publicly tied up with any single coolant/lubricant maker. You want to stay good friends with all your suppliers. Nicely refuse the request, making sure you stay on good terms with Levi Gate, too.

SY 4 (Request—Chapter 11). That testimonial from Al Youmin is too valuable to give up on using it. You won't necessarily want to print his letter *in toto* in your ads and direct mail but only to paraphrase parts and to use his name. By allowing this, Youmin will gain publicity for himself and his company, build his reputation as a leader in the field, and do other people a professional favor by telling them (through your advertising and direct mail) about a product (yours, admittedly) that will help them. Add any other arguments you think that you, as advertising manager of Levi Gate Specialties, might use.

SY 5 (Favorable reply—Chapter 5). That persuasive request from the advertising manager of Levi Gate Specialties is too good for you to turn it down. As Al Youmin, give him permission to use your letter and your name in advertising and direct mail. Make sure he knows you want to see anything he does before it goes into print, if it has your name in it.

SY 6 (Request—Chapter 11). After all the trouble you had getting Al Youmin's permission to use his name and letter, you hate to ask for more; but you need a good black-and-white photograph of him and one of his company buildings. Since he should already have these available, he ought to be able to send you copies. You will, of course, return them after use. And you want to thank him and promise photocopies before you use his materials.

SY 7 (Favorable reply—Chapter 5). That advertising manager at Levi Gate Specialties is pretty persistent. Now that you've gone this far, as Al Youmin send him a copy of your stock photograph of your building. For a picture of yourself, you have a snapshot taken a few years ago which may do. When does he expect to have the advertisement with you in it appear?

SY 8 (Request—Chapter 11). The photographs Al Youmin sent you were not too helpful. The photo of his building wasn't too bad, but the snapshot of him was barely usable. Taking a deep breath, you had it extensively retouched—it doesn't look much like him now, but it does look like a picture of a human being. By the time your advertising agency and your president, old Levi Gate, got finished, there wasn't much room left in the advertisement for his letter anyway, so all you could quote were a few generalized, congratulatory words. From what you sense about Al Youmin through your correspondence, he may not like all this, and he does have the right to pass on it before you print it. As advertising manager of Levi Gate Specialties, write Al, enclosing a photocopy of the proposed advertisement, and sell him beforehand on approving it as it stands. You'll need lots of resale and success-consciousness, as well as the rest of the letter-writing techniques you've learned.

SY 9 (Refusal—Chapter 7). As Al Youmin, you're sorry now that you ever let this thing get this far. The advertisement from Levi Gate is not the kind of thing you'd run. The headline ("Smooth Your Metalworking Path with Slick-Flo 1000") is unimaginative, the copy is dull, the picture of your building is so small the sign ("Youmin Company—Close-Tolerance Machining") can't be made out, and that picture of you doesn't look like you.

You know this will create difficulties for the advertising manager at Levi Gate, but you must disapprove the advertisement. But do it nicely.

SY 10 (Request—Chapter 11). The refusal from Al Youmin was a shocker. You know the advertisement featuring him is not a classic. But you have too much time and money invested to just drop the advertisement; so you elect for some quick revisions in the artwork: Make the sign on his building bigger so the "Youmin Company" at least pops out; heavily retouch the photo of Al again. As the advertising manager of Levi Gate Specialties, write another letter to Al Youmin. Subtly point out the changes in the art, explain that the headline and copy lead directly into his testimonial (economy and quality of work using Slick-Flo 1000), and finally, using all your talent and experience to keep his goodwill, point out that he has approval rights over only the two photographs and those words in the copy directly quoted from his letter. Get him to approve the advertisement.

SY 11 (Favorable reply—Chapter 5). When you (Al Youmin) receive the revised advertisement from the advertising manager of Levi Gate Specialties, his excellently persuasive letter and the changes in the pictures sway you. The picture of you, especially, is improved; it now looks like you; so you approve its appearance and the plan to use your letter and pictures. You still insist, however, on seeing a copy of anything using your stuff—*before* the ad goes out.

SY 12 (Sales—Chapter 8). You are the advertising manager for Levi Gate Specialties company. To merchandise your advertisement featuring Al Youmin's testimonial for Slick-Flo 1000, write a sales letter to go to all your customers and prospects. It will accompany a copy of the ad and a copy of Youmin's testimonial letter. Since you have the ad and the letter to carry the burden of detail, you can use your cover letter to sell Slick-Flo 1000's main advantages: won't break down or vaporize at machining temperatures; compatible with all metals, ferrous and nonferrous; easily cleaned and virtually infinitely reusable; economical price. Point up the technical advice your company can give, your long reputation for quality products, and your quick delivery. Offer technical literature and a sample of Slick-Flo 1000 on request.

SY 13 (Goodwill—Chapter 6). Since you got Al Youmin's approval to run the Slick-Flo 1000 ad featuring his testimonial, things have gone nicely. The plates have been made and sent to the trade magazines which will run the ad. Old Levi Gate (your president) is happy, and you're happy. Since you're the advertising manager of Levi Gate Specialties, to you falls the pleasant task of sending Al Youmin five copies of the advertisement, two of them mounted on easel boards. He will probably want to place them around his plant, and keep some to show his customers. If he would like more, you have a limited supply from which you can send him some.

SY 14 (Complaint memo—Chapter 11). You are Sam Lippery, West Coast sales representative for Levi Gate Specialties, and you're unhappy. Yesterday you called on one of your best accounts, Chip Braker Machining, and Chip threw a copy of *Technical Machining Magazine* in front of you, pointing to the latest Levi Gate advertisement, one for Slick-Flo 1000 that features another customer, Al Youmin. Chip, in his inimitable way, wanted to know first of all how Youmin got all the publicity and second, if Slick-Flo 1000 is so good, how come you never told him about it. You had a ticklish problem to remind Chip that you have been trying to sell him on Slick-Flo 1000 for the past two years; but you smoothed his feathers, promised him a generous sample, and got out. Write a memo to the advertising manager back at Levi Gate's home office and suggest strongly that an advertisement featuring the testimonial of a West Coast machine shop would be a good idea. You could use the help in your territory; since Youmin in Illinois was featured it would be only fair; and you have a real good candidate.

SY 15 (Refusal memo—Chapter 7). Being the advertising manager of Levi Gate Specialties is not all martini lunches and the glamorous ad biz. Take the memo you just got from Sam Lippery. After all the trouble you had with Al Youmin, you're not about to do another testimonial advertisement. They aren't all that great as a basis for advertising anyway. But you want to keep Sam happy, if possible; so point out to him that the Youmin testimonial was a one-shot deal, inspired by the purely unsolicited testimonial you got from him (attach a photocopy of Youmin's letter to your memo to Lippery). No plans have been approved to do more testimonial ads. If you do one for Lippery, you'll have to do one for each of the other representatives (all 32 of them!) to be fair. You can't be sure that everybody can come up with a customer who will write a strong testimonial. Tell him to explain all this to his customer, and also explain that to do an advertisement about that company would be unfair to all the other companies in the West Coast area. Be positive and success-conscious.

SY 16 (Personnel selector—Chapter 10). Put yourself in the shoes of Al Youmin. Your advertising manager just quit after a row with Engineering and left on short notice. You immediately thought of the advertising manager at Levi Gate Specialties, who ran that advertisement recently with that striking picture of you in it. He seemed imaginative, hard-working, persistent, pleasant, gentlemanly, and persuasive. On a hunch, write him to see if he would be interested in coming with Youmin Company. Be realistic when you describe the benefits, challenges, and opportunities—and be vague about the salary; no use chancing a too-high quote at the beginning.

SY 17 (Invited application—Chapter 10). When Al Youmin wrote to you about the possibility of being his advertising manager, you were intrigued. Things haven't been going well for you at Levi Gate Specialties lately, and a change might be a good thing. Putting yourself in the place of Levi Gate's advertising manager, write a very careful letter to Al Youmin guardedly expressing your limited interest, indicating that the salary area he talked about is too low, and asking whether he will pay your relocation expenses.

SY 18 (Job resignation—Chapter 10). Al Youmin upped his salary offer and agreed to split your relocation expenses. Along with everything else, it looks like a good opportunity. Now write your resignation letter to old Levi Gate, the president of Levi Gate Specialties, where (you reflect) you've worked for six years, had your ups and downs, learned a lot (and, you feel, contributed something too), made some hits and some errors (and a lot of friends—including old Levi, the devil, who at least always treated you right). Of course you won't *say* all of that, and you *will* remember one of Levi's first pieces of advice: "Always be kind to others on your way up the ladder of success; you may meet them on your way down."

| # Disappointing messages

[Character requires the courage to say no firmly
but pleasantly when saying yes or saying no
unpleasantly would be easier.]

EVERY NEGATIVE BUSINESS situation justifies taking the trouble to present your position effectively. Unless you recall clearly the suggestions about handling disappointing messages in Chapter 4 (pp. 79–81), therefore, turn back and quickly review them. What we said there is especially important as a basis for this whole chapter.

REFUSING REQUESTS

Most people are disappointed, irritated, or downright angry when told they can't have something, can't do something, or can't expect you to do something—unless you *first* give at least one good reason. If you make the psychological mistake of first saying no and then explaining, the emotional upset from your no will prevent the other person from listening reasonably.

Fortunately, back of most business refusals is some good reason dictated by known facts, fairness, sound business judgment, or even prior agreement. In effective refusals, therefore, you usually have to explain some facts, circumstances, or unreasonableness of which the reader is apparently unaware. Hence the central theme for writing effective disappointing messages is "explain *before* refusing."

Furthermore, one of the first lessons in good human relations any sensitive person learns is that when you take something away from or deny someone something, you give a reason, you give something else to compensate for the loss when you can, and you try to extend some gesture of friendliness.

Simply stated, the desirable pattern for refusals is therefore

—A buffer beginning (establishing compatibility; defined and illustrated below).

—A review of facts (reasons).

—The refusal itself, subordinated. ⎫ *or* A counterproposal which implies
—An off-the-subject ending. ⎭ the refusal.

Before studying an analysis of this suggested structure, however, read the following refusal of a request for a charitable contribution:

```
While we are primarily manufacturers of extruded plastic
products, we are well aware that we are also members of this
community and that we have real responsibilities for its
well-being.

Each year we therefore actively support the United Way.  One
of our chief officers usually serves on the Board of
Directors, as our Vice President of Finance presently does.
Many of our employees work in various capacities during the
annual fund drive, and we willingly give them paid time off
for this purpose when we can.  For the past five years Martin
Plastics has achieved its dual goals of 100 percent of
employees contributing and each contributing at least a fair
share.  In addition, we make a substantial corporate
contribution to the United Way each year.

Since the United Way apportions its receipts among the various
charities at work in our community, we are able to contribute
to all at one time and in one fund drive.  You can understand
how this maximizes our contributions and those of our employees
in the most efficient manner and with the least disruption of
business.  We strongly feel that the United Way is the fairest
way of fulfilling our charitable obligations and making the
biggest possible contributions.

Next year, when the annual United Way drive is on, we shall
take comfort in knowing that your charity, Homes for Homeless
Pets, will again receive a portion of the money collected
and can continue its valuable work for the animals that depend
so much on us.
```

The buffer beginning

Since people don't normally ask for what they don't expect to get, a reader opening your reply to a request almost certainly expects pleasant news. Probably that reader, in making the request, carefully figured out some seemingly good reasons why you should do as asked—and may have had some strong feelings about it. If you present a refusal immediately, you appear to ignore those feelings and reasons—and are likely to arouse a negative reaction, causing a mind closed to anything else you say.

On the other hand, if you pitch right in with a presentation of your reasons, you appear to be arguing—and dander, or at least suspicion, rises.

To prevent such mental impasses and emotional deadlocks, you need to show your reader that you are a reasonable, calm person by indicating some form of agreement or approval of the reader or the subject. Frequently you can agree completely with some statement made in the request. At least you can say something to establish compatibility, even if nothing more than that you have given the proposal serious thought. This is your buffer.

The turndown of a request for your company's manual (p. 80) could easily begin with

    You are certainly right about the pressing need facing most
    business firms for more effectively trained business writers.

Or it could start this way:

    Students attending Harwood College are fortunate to have
    teachers who try so conscientiously to correlate college
    training and business practice.

Both beginnings acknowledge the receipt of the request, clearly imply careful consideration, establish compatibility, and set the stage for a review of the facts in the refusal—*later.*

Six warnings deserve attention here, however, about writing buffers.

1. If you appear to be granting the request, you are building your reader up to an awful letdown! Such beginnings as these would mislead most readers:

    I certainly would like to see each Harwood student have access
    to a copy of our manual.

                                --

    You are right, Mr. Kolb, that abandoned pets deserve help from
    each of us personally.

In fact, anything you say in the buffer that seems inconsistent with what you say later will produce more resentment than effectiveness.

2. The *second* warning is against beginning irrelevantly or so far from the subject that the reader isn't even sure the letter is a reply. The buffer beginning must clearly identify the general subject. Otherwise, incoherence

and rambling will result. Even such a beginning as the following is irrelevant:

```
I well remember my first pet, a small white dog with an
irresistible sense of humor.
```

3. The *third* warning is against recalling any disappointment too negatively—for example answering a claim with "We regret your dissatisfaction. . . ."

4. As the *fourth* warning, you need to be careful about buffer length. You can easily go wrong either way—making the buffer too short to get in step with the reader and hence not really get off to a pleasant start, or too long to suit an impatient and resultingly suspicious reader.

5. As the *fifth* warning you need to phrase the buffer well so that it makes a smooth and natural transition to the next part (your explanation).

6. Despite the fact that many writers begin refusals with "I really wish we could. . . ," we do not believe it can do as good a job for you as a good buffer. It is stereotyped, it sounds insincere to many readers, and it invites the belligerent response, "Then why don't you?" But the greatest disadvantage (and the *sixth* warning) is that it defeats the whole psychology and strategy of B–plan letters—it establishes the refusal unmistakably in the opening before showing any reason.

To sum up, we can say that a good buffer will be *relevant, pleasant, equivocal,* and *transitional.*

Reasons rather than apologies

If you will apply the positive thinking and positive phrasing we talked about under "Positive Statement" (p. 88) and "Success Consciousness" (p. 90), you will resist the common impulse to apologize anywhere in a refusal *and especially in the beginning.* Apologies are no substitute for action or explanation. And they force you to phrase negatively the very ideas you should avoid—that you *will not, cannot, are unable to, do not have,* and similar negative expressions.

You will of course run into some situations where you have no satisfying reasons (nonexistence of certain information or simple unavailability). But in most cases when you have to refuse, that refusal depends on good reasons. *Those reasons—not some apology or policy—form the bedrock of your explanation.*

You want to emphasize those reasons which reflect benefits to the reader —if not directly, then indirectly by identification with a group with which the reader might be sympathetic. The writer of the charity refusal letter did a good job of relating reader benefit to the refusal. The following letter from a manufacturer refusing a dealer's request for samples also stresses reader benefits:

Congratulations on 25 years of service to your community!
Through continued association with retailers, we know that
only those whose businesses are based on sound managerial
policies and services succeed over so long a time.

We have tried to help in these successes by cutting costs
whenever possible and passing these savings on to retailers in
the form of lower prices. This aim led us to eliminate the
high (and often unpredictable) manufacturing and shipping costs
of special samples. You and hundreds of other druggists have
benefited from these cost reductions over the years.

Our favorable prices on quality products plus national
advertising and help with point-of-sale promotions are the best
ways we've found to increase your Walwhite sales.

If you'll fill in and mail the enclosed card, Mr. Robert
Abbott, your Walwhite representative, will be glad to arrange
a special Walwhite exhibit for your anniversary sale. This
attractive display will attract many customers.

You cannot, however, apply such reader-benefit interpretation in every
case. To attempt to would result in artificial, insincere talk. Better than
that is a thorough, logical explanation that is friendly and positive (without apology though basically selfish). The following letter refusing a request for permission to reprint some sales letters of a mail-order house is
quite acceptable:

You can count on a large, interested readership for the
article you are writing about the importance of sales letters
in business.

In our company, as you know, we depend upon letters exclusively
for sales. Of necessity, then, we have tested extensively to
find out the most effective procedures. Our highly paid
writers are continually revising, sending expensive test
mailings, and comparing the returns. The best letters
represent a considerable investment.

In the past we have had some of our standard letters used
without consent by rival companies. Because that use
decreased the letters' effectiveness for us, we now
copyright all our sales forms and confine them to company
use. Should we release them for publication, we would have
to incur the same expenses again.

I'm sending you some bulletins and a bibliography which may
help you with your article. Will you let me know the issue of
the magazine your article appears in?

If you establish such good reasons, you have no cause to apologize.

The derived, positive refusal

Ideally, your explanation and reasons so thoroughly justify you in refusing that anyone would infer the turndown. Thus prepared, your reader
is far more likely to accept your decisions without ill feeling.

But you cannot always afford to depend exclusively on implication to
establish the turndown unmistakably. The refusal must be clear; but even

when you have to state it, it need not be brutally negative. In fact, it need not be negative at all.

If you will look back at the sample refusals in this section, you will see that the writers established the idea of what they were not doing by a statement of what they were doing.

Not	*But*
We don't contribute to individual charities.	. . . the United Way is the fairest way . . . of fulfilling our charitable obligations. . . .
We do not supply special samples to retailers.	We . . . help . . . by cutting costs . . . and passing these savings on to retailers in the form of lower prices.
We cannot let you have samples of our sales letters.	We copyright all our sales forms and confine them to company use.

When you incorporate the limiting words *only, solely, exclusively* (even phrases like *confine to* and *concentrate on*), no doubt remains.

Saving some of your reasons until after establishing the refusal enables you to **embed** the disappointing news and thus reduce the impact of the refusal. In any event, you certainly want to take leave of your reader on a more pleasant note than the refusal.

The pleasant, hopeful ending

In some cases when you must refuse you can do little but reassure the reader through a few additional words that you are not utterly callous— or even merely indifferent. Good wishes for the success of the project, the suggestion of other sources, possibly the suggestion of being helpful in other ways, sending something other than what the reader has requested —all these are possibilities for ending your letter with a friendly gesture.

Sometimes you cannot comply with your reader's request but can suggest an alternative action, a counterproposal or compromise proposal, which will be of some help. In many instances it can successfully absorb the statement of the refusal and furnish you with the positive ending you seek. The following letter is an example of this technique:

Prudential's employees and clients will no doubt benefit materially from the reports manual you are planning, Mr. Lee— especially if it is the same caliber as the letters manual your staff prepared recently.

I'm sure many college teachers would be glad to furnish you illustrative material. And I am no exception. In the past fifteen years of working with business and college people trying to improve the quality of their reports, I've collected much HOW NOT TO and HOW TO teaching material.

For most of this I have only my single file copy, which I use in teaching a report-writing course three times a year and which I carefully keep in my office.

I'm sure my student assistant would be glad to photocopy it for
you during off-duty hours at the regular rate of $3 an hour.
Since the job involves no more than 50 or 60 pages, I feel
reasonably sure that securing the material this way would cost
you only about $10–15 (including cost of materials, copier
fees, and time).

I shall be glad to make the necessary arrangements if you
would like me to. I'm sure I can have the material to you
within four or five days after hearing from you.

Please note again that this writer does not resort to negative phrasing
or apologies. You too should resist the common tendency to resort to such
expressions as "I regret my inability to do as you asked," "I'm sorry to have
to refuse your request," or—much worse—"I hope you will understand our
position," especially at the end. For these weaklings, substitute appropriate
positive and gracious ideas such as those used in the examples given.

For writing goodwill-building refusals, check the reminder list of points
on page 211.

REFUSING ADJUSTMENTS

The letter refusing an adjustment is obviously a bad-news (B–plan)
letter. Your psychology of saying no is therefore important. So unless you
thoroughly understand it, review the explanation beginning on pages
79 and 205.

For your buffer-paragraph beginning, look for something in the situation which you and the reader can agree on and which is pleasant. Even
appreciation for the information you received could serve.

Although you may carefully introduce a sentence that serves as a transition and resale on the house, you need to get to your explanation or review
of facts and reasons fairly early. And you need to give the facts and reasons
fully in a clear system of organization.

Several special techniques are important if your explanation is to rebuild
goodwill while refusing to do what the reader asked. You already know
better than to hide behind the word *policy* or to give no reason at all. But a
flat-footed announcement of what a guarantee states is just as bad as
unsupported talk about policy.

Since you are refusing, obviously you are not charging responsibility
for the dissatisfaction to either the firm or the product or service. You must
clear that point up with adequate explanation as a basis for refusing. Resale
at this stage (before the explanation) in the area of the trouble is *not* the
way, but only a head-on collision with what the reader thinks. You *have*
to give the basic fact(s) on which your refusal depends. Doing so, of course,
makes the reader guilty; but don't accuse directly. Also, preaching or
belittling will only make matters worse.

Checklist for Refusing Requests

1. Your buffer opening must pleasantly establish compatibility.
    a. One of the poorest starts is talk about how pleased or flattered you are. It's vain and selfish. Shift the emphasis to your reader.
    b. Beginning too far away from the subject results in incoherence.
    c. Don't appear to be on the verge of granting the request.
    d. Nor do you want to intimate the refusal at this point.

2. Your transition must follow coherently and logically from your buffer.
    a. To avoid selfish-sounding turns, keep the emphasis on the reader.
    b. *Although, however, but,* and *yet* signal a turn for the worse. Avoid them as sentence beginnings.
    c. Avoid also the insincere "Although I should like to. . . ."
    d. Supply the bridging sentence showing why you are explaining.

3. Give at least one good reason before even implying the refusal.
    a. Emphasize reasons which are for the benefit of someone other than yourself if you can.
    b. Don't hide behind "our policy." Policies merit little respect; the reasons behind them merit a lot.
    c. For believability, you need specificness.
    d. Stick to what is plausible.

4. The refusal itself should be
    a. A logical outcome of the reasons given. Ideally, the reader should deduce the refusal before your definite indication of it.
    b. Presented positively—in terms of what you can do and do do.
    c. Preceded (and preferably followed) by justifying reasons.
    d. Unmistakable but implied or subordinated (maybe in a counterproposal).
    e. Written without negative words like *impossible, must refuse,* or *very sorry to tell you that we cannot.*
    f. Without apologies, which just weaken your case. Concentrate, instead, on what is hopeful.

5. Continue to convince your reader of your real interest and helpful attitude, without recalling the refusal, in the ending.
    a. Your ending must be positive and about something within the sphere of the reader's interest.
    b. Watch for bromides and rubber stamps in the end.
    c. Be wary of the expression "If there is any other help I can give you, please let me know." It can produce some sarcastic reactions.
    d. Follow through specifically with any wanted action.

Your best technique is to fall back on the passive, impersonal presentation (something "was not done" instead of "you didn't"), rather than accuse. The reader will be able to see who is responsible if you explain well that your goods and your firm aren't.

In fact, if you arrange your reasons and explanations carefully, they will probably make the negative answer clear by implication without the necessity of stating it. If not this way, at least you subordinate the refusal by burying it (that is, putting it in the middle of a paragraph where it doesn't stand out unduly).

After the refusal, which must be clearly there whether by implication or by direct statement, you may do well to add some more reasoning and explanation in support (thus embedding and further subordinating the refusal). Be sure you say enough to make your refusal convincing and justified.

Your ending then becomes an attempt to get agreement or the reader's acceptance of your refusal as justified. That is, you write with as much success consciousness as seems reasonable about the future outlook. This does *not* mean that you write and ask for an answer as to whether your action is all right. If it isn't, you will learn without asking.

Often the best ending assumes that the preceding explanation and decision are satisfactory and talks about something else. Rather than looking backward (and reminding the reader of the unhappy situation now cleared up), it may better look forward to the next likely relationship between writer and reader. The following letter illustrates most of the points:

> Your customers certainly do have a right to demand that all Neenah monogrammed stationery be letter perfect. One of the reasons we specify that all orders be typed or printed is to accomplish this aim.
>
> For that same reason, on the rare occasions when a shipment is not exactly as ordered, we print and ship corrected letterheads without question and without charge. To be sure your Neenah customers get exactly what they want, however, we need your careful help. If you'll check your orders of the past two months, you'll see that we have replaced six. A similar check of the enclosed photocopies will show clearly that we followed the original directions exactly on this seventh request.
>
> A corrected shipment for Mr. Washburn reading Freemont instead of Fairmont and for Miss Wentworth reading Montevallo University rather than Montevallo College will nevertheless go out to you within two days after we receive your approval of our two-part plan: (1) We'll debit your account for the new shipment at the usual prices, subject to our usual terms; (2) for greater profit for both of us, we ask you to again instruct your sales personnel to type or print all orders and verify with each customer every letter and every number to appear in the final printing. You can then rely on our providing you exactly what you order.

The checklist on page 213 reviews the highlights of refusing adjustments.

Refused-Adjustment Checklist

1. Make your buffer relevant, pleasant, equivocal, and transitional.
   a. But begin closely enough to the situation to acknowledge.
   b. Reflect pleasant cooperation (try to agree on something).
   c. Don't imply that you're granting or refusing the request.
   d. Avoid recalling the dissatisfaction more than necessary.
   e. Watch buffer length: neither too breezy nor too long.
   f. Early resale in the trouble area bluntly contradicts.
   g. Should you show appreciation for the report?
2. Make your facts and reasons courteous, thorough, and convincing.
   a. An immediate plunge (beginning of the second paragraph) into "our guarantee" or "our policy" is abrupt.
   b. Don't accuse the reader or preach. Phrase your explanation impersonally—and let the reader decide who's guilty.
   c. Establish the explicit, adequate facts—the basis for refusal.
   d. Even intimating refusal before reasons is bad psychology.
   e. When possible, interpret reasons to show reader benefits.
3. Make the refusal logical, subordinate, and impersonal but clear.
   a. Preferably the reader sees the refusal coming.
   b. Give it little emphasis. Consider implying it.
   c. Keep it impersonal and positive—in terms of what you do.
   d. Be sure it is there, however; unclear is as bad as too strong.
   e. Follow the refusal with reasons, showing any reader benefits.
   f. Customer education or counterproposal may imply the refusal.
   g. What about the returned product (if applicable)? Resell it?
4. Make your ending pleasant, positive, and success-conscious.
   a. When you need reader action, ask for it positively.
   b. Otherwise an off-the-subject ending about services, seasonal goods, or some other topic of interest is appropriate.
   c. Don't suggest uncertainty of your ground. Watch *hope/trust*.
   d. Apologies are unnecessary reminders of trouble; your explanation has already made the best apology.

For the COMPROMISE ADJUSTMENT, use these for Items 3 and 4:

3. Make your counterproposal as logical, helpful relief.
   a. Be careful to make a smooth transition from the explanation (which implies refusal) to the counterproposal.
   b. Offer it ungrudgingly, without parading your generosity, but let the service element prevail.
   c. Don't belittle it ("the best we can do") or make it sound like a penalty ("a service charge will have to be made").
4. Use a modified action ending.
   a. Ask permission; you wouldn't go ahead without agreement.
   b. Tell what the customer is to do, but don't urge acceptance.
   c. For service attitude, talk prompt satisfaction.

COMPROMISING ON ADJUSTMENTS

When you decide to try to compromise—usually because of divided responsibility, or uncertainty about responsibility or correction for the trouble—you may use either of *two* plans.

In the *first* you follow the refused-adjustment plan exactly down *to* the refusal. There you make your proposed compromise instead, explicitly. In effect, you are refusing the adjustment requested and are making a counterproposal—a compromise. When you ask acceptance of it, your success in getting a favorable reply will depend not only on how well you have presented facts and reasons to justify the compromise but on your success consciousness in presenting it and on your phrasing it to encourage rather than discourage acceptance.

The following letter in answer to a strong request for removal of the heater, cancellation of remaining payments, and refund of the shipping and installation charges illustrates the points. You will notice that it offers to compromise to the extent of canceling the remaining payments, but it proposes another action instead.

You are right in expecting your Warmall heater to heat a large
area such as your entire store, for that is what it was
designed to do.

To do so, the Warmall requires careful installation. It must
be located so that the air currents can carry its heat to all
parts of the room. Our engineer reports that the stove was
installed in the proper position but that later remodeling of
your store has blocked circulation of air with a half
partition.

Your stove can be all you want it to be if relocated; so
removing it would be useless. That would mean losing your
down payment and what you have paid for shipping and
installation, although we would of course cancel the remaining
payments. Moreover, you must have heat, and the Warmall will
do the job.

We have absolute faith in our engineer's judgment, but your
satisfaction is more important. So we want to do what is fair
to us both.

At your convenience we can move the stove to the position our
engineer suggested; and, if it does not heat to your
satisfaction, we will remove it and not charge you another
cent.

Will you suggest the most convenient time for the change that
will make your store warm and comfortable? We can do the job
so quickly and efficiently that your business can continue as
usual.

For a checklist following this plan of compromise adjustment letter, see page 213.

A *second* method of compromising—usually called the full-reparation beginning compromise—sometimes works better. You follow the plan of the letter *granting* an adjustment at the beginning, through the explanation. The facts, of course, will indicate divided or uncertain responsibility. Your resale talk will indicate that the repaired product (or a replacement up to par, in case the original was beyond repair) will give the service the customer wanted.

Since presumably the original desire for that service still exists, you ask the customer to make a choice—the refunded money or the product. And of course you word it to encourage choice of the product, because that way you have a customer satisfied with your product as well as your fair-minded practices.

Your main purpose is to restore goodwill and confidence. Your success depends on a start which offers everything requested and thereby pleases the customer, your explanation which shows the justice of a compromise, and your fair-mindedness in allowing the choice. The danger—not a very serious one—is that some people might try to keep both the money and the product.

Attached to this letter is a credit memorandum for $43.75, which we cheerfully send you for the five Bear Mountain hunting jackets you returned, as an indication that you'll always be treated fairly at Bowen's.

Under the assumption that these jackets would find a ready sale at a reduced retail price despite slight imperfections (a button mismatched, a crooked seam, or maybe a little nick in the fabric), we offered them "as is" and priced them at $8.75 instead of the regular $12.75. We felt that marking them "as is" indicated special circumstances.

Generally we follow the accepted business custom of making all such sales final for an entire lot. But as we evidently did not make the situation perfectly clear, we are leaving the decision up to you; if you feel that you're entitled to the adjustment, it's yours.

Many of your customers, however, would probably be glad to get nationally advertised Bear Mountains at perhaps $21 instead of the standard $25. And even if you sell these five at, say, only $16, your percentage of profit will be about the same as if you sold perfect jackets at full price.

Even though slightly imperfect, these jackets are still ready to stand a lot of hard wear. They are made to suit hunters' needs, with ample pockets for shells and with comfortable tailoring. Selling them should be easy, especially at a discount.

So if you'd like to reconsider and want to offer these jackets at a saving, just initial the face of this letter and send it to us with the credit memo. We'll absorb the freight charges. We'll look for your decision, but we think you can make a good profit on them at the special price.

Application of the checklist for compromises with full-reparation beginning (p. 216) to this letter will show that it is pretty good and will review the principles for you.

Checklist for Compromise with Full-Reparation Beginning

1. The beginning giving everything asked for is basic—to dissolve reader emotions and get you a reasonable hearing.
   a. Make it immediately, specifically, and completely.
   b. Build up the wholesome effect by a friendly, adapted expression to emphasize your reliability and prevent a curt tone.
   c. Don't apologize; Item 1a does lots more.
   d. Carefully avoid unnecessary negative reminders.
   e. Beginning with the compromise would infuriate readers. Since they think they're entitled to what they asked, you have to show otherwise before compromising.

2. The explanation (facts and reasons) must show that the claimant is expecting too much.
   a. Don't be too slow about getting to at least some of the explanation.
   b. Interpret it with a reader viewpoint and positive statement.
   c. Do not directly accuse; show blame impersonally (perhaps by customer education on the use and care of the article).
   d. Establish the facts to show that the claimant is at least partly responsible or is overestimating the loss.

3. Show the service attitude and your fair-mindedness in your proposal.
   a. As the foundation of your proposal, stress serving your reader.
   b. Recall the original desire for the service the reader wanted.
   c. Continuing the reader-benefit interpretation, state your proposal.
   d. Follow your suggestion with any other plausible sales points.
   e. Don't parade your generosity in the loss you take.
   f. Suggest—don't command or preach or high-pressure the claimant.

4. The modified action ending should give a choice but encourage the one you prefer.
   a. Tell what you want done: reject (return) the full reparation and accept your proposal.
   b. As in any action ending, make action easy.
   c. Do not bog down with apologies or emphasis on the full reparation.
   d. End with a short suggestion of reader satisfaction resulting from the proposal.

REQUESTS FOR CREDIT INFORMATION FROM CUSTOMERS

Many applications for credit do not give all the data you must have. You therefore write, asking for the needed information, and (as we explained on p. 106) in routine situations you normally would use a form.

The major problem is to avoid arousing the customer's suspicion or indignation because you have not approved credit forthwith. Where the danger seems great, therefore, you write a special B–plan letter with careful explanation and tone not possible in a form.

To soften the effect of the delay in approving credit and to quell suspicion, begin with buffer material, stress the benefits of complying with the request, show that you treat all customers alike, make action easy, and promise quick action. If character is not in question, be sure to say so. And to encourage response, use resale or sales promotion as the matrix for your explanation.

The following letter is typical in stressing "All our customers fill out this application . . ."; it is an appropriate covering letter for the form request discussed on page 107.

> Your interest in the conveniences of an Allen Tilby charge account is most welcome, Mrs. Lee.
>
> So that we may assist you as quickly and as easily as possible, will you please fill out the enclosed routine credit application? All our customers fill out this form as a help to both them and us. The information is strictly for our confidential files, to be used in setting up the best credit arrangements we can make for you.
>
> You can be sure that we will give your request our immediate attention. Just use the stamped, addressed envelope enclosed for your convenience in returning the application.

A letter to a dealer employs the same strategy:

> Corone fishing gear is a good line to handle. Dealers throughout the country report the favorable reaction of fishermen. And our advertising in <u>Field and Stream</u> and <u>Sports Afield</u> continues to create demand for Corone dealers.
>
> We're just as eager as you are to have your Corone sales start; so will you supply the usual financial information that all our dealers furnish us, along with the names of other firms from which you buy on credit? Most of our dealers use the enclosed form, but if you prefer to use your own, please do.
>
> This confidential information will enable us to serve you efficiently—now and in the future.

Occasionally such a request backfires, with a protest from the customer (sometimes quite vigorous). In such cases all you can do is write again, using a pacifying buffer, and then pointing out the value of credit and the importance (to you and your reader) of careful selection of credit customers. The letter reiterates the normalcy of the request and closes with a request for action. It is also a modification of the B–plan letter:

We're glad you let us know unmistakably how you feel about
sending financial information. And we're sure that as an
openminded business manager you'll want to look at your
supplier's side of the story. Only through complete frankness
can we work together successfully in a credit relationship.

We have some pretty definite ideas too—learned from selling
about 2,000 successful dealers like you several million
dollars' worth of Corone fishing equipment in the last 20 years
. . . about 90 percent of it on credit.

Because of our credit arrangements, Corone dealers can do a
large amount of business on a small investment. In effect, we
take the place of your banker, for the goods we send you on
credit are the same as cash. Like your banker, we can make
loans only when we have evidence of ability and willingness to
pay later. The only way we can protect all our dealers against
price rises due to losses from bad debts is to check every
credit applicant and select carefully.

If you applied for a loan at your bank, you'd expect to show
your financial statements to your banker. We are in the same
position—except that we have no mortgage to protect us, and
we are not so well informed as your banker about you and your
local market.

The confidential information we've asked for is strictly for
business purposes. It helps both of us. Since the peak sales
months are close at hand, I'm enclosing another form and an
addressed envelope so that you can get this information back
to us in time for us to get your fast-selling Corone fishing
gear started to you by the first of next week.

Because most requests for credit information from customers are simply modifications of direct requests and refusals, we run no checklists or cases.

CREDIT REFUSALS

In the light of poor standing on any or all of the four C tests for credit (p. 135) you will have to refuse some credit applicants. The most likely reasons are unfavorable reports from references or an unfavorable financial position. Your job will sometimes merely require suggesting some modification of the arrangement the customer has requested. In the case of an old customer it may be a refusal of a credit-limit revision or a suggestion of curtailed buying. All these situations are inherently disappointing; they are a reflection on the ability of the customer, who *may* interpret them as a reflection on honesty; and so they are fraught with negative possibilities.

As in any disappointing-news letter, you need to analyze the situation, search out any hopeful elements (especially character), line up your reasons, and write a B–plan letter.

The applicant may have receivables or payables out of line, or be too slow in meeting obligations, or be undercapitalized. *Whatever the reason, you have to establish it,* and in this function you have some educational work to do—without offense if at all possible.

You certainly do not want to close the door irrevocably on any debtor (except possibly deadbeats). A poor account at the time of writing may be a good one a year later (and if your wise counseling has helped in the improvement, you have established yourself as a helpful friend and are thus more likely to receive the customer's business).

For that reason, most good credit refusals establish good feeling in a short buffer, show the reasons in an analysis of the circumstances, identify the deficiency, refuse in positive fashion, suggest how the customer can remedy the deficiency, and invite a later application. Unless you can make a counterproposal, point out its advantages, and then ask for action on that basis, *the best ending is an attempt to sell for cash.* After all, the reader wants your goods and possibly can't get them on credit elsewhere either.

In the following instance, involving an order for $176 worth of work overalls, the dealer quickly responded with a financial statement and references in response to the request for them. Accounts receivable and payable were both too large; the trade association reported that strikes in the mines of the dealer's community affected all local trade. Since the references reported that the customer's payments were good enough during normal times, the credit writer sought to cultivate potential business while declining the account at present:

Your large order for Stalwart overalls suggests the prospect of an early strike settlement in your area. We're glad to hear that.

When the miners go back to work, the steady revival of business in and around Canyon City will no doubt help your collections so that you can <u>reduce both your accounts receivable and accounts payable</u>. In that way you can probably quickly <u>restore your current ratio to the healthy 2:1 we require</u> because we've found over the years that such a ratio places no burden on our customers. Such an improvement will enable us to consider your credit application favorably. Will you please send us subsequent statements?

You'll probably need your Stalwart overalls sooner than that, however; they're a popular brand because they wear well. Workers like the reinforced pockets and knees. They'll easily outsell other lines you might carry.

You can stock this popular brand and thus satisfy present demand by paying cash and taking advantage of the liberal discount we can give you. On this order, for instance, the discount at our regular terms of 2/10, n/90 would amount to $3.52—more than enough to pay interest for three months on a $100 bank loan.

Or you might cut your order in about half and order more frequently. But with a $100 bank loan at 8 percent and a stock turn of 12—which is a conservative estimate, Mr. Wolens— you'd make an annual saving of $16 after paying your interest charges. I don't need to tell you that that's 3 pairs of dependable Stalwart overalls absolutely free—overalls that you still sell for $7.80 a pair.

> Since we can have your Stalwart overalls to you in about five days, just attach your check to the memo I've enclosed and mail both of them back to me in the enclosed envelope to handle the order in this profitable way.

Usually you can specifically isolate the shortcoming(s) (in one or more of the four C's—p. 135) in an industrial or wholesale situation (as underlined in the preceding letter) and use impersonal, positive phrasing to save the customer's pride, suggest the remedy, and leave the way open for future negotiations.

In consumer letters involving a retail customer, however, nine times out of ten the reason for the refusal is the customer's failure to take care of obligations. This is a highly personal reflection, one which many retail credit people shy away from by feigning incomplete information and inviting the customer to come in and talk the matter over.

We do not agree with that dodging procedure. We think that a better method is the forthright credit refusal in the usual pattern of buffer, reasons, positive refusal, forward look, and counterproposal in the form of a bid for cash business.

> Thank you for requesting a credit account at Aiken's. We take it as a compliment to our way of doing business.
>
> For 50 years Aiken's has been bringing its customers quality merchandise at fair prices. This, as you realize, requires careful merchandising management. Not the least of these savings—the practice of paying cash for merchandise, thereby receiving discounts and eliminating interest charges, which we pass on to customers as lower prices—requires that we receive prompt payment from our credit customers.
>
> To assure that, we select our own credit customers carefully for both ability and willingness to pay. Though meeting all obligations promptly is often temporarily difficult, very likely you will soon qualify for a charge account at Aiken's by taking care of your other obligations.
>
> Meanwhile you will continue to receive the same courteous treatment that made you favor Aiken's in the first place. With our will-call, budget, or layaway plans at your disposal, you may own anything in Aiken's within a short time by making convenient payments of your own choice. Come in soon and let us serve you in this way.

The following letter refusing credit to a young man just out of college and with unsteady, low-income employment talks concretely and sensibly; it's a good credit-education letter. Note how the writer stresses the idea that character is not the basis for refusal.

> When you wrote last week asking for credit, as a member of the Illinois Credit Union we automatically asked the Union for your record. You can well be proud of the report we received.
>
> Such a complimentary report on your excellent character indicates a promising future. The fact that you have never defaulted or delayed in paying an account means that you will be able to get credit easily when your income becomes steady.

We could extend credit to you on the basis of your personal
record alone, for we know that you fully intend to meet any
obligations you undertake. But if some unforeseen expense
should come up, with your present fluctuating income you
probably could not pay your account. As a cooperating member
of the Credit Union, we would then be compelled to submit your
name as a poor credit risk. Such a report would limit your
chances of obtaining credit in the future—perhaps at a time
when you need it more than now.

For your own benefit you'll be better off to stick to cash
purchases now, but we shall look forward to the time when you
can comfortably and safely contract for credit with us.

Meanwhile you can make your dollars reach further by buying
from Bowen's for cash, for we buy in quantity, save on
shipping costs, take advantage of discounts and pass these
savings on to you in the form of lower prices. When you buy
at Bowen's, you therefore make the most effective use of your
income by getting quality merchandise at low prices.

Letters limiting the credit of an established customer are no different
from refusals to new customers; they just adapt the talking points.

Your $635 order for September delivery indicates a bright
outlook for fall sales. Apparently you are selling lots of
Carlton heaters. I'm glad to see that.

In trying to serve you well as always, we want to ask whether
this large order and the one you placed in March mean that your
business has outgrown the credit arrangement you now have or
that you may be overstocking Carltons.

With this shipment your account would stand about $500 beyond
the line of credit we agreed on when you first started dealing
with us five years ago.

If your ordering such a stock of Carlton heaters indicates an
extensive home-building program going on in Fairview, your
comments on local conditions and the information requested
on the enclosed form may serve as a basis for extending your
credit line to the point where it will take care of your needs.

Or if you want to continue the present line of credit and
receive the additional shipment, we will extend to July 10
the 5 percent discount on your $940 March order. By sending
us your check for $893, you will not only put your account in
shape for the present order; you will also mark up greater
profits on the sale of your Carltons.

We're just as anxious as you are, Mr. Skinner, to send you this
latest shipment. Please take one of these courses so that we
may ship your new stock of Carltons in time for the fall
season.

As in any good refusal, none of these letters apologize or hark back to
the refusal in the end. To do so indicates that you are not confident in
your decision. The checklist on page 222 incorporates the major suggestions for handling credit refusals or limitations.

Credit Refusal Checklist

1. Your opening:
   a. Your best beginning talks about something pleasant: the market; timeliness; the reader. . . .
   b. Beware the selfish note of "We are glad to receive. . . ."
   c. To keep your reader from considering buying elsewhere, get resale (product and/or house) early in the letter: consumer pleasure in use or dealer profit possibilities.
   d. References to the order, if there was one, should be worked in incidentally while you say something of more significance.
   e. Be careful not to mislead the reader.
2. Your explanation and refusal:
   a. Stick to the theme of a strong, healthy financial condition.
   b. Do not begin your explanation with writer-interest reasons.
   c. Give some justifying reasons before the refusal.
   d. Meet the issue squarely, making clear whether character is or is not the reason. Advantages in cash buying are not reasons for refusing credit.
   e. Avoid the negative, critical, nosey, or patronizing tone; state your reasons as helpfulness to the reader. Give just enough facts to show that you know without implication of FBI investigations.
   f. Be sure you've made clear that you will not now approve credit.
   g. Hiding behind "policy" evades the issue (and appears selfish).
   h. Phrase your reason in terms of your experience with others.
   i. Always leave the way open for credit extension later.
   j. But you can't make promises, except to reconsider.
3. Your counterproposal:
   a. Introduce a cash, reduced-shipment, or other plan as the solution.
   b. But first show why (help to the reader).
   c. If you propose cash with a discount, figure the savings.
   d. Possibly project the savings over a year's business.
   e. Can you suggest smaller orders? Local financing?
   f. Use the conditional mood in your explanation and proposal.
4. Your ending:
   a. Leave no details uncovered in your present proposal.
   b. In regular action-ending style, drive for acceptance.
   c. Success consciousness precludes the use of "Why not. . . ."
   d. You have to get approval before taking unasked action.
   e. Your last picture should show the reader's benefits.
5. Your tone:
   a. Throughout your letter retain an attitude of helpfulness.
   b. Sales promotion material on other goods is inappropriate.

ACKNOWLEDGMENTS OF INCOMPLETE OR INDEFINITE ORDERS

Any firm which sells by mail will receive some orders which can't be handled as the standard ("all's well") acknowledgments discussed on pp. 131 ff.). Some orders will be incomplete or vague, or for goods temporarily out of stock, or from people to whom you cannot sell, or for something a little different from what you have, or for several items involving a combination of these difficulties.

Keeping most of these problem orders on the books (and hence the profits from them) is often the difference between success and failure. While a firm may occasionally get into a situation where it can succeed in business without trying, smart competitors soon learn about such a gravy train and jump aboard. Those who don't know how to compete for problem-order business will lose it—and the profits that go with it.

For that reason, we devote the remainder of this chapter to disappointing (B–plan) acknowledgments of orders. And we do it in terms of letter writing—for good reasons.

In nearly all cases a well-done acknowledgment letter is the best way to keep the order on the books and the customer well served and satisfied. You could hardly expect to succeed with form letters because they cannot adapt adequately to highly varied circumstances and because their impersonality does not work well in handling negative situations. Telephone calls, while having the advantage of speed, lack two important advantages of a good letter:

1. They do not give the firm the chance to phrase the message so precisely, concisely, and persuasively as in a carefully done letter.
2. They do not provide a written agreement on the many details often important in the buyer-seller contract.

In acknowledging problem orders, you need a high level of know-how with various letter-writing principles and techniques. Since such orders are inherently negative (always delay and inconvenience, for example), you need to know how to keep the picture as bright as possible. You need resale to keep reader interest. Adaptation becomes important because of the varied and special circumstances. And since you often must ask the reader for a change of mind or for further action, you need all the principles of persuasion, including skill with action endings. None of these are likely to come out as well in form letters or telephone conversations.

     ❀   ❀   ❀   ❀   ❀

When you get an order that is incomplete (and therefore vague), you can either try to guess what the customer wants and thereby risk extra costs and customer dissatisfaction, or you can write for the needed information. Usually you write.

Since it is a *bad-news* letter (because of the additional trouble and delay), you will wisely use a buffer. Resale, thanks, and (if a new customer) a hearty welcome are all good buffer material for beginning the letter. A problem here is to avoid misleading the customer into believing that you are filling the order.

Very early—perhaps by starting to interweave some of it into the first part of the letter—you should stress the *resale* element. The more specific it is, the more emphatic it is. If you say the customer will like the product, make clear specifically why. Reassuring the customer that the product is good is resale that will help to overcome the drawbacks of additional trouble and delay. In this case it has a much more important role than in the standard acknowledgment. Although small bits of it may be scattered throughout the letter, at least some of it comes before the reader learns the bad news—to bolster the original desire in the moment of disappointment. It can be very short:

```
Fashion-conscious women everywhere are wearing Orlon acrylic
sweaters like the one you ordered, not only for their wide
color choice and style but because of their ability to be
tossed around and still keep looking nice.
```

When you have thus prepared the reader psychologically, *asking for* the needed information will reveal the bad news. Thus you save words, weaken the bad news by putting the reader's main attention on complying with your request, and avoid any goodwill-killing accusations. More specifically, your technique at this important crux of the letter is: *In one key sentence beginning with a reader-benefit reason for your request, ask for the information.* For example:

```
So that we may be sure to send you just the sweater that will
suit you best, will you please specify your color choice?
```

Now, if you add a touch of satisfaction-resale to motivate the requested action, do what you can to help the reader decide and answer (to overcome the extra trouble), and promise speed (to overcome as much as possible of the delay), you'll probably get the information you want, without ruffling your reader's feathers:

```
Coming in four subtle shades of harvest brown, lettuce green,
tile red, and sky blue, Orlon acrylic sweaters provide you
a pleasant color to match any complexion or ensemble.
Just use the handy return card, and you'll be enjoying the
sweater of your choice within two days after we receive the
information.
```

When circumstances permit, even a better idea is to get the customer to return your letter with the necessary information marked on it. Beyond making customer response easy, you get the desirable effect of removing your reminder of shortcomings from the customer's sight. The letter above could also have ended this way:

    Just check the box at the bottom of this letter to tell us
    what color you want, and return it in the stamped, addressed
    envelope. You'll be enjoying the sweater of your choice
    within two days after we receive the information.

Notice that although it treats an inherently bad-news situation, this letter uses no negative expression ("delay," "inconvenience," "incomplete," "regret," "sorry"). Most of all, the acknowledgment does not irritate by accusing with such expressions as "you neglected," "you forgot," or "you failed."

The following letter illustrates good technique for an acknowledgment when you can fill part of the order but have to get omitted information about another part. If you want to consider it as a simple acknowledgment of an incomplete order, however, you can read it without the first paragraph and the phrase *the file and* in the next-to-last paragraph.

    Soon after you get this letter you should receive the very
    protective locking and fire-resistant Chaw-Walker file you
    ordered October 2. It is to go out on our Meridian delivery
    tomorrow.

    The sturdy but light Model 94 Royal Electric typewriter you
    specified is our most popular one this year, perhaps because
    of its wide adaptability. Readily available in two type sizes
    and six type styles, it is suitable for virtually all kinds of
    work and various typists' tastes.

    To be sure of getting the type size and style you like best,
    please check your choices on the enclosed card of illustrations
    and return it.

    Although your letter was written in Executive style elite (12
    letters to the inch), you may prefer the more legible
    Professional style pica (10 letters to the inch) if you are
    buying for your reporters. It is the most widely used in
    newspaper work.

    All prices are the same—except $10 extra for the modish
    Script style, which you probably will not want—and your check
    exactly covers the file and three typewriters you ordered
    in any other choice.

    By returning the card with your choices of type size and style
    right away, you can have your three new Royals Friday, ready
    for years of carefree typing. We'll send them out on the next
    delivery after we hear from you.

For requesting additional order information in business-building fashion, apply the suggestions in the checklist for incomplete orders (p. 227).

DELAYS AND BACK-ORDERING

Sometimes the problem in an acknowledgment is that you can't send the goods right away. In the absence of a specified time limit, sellers-by-mail usually try to keep the order on the books if they feel they can fill it within a time that is really a service to the customer—that is, if they feel the customer would prefer to wait rather than cancel the order. After a buffer, they tell when they expect to fill the order and usually assume (without asking) that such an arrangement is acceptable. If the date is so far off that doubt arises, even within the 30-day maximum Federal law allows, they may ask instead of assuming. In either case the wise business writer will acknowledge the order promptly.

Again your main problem is keeping the order. This time, though, the only drawback to overcome is delay. Your main element is resale—to convince the reader that the product is worth the wait. It may include both resale on the house and resale on the goods (p. 72). If the order is the customer's first, resale is even more important and more extensive.

The plan and technique are the same as for the acknowledgment of an incomplete order, at least through the first paragraph and some resale talk.

```
Your order No. 5E361 (dated July 19) for 24 No. 536 boron
nitride standard 1/2-inch triangular inserts represents a
wise purchase.  This new material will let you operate at
higher speeds and take deeper cuts than you ever have before.
The resulting increase in productivity will mean increased
profits for you.
```

The parting of the ways comes where the incomplete order acknowledgment asks for information and the back-order acknowledgment explains the situation. The explanation should picture the goods on their way (and imply receipt of them) in the first part of a sentence which ends with a clear indication that that does not mean now (usually by giving the shipping date):

```
By going onto double shifts, we are confident we will have our
new sintering machinery set up and operating in time to get
these inserts, in the quality you expect, to you by the end
of August.
```

As always in letter writing, explaining in positive terms what you can do, have done, and will do is better than telling in negative terms what you can't do, haven't done, or won't do. As the writer of the preceding paragraph did, a good letter writer will avoid such unnecessary negatives as "out of stock," "cannot send," "temporarily depleted," "will be unable to," "do not have," and "can't send until."

Only a poor business manager gets caught short without a justifying reason. A good one will have a reason—and will explain it to customers to avoid the impression of inefficiency. Often it is basically strong resale material if properly interpreted. For example:

```
By performing our own sintering operation, we can exert a
higher standard of quality control and give you inserts that
have uniform density throughout, with no weak spots, and with
increased resistance to fracturing.  We have given your order
priority and are sure that by the end of August you will have
your inserts.
```

Checklist for Acknowledging Incomplete Orders

1. If you are sending any goods, say so immediately and give necessary details.

   a. If not, begin with a short buffer which is basically resale.

   b. Quickly but subordinately identify the order by date, number, and/or description.

   c. Slow: "We have received . . . ," "Thank you for your. . . ."

   d. Selfish: "We're glad to have. . . ."

   e. Provide some resale on the problem article before the bad news, but don't imply that you are sending the article now.

   f. Make the resale specific, not "We're sure you'll like these shoes." Say why.

   g. Use only brief phrases for resale on goods sent, or for any new-customer aspects, until you've asked for the missing information.

2. Ask for the information naturally, positively, and specifically.

   a. The natural transition to the request follows from preceding resale talk.

   b. Preface the request with a reader-benefit phrase—something like "So that you'll be sure to get just the X you want, please. . . ."

   c. To avoid puzzling, make the request fairly early—but not too quickly or abruptly.

   d. Avoid the accusation and wasted words of such phrasings as "You did not include" or "We need some additional information."

   e. Name the customer's options: color choices or different models, for example.

   f. Add explanations to help in the choice (or decision), to resell and to show your interest in satisfying.

   g. Keep the you-viewpoint: "You may choose from . . . ," not "We have three shades."

3. Close with a drive for the specific action you want.

   a. If many words follow the first indication of what you want done, repeat specifically.

   b. Make replying easy (maybe a return card to check).

   c. If appropriate, have the reader mark your letter and return it.

   d. Refer to the enclosure subordinately; action deserves the emphasis.

   e. Stress your promptness—preferably a date of arrival if you get prompt response.

   f. But keep it logical; post-office speed is not that of an automat.

   g. Try to work in a last short reference to reader satisfaction.

If resale on the house and/or sales promotion material would be appropriate—as the first surely would be in a new-customer situation —use Items 3 and 4 of the checklist for standard acknowledgments (p. 134) as additional Items 4 and 5 here.

More resale may follow the explanation to help make the reader want the product badly enough to wait. Because it has such an important job to do, it is probably more important in the back-order acknowledgment than in any other. It should be short, specific, and adapted to carry its full effect. It may include both resale on the house and resale on the goods (p. 72).

```
We're sure you want only top-quality tooling that will perform
to specifications—and that is what we insist on supplying
you. You have a right to expect the best—we have an
obligation to give it to you.
```

The ending of the back-order acknowledgment may go either of two ways:

1. You may ask outright whether you may fill the order when you have said you can. This plan is preferable if you seriously doubt that the customer will approve.
2. You may phrase it so that this letter will complete the contract unless the reader takes the initiative and writes back a cancellation. That is, you look forward with success consciousness to filling the order when you have said you can. Your assumption (that your plan is acceptable) will hold more frequently if you never suggest the thing you don't want your reader to do—cancel.

The following letter illustrates the handling of a back-order problem:

```
The women's white tennis dresses you ordered April 7—

4 dozen—style No. 16J7 women's tennis dresses, 1 dozen each in
sizes 8, 10, 12, and 14 @ $180.00 a dozen; terms 2/10, N/30

—are leading the summer sportswear sales of more than 400 of
our customers from Maine to California.

We are increasing production on this model and have booked
your tennis dresses for rush shipment April 27 by air express.

The unusual preseason popularity of this trimly cut tennis
dress owes much to its shimmering polyester and cotton fabric.
We used up our stock of the genuine combed cotton material;
and rather than use a substitute, we shut down production on
this model. A large stock of Glachine cotton fabric is
already en route here from Wancrest's famous North Carolina
mills; thus we are able to promise your shipment by April 27.

For this chance to prove once again Tropical's continuing
fashion superiority, we thank you sincerely.
```

Much of the back-order acknowledgment technique is the same as that used in standard and incomplete-order acknowledgments. The checklist for back-order acknowledgments points out the similarities and additional considerations (p. 229).

Back-Order Checklist

1. If you are sending any goods, say so immediately and give necessary details.
   a. If not, begin with a short buffer which is basically resale.
   b. Quickly but subordinately identify the order.
   c. Slow: "We have received . . . ," "Thank you for your. . . ."
   d. Selfish: "We're glad to have. . . ."
   e. Provide some resale on the problem article before bad news.
   f. Make the resale specific, not "We're sure you'll like. . . ." Why?
   g. Use only brief phrases for resale on goods sent, or for any new-customer aspects, until you've handled the key point.
2. Handle the bad news as positively as you can.
   a. Picture the goods moving toward or being used by the customer *before* indicating that you do not now have them.
   b. Avoid negatives: "out of stock," "can't send until. . . ."
   c. Do make clear when you can ship.
   d. Adapt to the one situation rather than a universal, like "In order to give you the very best service we can. . . ."
   e. Explain the reason for being caught short (if any)—preferably resale in effect—and clear up any money involved.
   f. To avoid cancellation of the order, some resale is important.
3. Resale on the house helps too, especially with new customers.
   a. For consumers: personal shopping, delivery, credit. . . .
   b. For dealers: sales representatives, manuals, displays, advertising aids.
   c. If you talk advertising, give publications or stations, amount of space or time, and schedules; show how it promotes sales.
   d. If you talk credit, invite application rather than promise.
4. Sales promotion material shows service attitude and builds sales.
   a. Keep it appropriate—usually on allied or seasonal goods.
   b. You-attitude and specificness are necessary to effectiveness.
   c. Emphasize service to the customer, not desire to sell more.
   d. In referring to enclosures, put the emphasis on reader action.
5. Look forward to future orders.
   a. If sales promotion is the basis, suggest specific action.
   b. If resale is the basis, talk of reader satisfaction.
   c. Guard against bromides and Greedy Gus wording as you close.
6. Word the back-order action phrase to stress the action you want.
   a. Ask only if you doubt that your plan is satisfactory.
   b. Be very positive and success-conscious.
   c. Suggest acceptance; avoid the idea of cancellation.
   d. Also avoid reminders of the delay.

ACKNOWLEDGMENTS DECLINING ORDERS

Only three likely reasons might make you decline an order:

1. The customer has asked for credit, and you are not willing to sell that way. In that case the problem is a credit problem (discussed on pp. 218–22).
2. You don't have the goods (or a suitable substitute), and you don't expect to get them in time to serve the customer. You then explain the situation, tell where to get the goods (if you know), maybe present resale on your company and sales promotion material on any other goods which seem likely to be of interest, and end appropriately.
3. You don't market your products in the way proposed. Most of these problems arise because (a) the orderer is an unacceptable dealer or (b) you sell only through regular merchandising channels and the orderer (usually a consumer or retailer) does not propose to go through those channels.

The following letter illustrates well declining an order for the second reason:

> Your order for us to repair your Keller 5,000 hp. electric motor is evidence that you have been satisfied with our repair work—and, I assume, that we have been doing our job right.
>
> At present we are equipped to rebuild just about any electric motor up to 500 hp. This is the capacity of our armature lathes and rewinding machinery. As you know, working on motors the size of your Keller is highly specialized work requiring large machines.
>
> We suggest you try Charles Lindgren & Co., 4018 Greenleaf St., Evanston, IL 60202. Lindgren specializes in repairing large electric motors and has the equipment to move your motor to the shop or to do the work in your plant. Because of its good name in the trade, we can confidently recommend Lindgren.
>
> Thanks, however, for offering us the job. For prompt, expert service on your motors up to 500 hp., you can still rely on us. We stock parts for and repair and rebuild most makes of motors, gear head motors, generators, alternators, electronic and mechanical variable speed drives and speed reducers, eddy current clutches, pumps, hoists, and welders.

Unacceptable dealer

A dealer may be unacceptable because (1) you sell only through exclusive dealerships and you already have a dealer in the territory or (2) because the orderer does not meet your requirements for a dealership. For example, the dealer may insist on consignment sales or unacceptable discounting.

The first part of the declining letter would be the same in each case and (except for the omission of resale) the same as the beginning of other bad-news acknowledgments we have discussed. In the first case your explanation (usually beginning in the second paragraph) would be how you operate and why you operate that way plus the simple fact of the existing dealership. In the second case it would be a simple explanation of your requirements, with justifying reasons. The ending for the one would be a purely goodwill ending of "keeping in mind" in case you should later want another dealer. The other would end with an offer to reconsider if a change or additional information shows the dealer meets your requirements.

Improper channels

Some buyers think that all manufacturers or producers should sell to anybody who has the money and omit jobbers, wholesalers, and retailers (who add so much to the cost of goods). Those who howl the loudest on this point also howl loudly when a producer from afar does not make the goods available in local stores. Both methods of merchandising have advantages and disadvantages. We must grant, however, that a producer of or dealer in goods or services has the right to sell any legal way, must make a profit to stay in business, and deserves to profit only from serving customers.

Assuming that your firm has taken the customer-service attitude, you are in a good position to acknowledge the order of a person who does not (through ignorance or intent) choose to follow your merchandising plan— usually a consumer asking for goods from a wholesaler or producer instead of through the regular retail channel, or a retailer attempting to bypass your wholesaler.

Some of the customer-service reasons you can point out for selling only through local retail stores are the advantage of being able to get goods quickly from local stores; of being able to see, feel, and try them; of being able to get adjustments and service easier—indeed, all the disadvantages a seller-by-mail usually has to overcome are now in your favor.

For a retailer, point out that going through your distributor means the distributor holds the big inventory and thus the retailer avoids an unnecessary capital investment in stock as well as high shipping costs. The local distributor knows local conditions and can give valuable advice as well as extend credit where you might not be able to. And the distributor's representatives are immediately available with advertising and merchandising help. If you maintained a national sales force, the retailer would ultimately see that cost added to the cost of the items.

Your bad-news letter begins in the same way as those acknowledging incomplete orders and orders you cannot fill immediately: with a buffer, including resale to help keep the customer interested in the goods (on which you *do* make a profit, of course, wherever you are in the marketing channels). As before, you are careful not to mislead.

After this beginning, you explain how you merchandise your goods (not how you don't, except by implication) and why you operate this way. As far as possible, you explain the *why* in terms of benefit to the customer (you-viewpoint)—not the benefits to you. At least a part of the reader-benefit *why* should come before the part of the explanation which conveys the bad news (by implication) that you are not filling the order.

If your explanation is good, the reader will decide yours is the best way. If your resale talk has been good, the desire for the product will still be there although the purchase has to be elsewhere. You tell exactly how and where to get it, and you give a last touch of resale to encourage ordering the way you suggest.

If you have several equally convenient outlets, you name them all to give a choice and to be fair to all. This letter follows the directions:

Karsol shower curtains like the ones you saw advertised will give you the wear you want for your motel units.

So that you will be able to select personally the exact patterns you prefer (from eight different designs offered), we have set up a marketing plan of bringing Karsol shower curtains to you through local dealers only. This way you will save handling, shipping, and c.o.d. charges. You can get your curtains at the White House, located at 300 Main Street in Boulder, thus speeding your purchases and avoiding unnecessary delays ever present when ordering by mail.

We have recently sent a large shipment of Karsol shower curtains to the White House, and you will be able to see for yourself that although these waterproof curtains are of exceptional strength and durability, they are soft and pliable.

Stop by the White House and select your favorite pattern of Karsol shower curtains that will satisfy your customers.

If you are really a good business manager, you will notify the retailers, so that they can write or call the interested prospect who doesn't come in (especially if the order is for a big-ticket item).

The reminder checklist on page 233 summarizes most of the guide points.

SELLING A SUBSTITUTE

Many times you will receive orders you can't fill exactly because you do not have the special brand, but you have a competing brand or something else that will render the service the customer obviously wants. You know that in most cases people buy a product not for the name on it but for the service they expect from it. If you think your brand will serve (and ordinarily you do, or you wouldn't be selling it), you remember your service attitude and try to satisfy the orderer's wants.

Checklist for Rechanneling Orders

1. Your buffer is a good place to work in resale.
   a. An exact reference to the merchandise ordered is a form of resale in that it attempts to etch the choice in the reader's mind. Other identifications (quantity, date of order, and the like) aren't so important here, since this is an outright refusal.
   b. But don't even intimate the refusal at this point.
   c. Nor do you want to imply that you are shipping the goods.
2. To avoid abruptness, continue the idea of reader benefit as you turn from the resale to your explanation.
3. Think—and write—positively in your explanation.
   a. As appropriate to your reader (a consumer or a dealer), focus on benefits (fresh stock, less inventory, savings on shipping costs, examination of all choices before purchasing, credit and adjustment services).
   b. Establish at least one good reason for your merchandising plan before stating it (the statement of the plan is the refusal).
   c. State the plan in terms of what you do, not what you don't.
   d. Make it clear; otherwise, you may get a second, more insistent order.
   e. Follow the statement of the refusal with additional customer advantages.
   f. Is there any advantage in pointing out benefits other than those for the customer?
   g. When a price difference exists (as is usual), admit it but minimize it.
4. Your action ending should urge the reader to place the order with the appropriate outlet.
   a. Be as specific as you can (name and address if only one place and hence no playing favorites), and build up the image of service.
   b. Work in specific resale material as a safeguard against the possibility of brand switching when the reader places the order again.
5. If fitting, have the appropriate outlet contact the reader.

As a point of business ethics, you should not try to sell a substitute unless you sincerely believe you can truly serve by saving the customer time, trouble, or money in getting wanted products or by giving service at least comparable to what is available elsewhere in terms of cost.

Once you decide that you are ethically justified in selling the substitute, you need to remember several working principles:

1. Don't call it a substitute. Although many substitutes are superior to the things they replace, the word has undesirable connotations that work against you. Burma Shave once used the connotation effectively in a roadside advertisement reading "Substitutes and imitations—give them to your wife's relations. Burma Shave."

2. Don't belittle the competitor's product. Not only is this questionable ethics, but it criticizes the judgment of the orderer who wanted to buy that product.

3. Don't refer to the ordered product specifically by name any more than you have to—perhaps not at all. Once should be enough. You want the would-be buyer to forget it and think about yours. When you use its name, you remind your reader of it—in effect, you advertise it. Conversely, stress your product, perhaps repeating the exact name several times.

Except for the fact that *the identification and resale are in general terms broad enough to encompass both the product ordered and the substitute*, and show their basic similarity, your beginning of the substitute-selling acknowledgment is the same as other buffers for bad-news acknowledgments. If you phrase the beginning well, you'll have no trouble making a smooth transition to further talk about the substitute.

```
Your repeat order of September 10 for 60 regular-duty
batteries suggests that you find your battery business
profitable.  We're glad to hear it, but we think we can show
you how you can do even better in the coming season.
```

You arrange to introduce at least one sales point favorable to the substitute *before* revealing that you can't send what was ordered. You need to convey the negative message fairly early, however, to keep the reader from wondering why all the talk about the substitute. Your best technique is the standard one for subordinating negative messages: Tell what you *can* do in a way that clearly implies what you can't.

```
In our continuous effort to provide you the best automobile
accessories and equipment at reasonable prices, we have found
that the new Acme battery excels others of its price class in
power, endurance at full load, and resistance to cracking.
Because of those desirable qualities, we decided two months
ago to stock the Acme line exclusively.  Although Powell of
Dayton still has the Motor King, we think your customers will
be ahead in service and you'll make more profits with the
Acme.
```

Once you are over that rough spot, clear sailing lies ahead. You continue your sales talk, concentrating on why you carry the substitute and what it will do for your reader, not on why you do not carry the ordered product. You give a complete, specific description of the substitute's good points in terms of consumer or dealer benefits (as the case may be).

A good test of the adequacy of your sales talk is whether it is all *you* would want to know if you were being asked to change your mind about the two products.

> Because of its 115-ampere power and its endurance of 5.9 minutes at full load, your customers will like the fact that the Acme keeps a hard-to-start engine spinning vigorously and increases the chance of starting. They'll also like the tough new plastic case that avoids the cracking and loss of acid sometimes experienced with hard-rubber cases.

Sometimes your price will be higher than that of the product ordered. If so, presumably you think your product is better. Your method of meeting the price competition, then, is to sell the advantages and then point to them as justifying the price.

> When you explain the advantages the Acme has over its competitors, you justify at least a $5 higher price in the customer's mind--and you produce a prompt purchase. The Acme battery will back you up, too, in the customer's long experience with it. It carries the usual 36-month pro rata replacement guarantee. And the fact that it wholesales to you at only $2 more means an extra $3 profit to you on each sale.

Sometimes you will have to admit (tacitly) that your product is inferior but adequate. Your technique then is to sell its adequacy and the fact that it is a good buy because of the price. If the customer had ordered a higher priced battery than you now sell, for example, you could replace the three preceding paragraphs with these:

> In our continuous effort to find the best automobile accessories and equipment at reasonable prices, we have found that the Motor King is a leading seller. Because of its low price, strong customer appeal, and complete range of sizes, we now offer only the Motor King for all cars. The fact that you could fit any car would give you a big advantage over competitors selling brands that come in only a few sizes.

> The $5 saving you can offer on the Motor King will have a strong appeal to many of your customers who are unwilling to pay higher prices for more than standard specifications for regular-duty batteries: 105 amperes, 48 plates, 5.3 minutes' endurance at full load. The Motor King meets these specifications, and it carries the standard 36-month pro rata replacement guarantee.

> And while your customers would be saving, we estimate that you would be making more profits because of increased volume that would almost certainly come from a complete line at favorable prices.

Usually, however, quality and price are about the same; and you simply sell the product on its merits and as a service or convenience because it is available.

When your selling job is done, you are ready to try to get action. You can do either of two things:

1. You can ask the orderer whether you may fill the order with the substitute, or ask for a new order specifying it.

2. You can send the goods and give the orderer the option of returning them at your expense—that is, you pay transportation both ways. Thus no question of ethics arises.

The first way, you would have an ending something like

```
May we help you increase your battery profits by filling your
order with 60 of these new Acmes in the same sizes you ordered?
```

The second way will sell more goods if you word the offer carefully to avoid any high pressure. You should use it, however, only in an attempt to give the best service you can—for example when the customer indicated pressing need, and transportation costs are small, and you are reasonably sure of acceptance. Indeed a recent Supreme Court decision may relieve the receiver of any responsibility for returning or paying for unordered goods.

If you do send the goods on option, you can greatly affect your chance of having them accepted by the wording of your offer. Note the difference between these two ways:

```
We believe you will find the Acmes satisfactory.  Therefore
we are filling your order with them.  If you don't like
them, just return them to us collect.

                           --

Because we are so thoroughly convinced that you will like
the Acmes, we are filling your order with them on trial.
When you see how they sell and satisfy your customers, we
believe you will want to keep the whole shipment and
order more.
```

The second puts the emphasis on the customer's accepting the merchandise, where it should be; the first, on returning the goods. The second way will sell more.

Whether your acknowledgment letter selling a substitute asks approval or explains that you are sending the goods on trial, you should merely ask or suggest the action and make it convenient. A last touch of resale may help, but you should not urge action—certainly not command it. This type of letter has the onus of suspicion on it from the outset. High pressure is out of place anywhere in it, especially in the end.

The checklist for selling substitutes (p. 237) summarizes the points you'll want to observe in writing successful letters of this type.

COMBINATIONS

In acknowledging orders, you will often find one for several items, some of which you have and others of which you don't. To answer such an order, you have to combine the principles discussed for different types of

Checklist for Suggesting a Substitute

1. Your opening:
   a. For acknowledgment, rely mainly on implication: maybe the date of the order and a general reference to the class of goods.
   b. Make the reference broad enough to encompass A (product ordered) and B (substitute).
   c. But don't call either by specific name, model, or number yet.
   d. Let the buffer be resale in effect, but not specifically on A.
   e. Intimating at this point that you're going to ship anything could mean only A to the reader.
   f. Establish early the kinship—the similar nature—of A and B, with emphasis on points in B's favor.
   g. Show gratitude for the customer's coming to you with business.
   h. The routine "Thank you" or the selfish "We're glad to have" is usually not the best way.

2. Your transition:
   a. Introduction of B should follow naturally from what precedes.
   b. Before revealing that you can't send A, introduce B and at least one of its strong points.
   c. Calling B a substitute or "just as good" defeats your strategy.

3. Your statement of unavailability:
   a. Stress what you can do, not what you can't; saying that you can send only B makes adequately clear that you can't send A.
   b. Identify A by name no more than once—when you clear it out of stock.
   c. Present the bad news early enough to avoid puzzling.
   d. Make perfectly clear that you can't send A.
   e. Stress why you carry B rather than why you don't stock A.

4. Your sales message on B:
   a. Sell B on its own merits; it's a good product; no apologies needed, and no belittling of A.
   b. Seek out the sales points, and apply them specifically.
   c. Interpret these points in terms of reader benefits.

5. Overcoming price resistance (see p. 118):

6. For your action ending to keep the order and goodwill:
   a. Make responding easy, as always.
   b. Work in a last plug about satisfaction with the product.
   c. High pressure is out of place in this letter, especially in the end.
   d. If you send the substitute, make returning it a free option.
   e. But emphasize keeping, rather than returning.

acknowledgments. The writer of the following letter to a new customer had to do so because the firm could send one item immediately, had to delay another shipment, couldn't provide another item, and had to substitute for still another:

> Your two dozen F78 × 14BW Firestone tires are already on their way to you. They should arrive by Motor-Van truck Thursday, ready for your weekend customers.
>
> Welcoming a new customer to our long list of dealers who look to us for automobile supplies is a pleasure. We shall always try to serve your needs by keeping up with the market and providing you with the best goods available.
>
> The GR78 × 15WS tires are a case in point. In another effort to assure our customers of the advertised quality of all products we handle, we returned to the manufacturer the last shipment of GR78 × 15WS Firestone tires because they had been slightly bruised in a shipping accident. Since we are assured of a new shipment in two weeks, may we fill this part of your order then?
>
> In trying to keep our operating costs and consequently our prices at a minimum, we have discontinued handling A78 × 13WS tires because of the small demand for them. Probably your best source for them is the Kimble Supply Company, 401 South State Street, Chicago 61382, which carries a large stock of obsolete auto parts and supplies.
>
> When our buyer was at the NAP Show last year, he found a new automobile paint that seemed superior to other paints he knew. It is a General Motors product in all colors, with the standard General Motors guarantee. Our other customers have been so well satisfied with its quality and price (only $2.85 a quart and $9.85 a gallon) that we now stock it exclusively. As I feel sure that you, too, will be satisfied with this new product, I am filling your order with the understanding that you can return the paint at our expense unless it completely satisfies. I think you will like it.
>
> Since I am awaiting the return of the enclosed card with your decision on the paint (sent with your F78 × 14BW tires) and the GR78 × 15WS tires to be sent in two weeks, I am holding your check to see how much the refund is to be.
>
> For your convenience and information, I am sending a separate parcel of our latest catalog and a supply of order blanks. We shall be glad to handle your future orders for high-quality automobile supplies.

Note the organization of that letter. The first topic is your most favorable piece of information (usually the best start). The next two topics (delayed shipment and the "no-got" response) are decreasingly pleasant. (If the orderer had been vague or incomplete about another item, this letter should have treated it in second place because the fault was the orderer's —who couldn't well feel very negative toward a request for clarification.) A substitute-selling part would come last in any combination acknowledgment—not because it is especially unfavorable but because of its own structure. Its ending—somewhat like the ending of other sales letters, just will not fit coherently anywhere else in a letter.

Now note (as another illustration of selling a substitute) how the letter would read if the order had been for only the paint (substitution). Read only the second, fifth, and seventh paragraphs.

The checklists on preceding pages for standard (p. 134), incomplete (p. 227), back-order (p. 229), rechanneling (p. 233), and substituting (p. 237) acknowledgments apply to the combination cases at the end of the next section.

CASES

Refusing requests

1.   As L. E. Sly, Jr., manager of General Selectric's Medical Systems Division, Post Office Box 987, Milwaukee, WI 53201, draw up a letter to turn down Sheldon Leonard, 3290 Claymount Circle, Joplin, Missouri 64801. Leonard applied for a job as X-Ray sales representative. You have had an incredible number of applications and have tried to give the most careful consideration to each one. Naturally, you appreciate the applicant's interest in your company but have filled the job with one whose qualifications seem specifically suited to your needs.

2.   With the high cost of printing and publishing, many book companies have to turn down requests for free copies to teachers. For your publisher, Richard D. Irwin, Inc., 1818 Ridge Road, Homewood, IL 60430, write a letter that turns down a request for a free copy of *Communicating through Letters and Reports* to Annette Mills, a teacher, San Diego State University, San Diego, CA 92111. Teacher's desk copy of book and manual are free when book is adopted as text and at least ten books are ordered. She can order on enclosed card and (if adopted) get charge canceled. Resale might stress that this text is used by over 200 universities and that it has been the leader in the field for 25 years.

3.   As the secretary of the math department at X University, you receive a memo from Professor Lynch in another department about taking a group of students (15 names listed) on a three-day field trip ten days hence. Professor Lynch asks that you inform math teachers and request that they excuse the student absences, though students will be expected to make up missed work.

Your department has 63 teachers and about 6,000 student enrollments in 95 courses (many of which have several sections). You aren't about to look through all the rolls to see what teachers have the listed students—or to pester all 63 teachers with a memo about the absences of the 15 students. Of course you won't tell all of this to Professor Lynch. You do want to help, but that's expecting too much. If Lynch wants you to notify the professors involved, then Lynch will have to tell you the math course (or courses) and section(s) each of the 15 students is taking. Send the list back and explain.

4. Assume that you are Governor Fob James of Illinois. You are asked by Ann Blalock, University of Illinois Young Independents Club, 11 Mueller Road East, Peoria, IL 61611, to debate campaign issues with two of your opponents for the nomination to run for the office of governor. As the incumbent governor you have too much official pressure that you have to face; do not have the time to campaign around the clock every day; daily receive challenges to debate Rufus Bank and Mrs. Mattie Lynn Edwards (the opponents); feel that if these two people want to debate between themselves, that is their business; and the dignity of the governor's office should not permit the incumbent to participate. For more than 30 years you have been a supporter of the University of Illinois and all activities and efforts of faculty and student body; you have been proud to be named an honorary alum. Your support of higher education is a matter of record; you would be happy to receive, as governor, an invitation from the proper authorities to address the student body.

5. Paul Liverman, librarian at Salt Lake City High School, 10 Exchange Place, Salt Lake City, UT 84101, replied to your promotional letter containing a reprint of "Inflation in the 1980s" by filling out your subscription blank for a year's subscription to *Wall Street* and requesting 90 more copies of the "Inflation in the 1980s" reprint, which you cannot send. One alternative you might suggest is Liverman's photocopying parts of the second copy of the reprint included with this letter. Give solid and believable reasons why you can't send 90 additional reprints (cost, paper shortage, etc.).

6. The person developing the program for the next national convention of your professional association has asked you to take an important part on the program, not as a speaker but to chair a session.
Your employer encourages employees to attend and participate in meetings of their professional groups by paying all or part of the expenses of attending when they are on the program. But the main speaker at that session (a good choice) would obviously be very uncomfortable with you in the chair (he/she is bitterly envious of you for winning out in competition for three much-wanted "prizes": your spouse, your present position, and recently your election to lead the most prestigious committee of the association). So you suggest a good friend (whom you name) for the chairing job.
Furthermore, the speaker you most want to hear at the convention is speaking at a concurrent session.

7.   Assume that you are the public relations director of a large paper mill (Southern States, Meadowbrook Road, Jackson, MS 39212). You have just received a request from the Dependent Children's Aid Society to use your company's parking lot area for a fund-raising cookout. After checking with your safety office, you find out that the firm's liability insurance policy does not permit the parking area to be used for "social affairs, games, recreation." There might be danger of injuries which might result from accidents on the paved surface. Write to the Dependent Children's Aid Society, 95 Rex Avenue, Shreveport, LA 71109, and tactfully refuse. Suggest that the group might use the local park, which has quite similar facilities.

8.   As a member (and secretary) of the trustees for the C. R. Anderson Research Fund of the American Business Communication Association, turn down the application for a grant to Bonnie Burroughs, Lewis Reed College, Portland, OR 97211. In her application, Bonnie gave no explanation of her qualifications or the set-up of her university to show that she is competent to do the job. She did say that she would use computer analysis in her research, but she did not say she had a computer available. Any proposal not approved may not be resubmitted for one calendar year except by encouragement by the trustees of the research fund. Because her project and her research approach sound interesting and promising, the trustees voted to encourage her to rework and resubmit her proposal before three months from today (when the trustees next meet).

9.   As director of the computerized census information at the University of Texas Libraries (Main Library, University of Texas, Austin, TX 78753), reply to Mardi Ferris, merchandising coordinator for Hudson Brothers, a large department store chain whose headquarters are in Dallas (45 Cockrell Hill, 75211). Mardi Ferris wanted a computer printout of the names and addresses of Texas residents who owned homes appraised at $50,000 or more. She told you that she was making up a storewide mailing list for all Hudson Brothers stores. Although it's legal to send her the list, you can't do it for free as she requested, even though she was right to point out to you that the University is a public-funded institution. The standard charge for census printouts is $12 per city and $16.50 an hour for computer time. You estimate that it will cost Ferris a total of $18 for every city with a population between 30,000 and 200,000. Write a letter in which you explain the charges clearly and ask her to submit, along with her check, a list of the cities she wants printouts for.

10.   To promote business during the slack season (right after Easter and before summer) your clothing store (Gordon's, Atlantic Avenue, Atlantic City, NJ 07177) selected its most valuable list (charge customers)

and mailed to each a $5 gift certificate to use any time within an 18-day period in May. No strings were attached. They could use the $5 for whatever in-stock merchandise they wanted. This would bring in not only the active charge customers but also those that had not bought—for whatever reason(s)—during the past months or years. Results were a return of 610 coupons over the 18 days (or a 15 percent return), the reactivation of dozens of inactive charge customers, and total business generated of $15,596 (an average increase of over $5,000 a week). But there were problems. Three coupons were mailed to Mrs. Jean Razzioli, Mrs. J. Razzioli, and Mrs. J. Razzoli (same person, same address, spelled differently). Mrs. Jean Razzioli lives 100 miles away (175 Ocean Boulevard, Cape May, NJ 07133). She does not want to come in and shop, but she wants to use the $15 (three coupons mailed in) to purchase a white polyester blouse, size 32, that she saw advertised in the Atlantic City newspaper. Write a letter to Mrs. Razzioli explaining that she was entitled to use one of the coupons and that she can charge the $10 for the blouse to her account. Apparently the computer made the mistake. Add appropriate resale on the blouse (hand washable, fine pearl buttons, stylish wide tie).

11. As sales manager of Kyle Office Supply, 987 Main Street, Bowling Green, KY 42101, write Staley Manufacturing Company. Staley has written you with a request for a sizable discount on purchases. The company is located 42 miles out of town. Your free delivery is limited by policy to within city limits, but to keep the account you have been giving Staley free delivery along with quantity discounts. Bill Cleino, new head of marketing at Staley, has been visiting the local Staley plant for the past four days, looking over all operations. He told the local Staley secretary in charge of ordering that at the company headquarters in Texas Staley receives a 15 percent discount on all office supplies. Now it is her job to get this discount. Your letter must say no.

12. Assume that (Case 19, p. 399) you have received a stern second notice from American Bank Credit Card telling you that you owe on your account (98765–90–74–98765) $250 for purchase No. 6576 of RTM stereo system from Knight's Music House, 985 Pine Street, your city, three months ago. You refuse to pay this amount because the stereo would not work right after three weeks. Explain that since then you have called Knight's twice and written once to come and get it or fix it but only got brushed off. You also wrote ABCC about a month ago—when you got the first bill. Write American Bank Credit Card (900 Bainbridge Avenue, Kansas City, MO 64109) again, making clear that you don't intend to pay. (A federal law effective October 28, 1975, holds a credit card issuer responsible for resolving disputes over which the credit card holder and a merchant honoring the card cannot agree—or stopping attempts to collect.)

Refusing adjustments

1. Assume that you are Robert Rickoff, marketing director of Rose Mary swim suits for women, 407 Hamilton Avenue, Brooklyn, NY 11229. Helen Ayres, 1215 Buchanan Avenue, Hollywood, Florida 32207, bought one of your swimsuits from Feline's, a large department store in Miami, two years ago. It cost $40 and was guaranteed for a season against defects in material and workmanship. The seams have now begun to rip and she has returned the suit to you (the manufacturer), two years after date of purchase. Ayres wants a refund or replacement, but she's not entitled to either. The hanging tag attached to the suit explained the one-season guarantee and made clear that any question about the guarantee was to be directed to the department store, not to the manufacturer.

2. *To:* Ms. Hattie Hudson, 900 Bay Street Road, Lawrence, Massachusetts 01841. *From:* You, Adjustment Manager, Linn and Scruggs, 340 Amsterdam Avenue, New York, NY 10006. *Case:* Last week Hudson charged at your store an off-white high-fashioned cocktail dress, priced at $150. This week she sent it back to you with a note saying that she really doesn't like it and it doesn't fit right either. She wants you to take the gown back and remove the charge from her account. Upon examination, however, you find traces of cigarette ashes 12 inches below the waist on the left side and traces of makeup around the neckline. Your company policy is that clothes cannot be worn and then returned; this is for the protection of your customers and to insure that all the clothes you sell will be fresh and new. Write a tactful, polite letter explaining that you cannot accept the dress for credit and that it is being returned to her separately. Don't lose her as a future customer! An off-white cocktail dress of this quality can be worn for years and all through the year.

3. John Walton enthusiastically bought a 24-inch three-speed tri-wheeler for $200 from you six months ago. You are the Swin dealer, the Cycle Shop, 7654 Broad Street, Columbus, OH 43214. Apparently John had been in an accident (the frame and front wheel are scratched and bent and two spokes broken). He brought the bike by your shop while you were out, but he told a serviceman that he wanted it fixed at Swin's expense and that he would pick it up in two weeks. You will not fix it at company expense because the warranty does not cover bicycles or tri-wheelers that have been abused or wrecked. You could have the tri-wheeler ready in two weeks at a cost of $46.39. Include some resale talk and ask Walton to authorize the repairs.

4. *To:* Mrs. Beverly Ellis, 46 Apple Hill Road, Barrington, IL 60010. *From:* You, Adjustment Manager, White Appliance Company, 4399 Avon-

dale North Avenue, Chicago, IL 60617. *Case:* 18 months ago Mrs. Ellis bought from your store an undercounter dishwasher (Model No. 78–7632). It cost $339.95 and carried a one-year guarantee against defects in workmanship or manufacture. Ever since she got the machine, it has persistently skipped the second wash-rinse cycle and consequently has failed to properly clean the dishes. In addition the energy-saver button has not worked sometimes. During the one-year guarantee period, your store made two service calls on the dishwasher, one to adjust the energy-saver button and one to replace the timer. Then about six weeks ago you went with the repair person and all three of you agreed the washer worked properly. Now Mrs. Ellis has sent you a letter that bitterly complains about the inferior machine and encloses a bill from a Barrington repair shop for $20.98 labor and $10.95 for a new timer, total $31.93. She wants you to pay this bill. Refuse to do so. Return the repair shop's bill to her and try to keep her goodwill.

5. As sales manager for Lawn-Power Inc., 2000 Schiller, Chicago, IL 60610, refuse the request of M. S. Westover, 3196 Beverly Road, Columbus, Ohio 43204 for a refund of repair charges. Your repair shop tells you that it was necessary to install a new motor and armature in his electric lawn mower. In most cases, failure of the motor and armature is caused by using a dull blade, which creates an extra drag on the motor. It may also be caused by using an abnormally long extension cord, which creates a voltage drop from the electrical source and results in damage to the motor. Lawn-Power's guarantee warrants for the life of the mower any defective parts and material. Normal wear, misuse, or abuse, of course, do not fall under the warranty policy. In reviewing the paper work on this transaction, you find that the repair cost as quoted was correct for both material used and labor costs.

6. Thomas Ryan, Director of Operations, Red Earth and Grits Railroad, 500 N. St. Augustine Rd., Valdosta, GA 31601, reported recently that some open-top hopper cars you supplied last year are developing severe weld fractures in the body bolsters and at the bottoms of the side posts. The cars will have to be removed from service for repair, and he wants your company to foot the bill. Your field engineers discovered the cars were hauling coal to a generating plant where a shaker unit was being used to empty the cars faster. As vice president, marketing, NCT Railcar Co., 1 E. Main St., Bozeman, MT 59715, write Ryan, enclosing (imaginary) a report from your field engineers. Point out that the hopper cars were not designed for shaker service (would require shaker bars on the top plates, special corner caps, bigger side posts, thicker side sheets, and special center sill and body bolster fabrication), that the order for the hopper cars didn't specify such, nor did anybody ever indicate that the cars would see shaker service. Thus your standard guarantee would not apply and you won't, therefore, contribute anything toward the cost of repairs and loss from the cars' downtime; but you will have your design engineers work with the RE&G people on the best way to make repairs and on possible modifications to the cars. Remember that, as a freight car manufacturer, your only important customers are the Class I railroads, and the RE&G is one of them.

7. For a couple of years now, your company, Pulver Fasteners, 12980 25 Mile Road, Utica, MI 48087, has been selling blind rivets to Ogden Trailers, 1545 N. Sedgewick St., Chicago, IL 60610. Ogden makes the small rental trailers people hook onto their cars to move furniture, etc. Last week you received a rather sharp letter from Larry Pierce, Ogden's purchasing manager, saying that the last batch of blind rivets you shipped are defective. The pins that should pull up the rivet and then break off are instead ripping all the way out, tearing up the rivet, and consequently slowing down production and jeopardizing shipping schedules. Ogden is using up some old rivets found in the back of the plant and wants to know how you plan to rectify the situation. Pierce hinted that beyond taking back the defective rivets, some sort of indemnity might be in order. An emergency call to your sales representative in Illinois sent him to Ogden, where he was able to get some of the rivets in question, some of the old rivets Ogden is using up, and a piece of aluminum panel with the rivets torn up from the pin ripping out. The salesman mentioned that Ogden was now using new Super-Puller pneumatic tools to pull the pins instead of the gentler hand-operated tools formerly used. A quick look at the material he sent revealed what happened: Obviously the new tools exert far too much clamping force and pull the pins from below the break line, thus yanking them through the rivet. The rivets are quite up to standard. The old rivets now in use are steel, not aluminum, and of course can take the punishment the new pneumatic tools hand out (but *not* the weather). Write Pierce, refusing to make any adjustment and pointing out where the trouble lies.

8. You are general manager of Singer & Olson, P.O. Box 15387, Agua Fria Station, Prescott, AZ 86312. Recently you supplied 700 three-ring binders, 2-inch capacity, blue vinyl, patent hinge, imprinted front and spine with company name and logo, with sheet protectors, to Ladders & Scaffolds, Inc., 1670 Babcock, Costa Mesa, CA 92627. L&S wanted the binders for sales representatives to use to hold their constantly changing price and specification sheets. Now you have one of your binders back from Henry Christensen, Ladders & Scaffolds Sales Manager, with a complaint: the rings spring (allowing pages to drop out), the covers are all becoming torn and bent, and the hinges are tearing. A cursory examination shows what happened: someone stuffed 2½ or 3 inches of paper in it and attempted to shut the binder; the paper sprung the rings apart, bending the locking mechanism and preventing the rings from ever closing completely, and exerting enough pressure on the covers to cause even your patent hinge to give way. Also, the sheet protectors are missing. Tell Christensen what went wrong (gently—he's a customer) and offer to provide 700 new binders at the same price as before, but without the one-time charge for the plate for the imprint, since you still have it on hand. Quote him prices for 3-inch and 4-inch binders, too. They appear to be what he really needs.

9. *Letterhead:* Bug-a-Boo Pest Control (611 Milledge, Athens, GA 30601). *Inside address:* Jason Hill (Rural Route 91, Box 509, Whitehall, GA 30689). *Signature block:* Sincerely yours, Neal Morris, Manager. *Situation:* When Hill bought three 100-pound bags of tri-nitre micrate, your combined fertilizer and bug killer (@ $50) for his two-acre truck farm, you told him to plow the stuff in at least 3 inches and to keep his livestock out of the field for at least three weeks. (The micrate poison becomes benign after three weeks.) You remember that you sold Hill the TNM yourself and were careful to explain how to use it as directed on the bag, and not to overdose. You even remarked that 200 pounds would be enough for his two acres and that he should hold onto the other 100 pounds until next spring.

About a week later, you got a nasty letter threatening to haul you into court and demanding that you "fork over" $200 to pay for his three hogs and 50 chickens that got into the field and were poisoned. When your entymologists investigated, they found that Hill had spread the entire 300 pounds over the top of the plowed field and hadn't bothered to plow it under. Naturally the chickens and rooting pigs got poisoned and died. Refuse to pay for Hill's livestock and reeducate him on the use of strong pesticides. Don't antagonize him; you want to keep his business. Besides, he has a reputation for gossiping; and he knows everybody in the county.

10. Adjustment Manager, Customer Service Department, Roster Corporation, Milwaukee, WI 53217, to P. M. Shoop, 498 Lochlomond Drive, Springfield, MO 65804. Shoop, a gourmet cook, returned an electric food slicer and shredder after two months (under one-year guarantee), saying that the slicer/shredder called Foodcrafter won't run and that the food pusher is so out of shape that it will not fit into the food hopper. He had taken the Foodcrafter to a local repair shop where the estimate of parts and labor to repair it was $20.95. The Foodcrafter retails for $60.95. He requests that you fix the Foodcrafter free and replace the pusher.

Write a refusal in the light of the following facts: The motor had been immersed in water and will have to be replaced. The food pusher had been subjected to intense heat (probably from a dishwasher). The 19-page booklet that accompanied Foodcrafter clearly said that the motor base was not to be immersed in water but was to be wiped clean (page 3). On the same page in large print is the instruction "Do NOT PUT PUSHER IN AUTOMATIC DISHWASHER." The Foodcrafter will have to have a new motor and the food pusher will have to be replaced. You'll need his authorization and check for $16.95 (including return shipping charges) to repair and return in a week after you hear from him.

11. For an additional case, see GS 19 (p. 304).

Compromise adjustment

1. You are Larry Lazarus of Lease-A-Lemon, Inc., of 1262 Resurrection Blvd., Houston, TX 77001. Your company rents clunkers at daily, weekly, and monthly rates, keeping them running as cheaply as you can. Lease-A-Lemon offers adequate transportation for about half the usual rates. Last week you rented one of your beauties to Petroleum V. Nasby, the Texas oil baron, who has a reputation for squeezing a nickel till Jefferson screams for help. Nasby ran out of gas on his way to a board meeting of Engulf Oil Corporation. He missed the meeting, at which a proposal of his was defeated by one vote. He blames your car and you for what he says is the $500,000 loss he suffered, and he's threatening to haul you into court. One of the clauses in your lease agreement covers you against this kind of lawsuit, but he's pretty powerful and can be quite vindictive when he sets his mind to it. Write him a compromise adjustment in which you calm him down, point out tactfully the clause in the lease agreement which he signed, and offer to reimburse him the $20 cab fare it cost him.

2. About two months ago you sold a mechanical watermelon picker to Bart Bledsoe of Archer, Florida (RD 26, 32618). Bart is the local watermelon king and does about $50,000 worth of business with your firm each year. Your company is Furrow, Harrow, and Plough Farm Equipment of Tallahassee, Florida (P.O. Box 1326, 32302). Bart wrote that suddenly the watermelon picker went berserk, pitching 20-pound melons into the air. The machine ripped a 30-foot swath through his melons and destroyed about $500 worth of fruit before it wedged against a fence post and stopped. When your service expert examined the machine, he noticed that the conveyor belt had been put in without crossing. When the machine began harvesting melons, the fruit could not move out of the picker, which became jammed full of melons, forcing the driver out of the cab, pushing the machine into high gear, and wedging fruit against the accelerator. The picker took off at flank speed, spewing melons and melon chunks as it tore across the field. Bart is really steamed and wants you to repair the machine and pay for the ruined watermelons. Compromise with Bart. You will repair the machine, but you won't pay for the melons. You will also

have to reeducate Bart and his hands about putting the conveyor belt in properly.

3. As customer relations manager for Radio House, 120 Garfield Avenue, Duluth, MN 55807, reply to a letter from Susan Byrdon, Dunleith Hall, Northwoods College, Grayling, MI 49738. Byrdon reports a radio purchased from your store blew up with sparks and pops in a cloud of smoke the minute it was plugged in; she is sending it back, demanding $31.45. The Service Department finds the plug wire had been pulled off its connection and bare ends had come together. The radio is unhurt, except the back is a little singed. The department reattached the wire and put a new back on—(no charge). The wire probably pulled loose in packing after you took the radio off the shelf. Byrdon got the $60 radio at the $31.45 discount since it was a display model. You make no refunds on sale items; all sales are final. But you do honor warranties. Resell Byrdon that the radio is now good as new, a bargain at $31.45. Use a full-reparation opening.

4. This whole situation is getting out of hand, but you don't want to anger Ladders & Scaffolds, a possible big customer (Case 8, p. 245). Henry Christensen didn't like your letter refusing responsibility for the unacceptable performance of your binders. He says that he specifically ordered 3-inch binders and that since you sent the binders direct to Ladders & Scaffolds's area sales offices, he didn't know until too late that they were 2-inch capacity binders. Your sales representative claims Christensen ordered 2-inch binders, and that's the way the order was processed. But Christensen gave your representative a verbal order; so if there was a breakdown in communication, there's no way to place the blame. But you're not going to give Christensen 700 new 3-inch binders (imprinted) for free; any of his area managers should have said immediately that the binders were too small to carry the load of paper. Write Christensen, offering to supply 700 new 3-inch imprinted binders at half price, since the blame appears to lie partly on each of your companies. Stress your fairness, not your generosity.

5. James O'Donnell, Rt. 2, Box 340, Lake City, MI 44651, claims that the roach powder your service man (Michigan Pest Control, 210 W. Bass Lake Road, Traverse City, MI 49684) spreads around his house has had no effect on the bugs. They line up to eat the stuff when they see him coming with it. Write a letter in which you subtly stress the necessity of keeping the premises clean and promise him that your service man will be out by the end of the week (no charge) to spread around a new pesticide, Zip 3–3, which kills roaches quickly by attacking their nervous systems. Together (he doing his part, you yours) you'll annihilate those bugs.

6. Leapards Interiors, 5905 Federal Way, Boise, ID 83714. On a dark, cloudy night you, William Leapard, went to Mrs. Ernest P. Hill's ranch, (Eagle Rock, Hansen, ID 83334) and measured for a padded headboard and matching draperies for her master bedroom. Together you selected the right shade of blue (No. 953), costing $400. While she was visiting her family in Hawaii, her house boy let you in to hang the new draperies and mount the headboard. Today you get a letter from her asking you to change the draperies and headboard. Instead of being the soft powder blue she thought she ordered, she has bright aqua blue draperies and headboard that clash with the walls. Because you showed her the color number, and she agreed to No. 953, you want to compromise—will furnish all the new material, but she has to pay $150 for the labor.

7. E. J. Bravata, Binghamton Realty, 3400 S. 1350 W., Ogden, UT 84403 (good customer for ten years) wrote you—"I'm returning the four file cabinets you shipped me in response to my order of two weeks ago. I specified No. 2R76 four-drawer steel files at $60, and you sent No. 2R78 at $80. Please refund the $20.87 shipping charges that I paid and send me a credit memo for $320. I'm returning the four, shipping charges collect. As far as I'm concerned you can forget the whole thing."

Several months ago you sent out a correction slip for your current catalog indicating that you no longer carry the No. 2R76. Since you notified everyone to whom you had mailed a catalog, you assumed that Bravata realized you'd fill his order with No. 2R78 (as your correction slip indicated). Possibly it didn't reach him; maybe some of the office help threw it away. Whatever the reason, you certainly want to sell him this superior file with its improvements: heavier steel, baked-on enamel instead of sprayed, polished aluminum drawer pulls (instead of chrome-plated), plus automatic stops that prevent drawers from rebounding or being accidentally removed. Before you can hope to convince Bravata, however, you'll need to refund the $20.87, assure him that you'll send him a credit memo for $320 as soon as you receive the file cabinets, and explain why you did not follow his original instructions. But most of all you want to sell him No. 2R78. You'll be willing to ship the four cabinets charges prepaid if he'll reconsider.

8. You (Standard Car Co., 205 S. Michigan Avenue, Chicago, IL 60604) delivered 30 subway cars to Washington, D.C., last year. A new problem has surfaced in those cars. Water is leaking into the air-conditioning control boxes, causing short circuits and distressingly acrid smoke. Your field engineer found that the controls for the air conditioning were installed improperly at your plant because the manufacturer of the controls had failed to supply you with proper instructions. Washington service men had repositioned the controls in the cars but had not properly rein-

stalled the gaskets on the control boxes (manufactured by Standard Car). Although the air-conditioning control supplier had accepted the responsibility (and the cost) of fixing the controls, the Washington subway people should have made sure the boxes were properly sealed after the job was done. However, since you are the supplier of the boxes, some responsibility may rest on you for seeing that the Washington people were properly instructed about the box gaskets. Offer to pay half the cost of the necessary repairs to the air-conditioning controls and boxes as a fair way of resolving the matter. Write to Operations Manager, Washington Public Transportation, City Office Building, 20010.

Credit refusals and modifications

1. In the credit card center of Texaco (P.O. Box 1322, Houston, TX 77001) you must turn down a request for a credit card (Christy D. Roberts, 13028 12th Avenue, Hartford, CT 06111). Reasons: employment irregular or too short; insufficient references.

2. As credit manager of Newson's, a beauty supply company (899 Ala Moana Boulevard, Honolulu, HI 96814), you have received a letter from Jeannie Roberts, asking for credit. She has been in Lahaina, Maui Island, for three months and is now in the process of opening a beauty parlor. She sends you an order for $400 worth of supplies (hair dryers, rollers, hair clips, customer smocks) and explains that this is her first beauty parlor since she has just recently graduated from cosmetology school. As references she cites the First National Bank of San Francisco, where she has an auto loan ("payments sometimes late"); Mrs. Baker Flowers, Dean of the Shelton Trade School in San Francisco ("pleasant, fair student; not always dependable on attendance and promptness"); and Harco Hardware Store, San Francisco ("few small purchases, none lately; account clear"). After checking her references, you decide that it would be unwise at this time to grant credit. Write her at 999 Anapalau Street, Lahaina, Maui 96754.

3. As manager of the Department of New Accounts, Rafer's New Point Mall, Winston Salem, NC 28305, turn down the credit application for a transient, Dean S. Mosshart, Apartment 11–B, Windemere East, Hinsdale, NC 28654. The principal reasons for adverse action concerning credit are: too short a period of residence, insufficient credit file (references, no bank account), and delinquent credit obligations. Mosshart works in construction when he can get employment. According to the little bit of information you can find, Mosshart has moved once a year for the past five years. He has a wife (unemployed) and three children. The only store reporting on his pay habits shows a slow-pay rating. Suggest he pay in cash and offer to review his credit at a later date.

4. As credit manager of Shillito's Department Store, 317 East Capitol, Jackson, MS 39205, you have these notes on a long letter from Mrs. Fred Ferris (RFD 2, Box 27).

Mother of three small children (ages eight, five, and ten months), has trouble making ends meet. Husband has a steady job, but doesn't make enough. Have to "juggle" the bills but some like the power and phone bill have to be paid or service cut. Have to let others slide on occasion like last month's car payment, and a doctor's bill three months overdue. Revolving charge account with us . . . past three months paid only the minimum $10 charge, a total bill close to your $300 credit limit. Wants new sewing machine. Could learn to sew and make all the children's clothes and most of own with the machine you sell for $135; three free sewing lessons come with purchase. Wants to raise credit limit to $400 so can charge the machine. Tell Mrs. Ferris no.

5. When you (Strong's Auto Parts, 1976 Collinswood Street, Cleveland, OH 44109) started five years ago doing business with Ronald Short, owner of Ron's Pit Shop (Coshocton, OH 45318, a high-performance center specializing in equipment for enhancing dragsters and custom cars), you agreed to a $1,500 credit limit. Ron's recent order, $500 worth of Treadrite tires, would put him over the limit you agreed upon. Ron hasn't paid his last two bills—$450 now 40 days past due and $800 now 10 days past due (terms 2/10, n/30). Tactfully refuse credit until he takes care of his outstanding bills. But try to get him to buy the tires on a cash basis. You want to keep his goodwill and his account, which averages about $600 a month.

6. The Be-Fit Salon, 908 Tenth Avenue, Emporia, KS 66801, ordered from your company, Herron-Parker, 200 East Washington, Indianapolis, IN 46204, two roller massagers at $80 each, No. YHF–76; two portable plug-in steam baths, No. YTM–98 at $150 each; two electric Progress-a-Cyzers, No. XTE at $60 each. After reviewing what two reliable sources said about its credit and after viewing the application, you have to deny credit (but maybe not decline the order). Two sources reported Be-Fit paid bills 30–60 days slow and the financial statement showed that it is undercapitalized. With a conventional loan it can take advantage of your 2 percent cash discount, which will at least offset interest costs. Drive for the order on a cash basis.

7. As credit sales manager of the Thompson Company, Kansas City, MO 64105, you have to acknowledge the order of Hector van Dalsem, who (according to the financial statements he sent with his application for credit and for his first order for work pants amounting to $300—he buys for $3 and sells for $6) is the sole owner of the Van Dalsem Dry Goods

Company, Eureka Springs, AR 72632. References he gave spoke well of his personal integrity and indicated that he is a reasonably good payer. Two sources said he pays within the terms; three said he was 15–45 days slow; one said "slow but sure." You are reluctant to extend credit to a man in a predominantly agricultural area who, at a time when farm income is high, has allowed his current ratio (quick assets to liabilities) to fall closer to 1:1 than to the desirable 2:1. Now is a poor time for van Dalsem to be taking on new obligations without straightening out his present ones. You suspect maladjusted inventories and lackadaisical collections. As much as you'd like to fill this order, you have to refuse. It's wiser for him to cut his order in half and pay cash (he'll still get the customary 2 percent discount). Since rush orders can be handled within four days, he can keep adequate stocks on hand. Perhaps later on when he has reduced his current liabilities and strengthened his cash position, your regular credit privileges of 2/10, n/30 can be made available. Offer a compromise solution as attractively as you can, and strive to convince him that Thompson pants are the best buy he can make.

8. Last week your company (Ray Lesser Paints, 123 Sullivan Parkway, Rahway, NJ 07065) received an order from John Prince, Brush and Roller paint store, 567 College Road, Manchester, NH 03156, for 100 gallons of Show-Glo Supertone latex paints, assorted colors (50 antique white, 20 shell white, 10 blue, 10 red, and 10 green). Show-Glo Supertone, the top paint in your line, sells for $8 a gallon to the dealer and $12 a gallon retail. This is the third credit order that King has asked for in the past three months, and he has yet to pay for the first two; one for $200 is 30 days past due, the other for $250 comes due in 2 days. When Prince assumed your dealership a year ago, you agreed to a $500 credit limit. He usually pays at the end of the net period, but twice he was ten days late. Refuse to extend credit for his new order until he takes care of his outstanding bills. Try to get him to pay cash for the new order when he sends in his check for the two unpaid orders.

9. For other cases, see GS 13 and 14 (p. 303).

Incomplete- and back-order acknowledgments

1. Paul Whitsett, Cruz Street 205, Old San Juan, PR 00672, orders from your well-established company, L. L. Ream, Inc., Freeport, ME 04033, one pair of men's blue denim sport jeans, $17 postpaid, size 40, two pairs of ladies' tan jeans at $17 each postpaid, no size specified, and two tattersall shirts, $14.50 each for men in extra large size. You can send the men's jeans and shirts but have to ask for the size jeans for the lady.

Tell Whitsett about your special this month on Ream's chino pants made of high-grade blended twill fabric. These washable pants for both men and women are on special for $9.50 (regularly $12).

2. As Brian Lucas, Director of Sales, King Manufacturing, Inc., P.O. Box 4598, Princeton, NJ 08540 (Case 1, p. 289), acknowledge the incomplete order from Murray White, 97 Windsor Avenue, Eugene, OR 97401. White ordered a King tennis ball machine from you but did not specify whether you should send the Little King ($332), which holds up to 60 balls and can be set at rate of 60 miles per hour; or the King ($595), which holds up to 100 balls and can be set at 120 mph; or the King Professional ($695, up to 150 balls, and 180 mph). For beginners you recommend the Little King. You can send the dozen cans of tennis balls he ordered at $36.

3. As M. T. Noonan, Director of Sales, Jet-Lube, Inc., P.O. Box 2158, Houston, TX 77026 (713/674–7617; TELEX 775393), write Harvey Sellers, Sellers Company (an area distributor, not a retail outlet), 11–U Northwood, East Lansing, MI 48690, that you have not been able to deliver point-of-purchase displays for your V–2 campaign. You want each retail outlet to have as many of them as necessary to do a good job of promoting V–2. Each display costs Jet-Lube $40. They are built to last. Jet-Lube is a special lubricant for oilfields, mining, and industry; and the company has been in business since 1952. You are extending the campaign a month, making 75 days from now to get those displays out and working. Dallas Displays (your supplier) just reported, today, expectation of delivering the displays in two weeks. The trouble has been an unexpected problem with the special color mix of luminescent paints you specified.

4. As manager of Harriet's at King's Alley, 131 Kauilani Avenue, Honolulu, HI 96815, acknowledge the order from Dr. Otis Lord, 345 River Road Medical Center, Dayton, OH 45401, for a typical men's sport shirt of Hawaiian design, medium size, and a matching dress, size 10. No colors are specified and no price. You will gladly make up the shirt and dress, but you want to be sure of color selection and design. Acknowledge the order and send along five swatches of material, asking the doctor to select the pattern of his choice. Prices vary somewhat, but generally a short-sleeved shirt (one or two pockets—which does he want?) runs $18.50 and a typical loose-fitting dress costs about $30. Postage adds another $2.50. You can have the shirt and dress made in two days after you receive his choice selection. Harriet's recognizes Visa or Mastercharge. Which does he prefer? (give card number and expiration date of the one preferred, if he wants to pay that way.)

5. As mail-order supervisor for the Redi-Frame Company (P.O. Box 998, Cucumber, WV 24826), acknowledge the order of Zelda Lincoln, historian of Gamma Omicron chapter of Sigma Epsilon Xi sorority (904 South Busey Street, Oxford, MI 38655). Lincoln forgot to tell you what sizes she wanted, or whether she wanted nailed corners or easy-clip corner assemblies on her 24 picture frames. Send her the ordered 12 sheets of off-white marbled mat-board (@ $.40 a sheet), ask her tactfully to tell you what kind of frames she wants, and acknowledge her check for $50.

6. As director of customer service for Me-Books Publishing Company, 11633 Victory Blvd., North Hollywood, CA 91690, ask Mrs. Victor Bliss, Rolling Hill Road, Skillwau, NJ 08558, for some missing information on her order of the Me-Book she wanted sent to her grandchild in Bloomington, Illinois. Children enjoy these books because they can see their own names, street addresses, phone numbers, and names of pets, siblings, friends, grandparents, parents, and givers. Mrs. Bliss failed to indicate the names of pets, siblings, and one set of grandparents. (Could the omissions have been intentional?)

7. Assume that you are in Mail Sales for Uniforms, Incorporated, 3618 Broadway, San Antonio, TX 78241. You must write Señor Juarez, manager of La Señora (a beauty shop catering to Americans), Circunvalacion Sud 136, Las Fuentes, Guadalajara, Jalisco, Mexico, that you can send (for the operators) five matching pant-set uniforms, blue, size medium, No. MP–765 in about three weeks, when you expect to catch up your production. You have mailed the two small-size uniforms today. Add resale about the garments (extra-strong seams, won't fade, handy two-patch pockets, double knit of polyester). Try to sell more of your uniforms and make ordering easy.

8. The Carter's Manufacturing Company, 50 Ellison Way, Independence, MO 64099, receives a first order (via your salesman, Albert Spiller) from Roy P. Miller, Miller Feed and Flower Shop, 999 Bonner Street, Abbyville, KS 67510, for a case (24) of Carter Anti-Pest Powder in 1-pound sizes at $9.60 a case. The Order Department passes it along to your (the sales manager's) desk because of the routine plan of having you write a letter to each new customer. On the bottom of the order is a note that says you cannot ship the powder for another two weeks because you have no 1-pound plastic containers; your next shipment of containers is supposed to arrive from Chicago in about that time. The government banned all the X–Y–210 containers for health/safety reasons. Write Miller welcoming him as a new customer and handling the back-order element positively, with emphasis on when he will receive the shipment.

9.   For Mallory, a prestigious mail-order house in Cedar Rapids, Iowa (1300 Elmhurst Drive, 52433), reply to Clarence Day, owner of the Green Door, an exclusive boutique and jewelry shop in Louisville, KY 40216 (Phipps Plaza). Day ordered six Karl Couturier wigs at $50 apiece and two dozen Montezuma imitation Aztec rings at $20 each. He included his check for $800 to cover the cost of the merchandise and shipping. You can ship him the rings; and though he indicated colors (two in each—brunette, blond, and red), he forgot to tell you the styles of the wigs he wanted. They come in shag, Afro, and standard (straight hair to the shoulders) styles. Get him to match up the colors and styles of wigs he wants.

10.   Yesterday you received an order from the Sand & Surf Boutique, 777 San Ladron Avenue, St. Augustine, FL 32816, for two dozen High 'n Dry giant beach towels at $2 apiece, six dozen pairs (size medium) of Sun-Yat-Sen zori at 50 cents a pair, and six Va-Va-Voom mini bikinis at $12 apiece. Eugene Bridgers, the owner of the S & S, included his check for $160.25 (cost of the merchandise and $4.25 shipping by UPS). Ship him the towels and zori, but back-order the swimsuits for two weeks. These new-this-year hand-crafted cotton-Dacron swimsuits (made in Italy and imported by Cosa Nostra Novelties of New York for exclusive distribution through member stores of the Coastal Boutique Association) caught swimmers' fancy more widely than the manufacturer planned for; but Cosa Nostra has promised to ship you a fresh supply of swimsuits by next week. Your firm (Ebb and Flow Supply of 43 Broadway, Bayonne, NJ 10106) can promise his swimsuits a week later.

11.   For other cases, see GS 8 and 10 (p. 301).

Declining orders

1.   Jerry Garner, 56 Woodacres, Portland, OR 97202 writes you, Sales Division, LeGout Foods, Franklin Park, IL 60131, wanting to buy direct from you one 7-pound can of LeGout pepper relish for $6. You do not sell direct to consumers for you have a contract to sell all you produce to Holiday Motels. Garner had eaten the delicious pepper relish at one of the Holiday Motels in Amarillo, Texas, and from the manager had learned the price of the can. Turn down Garner, but keep him sold on eating pepper relish at all your 1500 Holiday Motel locations in the United States, Canada, and Mexico.

2.   You are working in the Customer Service Department of the Fisher-Price Toy Manufacturing Company, East Aurora, NY 14052, and receive the following letter from Mrs. Alan Arkin, Cap-Haitien, Haiti: "Please use the enclosed check of $20 to buy some games or toys for a 12-year-old girl

and send them to me as soon as possible. The girl, my daughter, is confined to bed after undergoing extensive surgery on an injured hip."

Write to Mrs. Arkin, tactfully referring her to the nearest retail outlet of Fisher-Price toys, Rafer's, Biscayne Boulevard, Miami, FL 33139 (which has a catalog from which she may select suitable toys and games), and return the $20 check. Although Mrs. Arkin will be disappointed at not receiving the toys and games direct, be courteous and thoughtful, keep her goodwill, and produce a sale for your local dealer.

3. As head of public relations for Grosset & Dunlap, Inc., 51 Madison Avenue, New York, NY 10010, answer the request of Jeff Mathias, 1232 Montclair Circle, Saginaw, MI 48055, for "Crosswords from the *National Observer.*" Jeff reports that this is an excellent crossword puzzle publication. He was not able to get the paperback in Saginaw, Flint, or Detroit, and he has been looking for the past two years. Grosset & Dunlap's policy does not permit a solicitation of orders directly from consumers. Have him write to the Gateway Book Store, 45 Monroe Avenue, Cedar Rapids, MI 49501. Gateway carries a full line of crossword puzzles from the *National Observer* as well as from *Saturday Review.*

4. As sales director for King Manufacturing, Inc., P.O. Box 4598, Princeton, NJ 08540 (Phone: 609 452-8686) write Murray White (97 Windsor Avenue, Eugene, OR 97401), suggesting purchasing the Little King tennis ball machine ($332) from a local sporting goods store, Chuck's Sport and Court, 876 Trail Avenue, Eugene, OR 97401. You used to sell direct but changed your policy two years ago and sell only through authorized dealers. Resale: See facts in Cases 1, p. 289 and 2, p. 253.

5. As head of sales for Meadowcraft Outdoor Furniture, 923 Penn Avenue, Pittsburgh, PA 15219, decline the order from Safer's Department Store, 4301 North Charles, Baltimore, MD 21202, for $2,456.89. You have given the exclusive furniture franchise to City Furniture, 905 15th Street, Baltimore, for 12 years. (Since that has only two years to go, try to *hint mildly* of Safer's chance. You have thought of the need for another dealer in the big City—different section, where Safer's is—especially since your patio set of wrought iron won two Outdoor Furniture Association National awards last year—for design and for weather resistance, attributable to your patented mix of just the right amount of lead in the iron.) Perhaps Safer's could work out an arrangement with City to be a subdistributor. You have a store in Urbana, Illinois, that is the subdistributor for an exclusive franchise held by a business in nearby Champaign.

6. On your desk in the office of the sales manager of the National Cereal Company, 99 Beachfield Drive, Battle Creek, MI 49014, appears an

order for two cases of N&N (Natural and New, one of your popular new cereals), to be shipped direct to Jackie Simpson, Quick Food Shop, Five-Points, Hamburg, MN 55339. His check for the correct amount at your jobbers' prices is pinned to one of your current mimeographed jobbers' lists. You don't know how he got the list, and you don't propose to mention it in the letter. You cannot sell to him direct or at jobbers' prices, list or no list. Your exclusive distributor for his district is the Roberts Wholesale Grocery Company, St. Paul, MN 55143. Certainly you want Simpson to handle your popular new breakfast cereal; so you will return the check and ask him to place the order with Roberts. In the light of the ultimate advantages to retailers, make a presentation that emphasizes Simpson's advantages rather than your own or your jobber's.

7. You've just received an order from Dr. Gordon Shaver, the chief veterinarian for Macon County, Illinois, for six electric, continuous-flow vaccinating guns. There's been an outbreak of hog virus in Iowa and Missouri, and Dr. Shaver wants to help Macon County farmers innoculate their hogs before the disease spreads to Illinois. You'd really like to ship the guns to Shaver, but he can get them faster (although they will cost $2 more apiece) from Lincoln Feed and Grain, 1098 Gibbs Road, Kansas City, MO 64154, your local franchised dealer. Besides, you have an agreement with your franchised dealers that you will divert any orders you get from their territories to them. Write a letter to Dr. Shaver in which you divert his order to Lincoln in Kansas City. Give him the reasons first before you divert his order—e.g., quick delivery, service, a full line of veterinary equipment. (Your firm is Ortho-Vet, Inc., 504 Locust, San Antonio, TX 78206.)

8. When Delmar King graduated from junior college last spring and decided to open a variety store in his hometown (698 Main Street, Springtown, TX 76082), as sales manager of the Celluton Products Company, Ft. Worth 76102, you drove out (30 miles) to see him about paper products stock. He appreciated your suggestions; but, because of limited finances and the heavy expense of getting the business started, he cut your suggested order drastically.

You settled on a good stock of toilet and cleansing papers and your colorful Christmas papers. When the order totaled only 18 cases, you told King about your policy of not accepting orders for less than 25 cases; but you agreed to accept this first order anyway. But you asked for, and got, his promise of his financial statement at the end of the year.

King ordered 15 cases of school writing supplies and toilet and cleansing tissues in January, when you were in the hospital, and the order was filled by a clerk who saw that you had approved the previous order for only 18 cases. You wouldn't have filled it in view of the financial statement King sent January 4.

Now it is March, and you have an exact duplicate of the January order. There is no use to let him get by with this plan, contrary to your policy, which was established as much for his benefit as yours. Besides, he has not even tried some of your products.

In the spring and summer the need for school supplies will decrease; but the people of Springtown do lots of picnicking (at Lake Worth and Possum Kingdom) and use lots of paper cups, napkins, and plates.

For people in business, you have memo pads in various sizes and colors. Homemakers will be doing spring cleaning. Your decorative shelf papers might help. Your tough, chemically treated special paper for washing dishes and windows is catching on everywhere that homemakers have tried it.

Now financially able to order more heavily, King could easily make up an order of 25 cases of quick-selling paper products and not need to order so frequently, comply with your policy, and enable you to keep your prices to him down where they are by keeping your per-unit costs for handling, packaging, and transportation down to the minimum.

Instead of filling his order, hold it and write him a letter. He has your complete price list, unchanged since last fall.

9. For another case, see GS 11 (p. 302).

Substitute-selling acknowledgments

1. To Russell Engineering Associates, 477 Alamo Avenue, Portland, OR 97205, from Caulfield Wholesale Suppliers, 808 S.W. Broadway, Albuquerque, NM 87100. Order number: GJ–5032. You can not send the ordered five Craft electric wrenches, but you can substitute a new and improved Wannamaker wrench that is double insulated, has polymer motor housing ($25 each instead of discontinued Craft's $21.88). Motor develops ⅙ hp at 1,700 rpm and delivers 40 foot-pounds of torque in five seconds. Ask Russell for permission to send the improved electric impact wrench. Welcome this new customer with talk on quality of your service (been in business 50 years), your four research laboratories that are constantly finding new products.

2. Warner Inc., Townsend Way Southeast, Salem, OR 97303, Director, Western Sales Division, to Beverly Huff, Huff Music Company, 980 Main Street, Aberdeen, WA 98520. Huff ordered 12 sets of Palmer tape heads for reel-type tape recorders at $10 apiece (retail $15) and six Stanley A–622 sapphire needle cartridges for Girrard stereo turntables at $6 (suggested retail price $8). You carry the Stanley A–625, which replaced the A–622— better pick-up and tone quality. These new antimagnetic, synthetic diamond needles last almost twice as long as the old sapphire needles and cost only $7.50 (suggested retail price $10). Since Huff wanted you to bill

him at the usual 2/10, n/30 terms, sell him the A–625 on its own merits and ship them on trial along with the tape heads. Stress his keeping the substitute rather than sending it back.

3.   As director of sales for Green Pharmaceuticals, Alameda Road, Abilene, TX 79802, Cattle Care Division, reply to an order from George Lee, Smith-Lee Feed and Grain (800 South Main Street, Lawton, OK 73501). Lee ordered 50 one-gallon bottles of Terramycin X, an antibiotic used in calf feed to protect the young animals from viral and other infections. You don't sell Terramycin X any more, but you do sell Neo-Terramycin XX which replaced Terramycin X four months ago. Neo-Terramycin XX costs $15 a gallon; that's a dollar more per gallon than Terramycin X. And Neo-Terramycin XX is effective against more diseases than the old product, especially blackleg (the most dreaded cattle disease). Fill Lee's order with Neo-Terramycin XX. Sell the substitute on its own merits, and at its regular price.

4.   At Northern Hardware Wholesalers, 987 East River Road, Boston, MA 02119, you have an order from Roe Hardware, 6708 North Charles, Baltimore, MD 21231, for two dozen Flamet fire extinguishers, auto size. About 13 months ago you shipped Roe four dozen Flamet extinguishers in the larger sizes. Four months ago you acquired the Massachusetts distribution of the nationally advertised Stamp-Fire extinguishers and have sold out your entire supply of Flamets in the size ordered. The Stamp-Fire is a more effective and dependable instrument than the Flamet—fights all fires (flammable liquid, cloth, wood, paper, and electrical equipment); the clean, odorless carbon dioxide gas smothers fires and won't conduct electricity; approved by the Underwriters' Laboratories, Inc., and the Coast Guard. The 1-quart size has clamps for installing it on the automobile steering post (no holes or screws). This model is $6 a dozen higher than the Flamet, but sells better—vigorous national advertising. Ask permission before substituting the Stamp-Fire. If Roe still prefers Flamet, try Young's Hardware Company in Silver Spring, MD, the nearest distributor you know of.

5.   As mail sales coordinator for Kyle Stereo Components, 540 Audubon Avenue, New York, NY 10007, reply to an order from Alan Ritter, Apt. 605, Belle Meade Towers, 105 Lake Avenue, Knoxville, TN 37204 for two of your A–850 stereo speakers. Alan must have looked at a two-year-old catalog, since you stopped making the A–850 two years ago. You replaced the A–850 in your speaker line with the A–800. The A–800, unlike the A–850, comes in a solid mahogany cabinet. The A–850 was walnut. Of course you've improved the speakers too; the 10-inch double woofers and 6-inch triple tweeters produce a fidelity and clarity that the A–850 could not match (add some details). And Alan can have all this quality for only $20 more per speaker. Alan sent you a check for $160 to cover the cost of the speakers and shipping. Fill Alan's order with two A–800s and ask for $40 to cover the cost of these new improved speakers. Remember to sell the 800s on their own merits and be sure to give the option of returning them if not satisfied. However, stress Alan's keeping the 800s.

6. As sales manager for Chicago Business Center, 7179 W. Grand Ave., Chicago, IL 60635, write to Purchasing Manager, Pollack Industries, 3263 Flushing Rd., Flint, MI 48504. Your sales representative has been trying for two years to get Pollack as a customer, and now you have a first order: 300 floppy discs (for Xerox 850) with file storage jackets at $5.65, a total of $1,695. Apparently, while your sales rep's order was in the mail, also in the mail to your sales rep was your notice that you no longer carry floppy discs with file jackets (made of same paper stock as file folders), but have changed to floppy discs in vinyl jackets. These new floppy discs are certified error-free, and the vinyl jacket eliminates static interference. Jackets also have writing area and pressure-sensitive color-coded labels. Price for floppy discs in vinyl jackets is $6.20 each in lots of 50 or more. Total charge to Pollack will be $1,860. Save the order and this important new customer.

7. Dolan Luggage, Third Street, East McKeesport, PA 15035, to Ms. Irene Richter, 308 N. Sawyer Ave., Marcus, PA 19061. From your recent catalog (she said), Richter ordered for her husband's birthday (exactly one week from today) an all-leather brown molded attaché case D–765 at $35.95. Since Richter is on the list to receive your catalog, obviously she ordered from your catalog of two years ago—when you did have what she ordered. Since you dropped that line, you do not have an attaché case at that price, nor do you have one listed at that number. Your all-leather brown or black attaché case D–659 with aluminum frame, recessed spring-action chrome-plated metal locks, and three-pocket lid file runs $45.95. The all-leather cases have the approval of the National Luggage Dealers' Association. You'd gladly charge this case to Richter's account or send it c.o.d.—if you knew what case to send. You can't call—she added a postscript that she and her husband were going to Hawaii this week (wedding anniversary) but would be back for the birthday party. Whatchagonnado? Make up your mind and do something.

8. For an additional case, see GS 9 (p. 302).

Combinations

1. Vary the case (Case 11, p. 166) and assume that David Cavanaugh did not tell you the size of fur-lined gloves to send to Dodson. You have

sizes in small 8–8½, medium 9–9½, large 10–10½, and extra large 11–11½. Also assume that you have to back-order the shetland pullover No. 4356C sweater with the powder-blue yoke pattern. The cold winter plus the popularity of this attractive sweater seems to be the explanation. You can send the Eskimo parka to Mary Courtney.

2. Last Friday you received a rush order from Dr. Andrew Quigley, County Veterinarian of Alachua County (office in Alachua, FL 32616), for two gallons of equine encephalitis vaccine (V–211), six large syringes (B–201), and four continuous-flow vaccinating guns (V–316). Dr. Quigley neglected to tell you whether he wanted glass or plastic syringes or whether he wanted battery-powered or plug-in vaccinating guns (no differences in the prices of the syringes or vaccinating guns). Write Dr. Quigley to find out what kinds of syringes and vaccinating guns he wants and tell him you have only two plastic syringes until a promised new supply arrives ten days from now (a severe outbreak of equine encephalitis in the area has exhausted your supply). You are Director of Sales, Green Pharmaceuticals, Alameda Road, Abilene, TX 79803.

3. The Orange Shop, U.S. Highway 301, Citra, FL 32627 to Mr. and Mrs. Levert Killough, 908 Hickory Hill, Scrant, KY 40373. Notes on the order: Cannot send the ordered bushel and half-bushel boxes of navel oranges, but can send the fruit that is in season, the round, juicy Valencia oranges (smaller, travel and keep better, especially in hot weather). Do not have any Ruby Red grapefruit at this time—don't have any good grapefruit at this time of the year; but in about six weeks will have good ones. Want permission to send the No. 11 (bushel) and No. 22 (half bushel) Valencia oranges at costs of $16.95 and $11.25 now and back-order the bushel of Ruby Reds.

4. For your company, Caulfield Wholesale Suppliers, 808 S.W. Broadway, Albuquerque, NM 87100, handle this special letter involving a combination back order and substitute from Russell Engineering Associates, 477 Alamo Ave., Portland, OR 97205, Order No. GJ–5097. Because of the shortage of copper, you have to back-order the ten 60-foot coils of ⅜-inch copper tubing at $10 each for total of $100. Rally doesn't make the special cleaning powder for cars anymore. Your Super Satin Car Wax (only kind you sell) has a cleaner built into it. Most towns do not have places where cars can be waxed; so customers prefer the short-cut procedure of cleaner with wax for one operation. The ten cases 30-wt. oil, two cases of plastic funnels, and 50 rolls of repair tape went out this morning by Blue Bell Express. Tell Russell about your special on welders' goggles (NX 4215), usually $8.50 but $6 this month.

5. To your desk in the sales division of Holgate Manufacturing Company, 1599 North Sedgwick, Chicago, IL 60610, comes a letter from Horace P. Love, buyer, Washburn's Department Store, 900 Sycamore Street, Sunny Slope, MO 64110, authorizing the shipment of six dozen skate boards (Bv–986) with Chicago clay wheels at $2 each plus shipping costs of $3.89. Apparently Washburn's used an old catalog. When skateboards first came out, they were equipped with Chicago clay wheels which did not take turns well, thus injuring many young people. Skateboard technology has advanced, and the boards are now being manufactured with safe urethane wheels, which take turns exceptionally well; but they do not sell at $2. Prices range from $8 (retail) to $60 (suggested price), but to this department store $4–$30. Enclose your price list, ask for Love's action, and tell him that because of their popularity (especially in Florida and California) your stock is depleted. You should be able to fill his order in two weeks.

6. *From* General Wholesalers, Inc., Baltimore, MD 21224. Consigned to and destination Hopewell Stores, Inc., 3600 West Broad Street, Richmond, VA 23230. *Customer order No.* 985432A, *Delivering carrier* Eastern Trucking Co. *Car initial and No.* YM87643.

No.	Description	Cost	Total
4	Camera cases, leather	$ 2.00	$ 8.00
6	Flight bags, leather, 22″ × 13″ × 9″	15.00	90.00
8	Attaché cases, 18″ × 12½″ × 5″	15.00	120.00

Because of their popularity, you'll have to back-order the ordered 12 men's 42-inch travel bags. Delivery should be in two weeks. The sports bags (eight ordered in 12″ × 19″ × 11″) come only in vinyl (not leather as ordered). Gym suit, basketball, football uniform, or wet swimsuit can be put in this vinyl bag which resists moisture in and out. The reinforced hard bottom retains its shape after rugged use. The end-to-end zipper is for easy access to every corner. Ask for permission to send the vinyl bags. Retail price runs $5 for each bag. Terms 2/10, n/30.

7. Although it is midsummer, you, owner of Priester's Pecans, 227 Old Fort Drive, Fort Deposit, AL 36032, receive an order and check from Dr. Milton Rosenbush, 98 Holiday Terrace, Cedar Rapids, IA 52805 for the following:

1 No. 85 Natural Mammoth Halves	$10.25
1 No. 33 Toasted Pecan Brittle	6.60
1 No. 32 Pecan Pralines	6.10
1 No. 11 Jumbo Pecan Pieces (4½-lb. tub)	16.10
Shipping charges are included in prices.	$39.05

Dr. Rosenbush obviously ordered from a Christmas catalog, and at Christmas you had all four items. You won't have any pecan halves or pieces until October, and you'll be glad to send him the fresh nuts as soon as you harvest them. You are out of the pecan brittle but could substitute peanut brittle packaged in an attractive tin and for just $4.25 a pound. The doctor might enjoy trying pecan bark, which is made of four thin layers—three consisting of freshly roasted pecan kernels and creamy chocolate deftly blended and one layer of super chocolate brittle crunch—packaged in an attractive tin (1 lb. 8 oz.), $9.90. Write the letter sending the pecan pralines, offering to ship the pecan halves when you get them, substituting the peanut brittle, selling the pecan bark, and explaining that you are holding the check.

Persuasive messages: Sales

IF POTENTIAL USERS of a product or service realize their needs and desires, marketing it is a matter of making it available when and where wanted at an acceptable price, and filling the orders. Often, however, ultimate users are not conscious of their needs or desires until somebody else points them out. In those cases, marketing also involves sales promotion—pointing out needs and desires, and how the product will satisfy them—by personal selling, advertising, and mail. This chapter deals with advertising and selling by mail.

GENERAL SALES STRATEGY

Whether you sell by mail or in person, your procedures are essentially the same. You seek to gain attentive interest, convince your prospect that your proposal is worthwhile, and confidently ask for the action you want —usually an order.

In some cases you already have favorable attention, as when you answer an inquiry about your product or service. In those cases your job is to marshal your sales points and adapt them to your reader in a message that satisfactorily answers questions, convinces, and asks for action. You've already learned to do this in your study of invited sales (Chapter 5).

But in prospecting—or "cold turkey" selling, as many professionals call it—you have the preliminary job of getting your reader's attention and then arousing interest so that your reader will be eager to see what you have to say.

The surest way to get your reader to read, and ultimately to buy, is to *stress some reader benefit coming from what you have to sell.* To construct this benefit theme, you must know a good deal about your product or service, its uses, and the kind of people who can benefit from having it. From analyzing your product or service and your prospects comes the selection of the appeal to emphasize. And from a knowledge of marketing methods and people's buying habits comes the decision of what you want your prospect to do after reading your message.

Analyzing the product or service

Experienced, successful sales executives know that a thorough knowledge of the product or service is essential to successful selling. You will have a hard time convincing someone to purchase something unless you know it well. So you begin your sales effort by thoroughly analyzing what you want to sell.

Begin with some questions. Why was this product created? What was it designed to do? Was it to satisfy a need which existed and was recognized? Or was the product perhaps created for a need which does not yet exist or which is unrecognized? In either case, you must ascertain how the product meets the need.

Get to the designers and engineers, if applicable. What did they do in designing the product? What was their reasoning behind the overall design? What problems did they meet, and how did they overcome them? What are the outstanding features of the product? Get all the information you can. The more you have, the better (and more easily) you'll do your job.

Now you should have the tools you need to answer the most important question in marketing any product or service: *What will it do for people?* How will it make their lives better or their jobs easier, add to their security, increase their status, or otherwise satisfy a need or desire?

Although you need to know a great deal about the physical characteristics of a product (overall size, shape, color, length, breadth, height, composition, design, operation, for example), physical description of the product will not sell it. *The psychological description—interpretation of physical features in terms of reader benefits—is the effective part of selling.*

A pocket-size recorder, for example, has buttons, wires, battery, mike, and a motor. So what? It enables a business executive to record ideas, in or out of the office, it is true. But it also allows the executive to:

—Release the high-priced dictation time of a secretary for other duties.

—Dictate when and where desired—as time permits and as ideas occur.

—Arrange work for the office staff in the executive's absence.

—Have a record which does not get "cold," which anyone can transcribe with greater accuracy than is possible from shorthand notes.

—Have a record to play back without needing an interpreter.

Insulation is not just pellets or batts of certain sizes and materials. To a true marketer, it keeps houses warmer in winter, cooler in summer—and conserves energy. It thus reduces heating costs in cold months and cooling costs in warm months. It also deadens outside noises. Since it is fire-resistant, it reduces chances of fire and also decreases fire damage if and when fire breaks out. In view of all these reasons, insulation adds to the resale value of a house.

Even a child's tricycle (made of steel and chrome, with first-grade rubber tires) does more than provide pleasure for its youthful owner. It teaches muscular coordination, helps to develop visual perception and judgment, and develops leg muscles. It also releases parents from a certain amount of time spent in direct supervision.

Such analysis identifies the promises you can make your reader, the benefits you can point out that will result from using your product or service. Such psychological description helps the reader see your offer in terms of benefits to be received. That's what turns a prospect into a customer. (See pp. 33, 117, and 122 (4) for further explanation and illustration.)

Psychological description is interpretation, which deserves primary emphasis. Physical description is specific detail, evidence incorporated *subordinately* to bear out the promises established in psychological-description phrases and passages. Though physical description is necessary for conviction, in the final sales presentation it is subservient to psychological description—the interpretation of the thing to be sold in terms of pleasure, increased efficiency, increased profit, or whatever benefits you can most specifically promise your prospect.

Finding the prospects

True prospects are people who (1) need your product or service, (2) can pay for it, and (3) do not have it. In selling by mail, determining who these people are and their addresses involves making a mailing list. Of course you can easily get names and addresses; but are all those people *prospects?*

Some people who appear to be prospects will already be enjoying the benefits of your product or service—or one like it. But unless you know for certain, you need to find out. And the inexpensive way to find out is to solicit them (that is, try to sell them).

If you are selling a product everybody needs, all you have to verify is your prospects' ability to pay. But few products are useful to everybody (and when they are, direct mail is not the best way to sell them; direct mail is a selected-class medium rather than a mass medium like TV, radio, or newspapers).

In determining need, you have to start with logical analysis. For instance, you wouldn't try to sell bikinis to Eskimos or snowblowers in Puerto Rico. Nor would you try to sell a central heating unit to apartment dwellers or baby carriages in a retirement community.

You would seek to sell a piece of office equipment to some business owner or manager, aluminum cookware to homemakers and restaurant owners, insulation to homeowners.

Sex, age (and a close corollary, physical condition), family and dwelling status, vocation, geographical location, and financial situation are some of the more significant considerations in assuming that someone is a logical prospect for your product. In some cases you will need to go further than a logical analysis and make a marketing survey.

Logical analysis, and a marketing survey if necessary, will give you a list of characteristics that describe the most likely prospects for your product or service. If enough people share these characteristics to make it practical to approach them by sales letter, you have a direct-mail market.

Most sales letters have to go out in large numbers to secure the volume necessary for profit. But even when they go out by the thousands, you send them to a *selected* mailing list. As one direct-mail specialist put it, sales letters and direct mail are "not *mass* media but *class* media."

Assured of a direct-mail market, you next need a *good* mailing list. That means names and addresses that are *accurate* (no waste on incorrect or obsolete addresses), *pure* (all true prospects), and *homogeneous* (having the desired characteristics in common—the more the better for adapting your letter).

To get such a list, you can make your own, buy one, rent one, or—if you've already made one yourself—trade for one, but usually not with a competitor. Making your own list may be the best way *if* you know how and can afford the time and the money for necessary tools.

The obvious place to start compiling a list of prospects is your list of customers—people who have already bought from you. If your marketing plan includes advertisements, especially in trade magazines, inserting coupons in them offering free literature on the product or service will bring in names and inquiries of interested people.

Several directories (Dow's, Poor's, and others) classify names of companies by type of business and areas of operation. The Yellow Pages are a fertile source of prospects, especially if you are restricting your effort to a limited geographical area. Another alternative is to hire a clipping service to send you clippings of items (with names) printed in consumer and/or trade publications that deal with the type of people or companies you are seeking.

Like many other activities, however, *making* and *maintaining* a good mailing list requires not only more time and money but more **know-how** and facilities than most people can and will devote to the job. (Some of the best direct mail/marketing books devote whole chapters of 20–30 pages to mailing lists.) Therefore, unless you are going to study the subject to learn the procedures and techniques, and spend the money for the tools of the trade, you probably will do better to buy or rent your list from one of the many firms that specialize in them.

Hundreds of companies are in the business of making, selling, and renting lists (so many that the Department of Commerce publishes a directory of them). You can purchase virtually any list you want from list houses. Most of them have catalogs of the readily available lists they offer, giving the selection criteria, the size, and the cost of each list. If they do not have the list you want, they will build it for you according to your specifications, if you are willing to pay the price.

As a rule, the price is according to the difficulty in compiling the list, usually from 2 to 20 cents per name. A major factor is the number of common characteristics you specify. That same factor, however, affects directly the desirability and *purity* of the list. This last is important; it refers to the percentage of names that are not likely prospects.

An example will clarify the matter of varying list costs and purity. You can buy a big list of auto owners very cheaply (probably no more than 2 cents a name because of specifying only the one characteristic). But for promoting purchases of new Cadillacs, the list would have very low purity. Many of those people would have relatively new cars, and others would have too-low incomes. To purify your list considerably, you could add as specifications that the presently owned cars be at least four years old and that the annual incomes be at least $25,000. Your list would now be much smaller, and the cost might be just as much because of the much higher cost per name; but you would save lots of money you might have wasted on people who weren't prospects. Furthermore, you might sell more cars, especially if you made good use of the new information to *adapt* your letters by references to the financial status of the readers and the age of their cars. These facts point up an ever-present question in selling by mail: How far should you go in purifying the mailing list?

Another big problem is the list's *accuracy,* the percentage of incorrect names and addresses. About 19 percent of the people in America change their addresses each year. People who use old lists and are not aware of this situation are unpleasantly surprised at the number of undeliverable letters.

Mailing-list houses usually do not charge for incorrect addresses if you report them. This is how lists are qualified (the inaccurate names and addresses deleted). As a rule of thumb, any list that has not been qualified within the past year is suspect, and you can expect a good part of it to be useless. First-class mailings, or third-class with return instructions to the Postal Service, are how you qualify a list.

Whether you buy, rent, trade for, or compile your list, however, for sales effectiveness it must contain the correct names and addresses of people or companies with enough desirable characteristics in common to make them a group of likely prospects. Only then can you adapt your talking points and your references in persuasive fashion, as discussed on pages 85–88.

Choosing the appeal

From the analysis of your product will come your sales points. You know your product or service, and you know things about it that might convince people to buy. Obviously you can't put all of them in detail into one letter, or you'll have a cluttered message with so much in it that nothing sticks with the reader. Your next step is to select for emphasis the *central selling point*—the one big theme around which to build your letter. It is the answer to this question: *What one feature of the product or service is most likely to induce the prospect(s) to buy?* Your other sales points you can interweave, relegate to an enclosure, or leave for a subsequent mailing. In selling completely by mail, one incidental point that you may need to make clear (by explicit statement or implication) is *why* the reader should buy by mail instead of locally.

People buy for many reasons: to make or save money, to build or protect their reputation or status, to preserve health, to save time or effort, to protect themselves or their families or companies, for example. If you want to, you can find buying reasons listed in multitude in countless books on psychology, salesmanship, sociology, advertising, and marketing.[1] Pride, love, beauty, acquisitiveness, self-indulgence, self-preservation, curiosity, and sometimes fear play their parts in inducing interest and stimulating the final action—making the purchase.

People are both rational and emotional. They need a rational reason to support an emotional desire for something. Arguing the relative importance

---

[1] Abraham Maslow's writings provide the best classifications.

of rational and emotional appeals in selling, however, is comparable to a vigorous debate over which came first, the chicken or the egg. In writing good sales letters, if you remind your reader of a need your product will meet and supply evidence to back up your promise, if you stress what you think is the most important reason why the particular group of readers will buy, you won't need to worry about whether you are employing rational or emotional techniques. You'll be using both. And that's as it should be.

You may, however, need to vary the division of emphasis according to the kind of thing you're selling. Goods that are durable, tangible, expensive, and essential call for major emphasis on rational appeals. Conversely, selling things that are ephemeral (quickly used and gone), intangible, inexpensive, and nonessential (luxuries) calls for more emphasis on emotional appeals.

Certainly effective adaptation is necessary. Your choice of theme for your message will be affected by one or more of the significant considerations of the prospect's sex, vocation, location, age, source and amount of income, and social, professional, educational, or corporate status. One of the most obvious differences that affect your choice of theme is that between manufacturers and dealers on one side and consumers on the other.

Consumers buy for the various benefits the product or service will render. Manufacturers buy for the ultimate *profit* they will make by using your product or service to improve their manufacturing or other activities. Dealers buy for the *profit* they will make on reselling. That depends on the *number* they can sell and the *markup*, less any expense and trouble necessary in backing up guarantees with replacements, repairs, and service calls. The logic of selling to dealers lends itself to a formula statement as $P = VM - C$ (profit equals volume of sales times the markup, minus operating costs).

You can't always be certain, either, of the wisdom of your choice of theme. Testing two or more different letters on a part of your list in a preliminary mailing (about which we'll say more later) may help you to arrive at a choice, but sometimes even testing does not resolve your dilemma.

For example, in selling steel desks and chairs to fraternity houses, two writers came up with two different themes. One played up comfort and subordinated appearance, the other stressed appearance over durability and comfort.

Both these letters are well-knit presentations of their selected themes. Each establishes the same information about the product. But we suspect that the first version would sell more chairs to house committees, because on most campuses comfortable study conditions are more important than appearance, and for a longer time than rushing conditions. You would have to test to be sure. You don't have to test, however, to recognize the

First version	*Second version*
How many hours of each day do you spend at your desk? Three? Four? Maybe more?	Wouldn't you be proud to show your rushees uniform desks and chairs?
From experience you know how important it is that your desk be roomy and your chair comfortable. You can be assured of the comfort and convenience you need with Carroll steel desks and chairs. Especially designed as a study unit for college men, they are also sturdy and good looking.	Fine-looking study equipment will create an initial favorable impression. And they will realize, as you do, that following rush week comes work.
Since the desk is 31 inches high, you can cross your knees beneath the top. Or if you want to sit with your feet on the desk, propped back in your chair, you can do so without marring the surface or breaking the welded steel chair.	In Carroll steel desks and chairs you'll have study equipment that will stay good looking and provide years of comfortable use. The top has been chemically treated to avoid burns and scratches and to eliminate stains from liquids. Welded steel construction assures you that your Carroll desk and chair will retain their attractive straight lines. And a choice of battle gray, olive green, or mahogany enables you to select a color which will blend in well with your present furnishings.
Whether you choose the steel top at $140.75 or the laminated plastic top at $135.75, you don't need to worry about nicks and scratches. Either top, 28 inches wide by 42 inches long, gives you ample room for all the books and papers you have in use. Shelves at one end and a large drawer keep your other books and supplies at hand.	Either the steel top at $140.75 or the laminated plastic top at $135.75 will retain its attractive appearance over the years.
And you can have Carroll desks and chairs in battle gray, olive green, or mahogany.	The ample work space of the desk—28 inches wide, 42 inches long, 31 inches high, with shelves at one end and a generous drawer—and the swivel chair of body-comfort design mean comfort for study as well as for long bull sessions.
After you've had a chance to read over the enclosed leaflet (which explains the attractive quantity discounts available to you), you'll see why dormitories at Michigan, Iowa, and Princeton recently chose Carroll study equipment.	After you've had a chance to read over the enclosed leaflet (which explains the attractive quantity discounts available to you), you'll see why dormitories at Michigan, Iowa, and Princeton recently chose Carroll study equipment.

effectiveness of both the psychological description and dramatization in both letters. (If you didn't see them, read pp. 33, 117, and 122).

A letter addressed to the appropriate purchasing agent for the dormitories would wisely have stressed still a different possible theme—holding down maintenance and replacement costs.

Identifying the specific goal

You may know before you begin your prewriting analysis exactly what you want your reader to do. But you'll want to *be sure that the action you request your reader to take is logical* in the light of purchasing conditions, which are governed by the nature of the product, the circumstances of the customer, and authorized, organized marketing channels.

Many sales letters cannot and should not drive for completion of the sale. All they do is ask for a show of interest (and thus help to weed out everybody except true prospects). You may want your reader to request a booklet, come to your showroom, or give you some information; or you may want authorization for a sales representative to visit. In many instances, of course, you can logically ask for an order. Regardless of what the appropriate action is, decide on it and *identify it specifically before you begin to write.*

Any possible version of the letter about fraternity desks and chairs should have some type of action ending, identifying payment and shipping conditions if an order by letter is appropriate or—more likely in this case—inviting the reader to come to a display room or to authorize the visit of a representative. Whatever you decide is the appropriate reader action, you've already learned how to ask for it (back on pp. 119–21).

WRITING THE PROSPECTING SALES LETTER

After thorough study of your product and prospect, selection of theme, and decision on your specific goal, you develop your theme in a C–plan letter patterned by some adaptation of the standard sales presentation: Attention, Interest, Conviction, and Action. (If you want to substitute *Desire* for *Conviction* in letters appealing largely to emotion, go ahead; it won't alter your basic procedure. If you want to call it Promise, Picture, Prove, and Push, you won't go wrong because of your label.)

But don't think of a presentation in terms of four or five or even three parts. In a good letter, smoothly written for coherence and unity of impression, you can't separate the parts cleanly. Although we analyze the writing of a sales letter in terms of getting attentive interest, establishing belief and trust, overcoming price resistance, and confidently asking for action, the final version of it should be a presentation that is smooth be-

cause of its coherence and persuasive because of its singleness of purpose (giving it unity) and progression of thought.

If there is a key to selling, we think it is this: Help your prospects imagine themselves *successfully* using your product or service. Your readers
must clearly picture mentally how your product or service will contribute
some benefits wanted—status, well-being, self-satisfaction, and so forth.

You help your readers imagine themselves successfully using your product or service through psychological description in dramatized copy. (If
you don't remember how to dramatize, look back at pp. 117–18.) To help
them justify themselves logically in acting to get the benefits you have
made desirable, you interweave (or follow up with) physical description
and other evidence that they can get the wanted benefits.

The sales messages in this chapter all exhibit this fundamental pattern of
persuasion, and we will examine it in detail.

Getting attentive interest

If you believe in your product and what it can do for your reader,
you'll have no big problem starting a sales letter effectively. All you need
to do is *hold up the promise of the big benefit your product can contribute
to the reader*. If it's a genuine benefit and your message is to a real prospect,
you'll get attention.

Yet because of the clamor for attention which many advertisers talk
and write about, many advertisements and letters put on a show with the
bizarre, the irrelevant, and the irritating to make the reader stop and listen.
They seem to say: "We know you won't listen otherwise; so we're standing
on our heads to attract your attention. Of course, standing on our heads
won't tell you a thing about our product or what it can do for you, but it'll
make you sit up and take notice."

To that, all we can say is: "Sure! The freak at the circus commands
attention. And if sheer attention is all you want, walk naked down a busy
street. You'll get attention. But is it appropriate? Is it in good taste? Will
it really help to induce the reader to buy?"

Relevancy is essential. Without it, your trick or gadget will be only a
distraction and a detriment rather than an assist to your sales effort. Tricks
are legion, and they create talk, even notoriety, about you. But *unless they
lead naturally, plausibly, and shortly to what your product can do for your
reader, they're not worth the effort and expense.*

The American public is educated and sophisticated. It is quick to criticize or, worse yet, to laugh at poor advertising. It hasn't bought the Brooklyn Bridge for a couple of generations. The farmer's daughter has been to
town—even if it's only via TV. Smug patter about the 14-year-old men-
tality is beguiling—and dangerous. Even 14-year-olds recognize the difference between showing off and real selling.

You'll read much and hear much about tricks, stunts, and gadgets. Good-luck pennies, four-leaf clovers, keys that open the door to everything from business success to a happy home life with your dog, rubber bands (which most of the time only stretch the reader's patience), cartoons, faked bills in window envelopes, simulated handwritten messages, names of readers written at the top of the page in red, blue, gold ("the symbol of things precious, and your name means much to us!"), boldface numbers ("2,400,001! What's the 1 for? That's *your* copy!"), shorthand copy, Chinese writing, the early bird with the worm in its mouth, checkerboards, mirrors, alarm clocks—all these and many others may distract from your sales message rather than assist it unless they enable you to *cut through quickly to the benefit your product can render.*

You may dream up a trick or gadget occasionally that naturally, plausibly, and quickly illustrates or introduces the benefit your product can render. If it can meet the tests of relevance, plausibility, good taste, and speed, you may want to use it. A fire-sale letter typed in red may have salutary appeal. A check form made out to the reader, immediately followed by the lead, "What would it mean to you to get a *real* check like this *every month?*" may plausibly preface sales talk about an annuity or health insurance.

We do not mean to imply that all tricks, gadgets, and humorous letters are undesirable. Certainly you'll find occasional opportune times for the whimsical, the gracefully turned phrase, the chuckling at humanity's idiosyncrasies, and the outright humorous. But before you use what you think is a bright, clever, or punny approach, recall the old story of the woman who asked her husband if he had seen a certain clever ad. "What was it about?" her husband asked. "I don't remember," the lady replied, "but it was right next to that homely X, X, and Y ad."

If you can phrase an opening which is deft, novel, and catchy, use it —provided it paves the way quickly and naturally to the introduction of what your product can do for your reader. If you can't, forget about it.

The benefit-contribution-product beginning is always applicable and always good. Associate the benefit with your reader, then bring in the product as the provider of the benefit, and you have a good opening.

A business-reporting service used the following successful opening[2] in a letter to contractors:

```
A lot of money spent
now and later
on new construction

in your area—

—is going to wind up in somebody's pocket . . . and it might
as well be yours instead of your competitor's!
```

---

[2] Many large-volume sales forms, having no inside address and salutation, use this facsimile or faked layout to look like the usual letter and reduce readers' missing those parts.

Selling word processing equipment to office managers, the following opening (below a clipped-on photograph of a girl powdering her nose while surrounded by three of the machines referred to) pinpoints a real problem and its solution:

> What happens when a girl "powders her nose" in the offices of the Northeastern Mutual Life Insurance Company?
>
> When her typewriter stops, production ceases. And office costs go up.

A variation of theme for the same product went this way:

> "I've had five years' experience with the Mutual Life Insurance Company, can type 140 words a minute, am willing to work each day indefinitely, do not get tired, and demand no salary."
>
> Would you hire this typist? We did. And she typed this letter in two minutes.
>
> Of course, it isn't human. It's a machine—the Robo-Typist—which types any letter you want from a magnetic tape at 140 words a minute.

Note that in all these quoted openings *the lead is simply a reminder of a need for which the product comes in shortly as an agent for satisfying that need.* They do not command, preach, cajole, beg, or exhort. They do not challenge. They do not scream in superlatives (finest, amazing) with exclamation points! They do not begin with talk of the product itself ("Now you too can have XYZ dog biscuits!") or the company ("53 years of doing business . . ."). Here's an example of an opening that does just about everything wrong:

> Recently I was appointed Director of Sales—Midwest Region for the Hardly Used Tool Company and I will now have the pleasure of working with you in handling your used tool requirements with our company.

Good openings positively, specifically, and vividly, but believably, say or imply, "As help in handling this specific problem, I suggest. . . ." They get attentive interest through psychological description of the product in use benefiting the reader personally. Thus they cause the reader to want more information, especially on how the product can fulfill the promise.

Establishing belief and trust

Having made the promise, a letter must quickly supply evidence to back it up. If the opening is successful, it has established tentative approval or agreeableness rather than serious doubt. The next part of your sales letter—which ordinarily consumes the greatest amount of space—tells how your product does meet the need and *gives specific information that will make your reader believe you.* You thus maintain and continue the agreement you establish in the start of the letter.

Explanations and descriptions of the product or service *in use* are how you handle this part. Word pictures of how it works and how it is made, performance tests, testimonials of users, statistics of users, facts and figures on sales, guarantees, free-trial offers, offers of demonstrations, and samples are some of your most common devices. Note how the following letter supplies evidence to support its opening claim.[3]

The Carriage Return Lever
On a Manual Typewriter
Is Costing You Money . . .

. . . and it's money you don't have to spend any more.

Human Efficiency, Inc., has completed a series of exacting tests showing that you can save as much as one hour each day for each typist you employ when you install Speedo Carriage Returns on your manual typewriters.

Watch one of your typists. Every time she returns the carriage to the next line, her left hand makes three movements. When the bell signals the end of a line, her hand moves from the keys to the lever, throws the lever, and then returns to the keys. It looks fast and easy, doesn't it? It is—an expert typist can do it in just one second.

Just one second, but one second becomes one minute when your typist types 60 lines. And that one minute multiplies to one hour every 3,600 lines. From your experience as an office manager, you know that 3,600 lines aren't very many for an efficient stenographer to type, especially the short lines required for orders and invoices.

Using a Speedo, your typist performs one step—not three—to return the carriage to the next line. When the bell signals the end of the line, she presses a foot pedal; the carriage automatically spaces correctly and returns to the left margin. One tenth of a second—not one second—has elapsed.

And because her hands do not have to leave the keyboard, accuracy increases when you install Speedos. Human Efficiency tested 150 typists using Speedos for two weeks in 20 different large plants. They showed a 16 percent reduction in errors— and, naturally, a similar 16 percent reduction in time spent erasing errors.

Part of the explanation for the increase in output and decrease of errors is a reduction in fatigue. Throwing a carriage just once doesn't amount to much, but when your typist repeats hundreds of times she uses up as much energy as if scrubbing the floor. The Speedo not only reduces the strain by two thirds but shifts it to the leg and foot, which can bear it far better than the arm. Tests of 45 typists

---

[3] We have two comments before you read the letter: (1) Though the product sold is obsolete because of electric typewriters, the letter is an excellent one to illustrate the point of convincing the reader by detailed logic and facts about the product *in use*. (2) Yes, this letter is long—as most effective sales letters are. But don't confuse length with a lack of conciseness. If you're worried about length, remember that the firm which has tested more of its sales letters than any other, Time, Inc., never writes one-page sales letters any more—they always pulled less under test. Remember, too, the statement of one of the nation's most renowned consultants, Howard Dana Shaw, that in general a long letter will outpull a short one if it tells, in an interesting way, something of value to the reader.

employed by the Kenoya Wholesale Grocery Company of Columbus, Ohio, showed that after two weeks they increased by 9 percent the amount of copy produced daily.

Clamped to the carriage-return lever, the Speedo connects to the foot pedal by a thin wire. The adjustment is simple; you can put one on any standard typewriter in less than five minutes.

Turn to pages 1 and 2 of the enclosed folder and read the complete report of the tests. On page 3 you'll find comments of typists who've used the Speedo and the comments of their office managers. Read how the typists all agree that they had no difficulty learning to use the Speedo efficiently.

Page 4 gives you data on prices and shipping. Note that the Speedo with all its advantages—plus an unconditional 90-day guarantee—is yours for only $4.50 because we sell Speedo only by mail to help keep the cost down. And by ordering a dozen for $46 you save 70 cents on each one.

Fill out the enclosed order blank and send it to us in the return envelope provided. We'll immediately ship your Speedos by whatever method you direct, either prepaid or c.o.d. Within 10 days at the most you'll be able to see the increased output and accuracy of your typists.

Surely you remember that sincerity is essential to the reader's belief and trust, that you-viewpoint description is vital, that psychological description in terms of the reader's use and benefits is far superior to mere physical description of the product, that specific words in positive language are necessary to effective sales techniques, and that enclosures (properly introduced) can often supplement letters effectively. If not, turn back and review the persuasion principles in Chapter 4 and the analysis of the invited sales letter in Chapter 5. All we're suggesting is that you apply the same principles.

Overcoming price resistance

You've already studied effective ways of handling dollar talk too (back in the discussion of the invited sales letter, pp. 118–19). The principles are the same in prospecting sales.

Asking confidently and specifically for action

If we discussed again what we've already told you and illustrated for you repeatedly about action endings (indicate confidently what you want your reader to do and how to do it, make it easy and make it sound easy, and supply a stimulus to prompt action in a quick reference to the contribution the product can make to the life of the reader), we'd be using your time unnecessarily. Furthermore, the summary checklist (p. 279) itemizes the points specifically.

ADAPTING TO CLASSES

All good sales letters follow the basic procedures advocated in the preceding pages. Only in their talking points and in their interpretation and references do they differ as they go to farmers instead of bankers, to lawyers instead of engineers, to consumers as opposed to dealers or manufacturers. If you are a person of feeling and imagination and are unselfish enough to forget yourself in analyzing another person's (or group of persons') circumstances, you won't have much trouble writing successfully adapted letter copy.

As an illustration of how tone and talking points differ, study the following two letters. The first is to a homeowner, the second to a dealer. In both cases the product is a special kind of lawn mower which eliminates hand clipping.

Lawn-mowing Time

Extra Time for
Summer Rest and Fun!

You can cut your lawn-mowing time in half with an easy-operating Multimower because you can eliminate the hand clipping and trimming and the raking. The Multimower gathers all the grass it cuts.

So with just one run over the lawn with your Multimower, your lawn is in shape. And it's just a light workout. You can cut your grass flush against fences, trees, and flower beds. The interlocking rotary cutters enable you to mow tall grass and tough weeds with no more effort than it takes to cut short grass. And you're less tired when you get through because you handle only the minimum weight when you use this 58-pound mower. It's light enough for almost any member of the household to use.

Even though the Multimower is light, you have a precision mower of sturdy construction and strength-tested materials. The drive shaft is mounted on free-rolling, factory-lubricated, sealed ball bearings which keep dirt and water from rusting these parts. And the cutters are self-sharpening. So add gas and your Multimower is ready to go.

If the weather keeps you from mowing your lawn on schedule and grass gets a little too high, simply adjust the handle knob to the cutting height you want and drive your Multimower easily across your lawn, cutting a clean, even 21-inch swath.

Many of the 8,000 enthusiastic Multimower owners have been using theirs for over two years. Some of their statements, along with illustrations and the details of our 90-day structural guarantee, you can read on the two inside pages. You'll see, too, that we pay shipping charges to your door. Multimower is available only by mail at the economical price of $139.95. The time you save on the first summer's Multimowing is probably worth more than that.

Use the handy order mailer to send us your check or money order. Within a week after you mail it, you'll be able to cut, trim, and gather up the grass on your lawn in only one easy, timesaving Multimowing.

Prospecting Sales Checklist

1. Get started effectively and economically.
   a. Suggest or hint at a specific reader benefit in the first sentence.
   b. Show a need before naming the product as serving it; but usually use positive selling, not predicament-to-remedy pushovers.
   c. Concentrate on a well-chosen central selling point at first.
   d. Quickly get to the distinctive thing about your product (not just anybody's). Avoid unnatural or delaying gimmicks.
   e. Don't begin with an obvious statement or foolish question.
   f. Suggest, remind, but don't preach: "You will want. . . ."
   g. Don't claim too much for your product. Be reasonable.

2. Back up your opening promise with a persuasive description.
   a. Subordinate and interpret physical features in terms of benefits.
   b. You-viewpoint is not automatic from use of *you* ("you will find" and "you will note"); but as the subject or object of action verbs, *you* helps.
   c. Guard against stark product descriptions (beginnings like "Our goods . . . ," "We make . . . ," or "XYZ is made . . .").
   d. Specificness in description is necessary for conviction.
   e. Even in form letters, refer to some action or condition that applies and avoid references which brand them as forms.
   f. The history of the product or firm will bore most readers.
   g. Eliminate challenging superlatives.
   h. Guard against the trite "truly" and "really" and the indefinite "that" ("that important conference").

3. Be sure to cover all important points with proper emphasis.
   a. Develop the most appropriate central selling point adequately.
   b. Stress your central theme for singleness of impression.
   c. Give enough detail to sell your reader on reading an enclosure, when you have one, and even more when you do not.
   d. Provide adequate conviction through selected methods.
   e. Introduce any enclosure only after most of your sales points, stressing what the reader is to do with it or get from it.

4. Remember the price; it is an integral part of any sales message.
   a. Unless using a recognized-bargain appeal, minimize price.
   b. Keep price out of the ending, at least the last sentence.
   c. If you choose not to talk price now, offer to sometime and reassure the reader that it is not out of line.

5. Forthrightly ask for appropriate action (and tell why buy by mail).
   a. Name the specific action you want your reader to take.
   b. Be confident. Avoid "If you'd like . . . ," "Why not . . . ?"
   c. Avoid high-pressure bromides: "Why wait?" "Don't delay!"
   d. Refer *subordinately* to ordering aids (blanks or envelopes).
   e. End with a reminder of what the product will contribute.

6. Check for any unintentional promises of safety or warranty.

The letter to a dealer stresses the same points, to show *why to expect high-volume sales to customers;* but it does so more rapidly and concisely, in order to concentrate on sales aids, price spreads, promptness and regularity of supply, and service as parts of the profit-making picture. Remember the formula $P = VM - C$. And since V (volume of sales) is usually the main variable, give it the major attention it deserves by pointing out how the features of the product will appeal to buyers.

Still the approach is the same as in any sales letter: It seeks the answer to the ever-present question, "What will it do for me?" To a dealer the answer is always "profits," but profits depend on salability (the features of the product that cause people to buy), on serviceability, and on markup. Since salability—features attracting buyers—is usually the main point, the psychological description becomes *interpretation of those features in terms of consumer appeal.* A dealer is also interested in your promptness and regularity in filling orders, in guarantee and service arrangements, and (if you provide any) advertising or other selling aids to help sell more—as in the following letter:

When you show a customer a Multimower, a lawn mower completely new in design and principle, which cuts, trims, and "rakes" a lawn in one operation, you have a quick sale, a satisfied customer, and a $46.65 profit.

Your customers will like the Multimower because it gives them more time to spend in enjoyable summer recreation. It cuts right up to walls, fences, trees, and flower beds and thus eliminates the need for hand trimming in spots not reached by ordinary mowers. Its easily adjustable cutting-height regulator and self-sharpening cutters that slice down the toughest kinds of grass, dandelions, and weeds will assure them of having a trim, neat lawn in half the time they've formerly spent.

Both men and women like the Multimower because its light weight —only 58 pounds—means easy handling. The quiet operation of the interlocking cutters has won approval of 8,000 Multimower users. They like it, too, because it is permanently lubricated and self-sharpening. With a minimum of care it's always ready for use. So normally you just put in the gas and it's ready to go.

No doubt many of your customers have been reading about the Multimower in the full-page, four-color monthly ads that started running in Homeowners and Vacation magazines in March and will continue through July. A reprint, along with testimonials and conditions of our guarantee, appears on the next page. Note the favorable guarantee and servicing arrangements.

In these days of high prices, the $139.95 retail cost of the Multimower will be popular with your customers. Our price to you is only $93.30.

By filling out and returning the enclosed order blank along with your remittance today, you'll be sure to have Multimowers on hand when your customers begin asking for them.

In looking for differences that adapt the two versions of the Multimower letter to users and dealers, did you notice that the main differences are in the psychological description while the physical description is essentially the same—and subordinated? If not, perhaps you should read p. 280 again.

The helpful checklist on page 282 summarizes the significant points to keep in mind for selling to dealers.

LEGAL CONSIDERATIONS

Whether writing to a user or a dealer, a sales writer must keep in mind legal responsibility for what the message says. Recent court decisions have firmly placed the legal responsibility for product liability squarely on the manufacturers and designers of products. And they may still bear the responsibility even if an injured user admits reading and understanding the instructions supplied with the product. Clearly the ancient doctrine of *caveat emptor*, "let the buyer beware," is changing to *caveat venditor*, "let the seller beware."

As an example, suppose the Multimower letters above said

```
The unique spring-loaded on-off switch, cuttings-deflecting
exhaust, and rugged blade shield make the Multimower safe
to use.
```

If worded that way and the spring in the switch broke and hurt a user, or if the mower accidentally got on someone's feet, severely injuring them, that sentence would make Multimower's position in court indefensible. The letter would have made an absolute claim for safety, and the company would be legally responsible for making that claim good.

Better would have been to qualify the statements: ". . . safe to use while using normal safety precautions," or "In normal use, and observing proper safety precautions. . . ."

Warranties and guarantees are an area in which writers of sales letters are even more likely to get into trouble unwittingly by (1) implying a warranty where no warranty exists or (2) extending an existing warranty infinitely. As an example, the third paragraph of the first Multimower letter originally ended:

```
So your Multimower is always ready for you to use.  All you
need to do is put in the gas.
```

First, the writer implied a warranty unintentionally, saying that *all* that is needed is gas, and the mower will operate. Second, that word "always" extended the warranty or guarantee infinitely. The writer unintentionally made a legally binding promise that the Multimower will perform until time and the universe end, provided only that the user puts in gas!

Dealer Sales Checklist

1. A dealer sales letter opening has to move fast.
    a. Devote at least the beginning to the reader and benefits to come—not yourself or even the product per se.
    b. Picture the act of selling and the product's consumer appeal.
    c. Stress a distinctive point; avoid obvious, slow, general copy.
    d. Avoid exaggeration and questionable superlatives.

2. Though you might mention profits, the first point to develop is salability (volume). Without consumer appeal the product stays on the shelves and makes no profit regardless of price spread.
    a. To stress consumer demand, explain the product's points in terms of customers' reactions, demands, and approval—hence high-volume sales.
    b. Talk about the dealer's selling—not using—the product.
    c. Adaptation here means talking of sales demonstrations, wrapping up a purchase and handing it across the counter, ringing up a sale, answering customers' questions, and the like.

3. Show how the manufacturer helps to push the sale, if applicable.
    a. Refer to whatever dealer aids you have (advertising, displays, mats, cuts) with emphasis on how they build local demand.
    b. Give working ideas of size (quarter page, half page), extent (time it will run), and coverage (specific medium—magazine, newspaper, radio, and/or TV station—and type of audience).
    c. Interpret any advertising as promoting inquiries and sales.

4. Continue pointing to appeal and profitable selling in the price talk.
    a. Price is most appropriately handled late, most naturally as you ask for an order and talk payment details.
    b. Include a specific mention of price spread, percentage, or both.
    c. Terms and manner of payment have to be cleared up.

5. You will almost always have some enclosures to handle.
    a. Don't divert attention to the enclosure until near enough the end that the reader will complete the letter.
    b. Make the reference to an enclosure carry a sales point too.
    c. Don't depend too heavily on an enclosure to do the selling.

6. Make the action ending brief and businesslike too.
    a. Probably better avoid commands to the seasoned buyer.
    b. Exaggerated superlatives are out of place here too.
    c. Of course, you name the specific action you want.
    d. And you make that action easy.
    e. Use a whip-back suggesting prompt handling and profitable selling.

7. Check for any unintentional promises of safety or warranty.

Here's how those sentences could be rewritten to avoid the problem:

```
A minimum of easy maintenance will help keep your Multimower
ready for use.  Virtually all you need to do is put in the gas
and start it.
```

Words to watch out for when you are writing sales messages are *always, never, whenever, all, perfectly, trouble-free, simply,* and others like them. They signal that you may need to reword what you said, or qualify it.

TESTS AND TESTING

Testing a mailing to predetermine the returns (or the pull or the pulling power) of a letter is serious business among high-volume mailers. Testing means simply mailing the letter to a portion of the names on your list to see whether you can get a profitable percentage of people to take the action you want. You can see why a business executive would be wise to test a mailing before risking the money to send 10,000 letters, especially if the mailing pieces are expensive.

Suppose your mailing pieces cost 30 cents each (not unusual in a mass mailing) and you make $3 on each sale. Obviously, you have to make sales to 10 percent of the list to break even. Now suppose you have a 90 percent accuracy factor (that is, the percentage of correct addresses). Each 100 letters have to bring ten orders from every 90 people who get them. Further suppose the purity (how many names on the list are likely prospects instead of deadwood) is 70 percent. This means that your 100 letters have to bring ten orders from every 63 good prospects (70 percent of 90). This requires about 16 percent pulling power from your letter (10/63).

Most sales letters don't do so well. But you could change the situation into one that would be profitable by increasing any or all of the accuracy, the purity, or the pulling power—or by decreasing costs of the mailing or increasing the profit on the sale.

Other significant reasons for testing are to find out which of two or more messages has the greater pull or which of two times (day or week or month the mailing piece arrives) is more profitable. *But you can test only one factor at a time!*

You can test one color against another; but if you also vary size, copy, or time, your test doesn't mean a thing. You can test one lead against another; but if the rest of the copy and the time of arrival are not the same, you still have no basis for saying that one lead is better than the other.

Many published test results concern format and timing. If you talk with enough people in the field or read long enough, you'll be reassured— often vehemently!—that every color you've ever seen is the best color for a mailing. You'll find one person swearing by third-class mail and another at it. You'll find out, however, what all experienced persons with judgment discover: Because people and circumstances constantly change, so do the results of testing; what a test suggests this week may not be true next week and probably will not be next year. The only way to be safe is to test in each new situation and then follow through as fast as you can.

Even so, you usually expect only 5–10 percent pulling power. But especially effective copy, carefully selected mailing lists, or unusual offers often increase these percentages.

Even such apparently insignificant things as the time of arrival are important. Experience has shown that sales letters should not arrive in an office at the beginning or ending of a week or month or at the homes of laborers or farmers in the middle of the week. Around Christmas time and April 15 (income tax time) are especially bad times of the year. In general the fall and winter months are better than spring and summer. Of course, seasonal appropriateness of the goods and geographical locations can easily affect this. Even temporary local conditions may.

By keeping careful records on the tests and on the whole mailing, through the years users develop a considerable quantity of experience data that may help guide them in future work.

WRITING SALES SERIES

The sales letters we have been discussing are lone efforts to produce or promote sales. Because single sales letters frequently cannot do all the work a series can, probably *just as many* sales letters go in series as singly. Usually they are obviously processed (form) letters, sent out in large numbers by third-class mail. For further economy they often use some simulated address block instead of an inside address and salutation (like our examples on pp. 274, 276, and 278). By careful phrasing, however, a skillful writer can *make the one reader of each copy forget the form and feel that it is a well-adapted message that certainly fits personally.*

Whether a letter is a single sales letter or one in a series makes little difference in the techniques or preliminary planning, but in one of the three types of series (wear-out, campaign, and continuous) the letter's organization is more complicated.

The wear-out series

Probably the most widely used of sales series is the wear-out. In it each mailing is a complete sales presentation on a relatively inexpensive product (usually not over $25). The product almost has to be inexpensive, because one letter cannot hope to succeed in persuading most people to buy expensive items by mail from a complete stranger.

After the market analysis, preparation or purchase of a mailing list, and preliminary planning comes the writing of the letter. Probably you and several other executives, and perhaps a letter consultant, will spend hours preparing the letter, or several versions of it. These first few copies may cost several hundred dollars in time and consultant's fees.

Then you test your list, and perhaps several versions of the letter. If one letter seems to have the best pulling power (and that is high enough to make it profitable), you run off hundreds or thousands of copies and mail them out at a carefully selected time. Now that the big investment has been divided among so many, the cost per letter is not so big.

After an interval, usually of one to three weeks, you remove the names of purchasers (unless the product has frequent recurring demand) and send another letter (or sometimes the same one) to the remaining names on the list. Sometimes the third or fourth mailing brings better results than the first, even with the same letter, because of the buildup of impact. You continue to repeat the mailings until you reach a point at which the percentage of returns from each mailing no longer yields you sufficient profit to continue. Those left on the list are the "hard cases" that apparently won't buy no matter what. The list is worn out; hence the name.

The campaign series

What has been said about the cost of the first copy, the general preliminary planning, the testing, and the usual interval between mailings of the wear-out series also applies to the campaign series. But there the similarity stops.

The theory of the campaign series is that people buy some (usually inexpensive) items quickly, without much thought; but before buying certain other types of items (usually more expensive), most people ponder for a month or more and talk over the situation. To send one letter which first introduced such an item and, after only two minutes of reading time (as in the wear-out series), asked for the decision on an order card would be to pour money down the proverbial rathole. Instead of the wear-out, you would use the campaign series for such a situation.

Your preliminary planning is as different as the price involved. You decide approximately how long most people on the mailing list would want to think over your offer before making up their minds. Then you decide how frequently they should be reminded to keep them thinking about your product or service. On that basis you decide the length of the series—in time and number of mailings.

The essence of planning the series of letters (whether two or a dozen) is to make the whole series cover the parts of a complete sales presentation and knit them together. In any case the first letter will try hard to get attention and start working at interesting the prospect. Further letters will strive to develop interest in buying until the last makes the strongest drive for action. As people respond, you remove their names from the list.

The last letter is not the only one, however, to which a reader can easily respond. Sellers by mail know that they will not usually get any action from more than half of their prospects. But they also know that in almost any large group some people will be sold on the first contact. Consequently, they usually provide order forms with almost every mailing.

If you have ever let your subscription to a magazine lapse, you have probably received campaign series letters. To help illustrate further the differences between a campaign series and the single-letter sales presentations discussed earlier, however, we have included the skeleton of a typical campaign at the end of this chapter.

The continuous series

The wear-out and campaign series are different in many ways, but they are much more like each other than like the continuous series. Both the wear-out and the campaign series are usually complete sales presentations which try to bring in orders. The continuous series rarely does. Also the users (and uses) of the continuous series are most frequently department stores (as a goodwill or sales promotion medium) and oil companies and credit card organizations (as a direct-mail selling system). The mailing list for the continuous series is usually the firm's charge customers. The continuous series usually costs little because it rides free with the monthly statements.

Still, perhaps the biggest distinction is the rigid planning of the campaign series as compared with the more haphazard nature of the continuous series, which commonly includes special mailings at holidays but also on almost any other special occasion. It does not run for any set length of time or for any definite number of mailings; and it may *promote* a great *variety* of products while the campaign and wear-out series are *selling one*.

❖ ❖ ❖ ❖ ❖

The following direct-mail campaign directed to accounting firms, tax services, and law firms emphasizes the economy of making dry photocopies instantly with an Adeco Auto-Copier (costing about $2,000). The letters could go to only one city or over the entire country. A sales representative within a city could readily assemble a mailing list from the Yellow Pages, or buy the list. Certainly a nationwide mailing list would be more inexpensively purchased than assembled.

The mailings are planned for intervals of about three weeks. For economy they use a simulated address block (first few words of the copy set up like an inside address and salutation), are printed, and go third class. Each mailing includes a reply card which reads something like this:

> Yes, I would like to know more about how the Adeco Auto-Copier
> will help me. Please call me and arrange an appointment.

The card provides blanks for indicating name of individual, position, company, and address.

The first mailing includes a 12-page, two-color booklet containing illustrations, savings estimates and comparisons, and information about the company and its organization.

> You can save
> Up to 80 percent on
> Copying jobs . . .
>
> . . . by letting your typists make photocopies with the
> Adeco Auto-Copier.
>
> In less than 15 seconds an unskilled operator can turn out a
> legally acceptable, error-proof copy of an original—one that
> would take your typist at least 10 minutes to copy. If your
> office produces only 15 copies a day, the Auto-Copier can save
> you about $6 each working day. When you need to turn out
> large numbers of copies, the Auto-Copier makes them for you as
> fast as 200 an hour, at proportionate savings.
>
> Your Auto-Copier takes a picture without using a camera. So
> in turning out copies of complicated tax forms, accounting
> forms, government records, and deeds, it assures you of
> error-proof copies.
>
> The Auto-Copier is a fully automatic, continuous copier and
> processing unit combined. In just two simple steps you can
> turn out prints made from any original up to 11 by 17 inches
> whether printed on one or two sides. Since it dries its prints
> automatically, they're ready for your instant use.
>
> Just put the Auto-Copier on any convenient desk or table, plug
> it in, and you're ready to start. You can copy any
> confidential material right in the privacy of your own office
> in just a few seconds. Read the description in the enclosed
> folder of the Auto-Copier's easy, simple operation.
>
> The Auto-Copier will actually enable you to have one unskilled
> clerk do the copying work of six expert typists. Just return
> the enclosed card so that your Adeco representative can show
> you how to let the Auto-Copier cut the high cost of duplicating
> records.
>
> Auto-Copies of tax forms are fully acceptable and approved by
> the Internal Revenue Service.

The second letter accompanies a four-page, two-color folder headlined "Make photocopies of tax returns instantly!" In the upper left corner of the letter appears the picture of an office worker operating an Auto-Copier. To the right of the illustration is a SOLID CAP headline stressing the near-instantaneous copying. The five-paragraph letter then talks speed and IRS acceptance, reduced number of typists and costs, absolute accuracy without proofreading, and summary (as a demonstration can show).

Letter No. 3, accompanied by a one-page folder, offers a week's free trial (with the postcard altered in wording accordingly). It recaps previous points (in different wording), adds convenience (of light weight, small space, and easy plug-in), and pushes for a free-trial demonstration.

The fourth letter pictures an office worker turning out copies on the Auto-Copier while looking directly at the reader and saying:

```
I've typed thousands
of tax returns.

And I know the Adeco Auto-Copier can save you money because it
can reduce your tax copying work up to 80 percent.

For two years I have typed tax forms in the offices of
C. C. Putnam, CPA, 166 Stallings Building, Atlanta 30218.

Turning out an original copy of a complicated tax form is a
job in itself, but typing 10 or 12 clear, correct copies is
next to impossible.

Now just a minute! I'm not a poor typist. I can type 60
words a minute with no errors on a 10-minute test. That is
certainly as good as the average typist. But I still have
trouble aligning forms, making corrections, and typing perfect
copies.

With the Auto-Copier I simply type the original and run off as
many copies as I need. I can now turn out in one day reports
that used to take several days. Each detail of the original
reproduces accurately and legibly—and the only copy I have to
proofread is the form itself!

Our clients like Auto-Copied forms, and the government
accepts them without question.

In addition to tax form copies, I use the Auto-Copier for
letters, bank records, claims, graphs, or invoices. No more
costly retyping or hand copying!

My employer and I agree that the Auto-Copier is the answer to
our copying needs. Your Adeco representative would like to
show you how the Auto-Copier can solve your copying problems
too. Check the enclosed card today for a demonstration in
your office.
```

The letter carries the signature of the speaker and the title as secretary to Mr. Putnam.

The fifth mailing reestablishes the main talking points and stresses much harder the advantages of having the sales representative come in and demonstrate

```
Can your typists turn out
200 perfect copies an hour?
With the Auto-Copier they can!

The Auto-Copier will enable one unskilled clerk to do the
copying work of six expert typists.

In addition, you are assured of perfect accuracy—each detail
of the original is accurately reproduced without any
possibility of error. And there's no need for tedious,
time-consuming proofreading and checking either.
```

In turning out copies of complicated tax forms, legal reports
and records, and accounting data on the Auto-Copier, your
typist can run off up to 20 clear copies in no more than five
minutes. Since no errors appear, Auto-Copier eliminates
erasing time and messiness.

You can put your Auto-Copier on any convenient desk or table,
since it measures 20 by 11 inches. You simply plug it in,
and it's ready to use. No special installation is necessary.
Anyone can run it.

Since Auto-Copies are processed and dried automatically,
they're ready for instant use. You need no developing,
washing, drying, or printing space because the Auto-Copier
does everything in one simple operation.

Your Auto-Copier representative would like to talk with you
about your particular copying needs and show you how other
companies are using Auto-Copier to help cut copying costs.
Just sign and mail the enclosed card for a demonstration in
your office.

Mailing No. 6 (the last) is the booklet sent with the first letter. Attached
to the booklet is a memo in simulated handwriting:

If you didn't get a chance to read the first copy of the
booklet I sent you recently, here's another.

It will explain how the Auto-Copier can help you cut the high
cost of duplicating records.

For a demonstration in your office at a time you specify, just
fill in and return the enclosed reply card.

CASES FOR SALES

1. For King Manufacturing, Inc., P.O. Box 4598, Princeton, NJ 08540,
as director of sales write a form letter to be processed on a machine that
types in the inside address and salutation of members of tennis clubs in
Texas. *Product:* Three tennis ball machines (impersonal practice partner)
—Little King, $332; King, $595; and King Professional, $695. Little King
holds up to 60 balls and can be set to eject at up to 60 miles per hour;
King, 100 balls/120 mph; and King Professional (favorite of professionals),
150 balls/180 mph. Portable (30, 40, 50 lbs.); and have two cart wheels for
on-ground moving. (Assume one-page enclosure with pictures and physical facts.) All have plastic hopper and aluminum tube with plastic ends.
To operate: fill machine with balls, turn knobs to set speed, frequency, and
direction of the ball. All parts guaranteed for five years. Less expensive
than through local sporting goods store.

2. *Mailing list:* Prospective brides from newspaper clippings. *Product:*
Inexpensive stainless-steel flatwear (Dansing). Write a form letter selling
service for eight (8 knives, dinner forks, salad forks, soup spoons, 16 tea-
spoons, butter knife and sugar shell), or 50 pieces. Construction: tarnish-

resistant, heavy-gauge stainless steel. Dishwasher safe. Three popular patterns are Kenyon, a pistol-grip design in satin finish that sells for $44.99 (service for 12 at $67.48); Omega, mirror-finished 17th-century design, $35.98 (for 12, $53.98); Lady Sara, with oxidized finish to create depth and shadow in pattern, $35.98 (service for 12, $53.98). Along with your form letter assume a four-color brochure and a business reply envelope and order card. The brochure pictures a setting of each pattern and a five-piece serving set that includes a gravy ladle, serving fork, three serving spoons (two solid and one pierced).

3. Emergency Alarm systems from Res-Q Inc., 10617 W. Oklahoma Ave., Milwaukee, WI 53227, can be used in homes and apartments. Designed for elderly people who live alone, people with heart conditions or other health problems, handicapped persons, and shut-ins. The system for homes and other single-dwelling units consists of an outside, weatherproof warning horn and a portable, 3-ounce coded radio frequency transmitter with push-button control to activate the outside alarm. The apartment unit consists of the same transmitter and a receiving unit containing a warning horn and a red light that is mounted on the apartment entry door. Alarms have an operating radius of 150 feet and are certified by the FCC. Priced at $199.50. Your mailing list is made up of elderly people who live in houses and apartments in the Northeast. Write a letter and assume an illustrated brochure.

4. *Company:* Nyman Scientific Co., 380 Nyman Building, Rose City, MI 48654. *List:* Homeowners in Southwest (50,000). *Product:* Windmill replica built to scale of heavy-gauge steel. Lawn model can show wind direction, lends a rural charm to a lawn or garden, has a durable outdoor finish. As the wind blows, the wheel silently revolves on shielded ball bearings. Suggested as centerpieces for plants or flowers or as holders of yard lights, house numbers, signs. Aluminum color, has red trim, stands 4½ feet, has a wheel diameter of 22 inches, weighs 46 pounds, sells for $44.95 postpaid. Desk model stands 17 inches with a 5-inch wheel diameter, $10.85 postpaid. *Enclosure:* Folder with pictures and testimonials. *Assignment:* Assume the enclosure and write the letter, which will be processed on a word-processing machine.

5. In a brown paper bag envelope you are going to sell your "Brown Bagger's Special," a new $25,000 six-year term life insurance policy for budget-conscious families who are just starting out—need life insurance but can't pay a lot in premiums. The policy is renewable and convertible. No physical needed for persons below age 35. Sell only by mail or phone: (419) 354–3585. Premium rates by ages on card. Enclose reply

envelope. Sign as Jim Handley, agent. Your company, Educator & Executive Life Insurance Company, 4400 North High Street, Columbus, OH 43212.

6.   To conserve fuel, reduce bills, and increase comfort, you feel that now will be a good time to sell home insulation in Madison, Wisconsin, before the cold months get here. You used the census information in the University library to prepare a list of 3,000 names of homeowners whose homes have central heat and air and are valued at or above the $50,000 price bracket.

Your firm, Empire Industries, 4402 E. Washington Ave., Milwaukee, WI 53201, has developed a technique of pumping insulating materials into attics and walls by hoses and air pressure. Since most of the homes in Madison are block construction, you decide to concentrate on insulating the attics; 80 percent of the heat loss in a home occurs through the attic and roof. By applying a 7-inch layer of your special polyfoam insulator, you can cut the heat loss by two thirds and save the customer about 15 percent of the $50 average monthly cost of heating (or cooling).

It takes only two hours to fully insulate the attic of a three-bedroom house. Your three Madison dealers will subcontract any jobs you get. You will ask your customers to authorize a visit from your sales representative rather than send the $300 cost of doing the job. Write a prospecting sales letter (form letter) that can be sent to the 3,000 names on your list. Sign the letter with your name as Director of Sales and date it simply—Fall, this year.

7.   As vice president of Zoellner Bros., a division of Greyhound Armour, 3209 West District Blvd., Chicago, IL 60632, write a letter to major companies like General Motors, Ford, General Electric, and Scoville Manufacturing asking them to send a gift of Zoellner Brothers products this Christmas. Sending a gift of Zoellner's famous prime meat, poultry, seafood, or complete celebration dinner is like giving a friend an incomparable dining-out experience. Since 1945 Zoellner has built its reputation on prime steaks. You also handle related items such as veal, lamb, pork, gourmet chicken items, turkey, lobster tails, and shrimp. You have several precooked items called the Gourmet Convenience Food Line (Beef Stroganoff, Prime Boneless Short Ribs of Beef, Beef Burgundy, and Chicken Aloha). Zoellner has been supplying to luxury restaurants and private clubs for years.

To order, choose from the array of items in the brochure. Zoellner gift-boxes the items befitting their excellence, provides a personalized card with the purchaser's name, and ships in reusable styrofoam shipping containers with dry ice (perfect condition on arrival assured, fully guaranteed). Container holds meat frozen for seven days in transit to any place in the world. Just sent a box of steaks to an influential executive in Malaysia.

8. (*a*) As Jason Warfel, promotion manager, American Geographic Society, Columbus, OH 43216, sell your new book, *Wilderness, USA* ($9.95, 8¾″ × 12″, 344 pages of vivid, authoritative text) to members of the society. Its 302 full-color illustrations—90 percent never before published—include 25 double-spread panoramas and 22 maps; most show major roads to each area, main trails, and key points of interest. Readers can examine the book at no obligation. Assume that the mailing includes brilliant full-color photographs showing many of the country's most beautiful or breathtaking scenes displayed on an 18- by 22-inch full-color broadside, your letter, and a business-reply card. Somewhere in your letter use the quotation from John Muir: "Nature's peace will flow into you as the sunshine into the trees."

(*b*) As Bill Schoof, Vice President, Marketing, Richard D. Irwin, sell your text (this book) to each of the top five to ten executives in each of the *Fortune* 500—names available in directories.

(*c*) As Bill Schoof (preceding case) offer the text at a special reduced price, say 20 percent discount, to companies to use as a gift to prime customers or incentive rewards to employees deserving recognition (say leaders in sales).

9. (*a*) You, Larry B. Bucks, Executive Vice President—Marketing, have a mailing list of 200,000 frequent business travelers on your Continental Airlines, 7300 World Way West, Los Angeles, CA 90009, among whom you want to promote your Presidents Club—users of your airport lounges in major cities where your member travelers can check in, get their boarding pass, have a drink, make a call, or whatever in the club's quiet, luxurious surroundings. Initiation fee of $65 for the first year and then an annual fee of $35. Write them.

(*b*) Again as Larry Bucks (preceding case) you screened 400,000 people who live on your routes and were qualified based on their income ($13,000 or under) to receive your "Fly-Away" credit card. The recipient could use the card as cash to buy air transportation on Continental and also the six carriers you connect with (Aloha, Frontier, Golden West, North Central, Ozark, and Texas International). It includes a time-payment with 12 percent interest, which is 6 percent lower than most charge cards. If the customer runs a little bit short of cash, wants to extend payments, or deals directly with the airline rather than through an intermediate card, then this card is handy. Once customers get these cards, they'll use them (according to some tests you ran last year). You hope to open up a market for people who might not have another kind of credit card and who might not have as much "plastic" as the average frequent traveler has, so it's pretty specially targeted toward the family-type traveler and the up-and-coming young traveler. Ask the recipient to affix the peel-off label to the reservation certificate, then sign and return it to you. Because the certificate expires June 17, should return it right away. This "Fly-Away" card will give the receiver credit access to more than 46 cities and cover "Charge it" orders for super tours to places like Hawaii, Florida, ski country.

10. (*a*) *Company:* Zodiac Simplex, 315 West Allegon, Lansing, MI 48910. *Mailing list:* Subscribers to *Field and Stream*. *Product:* Inflatable boat you can stow in a closet, transport in a car's trunk, set up and launch at beach, riverbank, or dock. Unparalleled stability and load-carrying capability. Safe and seaworthy (avoid possible legal problems). The dinghie looks like an oblong doughnut, is called Zodiac Simplex. Floorboards stiffen the fabric bottoms and make them feel more stable. Rowing is easy because this model has a keelson (a separate, inflatable chamber running fore and aft the floorboards). It comes with oarlocks, outboard-motor bracket (or transom assembly), and floorboards. Can be set up in ten minutes by one person. Holds three people comfortably. Maximum motor, 6 hp. Price $531 (including floorboards and outboard bracket). *Action:* Ask reader to fill out a card for more information.

(*b*) Sell the Zodiac Simplex (preceding case) to resort owners in Michigan, Wisconsin, and Minnesota to pack into other lakes than the ones they're on. Saves hauling heavy boats to other lakes in spring and bringing them back in fall. Avoids theft/damage of boats left at other lakes.

11. *Company:* Glory, 3200 West Peterson Avenue, Chicago, IL 60659. *Mailing list:* Office managers of industrial plants. *Product:* Glory Coffee Service Plan. If the office manager buys just the Glory coffee, you furnish the Glory brewer, creme, sugar, and filters free. The coffee is Glory's finest —a gourmet blend found in elegant hotel dining rooms or exclusive restaurants. The free service is that you see to it that the office is fully supplied at all times, and you personally phone each month to make sure everything is running smoothly. The coffee costs just a few cents a cup. Ask the reader to fill out a card you'll enclose. The card brings 100 free cups of Glory's Finest Coffee and will introduce the reader to the finest, fastest, most attentive coffee service plan in the business. The employees will have more energy, production time, and appreciation than before Glory.

12. This case is a three-in-one (*a*, *b*, *c*). With a mailing list of (*a*) health food stores, (*b*) diet clubs, or (*c*) members of the Nationwide Spa in the Midwest, set up a form letter with a faked inside address. Your company, Greenwood Associates, Inc., Glenview, IL 60005, has a new product called the French Twist Automatic Calorie Counter which it hopes to sell individually by mail for (*c*) $14.95 or in quantity

(*a* or *b*) for $9.95. This watchlike device, which is clipped to a belt as you would a pedometer, automatically computes the calorie burn-off with each step the wearer takes. Walking, jogging, jumping, and similar activities cause a hand on the dial to revolve, and the measurements accumulate as calories are expended. A doughnut contains about 151 calories, equivalent to the energy expended by an average person jogging for about 14 minutes or walking for about 49 minutes. Pretend to enclose a folder with pictures of the French Twist Automatic Calorie Counter and an order card.

13. Ruud Manufacturing Company, 165 North Broad Street, Philadelphia, PA 19121. Attention Ms. Stella Johnson. From Captain's Travel Service, Inc., Edward E. Baskin, Manager, International Tours Division, 919 Linden Avenue, Minneapolis, MN 55403. *Subject:* Executive "Sea-School." Beginning next February 14, Captain's will launch another of its famous Schools-at-Sea for top-echelon executives. Leaving San Diego Harbor, Captain's sails on one of the most luxurious ocean-going vessels afloat. This 20-day cruise includes stops at Hilo, Kahului, and Honolulu, Hawaii. En route, seminar sessions, held in beautifully appointed meeting rooms, will be led by leaders of international reputation. Growing professionally while enjoying soft Pacific breezes is the deal of a lifetime! Complete details enclosed give dates, prices, seminar leaders, and social events—all planned with executive interests in mind. Action ending. Make it easy for Johnson to reply with an addressed, stamped card.

14. With the love-bug season approaching, you feel it will be a good time to introduce your new Bug-Off insect deflector screen. The Bug-Off screen fits across the front of any truck tractor and catches bugs before they spatter on the paint and windshield. Love-bugs take the paint off with them when you try to wash them off. The Bug-Off protective screen has a thin linen backing that catches the smashed bugs that pass through the ⅟₁₆-inch squares of the nylon screen, but the cloth is not thick enough to block the flow of air to the truck's cooling system. And the adjustable Bug-Off screen fits all trucks, from GM to White. The screen can be cleaned simply by spraying with a garden hose and scrubbing the bugs off with a broom or a stiff bristle brush. Write a form letter that could be sent to trucking companies, truck fleet operators, and truck owners in the Gainesville/ Orlando, Florida, area. In your letter, present and sell the Bug-Off screen to the prospects on the mailing list you purchased from the Florida Department of Motor Vehicles. The screens cost $17.95. All the customer has to do is take it out of the mailing tube and tie it on. Your company is Bugs-Off, 811 St. Johns Ave., Jacksonville, FL 32666.

15. Using the information in the previous case, write a form letter that you can send to auto accessories and hardware store owners in the Gaines-

ville/Orlando area. Point out to the dealer the advantages of stocking and selling the Bug-Off screen now that the love-bug season is approaching. The cost to the dealer is $11.95; the suggested retail price is $19.95.

16. *Company:* Middleton Design and Equipment Company, 409 Linton Avenue, Providence, RI 02908. *Mailing list:* Hospitals in the Southeast. *Product:* Fly-Grid, a unique, all-electric flying insect electrocutor; (1) a certified radiant energy black light fluorescent lamp that attracts flying insects, (2) a grid charged with high voltage that electrocutes insects, and (3) a removable tray to contain all insect remains. Five-foot tall "Big Boy" used around food processing plants, zoos, catering places; a small, light-weight portable unit for patios, small office areas, and dining rooms. The only system which health departments will allow to operate 24 hours a day; guaranteed for three years except the bulb. *Action:* Enclose a card so that a sales representative can call about prices. *Testimony:* Any fried chicken processing plant or quick-food eating chain.

17. The bicycle thief is probably the busiest person on most campuses these days. Despite proliferation of chain locks, yokes, and burglar alarms, the demand for high-cost, ten-speed bikes makes the thefts a lucrative business. Nearly impregnable, polyester-laminated fiberboard-box bike lockers have aluminum frames and pick-proof, seven-pin tumbler locks. They sell for $146 each and rent for about 25 cents a day. As director of sales for Rodney Corporation, 609 St. Charles Avenue, Los Angeles, CA 90041, write a sales letter to the purchasing agents of all major universities (not already sold) telling them about your Loka-Bike, suggesting they purchase directly from you, and then rent (coin-operate) the lockers to students. Within the past year Rodney Corporation has placed coin-operated units at bus and rapid transit stations, shopping malls, and many universities.

18. After seven years of preparation, the Book-of-the-Month Club, Camp Hill, PA 17012, developed a comprehensive home-study program for reading improvement. Reading speed can be increased as much as 50 percent in just two weeks' time without cost or obligation. For the first two weeks, the subscriber will use a portfolio ($5.75) and a Reading Pacer ($70.50) which will be used with other portfolios. If, after studying and using the first portfolio, the reader wants the others, they will be sent at the rate of one every three weeks. If the reader is not sure of improvement, then all the materials may be sent back within two weeks (no charge).

The first portfolio contains: Basic Instruction Guide, Training Manual, Eye-and-Mind Practice Section, Speed-and-Comprehension Practice Material, Practice Material for the Reading Pacer, Speed and Comprehension Tests, Reading Improvement Chart. Each of the portfolios takes up a different reading problem, and in each case the problem being covered is first explained, and then the particular weakness causing it is dealt with by means of specially prepared practice materials. The serious student need spend no more than an average of 15 minutes a day to keep up with the instruction. Psychologists have found that the ability to read swiftly and with complete comprehension is an acquired and not an inborn skill. Slow readers are almost invariably the product of poor training at an early age.

Write a special sales letter to your large membership list. Include (assumed) a picture of the Reading Pacer and the portfolios, along with an order form and envelope.

19. Already 80,000 users enjoy Hydro-Fin (by Hydro-Fin, Inc., 175 Ichthus Street, Detroit, MI 48224). Attaches somewhat like a small outboard. Operates with one hand. Leaves one hand free to troll or cast. Propels and directs boat silently, easily, up to 3 miles per hour. For fishing, duck hunting, sailing, $27.95, fully guaranteed. Try to get an order on the enclosed blank. Enclosed booklet shows pictures, details, and testimonials. How would you get a mailing list?

20. Your company, Stanley and Stroughton, Inc., 497 Newburg, Neenah, WI 54946, manufactures Firmaides, dinner napkins 17 inches square made of triple-ply, fine-quality cellulose. Market research shows that some commercial restauranteurs pay more for rented table linens than the cost of these napkins (one case of 2,000 napkins sells for $30). When they use their own linens, pilferage losses and replacements due to fraying and cigaret burns amount to a significant cost. Operators who are using most paper services are dissatisfied with the small size and poor quality of the napkins, but operators of fine establishments are interested in a luxury type of paper napkin for cocktail lounge or luncheon service. With economy and quality appeals, write a letter to hotel managers in the East. For our sample you write Mary Hunter, Hunter's Lodge, Portland, ME 04155. See whether you can convince your prospect that this snowy-white napkin is far superior to ordinary paper napkins. It is intended for use instead of linen in the finest inns, hotels, and clubs, where patrons expect the best.

With these large paper napkins that won't slide off laps, the hotel or lodge avoids laborious ironing, sorting, counting, bundling, and handling. Also Firmaides have no holes, no frayed edges, no rust spots, or stains. Besides calling Hunter's attention to the enclosed sample napkin, suggest ordering by filling out the reply card.

21. Your company—Samuels, Speery, and Sand, 5340 Delmar Boulevard, Saint Louis, MO 63196—perfected a formula for protecting tools from rot, rust, heat, and cold. Tool-Guard stops splitting of wooden handles, waterproofs joints, penetrates wooden surfaces, sets up a weather-resistant, glovelike coating, leaving no sticky surfaces, making tools grip easier, safeguards metals. As a test 5,000 tools were tested two years ago in Saint Louis. During the two years the tools were exposed to rain, snow, sun, and sleet, but they didn't rust, nor did the handles deteriorate in any way. In a short time this product pays for itself. A 1-gallon metal drum, $19.50 retail, is enough to protect 600 tools. Also available in a 4-ounce plastic bottle with applicator top (20 tools, $1) and 16-ounce bottle ($2.95). You're going to send a one-page letter to all contractors in the Missouri-Illinois-Wisconsin area. Your mailing will be a four-page folder: the letter on the first page; two-color illustrations, copy, and endorsements on the rest. (For class purposes just write the letter and assume the rest.) On the fourth and final page will be an order blank. To cut down on the expense of mailing, use a faked inside address imitative of the three-line inside address. Even your signature as sales manager can be processed.

22.   Try a mailing promoting Tool-Guard to hardware dealers in the area (see preceding case). A 4-ounce plastic bottle with applicator top wholesales for 50 cents, 16-ounce bottle, $1.75. To make ordering easier, you've enclosed an order blank along with pictures of the product. You can afford to send card displays and envelope stuffers to help promote Tool-Guard. You are running full-page ads in the monthly *Hardware Review*.

23.   (*a*)   A recent survey shows that 80 percent of the families living in homes assessed at $40,000 or more have outdoor cooking facilities. You know from your own experience and that of your friends that the most common (and much preferred—for food flavor) fuel is charcoal and that an almost universal problem is getting it started and the fire spread throughout, ready for use. Whether you (or anybody you know) uses kindling, a liquid starter fluid, or an electric starter, it takes at least 40 minutes before you're ready to cook. Your company, Holiday House, Inc., P.O. Box 62, Kansas City, MO 64133, has therefore put on the market a handy gadget called FireFly (a small blower). Eleven ounces, starts fires in minutes, revives fires in seconds. Hand-operated, directing a flow of air where you want it, Firefly has even a charcoal fire ready in ten minutes. Ideal gift, beautiful charcoal color, textured finish, hand-fitting handle. Fully guaranteed. $5.25 plus 50 cents for postage and handling. Write a letter to sell this needed, popular-where-used product to a large mailing list and attach an explanation of how you would get your mailing list. Assume an enclosure sheet with details and picture.

(*b*)   Sell the Firefly (preceding case) to hardware dealers in quantity at $4—as the manufacturer (Outdoors Specialties, 6340 South Jefferson, St. Louis, MO 63166) which also supplies Holiday House. Assume the enclosure.

(*c*)   As your teacher directs, writing from Holiday House or the manufacturer, sell the electric charcoal starter mentioned (preceding two cases) to appropriate mailing lists, assuming appropriate enclosures. It's a loop-like heating rod on cool wooden handle; 6-foot cord; uses 110 volt current; runs ten minutes. Then fire spreads in 30 minutes (or with blower in 10). No kindling or messy liquid starter required; hence no danger, objectionable odor, or chemical tastes in food.

24. Because of the high costs of cars and gasoline, your market analysts tell you that now is a good time to introduce your new Schwanz ten-speed, lightweight, Hillmaster bicycle to the public, especially to college students. Your Schwanz representative has gathered a fairly pure mailing list of University of Illinois students who do not own bikes by checking police department registration records against the new student directory. You need a letter introducing this latest design, racing-type bicycle to the students. Hillmasters come in a variety of colors and with a complete line of bicycle accessories (for all Schwanz bikes). The Schwanz Hillmaster costs $100 retail and can be purchased at Straight's Cycle Shop (804 West University Avenue). Although $100 is a good price for a 10-speed bike, most college students can't write a check for $100 immediately. Therefore, your action ending will ask them to show their interest by sending back the enclosed postcard that already has their names, addresses, and phone numbers. You will, in turn, forward the cards to your Schwanz dealer in Urbana (Straights). You supply the details about the bike.

25. For more sales-to-dealers situations, make appropriate modifications and sell the product listed in Cases 1, 2, 3, 4, 10, 16, 19, or 23 above.

26. For more cases in sales, see GS 1a–f in the following series.

THE GOLF SERIES (GS)

The following series of 39 cases involves 15 of the 17 chapters in the book (all but Chapters 14 and 15, on complete analytical reports). Their order as they come up in the book is (in Chapter 5) Cases GS 5, 6, 7, 16, 18, 21; (in Chapter 6) 17, 12, 25, 27, 30; (in Chapter 7) 19, 13, 14, 8, 10, 11, 9; (in Chapter 8) 1a–f, six cases; (in Chapters 9, 10) 31, 32, 33; (in Chapter 11) 4, 15, 20; (in Chapter 12) 28, 29; (in Chapter 13, 16) 3, 22, 24, 26; and (in Chapter 17) 2, 23, 34.

GS 1 (Sales—Chapter 8). You are the General Manager of Eagle Golf Company, 2800 Industrial Park, Fond du Lac, WI 54935, a medium-sized company manufacturing and selling golf equipment to golf course pro shops, sporting goods wholesalers and retailers, and discount stores and other mass merchandisers. Now Eagle is preparing to market a new golf ball, the Black Eagle, featuring a new patented liquid center that acts as an internal gyroscope to help keep the ball flying straight, a new oval cross-section rubber band wrapping that allows tighter wrapping than ever before (results in longer flight), and a new cover with aerodynamically designed dimples which help reduce slices and hooks. Your tests show the Black Eagle outperforms any ball presently on the market in distance of flight. In addition, Black Eagles come packaged in vacuum cans (three to a can) like tennis balls, ensuring that they reach the golfer factory-fresh and in peak condition for play. Suggested list prices are $7.50 a can or $26 for a box of four cans. The boxes come in cartons of 12 or 24 boxes. Black Eagle golf balls are to be sold only through golf course pro shops. You give 40 percent off to licensed pro shops and 55 percent off to recognized jobbers and wholesalers. Good advertising support (regularly scheduled advertisements in the leading golf magazines and selected sports magazines; Eagle's touring professionals will play and promote the Black Eagle).

(*a*) Write a letter to go to golf course pro shops soliciting orders for the Black Eagle golf ball.

(*b*) Write a sales letter to go to members of the PGA (Professional Golfers' Association) and the LPGA (Ladies' Professional Golf Association) telling them about your revolutionary new golf ball and inviting them to ask for a free can of three (they must furnish you their professional registration number).

(*c*) Write a letter to go to 18,000 leading amateur golfers around the country, telling them about the Black Eagle and suggesting that they buy the balls from their golf pro.

(*d*) Write a sales letter to sporting goods wholesalers, the companies who distribute sporting goods of all types to the thousands of small sporting goods stores. Sell them on carrying your new golf ball (to protect the pro shops, you have given the Black Eagle another name for marketing through sporting goods channels: "Par Straight"). Prices and packaging of the Par Straight are the same as for the Black Eagle. Minimum order is six cartons of 12 boxes, or six gross of balls.

(*e*) Write a sales letter to sporting goods retailers, which include the large sporting goods chains. Sell them the Par Straight. To buy direct from you, they must order at least six cartons of 12 boxes each (six gross of balls); this earns the 55 percent discount. Otherwise they can order in smaller quantities from their wholesalers at the 40 percent discount. Your standard terms apply to approved open accounts: 2 percent if your invoice is paid in 10 days, the net amount of the invoice is due within 30 days. All others must send a check with the order or accept shipment c.o.d.

(*f*) For discount stores and other mass merchandisers you are writing to, you give yet a third name to your new golf ball, "Red Lion." In its guise as the Red Lion, your golf ball is the same as the Black Eagle; but it does not come in the vacuum cans. You package them in the conventional cardboard and cellophane boxes, three balls to a box, four boxes to a dozen balls, 12 or 24 boxes of a dozen to a carton. Minimum order is six cartons, which earns a 40 percent discount off the suggested retail prices of $2 per ball, $5.50 per box of three, and $20 per box of 12. An order of 12 gross of balls earns 50 percent off list, and an order of 18 or more gross of balls earns the maximum discount of 60 percent.

GS 2 (Oral communication case—Chapter 17). Coincidental with the introduction of the Black Eagle golf ball to the golfing world, Ralph Nestor, the president of Eagle Golf Company, has called in Eagle's sales representatives from all over the country for a sales meeting. As general manager you have to make the presentation of the new ball to the sales reps. Since you want to get the reps as excited as possible about this hot new item, use all the audiovisual aids your circumstances permit. (You can get additional information about golf balls and the sport from magazines like *Golf Magazine* and *Golf Digest*, sold on most newsstands.)

GS 3 (Informative memorandum—Chapter 16). Write a memo to go to all the department heads at Eagle Golf Co., copy to the president. Outline the channels of distribution for your new golf ball (see Case GS 1 for the basic data). Explain why each channel is to work the way it is and the results you hope to get. Be as specific and realistic as you can when you add details.

GS 4 (Persuasive request—Chapter 11). PGA and LPGA have just released their lists of new golf professionals, those who have finished their apprenticeships. Persuade them to sign contracts with Eagle as "Pro Users" of the Black Eagle Golf Ball. They receive 36 balls to start with and 12 balls per month for the year of the contract. In addition, they will receive 12 more balls for each tournament they play in during the year. Make sure they do not confuse this with an offer to fully sponsor them. Your fully sponsored professionals receive annual retainers, just about all the free equipment they want, and expense money for tournaments, all in return for promoting your products. At best, you can only hold out the wraith of a hope to these new pros that someday they might achieve full sponsorship . . . after they prove themselves winners. Since new pros are inundated by offers of all sorts, you'll have to exert yourself to get and hold their attention in your letter.

GS 5 (**Favorable reply with no possibility of a sale**—Chapter 5). Reply to Howard Nieberg, Bishop Hall, St. Benedict University, Peotone, IL 60468, who is investigating recent changes in golf marketing for his Master's thesis. He wants your sales volumes of balls, tees, and golf clubs for the past 15 years, and any comments you might care to make about growth and reduction of various sectors of the golf market. You have the sales volume data he wants; it's just a matter of retrieving it from your computer. Make what comments you can, being realistic. What else might you send him?

GS 6 (**Favorable reply with possibility of a sale**—Chapter 5). One of the happier aspects of your job is receiving and acting on inquiries like the following. Personally You, Inc., 4220 Abram Court, San Leandro, CA 94577, is a mail-order seller of products personalized with its customers' names. The president, Pauline M. Saunders, wants to know if you can supply your new Par Straight golf ball in lots of one dozen, imprinted with her customers' names, which she will supply. She will order 12 lots at a time to be shipped to her. You will be glad to sell balls to Personally You, but you can't imprint them—no facilities. However, you have done business with Sneddon Press, P.O. Box 200, Oconto Falls, WI 54154, which is reliable. Saunders can make arrangements with Sneddon, and you can ship balls there as required, billing her. But, and it's a big *but*, what about packaging? You can't, at any reasonable cost, get balls imprinted with customer names back from Sneddon, keep them straight, can them, and mark each can for the name on the balls inside. Will she settle for your conventional but attractive cardboard-and-plastic box packaging? You can ship balls in bulk to Sneddon and supply the packaging folded flat for a real saving in shipping. Sneddon can imprint and then complete putting the balls in the boxes.

GS 7 (**Order acknowledgment**—Chapter 5). Orders are coming in now from pro shops for the Black Eagle ball. Draft a form letter to go to shops that order the balls for the first time. Fill-in inside address, salutation, and personalizing. Thank the shop for the order. Resell the ball and Eagle Golf Company. Sales promotion: Tufftee, your flexible plastic tees available in silver, gold, red, blue, and yellow. Expensive, but won't break like wood tees. Won't hurt balls or clubs. Packaged six to a plastic holder. Suggested retail is $2.50 per holder. Packed 12 holders to a carton. Minimum order is one carton ($30). Offer a sample tee on request, but try also for the more desirable (for you) order.

GS 8 (**Acknowledging an incomplete order**—Chapter 7). Robert S. Kowalski, golf professional at Sandy Greens Golf and Country Club, Route 1, Potlatch, ID 83855, ordered three 12-box cartons of Black Eagle golf balls, one carton of Tufftees, two dozen golf towels in assorted colors, and 12 sets of four vinyl wood covers (6 black, 3 blue, and 3 red). Your sales representative in Idaho considers Sandy Greens to be a most important account and wants its first order handled with kid gloves. Find out whether Kowalski wants the 100 percent cotton golf towels (retail $3.95 each) or the 60% Dacron/40% cotton towels (retail $3.50 each). The vinyl covers for woods come numbered 1–2–3–4, 1–2–3–5, 1–3–4–5; how many sets of each number arrangement does he want? His credit has been approved, with an initial limit of $2,500.

GS 9 (Selling a substitute—Chapter 7). You have an order from John Melisinas, manager of the pro shop at Prairie Country Club, P.O. Box 12390, Wichita, KS 67277. You shipped all he ordered except the mesh-back Handi-Par golf gloves in assorted sizes and colors. You have switched to all-vinyl construction instead of the former vinyl palm and fingers with a mesh back, and from a snap closure to a Velcro closure. New glove is less likely to stretch out of shape than the old design. Velcro closure is almost infinitely adjustable, unlike the snap closure. Overall, the new glove lasts longer, better helps golfer keep all-important control during swing. List price of $7.95 for the new glove is 50 cents more than for the old mesh-back model. Sell Melisinas on switching.

GS 10 (Back-ordering—Chapter 7). Norman Fredrickson is the golf buyer for a chain of 14 sporting goods stores (Hunt's Sporting Goods) headquartered at 9788 E. 55th Pl., Tulsa, OK 74145. He just ordered 360 "Pro Hold" vinyl golf bags from you, in assorted colors. Your Pro Hold bags feature Eagle's unique molded bottom cup, specially designed and reinforced to take the abuse of golf cart use. Right now the company that molds these cups is hit by a strike and is shut down, but advises that it should all be over in two weeks and Eagle's order will then receive priority. Altogether, this means about a three-week delay in getting the bags to Hunt's. Can you hold this big order?

GS 11 (Declining an order—Chapter 7). Empire Sports Shop, 6741 Midway Blvd., Broomfield, CO 80020, ordered one carton of 12 boxes (one gross) of Par Straight golf balls. Empire must order six gross from you to qualify to order direct and get the 40 percent discount. Further, you have no credit information on Empire, so cannot give credit. Best Empire order from its usual wholesale sources until it can meet the minimum order requirements. Rocky Mountain Distributors in Denver handles Par Straight balls; suggest Rocky Mountain to Empire. Resale: broad line of Eagle products, long reputation for innovation and quality. Sales promotion: any product described in this series of cases.

GS 12 (Conveying sympathy—Chapter 6). Mary Holland was a co-founder of Heckel and Holland, successful sporting goods wholesalers located at 400 Washington St., Billings, MO 65610, and one of the first women to break into the once all-male sporting goods business. Furthermore, she early showed the good judgment to take on and sell Eagle Golf's products. You have known Holland for years, met her repeatedly at trade shows and conventions. She died last week. Write a letter of sympathy to her partner, Carl Heckel.

GS 13 (Requesting credit information from a customer—Chapter 7). In the morning's mail came an order from American Golf Center, 770 Burr Oak, Westmont, IL 60559, a specialty golf shop. The proprietor, Richard Beulich, wants you to bill this, his first order, on credit. You cannot readily obtain any credit information on his store. Ask Beulich for the names of at least three firms in the sporting goods field from whom he has bought on credit. Though you cannot ship on credit until he has established some credit, keep this order and keep American Golf Center as a customer.

GS 14 (Credit refusal—Chapter 7). A few days later (see Case GS 13) you receive Beulich's single credit reference. Although it checks out, you must have three good credit references before you can be reasonably expected to ship goods on credit. So you'll have to tell Beulich that until he can come up with more substantial credit references, you can ship to him only c.w.o. (cash with order) or c.o.d. (collect on delivery). Sit down, have a cup of coffee, and find a way to do this and still keep American Golf Center as a customer.

GS 15 (Persuasive request for credit—Chapter 11). Now suppose that you are Richard Beulich, owner of American Golf Center (Cases GS 13 and 14). That credit refusal was certainly a gentle one. Maybe Eagle Golf Company just doesn't understand your peculiar situation. After all, you're new, been in business for only a few months, not long enough to establish much credit. Your personal credit is excellent, though. And you think you have sufficient capital to go into this business or you wouldn't have opened it up. Credit has to start somewhere—someone has to take the first step and trust you. You really need Eagle Golf products for your store, etc., etc. See if you can't get Eagle to bill that order on credit after all.

GS 16 (Credit approval—Chapter 5). That (Cases GS 13, 14 and 15) was a pretty persuasive letter Beulich sent you. How can you refuse? Write Dick (by now you're on a first name basis with Beulich) and grant him credit. His goods are on their way. For the time being you will limit American Golf Center to $800 credit, spell out your terms (2/10, net 30, 1½ percent interest charged cumulatively monthly after 30 days, billing on the 10th of each month for purchases made up to the 30th of the preceding month, and so on). Sales promotion: blister pack of two dozen golf shoe spikes with a combination spike wrench/spike cleaner; suggested retail price is $2.95; it's a fast-moving item; comes 12 blister packs to a carton (which unfolds into a counter display box); packs are also punched for pegboard display.

GS 17 (Letter giving praise—Chapter 6). Write an informal letter to Max Missner, Vice President for Marketing, Custom Golf Equipment, 7241 W. Madison, Forest Park, IL 60130, congratulating him on completing his year as president of the Golf Equipment Manufacturers' and Wholesalers' Association. GEMWA has had a good year, the annual meeting at the National Sporting Goods Show was successful, etc., etc. Add details as necessary, but be careful to be realistic.

GS 18 (Direct claim—Chapter 5). You are a "weekend golfer," and you are unhappy. Just a month ago you purchased a set of Eagle Golf Company "Red Diamond" irons from a local sporting goods store. Saturday, only the third time you had played with the irons, the shaft on the six iron bent badly. You expected rather longer life from the irons than this—the six iron is beyond repair. You sent in the warranty card when you purchased the clubs, and they should still be under warranty. Send the bent club to Eagle along with your claim. What exactly do you want Eagle to do?

GS 19 (Adjustment refusal—Chapter 7). As general manager of Eagle Golf Company, you get to answer the unhappy golfer's complaint (Case GS 18). You get to since you are going to refuse the claim. The head of the club is bent back on the shaft, indicating that the club was hit into something solid, like the ground, a tree root, or something of the sort, and hard enough to severely bend the club. You warrant your clubs to be free of any defects resulting from materials or workmanship, but not from damage resulting from misuse. Can you refuse the claim and do it in such a manner that this customer won't "bad mouth" you to all his or her golfing friends?

GS 20 (Persuasive claim—Chapter 11). Put yourself back in the shoes of the golfer with the bent six iron (Cases GS 18 and 19). If Eagle Golf Company won't respond to a normal claim, you'll just have to get persuasive about it. As a basic appeal you might point out to Eagle that golf courses are full of hazards, nobody's perfect (even the best golfers dub a shot now and then), if Eagle sells clubs through sporting goods stores it can hardly expect them to wind up in the hands of excellent golfers all the time, and so on. Marshal your arguments cogently and logically, and tell Eagle how to revive your faith in the clubs.

GS 21 (**Adjustment approval—Chapter 5**). The unhappy golfer's persuasive claim (Cases GS 18, 19 and 20) may not be entirely watertight but does make some valid points. Tell the customer that you are sending a replacement six iron. Furthermore, as a result of the claim, you are beginning an investigation of the trouble with an eye toward improving the abuse resistance of Eagle's golf clubs.

GS 22 (**Meeting memo—Chapter 16**). To Department Heads: Marketing, Research and Development, Engineering, and Manufacturing. Briefly review the problem in Cases GS 18–21 and schedule a meeting to discuss what can be done. Be specific about agenda, time, place, etc.

GS 23 (**Oral exercise—Chapter 17**). Set up a group meeting with students playing the roles of the department heads (Case GS 22). Keep in mind that in real life, each department would be likely to expend its initial energies in face-saving (remember the adage, "It's not whether you win or lose but how you place the blame."). This is the kind of behavior that will have to be overcome before you can expect any results from the meeting. Discuss the six-iron problem. The student taking the part of the general manager will lead the meeting.

GS 24 (**Interoffice memo—Chapter 16**). Assume the meeting (Case GS 23) was held. Realistically estimate the outcome of the meeting: More research and development? Better engineering? More careful quality control in manufacturing? Better materials purchased? Change in warranty? Whatever? You decide, and then write a memo to the department heads of finance and accounting, purchasing, and legal. Inform them, bearing in mind that they will be all too aware that they were not invited to the meeting. Think this one out carefully; poor handling of the situation could dislocate a lot of nose joints, with all the resultant ill feelings and bad effects on the company's operations.

GS 25 (**Expressing appreciation—Chapter 6**). As the Georgia-Florida sales representative for Eagle Golf Company, write to A. V. Sosin, Sports Buyer, Palmetto Family Stores, 201 Castlewood Rd., North Palm Beach, FL 33048, thanking Sosin for seeing you last week and attentively listening to your presentation on Eagle's Par Trot golf shoes for men and women. Naturally you may want to remind Sosin about Par Trot shoes' high-grade leather uppers, up-to-date styling, patented Never-Loose spikes, foam comfort arches, availability in lace or buckle-over styles, and so on. Don't forget to ask for an order, since you didn't get one last week when you talked to Sosin.

GS 26 (**Interoffice memo—Chapter 16**). As general manager of Eagle Golf Company you review any correspondence a new sales representative writes during the first three months on the job. As a result, this beauty comes over your desk:

Mr. Alvin V. Sosin
Sports Buyer
Palmetto Family Stores
201 Castlewood Road
North Palm Beach, FL 33048

Thank you, Al, for one of the most enjoyable sales calls I've ever made. Even if I hadn't been able to tell you about our Par Trot Golf Shoes, meeting you would have made it well worthwhile.

That was really some lunch we had, wasn't it, Al? I swear I still felt those three martinis the next day! I'll never know how you were able to cope with your office work that afternoon since you weren't feeling any more pain than I was!

As I said, Al, I'll be in North Palm Beach again July 18, and I'm eager to take you up on your invitation: do you really think we can make all the bars on Atlantic Avenue in one night? If you can get away from the little woman, we can sure try. I'm looking forward to really tying one on with you, Al.

Regards,

Eric Nelson
Sales Representative

In his youth and eagerness, Eric has committed an unpardonable blunder. Point out to him in a confidential memo just how much trouble his letter could cause Sosin should others read it. Give Nelson a good dressing down, but try not to break his spirit or scare him into being an ineffectual salesman. He should indeed attempt to get on a personal, friendly basis with his customers but must learn not to overdo it. Should he write an apology to Sosin?

GS 27 (Letter of apology—Chapter 6). Whether or not Nelson should write a letter of apology to Sosin (Case GS 26) would depend in real life on the company's way of doing business, and on Nelson and Sosin. For the purpose of this case, assume Nelson should apologize to Sosin for his letter. Write the apology for Nelson.

GS 28 (Collection appeal—Chapter 12). After seven months of paying his bills on time, and having his credit limit raised to $2,000, Richard Beulich (Cases GS 13–16) missed payment of his July invoice and is now overdue on August as well. Reminders and an inquiry have gone out, but to no avail. Write a collection appeal to Dick. You choose the appeal to use.

GS 29 (Urgency collection—Chapter 12). The collection appeal (Case

GS 28) prompted no answer. As you might expect, Beulich has not ordered anything since he got behind. Now write him an urgency collection letter. Can you get the money he owes and still keep him a customer?

GS 30 (Letter anticipating resistance—Chapter 6). Price rise coming on Black Eagle (and Par Straight and Red Lion) golf balls. New suggested retail prices will be $8 a can of three, $27.75 a box of four cans (12 balls). Reasons: increased labor costs, higher utility bills, more expensive production machinery, high raw materials, etc., etc. Be specific and realistic. Set this letter up for word processing or as a full form letter as directed. Signature will be that of the president of Eagle Golf Company.

GS 31 (Invited application—Chapter 10). Assume you are you, and you have seen a job you want listed in an advertisement by Eagle Golf Company. (Pick an ad from the classified section of a newspaper, the "Positions Available" section of *The Wall Street Journal,* or some other source for inspiration.) Write the invited application (make believe you're including a résumé). You can assume you are graduating from school or further advanced in your career, providing you remain realistic. New college graduates seldom attain vice presidencies!

GS 32 (Thank you letter—Chapter 10.) As a result of your application letter and résumé, you had an interview with the general manager of Eagle Golf Company, E. K. Shea, who told you the company would give you a decision in three weeks. Write to Shea, say thank you for the interview, and use the information about Eagle contained in this series of cases for specific things you can refer to.

GS 33 (Resignation—Chapter 10). Eagle Golf Company has hired you! Now write a resignation to your present employer, Kim Williams, President, Golf Plus, Inc., 3110 N.E. 65th St., Vancouver, WA 98663. Tell (be realistic) about your new job, and resign without burning any bridges behind you.

GS 34 (Oral exercise—Chapter 17). It's annual meeting time and all the executives and sales representatives of Eagle Golf Company have assembled, along with middle management and the scientific types, to discuss plans for the next year. Unexpectedly (or not, as your instructor specifies), your superior calls on you as a new employee of the company to get up in front, tell who you are, and give a short recital on your background, title, duties, and new ideas for the coming year. Do it.

| # Evaluating yourself and potential employers

UNLESS YOU ARE extremely fortunate (or unambitious), sometime in your life you will write letters to get work: summer jobs; jobs launching a career when you graduate; a change of jobs for more money, for a better location, for work that has greater appeal to you. . . .

And even if you never write such letters, the assurance and confidence from analyzing and realizing what you can do if you have to are good equipment for successful living. Too, from a practical standpoint the experience of job analyzing is essential preparation for interviewing—an inevitable part of the job-seeking procedure.

As in sales, when you seek work, you are selling; and as in any sales situation, you are simply marketing a product: your services. You market that product to prospects: business firms or other organizations which can use your services.

In some cases those firms make their needs known—through advertisements, word of mouth, placement agencies, or recruiting personnel. In these circumstances we call the application *invited*. In other cases firms do not make their needs known, so it's a case of *prospecting*. You'll find, then, that job-getting letters will be directly comparable to either the invited sales letter (Chapter 5) or the prospecting sales letter (Chapter 8). Both must convince someone of your ability and willingness to do something; the big difference between the two is in the approach.

Finding a job is a serious and very competitive business. If you are content to accept what life doles out to you, you will probably never write anything but invited application letters. But the *prospecting application* is the logical first choice for learning because you will write better applications of any type as a result of thorough analysis and writing of this kind. Moreover, in the job market the prospecting letter has these advantages over the invited:

—You have a greater choice of jobs and locations, including jobs not advertised.

—You don't have as much competition as for an advertised job, sometimes no competition, as when you create a job for yourself where none existed before.

—Often it is the only way for you to get the exact kind of work you want.

—You can pave the way for a better job a few years later after having gained some experience.

Of course you need to know what kind of work you want to do before you ask someone to let you do it. You may now know exactly what you want to do—that's fine! You may even know exactly the organization where you will seek employment and be thoroughly familiar with its products, operations, and policies. But if you don't know for sure, the following few pages will help you arrive at those important decisions.

And even if you *think* you know, you will profit from reading—and maybe revising your present plans. Life holds many changes, occupational as well as personal. In fact, the average American professional changes jobs every four years. One's goals at 30 often contrast sharply with those one had at 20. Many a job plum turns out to be a lemon. Columbia University even has a booming program for retooling college graduates who find, after a few years, that they don't like the career for which they first prepared.

Some of the reasons people give for changing jobs are that they want

—More prestige (bigger title), opportunity to advance, independence.

—Control over budgets, subordinates, work schedule.

—A bigger salary, new career, geographical location.

—More creative, challenging, mental/physical, or routine work.

—More/less excitement, pressure, travel, dealing with people, vacation time.

—Better fringe benefits, hours, office, or other working conditions.

—To own part of a business or follow a spouse.

—Less time to get to/from work.

For you, probably the most significant reason will be your ambition to get ahead: to assume more responsibility in work that is challenging and interesting and thus merits respect and prestige in the eyes of other people, with consequent increased financial returns.

The starting point in your thinking and planning, in any case, is yourself.

ANALYZING YOURSELF

If you are going to sell your services, you will do so on the basis of *what you can do* and *the kind of person you are*. Today we talk in terms of skills. What is your strongest skill, second strongest skill, third, fourth, . . . ? Your skills are marketable products and deserve careful analysis. The *education* you have, the *experience* you've had (which is not so important in many instances as college students assume it to be), and your *personal attitudes and attributes* are your qualifications which enable you to get along with and do something for someone by using the skills you've developed.

Early in your career, especially, attitudes and attributes may be the most important of the three. If you don't like a particular kind of work, you probably won't be successful in it. Of all the surveys of why people lose jobs, none has ever cited less than 80 percent attributable to personal maladjustments rather than inability to do the work.

Because your attitudes play such an important role in determining whether you will get the job you want, perhaps a good start in analyzing yourself is to consider reasons why some interviewed people are not hired. Professor Frank S. Endicott, long-time Director of Placement at Northwestern University, has given us the most frequent reasons (listed in order) from his survey of 153 companies. Because the list grows out of job interviewing, we have put it on p. 635.

No one but you can decide whether you will like a particular kind of job. Your like or dislike will be the result of such general considerations as whether you like to lead or to follow, whether you are an extrovert or an introvert, whether you prefer to work with products and things or with people and ideas, whether you are content to be indoors all your working hours or must get out and move around, whether you are responsible enough to schedule your own time or need regular hours under tight supervision, whether you want to work primarily for money or for prestige (social and professional respect and greater security can partially compensate for less money to some people). Certain kinds of work call for much traveling, entertaining after work hours, frequent contact with strangers, staying "dressed up" and "on call" physically and mentally; other kinds are just the opposite.

After you have had several years of work experience, you will know better under what conditions you work best and what kind of work you prefer. If you have yet to establish such preferences, the checklist on your abilities, skills, and interests may help you clarify your thinking about yourself (and at the same time give you some advice).

For most readers of this book, education is already a matter of record or soon will be. In some college or university you are laying a foundation

---

Checklist on Your Abilities, Skills, and Interests

1. Read the statements below and think before checking the one(s) which most accurately fit you.

   a. I prefer a job requiring: ___physical work; ___brain work; ___both.

   b. I would like to work: ___indoors; ___outdoors; ___both.

   c. I like to: ___work with things, tools, or equipment; ___work with people; ___work with ideas; ___work where I can think my own thoughts; ___work alone; ___work as part of a team; ___express my ideas; ___help others; ___see the results of my work; ___take on new duties; ___keep everything in good order; ___look for other jobs that need doing when my own work is finished; ___learn new things; ___fill requests fast and accurately; ___stay with a job until it is well done; ___keep a good appearance; ___do better than others performing the same work.

   d. I have: ___the ability to make friends easily; ___a good sense of humor; ___a strong sense of responsibility; ___a cheerful outlook.

   e. I am: ___energetic; ___a fast learner; ___good with words; ___good with figures; ___good with my hands; ___accurate with details; ___easy to get along with; ___careful to follow directions; ___dependable and prompt; ___neat in work habits; ___cooperative with others; ___not a clock-watcher; ___willing to do extra work; ___self-disciplined; ___imaginative.

   f. I want to: ___obtain more training after work hours; ___move ahead on the job; ___make my own opportunities; ___do an outstanding job for my employers; ___contribute to the support of my family.

2. Write down about five courses in school (or other training) you liked best and/or disliked most.

3. List any nonacademic activities you particularly liked and any accomplishments that made you feel proud.

4. Jot down any kinds of tasks you have done well or really liked in the past—at home, school, military service, or elsewhere.

5. Write down, as best you remember, good things people have said about you.

of courses pointing to job performance in some selected field. While graduation is a certification of meeting certain time and proficiency standards, the individual courses and projects have taught you to do something and have shown you how to reason with judgment so that you can develop on the job. Unless you intend to forfeit much of the value of your training (which for most people who go through college represents an investment of $10,000–30,000), you will want to find work in the field of your major preparation.

Experience, likewise, is already partially a matter of record; you've held certain jobs or you haven't. Most employers look with greater favor on the person who has already demonstrated some good work habits and exhibited enough drive to work and earn than they do on the person who has held no jobs. But if you've never earned a dime, don't think your position is bleak or unique. Many employers prefer a less experienced person with vision, judgment, and a sense of responsibility to some experienced plodder with none. And as you know, many employers prefer to give employees their own brand of experience in training programs. When you are young, then, you sell hard your creativity and talent in lieu of the experience you have yet to obtain.

Regardless of your status, when you show that you understand and meet the requirements for the job, you have an effective substitute for experience. Furthermore, if you discard the kind of thinking that brands your education as "theoretical" or "academic," you will begin to realize that it is as down to earth as it can be. And that is true whether you have stressed cost accounting or a study of people and their environment.

But since you may still need to come to a vocational decision, because your learning may apply equally well in many different lines of business or industry, and because you probably don't know as much about job possibilities as you could (most folks don't), you'll do well to do some research.

To get some idea, you may want to read a description of job opportunities, requirements, and rewards concerning the kind of work you are considering. Publications like *Occupational Briefs* and other job-outlook pamphlets published by Science Research Associates (155 N. Wacker Drive, Chicago 60606), and the publication *Occupational Outlook Handbook*, put out by the Bureau of Labor Statistics assisted by the Veterans' Administration, will help you. If you check in *Readers' Guide, Applied Science & Technology Index*, and *Business Periodicals Index*, or *Public Affairs Information Service*, you may find leads to more recent publications.

You may want to consult some guidance agency for tests and counseling. Most institutions of higher learning have facilities for testing vocational aptitudes and interests, as well as intelligence, and they are often free. So do U.S. Employment Service offices and Veterans' Administration offices. And in practically any major city you can find a private agency which, for a fee, will help you in this way. Reading and talking with other people—professors, friends, parents—can help you, but only you can make the choice.

Having chosen the particular kind of work you want to do, you should make an organized search for those who can use your services.

SURVEYING WORK OPPORTUNITIES

If you are dead sure that you have chosen the right kind of work and the right organization, that the firm of your choice will hire you, and that both of you will be happy ever after, this discussion is not for you.

Most job seekers, however, are better off to keep abreast of current developments as signs of potential trends in lines of employment and specific companies.

The publications of Science Research Associates (already referred to) give business and employment trends that can help you decide whether you are going to have much or little competition in a given line of work (as well as what is expected of you and approximately how far you can expect to go). The annual Market Data and Directory issue of *Industrial Marketing* and Standard and Poor's industry surveys analyze major industries, with comments on their current positions in the economy. (S&P also identifies outstanding firms in each field.) The *Dictionary of Occupational Titles* (U.S. Employment Service) and the *Occupational Outlook Handbook* help you to keep informed on vocational needs. (Our condensation on pp. 479–85 of the *Handbook* article, with projections to 1985, is a good starting point.) The special reports on individual fields which *Fortune* and *The Wall Street Journal* run from time to time are helpful also. And study of trade journals devoted to the field(s) in which you are interested can help you decide on a given kind of work.

Once you make that decision, you seek names of specific organizations which could use your services. You can find names of companies in *Career, The Annual Guide to Business Opportunities* (published by Career Publications, Incorporated, Cincinnati and New York), *The College Placement Annual*, Standard and Poor's manuals, Moody's manuals, and the Dow directories. Trade directories are also useful. If you are concerned with staying in a given location, the city directory—or even the classified section of the phone book—will be helpful. Even if there is no city directory, the local chamber of commerce and local banks can help you.

If willing to spend a little time, you can assemble a good list of prospects from reading business newspapers and magazines. When significant changes occur within a company—for example, a new plant, an addition to an already existing structure, a new product launched, a new research program instituted, a new or different advertising or distribution plan announced—some newspaper or magazine reports that information. Widely known and readily available sources of such information are *The Wall*

Street Journal and the business section of an outstanding newspaper in the region of your interest. *U.S. News & World Report* and *Business Week* (in their blue and yellow pages) give you outstanding developments; *Marketing Communications* summarizes what is happening in marketing.

Of special value are the thousands of trade magazines. No matter what field you are interested in, you can find a magazine directed to people in that field. The monthly *Business Publications* edition of Standard Rate & Data Service (SRDS) lists trade magazines by the fields they serve. If your library does not subscribe to SRDS, advertising agencies do, and a local one will probably be willing to give you an old copy or let you look at a current issue. Most trade magazines have student subscription rates (often free) and will also usually send a copy or two at no charge, or supply copies of specific articles. From such reading you can assemble a list of companies, the nature of each business, the location, and sometimes the names of key personnel.

Many large companies distribute pamphlets dealing with employment opportunities with the company and qualifications for them; all you have to do is write for one.

If you're interested in a corporation, frequently you can get a copy of its annual report from a business library in your locality. If not, you can get one by writing the company for it. The report will also often identify key personnel, one of whom may be the person you should direct your letter to.

Certainly other people can also help you. Teachers in the field of your interest and business people doing the same thing you want to do can make many good suggestions about qualifications, working conditions, opportunities, and business firms. Before taking their time, however, you should do some investigating on your own.

ANALYZING COMPANIES

The more you can find out about an organization, the better you can write specifically about how your preparation fits its needs. And remember, that's what you have to do in a successful application—*show that you can render service which fits somebody's need.*

For that matter, even if you are fortunate enough to have interviews arranged for you, you'll want to find out all you can about the company. Look into its history, financial and organizational structure, home office and other geographical locations; relative size in the industry (number of plants and/or other operations; array of product lines and services); growth picture (sales for the past five years; potential for new markets, products, or services; competition; growth in per-share earnings and stock prices); and the corporation as an employer (ages of top managers, typical career paths in your field, nature of developmental training, average time in nonmanagement assignments, relocation policies, pay scales and—often more important—fringe benefits like medical and life insurance, stock-purchasing plans, tax shelters, and retirement benefits).

Probably the best source of such information—and the easiest for you to obtain—is the annual report. Most annual reports summarize the year's overall activities in terms of products, employment, sales, stockholders, management conditions affecting the industry and the company (including governmental activities), and a wide range of other topics. Careful reading of the last five years' annual reports will make you well informed on almost any company. Or you might learn even more from reading a company's Form 10-K.

Standard and Poor's manuals and Moody's manuals summarize history, operations (including products or services, number of employees, and number of plants), and financial structure. These are usually available at stockbrokers' offices as well as libraries.

If you can't find the needed information in sources like these, you may be lucky enough to find it in some magazine. *The Wall Street Journal* is a basic source (see its index); and *Fortune,* for example, has published many extensive articles about specific companies. *Time* does regularly. Indexes—*Readers' Guide, Applied Science and Technology, Business Periodicals, Public Affairs Information Service*—may show you where you can find such an article.

We have mentioned trade magazines as a basic way of learning about the field you are interested in. Another source you should investigate is associations in that field. Such trade associations abound, and they are the medium for exchanging information about new developments, who's who and where, and who has job openings or is looking for a new position. If you have pretty definitely settled on the field you want to work in, you can do some invaluable spade work by joining the appropriate trade association, especially if you are still in school. Most associations welcome student members (often at reduced dues); and many run matchmaker services to get employers and prospective employees together. You can find the one you want in *National Trade and Professional Associations of the U.S. and Canada.*

If you want to get a head start on your competition, tell the officers of the association you want to get involved actively, perhaps by working on some committee. Associations need *active* members, and you are pretty sure to be welcomed with open arms. Such association work is generally not too demanding and will have the immediate benefit of giving you information useful in pursuing your major. But most important, people working with companies will get to know you, and they can provide entrée to job opportunities you might otherwise not learn about—and may serve as references.

From whatever source you can find, learn as much as you can about what the company does, how it markets its products or services, the trends at work for and against it, its financial position, its employment record, what kind of employees it needs and what it requires of them—plus anything else you can.

FITTING YOUR QUALIFICATIONS TO JOB REQUIREMENTS

Actually what you are doing when you analyze yourself in terms of a job is running two columns of answers. What do they want? What do I have?

The answers to both questions lie in three categories: personal attitudes and attributes, education, and experience—but not ordinarily in that order of presentation! In fact, as explained in greater detail in the section "Compiling the Résumé or Data Sheet" (pp. 321–44), you will put yourself in a *more favorable light if you follow an order emphasizing your most favorable important qualification in the light of job requirements. This rarely means little personal details like age, weight, and height. But remember that desirable attitudes and personal traits and habits are basic equipment in any employee (and for writing a good application). Without them, no amount of education and/or experience will enable you to advance in a job, even if you are lucky enough to get it.*

One way to maximize the benefits of your personal traits, education, and experience in preparing your résumé (and preparing for an interview) is to write for yourself an autobiographical sketch, starting with your earliest years. Tell about where you grew up, your parents, your interests, hobbies, and how they changed over the years; about your hopes, goals, satisfactions, your feelings regarding remembered events and situations, and about "special" people you remember and how and why you remember them. Account for your early work experience, school experience, and (if any) military experience. Write down your reasons for your college choice and curriculum interest. Try to formulate your career and personal goals. Try to recall dates and organize your autobiographical sketch for clear continuity.

Most of this material will not, and should not, appear in your résumé. You will distill the essence of the content into a one- or two-page summary which is effectively a summary of you, now! Preparing that summary can stand you in good stead if an interviewer asks you, a week or so later, what many of them do ask—"Tell me a little about yourself" or "Tell me your life story in two minutes." You will know how to stress attitudes and interests, education, experience, and goals.

The right work attitude

A company, other organization, or individual puts you on a payroll because you give evidence of being able and willing to perform some useful *service*. That means work. The simplest, easiest, and most effective way to think, talk, and write about work is in terms of doing something for someone. The only way you'll convince someone that you can do something is first to realize that you're going to have to be able and willing to produce; that hard work is honorable; that recognition in the form of more pay, more benefits, and flexible hours comes only after demonstrated ability; that you have to be as concerned with *giving* as you are with *getting*, and that you have to give more than you get, especially at first; that you know you can learn more than you already know, and are willing to in order to grow on the job; and that glibness does not cover incompetence or poor work habits—not for very long, at any rate.

The only way you can earn the right to stay on a payroll is to give an honest day's work and to give it ungrudgingly. That means punctuality, reliability, honesty, willingness, cheerfulness, adaptability, leadership, and cooperativeness.

Without a desirable outlook toward work and the conditions under which it must be carried on, competence can be a secondary consideration. Before you can ever demonstrate competence, you have to gain the approval of other people. You can be good, but if you don't get along well with people, your superior abilities won't be recognized. Even if recognized, they won't be rewarded.

You can be very good, but if you indicate that you think you are, you're going to be marked down as vain and pompous. One of the most frequent criticisms of college graduates is that they have overinflated ideas of their abilities and worth. Of course, if you don't respect your own abilities, no one else is likely to either. The key is to recognize you can do something because you've prepared yourself to do it, that you have the right mental attitude for doing it under normal business conditions, that you believe you can do it, and that you want to.

Confidence in yourself is essential, but so are reasonable humility and modesty. You can achieve a successful balance if you imply both in a specific interpretation of how your education, experience, *and disposition* equip you to perform job duties.

Specific adaptation of personal qualities

The work-for-you attitude in an adaptation implying confidence in yourself is basic in any application. The value of some other attitudes or personal qualities depends on the particular circumstance. Affability, for instance, is highly desirable for work in which a person deals primarily with people (saleswork, for example); it is not so significant in the makeup of a statistician or a corporation accountant. Accuracy is more to the point for them, as it is for architects and engineers. Punctuality, while desirable in all things and people, is more necessary for public accountants than for personnel workers; for them, patience is more important. While a sales-person needs to be cheerful, a sales analyst must be endowed with perseverance (although each needs a measure of both). Certainly in any position involving responsibility, the candidate for the job would want to select details from personal experience which would bear out the necessary virtues of honesty as well as accuracy.

While all virtues are desirable—and truth, honor, trustworthiness, and cheerfulness are expected in most employees—a virtue in one circumstance may be an undesirable characteristic in another. Talkativeness, for example, is desirable for an interviewer seeking consumer reactions; the same talkativeness would be most undesirable in a credit investigator (who also does a considerable amount of interviewing). Both would need to inspire confidence.

Indeed, finding the right balance between self-confidence/aggressiveness and humility to sit well with the reader and the job (and reflecting it in style and content) is one of the hardest things about writing good applications. Most employers want neither a conceited, cocksure, overbold and uninhibited, pushy extrovert nor the opposite extreme. They do not want new employees to take over their own jobs in a few weeks, but they know that the meek do not exhibit the leadership needed in future managers either.

In analyzing any job, estimate what you think are the two or three most important personal characteristics and plan to incorporate evidence which will imply your possession of them. The reader will then likely assume the others. You can't successfully establish all the desirable ones. Besides, you have to show that your education and experience are adequate in selling yourself to a potential employer.

Enhancing your college preparation

With the desirable work-for-you attitude, you'll think in terms of job performance. If your reading has not given you a good idea of the duties you would be expected to perform on a particular job, you'll profitably spend some time talking with someone who has done the work and can tell you. You cannot hope to anticipate everything you might be called upon to do on a given job (nor would you want to talk about everything in your application); but if you anticipate some of the *major* job requirements and write about your studies in a way that shows you meet these requirements, you'll have enough material for conviction.

Although recruiting ads often stipulate a level of academic attainment, your academic status (units of credit) or a diploma is not what enables you to perform a useful service. *What you learned in earning them does.* To satisfy the arbitrary advertised requirement, you'll need to establish quickly your graduation (or whatever the requirement is). But the *pri-*

mary emphasis in your presentation needs to go on those phases of your education which most directly and specifically equip you for the work under consideration.

Similarly, in planning your application (but not in writing it), you should list, as specifically as you can, job duties you can be reasonably sure you'll have to perform and, in a parallel column, the background that gives evidence of your ability to do them.

An applicant for work in a public accounting firm knows that the job requires analyzing financial data, preparing working papers, assembling financial statements, and presenting a report with interpretive comments. The direct evidence of having learned to do these things is experience in having done those same things in advanced accounting courses and/or work experience. The applicant must also communicate findings intelligibly and easily to clients, and (as evidence of ability to do so) should cite training in report writing (and letter writing) as well as in speech. If the applicant assumes that pleasant relations with clients are a desirable point to stress, citing study of psychology and sociology might be useful.

A secretarial job-seeker appears more valuable by talking in terms of relieving a busy employer of much routine correspondence as a result of having studied business writing. Since the job would involve handling callers both face to face and on the telephone, the applicant should cite courses in speech and in office procedures too.

If you are interested in sales as a career, your specific work in direct selling (both oral and written), market analysis and research, advertising principles and practice, and report writing needs emphasis (along with any other specifically desirable preparation that you know about).

In all instances, applicants need to be selective, concentrating on that study which most nearly reflects the most advanced stage of preparation. For example, a person who cites evidence of training in market analysis and research will certainly have studied marketing principles. Similarly, the successful completion of an auditing course implies a background of beginning and intermediate principles of accounting. Careful selection of the most applicable courses precludes the necessity for listing qualifying courses and thus enables you to place desirable emphasis on the most significant.

Making the most of experience

Any job you've ever held that required you to perform some task, be responsible for successful completion of a project, oversee and account for activities of other people, or handle money is an activity you can cite with pride to a prospective employer. You may not have been paid for it; that doesn't matter a lot. The college student who directs a campus unit of the United Way drive gets a workout in organization, delegation of authority, persuasion, systemization, persistence, punctuality, responsibility, honesty, and accuracy that is good work experience. It is experience which is more valuable than that of the student who operates a supermarket cash register four hours a day—and nothing else, though that indicates experience in responsibility for money and customer relations. Especially if both students are aiming at managerial work or some kind of contact work, the one who has earned no pay but has had more experience working with people and assuming authority and responsibility is more desirable.

You may not have held the job for any length of time—maybe for only a summer or over the holidays or briefly part time while in school. But didn't you learn something that increased your ability to render service?

You may have held a job that does not appear to be related to the work you hope to do. The checker at the supermarket, for example, may have punched a way through college because that was the only way to pay for an education in marketing. But hasn't that person demonstrated vision, perseverance, accuracy, the ability to work under pressure, the willingness to be cheerful and polite to customers, and—if observant—had a good workout in interpreting consumer demand?

Even the person of limited experience can interpret it in relation to job requirements, giving the most significant part the emphasis of position. The most directly related phase of experience is the one most nearly preparing you to do something. For example, if the supermarket checker had also been a fraternity or sorority house treasurer (involving handling and accounting for money), an application for accounting work would want to emphasize the treasurer's duties over the checker's job; but, an application to do selling would make the checker's job more significant.

If you are fortunate enough to have a wide range of experience, your problem is simply one of picking and choosing and presenting (in an order of descending importance to the job sought). Chronology (a time sequence) rarely should be your governing choice at graduation. Later as an experienced employee changing companies, however, you might wisely elect to present job experience in chronological order (or the reverse), emphasizing progress to your present state of preparation. Such order-of-time presentation suggests a well-defined goal and success in attaining it.

Whatever experience you elect to present, you want to show as directly and specifically as possible that as a result of this experience you come equipped with the skills to do the job or at least to learn how quickly. The surest way to present this information about yourself in the *most favorable light is to describe past-experience job duties related to the job you're seeking.* You will strengthen your application if you interpret the experience to show what it taught you about important principles, techniques, and attitudes applicable to the hoped-for job. Evaluating work experience is the same as evaluating education; it's matching up as far as possible the answers to "What skills do I have?" with the requirements under "What do they want?"

You will rarely, if ever, meet all job requirements; and you will always have some points that are stronger than others. Outright lack of a specific point of preparation or below-average standard are negative points to be handled in the same manner that any good writer handles them: embedded position and corollary positive language.

Determining a favorable order of presentation

After you have listed the necessary and desirable qualifications for the job and your own specific preparation as defined by personal qualities, education, and experience, you will then need to decide on an order of presentation that is most favorable to you.

Most people get their jobs in the first place because of competence, not personal charm or good looks. While undesirable personal attributes and attitudes can keep you from getting the job of your choice (sometimes from getting *a* job!) and may result in your losing the job even if you fool someone and get it, good personality will not ordinarily get you the job unless you *first show ability to do the work.* Competence stems from good education or worthwhile experience, or a combination of the two that produces the needed skills.

If your strongest point is thorough preparation, that is what you want to start with; if it is experience, begin that way. And within each of these categories, arrange your qualifications so that the best comes first (as any good seller does).

Without telling your reader what they are (surely your reader knows them!), be sure to give evidence that you meet all important job requirements. And write your evidence *not* in the order it occurs to you, or even in an order of what you estimate is of greatest significance in the evaluation, but in an order that stresses your strong points.

For this comprehensive presentation, a résumé (often called data sheet or personal record sheet) is the preferred form.

COMPILING THE RÉSUMÉ OR DATA SHEET

We emphatically recommend that you prepare your résumé *before* you write your letter. Making the necessary self-analysis and job analysis helps you recognize your assets and truly see yourself realistically in relation to the job you want. Thus it can bring you back into alignment if you have swung too far up (overconfident) or too far down (in the dumps). Perhaps more important, organizing your data usually shows you what to stress in your letter, the problems of which we will discuss more fully in the next chapter.

The purpose of a résumé is *to help sell you to a prospective employer.* So remember that, because a company's job-application form isn't trying to sell you, you should avoid filling out one (if you can graciously) and write your own *selling* data sheet. (Even if you do have to fill one out, you can put down the necessary personal details and then write "see attached résumé" for the rest.) You will find that a well-prepared résumé can help you gain appointments for interviews and serve as a useful tool during interviews. If several people are to talk with you at the job location, send a copy for each to whoever arranges your schedule. You might even give copies to friends and relatives to hand to their associates where jobs might be available.

Your résumé can accompany either a prospecting or an invited application letter—and often serves to start off an interview under favorable conditions. It tells your complete story—the little details as well as the big points—thus *enabling your letter to be shorter and to concentrate on showing how the high spots of your personal qualities, education, and experience equip you to do good work.*

As one authority said, a résumé gives your life's history in two minutes, indicates your organizing and language ability, and leaves your letter free to sell. It is a tabulation of your qualifications, giving pertinent, specific details concerning your education and experience, and sometimes supplying the names, addresses, and telephone numbers of references who can (and will on request) verify what you say about yourself.

Since the data sheet must carry a wealth of detail and condense the material into a small amount of space, it follows good outlining principles and form. The best form is the one that enables you to make the most favorable presentation of your qualifications, attractively displayed and concisely stated. You need to use the space-saving devices of tabulation and noun phrases (rather than sentences and conventional paragraphs).

To facilitate rapid reading, you should use headings, differentiate type for the various classes of information, and observe uniform indentions for rows and columns of information. Parallel construction in phrasing requires special care. (If you stick to noun phrases, you'll eliminate your problems in this respect.)

Impersonal style, without opinions and comments, is usually best for this concise, basically factual presentation (but be careful not to fall into unnatural, stuffy, pompous phrasing).

Usually the desirable tabulation form will be in three to five parts.

First, you need a selling, identifying, and informative heading. Specifically, for selling quality, conciseness, and easy finding of necessary information, we suggest

(your name)'S QUALIFICATIONS FOR (kind of) WORK WITH
(company name)

Write the heading in solid capitals, centered or at the left margin, about an inch from the top (or wherever necessary for the best uncrowded placement on the page). If the line is too long, break it near evenly and double-space the parts. If you're going to use the same résumé for several applications, of course you'll have to omit the company name (and lose some favorable effect of individualizing and specific adaptation unless you use word processing equipment to type it in later). If you feel like using a favorable adjective—like *effective, successful,* or *helpful*—before the kind of work, go ahead. It can do a lot of selling for one word.

To get the necessary information of your address and telephone number (with ZIP and area codes) in for easy finding but without undue emphasis, we suggest putting it parenthetically, single-spaced and centered, under the heading or at the left margin. If some of an extended series of letters or calls might come when you are at different places (home versus school or office, for example), you might well give both, one to the left and one to the right, labeled and with dates if known.

Second, if you can express your career plans and goals clearly and concisely, consider whether to state your objective (job or career) in your résumé. Most employers like it as evidence that the applicant shows ambition and maturity by thinking and planning specifically for an upward course. Others fear that the plans may restrict the applicant's adaptability to company needs, though this is a questionable objection.

We suggest that you consider:

1. Using the subheading "Job Objective" (centered or at or in the left margin, like your other divisional heads) when using the company name in the heading and stating your objective clearly and concisely with specific adaptation to that one job. To do so you of course must know quite a bit about the company.
2. Using "Career Objective" when preparing a résumé for several different companies and stating your objective a little more broadly (but still clearly and concisely).

One very successful applicant, who knew the receiving company well, cut both ways with simply "Objective" as the head and a statement that fit specifically but also applied broadly:

```
To work in a marketing line or staff job.  To handle projects
and assignments concerned with the various aspects of marketing
and offering cross training into other major functional areas.
To gain additional business knowledge, experience, and judgment
necessary for advancement.
```

Your statement of job or career objectives should be specific enough to show that you know where you want to go. Too broad a statement like "I want to use my talents and abilities in the best manner to advance myself and my employer" will present a damaging appearance of immaturity or naiveté. For optimum effectiveness (if you can do it briefly enough), you might make your statement a summary or abstract of your qualities, experience, and accomplishments in terms of their benefit to the potential employer. By implying the jobs/titles you qualify for, it could help an organization immediately to match you to a job opening it may have.

Third, you need to make an important decision before putting down the next part (and most emphasized by position, so presumably most important). Traditionally company application forms used to ask, *first*, for name, address, and then lots of personal information. And some sheeplike authors of textbooks suggested "Personal Details" as the first major division. We never considered such information deserving of that emphatic position, even for some parts that were sometimes relevant to the job. Some company application forms went so far that one secretarial applicant answered "Yes" in the blank by *Neck* in the measurements section.

Relatively recent Civil Rights legislation, however, now prohibits prospective employers from considering most personal-details information—specifically race, religion, age, sex, marital and family status, and photographs—unless they can show job-justifying reasons. Of course no law prohibits you from volunteering such information; but if personnel people cannot consider it, it at least becomes useless. Even worse, because many of them are scared by some of the not-yet-court-tested legislation, some say they prefer not to have the information lest they be accused of using it. Our advice on the topic therefore boils down to three suggestions:

1. Generally do not include the questionable personal details.
2. When the nature of the job does make a piece of the information a valid (and hence legal) consideration, put it in. The worst anybody can do is throw it out.
3. Take security in the practice of the U.S. government itself. Since 1978 it has taken recourse in the job-justifying exception and has not only used some of the generally "outlawed" criteria in some of its hiring but has actually specified them in some job descriptions.

Most personal details—even when job-justified—never were appropriate in the emphatic first position, except possibly in applications like that of the would-be chorus girl whose 38–24–34 measurements properly went there because they were her most important qualification. Though use of such physical details, photos, and the like in résumés is decreasing because of EEO legislation, her information was legally usable because it was job-justified. In setting up her résumé that way, she also called attention to two good points which we can use: (1) decide what is your biggest asset (qualification for the job) and (2) put it in the emphatic position.

For most college students ready to go on the job market, their education is usually the deserving topic; and any experience can follow. For applicants with extensive related experience that would weigh heavier than their education, the reverse would be true.

In presenting your education, give the section a heading, perhaps with a favorable adjective like *professional* or *thorough*. You waste an opportunity to sell yourself by labeling it just "Education." Then give a clear total picture (beyond high school, or including it if something there was particularly pertinent to the job), with emphasis on the most relevant parts. Quickly establish the main area(s) of study, your status in the program—any degree(s) received or to be received (with dates)—and the institution(s). To highlight your specific preparation for a particular job, you might then list (with descriptive titles or following explanations) several especially pertinent courses—particularly if they were electives.

Don't, however, try to "snow" the reader with a long list of courses required for your degree. You will only be insulting and look stupid, for most business employers know pretty well what's required for degrees they're interested in. They also understand the concept of prerequisites; so don't list any beginning or principles (prerequisite) courses along with more advanced ones in the same area. After all, to have taken advanced courses you *must* have taken the basic courses first. Worth more would be a list of several less directly specialized courses that are useful and/or broadening. For instance a few good courses in statistics and business communication (letters, memos, reports—the topics of this text) would be helpful in almost any salaried business job—and any prospective employer knows that.

Whether you should indicate your grade average depends somewhat on the nature of the work but more on whether your record is favorable or unfavorable. Work as a clerk or at something where physical action is more important than mental effort may not require good grades (or usually pay much money); but good grades will count for any kind of management, professional, or technical work. Contrary to much student excuse-making and/or ego-stroking, solid statistical evidence shows that grades have a high positive correlation with success in all fields checked except two—politics and athletics. Business employers know that and act accordingly.

So if your grades are low, forget them and hope the interviewer does. If they're favorable, say so—in a clear way. Perhaps best is the A, B, C . . . system, because everybody understands it. Point averages, on the contrary, are often confusing. What most college people call a GPA (grade-point average), some call a QPA (quality-point average). Perhaps more confusing is that some schools use a five-point system, others a four, and others a three. As a consequence, reporting a QPA of 2.78 from a three-point school (pretty good) will cause a reader from a five-point GPA school to wonder (after figuring out the meaning of Q) how you graduated with that D+ average!

If you put education as the first major subdivision (after job or career objective), then experience (if any) will follow it—or (in some very rare cases) combine with it. For instance, a successful applicant to a college-textbook publisher for a job as book representative (getting professors to adopt company books) wisely used a double heading, "Education and Teaching Experience." The reason was that the only relevant experience (too little to deserve separate-section listing) was two years of part-time teaching of beginning courses while getting the MA.

Usually, however, experience appears as the *second* (or first if the more important) division of qualifications. Again, the single word should carry justifiable qualifiers. We've seen these in successful applications: "Work Experience Requiring Accuracy" (an accounting applicant); "Experience Working with People" (a public-relations applicant, who stressed extensive leadership roles in campus activities); and "Business Experience Requiring Accuracy and Judgment" (the mature marketing applicant whose objective you read earlier).

Then follows the work experience—usually in reverse chronological order, to stress the most recent, most advanced, and usually most relevant. Items to cover in each job listed are beginning and ending (inclusive) dates, job title, duties performed, and name and place of employer and name of immediate superior.

In this section particularly, remember that the less experience you have to list, the more important even seemingly irrelevant work experience is if it taught you anything (good work habits, dealing with people, . . .). Even small jobs like part-time work while in school can carry impact on the important points of leadership and honesty, for example, if you had responsibility for directing other people or handling money. Similarly, though mere membership in a campus organization amounts to little, election to and accomplishment in officer roles in campus activities show two desirable qualities: general approval by others and leadership.

Together the dates given for your education and experience should cover your life since high school. If not, an alert interviewer may wonder what you're hiding—and may ask, as one did, whether you spent some time in jail or the pen.

In describing your experience, you want to show potential employers progress in your accomplishments. Using reverse chronological order will put your last (and supposedly highest status) job at the beginning of the section. In setting down your experience, remember that while you can't change your record, you can (truthfully) change how you describe it.

When talking about any experience you have had, the key word is *responsibility*. Evidence that you have been responsible also implies honesty, maturity, punctuality, and a host of other virtues. You will be wise to use this word often as you write up your experience. Writing in noun phrases rather than in sentences will have the desirable effects of shortening your résumé while simultaneously making it clearer, more concise, and more effective:

```
    Tobias & Olendorf, Inc., 520 N. Michigan Ave.,
Chicago, IL 60611 (312/555-7575), 12/60-5/64. Responsible for
media research and internal traffic functions; later promoted
to copy contact on major accounts. Prepared marketing plans,
```

developed marketing research procedures, oversaw production and directed preparation of print, radio, and television advertising; supervised media scheduling; conceived, presented, and implemented improved reader/viewer response techniques.

Note the heavy use of action verbs that imply creative, managerial, and customer-relations work—*prepared, developed, oversaw, directed, supervised, conceived, presented,* and *implemented*. These are the kinds of words you should strive to use (but realistically) in talking about your experience. Not only will you present yourself in a good light, but consciously using such vocabulary will keep you thinking in terms of management, professionalism, creativity, and, most important, *doing*. To help you, here is a partial list of such words:

administered	developed	introduced	recruited
advanced	directed	invented	regulated
analyzed	discovered	judged	reshaped
applied	employed	launched	resolved
approved	enlarged	led	restored
arranged	established	managed	revised
assigned	evaluated	negotiated	scheduled
awarded	executed	opened	served
began	expanded	operated	settled
commanded	extended	ordered	shaped
conceived	governed	organized	solved
conducted	guided	originated	stabilized
controlled	handled	oversaw	started
coordinated	headed	planned	steered
corrected	implemented	prepared	straightened (out)
created	improved	produced	superintended
decided	inaugurated	progressed	supervised
delegated	increased	published	systematized
determined	initiated	ran	trained
designed	installed	raised	

The rest of your résumé (after education and experience) requires even more discretion.

For the last division, a list of about three references (people able and willing, on request, to write or talk evaluatively about you to interested prospective employers) has long been the standard recommendation—including ours. Some people now, however, are omitting the list and adding only "References gladly furnished upon request" (with or without the heading "References").

That practice may be wise if any or all of the following apply:

1. You do not want (*a*) your friends to be bothered or (*b*) your present employer to know that you are considering leaving (and hence you can't list what is probably your best reference).

2. You do not trust any important references you could list to say anything helpful about you.
3. You (*a*) are in no hurry to get a decision and (*b*) trust your application to interest the addressee(s) enough to take the extra time and trouble to get the references later from you.
4. You doubt that the prospective employer would ask the references anything.

If you're applying for a job of any importance, you're probably wrong if you think Item 4. You're hurting your chances if you think 3*b* and an unusual case if you think 3*a*. If 2 is right, you had better change your ways and earn a better reputation or some better friends. If 1*b* is right, you need to work especially hard to get a different job (and more fair-minded employer); and if 1*a* is right, you need to earn some true friends. Your references will not usually receive inquiries until your prospective employer is considerably interested in you; and true friends won't mind the bother of helping a friend.

From that reasoning, we conclude that generally you should list references—except possibly in extreme situations—and further reasoning only convinces us more strongly.

After all, the thinking of an employer considering a recent university graduate usually goes about like this. (1) I hope to get a good employee who will stay on the job a long time. (2) Counting the recruiting and training costs with the employee's salary and fringe benefits for 40 years (more or less), I would expect to spend over $1,000,000. (3) Wise decision making calls for me to get all the information I reasonably can to select a good employee worth the money. (4) That means getting information not only from the applicant but from other people (references).

Whether or not we've convinced you that you should list references on your résumé, you will need to make them available some time before getting an important job; so here are some helpful pointers:

1. Select three or four people who (at least collectively) know well your personality, your education, and your job performance.

2. The more accomplished or prominent they are (as shown by their titles), the better; but don't make the mistake of listing a corporation president who barely knows you instead of a low-level supervisor under whom you worked three years (or a professor or dean who knows you only from a one-term/once-a-week big-lecture group you attended instead of an assistant professor who taught you the three most important advanced courses in your major).

3. Avoid any reference who is biased. That rules out (except for very unusual circumstances) relatives, lovers, and associates only through social or church organizations. Employers used to want a "character" refer-

ence and often got a church official. Now they have pretty much dropped the idea of a special character reference because, as one personnel manager said (and the seven others on the panel agreed), "At my company we won't write a minister because those people won't tell the truth—and we want the truth, the good *and* the bad." They also agreed that the best references are former or present employers and teachers—who also do a better job of covering the character traits that are important. Try to get one who will write a specific, analytical letter like that on p. 112.

4. When you've settled on your best references, get their permission. That is not only the courteous thing to do (because you *are* asking a favor); but it gives you a chance to help them, the employer, and yourself by telling them the main criteria for the job (points to cover in their responses).

5. List your three references with names, titles, and addresses and telephone numbers (with ZIP and area codes and with indication that you have their permission). Unless other information in the résumé (such as a reference's title and address) at least implies the relationship with you (say former employer or teacher), make the relationship clear. No listed reference should cause an interviewer to wonder—as one did, and asked, "Who is this Joe Doakes—your father-in-law, who would take care of you to help his darling daughter?"

6. Then, to help your references do the best job for you, send each one a copy of your résumé.

Having finished with the content, organization, and style of your résumé, you still have some important considerations of its general and specific appearance before you put it on the final paper. Until you get an interview, it is your representative. Make sure it has a quality appearance—like you.

Naturally you will consider the quality of paper and type, the margins and line balance for good layout, and the form and spacing of the section and subsection headings.

The big question is whether to type each copy individually or type one and make many. The individually typed copy is the most effective for several reasons. Employers are about as proud and subject to jealousy as people courting. They all want to assume—even when knowing better—that you are particularly interested in them. Furthermore, you can put the employer's name in your heading and thus gain the favorable effects of individualizing and better adapting—things you can't do with a broadcast message.

A change of company name in the heading, and perhaps other minor changes, will adapt the résumé to any number of other applications for the same kind of job. Even when the kind of work changes, you can quickly reevaluate your qualifications and reorganize and rephrase in the light of circumstances—things you would not likely do if you had a pile of the same (generalized, or worse, misfitting) résumé copies.

As a practical matter, however, you may have to run off multiple copies —because you don't have time or money to type or have typed all the copies you need. In that case, never resort to messy carbons, photocopies, or mimeographed or dittoed copies. They're like birdshot, which won't get you deer-size jobs. Instead, to be sure your résumé represents you fairly, get the best reproduction you can afford—to look as near as possible like the original neatly typed copy.

Modern word processing equipment allows you to provide each prospect with what is in effect an individually prepared résumé. You can have your résumé recorded on equipment which will then type it out repeatedly, at high speed, stopping at designated points so that an operator can add, for example, the name of the company that copy of the résumé will go to.

In addition, some of the machines allow you to justify (even up) the right-hand margin if you wish. You will find companies with word processing and composing equipment in the Yellow Pages under "Cold Type Composition."

If you elect to have your résumé printed, do *not* type in the company name or anything else. You can never satisfactorily match a typewriter (even electric with a one-time carbon ribbon) to printed material, and such an attempt is more damaging when it misfires than any poor effects from a printed résumé.

The following five illustrations vary considerably in content and form. Study them thoughtfully. Notice how the varied illustrations all still follow closely the suggestions for form and content.

The first illustration (Figure 9–1) is perhaps the most typical for college undergraduates. By careful selection, concise phrasing, and good layout, Jane Chase put on one page, in specifically individualized wording, just about everything employers want in a résumé. Jane knew she was to have an interview with one of Andersen's representatives; so she took the time and trouble to tailor-make her résumé and included references.

Because Milton S. Delbridge (Figure 9–2) had no particularly pertinent course work outside the standard major, he led with his objective and skills experience. In contrast to Delbridge, Roberta Klein (Figure 9–3) had a great deal to report. Earl Bostany, on the other hand, used a simplistic presentation with side heads and told less about himself (or perhaps had less to tell). (See Figure 9–4.)

The fifth résumé is a special situation. The applicant was a little older, more educated, and more experienced. Moreover, he was shooting for (and got) bigger game. He had a job and wanted a better one. He felt that the companies should know how old he was, his marital status, interests, memberships, and physical characteristics. Both companies he wrote were pleased with his individualized (tailored) résumé. He received two job offers and increased his salary by 25 percent. Yes, his résumés took time, but they brought the results he wanted. (See Figure 9–5.)

FIGURE 9–1   *9 / Evaluating yourself and potential employers*   **331**

JANE CHASE'S QUALIFICATIONS FOR

MANAGEMENT ACCOUNTING WORK WITH ARTHUR ANDERSEN, INC.

(P.O. Box 3815, University City, State ZIP, Phone: 305/555-0500)

Objectives

To work at an accounting or accounting-related job. To gain knowledge in other areas of business and to gain the experience necessary for advancement.

Thorough College Training

B.S. in Business Administration, major in accounting and minor in economics in the School of Commerce at State University. Expected graduation, August 2, 1980. "B" average in accounting courses and also the following courses important in all areas of business:

Report Writing   Business Statistics

Business Law   Marketing

Computer Science   Business Letters and Memos

Work Experience
(Paid 100% of college expenses)

1978 to present — Work with Potter and Bryant, CPA, as an assistant in preparing tax statements.

1974-1978 — Four years with Blue Mill Restaurant. Responsible for the kitchen and food preparation areas, maintained inventory, ordered products.

1973-1974 — Worked at Bruno's Supermarket as a stocker.

JANE CHASE'S QUALIFICATIONS, PAGE 2

Activities/Honors/Awards

College: Alpha Lambda Delta, first-year honorary

Beta Gamma Sigma, business academic honorary

Beta Alpha Psi, accounting honorary

Blood Drive, TB Detection Drive, Homecoming Committee

High School: Vice President of Senior Class

References (by permission)

Ms. Carol Bryant, CPA

Potter and Bryant, Accountants

706 First National Bank Building

Central City, State ZIP

Phone: (305) 555-3680

Dr. Joseph P. Bane

Professor of Accounting

State University

University City, State ZIP

Phone: (305) 555-4300, Ext. 845

Mr. Max Evans

Blue Mill Restaurant

900 University Avenue

University City, State ZIP

Phone: (305) 555-1770

MILTON S. DELBRIDGE

Post Office Box 1234, Main City, State ZIP — (325) 555-5678

OBJECTIVE

Writing/Editing — aiming for employment where a strong sense of responsibility, strong technical skills, and willingness to learn and grow are valued characteristics.

SKILLS, EXPERIENCE, AND ACCOMPLISHMENTS

Writing/Editing — Staff writer for independent weekly newspaper, writer for college newspaper, editor of high school yearbook.

Reviews — Reviewer of concerts, movies, television (reviews for the newspaper, class assignments).

Public Relations — Publicity Chairman for fraternity; active in 1980 Presidential campaign.

Copywriting — Advertising copywriter for weekly newspaper, college newspaper.

Advertising Sales — Sold advertising space for weekly newspaper, college newspaper.

EDUCATION

B.A., West State University, May 1980.

Major: Journalism and English   B average

ACTIVITIES/HONORS

College: Communications Achievement Award; Men in Communications, Inc.; Alpha Omega Fraternity; Student Government Association.

High School: Valedictorial; Society of Outstanding American High School Students; Student Council Vice President; History Award (1976); French Award (1976); Beta Club; Youth Legislature.

FIGURE 9–2 (continued)

MILTON S. DELBRIDGE, PAGE 2

EMPLOYMENT HISTORY

Summer, 1979: Staff writer and advertising space salesman for *The Maynard News*, Maynard, Texas.

Summer, 1978: Clerk for the U.S. Government Printing Office, Washington, D.C., under the Summer Intern Project.

Summer, 1977: Bookkeeper/Receptionist for the Robert Wayne Cattle Company, Maynard, Texas.

Summer, 1976: Traveled in Italy with Experiment in International Living (lived with an Italian family for five weeks).

REFERENCES

Will be furnished upon request.

ROBERTA KLEIN'S QUALIFICATIONS

FOR LAW SCHOOL ADMISSION

Educational Experience

Bachelor of Science, The University of X, College of Commerce

and Business Administration, major in accounting. Expected graduation:

May, 1980. Grade Point Average: 2.70 (3.0 scale).

Graduate, Scottsboro High School, Scottsboro, State, May, 1976. Graduated first in

class with an emphasis on college preparatory courses. Also attended

Monte Vista High School, Whittier, California (1973-1974), and Lloyd V. Berkner

High School, Richardson, Texas (1975).

Work Experience

Part-time work while attending college:

Since May 15, 1978 — Student assistant in the Accounting Office, Main Library,

The University of X, working from 15 to 20 hours per week.

1977-1978 — Research assistant, Research Center, Office of Development,

The University of X; worked 20 hours per week.

Summer employment:

1979 — Clerk, Inventory Control, Jim Walter Window Components (Jim Walter

Corporation), Hialeah, Florida.

1978 — Appraiser's assistant, John Ruhe and Associations, for the Jackson

County Tax Assessor, Scottsboro.

1977 — Disc Jockey, WCRI Radio, Scottsboro.

1976 — Manager, Tennis Pro Shop, City of Richardson Tennis Center,

Richardson, Texas.

Other work: Inventory clerk, grocery store checker.

ROBERTA KLEIN'S QUALIFICATIONS FOR LAW SCHOOL ADMISSION, PAGE 2

College Activities

Student Development Council, 1976-80

 Treasurer, 1978-79

 Publicity Director, 1977-78

 Founding member, 1976

The College of Commerce and Business Administration

 Academic Honors Committee, Leader, 1979-80

  Honors Proposal, Co-author, 1979

  Student Advising Report, Author, 1979

 Accounting Society, 1977-80

 Student Executive Council, 1977-79

 Peer Advisor, 1977

 Insurance Society, 1978-79

Student Government Association

 Student Senate, Off-Campus Senator, 1977-79

  Rules Committee, Leader, 1978-79

  Parliamentarian, 1977-78

  Off-Campus Task Force Leader, 1978

 Off-Campus Association Advisory Board, 1976-80

  Housing Supervisor, 1977

  Landlord Relations Committee, Leader, 1976-77

College Honors

Beta Alpha Psi, accounting honorary

Beta Gamma Sigma, business academic honorary

FIGURE 9–3 (concluded)

ROBERTA KLEIN'S QUALIFICATIONS FOR LAW SCHOOL ADMISSION, PAGE 3

Dean's List, 1977-79

1979 Dean's Service Award, College of Commerce

Mortar Board

Selected to *Who's Who Among American Colleges and Universities*

Permanent Address: 413 Martin Street

                         Scottsboro, State ZIP

                         Phone: 555-1353

References will be furnished upon request.

Earl G. Bostany

672 Idlewild Circle

Birmingham, Alabama 35205

Phone: 555-0746

JOB OBJECTIVE: Accountant/Auditor

EDUCATIONAL HISTORY:

Will receive B.S. degree in Business, University of Alabama, major in

accounting, in July 1980.

Minor emphasis in finance, investments and portfolio analysis,

insurance, and economics.

SCHOOL ACTIVITIES AND HONORS:

Alabama Accounting Society, Alabama Insurance Society, Gamma Iota

Sigma Insurance Honorary, and Dean's List.

EMPLOYMENT HISTORY:

Summers 1978	Baptist Medical Centers
and 1979	3201 4th Avenue South
	Birmingham, Alabama

Duties: General Accounting, Account Analysis, Property and

Construction-in-Progress Accounting, and Inventorying.

From 1976	Parisian Department Stores
to 1979	Eastwood Mall at Crestwood Boulevard
	Birmingham, Alabama

FIGURE 9–4 (*continued*)

Duties: Temporary employment (selling) on holidays and

semester breaks. Dealing with people and cash.

From 1974   Nohab Incorporated, S.C.M. copy machine dealer

to 1976   1705 29th Court South

Birmingham, Alabama 35209

Duties: Stock Clerk/Delivery. Complete control of inventory.

AVAILABILITY: August, 1980. Able to travel and/or relocate.

References available upon request.

DAVID SENNING'S QUALIFICATIONS FOR

REPRESENTING SEARLE RADIOGRAPHICS

3923 Shannon Lane

Birmingham, Alabama 35213   (205) 555-9103

Work Accomplishments

Medical: Represented the X-ray Division of E. I. duPont in Nashville,

Tennessee, July, 1975 – January, 1979. Assumed territory with

72% penetration and $1.4 million in sales. Ranked 4th in the

region in net gains the first year. Consistently realized $250,000

in net gains annually. Final penetration of 92% reflected over

$25 million in sales. Served and sold to radiologists, hospital

administrators, chief technologists, nuclear medicine

departments throughout Southern Kentucky, Middle Tennessee,

and Northern Alabama. Principal products included medical

imaging, film processing, and film handling equipment.

Designed departments for seven major hospitals to incorporate

the duPont equipment sold. Appointed Equipment Coordinator

for the district in 1978. Authored three technical presentations

for customer and field training. Originated an extremity

exposure technique that formed the basis for Dr. Thomas

Duncan's article on arthritic studies. Introduced three technical

representatives and two service representatives into the field.

Routinely serviced Kodak and duPont equipment.

FIGURE 9–5 (*continued*)

DAVID SENNING'S QUALIFICATIONS FOR REPRESENTING
SEARLE RADIOGRAPHICS, PAGE 2

Industrial: District Representative for Betz Laboratories from January, 1979,
to present, selling water treatment to engineers in paper, tire,
ammonia, and chemical plants. Improved customer relations at
Reichhold Chemical, General Tire, Southern Natural Gas, and
Gulf States Paper by thorough investigation of existing
treatment programs. Formulated water treatment guidelines for
these plants as well as Gulf States, Demopolis, Union Camp,
Hunt Oil, B. F. Goodrich, and Car-Ren. Drafted successful
proposals at all listed accounts.

Military: Commissioned as second lieutenant, 1973; discharged as first
lieutenant, 1975. Served as platoon leader over 44 men and six
E-6 sergeants. Duties included those of supply officer, pay
officer, motor pool officer, dispatcher. Became Brigade Legal
Officer advising all Fort Lee Company Commanders.

University: Worked under Dr. Wendell Hewitt as a graduate assistant while
earning Masters in Business Administration. Organized class
presentations, lectured classes, graded class work.

Additional: Worked four summers without absenteeism on shift work as a
summer laborer at Gulf States Paper Corporation, Tuscaloosa.
Worked part time after high school as a salesman in retail store
for two years.

Mastered Dale Carnegie course while working for duPont.

FIGURE 9–5 (concluded)

DAVID SENNING'S QUALIFICATIONS FOR REPRESENTING
SEARLE RADIOGRAPHICS, PAGE 3

Professional College Training

Master of Business Administration, 1974, University of Alabama, with 2.5 average

(3.0 scale).

Some courses that instilled practical sales skills: business communication,

financial analysis, statistics, accounting, economics, management, marketing,

report writing.

B.S. Chemistry/Mathematics, 1972, University of Alabama.

Electronics (by correspondence), completed May, 1980, Bell and Howell School,

Chicago, Illinois. The course objective: learn modern electronic principles for

field repair.

Personal Details

Born 1950, Austin, Texas   Interests: Photography

Married, 1972: one daughter, 4½   Tennis

           one son, six months   Hunting

Memberships: Woodcraft

    American Chemical Society   Physical Characteristics:

    Episcopal Church   5 feet, 11 inches

                             195 pounds

                             Excellent health

References

Will be furnished upon request.

Résumé (or Data Sheet) Checklist

1. Give your résumé an informative heading worded for the appropriate degree of "selling."
   a. Identify your name, the type of work desired, and (preferably) the company to which addressed.
   b. Be sure you apply for work, not a job title.
2. For appropriate emphasis, ease of reading, and space saving:
   a. Balance the material across the page in tabulated form.
   b. Use difference in type and placement to affect emphasis and show awareness of organization principles.
   c. Centered heads carry emphasis and help balance the page.
   d. Capitalize the main words in centered heads and underline the heads unless in solid caps.
   e. If you have to carry over an item, indent the second line.
   f. Remember to identify and number pages after the first.
3. Lead with whatever best prepares you for the particular job, but account for the chronology of your life since high school. (Gaps of more than three months may arouse suspicion.) When older and extensively experienced, such complete coverage is less necessary.
4. Education details should point up specific preparation.
   a. Show the status of your education early: degree, field, school, date.
   b. Highlight courses which distinctively qualify you for the job. Listing everything takes away emphasis from the significant and suggests inability to discriminate.
   c. In listing courses, give them titles or descriptions which show their real content or briefly give specific details of what you did.
   d. Give grade averages in an understandable form (letters, quartiles, or percentages; GPA systems vary too much).
   e. Avoid belittling expressions like "theoretical education."
5. Experience: for jobs listed,
   a. Give job title, duties, firm or organization name, full address, specific dates, *responsibilities*, and immediate superior's name.
   b. If experience is part time, identify it as such.
   c. Consider reverse chronology or other arrangement to emphasize the most relevant and important.
   d. Use noun phrases and employ action verbs that imply *responsibility*.
6. If you include a personal details section, it should present a clear, true picture. (Though law prevents employers from asking, no law prohibits you from volunteering information about race, religion, age, health, and marital status.)

Résumé (or Data Sheet) Checklist

(continued)

   a. Tabulate, but try combining ideas to save words:

Born in East Lansing, Michigan, 1960	Married, no children
5′11″, 185 lbs.	Member of (list appropriate organizations)
Good health, glasses for close work	Like fishing and reading

   b. Give your address(es)—and phone(s) if likely to be used— in minimum space where easily found but not emphasized.

7. List or offer to supply references. When you list references (to conclude your résumé or supply later on request):

   a. Give the names, titles, full addresses, and telephone numbers of references for all important jobs and fields of study listed.

   b. Unless obvious, make clear why each reference is listed.

8. Remember these points about style:

   a. A résumé is ordinarily a tabulation; avoid paragraphs and complete sentences.

   b. Noun phrases are the best choice of grammatical pattern.

   c. Items in any list should be in parallel form (See Para. in Appendix B).

   d. Keep opinions out of résumés; just give the specific facts. Use impersonal presentation, avoiding first- and second-person pronouns.

chapter 10

Letters about employment

WRITING THE PROSPECTING APPLICATION

IN SELLING as in fishing, you almost have to have a feeling of success consciousness and optimism—the ability to think positively. You can hardly force yourself to really try to catch fish or make sales unless you feel that you have an attractive bait or an appealing product or service. Other people (and seemingly even fish) quickly sense how you feel about yourself and respond accordingly. And since application letters are sales letters in every way—sales letters selling your services—you have to have self-confidence and positive thinking.

That, you remember, was one of the reasons we urged you in the preceding chapter to prepare a good résumé *before* writing your application letter. Especially if you're down because you are earning less than A's in courses or encountering questions about whether you'll graduate—or your present job is going sour (or worse, you've been fired)—*realistically assessing your strong points through preparing a good résumé can be a big step toward retaining and increasing your self-confidence and optimism.*

With a well-prepared résumé you will have done a good job of lining up your qualifications, of realizing what you can do, and of deciding on those qualifications that most nearly equip you for efficient performance. You are then in much better shape to write an application letter—a sales letter selling your services.

At times you may want to send a prospecting letter without a résumé. That's your decision. We don't think it's the better decision; most personnel people prefer to receive one. Even if you elect not to use one, you'll write a better letter for having prepared it. Having prepared it, you're throwing good money away if you don't let it work for you.

You're also being very foolish if you fail to capitalize on your investment of time and effort (and maybe even cash) by slavishly following the points and aping the style of another person's application letter. The good "model" application letter doesn't exist—and never will for applicants of average intelligence and above. They realize that *the application letter must be an accurate reflection of the writer's personality as well as aptitudes*. So they will write their own.

If you're smart about sending your prospecting application to a company, you'll also do some research to find out the name of the person it should go to. Except in applying for a very low-level job, sending a prospecting application to a personnel department or to a title is generally useless. If you want to work in a specific Purchasing Department, address your letter personally to the vice president of purchasing or director of purchasing. You can get that person's name from trade directories (see Chapter 9, p. 315) or by telephoning the company and asking for the name.

For some suggestions about format and mailing, see our comments under "Writing the Invited Application" later in this chapter.

Securing favorable attention

As in sales letters, the infallible way to secure interest in your application letter is to stress your central selling point in writing about serving the reader. Your central selling point may be an ability based on education, experience, or personal qualities—or a combination of them.

A 19-year-old secretary with two years of college summarized important qualifications for a position in an exporting firm in the following well-chosen lead:

```
As a secretary in your export division I could transcribe your
dictation accurately in attractive letters and memos at 50
words per minute—whether it is in English or Spanish.
```

Another student just graduating from college got favorable attention with this:

```
Because I have had an unusual five-year educational opportunity
```

```
combining the study of engineering and management, I feel sure
of my ability to do efficient work in your industrial
engineering department and to steadily increase in usefulness.

I could conduct a time study with a technical knowledge of the
machines concerned or work on the problems of piece wage rates
without losing sight of the highly explosive personnel
situation involved.
```

To state the central point, a more mature and better educated writer with more experience began as follows to a textbook publishing company:

```
With my college background of undergraduate and graduate work,
my teaching experience, and a temperament which helps me to
adapt easily to college people and circumstances, I believe I
could do a good job as a field representative for your firm.
```

Those openings have nothing tricky about them. They just talk work—and the education, experience, and/or personal qualities that point to doing a good job.

You may be able to capitalize on a trick in some situations—provided it shows knowledge of job requirements. The young advertising candidate who mailed a walnut shell to agencies with the lead "They say advertising is a hard nut to crack" got results from the message enclosed in the walnut. The statistical worker who drew a line graph showing the Federal Reserve Board Index of Industrial Production and in the opening lines commented on the significance of its recent movements certainly had a head start on other candidates for the job.

If you can think of a trick or gimmick which is pertinent, in good taste, and not stereotyped (such as the balance sheet from an accounting candidate), it may help you. But it is by no means a must and can do you more harm than good unless you handle it carefully and thoughtfully. Generally personnel people don't like gimmicks.

You *do* need to concentrate on rapidly and naturally establishing your qualifications with the attitude that you want to put them to work for the reader in some specific job. Having held out such a promise, you need to back it up.

Supplying evidence of performance ability

Your evidence in an application is simply an interpretation of the highlights of your opening and résumé. For persuasiveness, you phrase it in terms of skills that point to "doing something for you."

The secretarial applicant to the exporting firm continued in the following vein:

```
In secretarial courses during my study at Temple College, I've
consistently demonstrated my ability to handle material at that
speed.  And as a matter of practice in my course in conversa-
tional Spanish I take down what my teacher and my classmates
say.  I have no difficulty transcribing these notes later.
```

I learned a good deal about your markets and your clientele while doing research for a report I submitted this semester in marketing, "Some Recent Developments in International Markets." In the process I became familiar with such publications as The American Importer, Exporting, and The Foreign Commerce Yearbook.

I am by disposition neat and conservative in appearance. Early in my life mother impressed upon me the desirability of a low-pitched voice and distinct enunciation; and college speech teachers have further developed my speaking skills. The A I made in Business Communication suggests my tact, language facility, and persuasion. On the telephone, in person, or in letters and memos, I could communicate pleasantly and effectively with your employees and customers.

Various advanced courses (listed on the enclosed resume) have given me skill in operating office machines of different kinds and in filing and record keeping. Putting these skills to use as a part-time assistant secretary in the Marketing Department here at school the past two years has enhanced those skills and given me the confidence to serve you well.

An applicant for an apprenticeship in an architectural firm wrote a short letter, but it's packed with statements of accomplishments as evidence of desirable skills.

At this point in my career, I have two main qualifications to offer you: my job experience and my bachelor's degree in architecture from the University of Illinois.

My practical experience covers six years of part-time work with the same architectural firm, Mosely Architects. I started with Mr. Carl Mosely when I was a senior in high school, handling the firm's printing in the afternoons. My duties as well as responsibilities grew in proportion with my experience to include many aspects of drafting, together with design: stairs, cabinet and partition detailing, structural foundations, floors, roof framing, site planning, scheduling, and, in some instances, design and presentation drawing.

Projects I worked on ranged from $40,000 houses to $5,000,000 office buildings, with banks, churches, and small condominiums completing the spectrum. While working on these jobs I had the opportunity to associate directly with mechanical, electrical, and structural engineers, in addition to the six members of the firm itself.

Of course I could not have developed and advanced that way without furthering my education. To summarize my degree from Illinois, I graduated from the five-year program in architecture in the upper 5 percent of my class. While in school I competed in four major design competitions and received an award for each entry—one first prize, one second, and two thirds. Please refer to the enclosed résumé for additional information on my education and extracurricular activities.

I would like to show you my portfolio of school and job work and would be grateful if we could set up a time at your convenience. Please call me at 555-6360 so that we can talk about my working as an efficient apprentice for your firm.

Overcoming deficiencies is a difficult function of the letter, not the résumé. In almost any application situation you'll have one or more. If you feel that a deficiency is so important as to merit identification and possibly discussion, embed it in your letter and endow it with as much positiveness as possible.

The applicant wanting to be a publisher's representative (p. 347) faced a two-strike situation and knew it: education in a commerce school of a state university in the Southwest rather than liberal arts in an Ivy League school. The following fifth paragraph of the letter met the issue head on and capitalized on it:

> The fact that I have studied business at Oklahoma rather than liberal arts at an Ivy League school may actually make me a better representative, Mr. Dayton—especially if I'm assigned to the Southwest, where I already know the territory. I could serve happily as your representative in any district, however; I've traveled over most of the U.S. (and in Europe and the Far East while in the Navy) and can adapt readily to the fine people and country one finds everywhere.

Probably the finest example we've ever seen of turning an apparent handicap into a virtue is that of a young applicant who at first didn't know where to turn when confronted with the necessity of getting a job. Thoughtful analysis of accomplishments in college and how they could be used in business led to the following letter (to a large Chicago mail-order firm). The third paragraph is the epitome of positive thinking.

> Isn't one of the significant qualifications of a correspondent in your company the ability to interpret a letter situation in terms of the reader?
>
> Because I believe that I could express an understanding of a situation clearly and imaginatively to your customers (a degree in English from the University of Illinois, an A in Business Communication, and the editorship of my sorority paper suggest that I can), will you allow me to become a trial employee in your correspondence division?
>
> Learning your particular business policies and procedures in writing letters would come quickly, I believe; I am used to following assignments exactly, and I have no previous working experience to unlearn.
>
> I have a good background in writing. I can type 60 words a minute. And the varied extracurricular activities listed on the enclosed résumé are my best evidence for telling you that I've successfully passed a four-year test of getting along with people.
>
> Will you call me at 876–2401 and name a time when I may come in and talk with you?

It worked! And the same kind of positive approach to any handicap you may have—physical or otherwise—is probably your best way to treat it.

Talking the special language of the business also convinces your reader of your performance ability and helps to overcome any deficiency. In all the examples in this analysis, you've probably noticed that each incorporated specific and special references to conditions or products or activities peculiar to the given job. Such references certainly further the impression that you are aware of job requirements and conditions. The secretarial applicant for work in the export field referred to transcription in Spanish, recent developments in international markets, and to communicating effectively with employees and customers. The would-be publisher's representative (in parts not quoted) referred to books, teachers, college circumstances, and textbook adoptions (the end and aim of that particular job). The industrial management applicant referred easily and sensibly to time studies, piece wage rates, explosive personnel situations, and (later) to tractors and cotton pickers, two products of the company. The would-be architect apprentice referred to drafting, design, and various kinds of buildings.

From your research you can readily establish such references. If significant enough information, they may be good choices of talking points for your beginning, especially if they show knowledge of the company and its working conditions and requirements, along with a desire to serve:

> The marked increase in General Motors sales for the first two quarters undoubtedly reflects the favorable public reception of the new passenger car models and the new Frigidaire appliances.

> With a minimum of training I could take care of a man-sized share of the extra work these increased sales plus the increased production (announced in your annual report) mean for your accounting staff.

> --

> The regular Saturday night reports your retail dealers submit show consumer trends which I want to help you translate into continued Whirlpool leadership—as an analyst in your sales department.

The applicant who wrote the following for an accounting job showed obvious research on and adaptation to Texaco:

> I believe that I can perform the duties expected of accountants in your expanding financial department. The combination of a challenging undergraduate program at the University of X and much work experience will enable me to work effectively and be productive immediately.

> Upon completion of your required orientation program, I assure you that I could work in a way which would benefit Texaco and contribute towards achieving the company's goals. My advanced studies in cost accounting will equip me to analyze and communicate financial information which may benefit top management.

> Your increasing involvement in overseas projects is an area in which I am deeply interested. Through my studies in international finance, I have learned many things which may be incorporated into the plans of your company.

My work experience has enabled me to apply my education to actual working conditions while gaining insight into the total field of accounting. As a summer intern for Haskins-Sells, I was able to participate in audits and deal with numerous problems in costing procedures. I learned the value of hard work and developed an acute desire to excel. Serving as Treasurer for my fraternity helped me to gain valuable experience in financial budgeting and taught me many principles of organization.

As a conscientious person, I always strive to do my best for my employer. I am eager to learn, easy to train, and ambitious to be a productive part of your organization. I believe that I have a great deal to offer Texaco, and I know that Texaco has a lot to offer me.

At a time convenient for you, I would be most grateful for an opportunity to meet and discuss with you ways I could possibly best serve Texaco.

Just as each of these candidates continued to talk the terminology peculiar to the job, you want to show such knowledge of company activities, working conditions, and job requirements. But if you state it in independent clauses (obvious or flat facts which the reader probably already knows), you'll sound wooden and dull. Suppose, for example, that the accounting applicant had told Texaco the following points flatly, as stated here: Your financial department is expanding. I have taken advanced courses in cost accounting. You are increasingly involved in overseas projects. I have studied international finance. I have also been a summer intern with Haskins and Sells and treasurer for my fraternity.

The desirability of *emphasizing qualifications instead of analysis* will be clearer to you through comparing the following original letter (its flat statements underlined) with the revision.

Original	*Revised*
It takes a secretary who is versatile, accurate, reliable and dependable for a firm like the Brown Insurance Company. I realize the importance of your having such a secretary, and I believe I have the necessary qualifications.	My year's work as secretary, four years' thorough college training in commercial studies, and lifetime residence in Tuscumbia should enable me to serve you well as a secretary and further the friendly relations between you and your clients.
Having graduated from the University of Alabama with commercial studies as my major, I am familiar with such machines as the adding machine, Mimeograph, and Comptometer. Since my graduation I have been employed as a secretary with the Reynolds Metal Company. This has given me an opportunity to combine my knowledge with experience.	Whether you want to send a memo to a salesman, a note to a client, or a letter to the home office, I could have it on your desk for signing within a short time. While earning my degree at Alabama, I developed a dictation rate of 100 words per minute and a transcription rate of 45, which I demonstrated daily during my year's work as

Original (continued)

Insurance takes a lot of time
and patience. A large amount
of bookkeeping is required
because every penny has to be
accounted for. My one year of
accounting at the University
will enable me to keep your
books neatly and correctly;
and if it is necessary for
me to work overtime, I am
in good physical health to
do so.

The Brown Insurance Company has
many customers in different
parts of the country; so a
large amount of business
letters and transactions are
carried on. As your secretary,
I could take dictation at 100
words a minute and transcribe
your letters accurately and
neatly at 45 words a minute.

Even though accuracy and speed
are important, personality is
an important characteristic
too. Because of the many kinds
of people who are connected
with this type of business,
it is important to have a
secretary who not only can
file, take dictation, and type,
but who can be a receptionist
as well. Since I have lived in
Tuscumbia all my life, I will
know most of your clients as
individuals and can serve them
in a friendly manner.

I have enclosed a data sheet
for your convenience.

Will you please call me at
374-4726 and tell me when I
can talk to you?

Revised (continued)

secretary with the Reynolds
Metal Company.

To help with the varied kinds
of record keeping in a large
insurance agency, I can use
the knowledge and skills from
a year's course in accounting
and my study of filing systems,
office practices, and office
machines—all applied during my
year of work. You can trust
me to compute premiums
accurately, send notices on
schedule, and devise and turn
out special forms when
necessary.

I realize that in an insurance
agency everyone from the
janitor to the bookkeeper
affects the feeling of the
public and that all must
exercise friendliness and tact
in any contact with a client.
I anticipate the unexpected,
and I meet it calmly; so I am
prepared to handle a number
of duties and to adjust to the
demands of a busy, varied work
schedule (including overtime
work when it's necessary). I
would expect to maintain
cordial relations with all your
clients and prospects quite
naturally and easily because
most of them are the neighbors
and friends I've lived around
all my life.

Ms. Bills and the other
references I've listed on the
enclosed résumé will be glad
to confirm my statements that I
can work efficiently and
cheerfully for you. After
you've heard from them, please
call me at 374-4726 and name a
time that I may come in and
talk with you.

The original, you notice, is almost painful in its flat, obvious statements.
It also uses so much space stating requirements of the job that it fails to
establish qualities of the applicant. The revision eliminates the flatness and
preachiness through subordination, implication, or incidental reference.
Although the revision is a little longer, it accomplishes a good deal

more: It establishes qualifications in a good lead; it talks the special language of the reader; it establishes more qualifications. It also has a much better work-for-you interpretation. But the major improvement of the revision over the original is that it eliminates the preachy, flat statements (particularly at the beginnings of paragraphs) that made a smart applicant sound dull.

Asking for appropriate action

Whatever action you want your reader to take, identify it as specifically as possible, and ask confidently for it. Ordinarily it is to invite you in for an interview. As a self-respecting human being who has something to offer, you do not need to beg or grovel; but you do need to remember—and to show you realize—that the reader is under no obligation to see you, that giving you time is doing you a favor, that the time and place of the interview are to be at the reader's convenience, and that you should be grateful for the interview.

The full-fledged action ending of the sales letter, however, requires slight modification for the application letter. You cannot with good grace exert as much pressure. For this reason most employment counselors and employers do not advocate using any reply device (an employer is happy to pay the postage to reply to a potentially good employee, and writing and mailing a letter are routine actions). But your application action ending should still suggest a specific action, try to minimize the burdensome aspects of that action through careful phrasing, establish gratitude, and supply a stimulus to action with a reminder of the contribution you can make to the firm.

You've already seen several action endings in this chapter. But to drive home the point, let's look at some others.

A Red Cross applicant definitely planned a trip to Washington for job-hunting purposes; so the letter logically and naturally ended with:

When I'm in Washington during the first two weeks in August, I should be grateful for the opportunity to come to your office and discuss further how I may serve in filling your present need for Red Cross club directors. Will you name a convenient time?

The industrial-management applicant ended in this simple fashion:

Please suggest a time when you can conveniently allow me to discuss my qualifications for work in your industrial engineering department.

And the secretarial applicant confidently asked the exporter-reader:

Won't you please call me at 615–5946 and tell me a time when I may come to your office and show you how well my preparation enables me to serve your firm?

The publisher's-representative applicant was in a slightly atypical situation. Lack of both the money and the time right then prevented asking directly for an interview in New York. Here is the solution:

```
After you've had a chance to verify some of the things I've
said about myself in this letter and in the résumé, will you
write me frankly about the possibilities of my working for you?
Possibly I could talk with one of your regional representatives
in this area as a preliminary step. Or I can plan to go to
New York some time this summer to talk with you further about
my successfully representing your firm.
```

As it turned out, the applicant flew to New York at the expense of companies on two occasions within two weeks after sending the letters, but that was the result of further correspondence—and it's certainly not anything to count on!

One other item you should consider is whether to include an *availability date* in your prospecting application. If you are presently working for someone, you would want to give proper notice, and you can tell a prospective employer this in your résumé: "Available to come to work for you one month after giving my present employer notice." The other common reason for not being immediately available is pending graduation: "Available to come to work for you immediately after graduation on June 10." Otherwise we do not recommend you mention availability. To say "Available immediately" implies that you are presently out of work, something you would not want to mention.

If you mention availability in your résumé, you should also mention it in your letter as a point in good communication (clearing up all questions between you and the reader). Even if you feel that a stated graduation time implies an availability date, by skillful and brief wording you can reemphasize your knowledge of the company and add mild urgency to your letter with it. For example, suppose the publisher's-representative applicant had changed only the last sentence to:

```
Or I can plan to go to New York this summer—in time to get in
on this year's training program—to talk with you further about
my successfully representing your firm.
```

     ✿   ✿   ✿   ✿   ✿

Such letters as suggested in the preceding pages won't work miracles. They won't make a poor applicant a good one. They won't ordinarily secure a job; usually they can only open the door for an interview and further negotiations, but that is their purpose. To make yours do all it can, you may want to review the checklist of suggestions on pp. 356–57.

WRITING THE INVITED APPLICATION

Often a firm makes its personnel needs known by running an ad, by listing with an agency (commercial, where they'll charge you a fee, or governmental like the U.S. Employment Service offices and state-government equivalents), or simply by word of mouth. As you probably know, most large companies also list their needs for college-graduate personnel with college placement bureaus and have recruiting personnel who regularly visit campuses scouting for talented young men and women. Currently, however, less than 10 percent of managerial level jobs are advertised, a point in favor of prospecting applications later in your career.

Situations where the prospective employer actually goes out searching for new employees give you one drawback (you'll have more competition because more people will know about the job) and two advantages in writing a letter: (1) you don't need to generate interest at the beginning (you already have it!); and (2) the ad, agency, or talent scout will give you the job requirements or as a bare minimum identify the job category and principal duties.

Even when you hear of the job through other people, they will usually tell you what you'll be expected to do. So matching up your qualifications with the job requirements is easier in the invited situation than with prospecting applications, because your source will usually identify requirements in some order indicating their relative importance to the employer.

If you are equally strong on all points of preparation, you have no problem. You simply take up the points in the order listed. But such a happy condition you'll rarely find. Most often your best talking point is not the most significant requirement, and usually you'll be deficient in some way. The solution is to employ the same strategy you did in writing the invited sales letter: Tie in your strongest point of preparation with something the reader wants done; take up those points wherein you are weakest in the middle position of the letter and attempt to correlate them with some positive point.

Your analysis of job requirements and compilation of a résumé are exactly the same procedures as in a prospecting situation. Adaptation is simply easier. And once past the opening, supplying evidence and asking for appropriate action are the same. Since the beginnings in the prospecting and the invited applications do differ somewhat, we need to consider why and to make some suggestions that will help you write good ones.

Whether you learn of the job through an ad, through an agency, or via a third person, your beginning is pretty much the same. The first requirement is that it mention your main qualifications; the second, that it identify the job; the third, that it show a service attitude; and the fourth, that it refer to the source of the information (*subordinately* unless it is significant).

The reason for telling how you learned of the job is simply that the reference to the ad, or the bureau, or the person who told you about the job is an automatic attention getter which favorably reinforces the reader's willingness or even eagerness to read your letter. One good sentence can accomplish all four functions and point the trend of the letter.

Prospecting Application Checklist

1. The prospecting application must generate interest from the start.
   a. Establish early your central selling point of education or experience or both, in terms of doing something for the reader; later, develop them in the order mentioned. (You may also cite your research on the company or the field, or tell a human-interest story; but they postpone the real message.)
   b. Avoid the preaching or didactic, flat statement.
   c. Avoid implying that your up-to-date techniques are better, or telling the reader how to run the business.
   d. Make clear early that you are seeking work of a specialized nature, not just any job.
   e. Be realistic; talk work and doing, not "forming an association with" or *position, opening, application, vacancy,* or *opportunity.*
   f. You need verve and vigor, not stereotypes like "Please consider my application . . . ," "I should like to apply for . . . ."
   g. Don't let your biography drown out what you can do now.
   h. Don't give the reader an opportunity to shut you off with a negative response.
   i. Mere graduation (rather than the preparation back of it) is a poor lead anywhere, especially at first.
   j. Eliminate selfish-sounding statements or overtones of them.

2. Interpretation and tone are important from the start.
   a. Maintain a consistent, acceptable tone, neither apologizing for what you don't have nor bragging about what you do.
   b. For conviction, back up your assertions of ability with specific points of education or experience as evidence.
   c. Generalizing and editorializing are out of place: "invaluable," "more than qualified," even "excellent."
   d. Avoid needlessly deprecating your good qualifications.
   e. Project your education or experience right to the job.
   f. Use enough "I's" for naturalness, but avoid monotony.
   g. Show the research and thought which have gone into the project. Address the letter to the appropriate individual if at all possible; talk about company operations and trends in the industry; even a deft, tactful reference to a competitor can be a point in your favor.

3. Your education and experience are your conviction elements.
   a. Talk about your experience, schooling, or personal characteristics in terms of accomplishing something. For example, you may register for, take, attend, study, receive credit for, pass, learn, or master a course.
   b. The emphasis should go on a phase of work connected with the job you're applying for.

Prospecting Application Checklist

(*continued*)

c. Refer to education as work preparation (in lowercase letters) rather than exact course titles (in capitals and lowercase).

d. You need highlights rather than details in the letter.

e. But even highlights need to be specific for conviction.

f. Your résumé supplies thorough, detailed coverage. Refer to it incidentally, in a sentence establishing some other significant idea, just before asking the reader to take action.

g. A one-page letter may be desirable, but telling all of your story in the most effective way for you is more important.

4. Reflect your personality in both content and style.

a. Refer to the more significant personal characteristics affecting job performance, preferably with evidence that you have them.

b. Incorporate phrases which reveal your attitude toward work and your understanding of working conditions.

5. Ask for appropriate action in the close.

a. Name the action you want; make it specific and plausible.

b. Don't beg and don't command; just ask. And avoid the aloof, condescending implications of "You may call me at . . . ." Usually you ask for an appointment to talk about the job.

c. Eliminate references to application, interview, position. Use action references to work and the steps in job getting.

d. Clearly imply or state that you will be grateful. But "Thank you for . . ." in present tense sounds presumptuous.

e. Show success consciousness without presumptuousness.

f. A little sales whip-back at the end will help strengthen the impression of what you can contribute.

FOR WRITING INVITED APPLICATIONS

6. When writing an application in response to an ad or at the suggestion of an agency or friend:

a. Primary emphasis should be on putting your preparation to work for the reader. But since your reference to the source is an automatic way of securing attention, you should identify it early and emphasize it if it carries an implied recommendation.

b. Avoid stating what the reader would infer ("I read your ad").

c. Don't ask questions or phrase assumptions which are clear pushovers: "If you are seeking X, Y, and Z, then I'm your man." "Are you looking for an employee with X, Y, and Z? I have X, Y, and Z."

d. Postpone salary talk until the interview if you can. If the phrase "State salary required" is included in the description, your reply of "your going rate" or "your usual wage scale" is acceptable to any firm you'd want to work for.

The opening of the following letter puts emphasis on service through work, clearly identifies the specific kind of work sought, and desirably subordinates the reference to the source. Note that after the opening the letter reads much the same as a prospecting application (indeed, if you omit the lead in the faked address block and the first two lines, it could be a prospecting letter). Note also the adaptation of talking points—the stress on experience rather than on formal training.

I'm "sold
on insurance"
and I believe I can be the aggressive sales representative you advertised for in Thursday's Express.

Five years of experience in dealing with people very similar to your prospects—in addition to technical training in insurance and sales—would aid me in selling your low-premium accident policy.

As a pipeliner in Louisiana I made friends with the kind of prospects to whom I'd be selling your policies. I had a chance to study people, their hopes and fears and desires for protection and security, while doing casework for the Welfare Society in San Antonio. And while working as a waiter both in high school and in college, I learned how to work for and with the public.

The most significant thing I learned was to keep right on smiling even though dog-tired at the end of my 6—12 p.m. shift after having been to school most of the day. And I certainly learned the meaning of perseverance when I had to go home after midnight and get on the books for the next day's assignments.

The same perseverance that earned me B's in Insurance and Income Protection, Liability Insurance, and Personal Sales Principles will help me find leads, follow them up, persuade, and close a sale. I know an insurance representative makes money personally and for the company only by sticking to a schedule of calls. But I'm equally aware of the value of patience and the necessity for repeat calls.

Because I'm friendly and apparently easygoing, your prospects would like to see me coming. As you see on the enclosed résumé, I was elected a Favorite at Schreiner Institute; and at the University of Texas I was tapped for Silver Spurs, a service-honorary organization. Making these many friends has resulted in my knowing people from all sections of the state.

Dr. Fitzgerald and the others I've listed on the enclosed information sheet can help you evaluate me professionally and personally if you'll write or call them.

Then I would be grateful for your telling me a convenient time and place when I may talk with you further about my qualifications for being the hardworking sales representative you want.

Frequently your source—especially an ad—gives you an effective entering cue and provides you with useful reference phrases throughout the letter. From the key phrases you can almost reconstruct the ad answered in the following letter:

Because of my college training in accounting and my work
experience, I believe I can be the quick-to-learn junior
accountant for whom you advertised in the May Journal of
Accountancy.

Having successfully completed down-to-earth studies in tax
accounting and auditing while earning my degree, I should be
able to catch on to your treatment of these problems quickly.

And while working as assistant ledger clerk for the Grantland
Davis firm in St. Louis one semester, I developed a great
respect for accuracy as well as an appreciation of the
necessity for the conscientious, painstaking labor so essential
in public accounting. There, too, I saw clearly the necessity
for absorbing confidential information without divulging it.

My natural aptitude for analysis and synthesis, strengthened
by special study of the analysis of financial statements and
reinforced with a broad background of economics, law, and
statistics, should enable me to handle the recurring tasks of
compiling comparative statements of earnings and net worth.
And my training in writing reports will help me to tell the
story to my supervisors as well as to clients.

Realizing that the public accountant must gain the confidence
of clients through long periods of accurate, trustworthy
service, I welcome the offer of a long-range advancement
program mentioned in your ad. I'm not afraid of hard work;
and I enjoy the good health essential in the long, irregular
working hours of rush business seasons.

Will you study the diversified list of courses and the
description of my internship listed on the attached résumé?
Note also, please, the wide range of activities I took part in
while maintaining an A average. Then I would be most grateful
if you will write or call me so that we can talk further
about my qualifications for beginning a career of immediate
usefulness to you.

I can start to work any time after graduation on June 4.

A variation of source doesn't affect your procedure—except that you
*emphasize a source that would be influential in your getting the job; other-
wise, subordinate the source.* If you learn of the work through an agency
or a third person, the procedure is still the same. Here are some openings
bearing out our statement:

Since I have the qualifications necessary for successful
selling that you listed in your recent letter to the dean of
students here at the University of Nebraska, I believe I could
serve you well as a . . . .
--
When I talked with Ms. Sarah Lomer this morning, she assured
me that I am qualified by experience and professional training
for the duties of a field auditor with your firm.
--
During the four years I worked as a branch-house auditor for
the L. B. Price Mercantile Company to put myself through
school, I became thoroughly familiar with every phase of
accounting work necessary for a branch office of a large
installment concern and with the reports required by the home
office.

> I'd certainly like the chance to prove that my education and
> personal characteristics parallel the description of the
> desirable management trainee that you gave to Dr. Morley, head
> of our placement bureau, when you visited the campus last week.

Two warnings need sounding, however. The *first* is to guard carefully against stupid questions, questions made perfectly clear from the ad or the situation. One applicant to a legal firm began with:

> Are you looking for a college-trained secretary who can do the
> work in your law office efficiently and accurately and who is
> eager to learn law work? If so, I think I can meet your
> exacting requirements for a legal secretary.

The ad had made the answer perfectly clear! And an efficient candidate only looked silly.

The *second* warning is against showing signs of selfish glee over having discovered a job possibility of your choice. When you read or hear about a job, you may rightly think, "That's just what I want!"—but don't write this or any variation of it. Start writing in terms of doing something for the reader: what you can give instead of what you hope to get.

Perhaps a *third* warning is in order—against assuming that you don't have much of a selling job to do because the reader is on the asking end. Nothing could be further from the truth. The competition you're up against for an advertised job is keen even in the heyday of prosperity. And because many others will apply, you'll have to write a superior letter to be chosen as one of the final few for interviewing.

In fact, the reader may face such a heap of letters that yours may not even get read. For that reason you may want to do something so that your letter will be selected for reading:

1. When competition is keen, you may want to get the first edition of the newspaper and have your material in such shape that you can have a complete, well-written letter and résumé in the employer's hands hours or even days ahead of other candidates. Even though you may not get the immediate response you want, your letter (if it is good) becomes better in the eyes of the employer as poorer ones come in through the mail. Remember, too, that people are relieved by the first application that comes in and feel kindly toward it. It relieves the fear of every such advertiser—that maybe no one will answer the ad.

2. As an alternative strategy, you can wait 10 to 16 days after an advertisement appears before sending in your application. Two reasons for this are (1) companies are usually slow and careful about filling a job; and if your application is superior to those that have arrived earlier, you will stand out; and (2) roughly 82 percent of the answers to a job advertisement will come in during the first week after the ad appears; why have yours arrive with so many others? (For maximum effect, mail so yours arrives on Tuesday or Wednesday.)

3.   A favorite device is sending the letter by special delivery. Few personnel people object. If you are in the same town, you can deliver the letter yourself, with the request that it be turned over to the appropriate person.

4.   If you insert the letter in an envelope large enough to accommodate an 8½- by 11-inch page without folding and put a piece of cardboard under it to keep it smooth, the contrast between your letter and all the others that have been folded will call attention to yours.

But none of these devices will make much difference if you do not write from the viewpoint of contributing to the firm through effective, efficient work.

While the advertisement or other source of information usually gives you some advantages in writing invited instead of prospecting applications, ads often give you one or more of three special problems.

1.   When the ad asks you to "state salary expected," "give salary history," or "give salary on last job," take the advice of eight personnel directors on a panel: Don't do it. You hurt your chances if you shoot too high or too low. Instead, say something like "Your usual salary range," "Negotiable in the interview," or the like. A company should want to hire you for what you can do for it, not because it can get you cheap.

2.   Ads often say "Send résumé." Again, don't do only that. These ad writers want to save time by screening only factual résumés; and they are not interested in selling you on the job, but *you* are interested in selling yourself. An interpretive letter is a much better selling instrument than a résumé. (Does anyone buy a new car after just receiving a window sticker in the mail? Selling a car usually takes a sales talk followed by a demonstration, or in job-hunting parlance, a letter and résumé followed by an interview.) So send your letter *and* your résumé.

3.   What we said (p. 354) about availability date also applies in an invited application letter, but to a lesser degree. When a company advertises for help, it needs someone right away. You can assume that you must be available immediately (or very soon) and should give the earliest date you can start work (which can eliminate any of your competition who cannot start that soon).

As you already realize, most of the items we suggested to you in the prospecting application checklist (p. 356) apply equally when you write an invited letter. Study them again, and review the additional items at the end of that checklist which are peculiar to the invited situation.

CONTINUING THE CAMPAIGN

Regardless of the results from your application, you have some follow-up work to do.

If you get an invitation to an interview, you know how to handle it. Accept promptly, pleasantly, and directly (if that's your decision) as suggested in Chapter 5. Just remember to continue your job campaign by indicating continuing interest in serving. If you decide to turn down the invitation, Chapter 7 has shown you how; but remember, also, the adage about never burning your bridges behind you.

If within a reasonable time you do not hear from the person or firm you've applied to, you'd probably better send a follow-up letter indicating continuing interest.

Follow-up letters

A good salesperson doesn't make one call and drop the matter if that doesn't close the sale. Neither does a sales-minded job applicant.

To have a reason for sending a follow-up letter two or three weeks after the original application, some applicants intentionally omit some pertinent but relatively insignificant piece of information in the original.

> I noticed in rereading my copy of the application I sent you three weeks ago that I did not list Mr. Frank Regan, manager, Bell's Supermarket, Rome, Georgia 30161

> Since I have worked under Mr. Regan's direct supervision for three summers, he is a particularly good man to tell you about my work habits and personality. I hope you will write to him.

Such a subterfuge we cannot commend, if for no other reason than that so many other approaches are available to you. Election to an office or an honorary society, an extensive trip that has opened your eyes to bigger and better possibilities of the job, a research paper that has taught you something significant to the job, and certainly another job offer are all avenues of approach for reselling yourself and indicating continuing interest.

Even if you receive the usual noncommittal letter saying that the firm is glad to have your application and is filing it in case any opening occurs, you need not hesitate to send another letter two, three, or six months after the first one. It should not be another complete application (yours will still be on file); it is just a reminder that you are still interested. One acceptable one is this:

> I know that many organizations throw away applications over six months old.

> Because that much time has elapsed since I sent you mine (dated April 15), I want to assure you that I'm still interested in working for you, in having you keep my record in your active file, and in hearing from you when you need someone with my qualifications.

Only a lackadaisical applicant would end the letter there, however. Just a few more words could bring the information up to date and perhaps stimulate more interest in the application, like this:

```
Since graduation I have been doing statistical correlations at
the Bureau of Business Research here at the University. I've
picked up a few techniques I didn't learn in class, and I've
certainly increased my speed on the computer keyboard and
calculator.

I still want that job as sales analyst with your firm, however.
```

Thank-you letters

Following an interview, whether the results seem favorable or unfavorable, your note of appreciation is not only a business courtesy; it helps to single you out from other applicants and to show your reader that you have a good sense of human relations.

Even when you and the interviewer have agreed that the job is not for you, you can profitably invest about two minutes writing something like this:

```
I surely appreciate the time you spent with me last Friday
discussing employment opportunities at Monitor and Wagner.

The suggestions you made will help me find my right place in
the business world.

After I get that experience you suggested, I may be knocking
at your door again.
```

When you are interested in the job discussed and feel that you have a good chance, you're plain foolish not to write a letter expressing appreciation and showing that you learned something from the interview.

```
Your description of the community relations program of Livania
has opened new vistas to me, Ms. Lee.

The functions of the public relations department in your
company as you described them made me much more aware of the
significance and appeal of this work.

As soon as I returned to the campus, I read Mr. Fields's book
that you suggested and the pamphlets describing U.S. Steel's
program.

Many thanks for your suggestions and for the time you took
with me.

I shall be looking forward to hearing the decision about my
application as soon as you can make it.
```

Job-acceptance letters

When an employer offers you a job and you decide it's the one for you, say so enthusiastically in a direct A–plan letter that keeps you in a favorable light—perhaps by restating your interest in serving well. Just remember, also, to seal the contract by brief accepting references to (not flat repetition of) the terms—or by filling out and returning supplied contract forms, as in the following:

```
I certainly do want to work with Franklin & Franklin—
and I didn't need a week to think it over, Mr. Bell,
although I appreciate your giving me that much time to decide.
```

```
I've filled out the forms you gave me and enclosed them with
this letter.  Anything else?
```

```
Unless you tell me differently, I'll take off two weeks after
graduation.  But, as you asked, I'll call you on Friday,
June 11, to get report-to-work instructions for Monday,
June 14.
```

Job-refusal letters

Sometime in your life you'll have to tell somebody that you don't want to accept an offer. You may feel that it's routine, that it doesn't mean anything one way or the other to a busy person who interviews many applicants and has many other people available. Remember, though, that a human being with pride and ego is going to read your letter. So make yourself think, "I don't want that job *now*," for you may want to reopen negotiations at some future point.

To wind up negotiations pleasantly and leave the way open for yourself, write a B–plan letter with a pleasant buffer of some favorable comment about the company or the work, some plausible and inoffensive reason, the presentation of the refusal as positively and subordinately as you can phrase it (possibly with the statement of where you are going to work), and an ending expressing good feeling and appreciation or both. The following letter is a good example:

```
Meeting you and talking with you about working for Bowen's was
one of the more interesting job contacts I have had.
```

```
The opportunity to learn the business from the ground up and
to grow with an expanding company is a challenging one, one
for which I am grateful.
```

```
As you will remember from our discussion, I am still primarily
interested in product research.  Since I feel that my abilities
will be utilized best in that way, I am going to work for (a
company) that has offered me such employment.
```

```
I shall certainly continue to watch your company's progress
with interest, and I shall look forward to reading or hearing
about the results of your new prepackaging program.
```

Letters of resignation

Resignation letters, like job-refusal letters, are modified B–plan letters. Remember, however, that you want to stay in the good graces of the individuals who have assisted you in your career. You will be wise to give ample notification and to give credit where credit is due. The suggestion "Be kind, courteous, and considerate to the people you pass on the way up the ladder of success; you will likely meet them on your way back down" is good advice to keep in mind when you leave a job.

When you have worked for a firm, you have benefited in some way (in addition to the regular pay you have drawn). Regardless of how you may feel at the time, remember that you can say something complimentary about how things are run, about what you have learned as a result of your experience, or about the people with whom you have associated. By all means, say it!

Then announce your plan to leave, giving consideration to the necessity for ample time in which to find a replacement. In some cases no more than two weeks is enough advance notification; sometimes it should be long enough for you to help train the person who will take your place.

In many circumstances your resignation can be oral. And in many circumstances it may be better that way. But when you need to write a letter, consider adaptations of the following:

```
I've certainly learned a great deal about the clothing market
from my work as sales analyst at Foley's the past 18 months.

I shall always be grateful to you and the other personnel who
have helped me to do the job and to prepare for a more
challenging one.

You will perhaps recall that when I had my interviews with you
before starting to work, I stressed my interest in working
toward a job as a sales coordinator.

Since I now have such an opportunity at Sakowitz, Inc., I am
submitting my resignation.  Apparently it will be some time
before such an opportunity is available for me here.

I should like to terminate employment in two weeks.  But I can
make arrangements to work a little longer if this will help to
train the person who takes my place.

My thanks and good wishes.
```

Often when another offer comes your way, you'll feel free to discuss the opportunity with your current employer before making a final decision. Such a conference has many advantages for both employee and employer. Often a counteroffer results, to the mutual satisfaction of both, and the job change doesn't take place. If, despite a counteroffer, you still decide to make the change, you can resign in good grace with a letter somewhat like this:

```
Your recent offer is one I appreciate very much, and it made
me give serious thought to continuing at Bowen's.

Let me say again how much I have appreciated the cooperation,
the friendliness, and helpfulness of everyone with whom I've
been associated here.

After considerably more evaluation, however, I believe I can
make a greater contribution and be a more successful business
manager by accepting the position offered me by Lowen's.

I hope that I can leave with your approval by (specific date);
I feel sure that all my current projects will be complete by
that time.
```

You'll hear from me from time to time—if for no other reason
than that I'll be interested in how the new credit union works
out.

But I'll always want to know how things are going for Bowen's
and the many friends I've made here.

When appropriate, a possible talking point is the suggestion of a successor to you; often this is a big help. A constructive suggestion, phrased positively, implies your continuing interest in the organization.

Letters of resignation written by college students who resign after having agreed to work for someone but before actually reporting for work are quite different—something we take up with reluctance. Many personnel people regard them as breaches of contract. Certainly a practice of sliding out from under such agreements will soon give you a black eye employmentwise.

We would urge you to give serious thought before definitely accepting a job offer. Don't make the mistake of grabbing the first job offered you, only to have something infinitely more to your liking come along later. We'd further urge you never to let yourself get caught in the position of being committed to two employers at the same time. If you have agreed to go to work for a firm and then you have a later offer which you want to accept, do not accept it until you are released from the first contract. To the second potential employer, reply in some vein like this:

I certainly would like to accept your offer to come with your
firm. As attractive as your proposal is, however, I must
delay accepting it until I can secure a release from the
Jenkins firm in Blankville. After my interview with you, I
accepted this position, which at the time appeared to be the
most promising available.

Can you allow me enough time to write the Jenkins personnel
manager, explaining my reasons and requesting a release? (I
can give him the names of two friends who might be suitable
replacements.)

This problem shouldn't take longer than a week to settle. I
appreciate your offer, regardless of how things work out.

If necessary, phone the second potential employer, explain frankly, and get approval to wait. But for your own protection, do it *before* writing a letter like the following:

As you know, I am now planning to report to work as an
executive trainee shortly after the first of June.

Before I made this agreement with you, I had talked with a
representative of the Larkin organization in Sometown
concerning the possibilities of my working there as an analyst
in the quality control division, which is the kind of work I
have specifically trained for and know I want to do.

I believe I'd be a better adjusted and qualified employee in
the Larkin job. That is the main reason I ask that you release

```
me from my commitment with you.  The fact that Sometown is a
considerably larger city and that the starting salary is
somewhat larger are only secondary considerations.

No doubt you have other people you can call on to take my
place, but you may be interested to know that Don M. Jones and
Peter Lawson are interested in the Jenkins program.  You can
get portfolios on both of them through the placement bureau
here at school.

Since the Larkin people have agreed to postpone a decision
until I have heard from you, I would appreciate a quick reply.

You can rest assured that I shall keep my word with you and
that if your answer is no, I shall report to work as promised
and do all I can to be an efficient, cooperative, and cheerful
employee.
```

Only a Simon Legree would say no to the foregoing letter. If the company releases you, you'd then write the appropriate acceptance letter to the second firm; but you should, as a matter of business courtesy, write a short thank-you letter to the first company.

TWO USEFUL MODIFICATIONS OF APPLICATIONS

The following two letter possibilities for helping you get the job of your choice are *not here with the implication that they will take the place of the complete sales presentation* we have suggested to you. Only because they may help you some time do we even remind you of them.

The job-anticipating letter

Most personnel people are willing to give advice. And most of them are pleased with a show of interest in their companies and evidence of long-range planning on the part of a student. With that in mind, several of our students have had successful results from letters like the following, sent in the junior year of college:

```
A course in the operation of business machines under Mrs. Lora
Osmus in the Statistics Department at school gave me skill in
their operation and showed me the tremendous possibilities of
Burrows equipment for business use.

After comparing Burrows and ABL equipment that was on exhibit
on Commerce Day and talking with the Burrows representative in
charge of your display, I am coming to you directly and
frankly for some help.

Since I have completed practically all the courses required
for the B.S. in commerce, I am free to elect practically all
courses I shall study next year before June graduation.  On
the attached sheet I've listed the courses I've completed and
those I'm contemplating.  Will you please rank the ones you
consider most beneficial for a prospective Burrows
representative?
```

Naturally, I will regard your suggestions as off-the-cuff
assistance that implies no commitment. I'm just trying to
equip myself as well as I can to meet the competition for the
first available job with your company after I graduate.

I shall be most grateful for your comments.

The telescoped application inquiry

We realize that good applications take time. They're worth the time, however.

But we also know that sometime, somewhere, you may need to send some inquiries in a hurry and simply cannot write a complete one. You may be able to make profitable use of the services of your college placement bureau in a letter, as one student did. The applicant was too busy writing a thesis and sitting for graduate examinations to prepare a thorough application. So six firms received the following request and reply card:

With completion of an M.S. degree in accounting at the
University of North Carolina and two years of retail merchandise
accounting experience, I believe I could make you a good
accountant with a minimum of training—and be able to advance
more rapidly than the majority of accountants you could hire.

I am not just an accountant: A well-rounded background of
finance, transportation, economics, and other related subjects
will enable me, in time, to do managerial work as well.

May I have the Placement Bureau here at the University send
you a transcript of my college record together with a detailed
record of my experience, faculty rating statements, and names
and addresses of former employers?

I shall be happy to furnish any additional information you may
want and to be available for an interview at your convenience
later if you will check and return the enclosed card.

All six firms replied, but only one resulted in an interview.

This kind of quick note may be a stopgap measure sometime. But this person's experience simply reconfirms the fact that you must tell a complete story if you expect to get a show of effective interest.

✿　　✿　　✿　　✿　　✿

Although letters exchanging information about applicants are a part of the employment routine, applicants themselves do not write them. For that reason, and because you studied them in Chapter 5, we see no point in taking them up again here. They are A–plan letters, characterized by directness and conciseness.

Likewise, we do not think you need to study or write the kinds of letters an interviewer or employer writes offering an applicant a position (clearly an A–plan good-news letter) or turning down an applicant (a B–plan disappointing news letter). With but simple changes of talking points and references, they follow the principles of their basic plans (Chapters 5 and 7).

CASES FOR APPLICATIONS

Preliminaries to preparing résumés, applications, and interviews

1.   After reading Chapters 9 and 10 and in Chapter 17 the first section and the "Interviews" section, make an appointment with a personnel director or other hiring decision maker of a firm. Interview that person to determine what the firm feels is vital to include in an unsolicited application letter and résumé. Find out the best methods for securing a job there. Then report your findings to the class in a written or oral presentation (as your instructor directs).

2.   Write out ten questions which you feel you should (or could) ask a corporation's campus recruiter who might interview you.

3.   Write out ten points which you would try to bring out about yourself in an interview for a desired job.

4.   Before you write your application letter and résumé, but after reading Chapter 9, write a memo to your instructor answering the following questions:

   a.   What are your career plans?
   b.   What training, attributes, or attitudes does one need to obtain a job and succeed in your chosen field?
   c.   What will you be required to do on the job? (Give a job description.)
   d.   What is the demand for people in your field this year? What is the future outlook for availability of jobs in your field?
   e.   What company would you like to work for? Why?
   f.   What do you need to know about this company before applying for a job? (Give the pertinent information about the company you have chosen.)

Since you will be using library materials, refer to pp. 488–92 for the way to tell how you got your information.

5.   Split into groups of four and concurrently conduct mock job interviews. One student in each group should be the interviewer, one the job applicant, and the other two observers and (later) commentators. The interviewer needs a copy of the applicant's résumé (and two minutes to read it) before the interview. The observers should each give a critique of each performer at the end of the interview.

Prospecting applications

1. Assume that you are in your last term of school and graduation is around the corner. Your interest is in finding work which you like, for which you have been preparing, and in which you could support yourself now and support (or help support) a family later as you win promotions.

Newspapers, trade magazines, and placement bureaus list no job of your choice. So you decide to do as any good seller does: analyze the product (yourself); then appraise the market (companies which could use a person who can do what you are prepared to do); then advertise (send the companies an application letter and résumé). Such a procedure sometimes creates a job where none existed before; sometimes it establishes a basis for negotiations for the "big job" two, three, or five years after graduation. And very frequently it puts you on the list for the good job which is not filled through advertising or from the company staff.

To analyze the high points of your preparation, you will need to consider the courses you have had and make plausible assumptions (don't go daydreaming and woolgathering; stick to probabilities) about the courses you will have completed on graduation. *This means you'll have to study your college catalog.* It also means that you will have to make a temporary decision about the kind of work you want to do. If you haven't the faintest idea of what you'd like to do, follow the suggestions in Chapter 9.

Distinguish between those courses that actually qualify you to do the type of work you are seeking and those that give you background education. If you've had experience directly related to the job you want as a career, that's fine; but any work you've done means qualifications (military experience—active duty—is in almost the same category as on-the-job experience). With these training and work sections mapped out, complete a tentative résumé with appropriate personal details and references.

Then study the market, as suggested under "Analyzing Companies" (p. 314). In actual practice you might compile a list of companies and send them an application. For this assignment, after some preliminary digging around, select one company and plan a letter-résumé combination addressed to that company. Adapt it as specifically as possible to the one company. You may or may not be able to find out the name of the specific individual to address it to. If not, address it to the personnel department or to the head of the particular department in which you are interested.

You will benefit from this exercise in application letter writing only if you approach it earnestly and seriously. *It should be a job utilizing your college training.* It should be a job geared to what you could reasonably assume will be your level of performance at graduation. Few just-out-of-college folks can expect to be sales managers, chief buyers, senior accountants, copy chiefs, and the like; you'll have to begin at a subordinate level and work up; you'll want to *show in your letter that you realize this fact.*

On the other hand, don't waste your time and your instructor's applying for something that you could readily do if you had never gone to college.

You will sometimes hear advice to confine your presentation to a one-page letter and a one-page résumé; but don't be afraid to go to two pages for either. As in sales letters, some highly successful ones run to two and sometimes even three pages. What is important is that you make your presentation fully, and in the way that is most favorable for you. Take as much space as necessary to present the facts about yourself in the best light, remembering that employers don't like to buy pigs in pokes but don't like padding either.

2.   You have learned of a $500 scholarship that is available for somebody with your major who (*a*) has at least a B average, (*b*) can attend a week-long, expense-paid convention in Dallas during the summer, and (*c*) will write a letter of application. Assume *a*, *b*, and *c* and address your letter to the American (your major) Association, 753 West Market St., Akron, OH 44312.

The Association has several reasons for and restrictions on giving you $500 plus another $400–500 in trip expenses:

a.   It wants to encourage good people to get into the line of work (and, it hopes, the association).

b.   It wants to help with the professional education of selectees by giving them additional early insights into the ways the professionals work and talk.

c.   It will spend only about $5,000 a year on the five scholarships to be granted by making them nationally competitive.

The basis of the selection is solely the letter you send in (with or without a résumé—your choice, unless your instructor makes it for you).

3.   Since you will be graduating in June, you feel that now is the time to prospect for a job. You have already spent two months researching likely corporations, and you have asked the campus placement center to keep a file of your transcripts and reference letters. Write a letter to Jonathan Renolds, personnel director of Universal Products, a large conglomerate. Use your own experience and educational background to request an interview at Universal's nearby branch (select a city near you) for work that your own qualifications best fit. (You will want to do a thorough job now, so you can use this letter for real later on.)

4.   You have read recently that next year's budget for your school will be cut back extensively. To offset the increased class size that will result from the funding cutbacks, the Board of Regents has authorized departments to use advanced undergraduates who have made A's in first- and

second-year survey courses to act as teachers (guiding students through a well-planned program) for those courses. The salary will be $2,500 for nine months. Since you made an A in _____ (use your own major), you feel you can qualify. Write a prospecting job letter to Dr. Doris Davidson, head of the _____ Department, outlining your qualifications and asking for an interview.

5. You've decided that you want to earn some money, see some new places, and have some fun this coming summer. So you're going to address an application for summer employment to a summer camp or an inn at a resort (possibly one of the national parks). You'll have to indicate a willingness to do housekeeping duties (including kitchen and dining room work), although if you have enough maturity and the right kind of experience you may be able to get some kind of clerical or even more specialized assignment. Since college students chosen for such jobs are really hosts and hostesses to the guests, stress poise, dignity, and cheerfulness, as well as any talents for entertaining.

6. Modify the preceding problem to this extent: You want to be a counselor at a summer camp for children of any age group at least eight years younger than you. Choose a camp with which you are familiar, or find out about one. Address the letter and résumé to the camp director (by name if you can get it). Note here the importance of understanding and getting along with youngsters, the ability to direct activities, and the emphasis on leadership, athletic, and teaching abilities. Apply to a camp which is not in your home town or your college town; it should be a residence camp, not a day camp.

7. Look over your local situation for part-time job possibilities, perhaps on your college campus or in the college community (close enough for you to arrange a schedule of classes that would permit you to work in the afternoons). Word the application so the reader will understand about how many hours a week you can work. Prepare a résumé and letter that summarize and interpret your background up to the time of writing.

8. Assume that you are *not* graduating this year and write a job-seeking letter for full-time work next summer. It should not only enable you to earn some money to apply on your college expenses; it should also be work which will be good preparation for the career you plan when you finish your degree and/or leave college. Too, consider the prestige value of the company name on résumés you will prepare later in your life.

This may well be the company to which you would send an application upon graduation; if so, shape your letter presentation accordingly.

9. With plausible assumptions and appropriate modifications, write a job-anticipating letter to the company of your choice. Assume that you have one more year of college before graduating.

Invited applications

1. A good starting point in job getting is the want-ad columns of newspapers and magazines (especially trade magazines). Study the ones of your choice and find an ad that describes a job you would like to have, requiring qualifications you could reasonably assume at the time of your graduation (or some other assumed time as affected by your intentions). It should be a job utilizing your college training. And it should clearly call for letter—not telephone—answers. Clip the ad neatly to your letter; or if you find the ad of your choice in a library copy, make an exact copy, with exact reference: name of publication, date of the issue, and page on which you found the ad. You may instead choose one of the ads listed later in this case.

Draw on imagination, experience, and whatever information you can find out to bring the situation as close to reality as you can. Read the ad thoughtfully for what it says, and search mentally for those qualifications it only implies. Then evaluate your own training and experience in the light of the specific job. You can readily distinguish between courses that actually qualify you to do the job you're considering and those that are only background. You can certainly classify your work experience in an order of applicability to the given job. Further, analyze significant personal factors. And finally, decide upon references. You will need to send along a résumé (and refer to it in your letter) unless you have contrary instructions.

Submit the letter trying to get the one job for which you are best suited, either from an ad you've found or one of the following:

(*a*) Administrative Assistant—Large Dallas clinical laboratory seeking individual with degree in business administration and interested in getting experience in collections and third-party reimbursement. Salary commensurate with education and experience. Send letter and résumé to Y–7380, *News.*

(*b*) Programmer, 370 Cobol. Westchester-based company, an industry leader in technology, requires programmer with ability to work on own. Good company benefits. Excellent working conditions in new modern plant. Send letter and résumé to P. Barbato, Westchester Rockland Newspapers, Inc., 1 Garnett Drive, White Plains, NY 10604.

(*c*) Marketing Trainee—$16,000 Yr. Large national *Fortune* 500 corporation seeks sharp, aggressive degreed applicant to enter administrative management program with career path leading to wholesale tangible marketing. Dallas based, rapid advancement, excellent compensation & super benefits. Jack Bundy, First Bank & Trust Building, Suite 302, Richardson, TX 75080.

(*d*) Accountant Management Candidate. Middle-West consumer-oriented concern seeks self-starting accountant for home office assignment. Prepare management reports, work heavily in financial analysis. All aspects of accounting for company and subsidiaries; challenging career opportunity. Above average salary and benefits. Write Management Personnel Service, 6060 North Central, Peoria, IL 61617.

(*e*) Public Oriented Person needed with ability to perform in a customer relations and sales capacity for multimillion-dollar company. Handling customer problems and complaints, acting as goodwill ambassador and selling. Limited travel and a 5-day work week required. Write Mr. Cawthorn, Wherry Minivac, Marketing Dept., 2 Metroplex Drive, Suite 1100, Atlanta, GA 30304.

(*f*) Assistant Manager Trainee, genuinely interested in a career in food service industry. After six weeks professional training, become an assistant restaurant manager and work way into a restaurant manager's position. No experience necessary. Incentive bonus plan. Paid vacations. Group insurance. Employee stock ownership plan. Retirement benefits. Opportunity to grow. Write Gene Purvis, Box J–121, *Times.*

(*g*) Exec. Sec'y. Opening for Executive Secretary to Pharmaceutical Sales Division Manager. Must have ability to utilize office procedures, proficiency in handling telephone communication w/sales personnel & public, ability to supervise and schedule work load for office. Submit letter and résumé to Ms. M. Hischer, Wyeth Laboratories, P.O. Box 35213, Dallas, TX 75235. Equal Opportunity Employer.

(*h*) Assistant Managers, Tenneco Food Stores. Gain management experience and a chance for advancement. 5-day work week, vacation, and other benefits. Apply 2374 Briarcliff Road, Chicago 60658.

(*i*) Decorating Consultant. National concern. Good starting salary, many company benefits. Apply William Sherwin Co., Lubbock, TX 79408.

(*j*) Sales Representative—needed for progressive Philadelphia-based food service company. Excellent salary, commission, benefits and bonus arrangement for aggressive individual. Write Richard Levin, Blue Ribbon Service, Oxford Ave., Philadelphia, PA 19111.

(*k*) Excellent Business Opportunity as manager, well-established dress shop, Bay Area, ideal mall location. Salary plus profit sharing. Reply P.O. Box 85162, Clearwater, FL 33518.

(*l*)   Customer Relations—Position open for person with farm background or farm sales experience. Neatness and ability to talk to people essential. College graduate desirable. Person selected will interview farmers and do limited travel in North Carolina. Earnings range $11–15,000 first year, depending on individual selected. Benefits include stock options and substantial yearly increases in income. Write Manager, Box 79, c/o *Herald.*

(*m*)   Computer Programmer—Must have experience in Cobol & Bal languages. Immediate requirements. Competitive starting salary, excellent benefits, fast-growing company. Send résumé to: Central Computer Services, Box D–90, c/o *News.*

(*n*)   Office Manager. Knowledge of office machines; knowledge of accounting desirable. Must have initiative, ambition, adaptability, eagerness to learn. State full details, salary expected in letter. Large firm with sales-service outlets in key cities of the United States, Europe, Canada, Mexico. Local Box 70.

(*o*)   Insurance Manager—American Life Insurance Company. Must be able to hire and train sales personnel. Prefer college graduate with knowledge of insurance and business. Salary override commission and renewal bonuses. Apply with letter and data sheet, Box 98765, *Times.*

(*p*)   Immediate Opening—internal auditor. For young college graduate with major in accounting to train as internal auditor with growing national manufacturer in Iowa. Excellent opportunity for person with executive potential, ambition, attractive personality. Experience helpful but not essential. Established concern. Up-to-date employee benefits. Write giving full details of qualifications and salary requirement. All replies will be kept confidential. Write C–90, c/o *News.*

(*q*)   Accountant—expanding national concern. Traveling. Good opportunity for person with ambition, personality, hard-work habits. State training and experience in confidential letter to P–87, c/o *News.*

(*r*)   Executive Secretary—Outstanding position for friendly and aggressive person. $475. Write Box 987, c/o *Press*, stating training and experience.

(*s*)   Credit and adjustment manager of national shirt manufacturer needs assistant. Handle routine correspondence, supervise clerical help. Bright future for right person. College training, business experience, mature judgment necessary. Salary $7,500 to $10,000, depending on qualifications. Box R–88, c/o *Press.*

(*t*)   Sales Representative—P. Q. Holcomb Manufacturing Company— has a new local opening. A local semiestablished high income potential territory will be available within the next 30 days. The individual will call on industrial, institutional, and commercial accounts. The right person for this career opportunity should have successful sales experience and have a keen desire to earn more. In addition to high earning potential we offer an expense-paid training program, no overnight travel, and ample opportunities for advancement. An Equal Opportunity Employer. Write Box T, *Herald*.

2.　When you went past your department bulletin board yesterday, you noticed that the Ridan Corporation was advertising for a _____ (put in a job for which your experience and training can qualify you). Your adviser thinks you can fill the job. Write a letter to Maxwell Moody (personnel director of Ridan, 444 Hill Road, Amarillo, TX 79105) in which you present your qualifications and ask for an interview during a short span of days you plan to be in the Amarillo area.

3.　Your college adviser (use the name) just mentioned to you that a good friend (provide the name), the personnel director of Superior Petroleum (856 Faisel Avenue, Houston 77020), has asked that good prospects be steered Superior's way at the on-campus interviews coming up next month. You like Superior's positive view toward protecting the environment and had thought of writing a prospective job letter. Now, however, you can write an invited job letter. Your adviser told you that Superior needed people with your qualifications. Write an *invited* job application letter that shows your qualifications for going to work for Superior and asks for an appointment during the interview period. Assume that your résumé goes with the letter.

4.　This morning you had a walk-in interview with the representative of a firm you'd like to work for. After half an hour of talk which appeared to be mutually satisfactory and during which time you found out a lot about the company, the representative handed you one of the company employment forms for applying, shook your hand, and ushered you out of the room, saying, "Fill this out and return it to me with a letter of application." *Assuming* the form is filled in neatly and completely, draft your earnest but enthusiastic letter of application. Be careful to talk work rather than employee benefits. Assume specific names for the representative and the company.

5.　From the head of the department in which you are majoring, this morning you learn that a firm you hold in high regard is seeking a person with substantially your qualifications for a particular job you want—*a job calling for an unusual combination of qualifications that you have.* Fill in with the necessary specific details and write the letter you would send, assuming that your résumé presentation will accompany it.

6.   The director of your college placement bureau (use name) has just told you about the training program of a large corporation. The personnel director indicated in a letter that the company seeks college graduates to train for managerial positions throughout the organization. During a year trainees work in every division under close supervision and attend a series of classes. Assume a specific company, indicate your particular field of interest, but reflect a receptive attitude toward the various phases of the training program, showing your realization of its benefits regardless of the specific work you'll eventually perform, and send an application letter and résumé.

7.   For another case, see GS 31 (p. 307).

Follow-ups

1.   In response to your application you receive an invitation to come in for an interview at a time and place convenient for you. Write the acceptance confirming the circumstances.

2.   Assume that in response to your prospecting application you receive an invitation to come in for an interview at a time which would be convenient if you had the money for traveling to the distant point. Write the letter which reaffirms your interest. Admit your lack of funds and ask if you might see a representative of the firm at a place which is more accessible to you.

3.   Assume that you have had an interview as a result of your letter and résumé. You know the company representative interviewed several other candidates for the job. In a thank-you letter, confirm your interest in employment by the company and add other details to show that you picked up something from the interview. The representative promised to get in touch with you in a week or ten days.

4.   Not having heard from the application letter you have sent, write a letter reemphasizing your desire to work for the firm. You may want to send it as soon as three weeks after the initial letter; you may prefer to wait longer. Clearly refer to the original application by date and type of work discussed. Include any additional data you think will help sell you. This letter, however, should not be a rehash of what you have already written. It should identify the action you want the reader to take.

5.   Assuming that almost a year has passed since you sent your original letter, write a follow-up letter that reassures the firm of your desire to work there. In the meantime a good deal has happened to you (or should have!).

Account for the way you have spent the time in such a manner as to show that it is preparation for the job you seek.

6. Although you were offered a job in response to your application, you have decided that you do not want to accept it because it is not in the field of your primary interest and for other plausible reasons—not salary. Write the tactful letter that expresses appreciation for the time spent with you and the interest shown in you and that leaves the way open for you to resume negotiations later if you care to. Comment favorably on some aspect of the company.

7. You have just been informed that you were not chosen for the job you have worked so hard to get—and still want. Remember, however, that you were considered; that someone spent a good deal of time with you; and that, employmentwise, nothing is ever final. Write the letter expressing appreciation for the courtesies extended you, revealing how you have profited from the contact, and showing your determination to reach your intended goal. Above all, the letter should reflect a friendly feeling toward the company and the representative addressed.

8. As a result of your determined efforts and good showing, you've been offered the job of your choice. The letter so informing you requests you to fill in an employment form and return it and names a starting date that fits in with your plans. Write the acceptance.

9. Assume you have an intolerable situation where you are employed. Your boss lies, covers up, misleads, is basically dishonest. Although physically attractive, a money-maker for the firm, this person is most difficult to work for, and you cannot take the situation any longer. Write a letter of resignation and assume you have another job to go to. You assume names of company and people.

10. For other cases, see GS 32 (thanks) and GS 33 (resignation), p. 307.

chapter 11 # Persuasive messages: Requests

SPECIAL REQUESTS

ALTHOUGH MOST INQUIRIES people in business make are for information about products, services, or people—and therefore the receiver is usually willing if not glad to reply—some of them ask *special favors of receivers who have no built-in motivation to reply.*

These special requests are more difficult than the direct inquiries discussed in Chapter 5—and for a readily understandable reason: Most people, when asked to do something not obviously beneficial to themselves, can think of two reasons why they should not for every one reason why they should. The ability to make effective special requests is therefore one of the most important you can develop—for both your business and non-business use.

Each person comes into the world with certain abilities—and some with the proverbial silver spoon in their mouths. The important question is not what you were born with but what you do with it. As a worthwhile person you should use at least some of your time and abilities to make the world better instead of just taking what you can get from it; and, since you can do little alone, the extent to which you can contribute—in business, education, government, science, or a profession—will depend more on your ability to create ideas and persuade other people to help you implement them than on any silver spoon or almost any other asset you may have.

In enlisting the help of others, you need to realize that no one ever has enough money or time to give either of them spontaneously and unquestioningly. No one is willing to reveal certain kinds of information without knowing its intended use and deciding that the purpose is good. To put the question directly in these cases is to get an immediate turndown. So the special request has to be persuasive. Like the simple inquiry, the effective special request is specific and concise, but it is not direct; and because it usually requires more explanation, it is usually longer.

Favor-seeking messages are, as already explained briefly in Chapter 4, C–plan messages. The secret to their successfully persuasive copy is to (1) secure interested motivation first by offering, suggesting, or implying a benefit—the you-attitude as explained on page 82 and under **YA** in Appendix B—or at least talking about something of interest; (2) justify the request by interweaving necessary information with explanations and reminders of the benefit(s); (3) try to foresee and preclude or minimize objections; and (4) after giving the necessary information and persuasion, confidently ask for the desired action.

Before we go further in telling you how to phrase persuasive requests, however, a point of caution deserves your attention: *You should not be making such requests unless you cannot get what you want by your own efforts.*

Securing interest

If you are going to strike the appropriately persuasive theme, you need to analyze the situation to select the most pertinent and applicable *motive* as the beginning.

Money being what it must be in business thinking, the strongest appeal is one that holds out the prospect of sales, of saving money, or of promoting goodwill with an audience wherein sales may ultimately materialize. Such potential-dollar themes offer the most concrete form of benefit and are responsible for this opening to an advertising manager of a manufacturing company:

```
What would it be worth to Field's to add some 8,000 potential
customers to its prospect list?
```

and this opening to the circulation manager of a magazine:

```
Who will be your subscribers ten years from now?
```

If you can apply such reader-benefit themes appropriately and remain within the realm of good taste (avoiding the suggestion of bribery), you undoubtedly have the strongest appeal you can make.

In many instances, however, such dollar-minded talk would arouse indignation or would not apply. But you need not despair of finding a talking point which will stress the reader's benefits or interests rather than your own. The letter to the correspondence supervisor (on p. 82) that begins

> How often have you received—even from well-educated people—
> letters that are not worth your attention?

clearly holds out a benefit by talking in terms of making the reader's job easy. Many times the basis for a busy person's filling out a time-consuming questionnaire (or one that asks for information ordinarily restricted to the firm) is the realization that a result of the information thus gathered and made available will be improved efficiency.

Indirect benefits may serve too. When you can show how your project will promote the welfare of a group in which your reader holds a membership or other interest, you can make a strong appeal. On this basis you might persuade a public accountant to speak to a college accounting club, an alumnus of a professional fraternity to take on a responsible office in the organization, or a correspondence supervisor to address a group of teachers or students of business writing.

The following letter written to the founder of the successful *Direct Marketing/Mail* magazine got results (the founder came to Gainesville and talked to two groups of students):

What can I do with students who consistently turn in sales letters with the same old overused and misapplied tricks as the dominant message?

Year after year I lecture to my students in Business Communications on how to write a good sales letter. I put my book (Communicating Through Letters and Reports) in front of them, give them outside readings for additional help, and still a few repeatedly miss major points.

Don't you agree that all of them would benefit and more thoroughly understand the techniques of writing sales letters if they could hear an explanation from a specialist with a flair for speaking to groups and winning their attention?

Next Monday (February 26) at 1:20 p.m. and 7 p.m. I have scheduled the first of two 50-minute lectures on sales letters to the two groups. I can always count on the attendance of at least 200 students in each group; and with the announcement of a guest speaker who is the past editor of a popular magazine and specialist in this area of communications, I'm certain their enthusiasm would soar.

Since they received their assignment last week, they will have been exposed to the material in my book by the Monday lectures, and I will be able to notify them in their discussion classes of your arrival. Of course, I'm looking forward to having you as my overnight guest, and my wife is a splendid cook. She's been looking forward to meeting you for years.

The students on the campus this year are an eager, active group. They respond particularly well to visiting speakers. Won't you call or write me within the week to let me know I can expect you on Monday? I would appreciate having my students hear from an expert before they become tomorrow's sales letter writers.

Although many special requests such as the preceding letter appeal to friendship, interest in a particular field, or altruism,[1] in most business situations you will do better if you select and emphasize direct benefit talking points—such as the three one-sentence beginnings at the start of this section imply.

As you look back at the beginnings quoted so far in this section, you will also note that in addition to highlighting benefits (or at least supposed interest), these openings are questions. You will note, too, that the questions are rhetorical (asked not to get their answers, as in inquiries, but to promote thinking and encourage reading on).

We do not mean to imply that all persuasive requests must begin with a question. But a question beginning commands greater attention than a declarative statement, is never as challenging as some statements are, can be subtly flattering, and more readily *leads to thinking about your suggestion*. In phrasing such questions, however, you will be on safer ground if you eliminate the possibility of either a "Yes" or "No" answer because such an answer stops thought about the mentioned or implied benefit. To promote thinking about the circumstances that will lead up to the request, each of the preceding openings employs the strategy.

Neither do we mean to imply that to secure interest you must studiously avoid *all* yes or no questions. If the answer leaves an intriguing wonder about how to get the mentioned benefit, you've achieved your purpose of leading into interested contemplation of your message. The following opening addressed to a national retailer contemplating entering the Texas market, for example, is certainly a good one:

```
Wouldn't you consider the respect and attention of some 200
key Texas retailers a valuable opportunity to test the true
business conditions in that state?
```

The mental response to such a question is positive and pursuing; and as long as you can be fairly sure of a positive reaction, you are probably on safe ground.

The danger lies in getting an irritated answer—whether that answer is a yes or a no or any of the variants of "So what?" The student who invited the head of a large public accounting firm to speak to a college group and began with

```
Do you believe in preparing for the future?
```

---

[1] Though letters seeking funds for worthy causes are special-request letters and thus within the scope of this analysis, we do not take them up here because they are too highly specialized and often have civic, religious, and fraternal manifestations. When faced with such problems, you can be sure that the fundamental principles we present here will apply; but for more detailed techniques and "tricks of the trade," check some books like Margaret Fellows and Stella Koenig's *Tested Methods of Raising Money for Churches, Colleges, and Health and Welfare Agencies,* Harper & Bros., New York, 1959.

apparently gave little thought to the probable snort that would result from such a question. To eliminate the irritating aspects (and get closer to the subject) a supervisor changed the opening to read:

```
What, in your opinion, are the desirable personal
characteristics of the successful public accountant?
```

True, that beginning implies no benefit; but it is certainly a subject of practical interest. Of possibly greater benefit implications is this one:

```
What does it cost you when you have to dismiss a well-grounded
junior accountant because of poor personal characteristics?
As you know, the actual cost of additional recruiting and
training isn't the only loss either:  The loss of prestige and
possibly of clients is a greater threat.
```

Careful study of the preceding beginnings will show three other advantages that come from question beginnings implying reader benefits: (1) they are more likely to keep the reader in the picture, (2) they almost prohibit you from making the serious mistake of beginning with explanations or details of circumstances, and (3) they make the transition to the explanation easier.

Justifying the request

Having secured interest with a beginning which holds some promise of benefit or at least talks of interesting things, you usually need to devote the greater part of your letter to explaining what your project is and what good comes of it—particularly the *good* (benefit) coming to the person you're trying to persuade. Thus and only thus can you keep that person involved —and you can't persuade without that involvement.

In almost any request, details concerning who, what, when, where, why, how (sometimes how much) need clarification; but they do *not* deserve first place. And even in this second section (where they belong) you need to *subordinate* them to reminders of benefits coming from granting the request. In inviting a speaker, for instance, you need to tell the nature and size of the audience, the time and place, the facilities available, the amount of time allotted, and the topic (if you are assigning one). Sometimes knowing about other speakers who will precede and follow would be helpful. But even after a benefit-oriented beginning such details should come in *subordinately* as much as possible.

A common mistake is ignoring the reader and the benefit beginning just to write about the project. The following, for example, would be laughable if it weren't so pitiful. Written by a Texan too immature to have outgrown chauvinism and too lazy to have studied this book, it sounds like a candidate campaigning for a county judgeship:

The Texas Business Conference will be held the 28-30th of next month at the Lakeway Inn just outside Austin where we again expect 200–300 business executives to convene for our twenty-fifth annual meeting.

We boosters of the great Lone Star state are interested in her future. We have observed her vast resources being utilized more and more through the years and have seen her taking her place in the vast industrial economy of our country. . . .

What should the Texan have said in view of these known facts?

—The purpose of the letter was to get a big-name speaker for the retailers' group of 50 to 100.

—In *Time* the week before, an article about one of New York's biggest retailers explained that Mr. Hoving (our fictional name) was considering branches in the Southwest.

After following some advice to study a previous edition of this book, the same Texan wrote this:

What was your final decision regarding the installation of an employee bonus system in your stores, as mentioned in last week's *Time*?

Leading Texas retailers are eager to hear how you solved this problem and others like it, and the reasons behind the solutions. They'd look forward with interest to sharing ideas with you. And you'd get a very accurate reflection of Texas retail conditions if you'd talk to the group from 2:00 to 3:00 on the 29th and then lead a half-hour's informal discussion when the 50-100 members meet for the 25th annual Texas Business Conference at the Lakeway Inn just outside Austin on the 28th to 30th this month.

Your ideas on sales promotion, ways to meet the competition of discount houses, and personnel-management problems distinctly applicable to department stores would be eagerly received, shared—maybe even contested if you care to invite a vigorous discussion—by these men and women. And they'd certainly be appreciated more than usual because our members are fully aware that prominent speakers appear at their own expense— that the pay they receive is the self-satisfaction one feels in having his ideas accepted by others and the benefits of other successful men's experiences and viewpoints.

To help us get the desirable publicity for your appearance, will you write us by the 10th that you'll be with us? We anticipate your "Yes" with gratitude and enthusiasm. And we're certain that you could pick up some useful ideas and information about a section of the country that is expanding rapidly.

By casting the proper bait—a package of just about all the principles explained in this chapter and epitomized in the checklist—the Texan caught the particular big fish he wanted. The well-chosen appeal, taken from the *Time* story, is the chance to learn more about Texas business waters before coming in. Of particular note is the skillful way of telling

Hoving he gets no fee. By such know-how—including the legitimate use of several passives in the third paragraph to put the emphasis on Hoving and his ideas rather than on *we*—the Texan talked a busy man into leaving his business to prepare a speech and fly from New York to Austin and back at his own expense to give it (something $1,000 would not usually do).

Conversely, nobody would be enthusiastic over a beginning like this:

```
As a Master's candidate at Harvard University, I am planning a
thesis on palletization.  Professor H. D. Brunham of our
marketing department has suggested that I write to you to find
out the results of your experience.
```

Notice in the following copy how the student seeking this information not only changed the opening to an interest-arousing question but also *subordinated* the necessary but uninteresting details of the original opening:

```
Just what economies are you experiencing from your installation
of palletization?

Are they as great as my limited experience has led me to
believe?

Has palletization been adopted by an increasing number of
business firms in recent years?

Regardless of your experience in using pallets, your comments
in answering these questions could contribute materially in
making a worthwhile, authentic, down-to-earth thesis of the
one I am preparing as partial requirement for an M.S. degree.
Too, the finished thesis may well be of practical interest to
all users and potential users of pallets.

Perhaps you have some printed material which you can simply
enclose in the stamped, addressed envelope I've included.  If
not, will you take a few minutes to tell me your experience
with pallets, the cost of palletizing (with particular
emphasis on warehousing), current uses or ideas in
palletization, and/or possible sources?

Although I don't have to, I'd like to be able to quote you;
but I'll handle the material with whatever degree of
confidence and anonymity you specify.  And no part of this
correspondence will ever be used for any purposes other than
research, I assure you.

Since I have to assemble material and start writing by June 1,
I'd be most grateful if you'd let me hear from you before that
date.

If you would like to read the finished thesis for a new idea
or two that you might be able to put to work, I'll be glad to
lend you my personal copy shortly after August 25.
```

Why—besides the interest-arousing question beginning and the skillfully subordinated facts justifying the request—did seven copies of that letter bring five detailed replies? Did you notice (second, fourth, and last paragraphs) the prospect and reminders of the reader's possible benefits—the last a usual one (where fitting) of offering to share ideas? Did you notice (fifth paragraph) how clear and specific the writer made the requested action and how easy it seems? And did you notice (sixth paragraph) the reassurance against any fears as to how the information might be used? And how (next-to-last paragraph) the writer avoided seeming to push the reader around by justifying the request for action by a necessary end date? Any one of these points may make the difference between your getting nothing and getting what you want in a persuasive favor-seeking situation.

Minimizing obstacles

Even though your interest-arousing first sentence and justifying explanation may have supplied good reasons which highlight the reader's advantage or interest, in most circumstances some fly is in the ointment: a negative factor you have to overcome. It may be a sum of money you are asking for. Then you break it down into several payments. It may be that you can offer no fee or a smaller fee than a program speaker is accustomed to receiving; then you cite other (perhaps intangible) rewards. It may sound like a lot of trouble or work (say, a questionnaire). Then word it to sound as quick and easy as possible. It may be that you're asking for secret information. If so, give assurance that you will do all you can to protect the reader's interest. Regardless of the case or the circumstance, you can usually find some positive corollary to the drawback.

As added inducement, you want to make the job sound as easy as possible and as pleasurable as possible. Phrasing can do a lot here. At least you should reduce the mechanical aspects of complying with your request to the minimum of detail, time, and money. That is why most questionnaires are fill-in or checkoff forms and why a return-addressed reply device requiring no postage ordinarily accompanies such requests.

Positively anticipating acceptance

After establishing the reader's benefit or contribution, making clear exactly what you want and why (along with reminders of the benefit), and minimizing obstacles, you should confidently ask for the response you want. Hesitant, apologetic expressions belittle the request itself and have the disadvantage of suggesting excuses as reasons for refusal. Such expressions as the following hinder rather than help:

```
I realize you are very busy, but . . . .
I'm sorry to trouble you for such an apparently insignificant
matter; however . . . .
I hesitate to bother you with such a request . . . .
If you consider this a worthwhile project, . . . .
```

Eliminate such thinking (maybe by rereading the discussion on "Success Consciousness," p. 90) and forthrightly name the specific action you want. Although you may have referred to it earlier, be sure to ask for it or at least refer to it near the end.

In your favor-seeking letters apply the summary of points on page 388.

PERSUASIVE CLAIMS AND POLICY COMPLAINTS

Sometimes you will have good reason to believe that you need to be rather persuasive to get results on a claim. Your reason may be that you know the other person to be rather reluctant to grant claims, that your case is subject to some question and you need to make as good a case as you can within the facts, or (most frequently) that you have already tried a direct claim (pp. 141–44) and have been turned down.

Whatever the cause, you use C–plan organization and psychology (similar to the special request) when you need to be persuasive, and you can appeal to any desire that might motivate. Some of the main appeals (more or less in ascending order of force and objectionable tone) are to the desire for (1) customer satisfaction, goodwill, and favorable publicity; (2) a continued reputation for fair dealing; and (3) legal meeting of a guarantee.

Again your message divides rather distinctly into three parts, but their contents are somewhat different from those of the direct claim:

1. You begin by stating and getting agreement on a principle which is the basis of your claim. (In logic, it is the major premise.)
2. You explain all the facts in detail, as in any claim. (The term in logic is the minor premise.) This part may be several paragraphs long. In it you show clearly the other's responsibility.
3. You apply the facts or minor premise to the principle or major premise so as to draw a conclusion, as the logician would call it. The conclusion will point clearly to a certain action. You then request that action.

Here are two examples of how the system works. The first was an initial claim. It was successful, in spite of the fact that a glance may suggest that the writer had no justified claim. A closer look, however, will make the justification clear. The situation was quite different from a person's just buying something and finding a few days later that the seller has reduced the price. The key difference is the sales clerk's assurance to the claimant—you save no money by waiting. The appeal is therefore to the desire for customer confidence.

Going to a lot of trouble and expense in selecting and training your sales personnel doesn't do much good, does it, Mr. Barnes, unless your customers trust them? That's why I'm writing to you.

On July 5 I was in your store looking at an XXXX suit priced at $157.75. I decided to leave and wait for a late-summer sale, but your salesclerk assured me that you would have no sale on XXXX suits, that the manufacturer had never allowed

Special-Request Checklist

1. Your opening should be dominated by something of reader interest.
   a. When you can, develop a benefit theme.
   b. A subject line (unsound in any C–plan letter) or unmotivated request is likely to defeat your purpose.
   c. Though a rhetorical question is usually best, one with an obvious yes or no answer stops rather than starts consideration.
   d. Are you promising too much (like total attendance of a group) or so bluntly as to be suspect?
   e. Don't appear to suggest a bribe or depend on obvious flattery.
   f. Explanations do not arouse interest; put them in the middle.

2. Keep the addressee(s) involved as you shift to your explanation.
   a. Give necessary details to prove that your project deserves consideration and to enable informed action on your request.
   b. But subordinate these details to reminders of benefit(s).
   c. Adapt your message; when you can, personalize it.
   d. If it is long, consider using name(s) in the second half or referring specifically to the city, work, or . . . .
   e. Don't phrase the exact request until after most of the benefits.
   f. Make participation sound easy—maybe even fun!

3. Any potentially negative element requires careful treatment.
   a. Elimination of a negative element is unethical and wasteful.
   b. Minimize it by positive statement, embedded position, and minimum space.
   c. Maintain a tone of confidence; avoid apologies; but, to avoid presumptuousness, also use the conditional mood in talking about requested action: *not* "you will be scheduled to speak . . ." but "you would (or could). . . ."
   d. Don't supply excuses for nonacceptance.
   e. Give assurance that you will handle confidential or other restricted material in whatever limited way specified.

4. Introduce any enclosure skillfully:
   a. Not too early—until you have finished your message.
   b. With emphasis on what to do with or get from it.

5. After justifying it, ask confidently for the desired action.
   a. Good action endings indicate specifically what to do, how to do it, helps and/or suggestions for ease of action, and reason for prompt action. Make specific and clear the action wanted.
   b. Justify, and establish specifically but subordinately, any time limits.
   c. Establish appreciation cordially in first-person future conditional. Offer to reciprocate if appropriate. Don't "thank in advance."
   d. When you include a return envelope, subordinate it.
   e. Inject a last punch line on the available benefit(s).

its suits to be sold at reduced prices and would not do so
this year. So, since I wanted the suit, I bought it.

Now I notice that you have reduced the price to $135.88. My
plan, you see, would have saved me $21.87. Because your sales
clerk induced me to buy through assurance that I could not get
the suit cheaper by waiting, I believe you will agree that I'm
entitled to a refund of $21.87.

I am sure that you want me to trust your salespeople. You can
renew my faith by standing behind what they say.

The following illustration is a persuasive claim written after a first
claim brought a proposal to compromise. It got the money, the full amount
without compromise, by appealing to fair-minded analysis of the facts (and
hence the injustice of compromise in the case).

Gentlemen:

Subject: Claim No. 070-6289

Do you think a sales representative for the XXXX Casualty
Company would sell me a policy if I offered to pay half the
premium requested? I don't. That would be a compromise on
the value of the policy.

Compromises in the adjustments on policies likewise are for
cases involving doubt about responsibility or about the amount
of damage done. In my claim no more doubt arises about either
than about the value of the policy.

Analysis of the facts will show that Mr. Hall ran up behind me
so fast that he could not control his car and hit the left
rear part of the side of my car. Clearly he was responsible.
Three reputable repair shop estimates of the repair job make
sure of my having a fair appraisal of the damages. The lowest
of the three is $186. So no doubt exists about the damage.

Therefore I am returning the Release and Settlement form you
sent and asking that you send another based on one of the
estimates I formerly sent in. That is the only fair
settlement.

Since your job is to keep your loss ratio down as low as
possible while being fair about the obligations the company
assumes in insuring clients, the solution is to settle on the
basis of one of the estimates submitted.

I look forward to receiving that settlement.

Whereas claims ask restitution for mistakes, damage, or unsatisfactory
products, *policy complaints* request correction of poor service or unsatisfactory policies and practices. A policy complaint may be like a direct
claim or a persuasive one, but it is more likely to be persuasive, as in the
following example:

Am I right in thinking that Racine Motors wants its policy on
direct-sale commissions and cooperative selling campaigns to
promote long-range goodwill and increased sales in this
territory?

Because I think so but find the present practice is not
working out that way, I think you will want to review your
policies in view of my experience.

Recently one of our sales representatives called on a prospect
in our territory and found "the prospect" already enjoying the
reliability and efficiency of a 20-hp Racine motor, which we
normally stock. Further investigation revealed that you sold
the motor directly at a price below our selling price. Yet
we have received no dealer's commission on this sale. This
is one of several occasions brought to my attention in the
past year which prompt me to ask you for a clarification of our
agreement.

Admittedly with the helpful assistance of your missionary
sales personnel, we have been able to sell a substantial group
of the industrial users in this area on the economy and
dependability of the Racine electric motor. We want to keep
and expand this patronage, but that will be difficult if we
are working at cross-purposes with you.

For our mutual good we and you should quote uniform prices,
and we should get our dealer's commission on any direct sales.
You would gain by being relieved of the marketing functions and
by having a ready-made market for your motor, and we would gain
by getting our just profits and keeping the goodwill of our
customers. That, I thought, was the intent of the exclusive-
dealership contract you signed with me.

We have been contemplating an expansion of our stock to include
your 60-hp motor, which would play an important part in our
sales program. Please give us a definite working policy so we
will know where we stand.

PERSUASIVE REQUESTS FOR CREDIT

You can apply for credit in direct, brief style when you are reasonably
sure you can meet the firm's credit tests (see p. 106). When you know
you are going to have to ask for special concessions, however, a persuasive
application patterned after the special request may be in order. The presentation establishes interest by stressing potential profitable business,
stresses your capacity for management, establishes a sensible plan for
meeting the obligation, and confidently asks for action. Like all the other
messages in this chapter, it is a modification of the AICA (Attention, Interest, Conviction, Action) of sales presentations.

In the following example the applicant asks for 150 days' credit, knowing that 30 days is the usual time allowed by the Long-Shearer Company.
*Although the letter is unusually long, detailed, and persuasive for a credit
application, it is for an unusual situation.*

Lots of auto-accessories dollars are floating around in
booming Lubbock. Yet the chains sell only a standard line.

An alert independent retailer offering a complete line of parts
and accessories could certainly count on the reputation of
Long-Shearer accessories to give a rapid turnover and a good
share of this increasing market.

Hence I am optimistic about the store I plan to open on June
24. Right on Main Street, near several garages and body shops,
the 50-foot-front store is out of the high-rent district, yet
accessible enough to get me my share of the walking trade.

The market survey I made last week indicates that conservatively I can expect 300 people in my store every day. And the managers of all the garages and body shops in the area of my store have promised me they'll buy from me.

They got to know me while I worked in my father's Ford service shop during and after high school. We became better friends in the year and a half I spent in the parts department after serving in the Navy and before returning to the University of Texas to complete my degree in marketing. I made friends with them—and I learned a lot about the business. I also made friends of most of the young business leaders in town through membership in Rotary and serving a term as president of the Jaycees.

I'm willing to put every bit of the $20,000 insurance money my father left me into the new store. I have no illusions of getting rich quickly and am fully prepared to plow profits back into the store so that it will get started on the right foot. You can see from the following allocation of the $20,000 that the store will be financially sound.

With $2,000 for store equipment, $3,600 for rent and operating expenses, and $3,600 plus a small personal fund for six months' personal expenses, I'll have about $10,000 left to buy an initial inventory. For the sort of stock I'll need to have an edge on my competitors, however, I should have an initial inventory of $20,000. I would therefore like to finance a $10,000 Long-Shearer accessories stock by paying $5,000 now, $2,500 in 120 days, and the other $2,500 30 days after that.

I plan to finance a $10,000 parts stock from the Auto-Life Company in the same manner. With Long-Shearer accessories selling as well as they do, plus living close to my budget, I'm confident that these estimates allow an adequate margin of safety.

An accessories stockturn of 3 and a markup of 50 percent should give me a gross profit on accessories of $10,000 in 120 days. Since I've budgeted my own money for operating expenses for six months, almost all of the $10,000 should be left to pay for the credit stock and to reorder another $10,000 of accessories stock. Look over the enclosed order and see if you don't agree that the accessories I've ordered will sell quickly.

You'll notice that the enclosed list of references is a diversified group of Lubbock business executives, ranging from the president of the Lubbock National Bank to the manager of the largest auto repair shop, the Fix-um Garage. Any one of them, as well as the Lubbock Retail Credit Bureau, will be glad to tell you about me.

I shall be grateful for your help in starting my new store. With business progressing as it is in Lubbock, and with fast-moving Long-Shearer accessories to sell, I feel certain that the new store will be a success.

CASES FOR SPECIAL REQUESTS, CLAIMS, AND CREDIT

1. When you graduated from high school six years ago, at your parents' insistence you went to the University of Illinois, Urbana, where—

after a disastrous academic year (D average)—you left school to take a job in a grocery business in Peoria, Illinois. You spent the next four years (you might add military service, if applicable) with World Food, a national supermarket chain, during which time you worked your way up from bagger to grocery manager. You recently asked your personnel manager about World Food's manager-trainee program, but he told you that you need a bachelor's degree to qualify.

That did it! You realized that you can't advance further in your present job; therefore, you decided to take a three-year leave of absence from World Food and finish your undergraduate degree at Southern Illinois University at Carbondale. After completing your degree, you could enter the World Food manager-trainee program. With your practical experience, you would be certain to succeed.

Your application to Southern Illinois University was turned down because of your below-average performance at Illinois. To be accepted at Southern Illinois University, a transfer student must have a C average in all subjects. According to the catalog, however, you can appeal to the admissions board for a waiver of the C requirement. Write Professor Frank P. Foster, Chairman of the Admissions Board, requesting the waiver. Stress your maturity and work record. Admission boards like this or any other evidence of responsibility and motivation (e.g., family, good military record, church, etc.).

2. As the person in charge of "Funds for the Library" of The University of the South, Sewanee, TN 37375, write a form letter to parents of graduates of this fine institution. Facts: Publishers give "educational discounts," but to catalog a book and ready it for use costs an average of $17.39 per book. Every day, 1,000 books are published. Every year, 60 million pages of new scientific and technical data are released. Books are the scholar's tools and the library a workshop. Unless the University of the South continues to acquire books (on a selective basis) the library will be outdated. Scholarly journals as well as books must be purchased. The journals now cost from $28.52 to $37.50 per year. A library also has microfiche, microfilms, and other forms of film so small that an entire newspaper page can be reproduced on an area smaller than a postage stamp—and that requires special viewing equipment to enlarge the image for reading. Microforms save money because they consume so little space, but they cost almost as much as—sometimes more than—the book itself. The library is an excellent investment (tax deductible) because it has helped attract and retain good students and good professors. Ask for a contribution to help the library get new books, periodicals, microforms, and viewers.

3. For a bulletin you are writing on various machinery, procedures, and techniques in the processing of forest products, you have devised a two-page questionnaire to be sent to a sizable mailing list of small mills. The bulletin, to be published by your state university extension service, is to cover your three years of research on the best methods of processing different forest products for different purposes. You are a professor of forest products in the state university—half-time teaching and half-time research through the extension division.

In return for each filled-out questionnaire, you will send the small mill a marked copy of the bulletin—plus a brief statement of recommended changes for improving its operations.

Your research is completed and written up except for a section on current practices and problems. You and the bulletin editor have therefore scheduled your bulletin to go to press in two months—two weeks to get the questionnaires back, four weeks for analysis of the data, and two weeks for writing and editing. The data from mills will be presented statistically —no names attached—and you will later get specific approval before writing about any individual mill's problems your questionnaire asks for.

4. While trying to work out a good questionnaire (see preceding case), you decided that a questionnaire really couldn't get the information you need. So instead of sending one, you worked out a series of one-day visits to a sound sample of 15 mills on your list.

You still need to write a persuasive-request letter, however, to go to each of the sample mills to get approval of your coming and snooping and asking a lot of questions. You'll use essentially the same letter (changing names, addresses, and dates for the visits). You will want the mill to provide a well-informed company officer to go along with you through the plant and answer questions.

Of course you'll still send a copy of the completed bulletin; but worth more, you think, will be your willingness to answer questions as well as ask them and to make suggestions on the spot for improving operations. In effect you are offering your services as a consultant for one day free—the kind of thing for which you usually charge $250 plus costs.

5. At Iowa Power and Light, Des Moines, IA 50310, your meter readers have been having trouble with biting dogs. In fact, about ten readers sustain dog bite injuries each month, and that doesn't count the near misses. As the director of public relations, set up a form memo that is to go along with the monthly statement asking your customers to please be sure that their animals can't harm IPL meter readers when they come to read the meter. Unless these readers have safe access to the customer's electric meter, IPL has to estimate the electrical usage for the month. This practice is as inconvenient to the customer as to IPL. You do not want to continue the present system (good people are hard to replace, and three have quit in the last three months because of dogs). Still some people have ignored your two former little barks about this situation. See if you can, without really drawing any blood (or even fire in their eyes), convince these people that you too could become a "biter." That is, show some teeth in this bark, but don't bite—at least not yet. Be persuasive but not mean or nasty.

6. *Letterhead:* University of Puerto Rico, Rio Piedras, PR 00601. *Mailing list:* 10,000 students from the university directory. *Date:* January 10, 19—. *Information:* As a member of the student government you have been concerned about the recent rumblings from the legislature about tuition increases. And these noises come close upon a large increase last year. Fellow students have been complaining about dorm facilities, lack of parking, poor advising, and class scheduling.

One legislator, Senator Anasco, has introduced a bill whereby students will be charged for half the cost of their education. What you and your concerned students committee (called SART—Students Against Rising Tuition) have in mind is to set up some kind of campus organization (a student union) to look after the rights (and some suggest the wrongs too) of students and perhaps, after you have gained support and influence, to ask the administration to give you representation on university committees. It seems logical to you that students ought to have some say in formulating the policies that will affect them for four years, and even longer if they go on to graduate school.

Your immediate problem, however, is organization. How do you overcome traditional student apathy about student government? Write a form letter that can be sent to students inviting them to come to an organization meeting January 22, at 5 p.m. in Center Comercio on the main campus. Dean Jesús Garrachales has given your organization permission and encouragement to start such an organization.

7. Your appeal to the Denver, Colorado, public for monies to fund DEF (Denver Ecology Fund) was successful. Your several mailings drew in about $150,000. Now you need volunteers to help on various projects around town similar to the clean-up campaign of the roadside parks that you organized. In one day 400 people picked up cans, bottles, and paper that picnickers, campers, and travelers had strewn along. There seem to be many ecology-minded people in Denver; 200 of them showed up last week to work on the DEF project to remove trash from the approaching highways. Rather than rely on public spontaneity, which has a way of suddenly disappearing, DEF wants to set up a standby list of citizen workers who are willing to give one Saturday a month to various clean-up projects.

Write a persuasive request to mail out to your list of contributors that demonstrates the value of community action to clean up Denver and convinces them to pledge one Saturday a month to DEF clean-up programs.

8. When you went home last weekend your family told you that they would not be able to help you pay your tuition costs for the next term. You didn't want to quit school; so you went to talk with Mary Ball, Director, Loan Department, First National Bank, about a federally insured NDEA loan for $600 to help cover your education costs for next term. You didn't expect any difficulty; your family has an excellent credit record, and you figure you can repay according to the terms. Besides, your B+ average demonstrated your seriousness about getting an education.

Ball assured you that you would get your loan about a month after she put through the papers. She suggested (and you agreed to) a 60-day note for $300 for now. You should pay off the note and get the other $300 when your loan came through. That was about two months ago. You got your $300, 60-day note on December 20. Although you've been patient about it, your loan hasn't come through. You called Ball three times and were assured that your money was on its way. During your last phone conversation on February 15, Ball told you that she had the money and was sending it out to you the next day. It's now February 25, and you still haven't gotten your check; but you have received a due notice and a past-due notice on your $300 note.

Evidently something went wrong with your federally insured loan. You realize that money is tight and that educational loans are high-risk investments for banks. Write Ball asking for the money she promised you and an explanation for the delay. The threat to your credit record is obvious, since the bank will no doubt alert your local credit bureau. Also indicate that you have sent a copy of your letter to John McGuire, the bank president, who is also a good friend of your father.

9. As the letter-writing consultant for a local community improvement association, write the copy for a form letter to local merchants for donations of money, clothing, candy, toys, canned goods, or other products to go in Christmas baskets to be distributed to needy families. The major emphasis is to be on money, but invite other contributions too. Except for the money (which they are to mail in), you will offer to pick up contributions at the merchants' convenience (they are to tell you time and place). You have arranged with the local newspaper to list donors, without specifying what the donation was, in a story about the results of your drive.

10. As a graduate student in the School of Law Enforcement and Administration, Utah State University, you are writing a thesis on the use of photography in law enforcement. A part of your research method is a questionnaire which you will send to a large number of reputable law-enforcement agencies.

Write the covering letter you will send to induce Paul Herzog, a lawyer who is secretary to the Vermont Chiefs of Police Association, to fill out the three-page questionnaire. Data from returned questionnaires will be largely statistical (no specific names attached); but for any quotes you want to use, you will write to get specific permission. The questionnaire takes only ten minutes (it's largely a checkoff form), a return envelope is enclosed, and you're sure Herzog has information that will be helpful and appreciated. You suspect he will be interested in your findings, an abstract of which the *Police Magazine* has already said it wants to publish. Your schedule means that you'll have to start tabulating and interpreting results in two weeks to meet both university and *Police Magazine* deadlines.

Herzog's recent speech before a national convention of law-enforcement officers, reprinted in the current *Police Magazine*, shows his concern for the bad reputations some law-enforcement agencies have developed and his interest in improving methods of investigation and data collection for courtroom use.

11. As associate dean of the College of Business, Eastern Kentucky University, Richmond, KY 40475, write a form letter that can be sent to deans of schools of commerce and business administration. The letter will be typed on the CRT machine so that it will have the appropriate inside address and salutation. You are interested in finding a professor to spend next year as a P. M. Meacham Distinguished Professor. (The American Assembly of Collegiate Schools of Business [AACSB] has agreed to pay the salary as a scholarship if it, you, and a selected professor can all agree on the deal.) One source for these highly talented individuals is from those faculty members who retire each year. Perhaps one could be recommended from the retiring faculty.

Eastern Kentucky University is located in the southern part of the Blue Grass region of Kentucky—a truly lovely area to live. The university enrolls approximately 13,500 students, of whom nearly 2,000 are majoring in the College of Business. Within the college, you offer 15 majors for the BBA degree and an MBA program. The faculty of the four departments—accounting, economics, business administration, and office administration/business education—now number 55. The college nearly meets the accrediting standards of AACSB, and you plan to apply for accreditation in the near future. A Visiting Distinguished Professor may well assist you in gaining the momentum necessary to achieve this objective and to further your educational mission. Anyone interested should contact you at the school address or by phone (606) 555–9876. A vita of the individual's professional activities will be needed subsequently. While the final application for the professional scholarship to AACSB is not due for some time, the Eastern Kentucky administrative processes are sufficiently lengthy so that you should begin the review not later than two months from now.

12. You know that your insurance company (offices in another city)

wants to make its own descriptions and appraisals of gems before insuring. That's the answer you got to your former letter. But you want to avoid the folderol and expense by writing another letter to ask an exception to the policy for a diamond you've just bought your wife and had set in a small heart-shaped pendant necklace. You see no use in the policy in your case— and in many similar cases, where it simply causes extra trouble and expense, runs rates up, and hence deters business. Any fool buying an expensive gem would have it on record, described and appraised by a competent person (a member of the American Gem Society). That's what you did—by two registered members. Their appraisals and descriptions were exactly the same, as shown on the signed, certified, and recorded sales ticket, photocopy of which you're attaching this time: $1,875; class 1 in each of the criteria of color (blue-white), clarity, and cut; weight 0.64.

13.   Three weeks after you moved into your new apartment at Highland Apartments, 1200 W. Bancroft Street, Toledo, OH 43606, you called Peter Lowe, your Superior Insurance agent to have your address changed on your renter's policy. The difference in price was $60 (from $25 to $85 a year) because of the all-wood construction of Highland Apts. Your check has already cleared the bank. A week after the check cleared, Highland burned to the ground. When you called Lowe, he simply mumbled something about making a list of what you lost and sending it to him so he could process your claim. Your total possessions, for which you have the itemized list and most of the sales slips, came to $5,000, which included small appliances, stereo-tape deck, books, clothes, etc. You didn't expect to get the full $5,000 back, but you felt that Superior would pay about $4,000. You could understand about $1,000 depreciation, particularly since some of your appliances and clothes were pretty old. But you were surprised when Superior sent you a check for $1,000 and a release form to sign and return. The letter said usually the refund was about four fifths of the total on complete losses such as yours, but it was hard to believe that a student at the university had $5,000 worth of possessions in an apartment. Although you had offered to let Lowe have copies of your records and sales slips, "I don't feel," he said, "they would be necessary." Your job now is to convince Superior that it should reimburse you the full four-fifths value ($4,000) of the goods you lost. Write direct to Superior Insurance, P.O. Box 2000, New Haven, IN 46774. Include copies of your evidence (assumed).

14.   You bought a $950 Aero-Cool central air unit from Chester Heating & Cooling, 220 Willow Crossing Road, Greensburg, PA 15601, and it was installed five days later. The people who installed Aero-Cool explained that they would have to come out the next day and check the Freon level in the unit. When you arrived home from work the next day, you naturally assumed that they had done so, turned the unit on, and it caught fire and

almost burned your house down. After much effort, you extinguished the fire and called Chester Heating & Cooling. You were told that the Freon had not been put in because no one was able to come to your house today and with the absence of Freon the unit caught fire. Also you learned that the terms of the warranty apply only after the Aero-Cool has been fully installed and OK'd. If the Chester Heating is in business to make the citizens of Greensburg comfortable, as advertised, you want your money back or a new $950 unit—installed.

15. When you bought your house about three months ago, the fellow who sold it to you was forthright about the leak at the base of the living-room wall. The house was built into the side of a hill, and the contractor must have hit the wall with his backhoe when replacing the earth against the living-room wall. Ernie Hill, the former owner, told you that he had to plug a hole in the cinder blocks about the size of a football before applying waterproofing compound to the wall and replacing the earth. The chap who actually did the repair work was Hamilton "Scoop" Riggs of Riggs Construction, and he guaranteed his work for a year.

The four-inch downpour you had last Friday night was the first real test of Riggs's waterproofing and repair job, and it failed the test. Your living room was dry, but the kitchen and utility room, both of which back up to the same wall that Riggs "fixed," looked like Lake Michigan. You called Riggs about the guarantee, but he was out. He was out all through the next week, and he wouldn't answer his home phone either when you called him there. Legally, you've got him; you have his signed guarantee that the wall will not leak for a year.

Before you dump a pound of sugar into the gas tank of his backhoe, or hire a lawyer to haul Riggs into court, write Riggs a persuasive claim in which you convince him to honor his guarantee and to come out to fix your leaking wall. Maybe he's simply embarrassed that his waterproofing didn't work. Hill said he seemed conscientious, and he came highly recommended.

16. From Rafers, New Point Mall, Winston-Salem, NC 28305 you receive at your school address a printed form from the Department of New Accounts signed by Meredith Pendleton. The form began, "We regret to inform you that the following action has been taken concerning your credit application. The principal reasons for adverse action concerning credit are that we are unable to verify your income, we have an insufficient credit file, and we see that you have delinquent credit obligations."

As you read the form closer you see that according to the Fair Credit Reporting Act, you can make a written request within 60 days of receipt of this notice for disclosure of the nature of the adverse information. You don't need this information; you need credit. Write Rafers a persuasive letter from your school address explaining that you are starting a new job next month in Winston-Salem earning $1,200 a month (name the place). Your credit file is probably incomplete because you had a difficult time getting credit in your own name after your divorce. Your ex-spouse was a free spender, ne'er-do-well, lazy person who ran up bills. You did not have credit established before your marriage, so the only credit you had was when you were living with your extravagant spouse. Explain that you are economical, can budget, and want to establish a good credit rating. You have no children or parents as obligations. You are buying a condominium (14 Belvedere Place) and moving next month. You bank with First National.

17. A developer's ad in the mail induced you to go see some property because of (1) a discount price on land bought that weekend and (2) a promise of (free) the beautiful 45-piece dinnerware set pictured on the reverse side of the ad, whether making a purchase or not. On departing (without purchasing), you asked for the dinnerware and was told it would come later by mail from headquarters. Next thing you heard was a letter from headquarters (any name and address you want to use) asking you to sign and return an enclosed gift certificate together with $8.95 handling charge on the dinnerware. Write the appropriate policy complaint letter.

18. Write a policy complaint to (any insurance company) on your Homeowner's Policy 382163 following the company's payment of $69.50 (fair) as coverage of other damages and losses you recently reported concerning a break-in at your home, but refusing payment for the reported $15.50 you paid a bonded locksmith for resetting your door locks and cutting new keys.

Significant facts: (1) As you first reported, the burglars took one set of your keys; so your four $29.50 locks became useless (until you saved the company money through the locksmith). (2) The adjuster says the policy doesn't cover the locks (which were not taken).

19. While attending school, you purchased and put on your American Bank Credit Card a RTM stereo system with an eight-track player recorder for $250 from Knight's Music House, 985 Pine Street, your city. Three weeks and six weeks later you called Knight's and reported that the stereo refused to work and asked that it be fixed or removed from your apartment. Now that you have the credit card bill, write Knight's a letter. The stereo turntable just won't turn. (You'll need to send at least a postcard to ABCC, too—but not for this assignment.)

20. For additional cases, see GS 4, 15, and 20 beginning p. 300.

Persuasive messages: Collections

THE MAIN PEOPLE who cause collection problems are the "credaholics" among us—people who can't resist buying more than they can afford and who, if they do not immediately hand over cash, do not see the debt as real. Frank M. O'Byrne, president of the National Credit Exchange, says they are often trying to catch up with the Joneses—but so are the bill collectors, for a different reason.

Credaholics, according to O'Byrne, typically are repeaters who fall into personality types with traits like poor sales resistance, immaturity, rationalization, poor budgeting, job jumping, and multiple marrying. Gerard Lareau of New York City's Consumer Counseling Service says they're like gamblers who won't admit they have a problem. Prime candidates are young couples with children and poor in-family communication. Two big danger signals are (1) debt payments calling for more than 20 percent of take-home pay and (2) taking out debt consolidation loans.

The only sure way for a business firm to prevent collection problems is to sell strictly for cash. Even with the most careful selection of credit customers, a credit manager will make an occasional mistake and will allow a credit sale to somebody who will not pay promptly—most likely a credaholic.

Unfortunately, however, strict cash selling is also an almost sure way to keep sales and profits unnecessarily low. For that reason the old battle among sales personnel who wanted to sell to everybody, credit departments which would approve sales only to gilt-edged credit risks, and collectors who insisted on prompt pay regardless of consequences has ended in compromise.

Today the thinking sales representative accepts the fact that you make no profit if you can't collect, does not try to sell without a reasonably good chance of collection, and helps the credit department find out about the chances. The credit manager accepts the fact that every sale turned down for credit reasons is a lost chance for more profit and approves sales to some marginal credit risks. Collectors remember that they not only must collect the money but must retain the goodwill of customers or see them drift away as fast as the sales department can bring them in.

Indeed, modern credit theory stresses selling not only to good risks but also to marginal risks as a means of increasing sales and profits. If a business firm follows this theory, as most do these days, its collection problems will be numerous—but expected and manageable, as we explain here.

DEFECTS OF OLD–STYLE COLLECTION PROCEDURES

In the early days of credit sales, only the best risks could get credit. When one of them did not pay promptly, the person in business was surprised, disappointed in a trusted customer, and irked because the bookkeeping routine was broken. All these emotions usually showed up in the efforts to collect the money—especially in the letters, then and still the main collection means, despite some use of telephone calls and professional collection agencies. Combined with stock letter-writing phrases, these emotions led to letters characterized by curt, exasperated, injured, accusing, or self-righteous tone and ineffective appeals to sympathy, fear of getting one's nose broken, or fear of a legal suit.

Indeed, you still see such letters from people who learned all they know about letter writing years ago only by reading and imitating the poor letters of others.

Besides the old faults, all too frequently collectors send obvious form letters to collect long-overdue accounts where a form hardly has a chance, or write many short letters when a good one only a paragraph or two longer would do the job. They then defend themselves by claiming that they don't have time or money to spend on individualized letters or long letters, or by saying (without testing to find out) that debtors won't read long letters. (But tests have shown repeatedly that longer letters nearly always pull better than shorter ones, and individual-sounding letters always pull better than obvious forms in collecting accounts that are very long overdue. The apparent reason is that in the longer letters you can present enough evidence and reasoning to be persuasive, and individualized letters convince the debtor that you will not overlook the debt.)

The approach of "several poor letters" delays collections and leaves the business to be financed through borrowing instead of through current collections. Thus it loses one of the main values of promptness, an improved cash flow.

The loss, however, is a small consideration in comparison with the main shortcoming of poor collection correspondence—its disposition to drive away customers that the sales department has brought in only at great expense for advertising and sales promotion. Here is a typical example:

```
We are trying to avoid getting impatient over your delay in
settling your account amounting to $18.00.  The amount is
considerably past due, and your failure to answer our letters
(all of which we believe have been polite) has been very
annoying as well as discourteous.

It is therefore our intention to seek other means of collection
of this account as we do not intend to let you beat it if at
all possible to prevent.  Just remember, the time to settle a
debt is before it gets into court.

It will be to your benefit to communicate with this office at
once.
```

Notice that the only reason given for payment is the implied threat to sue (for $18?). Such letters increase the difficulty of collecting because they make the reader hate to pay someone so thoroughly disliked, resolve never to do business with the writer again, and tell all their friends how they were mistreated.

After seeing the losses and other ill effects of their own inept collection procedures, such as the preceding letter, many business firms began to turn long-overdue accounts over to outside collection specialists. That, however, was in many cases jumping from the frying pan into the fire. Often the specialists charged 30 to 70 percent of the debt for collecting it. But worse—as they prospered and grew into some 5,000 professional collection agencies in the United States—many of them developed more and more distasteful, goodwill-killing methods that made debtors hate them and the firms that used them.

Gradually state laws in most states (37 at the present, particularly detailed in Florida) clamped down on the most unfair or annoying practices. For lack of uniformity, complete coverage, and enforcement in state laws, the federal government passed two significant acts (effective October 28, 1975, and March 20, 1978) that make unfair and annoying agency procedures illegal. Collection agencies can no longer use abusive or obscene language, threats of violence, extortion, harassment, "shame" lists, debt-revealing inquiries to friends or employers, pretense (of being an attorney, police officer, or government official), or other misrepresentation (like the threat or even implication of suing without clearly intending to do it).

Thus the laws encourage essentially what we have been teaching for 40 years in hundreds of university classes and in all six previous editions of this book—learn effective but gracious collection procedures that avoid the following unnecessary losses from poor practices:

1. A series of costly collection letters when one good one would do the job.
2. Delayed collection of money needed for operating expenses.
3. Additional purchases which may be added to the account before it is closed (and thus will increase the loss if the account is uncollectible).
4. Loss of sales (customers with overdue accounts commonly trade elsewhere rather than face the embarrassment of buying where they owe money).
5. The declining chance of ever collecting (33 percent of accounts are uncollectible when 6 months past due, 55 percent are uncollectible after one year, and 77 percent are uncollectible after two years).
6. Permanent loss of many disgusted customers.
7. The unfavorable attitudes these customers pass on to other customers and prospects.

These are high prices for any firm to pay for keeping a poor collector— higher than necessary to employ a good one.

ATTITUDES AND OBJECTIVES OF MODERN COLLECTION WRITERS

Modern collection methods can usually prevent these undesirable consequences. The trained collector takes the attitude that the debtor should pay because of a promise to do so by a certain date—which has come. So a collector need never apologize about asking for money due.

In asking, however, a good letter writer realizes that *people pay because of benefits to themselves rather than sympathy or any other reason.* The collector therefore not only associates the obligation with the goods through resale talk but, in persuading the debtor, points out the benefits of paying now.

The modern collector's thinking is quite analytical:

—I'm not the bookkeeper irked by broken routine. *Avoid a tone of exasperation and self-righteousness.*

—A delinquency is no surprise. Most people who do not pay promptly are still honest, and some are in temporary financial difficulty (needing only a little more time). *Avoid a curt tone. Be understanding and cooperative but firm.*

—Feel no hurt or disappointment as if let down by a trusted friend. *Avoid an injured, pouting tone.*

—Some delinquents withhold payment because they are dissatisfied with the goods or charges. *The job is one of adjustment, not collection.* (Federal law requires that sellers cannot even try to collect on customer-disputed goods or billings of $51–up for purchases within the state or 100 miles of home. The law applies equally to a holder in due course— that is, somebody like a credit-card company who has bought the original seller's rights in the accounts.)

—Some will have to be persuaded to pay. *Use the you-attitude.*

—A few, but only a few, are basically dishonest and will have to be forced to pay or marked off as losses. *Forcing payment does not include even threats of physical violence, extortion, or rumor-mongering (all of which are illegal). Civil court suit, the only legitimate forcing method, is so destructive of goodwill that it should not even be mentioned until you say (and mean, according to present law) it is the next step.*

Most important of all, the modern collector (unlike some predecessors) recognizes the true nature of the job and expects letters to do *two* jobs:

1. They must collect the money, promptly if possible.
2. They must also retain the goodwill of the customer if at all possible.

By adding the second job, the collector hopes to retain the customer, prevent the unfavorable publicity inevitably carried by a disgruntled former customer, and make each letter more likely to succeed in its first job—that of collecting. In many cases the second job is more important than the first. Certainly to collect $9.50 but lose the goodwill of a customer who has been buying hundreds of dollars' worth of goods a year is stupid.

If the collector has to sacrifice anything, promptness goes first despite the inherent losses (previously listed).

For effectiveness in both collection and goodwill, the modern collector cooperates with the sales department and may even inject some sales promotion material into *early* collection letters to a good risk when it might be of interest to the customer. It not only promotes future sales, but it shows confidence in the debtor and willingness to sell more on credit. Thus it is a subtle appeal to pride which helps to save the reader's face and goodwill. If used at the end of the letter, it relieves the sting and solves one of the correspondent's touchiest problems—how to provide a pleasant ending for a letter in which some element is displeasing.

Even when resale is not the basic collection appeal (as we discuss later), the collector can introduce into letters a few phrases of resale talk to keep customers convinced of the wise decision in buying *those goods* from *that firm*—and to make the obligation to pay concrete by attaching it to the goods. The following letter includes both resale and sales promotion talk:

> You probably remember your first feeling of pleasure when you saw the dark, gleaming wood and the beautifully proportioned design of the Heppelwaite bedroom suite you bought here a few months ago. The suite was one of the finest we have ever had in our store, and we were well pleased—as we thought you were —when you selected it for your home.
>
> At the time, we were glad to arrange convenient credit terms so that you could have your furniture while paying for it. Now if you will look over your bills, you will notice that those for October, November, and December have not been marked paid. The sooner you take care of them, the more you can enjoy your furniture because each time you use it or even see it you will subconsciously remember that you are up to date on your payments.
>
> When you come to the store to make your payments, be sure to see the home furnishings department as well as the time-payment desk. An entire new line of curtains, slipcovers, bedspreads, and scatter rugs is there for your inspection. You'll find a great variety of colors and fabrics made up in the latest styles. From the wide selection you can choose a beautiful new setting for your Heppelwaite suite.

This letter pretty well exemplifies the attitudes and objectives of modern industrial and retail collection writers: Ask for the money without apology because it is due, persuade by showing the reader benefits, use calm understanding and patience, collect but retain goodwill, and cooperate with the sales department.

CHARACTERISTICS OF THE COLLECTION SERIES

In trying to collect and retain goodwill, the efficient collector classifies delinquent accounts and prescribes the best treatment for each. The method is like a process of repeated siftings or screenings. Classification determines which and how many screenings each debtor will get. The procedure is a series of mailings, each of which eliminates some names from the delinquent list as they pay and aids in reclassifying and prescribing for those remaining.

To do its two jobs best, the collection series should have the following characteristics:

1. *Promptness.* Credit and collection people know that the sooner they start trying to collect after an account becomes due, the better the chance. The U.S. Department of Commerce has found that a dollar in current accounts is worth only 67 cents after six months (67 percent chance of collecting), 45 cents after a year, 23 cents at two years.

2. *Regularity.* Systematic handling of collections increases office efficiency and has a desirable effect on debtors. They see quickly that they are not going to slip through the holes in a haphazard procedure.

3. *Increasing forcefulness.* Wanting to retain the goodwill of the customer as well as collect the money, the collector starts with as weak a letter as is likely to work. Like the doctor who uses stronger and stronger medicine or resorts to surgery only as the need develops, the good collector applies more and more forceful methods and goes to court only after weaker methods fail.

4. *Adaptation.* Not all credit and collection people classify their customers into neat categories of good, medium, and poor risks as suggested by some books; but all competent ones vary their procedures according to the quality of the risk (as well as according to the general bases of adaptation already discussed). Usually the poorer the risk, the more frequent the mailings and the more forceful the messages. Whereas three months might pass·before anything stronger than a few statements go to a good risk, much less time might run a poor one through the whole sifting process and to court.

5. *Flexibility.* The collection procedure has to be flexible to take care of unusual circumstances. The collector would look silly to continue sending letters every 15 days to a debtor who had answered an early one with the message of being financially two months behind because of an automobile accident but able to pay the bill by a certain date.

STANDARD COLLECTION PROCEDURES

Collection plans and procedures vary so much that only a specialized book could discuss all variations. Also, various collection theorists and practitioners use different terms to mean essentially the same things. The befuddling complexity is more apparent than real, however. Many of the differences are only minor ones of mechanics rather than significant ones of substance. Most well-planned series apply essentially the logic and psychology explained in the next few pages to a screening process somewhat like the six-screen one shown in Table 12–1.

Of course, you would send only one mailing at each of the notification, inquiry, or ultimatum stages. The nature of the letters makes repeating them illogical. The number and frequency of mailings in the other stages vary from firm to firm, and often within firms according to the class of customer and other circumstances, such as the type of business (retail or industrial) and type of sale (open account, installment).

In general, the better the credit risk, the greater the number of mailings and the longer the intervals between them. A typical retail series might be two to four reminders, two or three appeals, and one urgency letter at 10- to 30-day intervals (which usually become shorter near the end).

TABLE 12–1

Stage	Assumption	Nature	Gist
Notification	Will pay promptly	Usual statement	Amount due, due date, terms
Reminder	Will pay; overlooked	Statement, perhaps with rubber stamp, penned note, or sticker; or form letter or brief reference in other letter	Same as above, perhaps with indication that this is not first notice
Inquiry	Something unusual; needs special consideration	One letter	Asks for payment or explanation and offers consideration and helpfulness
Appeal	Needs to be persuaded	One or more letters	Selected appropriate and increasingly forceful appeals, well developed
Urgency	May be scared into paying	Letter, sometimes from high executive or special collector	Grave tone of something getting out of hand; may review case; still a chance to come through clean
Ultimatum	Must be squeezed	Letter	Pay by set date or we'll report to credit bureau (or sue, now illegal to threaten and not do); may review case to retain goodwill by showing reasonableness

The assumption, nature, and gist clearly call for modified A–plan messages in the first two collection stages (where no persuasion seems necessary) and for C–plan letters in the last three. The inquiry stage is middle ground, where one might well use either. B–plan letters would be appropriate in collections only if the debtor had asked for an unapproved concession, such as an unearned discount (discussed later).

Notification (usually a form telling amount, date due, and terms)

On or about the due date, you have no reason to assume anything except prompt payment if the customer knows how much is due, what for, the due date, and the terms. Most people will pay in response to form notices—the first sifting—which give these facts. A personal letter at this stage would insult most people by implying distrust and concern over the account. Instead of a costly letter, then, the notification is almost always a statement (bill) sent on or about the due date. The forms have the advantage of avoiding insults and saving lots of money on the large mailings while reducing the mailing list for the later, more expensive stages.

Reminder (usually forms giving basic information and adding a push)

If the notice brings no response, the collector gives the customer the benefit of the doubt, assumes oversight, and sends one or more reminders —the number and frequency depending on the circumstances (Item 4 below). The collector knows that most of the remaining delinquents will respond at this stage and further reduce the list. Therefore avoiding offense while giving the necessary information (amount, what for, due date, and terms) is an important concern.

Reminders are usually forms, in order to save both money and the customer's face, but they may be of four types:

1. The form may be an exact copy of the original notice, or a copy plus a penned note, rubber stamp such as "Second Notice" or "Please Remit," or colorful gummed sticker. Effective examples are "Don't delay further; this is long overdue," "Your prompt remittance is requested," "*Now* is the time to take care of this," "Prompt payment ensures good credit," "Prompt payments are appreciated," "Don't delay—pay today," "Remember, you agreed to pay in 30 days," and "Have you overlooked this?"

Less effective wordings (with the apparent reasons for ineffectiveness in parentheses) are "We trusted you in good faith; we hope we were not mistaken" (undesirable implications and tone, stressing *we*); "We are counting on you; don't fail us" (selfish view); "If there is any reason for nonpayment, write us frankly" (suggests finding something wrong; lacks success consciousness); "If this checks up clear, clear it up with a check" (same criticism as preceding; the word play is questionable).

2. The second type of reminder form is a brief gadget letter:

We enclose a small piece of string, just long enough to tie around your finger to remind you that you should send your check today for $48.50 in payment of . . . .

--

The little alarm clock pictured in this letterhead, like any alarm clock, reminds you that it's time to do something you planned to do. This is a friendly reminder that you intended to send your check today for $28.65. . . .

3. An incidental reminder (underscored in the following example) may be included in a personalized letter mainly about something else:

With school starting soon, no doubt you have been planning to order some more fast-selling Queen candies to have plenty on your shelves before the fall rush begins.

By this time you have surely realized the advantage of handling Queen products in your new store. You will want to take advantage of our special Back-to-School offer too. It includes many delicious assorted candies popular with children.

<u>When you mail your payment of $126 due July 30, covering our last shipment under our invoice No. 134, dated June 30</u>, won't you include your next order, so we can assure you an early

delivery of factory-fresh candies? Notice the variety in our
complete line, as shown in the latest catalog, a copy of which
I'm enclosing for your convenience in making your selections.

If we let XXXXX represent collection talk and _____ represent resale
or sales promotion talk, the reminder letter may look like either of the following (usually the first, as in the preceding letter):

This	or	*This*

XXXXXXXXX

XXXXXXXXX   XXXXXXXXX

Up through the reminder stage in the collection procedure the assumption is that little or no persuasion is necessary. Thus forms or incidental
reminders can do the job more cheaply and avoid the sting that personalized, full-length collection messages would carry. You may have noticed
that even the incidental reminder in the Queen candies letter is in dependent-clause structure to avoid too much sting.

4. An individual-sounding letter solely about collection is the fourth
type of reminder form. For greater force in the last reminder, or to poor
risks, or about large amounts, the collector may, however, decide to write
a letter that talks collection all the way and seems to be individualized.
Since most delinquents have so much in common, it still may be a relatively inexpensive fill-in form if the writer watches the tone and content
carefully, typing each copy (perhaps made of form paragraphs) or using
word processing equipment.

The following letter for a wholesale concern, for example, adapts easily
to a large number of customers. With only one fill-in (for the underscored
part, conveniently placed at the end of a paragraph) besides the inside address and salutation, it will serve for a large mailing list. It has a touch of
pride appeal along with the reminder to reduce the sting of the apparently
individualized message.

As owner of a successful business, you know what a good credit
reputation means. You have one.

That's why we immediately extended you 30-day credit on your
recent order. We know that the reports of your good credit
reputation are correct. And we likewise know that you'll
send us payment as soon as this letter recalls the fact that
you owe $85 due November 15 for. . . .

Beyond the reminder stage, however, *obvious* form letters can hardly do
the job. In the inquiry stage and beyond, the very nature of the collector's
working assumptions calls for individualized messages.

For the later stages of the collection procedure the collector fortunately
has ample information on the credit application form and in the credit records to adapt an individually dictated letter. And earlier mailings usually

have reduced the list of delinquents so that giving some personal attention to each letter late in the collection procedure is both possible and productive.

Inquiry (giving the debtor a chance to pay or explain; offering help)

When the collector has sent enough reminders to decide that oversight is not the cause of delay, another assumption comes into play. With a new customer or a poor risk it may be that persuasion or force is necessary—and thus may lead to skipping a stage or two in the usual procedure.

With an old customer who has paid regularly, however, reason says that unusual circumstances must be the cause. The collector still has confidence in the customer (based on past favorable experience), still wants to retain goodwill, and is always willing to be considerate of a person temporarily in a financial tight spot.

The logical plan, then, is to write *one* letter in a spirit of friendly understanding and helpfulness, asking for the money *or* an explanation. Because the money is the real goal (not the explanation of what's wrong, or possible ways to help), it deserves the major emphasis. Care not to offend this formerly good customer apparently in a temporary jam, however, is important. So is care not to suggest that something is wrong with the goods or the billing (for reasons explained later). The only persuasion is in frankness, the offer of help, and a considerate attitude. Most people react favorably to requests presented in such a spirit.

The letters below illustrate the technique for the inquiry stage. The first (using form paragraphs) is designed to go out over the sales representative's signature.

In the three years I have been calling on you and we have supplied you with truck and trailer parts, Mr. Kingman, we have sincerely appreciated your business. We have also appreciated the way in which you have consistently kept your dealership's account paid up.

To a good customer and a friend, then, can I offer some help? We're sure you want to settle your account; and since some unforeseen circumstances appear to have come up, your agreement to one of these plans will give you an easy way to pay your account and maintain your good credit rating:

1. If you can, please send a check today for the full $823.40 to bring your account up to date and clear the outstanding April and May balances.
2. As an alternative, send a partial payment now for half the full amount and agree to pay the remainder in two equal installments within 30 and 60 days. If this is acceptable, just sign your name next to this paragraph and return it right away with your first check. Your signature will indicate agreement to this contractual arrangement.
3. Third, we can put you on a revolving credit plan, like many of our smaller and less well-rated customers. You

may continue to keep your open account, subject to a limit of $1,000.00 on your open balance. The finance charge will be 1½ percent per month of your previous balance after deducting current payments, credits, and past-due insurance premiums. This finance charge becomes part of your outstanding balance. The annual interest rate is 18 percent.

4. If for some reason you cannot accept any of these three plans, tell me what the trouble is, what we can do to help you, and how you propose to settle your account.

Please answer as quickly as possible, so I can report your decision to my management.

--

I wish I could sit down and talk with you for a few minutes about the circumstances that leave January and February charges to you on the books.

But because of the distance, I can only study our past experience with you, and various kinds of credit information. Your past record of prompt payment leaves me unconcerned about ultimate collection, but it also leaves me wondering what's wrong now.

Please either make immediate payment of the $157.47 balance due or drop me a note today telling just how you intend to handle the account. You'll find me cooperative in accepting any reasonable proposal for your taking care of it—or better, the $157.47.

You may have noticed that these letters avoid *two common collection-letter errors* that have their first chance to come up in the inquiry stage:

1. The *first* is that in writing inquiry-stage letters, collectors sometimes ask *questions about the customer's possible dissatisfaction with the goods or charges or both.* The apparent purpose of the questions is to secure some kind of answer—to keep the debtor thinking about the obligation and renew acceptance of it.

But aren't such questions psychologically unsound? If anything was wrong with the goods or the billing, would not the debtor have made a claim? Isn't the collector practically suggesting that the debtor, by claiming something is wrong, can gracefully postpone payment and perhaps even produce an unjustified adjustment? Certainly such a suggestion works in the opposite direction from both resale talk and success consciousness.

2. The *second* common error is *backtracking*—that is, going back to the assumption of an earlier stage in the collection procedure (see Table 12–1 above). Apparently in an effort to save the delinquent's face, a timid collector sometimes grabs back at "oversight" (the assumption of the reminder stage) after starting a letter in the inquiry stage. If oversight is still apparently the reason for the delay, the collection series should not advance to the inquiry stage.

The same kind of nerveless collector sometimes shows the same tendencies in two other places in the collection procedure. After an inquiry-stage offer of special consideration gets no response, it sometimes incongruously comes up again in letters of the next stage.

Not many collectors will send an ultimatum and then back down on it —the worst kind of backtracking. Those who do now violate federal law as well as spoil customers and lose their respect, just as many parents do with their children by issuing ultimatums and not carrying them out.

Appeals (basically reader benefits, made increasingly forceful)

The delinquent who does not respond to a friendly inquiry evidently is taking the wrong attitude toward the indebtedness. The collector's new assumption is that now the debtor must be persuaded to pay.

Basic considerations. The appeal stage is the collection letter writer's main work. Four important points are guidelines:

1. *For persuasiveness, write individualized messages.* The earlier brief notices, reminders, and inquiries will have collected most of the accounts (the easy ones) as inexpensively as possible in terms of time and goodwill. The remaining few will be harder to collect. Usually they will require individualized (or at least individual-sounding) letters rather than forms, because of the need to be persuasive. By using information in the credit records, the collector can write individualized messages that are specific and therefore persuasive to a degree impossible in a form.

2. *Develop only one or two points.* Scattering shots like a shotgun over several undeveloped appeals weakens the message too much to reach the remaining hard-to-collect-from delinquents. Something like a rifle bullet, with all the powder behind one fully developed central theme, will be more forceful. This usually means longer letters because they must be specific and say enough to make the point emphatic, but they pay off in results.

3. *Retain goodwill as far as possible.* Because they are individualized, pointed, full-length collection messages, appeal-stage letters necessarily carry some sting. Like doctors and patients, however, collectors and debtors have to accept the fact that the needle carrying strong medicine for advanced stages of a disease often has a sting. Still, the wise collector, like the humane doctor, will minimize the sting as much as possible without weakening the medicine.

You want to be firm without being harsh. By skilfully stimulating the customer's desire to pay, you'll both be happy.

4. *Select a reader-benefit appeal.* Successful collection, like successful selling or any other kind of persuasion, involves showing that the debtor will get something wanted or avoid something not wanted—in other words, using the you-attitude.

Appeals to sympathy (variously called the "poor me" appeal or the appeal to cooperation) do not meet the requirement. They are fundamentally selfish.

Though a cleverly and humorously overdrawn picture of the writer's family in need might bring the money (indeed did in one well-known case), it is more likely to bring a wisecrack answer. For instance, one man built a letter around a picture of his hungry-looking wife and 11 children, with the note below: "This is why I *must* have my money." The answer was a picture of a beautiful blonde with the note "This is why I *can't* pay."

Basically, people want

1. To get the service the product supposedly gives.
2. To have self-respect and the approval of others (they have to live with both themselves and others).
3. To avoid loss of what they have and add to those things (money, property, and the credit privilege, for example).

So a collector can be persuasive by reminding debtors of their obligations to pay for what they got and by showing how they benefit in self-respect or in economic self-interest.

The true collector is therefore really a seller of those ideas—by a careful analysis of the customer, selection of the appeal most likely to succeed with the particular individual in the specific situation, and selling the idea of paying by showing the benefits. The resale, pride, and fair-play appeals show the reader how to retain a clear conscience, keep self-respect, and preserve good credit.

The resale appeal. Touches of resale belong in every collection letter to keep the debtor satisfied with the purchase and to show what came in exchange for the promise to pay, but resale may also be the theme of a whole appeal letter. Essentially it goes back and almost repeats the points a good presentation would make in selling the product. By the time the collector is through reselling, the debtor will see the good value received. That can motivate payment as the way to a clear conscience.

Although inept phrasing may make any appeal ineffective or kill goodwill, the danger is not great in the resale appeal. Really effective use of it, however, requires imagination enough to paint a vivid, interesting *picture of the product in use*—and willingness to make it complete, detailed, and long enough to be persuasive. The following letter illustrates the type:

```
Now that Asbex and Asbar have had time to prove their profit-
making ability to you, can you say that we were right?  We
said that they would be a good selling team for you.

When you followed up your original Asbex order of April 15
with the April 27 order for 20 gallons each of Asbex and Asbar,
you showed that you thought the fire-retarding twins would
move quickly together.  With your good reputation for prompt
payment as our guide, we were glad to have such a desirable
outlet as your store for this pair of fast sellers.  Although
your payment of $39 for the first shipment, invoice BT-41198,
is now ten days overdue, you can keep your record intact by
```

sending us a check in the next mail. If you make the check
for $273, you can also pay for the second shipment, invoice
BT-41390, on its net date.

From all reports on the way business is in Ardmore, you'll be
sending us repeat orders before long. We'll be looking
forward to serving you now that you have learned that Asbex
and Asbar fill a recurring need of your customers.

The following letter from a building and loan collector who made the
loan originally and knew the family quite well is even more personal in its
resale appeal. The reference to passing pleasures in the second paragraph
is a subtle way of telling Barnes, without preaching, that the collector
knows where the money went—into expensive parties designed to keep
up with the Joneses.

When you and Mrs. Barnes moved into your new home two years
ago, I was very proud that I had something to do with it.
If anything contributes to the pleasure of life, it is a good
place to live—and especially if that place belongs to the
occupant. I feel that much more than mere sentiment is
behind the words "There's no place like home."

Indeed, so much of comfort, security, and pride comes with
home ownership that anyone should forego passing pleasures
that eat up income, take the savings, and invest in a home
—just as you decided to do.

The importance to you of keeping up your payments on your loan
deserves your serious attention. Perhaps by now you are used
to your home, and you take it as a matter of course. But take
a walk around the lawn. Note the landscaping; note the
beautiful architectural lines of the building. Then go inside
and think for a minute how comfortable you, Mary, Jim, and
Jane are there.

Think where you would be without it. And suppose you were
going to build today. Instead of the $38,000 you paid, you
would now have to pay about $50,000 because of increased
prices. Really, you cannot afford to stop enjoying those
comforts.

So will you please come in and take care of your March, April,
and May payments as soon as possible?

Pride appeal. Often resale talk joins a subtle appeal to pride, or the
appeal to pride may be more or less independent of resale on the goods.
In either case the writer uses practical psychology to know when to encourage pride by sincere compliments, when to needle it, and when to
challenge it. A bungled approach may get a surprising answer, as did the
collector who asked (some years ago; illegal now) what the neighbors
would think if the seller repossessed the debtor's new car. The answer was
that the neighbors all agreed it would be a low-down, dirty trick. The collector had erred in challenging instead of encouraging pride.

One collector succeeded by quoting from a highly favorable credit report on the debtor, asking if the description fit, and encouraging prompt

action to retain the good reputation. Others have given percentages of customers who pay at different stages in the collection procedure and said that of course the debtor does not want to be in the minority groups at the end of the list. The essence of success with the pride appeal is to *encourage the debtor toward prideful actions* and to avoid the use of accusations and implications of shame as far as possible.

The following example shows the method. Note that it ends with sales promotion.

> Your choice of the navy-blue suit and the light tan suit with matching shoes, purse, and gloves, for a total of $182.95, shows the care and pride with which you select your clothes.
>
> We feel sure that you want to show the same pride in maintaining your preferred credit rating. Drop your check for $182.95 in the mail today, and your account, due on November 10, will be paid in full.
>
> The next time you are in town, come by and look over our completely new line of Mary Margaret furs. Whether you want to make additions to your wardrobe or merely to see the latest fashions, you will be welcome.

Another example (to a university senior) incorporates a reference that is as effective and legitimate in collecting as a left hook is in fighting:

> Twenty-seven other Lansing residents bought Monora television sets the same week you got yours.
>
> That was just a little over three months ago. Yet 23 of them have already been in to take care of their payments as agreed. We made a note of their prompt payments on their records. And they walked out pleased with themselves, their sets, and us.
>
> When you stop to think about it, the good credit rating you establish by promptly paying as agreed is more than a matter of personal pride. It adds to the value and desirability of your account with any store in Lansing. It's a personal recommendation too, for employers often check the credit record of an applicant for a job.
>
> Take the two minutes now to send us your check. Or bring your payment to the store tomorrow.

Fair-play appeal. By using slightly different wording, you can turn the basic pride appeal into an appeal to fair play. The wording may recall the debtor's sense of respect for a contract, feeling of duty to do as promised, or conscience that commands doing the right thing. It develops the feeling that the debtor should carry out the buyer's part of the bargain, since the creditor has been fair in carrying out the seller's. Integrity or honesty may be as good a name for the appeal. Some people call it a request for cooperation.

Whatever the name, a well-developed, positive presentation (without accusations), showing that the reader should pay to be fair, is an effective appeal. It goes back to the fundamental idea that the debtor promised to pay by a certain time for certain goods or services. Having received the benefits, the debtor knows the fair thing is to pay for them. Almost everybody wants to be thought of as fair in dealing with others. Here are two examples of the appeal:

> On the basis of your urgent need for drive rivets, and because you supplied us with references, we were happy to fill your order February 6 for eight gross of our "Stellar" ½-inch diameter drive rivets.
>
> When we filled your order, we explained that our terms on open accounts call for payment within 30 days. Our suppliers have faith that we will pay them on time, and we have faith that our customers will pay us on time, enabling us to do so.
>
> You know that your account is now past due more than 60 days.
>
> When we shipped you the drive rivets, we had faith that you would do the fair thing and pay for them promptly. Won't you renew our faith?
>
> Make out a check today for the amount past due—$921.60—and mail it in the enclosed stamped, addressed envelope. That's the fair thing to do, isn't it, Mr. Spiegel?
>
> --
>
> How would you feel next payday if you received no paycheck?
>
> I'm sure you would feel that you had given good service and that your employer should pay for it.
>
> When we ask you for the $84.95 for the coat you bought on November 18, we are only asking for what is due us.
>
> At the time we placed your name on our credit list, we made clear that accounts are due on the 10th of the month following purchase. Perhaps more important, you accepted the terms in accepting that becoming coat.
>
> In fairness to us and to yourself, won't you please come in today and give us our paycheck according to our agreement?

Appeals to economic self-interest. Even those who have no sense of obligation to pay for value received (as developed in the resale appeal), or of pride, or of fair play in treating decent people fairly will likely pay if their own economic self-interest is clear. You may therefore write forceful collection appeals to a debtor's desire to retain the valuable credit privilege. In fact this is the main appeal in commercial and industrial credit collection.

> Why is a prompt-pay rating like money in the bank?
>
> Both are able to command goods and services immediately when you want them.
>
> On the basis of your ability to pay and your reputation for meeting payments promptly, we extended credit immediately when you asked for it. Now we ask that you send your check for $898.76 to cover your August shipment of small jewelry, sold to you on credit just as if you had drawn on your bank account for it.

Then look through the enclosed booklet. Notice the color
pictures of things you'd like to have in stock for Toledo's
Christmas shoppers. The heavy hollow silver plate described
on page 3 is a line for moderate budgets. It's durable as
well as handsome, since it's triple-plated silver on copper.

Should you care to order on our regular terms, enclose a check
covering your balance of $898.76 and order the new stock; use
your credit as if it were another check drawn on money in the
bank.

Though the following letter speaks of fair play, it is an appeal not to
fair play, as explained before, but to the debtor's economic self-interest in
enjoying the benefits of the credit privilege:

Are you playing fair—

—playing fair with yourself, I mean?

You want to continue to get what you need promptly by merely
mailing orders to your suppliers. Rightfully you can expect
the best of service along with good-quality products when you
arrange a businesslike transaction. You will agree that your
company would not be fair to itself if its actions caused it
to lose this privilege.

The Reliable Paint and Varnish Company has continued to honor
this privilege because in the past you have always settled
your account satisfactorily. At present, however, you owe us
$4,723.00, now three months overdue, on invoice 362773
covering a shipment of 575 gallons of Reliable Dual-Coat Zinc
Primer.

To treat yourself fairly and to preserve your company's good,
businesslike reputation, you will want to get your account
balanced promptly. Please use the enclosed envelope to send
your check today and put your account in good condition again.

Urgency

When the regular collector is getting nowhere with appeals like those
in the preceding letters, the next step may be stronger letters, perhaps
from a higher executive taking over for the final few.

When the treasurer, president, company lawyer, credit bureau, or collection agency signs letters, the psychology is to give the reader the feeling
that things are getting pretty serious. Although urgency-stage letters are
not actually the end of the collection procedure, they should seem close.

Actually the letter sent over the signature of the higher executive is
usually a forceful development of one of the appeals already discussed.
It may go a bit further on the economic interests of the debtor and talk
about the cost of facing suit (since the debtor would have to pay the bill
and court costs), but usually not—especially since it has become illegal
for professional collectors unless really intended. Any executive knows that
mentioning a court suit drives customers away—and hence will postpone
it as long as possible. Even now the firm is still interested in goodwill. It

knows that a chance of retaining the customer remains—if not as a credit customer, as a cash customer who may still speak of the firm favorably. So the executive more frequently plays the role of helper who allows a last chance and still does not turn the screws all the way down by setting an end date. The following letter, signed by the company treasurer, illustrates:

> When you began your business, a good reputation in Ardmore made it possible for you to get loans, and your hard work and prompt payments—good reputation again—got you credit on your purchases.
>
> This reputation is more important to you now than ever before, for with unsettled world conditions causing wide fluctuations in the securities market, credit agencies are becoming more and more strict in their policies—and businesses are learning to be more insistent on their terms.
>
> We have not received your check for the $234 for our invoices 69507, covering our shipment of 10 gallons of Asbex on April 10, and 76305, covering the shipment on April 20 of 10 gallons of Asbex and 20 gallons of Asbar. Some arrangement for this settlement is necessary right away. We are willing to accept your 90-day note at 12 percent for this amount so that you can retain your credit rating without lowering your cash balance.
>
> We would of course prefer to have your check; but for the benefit of your business, your customers, and your creditors, please settle your account some way with us today.

Ultimatum

If the serious mood, the strong appeal, and the bigheartedness of the executive's offer of still another chance do not get the money, the collector will give the screw its last turn—now assuming that the only way is to squeeze the money out of the debtor. Apparently as long as any slack remains, this debtor will move around in it. The collector therefore says calmly and reluctantly but firmly that on a definite date, usually five to ten days later, the account will go to a lawyer to institute suit—unless payment comes before that time. (The tendency of some collection agencies to use this approach as an insincere threat is surely one of the abuses the 1978 law will stop.)

Though the language of the ultimatum should be firm (and sincere), it should not be harsh. To minimize resentment, the collector commonly reviews the case at this point. Carefully worded, this letter may collect and still retain goodwill because of the fair-play appeal in the whole review. Usually it will at least collect.

It is more likely both to collect and to retain goodwill, however, if the writer is careful about these points:

1. Show your reasonableness in the past (without becoming self-righteous), your reluctance to take the present action, and the justice and necessity of it.

2. Word the ultimatum clearly, precisely, and calmly—not as a form of vengeance, penalty, or threat but as a progress report (including the usual future plans).

3. Stress the positive side (pay and keep all the advantages of your credit) instead of the negative (if you don't pay, you'll get a bad credit record—and lose in court).

As you read the letter below, notice how the writer did all of those things.

> When we sent your first credit shipment, $95 worth of Christmas supplies under invoice CA-872 on December 4, we took the step all stationery wholesalers take when approving credit: We verified your good credit reputation with the National Stationery Manufacturers Guild, of which we are a member.
>
> The Guild's certification meant that you invariably pay your bills. When we received a second order on January 26, we were happy to serve you again by shipping $42 worth of Valentine cutouts and art supplies, under invoice CB–345. Since then we have tried to be both reasonable and considerate in inducing you to pay by our usual collection procedures. Now we shall be compelled by the terms of our membership agreement with the Guild to submit your name as "nonpay" unless we receive your check for $137 by April 15.
>
> I ask you to consider carefully the privileges and conveniences you can retain for yourself by making that payment—the privileges and conveniences you get from your hard-earned and well-thought-of credit rating. You can continue buying from your old suppliers (including us). Credit requests to new supply houses will be approved on the basis of the Guild's favorable reports. You will save the extra costs of a court suit to collect, in which you would pay not only the $137 but the court costs.
>
> All the advantages of an unmarred credit standing among suppliers are yours now, insofar as we know; and we want to help you keep them so that you can continue to stock your shelves on credit. Mail us your check for $137 by the 15th and retain those advantages.

If an ultimatum like that above does not bring the money by the date set, the only remaining letter to write is a courtesy letter, not a collection letter, telling the customer of the action taken. Then the case is out of the collection writer's hands and in the hands of a lawyer.

The trouble with that arrangement is that your public relations went with the case—into the hands of the lawyer—and most lawyers don't seem to understand public relations. Therefore you should go as far as you can with your own good collection letters.

BEGINNINGS AND ENDINGS

For most writers the beginnings and endings of letters, including collection letters, are trouble spots. Beginnings are more difficult than endings because the background, point of contact, and theme vary more than the desired action; therefore the beginnings require more imagination and care if they are to be adapted and effective instead of dully standardized.

This much, however, we can say: You have to capture the reader's attention and interest and hold it through the letter. Identification of the account (the amount due, what for, and when due) should be clear in every case, *but these facts do not make good beginnings for persuasive letters* (those after the notification and reminder stages); the reader has already shown lack of interest in them.

Neither are references to former collection efforts good as beginnings. Such references may sound like whining or may suggest that the debtor can *again* ignore the request with impunity. Since collection letters are basically sales letters—selling the debtor on the benefits of paying—the collector will do well to reapply the principle of reader-benefit beginnings discussed in Chapters 8 and 11.

Just as the sales writer drives for an order at the end, the good collection writer strives to bring in a check or an explanation that will name a payment date. So the standard action ending—telling what to do, making clear how to do it, making action easy, and providing a stimulus to prompt action—is always proper except in the early stages of the series, where it would be too forceful. There, resale or sales promotion talk rather than the request for payment usually ends the letter to imply faith, appeal to pride, perhaps promote sales, and remove the sting.

Although the collector always writes with success consciousness, expecting each letter to bring results, all except the one serving notice that the account has been placed in the hands of an attorney should leave the way open for more severe action.

Whenever feasible, the collection writer should make response easy for the debtor. An addressed and stamped envelope does this, provides a strong stimulus to prompt action, and pays off. (An extensive research project found an increase of 12.29 percent in responses.) Even the casual "Don't bother to write a letter; just slip your check into the enclosed envelope . . ." will show the debtor your friendly attitude and will frequently produce the check.

HUMOR IN COLLECTIONS

Generally, past-due accounts are not laughing matters for either the debtor or the collector. But small amounts early in the collection procedure are not deadly serious matters either (though some inept people make themselves look silly by writing as if they were). In the early stages, where little or no persuasion seems necessary or even desirable, the main job is to gain attention and remind the debtor. Under these circumstances a humorous touch may be just the thing. Its sprightliness will supply the attention and memory value needed. The light mood will take the sting out and make the collector seem like a friendly human being instead of an ogre.

A widely known and highly successful collection letter, the famous "Elmer" letter by Miles Kimball, pictures both kinds of collector. The writer, a friendly human, warns the debtor against the ogre Elmer, treasurer of the company, who sometimes gets out of hand and writes letters that destroy a reader's will to live. The whole thing is a detailed and ridiculous account of the kind of ogre Elmer is and the disastrous effects of the letters, plus a brief warning to pay now before Elmer writes.

Shorter humorous letters are more usual. One merely asks for the name of the best lawyer in the debtor's town, in case the collector has to sue. One collector simply mailed small, live turtles to slow payers. *Time* has long used two humorous letters for people who don't pay promptly for their subscriptions. One, as the only thing on the back of the front picture cover of the current issue of *Time,* begins "I'm sorry—sorry I can't send you any more than the cover of this week's *Time.*" It then goes into a brief resale appeal. The other begins with the assertion of how much is due, pokes fun at the usual collection letter that breaks into tears in the first paragraph and yells for the law in the second, shows how large numbers of small accounts add up, and ends with the pun that "procrastination is the thief of *Time.*" Another journal begins a subscription collection with

"CHECKING, JUST CHECKING,"

said the telephone line worker when the lady jumped out of the bathtub to answer. I'm just checking to find out whether you want to continue to receive. . . .

The rest of the letter is the usual resale appeal with a standard action ending.

Another device is that called the one-sided or half-and-half letter. The writer presents what is essentially an inquiry-stage collection letter in a narrow column on the left half of the page and asks the reader to use the right half to attach a check or explain.

Though humorous touches (usually inexpensive forms) may be effective in collecting small amounts early in the series, they are too flippant for large amounts or late-stage collections. The exception is that they might serve just before an ultimatum to jolt the debtor. But we must not forget that

1. The credit obligation is a serious responsibility, and we can't expect the debtor to take it seriously if we are undignified about it.
2. Written joshing is more likely to offend than oral banter.
3. Gadgeteering and humor in letters of all kinds are likely to be overrated because we hear more of the occasional successes than of the numerous failures.

COLLECTING UNEARNED DISCOUNTS

A special problem which does not fit into the regular collection procedure is that of collecting unearned discounts (that is, discounts taken when sending payment *after* the end of the discount period). The fact that the amount is usually small—always small in comparison with the volume of business the collector risks in trying to collect—complicates the problem. Moreover, some large purchasers know the collector would think twice before losing their $200 or $200,000 orders to collect an improper $4 or $4,000 discount.

Fortunately the collector usually has some advantages too:

1. When the occasion arises, the debtor is almost certainly an experienced person who will understand a reasoned business analysis. For instance, if the collector cannot get the money in early and has to pay interest on money borrowed for financing, the debtor will understand that the end result will be a revised system with no possibility of discount.
2. The sizable purchaser has almost certainly investigated various sources of supply and might be as reluctant to change suppliers as the collector would be to lose a customer.
3. The fair-play appeal can include playing fair with all the collector's other customers. That is, you cannot well allow one to take the unearned discount while requiring others to pay according to terms.

Armed thus, the collector is ready for the taker of unearned discounts. First, assuming a little misunderstanding of the terms is a reasonable start. Then make the terms clear, and overlook the improper deduction *the first time*.

When no doubt exists, the collector can certainly assume (reasonably enough) that the unjustified deduction comes from failure to check the dates—an unintentional chiseling—and that the additional money will be forthcoming after a little reminder. One writer used an analogy for the reminder by telling the story of the boy who presented nine apples as his mother's offering for the church's harvest festival. When the pastor proposed to call to thank the mother, the boy asked that the thanks be for ten apples.

If neither misunderstanding of the terms nor failure to check dates is the reason, the collector has a real letter-writing job. Although well armed —with justice, legal advantages, and some psychology on their side—some collectors fear to go ahead. The almost inevitable result is chaos in the collection department, or at least in the discount system. Word gets around.

The bold do better. Their appeals are Item 1 above (the economic justification of discounting practices) and Item 3 (the broadened fair-play appeal). Often a good letter combines both, as in the following illustrations:

From your letter of May 25 we understand why you feel entitled
to the 2 percent discount from our invoice X-10 of April 30.
If some of our creditors allowed us discounts after the end of
the discount period, we too might expect others to do the
same.

The discount you get from us when you pay within a definite,
agreed-on period is simply our passing on to you the saving
our creditors allow us for using the money we collect promptly
and paying our bills within 10 days after making purchases.
It's certainly true that your discount of $4.57 is small; but
large or small, we would have allowed it if we had had your
payment in time to use in making a similar saving in paying
our own bills. If our creditors gave us a longer time, we'd
gladly give you a longer time.

Since they don't, the only solutions besides following the
terms are (1) stopping all discounts, (2) taking the loss on
all our sales, or (3) being unfair to our many other customers
by making exceptions and showing favoritism. I don't think
you want us to do any of those things, do you, Mr. Griggs?

When you mail us your check for the full invoice amount of
$228.57, we know that you will do so in the spirit of good
business practice and fairness.

Thank you for your order. You will find that our
merchandise and attractive prices will always assure you of a
more-than-average profit.

The letter above did both its jobs of collecting the money and retaining
the customer. Certainly the writer was not the distrusting merchant who
told a new employee that if somebody wanted to pay a bill and somebody
else yelled "Fire," the proper procedure was to take the money first and
then put out the fire.

The problem of unearned discounts sometimes becomes particularly
difficult because you have allowed one exception, explained the terms
carefully, refused to allow a second exception, and received a reply including statements like these:

. . . I thought that an organization such as yours would be
above such hair-splitting tactics . . . and I resent your
hiding behind a mere technicality to collect an additional
$3.69 . . . oversight. . . . If you wish . . . a new check
will be mailed, but . . . it will be your last from us.

Here's how one collection writer handled this hot potato—successfully:

I appreciate your letter of December 5 because it gives me an
opportunity to explain our request that you mail us a check
for $184.50 in place of the returned one for $180.81.

Our sincere desire to be entirely fair to you and all our
other customers prompted the request. For years we have
allowed a discount of 2 percent to all who pay their bills
within 10 days of the invoice date. Such prompt payment
enables us to make a similar saving by paying our own bills
promptly. Thus we pass on to you and our other customers the
savings prompt payments allow us to make.

But if our customers wait longer than the 10 days to pay us, we make no saving to pass on. Of course, an allowance of $3.69 is a small matter; but if we allowed it in one case, we would have to allow similar discounts to all our customers or be unfair to some.

I feel sure that you want us to treat all customers alike, just as you do in your own business. Certainly I do not think you would like it if you found that we were more lenient with somebody else than with you. Our request for the additional $3.69 is necessary if we are to treat all alike.

Thank you again for writing me and giving me this chance to explain. May we have your check—in fairness to all?

This—a letter refusing to allow an unearned discount or some other concession when forcefully requested—is the only likely kind of situation for B–plan collection letters. But it is not the usual B-situation. Here you're not just refusing to do something for the other person (give a discount). You're refusing to *let* that person *not* do something (send you the extra money). That is, you have to say both "I won't do what you ask" and "Now you do what I ask." It's a combination of the two most difficult kinds of letters—the B–plan and C–plan—and hence an appropriate culmination of your study of letters and end of our treatment of them.

❖   ❖   ❖   ❖   ❖

Because collection letters vary so much, they have few universal truths suitable for a specific checklist such as we have provided for some other kinds. The broader suggestions on p. 425, however, will be helpful as a partial checklist.

COLLECTION CASES

1. Six months ago Mrs. Cora Mayer bought the Riverside Motel, Fulton, KY 42006, with the hope that the new interstate running close by would soon be finished and that her investment would pay off. The place was run down, but Mrs. Mayer and her four children and one son-in-law had hope that they could get things in order and restore business. Mrs. Mayer has been a steady customer of your company, the Curtis Linen Supply Company, 1199 Grandview Drive, Fulton, TN 37206. You own and supply the entire linen and laundry service for the motel. Each day one of your drivers stops there, collects the soiled linens, and leaves a clean supply. Billings are made monthly. The Riverside Motel account now has a 20-day past-due balance of $255.98. You have continued to supply linens during the delinquency. Having sent the bill, and 15 days later a reminder, write an appeal letter to collect the $255.98.

2. You were so nasty and inept in trying to collect that $255.98 laundry bill from Mrs. Mayer (preceding case)—and the following month's bill for $263.25—that she made other arrangements, then paid you off and sent

Collection Letter Checklist

1. Follow a reasonable philosophy and adapted procedure.
   a. Associate the specific goods with the obligation to pay for them, and show that you expect payment because it is due.
   b. Always identify how much is due and how long overdue.
   c. Except in the first two stages and the ultimatum, the points in *b* and *a* are not good beginnings.
   d. Stick to your sequence of assumptions for different collection stages; backtracking shows weakness and loses reader respect.
   e. Try to get the money and keep the customer's goodwill.

2. Fit the tone carefully to the circumstances.
   a. Avoid seeming to tell the reader how to operate.
   b. Nasty, curt, injured, pouting, exasperated, or harsh tone doesn't help; it turns the reader against you instead.
   c. Scolding or holier-than-thou attitude brings resentment too.
   d. To avoid credit platitudes, relate credit principles and regulations to the particular case.
   e. Show confidence that the debtor will pay, by
      (1) Avoiding references to past correspondence (except in late-stage reviews).
      (2) Stressing positive benefits of payment.
   f. Be sure any humor avoids irritation or distraction.
   g. Avoid (1) accusations, (2) apologies, and—except in the reminder and inquiry stages—(3) excuses invented for the reader, including any hint of fault in the goods or billing.
   h. To increase the force, use more collection talk (and less sales promotion—good only in early letters to good customers).
   i. To decrease stringency and apparent concern, reverse *h;* watch proportions.

3. For persuasiveness (after the first two collection stages):
   a. You have to stress what the reader gains by doing as you ask.
   b. Remember the effectiveness of a developed central theme.
   c. Select an appeal appropriate to the circumstance and reader.
   d. Remember that any kind of antagonizing works against you.
   e. Individualize your message for stronger effect, even in forms.

4. Guard against the legal dangers.
   a. Reporting the delinquent to anybody except those requesting information because of an interest to protect is dangerous.
   b. Don't threaten physical violence, blackmail, or extortion.
   c. Be careful about your facts, and show no malice.
   d. Be sure that only the debtor will read (seal the envelope).

5. Adapt your drive for action to the stage of the collection.
   a. A full-fledged action ending is too strong and stinging early.
   b. But later, anything short of it is too weak.

you packing. Your boss (Curtis) found out about it and also sent you packing. But you soon got another job.

Now you know the other arrangements Mrs. Mayer made for her laundry. Your new boss (Nelson Byrne, Byrne Appliances, 2200 Manchester Road, Louisville, KY 40213) assigned you the job of handling collections, and one of your first cases turns out to be Mrs. Mayer. She had three $300 washing machines and one $370 dryer installed in the laundry room of her newly acquired motel (special sale, prices rounded in group purchase). She paid $70 down and agreed to pay $100 a month until the debt was paid. She made the first two payments on time; then two months ago, when winter had set in and business fell off, she stopped; so $300 of her $1,000 debt is due now. One of the problems, you suspect, is that the interstate did not get finished and the Riverside Motel is far away from any high-volume traffic pattern—but you're not telling Nelson what you know. Instead, you're going to get the $300 soon (and each of the seven $100 payments on time)—without more hassle with Mrs. Mayer. You *were* too nasty and stern before; so you're going to start with a nice inquiry.

3. Assume Mrs. Mayer (preceding case) does not respond to the inquiry. Write (*a*) an appeal letter—and (if that doesn't work) (*b*) an ultimatum.

4. As treasurer for your fraternity or sorority write a persuasive middle-stage collection letter dated June 20 to another member to collect $855.69. On March 30, the debtor owed $617.69 and signed a promissory note promising to pay on or before May 1. After March 30 not only was the $617.69 not paid, but the member failed to pay the April bill of $168.50 and the May bill of $69.50. The chapter needs the money in order to operate its summer rush and to open next fall. The chapter is highly reluctant to sue its members, but it cannot afford to forget sums as substantial as this one. You add the specifics as far as addresses and names and any other appropriate details are concerned.

5. For your fraternity or sorority's law firm (Pitts, Owens, Junkin, & Given, Suite 426, First Federal Building, your university city), write a follow-up to the preceding case explaining that you have talked with the treasurer and the president about the case. Ask the debtor to pay the house upon receipt of the letter. If you do not hear from the member, you will assume that he or she does not plan to meet this obligation and you will have no alternative but to tell the fraternity to forget the debt or to file suit upon the debt. Write the ultimatum.

6. As credit manager of Gilberg Fabrics, Upland Road, Charlotte, NC 28201, you have noticed that one of your regular customers takes dis-

counts to which she is not entitled. She (Billie Jean Young, Youngs Fabrics, Kenwood Mall, Cincinnati, Ohio 45236) has been sending in payments before the 30-day limit but has been deducting the 2 percent discount given to those who pay within ten days. Last month and the month before, you added the amounts of formerly taken unearned discounts to the statements sent. She paid the amount of the statements less the figure labeled as "unearned discount for preceding month." Write a letter to collect the $23.89 in unearned discounts formerly taken and to persuade Young to start paying within ten days or stop deducting the discounts.

7. Five months ago Henry Jackson (barber) bought a 22-cubic-foot golden-wheat-colored frostless side-by-side refrigerator-freezer for $659.95 and a two-speed golden-wheat eight-cycle washer for $319.95 from your appliance shop, White Brothers, 900 Warsaw Avenue, Cleveland, OH 44137. Tax and installation charges were $25.04. Jackson paid $300 down and agreed to make monthly installments of $23.98. In the three months since that, you have mailed him a statement with a friendly sticker attached (when he missed the first payment) and sent him a reminder letter when he missed the second. Develop a good appeal that you think will work, and apply it to some well-thought-out letter copy.

Facts about Jackson: age, 30; income varies but generally around $650 monthly take-home pay; marital status, divorced; no children; address, Apartment 11–B, Cleveland Heights, Spencer Road, Cleveland 44146.

8. Dr. William Merriweather, dentist, 19 Pike Road, Grassy Butte, ND 58001, bought $10,000 worth of equipment from you, Supreme Manufacturing Company, 90 Academy Place, Passaic, NJ 07013, two months ago. He paid $2,000 down and the rest was to be paid in $1,000 monthly installments. After making the first monthly payment, he stopped paying. A reminder and an appeals letter have brought no response. Your credit file on Merriweather shows that he practiced dentistry while in the Army shortly after he graduated with honors from Illinois Dental School, Chicago. He has a wife who comes from a prominent and wealthy Chicago family, two sons, brick home worth $60,000, two cars, and has never been arrested. Write (*a*) another appeals letter—and, if necessary (*b*) an urgency and (*c*) an ultimatum.

9. *From:* Inter-Galactic Corporation, Coomaraswamy Road, San Francisco, CA 94107 *To:* John Shellabarger, Office Machines, 9200 Evergreen, Chicago, IL 60627. Write an inquiry-stage collection letter over your signature, Credit Manager. Shellabarger sells your WPM word processing machines. In addition to collecting the amount due ($4,200), this letter must also provide a reasonable amount of goodwill for I–G. Shellabarger purchased three Model I WPMs three months ago on terms 2/10, n/60, but he

has not paid anything. You have sent the usual discount-reminder note, then the usual due-date statement, and another statement with a penned friendly reminder on the bottom 15 days later. Office Machines has been a regular discounting or prompt-paying customer of yours for six years, but Shellabarger has been manager just two.

10. Although you also wrote an excellent appeal-stage letter when the account was 110 days old (50 overdue), Shellabarger (previous case) did not reply. Now that the account is 130 days old (70 days overdue), write him an urgency-stage letter suggesting he get a bank loan or that he pay you in partial payments ($1,400 spaced over the next three months). Should you have some specific resale on the house and/or on WPM Model I?

11. Since the urgency letter (previous case) still brought no results from John Shellabarger, write a second urgency-stage letter. Use the approach you think will get him to pay up without losing him as a customer. The account is now 90 days overdue, but you're not ready for an ultimatum to Office Machines.

12. Still Shellabarger (previous case) ignores your letters; so today when the account is 110 days overdue, you write him the ultimatum. He has ten days to pay or you will turn his name over to the Manufacturer's Guild (but don't let it sound spiteful). Stress the positive side (pay and keep all the advantages of credit). Show your reasonableness (not your holier-than-thou-ness) in the past, your reluctance to take the present action, and the justice and necessity of it. Word the ultimatum clearly, precisely, and calmly. When his name is listed with the Manufacturer's Guild, he will have a difficult time getting new credit—and his old ones may dry up unless he waters them regularly.

13. Today it falls to your lot to write Mary Regan Butler a letter pointing out that she has missed three monthly home payments of $500 each on her $65,000 home to First Federal Savings and Loan (nearby city or your home town). Six weeks ago when one payment was 15 days past due, you sent Butler a deftly worded reminder. Fifteen days later you mailed a somewhat stronger message pointing up the delinquency and reminding her that two payments were now due. So having no response when the third payment comes due, you will write a rather strong letter urging payment or an explanation. Though this is an inquiry letter, it needs to be a forceful one ($1,500 due and all you get is silence).

14. Since Mary Butler (previous case) ignored your inquiry as she has all the rest, today (15 days after the third missed payment became due) you will write a letter that gives her one last chance before you institute foreclosure proceedings (in strict accord with the mortgage contract). She has ten days to meet the deadline.

15.   As credit collection manager of John Lear Farm Implement Company, Old Indianola Road NW, Topeka, Kansas 66619, you must write Felix Mostellar, dealer in Lear equipment, New Castle Drive, San Antonio, TX 78202, a dependable customer for the past five years, who still owes $3,500 for equipment purchased four months ago on terms 2/10, n/60. You have sent a regular due-date statement and a reminder letter from your form series on the 21st day of delinquency. Mostellar ignored them. Though you suspect the reason—in southwest Texas the drought has hurt the crops and thereby hurt the farmers—in view of your past experience with Mostellar, you will send an inquiry mixed with some appeal containing short resale on Lear farm equipment.

16.   Thirty more days go by and you have no word from your considerate inquiry to Mostellar (preceding case). Write a full-fledged appeal letter urging him to pay the $3,500.

17.   Thirty more days pass. Write an urgency-stage letter suggesting Mostellar make a series of partial payments or get a bank loan.

18.   Ten days later you *do* hear from Mostellar—a high-spirited, joshing, joking letter blaming the weather, no crops, and the laborers who won't work. He tells you that he can't collect from the farmers who owe him. You admire his good spirits in view of the hard times, you are sympathetic, and you feel like entering into his jovial mood (probably a case of "whistling-in-the-dark psychology")—but you can't afford to lose the $3,500, or even to forgo payment much longer. Write Mostellar the best you can. You are not hard-hearted enough for an ultimatum. You might want to read the text section on "Humor in Collections" and see if you want to use the old collector's joke with him—that you love him but since you aren't his mother he can't expect you to carry him a whole nine months.

19.   Assume that you are employed in the collection department of Gaver's Department Store (branches in 20 states but home office at 132 Vreeland Avenue, Jersey City, NJ 07307). Write a guide letter that Gaver's could send in each of the reminder, inquiry, appeal, urgency, and ultimatum stages. (A guide letter is like a blank key; before it's any good you have to cut and file it to fit the particular situation—lock/customer.)

20.   As Torrey Jemison, Credit Manager, Rudolph Publishers, 985

Second Avenue, New York, NY 10017, write an appeal-stage collection letter to Mrs. Clarence Hague, The Book Nook, 987 Green Arbor Road, Winnetka, IL 60093. Enclose a statement that shows The Book Nook owes $575.56 for books purchased 90 days ago. Rudolph's terms are net 30 days. Enclose an envelope for Hague's convenience and appeal to her to pay. She has been a faithful customer for three years, has an excellent location, but has been affected by a competing bookstore three doors down and by recession.

21. No word from Mrs. Hague and The Book Nook, but according to your field representative, John Spache, she said she would pay when business picked up. Point out the value of keeping her good-pay record in time of recession. Her account is 80 days past due.

22. After several phone calls to Mrs. Hague with no result in collecting the $575.56 (see preceding cases), you must write an urgency collection letter and explain that your past-due accounts are placed with MTD Incorporated, an international collection service since 1913. Urge Mrs. Hague to pay the 110-day old account and keep you from turning her name and the name of the book store over to MTD.

23. For additional cases, see GS 28 (appeal) and GS 29 (urgency) p. 306.

PART THREE

Reports—written and oral

WHY STUDY REPORT WRITING?

Two BASIC FACTS about report writing, as about memo and letter writing, are that (1) regardless of the work you do (except work for yourself or for wages), your ability to prepare good reports will be an important consideration in whether you get a good job and how fast you move up on the job; and (2) most people who have not studied how to prepare and present reports do it rather poorly.

The basic language of good reports differs little from the standard English used in any good functional communication. *Good reports, however, require the use of certain supplementary communication techniques and devices rarely learned except in reports courses.* Though report forms deserve some attention, you can learn them easily. Even the bigger job of learning to phrase the things you want to put on paper is only the last part of the overall problem of putting together good reports.

If you consider the meaning of *communicating through reports,* you'll realize that it involves *preparation.* Preparation for a report means mak-

433

ing a plan, getting the facts or evidence (research), organizing for meaning and coherence, analyzing this material to arrive at an interpretation and solution to the problem, and *then* presenting your analysis clearly and concisely.

You'll realize, too, that improving your ability to do all these things is an important part of a liberal education and especially the kind of education needed to cope with today's information-oriented world. Educated people now usually go into one of the professions (education, medicine, law, engineering, the ministry) or into jobs in government, industry, or business. Today reports serve so many important purposes in all those fields that an educated person needs to know how to prepare them well to perform effectively. Study and practice in preparing and presenting reports *will* help you, therefore, when you're a job candidate and when you're on almost any job.

History, functions, and present need of reports

In early history nobody needed reports. Almost everybody operated a complete one-person business or directed a small group of people under an on-the-spot manager, who had all the facts needed for making decisions. For example, when a shipowner captained a small ship, observation provided all the information needed and thus served the one general function of most reports—*to help the receiver make a decision by providing needed facts and/or ideas.*

Later, as society became more complex, some individuals gained power over large groups as tribal chiefs, masters, or employers—and found reports essential. When one of these bosses sent an underling to scout an enemy tribe or do some work, the boss wanted a report indicating difficulties encountered or to be encountered and the underling's suggestions on such things as materials, personnel, necessary time, and plans for overcoming the difficulties. For example, when a successful shipowner built a second ship and put a hired captain on it to develop trade along a different route, the owner needed reports to make wise decisions about future operations. Thus the ship's log came into being as one early form of written report.

Specific ways reports now serve. The impossibility of a manager's being in two places at the same time made reports necessary. Overcoming the problem of *distance*, then, is the first specific function reports may serve in achieving their general purpose of helping the receiver make decisions by providing needed facts and ideas.

When organizations grew to where the manager could not find time to oversee all operations (sometimes even under the same roof) and some of the processes became so technical that the manager did not have the knowledge to evaluate all of them, reports became more and more widely useful to solve two more specific problems: *time* and *technology.*

With the increasing complexity of society, *records* became more important too; and as their fourth specific function, written reports provided permanent records. Thus they became important in preparing tax returns, in preventing later repetition of the same work, and (through extra copies) in informing interested secondary readers.

As executives became responsible for more and more varied activities, the wiser ones realized that they could not do all the desirable thinking about new products, processes, and procedures. They therefore invited employees with initiative to submit ideas in reports. Hence reports began to serve management in a fifth way as vehicles for *creative ideas*.

As managers became responsible for numerous employees, some of whom they rarely saw, they often found that submitted reports were the best indicators they had of how well an employee was doing an assigned job. Thus reports began to serve in a sixth way—as a basis for *evaluating the employees* who presented them.

You see readily that reports have become essential tools of modern management if you bring these trends up to the present world of large and complex organizations, where

—Top management may be thousands of miles from some operations.

—Management cannot possibly find time to oversee all the activities (even in one location).

—Some of the processes are so technical that no one can be competent to decide wisely about all of them without guidance through reports from specialists.

—Numerous records must be kept and many people informed.

—Competition pushes a manager to use all the creative brainpower of all employees in developing new ideas, through suggestion boxes and reports.

—Personnel managers may never see employees they have to evaluate.

Questions reports answer.   In helping managers in those six ways, reports help with decision making by answering one or more of three key questions:

1. *Is the project under consideration feasible?*   In thinking about any proposed action that is not obviously possible, the decision maker's only logical first question is whether it *can* be done. Can you imagine spending time or money considering the other questions about any project until the necessarily first question of *whether it can be done* is answered favorably —by prior knowledge or by a report (or the first part of a report)? Michigan could not, in thinking about building the bridge across the Mackinac Straits; nor could the U.S. government in thinking about trying a landing on the moon.

2. *Should we take a certain proposed action?*   With feasibility established, decision makers trying to decide on a proposed new product, plant,

or other project will want—in answer to a second question—a report showing whether expected benefits will result in higher profits, better quality or quantity, or less time, material, or effort expended. That is the cost-benefits question. Particularly in reports for public institutions, at least some of the benefits are likely to be in terms of better service, safety, goodwill (including international relations), law enforcement, ecology, health, or education.

3. *Which is the best (or better) way (or solution)?* Only with the feasibility and payoff established can one logically consider this third question. Then the study and report may consider a choice between or among proposed ways, or it may have to propose and evaluate different ways to lead to a choice. Often the answer is a choice between the present way and a proposed new way. But it may be between or among products: IBM or Royal typewriters for our offices? Chevrolet, Ford, or Plymouth for our fleet? Repair the old or buy a new . . . ?

Any board of directors, president, governor, manager, superintendent, or department head in any organization—public or private—wants satisfactory answers to all three questions before approving substantial expenditures, changes in operations, or new regulations. Many times those questions lead to the assignment of reports. For this reason management today expects all employees (except possibly day laborers) to be able to prepare and present reports.

If you need more evidence that learning to present better reports will be a worthwhile activity for you, consider how your study of reports can help you as a student, as a job candidate, and later as a full-time employee on the job.

Help when you're a student and job candidate

Learning the things necessary for a good report can help you to earn better grades. Increased familiarity with sources of information—not just published sources and how to find them in libraries, but also methods of securing original data—enables you to do research more efficiently for papers required in other courses. (Reports are certainly not like term papers in objective or in some phases of treatment, but the research behind them is similar.)

Documenting—that is, backing up what you say with factual evidence, citing publications you use as authorities or sources of information, and explaining your research methods to assure soundness—is also similar in reports and term papers. And certainly you'll profit from the carry-over of organization principles and improved language ability. For these reasons students who have studied and applied reporting principles usually earn better grades on term papers in advanced courses and hence better grades in the courses.

If you go on to graduate school, you will find that your study of reports has been your most useful preparation. When you have to write the many long research papers and a thesis, you will already know how to collect, organize, and interpret data and to write up your findings in good style— using techniques and readability devices learned only in studying reports. Indeed, you will probably join the many graduate students we have heard make comments to the effect that "Thanks to my reports course, I know how to go about writing course papers and my thesis."

When you apply for a job, you'll find that employers put a premium on the services of people who can produce good letters and reports. Because reports play such a prominent role in most businesses (for reasons explained earlier), prospective employers often give preference to those applicants who have learned how to prepare and present reports. They prefer to hire people who can already do so rather than to spend vast sums of money on company-sponsored reports courses (as hundreds of companies do of necessity for people who have not had such preparation for their jobs).

One director of a college placement service reports that an increasing number of talent scouts (recruiters) ask, as one of the first questions, what grade a prospective employee earned in reports. (Note that they assume students have taken the course.) These recruiters apparently regard the performance of the student in a college reports course as an indication of ability to do something that is important to their organizations.

Help when you're on the job

If you are surprised by the interest *prospective* employers have in your ability to produce good reports, you may be even more surprised by their interest as employers. The reports a trainee on a new job usually has to submit may not only help to determine assignment to a division of the company but they also often determine whether to retain or drop the employee at the end of the training period.

Even after one becomes a full-fledged employee, management studies submitted reports not only for information and ideas in the solution of problems but for evidence of the employee's ability to communicate clearly, quickly, and easily. To an immediate superior, an employee will often report orally; but the immediate superior is not usually the one who makes the final decisions about salary increases and promotions. Since those who do may never have met the employee, they often consider equally important the immediate superior's evaluation and the *written* reports of the employee being evaluated. Employers often regard reports as the best (and sometimes they are the only) indication of how well an employee is doing the job.

Your study of reports, as you see, can help your grades in school, your chances at a desirable job, and your effectiveness and status in your career. You can hardly find a better set of rungs for the ladder to success than a series of good reports.

DEFINITION, NATURE, AND CLASSIFICATION OF REPORTS

In the earlier discussion of the general and specific functions reports serve, you have seen several implications of their nature. Yet the word *report* is such a broad concept that we feel the need to define it carefully. And since most attempts at one-sentence definition are either incomplete, too general to be useful, or not quite true, we give you an *extended definition*. An extended (or expanded) definition starts with a *standard definition*—that is, one sentence involving the term to be defined, a copulative verb (usually *is*), the genus or general class to which the term belongs, and the differentiae (the specifics that distinguish the term from others in the same general class). Then the extended definition explains more fully with such things as analyses, etymology, characteristics, and different species or classes; history, uses, and importance; and construction and/or method of operation and example or illustrations.

To make clear what we mean by *report*, we now define the term by all those methods except the three already used (history, uses, and importance) or the three to be used later (construction, method of operation, and examples).

The best *standard definition* we know for *report* is this: **A report is a presentation of facts and/or ideas to people who need them in decision making.**

Analysis of that definition involves several points: A presentation may be oral or written (as reports may be). "Facts and/or ideas" covers the possibilities of just facts without interpretation, facts *and* interpretation, or just interpretations of already known facts—and that statement fits.

Perhaps the most discriminating part of the definition, however, is the last part. As we use the term here, a report *does* go to somebody who faces a problem of making some kind of decision, and the purpose of the report message is to help in making a wise decision. That, you recognize, rules out such things as term papers and write-ups about books read—things often referred to in academic circles as reports.

Etymology can help in defining *report*. One meaning of *re* as a prefix is "back," as in *recall*. The *port* is from *portare* ("to carry"). Hence the Mountain States Telephone executive who explained a problem and assigned a report-writing job quite properly said "Find the answer, Jim, and bring it back."

Still, the best way to get a clear idea of the meaning of the word *report* —as of many others—is to consider the *usual characteristics* of reports, along with the special characteristics of different classes. Here, therefore, we give you those *characteristics*.

Usually, but not always:

1.   A report is a management tool designed to help an executive make decisions. Thus it is *functional* communication for the *benefit of the receiver*. The important person involved is the receiver, who wants some useful information which is not already available—quite a different situation from a professor's receiving a term paper from a student.

2.   A report is an assigned job. Usually the assigner will make clear the kind of report wanted; if not, the reporter should find out by asking.

3.   A report goes up the chain of command. A few reports go between people of equal rank, as between department heads, and some (usually better called directives) go downward from executives (but most reports executives prepare go to still higher authorities—boards of directors, legislatures, or the people who elected them).

4.   A report is for one person or a group (usually small) unified by a common purpose or problem, and usually having a spokesman who authorizes (orders) the report and thus becomes the primary addressee. A primary reader, however, may then send a written report on up the chain of command to just a few higher executives or reproduce it and send copies to the whole group. Corporation annual reports, aiming primarily at groups unified as stockholders or employees, have unusually large readership for a report.

5.   A report gets more than normal attention to organization. Of course, all good communications are organized; but because reports are usually expositions of complex facts and ideas for practical purposes and for busy receivers, reporters work harder at organization than most other communicators. Still the most common serious criticism of reports is their poor organization.

6.   A report makes more than normal use of certain techniques and devices for communicating clearly, quickly, and easily: commonly understood words (details on pp. 44 and 442); short, direct sentences and paragraphs (p. 44); headings, topic sentences, and brief summaries (p. 469); itemizations (p. 45); graphic presentations (p. 477); and specific, concrete, humanized wording (p. 45). (Though these techniques and devices can be very useful in almost any kind of communication, good courses on reports seem to be about the only places they get adequate attention, as on pp. 468–87.)

7.   A report should be accurate, reliable, and objective. No executive wants to base decisions on a reporter's errors, assumptions, preconceptions, wishful thinking, or any kind of illogic. Therefore a good reporter strives to be as objective as possible—though nobody can be strictly objective because selection of facts to include and evaluation of them will vary ac-

cording to who (what kind of person, as a product of background) is doing the selecting and evaluating. (See pp. 465–66.) And where the receiver might otherwise question the validity, the reporter explains sources and methods of collecting data to show the soundness of the facts presented.

8. Good reports—like good buildings, pieces of furniture, or anything else—vary in design according to their functions and conditions of use. People who deal with them have naturally given names to the different "designs" and then tried to classify them—and there they have run into trouble. A strictly logical classification of reports is impossible because the "namers" have shifted bases for their names. To remove some of the confusion, however, we give you the following *classification* as the best we know for (*a*) clarification and (*b*) use of names widely accepted (though we can't say universally).

From the reporter's standpoint the most important *classification* is **on the basis of content**—whether the report includes only facts (an *informational* report) or whether it goes further into interpretation (conclusions and/or recommendations) and becomes an *analytical* report (sometimes called *recommendation* or *improvement* report). A reporter can go wrong, and probably be embarrassed, either way. If the person who authorizes a report does not indicate which kind, the reporter should therefore ask.

Two kinds of confusion often attend that important two-part classification. Since an *analytical* report has more in it than one giving the bare facts on a subject, it is naturally longer. Hence some people refer to any *long* report as *analytical* and (at least by implication) think of *short* reports as *informational*. They may be wrong in all directions; *long* or *short*, a report may be *analytical* or *informational*.

Similarly, since long reports are more likely to be somewhat formal than are shorter ones, we often see an analytical report on a sizable subject referred to as a *formal* report and shorter ones as *informal*. In fact, no necessary relation exists between the length of a report and its formality. The only legitimate basis for calling any report *formal* or *informal* is the degree of formality in its style; and that should be a reflection of the relationship between reporter and receiver(s). The difference is the same as that between the appropriately familiar language and tone in conversation between long-time equal friends and the formal talk between strangers or people of different status.

Since we deal almost wholly with analytical reports (on the principle that anybody who can prepare them can leave out the interpretation and make informational reports), the **primary basis of classification in our treatment in the following chapters is length.** We call them *complete analytical reports* (or long reports, usually ten or more pages), *short analytical reports* (usually six to ten pages), and *short reports*.

Admittedly our naming is imperfect, but we think it is functional. By "complete" we mean not only "with interpretations" but also including all the standard parts; hence such reports are usually long. The short analytical report still has interpretations, but it may omit certain standard parts or combine them as explained in Chapter 16.

We see **no use for classification on the basis of subject matter** that produces such names as engineering reports, business reports, or technical reports. After all, report writing is report writing; regardless of the subject matter, the principles don't change, though the subject matter and sometimes the formats do. Furthermore, nobody ever completes such a classification (perhaps because doing so would serve no purpose and would require some detailed identification system such as the Library of Congress or Dewey Decimal systems used in libraries).

Other minor classifications are all more clear-cut than the foregoing. Perhaps the neatest is that on the basis of the issuing schedule. *Periodic reports* (coming out regularly—*daily, weekly, monthly, quarterly,* or *annually*) are the counterparts of *special reports* (prepared when a special occasion arises). Similarly the names of two other two-part classifications make their bases clear: *private/public* and *internal/external reports.*

Somewhat similarly, the names *letter* and *memo* (or *memorandum*) *report* mean that the reports are written in those forms (of any length, though usually short; informational or analytical; and about any kind of subject matter).

At that point, however, form as a basis of naming and classifying reports stops—unless you want to consider the *credit report* as a special form. In actual practice it usually is, because the sameness of subject matter and purpose have led to a nearly standard form. But variations are enough that you cannot use the name to mean necessarily a certain form.

Three other often-used names of reports clearly indicate their bases of classification and refer to true independents—two of them well identified by name and the other ambiguous. *Progress reports* explain what has been done on a project and usually try to predict the future (both in relation to any preset schedule). *Justification reports* (usually short and sometimes called *initiation reports* because the reporters usually initiate them) propose certain specific actions and provide evidence to show the wisdom of those actions. As such, the *justification report* is much like a well-prepared suggestion that might be dropped in a firm's suggestion box. The term *research report* may mean merely that preparation required some research (as most reports do). Most authorities, however, restrict the name to mean a report of research done to push back the forefronts of knowledge (often called pure or theoretical research) and perhaps without any immediate, practical applications in mind. To avoid being misled, you have to know who is talking. (We use the second meaning.)

For the reporter, much more important than knowing the names and classifications of reports (except possibly the distinction between *informational* and *analytical*) is close attention to the characteristics reports should have: *They should be full of useful information that is accurate, reliable, and objective; presented in functional rather than literary style; adapted to the receiver(s); carefully organized; and clearly, quickly, and easily understandable.* That relates directly to the preparation of reports. To give you a further and more important brief preview of what is coming, therefore, we give you the highlights of the preparation process.

REPORT PREPARATION

Preparing an analytical report is a five-step process. First the reporter *plans* the attack by getting a sharp concept of the problem, breaking it down into its essential elements, and raising questions to be answered about those elements.

Then the reporter *collects* appropriate facts, using the most suitable of the following methods and checking for reliability: library research (reading), experimentation, observation, and survey (of an adequate sample, by mail questionnaire, personal interview, or telephone interview).

Then comes *organizing* the facts according to the most suitable one of *chronological order, order of importance,* or (more likely) a fast, interesting, and clarifying *deductive order* if the reader is likely to be sympathetic, or a slower, duller, temporarily puzzling but finally more convincing *inductive pattern* if the reader is unsympathetic.

While *interpreting* the facts into logical conclusions and workable recommendations (omitted in informational reports), a good reporter attempts to be objective by avoiding all possible prejudices, preconceptions, wishful thinking, and fallacies.

Finally, the reporter puts the report into *words, symbols, and graphics,* using all suitable techniques and devices so that it makes clear what the problem is, shows that the information is reliable by explaining the sound research methods, and presents the facts and what they mean. To make understanding the message clear, quick, and easy, a good reporter:

1. Uses commonly understood words (uneducated, technical, and educated people all understand them and all appreciate the ease of comprehending everyday English).
2. Keeps sentences so direct and short (average about 17 words) that they need little punctuation except periods at the ends (or the oral equivalents).
3. Keeps paragraphs direct and short (questioning those of more than eight lines because short ones seem easier, are easier, and need fewer transitions).
4. Uses headings, topic sentences, and summarizing sentences to show the reader the organization (that is, where the line of thought is going and where it has been).

5. Itemizes (as here) to call attention to important points and to force concise and precise phrasing.
6. Uses all kinds of nonverbal means of communication (charts, graphs, tables, pictograms, maps) to assist words in presenting ideas clearly, quickly, and easily.
7. Chooses specific, concrete, humanized wording rather than generalizations and abstractions by showing how the facts affect people (preferably the receiver), thus making the report both clearer and more interesting, and thus meeting the two requirements for effective communication—that the message be *interesting enough to get attention* and *clear when attended (read or heard).*

chapter 14

Preparing complete
analytical reports

*[To think you know something that isn't so is
worse than not to know.]*

Planning the attack
Collecting the facts
  Library research
  Observation
  Experimentation
  Surveys
Organizing the findings
Interpreting the facts
Using effective report style
  Basics of report style
  Headings and subheads
  Objectivity in presentation
  Presentation of quantitative data
  Graphic aids as supplements to words
  Documentation

HAVING SEEN from the preceding chapter what a report *is*—along with the main report uses, characteristics, and classes—you should be ready to learn *how to prepare one.* You should realize, too, that a good course in business reports is a course in research procedure, a course in the organization of ideas, a course in logic, a course in English composition, a course in supplementary communication devices, a course in organizational behavior and communication, and a course in human relations—all in a current and *practical* setting.

Since we are concerned primarily with analytical reports, because they (if comparatively long ones) involve much learning that others do not, we take up first the complete analytical report—the granddaddy of reports. We are aware that today's efficiency-minded organizations make much more frequent use of short reports than of complete analytical reports. We cover the major reports first (in Chapters 14 and 15), nevertheless, because (1) they are very important when they do come into play (and are usually not well done unless by people who have studied them), and (2) by studying the complete reports, you learn most of what you need for preparing short reports. So (3) we can cover all the various kinds of short written reports in Chapter 16 (and the oral ones as part of Chapter 17).

Preparing a complete analytical report, whatever its length, is a five-step process: (1) planning the attack on the problem, (2) collecting the facts, (3) organizing the facts, (4) interpreting the facts, and (5) presenting the report in appropriate form and style. Since any or all of these five steps may be necessary in varying degrees in the preparation of a particular report in any form, we present the steps in this chapter before explaining and illustrating different forms in the next three chapters.

PLANNING THE ATTACK

Whether a report is oral or written, planning the attack is a job to be done at the desk—the headwork before the legwork. It involves six procedures, in the following sequence:

1. Get a clear view of what the central problem is. If you can't see the target you're shooting at, you're not likely to hit it.

This procedure requires reflective thinking. It may also require a conference with the person who needs the report. As a check, you can try writing a *concise* and *interesting* title that *clearly indicates the content and scope* (see p. 496). If you can also put in one sentence a precise statement of the purpose, clearly indicating what problem you are trying to help solve, you have the necessary clear view.

2. Consider conditions that influence the report—the attitude, degree of interest, knowledge, and temperament of the reader or audience; the use to be made of the report; and its importance.

The reader's or listener's temperament and knowledge of the subject have considerable influence on how much background and detailed explanation you need to give, and whether you can use technical terms. Your reputation as an authority and the reader's or audience's attitude will influence how persuasive you need to be (whether you use the convincing inductive plan or the faster, more interesting, but possibly less convincing deductive plan). Any known biases and special interests may influence what you should stress and whether you must use impersonal style. Your relationship to the primary receivers will indicate how formal or informal the style should be.

In considering use, remember that reports commonly go in the files for future reference after they have served their immediate purpose and that therefore they need to be clear to various people years later. Also, the immediate superior who asked for a written report may have to send it on up the chain of command for approval before anything can happen. So it needs to be intelligible to possible readers other than the one who asked for it.

Limitations on time, money, or availability of data may affect how thorough you can be and whether you can use costly plates and charts.

3. Divide the central problem (the *text* of your report) into its elements, the main divisions in an outline of the topic. The idea of dividing to conquer applies in report organization as well as in military strategy.

Whatever you do at this stage toward outlining will probably be only tentative and skeletal. You'll probably change it later, after you have the facts. At this point you merely need a starting guide to what kinds of facts to collect. So don't worry too much about form and accuracy; specific instruction on the finished outline comes later (pp. 461 ff. at which you might well glance now, to avoid some false steps).

Of course, not all problems divide alike, any more than all jigsaw puzzles do; but the dividing process is a job of finding the natural divisions of the whole. Since an introduction will be I in your final outline, for now you can skip it and begin listing your criteria or other major divisions as II, III, IV, . . . or (as we explain later) 1.0., 2.0., 3.0., ...

If the problem is one of deciding between/among two or more things, the *criteria* are usually the best major division headings. For example, if you are trying to decide which of several jobs to take, on what bases (criteria) do you decide? Maybe

II. Kind of work			2.0 Kind of work
III. Location			3.0 Location
IV. Beginning pay	or		4.0 Beginning pay
V. Chances for advancement			5.0 Chances for advancement
VI. Working conditions			6.0 Working conditions

Some topics common to many business problems are history, disadvantages of present system, advantages of proposed system, costs and means of financing, taxes and tax effects, personnel required, effects on goodwill, transportation, method of installation, utilities available and their costs, materials required, time involved, safety, increases or decreases in quality, market, competition, convenience, and availability of land.

4. Raise specific questions about each element. These questions further divide the problem, lead to subheads in your outline, and point more directly toward collecting data for answers. For instance on the job-choice problem under III (location) you might want to put subheads about moving, housing, climate, educational and recreational facilities, and perhaps others. Under IV (pay) you would surely think of beginning pay, chances for advancement, and retirement and other fringe benefits.

Put down all you can think of in this planning stage. But, so long as you have three to five major divisions between the introduction and the conclusions, don't worry too much about completeness. As you do your research, you'll think about (and add or combine) other major and/or subdivision topics for completeness in the final outline.

If cost is one of the elements in a problem, for example, you want to ask what the costs are for operating one way and what they would be under a revised system. You would then want to question further about how to find the costs in each instance. And you might do well to break the questions down further into first costs, operating costs, and depreciation; costs for personnel, for upkeep and for power; and the like. Specific questions on goodwill might include those about customers, stockholders, workers, and the general public.

5.   Take stock of what you already know. You may pose a hypothesis, but don't let it close your mind to other possible solutions. Don't assume that you know the answer until all the facts are in. *You certainly don't want to start out to prove a preconceived notion* (a blinder on the truth).

Get a clear concept of the assumptions you are willing to make, and separate those that you can hold without further checking from those that you must check and perhaps validate by supporting evidence.

Jot down answers known for the questions raised. Clearly indicate information gaps you need to fill, and jot down what you think tentatively are the best sources and methods for getting the missing data—experts, books and articles, and maybe the person who faces the problem you're helping to solve. You might even have to devise some kind of experiment. Or perhaps you need to plan a survey and must decide on the kind and size of sample, kind of survey, and the like.

6.   Make a working schedule. Assign estimated time blocks for each of the remaining steps in producing the report: collecting remaining data—and organizing, interpreting, and wording the final report. If you plan a survey, remember that mail requires time and that people don't always respond to questionnaires immediately. For any except the most routine kind of reports, be sure to allow some time for revising early drafts to put the final report in clear, interesting, and inconspicuous style and form.

The first item on the working schedule is the next step in report preparation—collecting the facts.

COLLECTING THE FACTS
[The ladder of success must rest on
   something solid.]

For collecting complete and reliable facts, you may use any or all of the four basic methods of securing information: (1) library research (reading), (2) observation, (3) experimentation, and (4) surveys. The first provides secondary (secondhand) data, and the others provide primary (firsthand or new) facts. In most cases you should use at least two of the methods in such a way as to get at the essential facts and assure their reliability.

Library research

While we know that many (even most) reports in business and industry are short ones dealing with day-to-day operations and not making much use of library research, we also know that high-level managements making major decisions nearly always do depend partly on major reports. For them, library research is almost invariably a part.

Indeed study of published books, articles, theses, brochures, speeches and other reports is the most universally useful method and is *usually the best first step*. When you face any problem of consequence, somebody else has probably faced the same or a closely related problem and written something worthwhile and relevant to your problem. And when pertinent data are already written, getting the facts by reading is nearly always easier and quicker than the laborious process of getting primary data by any of the other research methods.

Besides being the quick and easy way to collect facts, reading may also give a bird's-eye view of the whole problem, acquaint you with terminology and methods you may not have thought of, refer to other good sources, show formerly overlooked natural divisions and aspects of the problem, and in general help you to revise your tentative outline and plan of attack.

Reading about almost any topic, however, can be so extensive as to bog you down. Fortunately, you have good reasons to avoid that pitfall in doing research for a report. A report is a practical communication concerned with *currently* and *foreseeably pertinent* data. *It is not* a compendium, an encyclopedia, or a definitive treatment. Hence you can and should be *selective* in your reading for a report—ignoring the long ago and far away that is outdated or otherwise irrelevant. A good start is to weed out bibliographic materials by looking at their dates.

In what we give you here, to be helpful in your bibliographical research, we are selective on the basis of dates and on other bases. Instead of giving you even a large sample of the mind-boggling and space-wasting quantity of constantly obsolescing business-oriented publications in a good library, we give you the essence of library-research procedures or approaches and the main *keys* (guides) to finding what you need. With them—plus a little effort and help when needed from reference librarians (and sometimes a little bit o' luck)—you can find what you need for your report.

Fortunately, libraries are pretty well standardized. They nearly always have at least three broad categories of materials—reference books, books in the stacks, and periodicals. Some main ones of the great variety of *regular reference books are:*

Encyclopedias (*Americana, Columbia, Encyclopaedia of the Social Sciences, Encyclopedia of Science and Technology*, and the definitive *Encyclopaedia Britannica*).

Collections of generally useful, up-to-date statistical and other information, surprising in variety and amount (*The World Almanac* and *Facts on File*).

Census reports (U.S. government censuses of agriculture, business, government housing, manufacturing, population, minerals, and other breakdowns).

Yearbooks of various countries, trades, and professions (commerce, shipping, agriculture, engineering, and others).

Atlases (especially those by Rand McNally, the *Britannica, National Geographic*, and Hammond).

Dictionaries (*American College Dictionary, Standard College Dictionary, Webster's Collegiate Dictionary, Webster's New International Dictionary* [unabridged], and the *Oxford English Dictionary*—for etymologies).

Directories (such as Thomas' for American manufacturers and Ayer's for newspapers and magazines).

Who's who in various fields (including the *Directory of American Scholars, American Men of Science, World Who's Who in Commerce and Industry*, and Poor's *Register of Corporations, Directors and Executives*).

Statistical source books (*Statistical Yearbook, Statistical Abstract of the United States, Survey of Current Business, County and City Data Book*).

These are just a few main examples of the numerous reference books usually in a library. Constance Winchell's *Guide to Reference Books* (recent editions revised by Eugene P. Sheehy) tells about them and many more. Other helpful guides are *How to Use the Business Library*, Robert W. Murphy's *How and Where to Look It Up*, Gale Research Company's *Encyclopedia of Business Information Services*, and Rae E. Rip's *United States Government Publications*.

The standard key to *books in the stacks* is the card catalog, arranged alphabetically by author, subject, and title. But because libraries available to most researchers will not have all the books published on their subjects; because it takes months for books to be published, bought by libraries, and cataloged for distribution; and because not all topics appear in full-book treatment, for reports often the best up-to-date printed sources are periodicals.

Fortunately, one or more of the numerous periodical indexes, both general and specific for almost any field, cover most periodicals. Table 14–1

TABLE 14–1 Main current indexes

Title	Coverage	Publication facts (most frequent issue and cumulation)
Accountants' Index	International; technical books and magazines	Annually
Applied Science and Technology Index	Scientific, engineering and technical American and Canadian magazines	Monthly except August; annually
Biological and Agricultural Index	International; books and magazines	Monthly except August; annually
Business Periodicals Index	Business, industrial, and trade magazines	Monthly except August; annually
Chemical Abstracts	International; all phases of chemistry	Biweekly; semiannually
Education Index	Professional literature	Monthly except July and August; annually
Engineering Index	Domestic and foreign literature on engineering	Monthly; annually
Index Medicus	International; medicine and related fields	Monthly; annually
New York Times Index	The news in the paper	Semimonthly; annually
Public Affairs Informaiton Service (PAIS)	Periodicals and government documents and pamphlets of general, technical, and economic interest	Weekly except only two in August and three in December; annually, 5 yr.
Readers' Guide to Periodical Literature	General American magazines	Semimonthly; annually and/or biennially
Social Science and Humanities Index	Emphasis on history, international relations, political science, and economics	March, June, September, December; annually
Wall Street Journal Index	Corporate and general business news	Monthly; annually

describes the main current indexes; but if you do not find one for your specific field, look around and/or ask the reference librarian. And if the abbreviations or the system of indexing is not immediately clear to you, the preface always explains.

Whatever library key you use, you need to develop *resourcefulness*. Often when you look under one topic (say "Business Letter Writing" or "Report Writing"), you will find little or nothing. Don't give up. You have to match wits with the indexer and try to think of other possible wordings for the topic. "Business Letter Writing" might be under "Business English" or "Commercial Correspondence" and "Report Writing" under "Technical Writing" or something else.

When your resourcefulness brings you to a book or article that seems to be useful, scan it to see what portion (if any) of it is grist for your mill. A look at the table of contents may tell you whether it will be helpful.

If it seems pertinent, check its *reliability*. Remember that no decision maker wants to base decisions on unsound data, yours or anybody else's. Consider whether (1) the material is outdated, (2) the textual evidence and the reputation of the publisher and of the author reveal any possible slant or prejudice, and (3) the author is a recognized authority in the field. Reading a review in a related journal can help in judging the worth of a book. A sound reporter will not be duped by the usual undue worship of the printed word; just realize that something's being in print does not make it true.

If the material meets the tests for reliability and relevance (including its date), take notes—*a separate card or sheet of paper for each important note*. If you put more than one note to the card, you will have trouble in arranging the cards later because the different notes on a card will not all fit at the same place in your report, and hence some multinote cards will belong in two or more places in your arrangement. To save time later in arranging notes, put a notation at the head of each note card (that is, one which indicates where the information fits in your plan). It may well be the heading in your outline or the divisional symbol from your outline, say Section 3.3.

Of course, if you take a needed note on some topic not in your tentative outline, you make a slugged card for it and add the topic to your outline. Using cards for your notes gives several advantages:

1. They encourage taking concise rather than wordy notes. (Most notes should be mere jottings. But don't let them get you into trouble.)
2. You can handle them better than sheets of paper—and move them around better for adding to, subtracting from, or reorganizing your original (tentative) outline.

When in doubt, take fuller rather than scantier notes than you think you need; it's easier to omit later than to come back for more.

Some notes you may want to take in verbatim quotations, but usually not. Good researchers do not use many direct quotations—only (1) to gain the impact of the author's authority, (2) to be fair by stating exactly before criticizing, or (3) to take advantage of the conciseness, exactness, or aptness of phrasing. If you do quote, be sure to quote exactly and not change the original meaning by lifting a small part from a context in which it means something different.

In most cases you can save words and express the idea better for your purposes if you paraphrase. When you paraphrase, however, be sure not to change the original meaning.

In some cases you can save time later by writing your notes as a review of the article or book—that is, from your own point of view, giving the essential content of the article along with your comment on it—because that seems to be the form it will take in the final report. In other cases you will condense, digest, or abstract the article.

Whether you quote, paraphrase, review, or abstract the article or book, list in your bibliography *all* printed sources used directly in the preparation of the report; so you need to take the necessary bibliographic information while you have the book or magazine in hand. Although bibliography form is not standardized, the usual information is author's name (surname first, for alphabetizing), title of book or article and magazine, publisher and place of publication for books, edition if not the first for books, volume and inclusive page numbers for magazine articles, and the date. (The exact form comes later, p. 489.) For use in citations in the text, record the specific pages used for each note.

What we have suggested here are sound, basic library research procedures. If you follow them, you will make your library research effective, efficient, economical—and painless.

Observation

The second method of collecting data—observation—includes not only its usual meanings but also investigation of company records of finances, production, sales, and the like. As such, it is the main method used by accountants and engineers for audit, inspection, and progress reports.

The job of collecting data by observation usually involves no particular problem of getting at the facts. The important part is more likely to be *knowing what facts to consider.* This requires keeping in mind what your purpose is, so as to notice everything relevant and to relate each pertinent fact to the whole situation.

A skilled police officer's investigation of a murder scene or of an automobile accident site exemplifies the technique. Camera, measuring tape, and note pad are standard equipment for outside observation, just as the accountant's special paper, sharp pencil, and calculator are for inside inspection of the records. Still, the most important pieces of equipment are sharp eyes to see the situation, judgment to evaluate it, and (most important) imagination to see the relevance of a particular observed fact to the whole problem.

Observation has the advantage of being convincing, just as the testimony of an eyewitness convinces a jury more than circumstantial evidence. But it has the disadvantage of not getting at motives. That is, it may answer *what* but not find out *why.* For instance, an observer stationed in the aisle of a supermarket may tabulate which brand of detergent each shopper chooses, but that will tell nothing about *why* each shopper made that choice. And an observer who is not careful may put too much stress on a few isolated cases or may ignore factors (weather, place, time of year, month, week, or day) influencing what was visible for recording.

Experimentation

For the most part, experimentation is useful in the physical sciences rather than in business and the social sciences, and in industrial rather than commercial operations. And of course, the methods used vary almost infinitely according to the particular experiment to be done. Hence some of them are best taught by a specialist in the particular field, in the laboratory with equipment, rather than through a small section in a textbook mainly about something else. Regardless of field or problem, however, an experimenter should be as zealous as a reporter about the reliability of results. The basic requirements for reliability in experimentation are three:

1. *Accurate equipment (if used).* If a laboratory balance is inaccurate, or if a tachometer or thermometer misrepresents the facts, the results of an experiment using them will be unreliable.

2. *Skilled techniques.* A technician who doesn't know how to set a microscope won't be able to see an amoeba; and if unable to pipette both accurately and fast, will be no good at Kahn tests. Skilled techniques also include proper selection of specimens for study.

3. *Sufficient controls or repetition of results.* If an experimenter takes two specimens just alike and treats them exactly alike except in one way (perhaps inoculates one, keeping the other for a control), different results (say one gets a disease and the other does not) make a strong start toward convincing us. If repeating the experiment produces exactly the same thing every time (100 percent), only a few repetitions are thoroughly convincing. For every drop from 100 percent, however, the experimenter has to multiply the number of tests many times to produce similar faith in them.

Testing only one variable at a time is basic. If soil, seed, and temperature all change in two runs of an agricultural experiment, you cannot attribute different results to any one of them. If you clean your tank and refill with different gasoline, repair your carburetor, and adjust your ignition system all at the same time and your car runs better, you won't know what caused your troubles before.

Experts in certain phases of business can use experimentation that closely parallels laboratory methods if they are careful about their *equipment, techniques,* and *controls.* For example, marketing specialists can test the comparative effects of different advertising campaigns and media, sales promotion devices, prices, and packaging. Their problems of equipment and technique may be more psychological than mechanical and manual, and their controls can be difficult to set up to make sure that only one element changes; but experts can and do manage all three to assure reasonable reliability. (See pp. 283 ff. on testing sales campaigns.)

Surveys

Often the quality to be tested is not subject to exact laboratory-type examination—the sales appeal of a new car, for example. The only place to get an answer to that is from people. In fact, the survey for fact and opinion is a major method of collecting data for business and social science reports. It is particularly useful in discovering *why* people do certain things and in *forecasting* what will happen (both frequently important jobs of reports).

Regardless of which of the three kinds of surveys you use—mail questionnaire, personal interview, or telephone interview—research by survey involves certain basic problems, principles, and techniques.

Determining what people you will survey is the first problem. In some cases you may decide that the opinions of a few experts will be worth more than the answers of thousands of the general public, as they will be if the problem is technical or professional (say medical or legal). In that case, Chapter 11 and the "Interviews" section of Chapter 17 will help you more than the discussion of sampling here. If the whole group involved (called *the universe* by statisticians) is small, you may decide to ask all of them. But in most cases you take a sample.

How large a sample you need for sound results then becomes your next problem. The answer will depend on the degree of accuracy required and on the variety of possible answers. For instance, if plus or minus 10 percent is close enough, your sample can be much smaller than if you have to be accurate within a range of 1 percent. And if you have to forecast election returns only in terms of Democratic, Republican, and other votes, your sample can be much smaller than if you have to forecast the purchases of the 50 or more makes and body styles of cars. As an even simpler illustration, you can certainly better predict the fall of a coin (only two choices) than of a pair of dice, with 11 possible readings.

Although a full treatment of sampling theory would require a complete book, statisticians have provided us with some *simple devices for determining adequate sample size*. The simplest is the split-sample test. You break your sample arbitrarily (that is, to avoid any known differences) into two or more parts. You then compare the results from the various parts. If the results from the partial samples are acceptably close together, the results from the total sample will be acceptably reliable.

More precise checks on the adequacy of sample size require only a little mathematics and procedures explained in any beginning book on statistics.

We do not present them here because judgment, a study of statistics, and our observation of professional pollsters' accuracy based on surprisingly *small* samples show two things: (1) most people think a sample must be larger than it (statistically) needs be and (2) most people give too little attention to the other equally important requirement for a sound sample—stratification.

Even your adequate *sample must be stratified* (sometimes imprecisely called *representative*) or your results can go wild. That is, *each segment of the universe must appear in the sample with the same percentage as in the universe.* According to sampling theory, this will be the result if you take a large enough *random* sample (one in which each item in the universe has an equal chance of getting into the sample). In practice, however, you often have trouble making sure you really have a random sample. Unsuspected selective factors may work to produce an unstratified (and hence unsound) sample.

To avoid such a possibility, you can (as professionals usually do) use stratified sampling if you have data showing the proportions of different segments in your universe. Fortunately, you usually do. Just as a college registrar's office knows the number of students in different classes, majors, age groups, grade-point groups, and the like, the statistical source books provide breakdowns of people in nearly every imaginable way. Whatever group you may want to sample, you probably can find the proportions of the different segments making up the universe. The U.S. Census Bureau breaks its population figures down in almost every imaginable way. Remember, though, that the bureau's real head count is every ten years (those ending in 0—1970, 1980, 1990, . . .). Figures *between* those years are only estimates—but good ones. If 50 percent of your universe are farmers and 70 percent telephone subscribers, half your sample must be farmers and 70 percent telephone subscribers.

Adequate size and stratification together make a sound sample.

A sound sample can still produce unsound results, however, unless your techniques of getting answers from it are also sound. If you start out by surveying a minimum sound sample but get answers from only half of it, the sample of actual answers is unsound because it is too small. If you survey more than enough and get a large enough sample of answers, but 100 percent of one stratification group answers and only half of another group answers, your returns are not stratified and hence are not reliable. Of course, the best solution is to get 100 percent returns from all groups—an ideal rarely accomplished.

How can you induce people to answer survey questions? Sometimes a respondent is already so much interested, because the benefit is obvious, that you need not point it out. You can therefore begin directly with the request for help, as in the direct inquiry letters discussed on page 104 ff. At other times you have a selling job to do, as in the persuasive requests discussed on page 379 ff. Whether you are using a mail questionnaire, a personal interview, or a telephone interview makes little difference in the approach. Neither does the amount of information you want make much difference—whether you want to ask just one or dozens of questions. But to misjudge the situation and make a direct inquiry when you need a persuasive request may result in decreased returns and hence an unreliable sample.

Fundamentally, your persuasive method is the same as in persuading people to do anything, as in sales and collection letters: *Show them a benefit to themselves.* It may be a gift or reward, direct payment of a fee, or less obvious and less material benefits such as appeals to pride and prestige (but not obvious flattery), appeals to their desire for better service or more efficiency in their kind of work, or the possibility of their getting answers to some questions or solutions to problems they encounter in their own work.

The last two are frequently the best (because they avoid suggesting a bribe or being too mercenary, as the first two might), and they are more immediate and tangible than the others. For instance, personnel officers who read lots of poor application letters are likely to answer a textbook writer's or a teacher's questions about preferences in application letters—because of the possibility that they may as a result get more good applications and thereby make their work easier. A frequent method of inducing answers is the offer of a copy or digest of the survey results.

A big point to remember in making persuasive requests is to show a benefit *before* making the request. Then if you explain who is making the survey and why; make answering as easy, quick, and impersonal as possible; assure respondents that you will honor restrictions they put on use of the information; and tell pointedly just what you want them to do, enough people will usually do it to make your results reliable. Skilled approaches, both oral and written, often bring percentages of answers that surprise the untrained who have tried their hands and failed.

Chapter 11 explains in detail how to induce reluctant people to respond as you wish. If you feel more adept at talking on the phone than at writing a persuasive letter, you might consider calling people in your selected sample and asking them to cooperate in answering questions you plan to send. If you do, the principles in Chapter 11 apply to the oral persuasion too. It has been very successful in several situations that we know.

The approach you use will be a major factor in determining your success in getting returns by personal interview, telephone interview, or mail questionnaire; but *the questions you ask and how you ask them will affect both the percentage of returns and the worth of the answers.* For that reason, writers of questionnaires and people planning interviews need to keep in mind the following main principles used by professionals:

1. Ask as few questions as you can to get the necessary information.

Don't ask other people for information you should have dug up for yourself, possibly in the library. And don't ask a question when you can figure the answer from the answers to others. To avoid unnecessary questions—which reduce returns—write down all you can think of, group them, and then knock out the duplicates. (One kind of duplication is permissible: double-check questions which get at the same information from different approaches as a check on the validity of answers.)

2. Ask only what you might reasonably expect to be answered. Requests for percentages and averages are either too much work or over the heads of many people. Questions requiring long memory may frustrate and bring erroneous results. And most people don't even know *why* they do many things.

3. Make your questions as easy to answer as possible (perhaps by providing for places to check); but provide for all likely answers (at least the "no opinion" answer and perhaps the blank to be filled as the respondent wants to because no one of your suggested answers is suitable).

4. Make your questions perfectly clear. To do so, you may sometimes have to explain a bit of necessary background. If you ask "Why do you use X peanut butter?" you may get "It is cheapest," "A friend recommended it," and "I like its smooth texture and easy spreading" from three respondents. If you really want to know how the customer first learned of X, you should phrase the question in such a way as to get answers parallel to the second. If you are interested in the qualities that users like (as in the third answer), you should ask that specific question. Questions about *how* cause as many different interpretations as those asking *why* and require the same kind of careful wording. Also, double-barreled questions ("Did you see X, and did you like it?") frustrate the reader who wants to answer one part one way and the other part another way.

5. Carefully avoid leading questions—questions which suggest a certain answer, such as one to agree with the questioner's obvious view.

6. Insofar as possible, phrase questions to avoid the "prestige" answer—the respondent's answering according to what apparently would make the best impression.

7. Avoid unnecessary personal prying. When your question is necessary to your basic purpose, make it as inoffensive as possible (for instance, by asking which named *income* or *age* or *educational group* the respondent falls in, if that rather than the exact figure will serve your purpose).

8. Arrange questions in an order to encourage response—easier or impersonal ones at first, related ones together in a natural sequence to stimulate interest and aid memory.

9. Insofar as possible, ask for answers that will be easy to tabulate and evaluate statistically; but when they are important, don't sacrifice shades of meaning or intensity of feeling in the answer for easy handling. Often the most helpful answers a survey brings are those to open-end questions;

but if you ask many of them, you will reduce your returns. Such questions require time and thought to answer as well as to analyze.

Often *scaled* answer forms can bring responses desirably showing intensities of feelings that are still easy to tabulate and evaluate statistically. For example, a form asking for students' evaluations of professors might use a labeled continuum, thus: "On (a certain aspect of teaching), how would you rate Professor X?"

Excellent	Very Good	Good	Average	Poor	Bad	Terrible
+3	+2	+1	0	−1	−2	−3

After you have decided on the questions you want answered, your next problem is deciding *which type of survey* (mail questionnaire, personal interview, or telephone interview) will best serve your purposes. No one type is always best. The main *bases for your decision* are:

1. *The kind and amount of information requested from each respondent.* People are more willing to *tell* you personal information—and more of it—than they are to put personal facts in writing or to do very much writing. So if the requested information is personal or extensive, the personal interview would probably be the best form. The comparative anonymity of the interviewer and reluctance to talk long over the telephone with strangers are against the telephone method for such a situation. On the other hand, factual information (especially statistics, percentages, and averages) which the respondent may not know at the moment would come best in writing because the respondent can take a little time to dig up the information for a mail questionnaire.

2. *Costs.* Two facts about the sample to be surveyed affect the choice of method on the basis of cost—its size and dispersal. Within one telephone exchange, if your group is not large, the telephone is the cheapest method; but if it involves long-distance charges, they become prohibitive unless the group is small. The mail questionnaire has the advantage of wide geographical coverage at no additional cost; and the bigger the group, the greater the advantage, because duplicating and (even two-way) mailing of copies of a good set of questions costs little. The personal interview is almost always the most costly (mainly in interviewer's time) unless the group is both small and close together.

You need to consider cost per return, however; and since the mail questionnaire usually brings in the lowest percentage of returns, its advantages may not be so great as at first thought unless a good covering letter and set of questions mailed at an opportune time induce a high percentage of answers.

3. *Speed in getting results.* If you have to have the answers today, you can get some of them by telephone (and by personal interview if your

sample is not too large and the people are close together); but you can't get them by mail. Mail answers will flood you in about four days and dribble in for a week or more after that, unless you make clear that you need the information by a certain time (a point which needs careful justifying to avoid the bad manners of rushing a person to do you a favor).

4. *Validity of results.* Each of the three kinds of survey has advantages and disadvantages in terms of validity. Personal and telephone interviews, both being oral, have more traits in common than either has with mail questioning. Either the personal or the telephone interview can better clear up any confusion about questions and thereby get appropriate answers. In addition, the personal interviewer may pick up supplementary information (such as the general look of economic conditions around the home and incidental remarks of the talker) that will provide a check on answers given—an impossibility by mail.

On the other hand, in personal and telephone interviews people may give you offhand answers to get rid of you because the time of the call is inconvenient; and they may answer according to what they think is your view (playing the prestige-answer game). Moreover, high-pressure personal selling, obscene phone calls, and other abuses have made many people wary of personal and telephone calls, thus making oral surveys increasingly difficult and complicating the job of keeping samples stratified (and thus valid). Also certain segments of the population have fewer telephones than others and thereby skew a telephone sample—just as certain kinds of doors (maybe apartment dwellers'), being especially hard to get into, skew samples for personal interviewers.

Perhaps the biggest advantage of mail questionnaires is that people can choose the most convenient time to answer and are therefore more likely to answer thoughtfully. That includes taking time to check records for information not on the tip of the tongue. Moreover, everybody has a mailing address where a mail questionnaire can "get in"; so in view of costs and time, the mail questionnaire is less likely to be limited to a too-small group or one that is geographically or economically limited. But those who choose not to answer may be a special group (say the less educated who don't like to write) and may thereby unstratify your carefully planned sample.

5. *Qualifications of the staff.* Some people who can talk well and thus get information may not be able to write a good questionnaire and covering letter; and, of course, the opposite may be true. Even some good talkers have poor telephone voices that discourage that method. And others have appearances that discourage personal interviews.

If you select an adequate and stratified sample, induce people to answer by showing a benefit, ask good questions, and use the type of survey most suitable for your situation, surveys can get you a great variety of valuable information for your reports.

ORGANIZING THE FINDINGS

However you collect and record the necessary facts for your report, you have to organize them for interpretation (in an analytical report) and for presentation. Good organization is the marshaling of statements and supporting details, the orderly procession of paragraphs, the disposition of parts so that each finds its proper place.

Fundamentally, organization is the process of grouping things according to likeness and then putting the groups into an appropriate sequence. For example, if you explain in your letter or report how something is made, you should treat that part fully before going on to explain how it operates. Either of these topics may be just one paragraph, or it may be several. But you do want to group together all the details about how it is made before proceeding. Thus you achieve unity of that topic.

Having grouped according to likenesses, you have several choices of sequence for a whole letter, memo, or paragraph. Common paragraph sequences are (1) general to specific, (2) cause to effect, (3) order of importance, (4) nearest to farthest (space relations), and (5) order of happening (time relations). All of these may be reversed.

Your problem of organizing is probably easier than you suspect, however, because conventional practice (or someone who set up a standard plan of reports where you work) will have done most of the job for you. If you have no set plans to follow where you work, Chapter 16 gives help in organizing the widely varied kinds of short reports; and as explained and illustrated in Chapter 15, almost any long analytical report uses something approaching conventional practice for its overall organization.

Your only problem—and the only one we are talking about here, therefore—is the final organization of the *text* of complete analytical reports. The introduction is the first major division (1.0) of your final plan, and the conclusions and recommendations (together or separately) are usually the last one or two. The text includes the several major divisions between the introduction and the conclusions.

For a graphic, bird's-eye view of what we're saying, look at page 493. We're saying that you now must revise your earlier tentative outline for a final one whose skeleton is like ours, but you must put "flesh" (the "meat" of your report) on your skeleton.

Because the text is the essence of the report, *you do not have a section heading for it.* (If you did, it would be the same as the title of the whole report.) The divisions of the text, then, usually constitute sections 2.0., 3.0., 4.0., and so on—where you present all your facts, explanations, and reasons leading to your conclusions and recommendations. According to the instructions in "Planning the Attack" (Items 3, 4, and 5, pp. 445–47), you should already have set up the organization of your text as a tentative and probably incomplete plan to guide you in collecting data. If you didn't read and follow those instructions, you need to do so now.

That preliminary outline is the starting point for doing the present job—making a final outline as a guide to interpreting and presenting the facts.

Basically, organizing (outlining) is the process of putting related things into groups according to common characteristics *and your purpose* (playing poker instead of bridge, for example), and then putting the groups into a desirable sequence. In the process you may find that you need to revise your tentative outline because the information classified according to your first plan is not logically or psychologically arranged for good presentation. For instance you will want to *make sure that things the reader or audience needs to compare are close together.*

Certainly you need to check your tentative plan before going further. You may now be able to see enough interpretations of your data to make a sentence outline, as you couldn't earlier, because sentences require you to *say something about* the topics. If you can, it will be easier to follow while wording the report, it will force more careful thinking, and it will give the essence of your report (not just the list of topics discussed but the key statements about those topics). Because of its helpfulness in phrasing the report, you may want to make a full-sentence outline (like a lawyer's brief or a précis) for close-knit, logical wording, and then change it to one of the less cumbersome forms (later discussed) for final presentation.

Whether you use full sentences or noun-phrase topics, close adherence to the following principles is necessary for a good final plan (outline):

1. Stick to the *one basis of classification* implied in your title and purpose as you break down any topic (such as your text) into its parts. For example, on the basis of credit hours earned, college students are freshmen, sophomores, juniors, seniors, or graduates. You can't logically classify them as juniors, Protestants, and Democrats. Such a procedure shifts bases in helter-skelter fashion from credit hours earned to religion to politics. You would have overlapping topics, whereas the divisions of an outline should be mutually exclusive.

If your title is "Reasons for" (or "Why") . . . , the major divisions of your text can't logically be anything but the list of reasons. If the title is something like "Factors Influencing . . ." or "Ways to . . . ," each major division will have to be one of those factors or ways. The title "Market Factors Indicating Why a Rexwall Drugstore in Savannah Would Sell More Than One in Charleston" commits you to show for each subject—Charleston and Savannah—market factor evidence supporting your thesis. (This does not forbid giving the introduction, conclusions, and recommendations similar major-division status. They are not parts of the text you're organizing.)

Your proper basis will depend on the nature of the problem. It may be the parts of a whole, the factors to be considered, time periods, space areas, and many others. Cost-benefit and before-after analyses sound good but are too simplistic, and they defeat juxtaposition too much, for good report writing about more than simple problems. Organizing on the basis of how or where you got the information is never desirable—except possibly in a simple comparison study to evaluate the method or source. Even then, however, you have a better way.

In outlines of comparison leading to a choice, use the criteria (bases on which the choice depends) rather than the subjects (the things between or among which you must choose) as the major divisions. Your criteria are the things on which your choice will stand or fall, and hence they deserve the emphasis. In evaluating a Ford and a Chevrolet, for example, you should use both names frequently in your organization scheme, but neither would be a major heading as such. Your major headings would be the tests you decide to apply: costs (initial and operating—and possibly trade-in value), performance, comfort, and appearance. Under each head you would have to analyze each subject (Ford and Chevrolet).

2. Follow one good system to show the relationship of all the parts. The increasingly used system in business and industry is the decimal (sometimes called scientific) system, which has become popular because it immediately tells exactly where a reader is in a report and (because it developed in the physical sciences) it is thought to lend an air of "scientific authority." The older Roman system of outline symbols still appears in business use, and is still popular in many areas of education.

Decimal		Roman	
1.0.		I.	
	1.1.		A.
	1.2.		B.
	1.3.		C.
2.0.		II.	
	2.1.		A.
		2.1.1.	1.
		2.1.2.	2.
	2.2.		B.
3.0.	(etc.)	III.	(etc.)

You can use the decimal system without indentation if you wish—with or without is a matter of preference, but you can save time and space if you do not indent.

3. Cover all categories—that is, all the divisions at any level must add up to the whole indicated by your heading over those divisions. All the roman-numeral divisions together must add up to everything covered by the title, and all the capital letters under Section II must total the II data (and the same if you use decimal notation). If you classify students according to political affiliation, you would most certainly have Republicans as well as Democrats, in addition to others. If you classify according to religion, you would have to include non-Protestants along with Protestants (or word the title to show the limited coverage).

4.   Use no single subdivisions. If you start to divide section 2.1 by putting a subhead 2.1.1, you must logically have at least a subhead 2.1.2; you can't divide anything into one part.

5.   Use parallel grammatical structure for parallel things. All the roman-numeral divisions are parallel things; all the capital-letter divisions under one of them are parallel, but not necessarily parallel with those under another roman-numeral division. They may all be complete sentences, all nouns or noun phrases (probably the best), or all adjectives. In discussing the five sections of the usual application data sheet, for example, you would not list "Heading and Basic Facts," "Education," "Experience," "Personal," and "References." All except "Personal" are nouns, but it is an adjective. "Personal Details" would be all right.

6.   Consider the psychological effects (reading ease) of the number of parts in any classification. Three to seven is the optimum range. Of course, the nature of the topic may dictate how many you have. For instance, according to credit hours earned, the classes in a university are just five—from freshmen to graduates—no more and no less. In breaking down some topics, however, you have some choice in the number, depending on how broadly you name the parts. Having too few suggests that you didn't need the breakdown or that you have not completed it; having too many puts a strain on the reader or listener to remember them. In some cases you may be wise to shift to a slightly different basis of classification that will lead to a more suitable number of divisions. In other cases you can group some of the less important classes together (perhaps as "Others" or "Miscellaneous"); but this practice may appear sloppy to critical observers.

7.   Organize for approximate balance. That is, try not to let some of your divisions cover huge blocks of your subject and others almost nothing. You probably need to reorganize on a different basis if you have five major divisions and any one is more than half of the whole report. Of course, the nature of your subject may force you to some imbalance. If you are writing about American politics, for example, the Democratic and Republican parties will each be bigger parts than all the rest, which you might group together for approximate balance.

8.   Put the parts of each breakdown into the sequence most appropriate for your purposes and the situation. The *overall sequence or plan of a report* is usually one of the following:

a.   Direct (sometimes called deductive), giving the big, broad point first and then following with supporting details. This plan arouses more interest than some other plans because it gets to the important things quickly, saves the time of the busy person who wants only the big idea, and provides a bird's-eye view that helps in understanding the rest more intelligently. It is therefore desirable if the report's conclusion is likely to be welcomed or if the reporter is an authority whose unsupported word would be readily accepted, at least tentatively. But it is psychologically unsound where it risks the danger of objections at first and continued resistance all the way through.

b. Inductive (sometimes called scientific), giving a succession of facts and ideas leading up to the big conclusions and recommendations at the end. The inductive plan is slow and sometimes puzzling until the conclusion tells where all the detailed facts lead; but it is necessary in some cases for its strong logical conviction, especially when you expect opposition to the conclusions and recommendations that are coming.

c. Narrative (usually chronological accounts of activities). If no good reason argues against it—but usually one does—the narrative style of report is both the easiest to organize and the easiest to follow. The main objections are that it doesn't allow you to stress important things (it may have to begin with minor details, and the biggest things may be buried in the middle), and it doesn't allow you to bring together related things that have to be seen together for clear significance. The somewhat similar spatial arrangement (from top to bottom, front to back, left to right, or by geographical area) is usually the obvious choice if it is appropriate for the material at all.

d. Weighted (that is, according to importance). The weighted plan's basic advantage is that it enables you to control emphasis by putting the most important points in the emphatic positions, first and last.

For certain kinds of material and conditions, arrangement according to difficulty or from cause to effect (or the reverse) may be the wise choice. Similarly, some kinds of things almost have to appear in a definite order for the necessary logical sequence (the way proving a geometry proposition does).

Whatever the plan of organization, in the final presentation you will need to use meaningful headings and subheads, topic sentences or paragraphs, standard transitional words and sentences, and summarizing sentences to indicate organization, to show the coherence of parts in the organization, and to tell the hurried or half-attentive reader or listener the essence of the sections. The summarizing sentences, however, grow naturally out of your interpretation of the facts.

INTERPRETING THE FACTS

If the report is just informational, you are ready to put it in final form when you have organized the facts; but if it is to be analytical, you have to study the facts and interpret them into conclusions and/or recommendations for the boss, as required.

Interpretation is probably the hardest part of report preparation to teach —or to learn. Realization of six points, however, can help:

1. Without substantial, verifiable facts, you have nothing worthwhile to interpret. The solution is to go back to the data-collecting step and get the facts.

2.   A fact alone is not worth much. Significance comes only from *relating* two or more facts. *Seeing* formerly unknown relationships requires *imaginative intelligence* and *careful analysis of two or more different sets of facts at the same time.* Whether the analysis is simply logical reasoning or mathematical (usually statistical) figuring, a necessary ingredient is *imagination.*

For example, consider how George J. Van Dorp, water commissioner of Toledo, developed his method of determining the public interest in TV programs. As a fan of the "I Love Lucy" program, Van Dorp noticed that pressure in the water mains ran consistently high during the program. When commercials interrupted the show, the water pressure dropped appreciably—for about the length of the ads—then went up again when the players returned to the screen.

Many people seeing the changes in water pressure *and* the beginning, interrupted, and ending times of "I Love Lucy" would never have *seen* a relationship between the two sets of clear facts. Van Dorp had the *imaginative intelligence* to *see* the relationships—to interpret facts.

3.   Since the report user wants a sound rather than a prejudiced or illogical basis for decisions, your first consideration (beyond the ability to see relationships) in making the interpretation is *objectivity.* Nowhere else in report work is objectivity more important—or harder to achieve. Since you are a human being, your whole background and personality influence your thinking; you therefore must strive to be as objective and logical as possible and to avoid the temptation to stretch the truth a bit for dramatic effect. The following two basic kinds of unobjective attitudes require attention if your report is to be unbiased:

a.   Preconception.   A reporter who jumps to conclusions and closes out other possibilities before collecting and evaluating the facts will, under the influence of that preconception, overlook or undervalue some facts and overstress others. Such is the danger of working from hypotheses—unless you check results by pursuing a directly opposite hypothesis.

b.   Wishful thinking.   If you have a strong desire that the investigation turn out a certain way (because of a money interest or any other kind), you will find it hard not to manipulate facts (like the referee who has bet on the game) to make them lead to the desired result. Such attitudes can also lead to unintentionally slanted wording, since they will unconsciously affect your choice of phrasing.

4.   In addition to these dangerous attitudes to shun if you are to be a sound reporter, you must avoid the pitfalls to logical thinking (called *fallacies*). Although some of them—like circular argument and shifting the meanings of terms—are not likely to trap an honest reporter, avoiding these pitfalls requires constant alertness (especially if you've never studied logic):

a.   Avoid using sources (both books and people) which may be unreliable because of basic prejudice, because they are uninformed, or because they are out of date. Further, your sources may have misquoted or misinterpreted *their* sources—a common occurrence. Although you should have checked these things in collecting your data, you might well examine them again in the interpreting process.

b. Avoid making hasty generalizations—that is, drawing conclusions on the basis of too little evidence (maybe too small a sample, too short a trial, too little experience, or just too few facts). The temptation to make hasty generalizations will weaken if you remember that sometimes you can draw no logical conclusion from the available facts. Certainly you need to remember that lack of evidence to establish one hypothesis does not prove its opposite.

c. Avoid using false analogies. True analogies (comparisons of things that are similar in many ways) are effective devices for explaining unknown things. You simply teach the unknown by comparing it to a similar known. But, even at their best, they are weak as logical proof. Because no two things are identical, the truth may escape through one of the holes of difference. And false analogies (applying principles valid in one case to another case where they don't belong) are tools of the dishonest and traps to the careless thinker. Essentially the same error results from a person's putting a thing in the wrong class (say a persuasive request situation misclassified as a direct inquiry) and applying the principles of the wrong class to it.

d. Avoid stating faulty cause-and-effect relationships, such as

1) Assigning something to one cause when it is the result of several. Comparisons which attribute the differences to one cause need careful controls to be valid. Otherwise, some unseen (or intentionally ignored) cause may deserve much of the credit for the difference.

2) Attributing something to an incapable cause (for instance, one that came later).

3) Calling something a cause when it is merely a concurrent effect —a symptom, a concomitant.

e. Avoid begging the question—just assuming, rather than giving evidence to support, a point that is necessary to the conclusions drawn.

f. Avoid using emotional suasion (usually characterized by strong and numerous adjectives and adverbs, or any kind of emotionally supercharged language like that of a defense attorney pleading with a jury) to win your point, instead of depending on logical conviction through marshaling facts.

g. Avoid failing to distinguish, and make clear, what is substantiated fact, what is opinion, and what is merely assumption.

5. Another important *consideration* in making your interpretation is discovering the really significant things to point out. If you avoid basic prejudice prompted by preconception or wishful thinking, avoid the pit-

falls of various fallacies, and know what to look for, you should be able to interpret the facts and draw sound conclusions.

When you do, you should be sure they grow out of the facts, state them pointedly, and itemize them if they run to more than three or four. You can then turn them into practical recommendations that are general or concrete and specific, according to instructions you get with the report assignment. Itemization will usually help to make the recommendations desirably pointed too.

Some bosses want answers to all of what to do, how to do it, who is to do it, when, and where; others feel that the reporter with so specific a solution to the problem infringes upon their prerogatives of making decisions. But all expect you to show the significance of your facts to the problem. In addition to an organization and presentation of facts that lead to the conclusions, you have a duty to point out lesser interpretations along the way. Avoiding doing so is not, as some people (bureaucrats) think, the "safe way." It is failing to do the job properly.

Causes, symptoms, effects, and cures are always important—in report problems as in medicine. So (in terms of graphic statistical data) are high points, low points, averages, trends, and abrupt changes (especially if you can explain their causes). Without going into disturbingly technical statistics, you can probably hold interest with such measures of central tendencies as the mean (call it average), median (midpoint), and mode (most frequent item). Sometimes you might well use indicators of dispersion, such as standard deviation, range, and the *-iles* (percentiles, deciles, quartiles).

Appropriate comparisons can give significance to otherwise nearly meaningless isolated facts. For instance, the figure $7,123,191 given as profit for the year has little meaning alone. If you say it's 7 percent above last year's profit, you add a revealing comparison; and if you add that it's the highest ever, you add another. If your volume of production is 2 million units, that means less than if you add that you're now fourth in the industry as compared with tenth two years earlier.

Breaking down big figures into little ones also helps to make them meaningful. For instance, you may express capital investment in terms of so much per employee, per share of stock, per stockholder, or per unit of production. The national debt becomes more meaningful if you give it per citizen; the annual budget makes more sense as a per-day or per-citizen cost; library circulation means more in terms of number of books per student. Often a simple ratio helps, such as "Two fifths (40 percent) of the national budget is for defense." A pie chart showing the percentage going to each category in the whole budget would be especially meaningful.

6.   Whatever the analysis reveals, you need to state it precisely. Guard carefully against stating assumptions and opinions as facts. And select graduations in wording to indicate the degree of solidity of your conclusions.

The facts and analyses will sometimes (but rarely) prove a point conclusively. They are more likely to lead to the conclusion that ..., or indicate, or suggest, or hint, or point to the possibility, or lead one to wonder—and so on down the scale. Usually you can do better than stick your neck out (by claiming to prove things you don't) or draw your neck in too far (with the timorous last three of these expressions).

    ✻   ✻   ✻   ✻   ✻

But phrasing the ideas well is a problem for the fifth and last step in preparing a report—writing it or speaking it.

We want you to understand clearly that everything we have said so far is applicable to both written and spoken reports. Whether you type up a report and package it in a folder or deliver it in the form of a speech, the steps in preparing it are the same. You must plan your attack, collect the facts you need, organize your findings, interpret the data if appropriate, and finally put your report in the proper style. Only in this last step do written and oral reports begin to differ materially.

So don't think you should put an oral report in fully written form and read it. As we point out in Chapter 17, reading a speech is usually the worst kind of oral presentation. As you develop your outline and assemble notecards, you will be generating the notes from which you should speak. In fact, your speech notes should be all of your divisions and subdivisions, with enough information on each so that you will remember all you want to say. Since your report notes are in essence your speech notes, the next section of this chapter deals mainly with written reports.

USING EFFECTIVE REPORT STYLE

Your final phrasing of the report will not be difficult if you have done well the preceding four steps of preparation. But if your methods of planning the report and collecting, organizing, and interpreting data have been faulty, you're trapped. Our suggestions for a good report style will help only if you have something worthwhile to say and a pretty good idea of the sequence of points.

You will notice that our suggestions relate more to the *effectiveness* than to the *correctness* of your style, for two reasons:

1. Correct spelling, grammar, punctuation, sentence structure do not assure effectiveness—we assume that you have pretty well learned these aspects of your language before studying reports. And if you haven't, a more basic study of composition—or a careful review of Appendix B or some other good handbook—may be advisable.

2. Effective presentation presupposes reasonable correctness of language as well as information but also requires that you help your reader or audience to get your message clearly, quickly, and easily. How to do this is our next concern.

Basics of report style

Because almost everything we say about letter style in Chapter 2 and about communication in Appendix A applies equally to report style—and the few exceptions are obvious—we recommend that you read that material carefully before going on to the special points about report style.

As you have already seen in Item 6, page 439, effective reports use various techniques and devices for communicating clearly, quickly, and easily: commonly understood words, short sentences so direct that they require little punctuation, short paragraphs so direct that they require few transitional words, itemizations, graphics, and headings.

Even though you have read those other parts of the book, several points of basic style and some of the special techniques deserve a bit fuller treatment for preparing reports.

Adaptation requires that you consider not only your primary reader but likely secondary ones. Even though some may know the background of the problem and the technical terms of the field, others may not. The good report writer must therefore provide the explanations necessary for the least informed of important readers. This includes restricting your vocabulary to words they will understand readily. If you feel that you must use specialized terms, you had better explain them. Usually a parenthetical explanation right after the first use of a technical term is the best way. But if your report includes many such terms, it should provide a glossary in the introduction or in an appendix—to keep it from being "all Greek" to nontechnical readers.

Coherence becomes a greater problem as the length and variety of points in a report increase. Hence as a report writer you need to observe carefully the use of transitional words, previewing topic sentences and paragraphs, and summarizing sentences and paragraphs in the illustrations in the next two chapters. **Coh** in Appendix B and items S5–7 in the checklist for complete analytical reports (see Chapter 15) should also prove helpful.

Here is how one writer helped keep readers on the track with good headings, topic statements, summary paragraphs, and transitional ideas. (For economy of space, we have quoted only some of the *transitional* parts from various places in the 27–page report. The bracketed parts are our commentary.)

II. NASHVILLE'S LARGER MARKET AREA

Since women often will travel long distances to buy clothes, the secondary area surrounding the metropolitan area is important in determining the location of a Four Cousins retail store. [After this topic lead-in, several paragraphs followed identifying for both Nashville and Knoxville principal communities and number of people in them.]

Even though 370,000 more possible customers live within the market area of Nashville, most of the sales will come from the people within the immediate metropolitan area. [Summarizes II and makes transition to III.]

III. BETTER POPULATION FACTORS IN NASHVILLE

The total population and its rate of growth, number of women, and number of employed women show more clearly the potential buyers of women's clothing. [This topic statement preceded A, B, and C headings of subsections giving the facts about and the interpretation of the topics as announced.]

Even though Knoxville has a larger population and about the same growth rate, Nashville has more women and a significantly larger number of employed women. Thus it furnishes the kind of customer Four Cousins sells to. [Indicates what A, B, and C add up to.]

Potential customers are buyers, however, only when they have sufficient buying power. [Clearly foreshadows a topic coming up and why.]

IV. MORE BUYING POWER IN NASHVILLE

Effective buying income (total and per capita), income groups, home ownership, and automobile ownership give estimates of ability to buy. [The information as presented then follows in four sections.]

[This summary statement comes at the end of the section.] The Nashville shopper has more dollars to spend, even though home- and auto-ownership figures imply more favorable financial positions in Knoxville families. Higher expenditures for homes and cars in Knoxville explain, in part, why Nashville merchants sell more.

V. GREATER RETAIL SALES AND LESS COMPETITION IN NASHVILLE

[The writer continues the use of these coherence devices throughout the report.]

Parallelism is a special pitfall to the unwary report writer because reports so frequently involve series, outlines, and lists. Each is in effect the partition of a whole, the sum of the parts equaling the whole. Hence the law of logic and mathematics—that you sum up, or add, only like things—applies. Thus the breakdown of anything must name all the parts in similar (parallel) grammatical form—usually all nouns or noun phrases, adjectives, or complete sentences. (See Item 5, p. 463, for parallelism in outlines, and **Para** in Appendix B for a more comprehensive treatment.)

Timing of the verbs (tense) in reports also often trips a careless report writer. One simple rule answers most questions of tense: *Use the present tense wherever you can do so logically.* It applies to things that existed in the past, still exist, and apparently will continue to exist for a while (the universal present tense). Otherwise, use the tense indicated by the logic of the situation. Thus in talking about your research activity, you say that you *did* certain things, like conducted a survey (past tense in terms of the time of writing). But in reporting your findings, you say "70 percent answer favorably, and 30 percent are opposed." The universal present tense implies that the findings are still true. Surely you would not want to imply doubt on that point by using *answered.* (See **Ten** in Appendix B for further applications of the universal present tense.)

Ten common faults listed in American University Professor William Dow Boutwell's study of government reports (and printed in the *Congressional Record,* Vol. 88, Part IX, p. A1468)[1] occur frequently in business and industry reports too:

1. Sentences are too long. Voted unanimously as one of the worst faults in nearly all writings analyzed. Average sentence length in poor government writing varies from 65 to 80 words per sentence. In exceptionally good government writing . . . average length is from 15 to 18 words per sentence.

2. Too much hedging; too many modifications and conditional clauses and phrases. The master writer will say, "A third of a nation ill-clothed, ill-housed, ill-fed." The amateur will write: "On the whole it may be said that on the basis of available evidence the majority of our population is probably not receiving the proper type of nutriment. . . ." Psychologists say that "conditional clauses cause suspension of judgment as to the outcome of the sentence, and therefore increase reading difficulty."

3. Weak, ineffective verbs. *Point out, indicate,* or *reveal* are the week reeds upon which many a government sentence leans. Writers overuse parts of the verb *to be.* Hundred-word sentences with *was* or *is* as the principal verb are not uncommon.

4. Too many sentences begin the same way, especially with *The.*

5. An attempt to be impersonal, which forces use of passive and indirect phrases. Example: "To determine whether retail sales have been out of line with expectations based on the past relationship of retail volume to income, estimates of retail sales in the first half of each year . . . have been charted against income payments for the same periods, and a line of estimate fitted to the resulting scatter." The good writer would say: "Our statisticians have charted estimates of retail sales, etc., etc."

6. Overabundance of abstract nouns. Such nouns as *condition, data, situation, development, problem, factor, position, basis, case* dominate the writing of too many government documents. How bright and real writing becomes when picture-bearing nouns take the place of vague ones may be seen from this sentence: "During the lean years when salaries and wages were low and irregular, the people who drifted into the credit-union offices came around because they had dropped behind in their personal and family finances and had to get a loan."

7. Too many prepositioned phrases. In a study of reading difficulty, investigators (Drs. Leary and Gray of Chicago University) found that prepositional phrases ("of the data," "under the circumstances," etc.) add to reading difficulty. Yet, samples of government writing show that many officials use at least one prepositional phrase to every four words. Samples from good writing contain only one prepositional phrase to every 11 words.

8. Overabundance of expletives. "It is" and "there are" and their variants ruin the opening of many good paragraphs.

9. Use of governmentish or federalese. "Shop words" serve a proper purpose for "shop" audiences. But many government writers make the mistake of talking to the public in technical, office terms . . . .

---

[1] An AP Newsfeature, "Gobbledygook; Language of Government," by Richard E. Myer, September 5, 1971, stresses many of the same points.

10. Tendency to make ideas the heroes of sentences. People think in terms of people and things for the most part. The government official writes in terms of ideas and phenomena only. Hence, when a writer means "Employers refuse to hire older workers in defense industries," he writes instead: "Refusal of employment of older workers continues." In other words, the writer has substituted "refusal," an idea or phenomenon, for "employers"—living people.

Headings and subheads

Because written reports are sometimes long and because readers may want to recheck certain parts, they use headings and subheads, in addition to topic and summarizing sentences, to show their organization and coherence. As you'll see in Chapter 17, a good oral reporter will use the oral equivalents for the same purposes. Also, for the same purposes, we have used headings in this book. If you have not thought about them already, for illustration flip back through some parts of the book with which you are well acquainted and see if they don't serve these purposes.

Skill in using heads and subheads can be a valuable technique in your presentations, not only of reports but of anything else that is very long— even long letters.

The only reasonable test of how far to go in putting in subheads is this: Will they help the reader get your message? If so, put them in; if not, leave them out.

Despite the fact that headings and subheads are often great helps, no single system of setting them up is in universal use. More important than what system you use is that you *use some system consistently* and that the reader understand it. Most readers understand and agree on the following principles:

1. A good heading is a title for its section. As such (and as explained on p. 496), it should indicate clearly the content below it, should have reader interest, and should be as brief as possible without sacrificing either of the other two requirements.

Trying to keep titles too short, however, frequently leads to sacrifice of exactness and/or helpfulness. Usually a short heading is too broad (includes more than the discussion below it covers), or it tells nothing about the topic. Note the difference, in examples from annual reports, between "Profits" and "Profits Up 8 Percent from Last Year," and between "Position in the Industry" and "Position in Industry Changes from Eighth to Fourth." Particularly in reports where some readers might only skim, you can help them a lot by *making your headings tell the big point about the topic instead of just naming the topic.* You've already seen some good examples of such helpful *informative* headings (which J. H. Menning first named "talking heads," as opposed to merely *topical* ones) in the quoted illustration on page 469. The headlines in any newspaper or informative magazine article provide others.

2. The form and position of the head must make its relative importance (status in the outline) clear at a glance. That is, headings for all divisions of equal rank (say the roman-numeral heads in an outline) must be in the same form and position on the page, but different from their superiors (of which they are parts) and from their inferiors (their subdivisions). Putting heads of different levels in the same form and position is confusing; it misrepresents the outline.

3. Centered heads are superior to sideheads in the same form (compare second- and third-degree heads in the following illustration); heads in capitals are superior to those in caps and lowercase; and heads above the text are superior to those starting on the same line with the text (compare third- and fourth-degree heads in the illustration).

4. You should not depend on headings as antecedents for pronouns or as transitions. The one word *This* referring to an immediately preceding head is the most frequent offender. Transitions between paragraphs and between bigger subdivisions should be perfectly clear even without the headings.

5. In capital-and-lowercase heads capitalize the first word and all others except articles (*a, an,* and *the*), conjunctions (for example, *and, but, for,* and *because*), and prepositions (such as *to, in, of, on,* and *with*).

The following not only illustrates *one good system* but further explains the principles. Note that *above* second- and third-degree heads the spacing is more than the double spacing of the discussion.

FIRST-DEGREE HEADINGS

The title of your whole report, book, or article is the first-degree heading. Since you have only one title, no other head should appear in the same form. As illustrated here, the title uses the most superior form and position (as explained in Items 2 and 3 above). If you need more than this five-level breakdown for your report, you can type the first heading in spaced C A P I T A L S and move each level of heading up one notch.

Second-Degree Headings

If you use solid capitals centered on the page for the first-degree heading (title), a good choice for the second-degree headings (the major divisions in the outline) is centered caps and lowercase. Preferably, in typewriter face they and any other uncapitalized head should carry underscoring to make them stand out. If you do not need the five-level breakdown illustrated here, you could start with this form.

Third-degree headings

To distinguish third-degree headings from their superiors, you may put them at the left margin above the text, underscore them to make them stand out, and write them in initial-cap form (as here) or in cap and lowercase (which would require capitalizing the D in Degree and the H in Headings).

Fourth-degree headings.—For a fourth level, you may place headings at the paragraph indention on the same line with the text and write them as caps and lowercase or as straight lowercase except for capitalizing the first word. These headings definitely need underscoring and separation from the first sentence, preferably by a period and dash, as here. Some people drop the dash or the period.

Fifth-degree headings can be integral parts (preferably beginnings) of the first sentences of the first paragraphs about topics. Underscoring (italic type when printed) will make them stand out sufficiently without further distinctions in form.

Objectivity in presentation

Clearly a report user expects a writer to be as nearly objective as is humanly possible in collecting the facts, in organizing and interpreting them, and finally in presenting them.

That does not mean, however, that you must use impersonal style (which some people erroneously call *objective* style). You can be just as objective when saying "I think such and such is true" as when saying "Such and such seems to be true" or even "Such and such is true." The second and third versions mean only that the writer/speaker thinks something is true. The only sound objection to the first version is that it wastes two words, not that it is *natural* style.

The only real justification for recommending impersonal style in reports, as many books do (meaning no use of the first or second person—i.e., pronouns referring to the sender or receiver of the message), is that methods and results are usually the important things and therefore they, rather than the person who did the research, deserve emphasis as subjects and objects of active verbs.

But, since most things happen because people make them happen, the most natural and the clearest, easiest, most interesting way to tell about them is to tell who does what. A report about research done by its writer therefore naturally includes *I*'s; and, if it keeps the reader(s) or audience in mind properly, it also naturally includes *you*'s. To omit them is unnatural and usually dull, because it goes out of the way to avoid the natural subjects of active verbs or uses too many inactive ones and leaves out the most basic element of an interesting, humanized style—*people doing things.*

Because they are professionally trained, constantly practicing, and usually writing about people doing things (although in the third person, a part of impersonal style), newspaper reporters often write well. An equally trained and practiced business report writer (a rarity) *can,* by great care, write well in impersonal style. But most business report writers find it unnatural and difficult. Unless they exercise great care, it usually leads them into awkward, wordy, and weak passive-voice constructions; it gives away the third leg (frequent personal references) to Rudolf Flesch's three-legged stool of easy readability, so that the stool falls; and it *does not* gain objectivity.

Strangely, the strongest promoters of impersonal style are people who pride themselves on being scientific. They usually also insist that their style should avoid any kind of exaggeration about the true state of things. But they then argue that impersonal style gives the reader more confidence in their statements. When one of them draws a conclusion, therefore, it comes out as "It was concluded that . . . ," as if (falsely) some omniscient oracle had drawn the conclusion, when the true meaning is "I conclude that. . . ."

Actually, more destructive to objectivity than the use of a natural style is the use of too many or too strong adjectives and adverbs, or any kind of feverish, high-pressure, hot-under-the-collar wording. Such a heightened style—using emotional connotations, fancy figures of speech, and other techniques of oratory—has its place where the author feels deeply and wants the reader to feel deeply about the subject; but it leads to distrust and is inappropriate in reports anyway, where both parties supposedly think hard rather than emotionalize.

Simply put, then, our advice on natural versus impersonal style is this: Find out whether your primary reader thinks reports have to be in impersonal style. If so, accept the burdensome restrictions and do the best you can by

1. Avoiding "It is" and "There are," especially as sentence beginnings (**Exp** in Appendix B).
2. Putting most of your verbs in the active voice (**Pas** in Appendix B).
3. Picturing people (other than yourself or the reader/listener(s), of course) taking the action of as many as possible of your verbs.

But any time your primary reader/listener(s) will let you, *phrase your report naturally but calmly and reasonably.* Where the natural way to express an idea involves an *I* or a *you,* use it. Don't let anybody talk you into referring to yourself as "the writer"—or "the speaker."

Except for the fact that letter style allows more use of emotional suasion than report style does, the discussion of style in Chapter 2 applies to reports as well as letters.

In addition, reports also make more extensive use than letters of certain other techniques of presenting ideas clearly, quickly, and easily: using headings and subheads, presenting quantitative data skillfully, and using graphic and visual aids to effective communication.

Presentation of quantitative data

Most reports make considerable use of quantitative data. Consequently, in a report you need to know how to present figures for clear, quick, and easy comprehension. Most people will want the figures on measurable topics you discuss; and unless they have made clear that they want only the facts, they probably will want your interpretations showing what the figures mean (conclusions) and what you think should be done about them (recommendations). Even if those people have the ability to make the interpretations themselves, they likely will want you to make them—for possible ideas they might not see and for economy of their time.

The following brief suggestions will help you present quantitative information the way most people want it:

1. Make sure your figures are reliable by checking your sources and derivations of them. And when you present an average, make clear whether it is the mean, the median, or the mode.

2. Write isolated quantities in one of the standard ways explained under **Fig** in Appendix B.

3. Insofar as possible, avoid cluttering your paragraphs with great masses of figures. Tables are better if you have many figures—say more than six, as in a table of two lines and three columns (or vice versa). Ordinarily, however, extensive tables are not necessary to clear understanding of the text but are in a report to show that you really have the facts. In that case put tables in an appendix and refer to them specifically in the introduction or text; then follow Items 4–7 below for presenting necessary figures in the text.

4.   Put necessary statistical information as close as possible to the place in the text where it is most pertinent. Readers will likely refuse to flip pages back and forth to find a table, or at least will resent having to do so; and their concentration (and comprehension) will suffer.

5.   Small tables (usually called spot tables), perhaps using key figures based on extensive data in an appendix, are not only easy to read but can appear close to the relevant discussion on a page. Use them freely.

6.   Present key figures as simply as possible. Usually some ratio, rank, difference, or correlation is more important than the raw data. Instead of a gross of $2,501,460.70 and expenses of $2,124,101.40, the simple figures $2½ and $2⅛ million tell the story better. The ratio 1:7 or about 15 percent for the net certainly reads easier than $377,359.30 and is probably the more important figure. Moreover, except in bookkeeping and highly technical research, such rounded and simplified figures are precise enough for most purposes. Indeed, rounded figures in most cases are as accurate as the unrounded ones which are their bases. The means of arriving at most large figures are not accurate enough to make the last few digits anything but a bogus precision and a hindrance to readability.

Another way of increasing readability is to break big figures down into so much per . . . (whatever is an appropriate divider). If the divider is the number of persons involved (employees, students, or citizens, for example), you also gain interest by humanizing the presentation.

7.   Help your reader by pointing out (in terms of line graphs) highs, lows, averages, trends, ranges, and exceptions or extremes. They are not always readily apparent, especially to the many people who are not accustomed to analyzing statistical data; but they are usually important, especially if you can also explain their causes and/or effects.

Graphic aids as supplements to words

Various studies have shown that graphic aids (and visual aids in oral communication) help readers/listeners to understand and remember. Though the impact varies with kinds of people and kinds of material (quantitative data versus ideas, for example), the rounded figures go about like this:

	After 3 Hours	*After 3 Days*
Read or hear	70%	10%
See	72	20
Both	85	65

Since reports so frequently treat quantitative data, designs, organizational plans, and the like, you often almost have to use charts, graphs, pictograms, drawings, and maps as well as tables to present your information well, especially in oral reports. But in most cases—even for engineers and architects, who have to study drafting—these devices *only assist, not replace, words*. And since interpretation of graphics is not one of the three R's everybody learns, most graphics help to explain and/or support the text *only if the text helps them by telling how to look at them and what they mean*. Good communication therefore often involves care and skill in *interplaying* words and graphic aids.

Complete discussion of the uses, advantages, disadvantages, and techniques of preparing different kinds of graphic devices is beyond the scope of this book. And extensive illustrations—which are costly to reproduce and are not very helpful except when accompanied by the relevant text—would quickly run up the size and cost. Anyway, if you haven't already, you could get a better sampling of them in current use by observing as you read other books, newspapers, and especially news magazines like *U.S. News & World Report* and *Time.*

Still we think our handy, economical, minimum introduction to the commonly used types will help. We give explanations and enough related text to show how to interweave the graphics as assistants to words.

As you study our explanations and illustrations, look not only at the graphics; but notice what kinds of information call for them, whether the graphics really help, and how the authors *interrelate them and words* so that each aids the other. Besides that key point of interplaying graphics as aids, keep in mind the five other most important points about using them:

1. A graphic device should not call attention to itself until *after* an introduction to it (some discussion of the point and reference to the graph); in most cases it would otherwise only confuse and break continuity of the thought.

2. The existence of the graphic aid, or where it is, is *not* the important thing and does *not* deserve the emphasis when you refer to it. So refer to it *subordinately* and use the main clause of your sentence to make the significant point. "Twice as many men as women like X, as shown in Table 2" is one good way.

3. Insofar as possible, place graphic aids close to (usually between) comments on the same point. In written reports, that means (preferably) right before the reader's eyes. Unless the device is staring the reader in the face when you mention it, tell precisely where it is—*subordinately* (for example, "As Fig. 1 on the next page shows, X goes up as Y goes down").

4. Carefully label each graphic device (unless obvious) as a whole (title, and easy-reference number) and by parts, and provide a key (legend) if necessary. (Some people insist that at least major tables should carry titles and Roman capital numbers and other graphics, Arabic numbers below the display.) Variations in color, shading, crosshatching, and kind of line (solid versus broken, for example) are common means for distinguishing the different kinds of data in lines, columns, bars, and the like.

Where precision of quantified data is important, help the reader with grid lines (such as on graph paper) and by labeling significant points with the exact figures. And remember that percentages or other ratios are often more important than the raw figures from which they come.

Avoiding two kinds of possible distortion deserves particular caution.

a. Unless you are interested only in the comparative values rather than the individual changes in several lines or bars you are using, *be sure to start at 0 as the base.* If, for example, you use 0 as the base of the quantity scale and the first year presented has a volume of 50 and the second 60, the second year will look like what it is (a 20 percent increase, from 50 to 60). If you start at base 40, however, the second year appears to have doubled the first (20 above the base 40 and thus twice as high on the scale as the 50 of the preceding year, which was only 10 above the base).

b. If you handle the preceding situation properly in a line graph on a vertical scale of 0–70 and horizontal scale of 24 months that is 3½ by 4 inches, the line will appear to rise at about the proper incline—ten points or one-half inch in 2 inches (12 months). If you shorten the base to 2 inches, however, the incline will be twice as steep (one-half inch in 1 inch) and will give the distorted impression of a much faster rise.

5. Interpret your graphics (usually right after them) unless doing so would be insulting because the meaning is so obvious.

To begin seeing what illustrations of graphics we have provided, start flipping the pages of the book from the front. You'll notice that they illustrate (more or less in order) special layouts like the title page, tables of contents, boxed checklists, outlines of chapters, photolike reproductions (of letter, envelope, and memo layouts), parallel-column presentations, symbolic drawings (of A–, B–, and C–plans), résumés, regular tables—and literally dozens of other special arrangements on the page that help you to *see* the information.

You'll also notice that the best procedure in using graphics begins by (1) introducing the topic, (2) subordinately referring the reader to the graphic aid at the point where it will be helpful, (3) using the best type of graphic for the purpose, and (4) further commenting on (interpreting) the graphic device.

If you've made the observations we've suggested, you've seen how useful graphics can be and have also learned the basic principles you need to know to use graphics skillfully. You've noticed that even in a book emphasizing the psychological, linguistic, and business procedural aspects of effective business communication, we have made extensive use of many forms of graphic presentation. In most other aspects of business, which are more easily quantifiable, graphics of a few specific types can play an even bigger role.

For purposes of illustrating our specific explanations of the most commonly used quantitative-data graphics, we have chosen the following five from an article in the most recent *Occupation Outlook Handbook* (U.S.

480

Department of Labor, 1979) and have paraphrased enough of the text to interplay the two.

Bar charts are among the easiest graphics to make and to interpret. In their simplest form, you set up a row of bars (usually on a horizontal base of time periods, but it may be on a vertical base and represent time or any other function). The varying heights of side-by-side bars show changes in the other variable. (Scale-marked grid lines and the exact figures at the top of each bar will help the reader.)

A skillful writer can, by modifications of the simple structure, use segmented or subdivided bars (the parts distinguished by color or shading) to show additional information. A frequent use is to show the percentages of different components of a (or each) single bar (though a pie chart, discussed later, is a more "graphic" method). By using the standard solid lines for established data and broken lines for projections (future estimates), a graphic artist can legitimately add another dimension (but little complexity) to bar charts.

Facing a choice among the 20,000 kinds of work the *Dictionary of Occupational Titles* now lists and a variety of preparatory education and training programs, a career planner now needs to consider more questions than native abilities and interests. Though job opportunities and pay scales in different fields do change, their comparatively slow changes make current and even projected information important. For instance, the U.S. civilian labor force has increased noticeably and probably will continue to do so (a 19% change from 87.5 million in 1976 to an estimated 104.3 million in 1985, as shown in Chart 1).

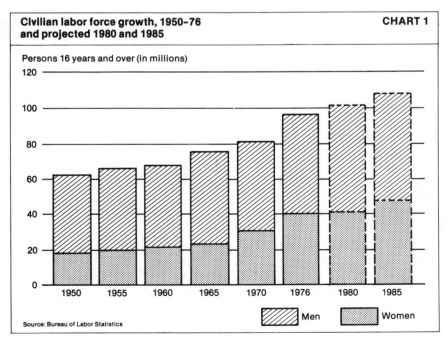

Civilian labor force growth, 1950-76 and projected 1980 and 1985 CHART 1

Persons 16 years and over (in millions)

Source: Bureau of Labor Statistics

Men   Women

You recognize that drawing a line connecting the upper left corners of the bars in Chart 1 would produce another simple and widely used kind of graphic—a line graph or line chart. In this case it should be a faired (smoothly curved) line because the data change more or less smoothly (instead of in jumps at intervals, which would call for straight-line connections between the jumps). You should recognize, too, that like the simple bar chart, the simple line graph can present projections (broken lines) and several concurrently changing kinds of data on the same base. If they might otherwise become confused, you would distinguish the different functions by lines of different color or form (such as - -, —, or . . . .); and you should limit their number to the range of easy comprehension/comparison. A frequent two-line business chart pictures one line labeled *costs* and the other labeled *income*—where they cross being the break-even point (or the owner's nightmare, the going-broke point).

Perhaps more significant are the facts that (1) more women entering the labor market are the main reason for the increase and (2) the percentage of women workers continues to rise while the percentage for men declines (Chart 2).

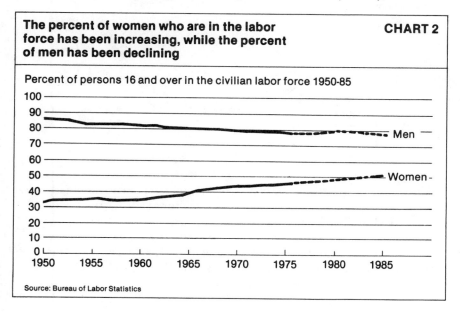

The percent of women who are in the labor force has been increasing, while the percent of men has been declining   **CHART 2**

Percent of persons 16 and over in the civilian labor force 1950-85

Source: Bureau of Labor Statistics

Pie charts are specialists in showing the parts of a whole—preferably with different colors or shading to distinguish the parts, labels to identify them, the raw figures for precision, and (usually the most important figures) their percentages for quick, easy comparison. Even they, however, can broaden their service by showing more than one breakdown.

In two broad categories, more than twice as many people (68%) work in five sub-groups producing services as in four subgroups producing goods. Though the biggest subgroup is goods-producing (manufacturing, 23%, as shown in Chart 3), it is only slightly larger than each of three service-producing subgroups (including general services such as education, health care, and repair and maintenance—18%).

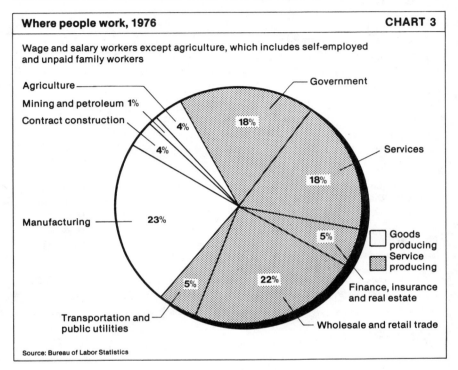

Where people work, 1976   **CHART 3**

Wage and salary workers except agriculture, which includes self-employed and unpaid family workers

Agriculture
Mining and petroleum 1%
Contract construction
Government
4%
18%
4%
Services
18%
Manufacturing   23%
5%
Goods producing
Service producing
5%   22%
Finance, insurance and real estate
Transportation and public utilities
Wholesale and retail trade

Source: Bureau of Labor Statistics

Since pie charts are stationary rather than moving partitioners (i.e., pictures breaking a whole into its parts at a given time), they cannot well present projections. The authors of the *Occupation Outlook Handbook* article we're paraphrasing therefore turned to two better ways of presenting such information—a *line graph* (two lines, projected, for the emphatic picture) and words for precision and details (mostly omitted here) as they traced the expected trends of all the subgroups.

More specifically, projections are that service-producing industries will continue to increase faster than their goods-producing counterparts (26 percent, from 56.1 million workers in 1976 to 71.0 million in 1985, versus 17 percent, from 26.6 million to 31.1 million). (See Chart 4.)

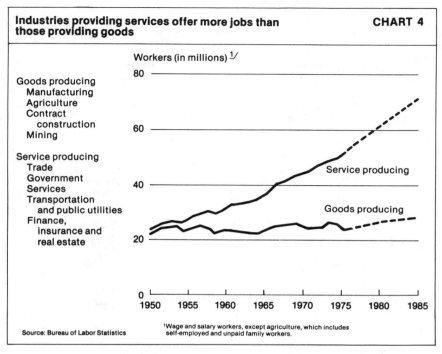

Industries providing services offer more jobs than those providing goods   CHART 4

Workers (in millions) ¹/

Goods producing
  Manufacturing
  Agriculture
  Contract
    construction
  Mining

Service producing
  Trade
  Government
  Services
  Transportation
    and public utilities
  Finance,
    insurance and
    real estate

Service producing

Goods producing

80
60
40
20
0

1950 1955 1960 1965 1970 1975 1980 1985

Source: Bureau of Labor Statistics

¹Wage and salary workers, except agriculture, which includes
self-employed and unpaid family workers.

General services have been the fastest growing service group (doubling between 1960 and 1976 because of the demand for health care, maintenance and repair, advertising, and commercial cleaning services). They will probably continue—from 14.6 million workers in 1976 to 20.6 million in 1985, a 40% increase that is nearly twice the rate of other service producers. . . . Automation, improved machinery, and hybrid crops are enhancing goods production without many additional workers. But the effects are not the same in all subgroups.

Though agricultural production has increased greatly, a continuing decline in agricultural workers since the 3.3 million in 1976 projects to 2.3 million by 1985, a 29% drop—the only projected decline. As a reflection of our increasing need for energy, employment in mining and petroleum production will probably continue rising—from 0.8 million in 1976 to 1.1 million in 1985 (39%). Projections of employment in contract construction. . . . ·

Because their projections of goods production involved a significant negative quantity, the *Occupation Outlook Handbook* authors wisely chose a good graphic form for the purpose—a *bilateral bar chart* (No. 5). We are not showing it to you because we show a more significant one below (Chart 9). Similarly, we're skipping No. 6 (a simple bar chart) because it shows nothing additional about using graphics, No. 7 (a four-part projected-line graph), and No. 8 (a complicated and not very significant bar chart).

Breakdowns of employment by the four standard occupational groups give the same picture from a different angle. White-collar workers (professional, technical, clerical, sales, managerial) constitute the biggest number and are the fastest growing group. Projections in millions, 1976 to 1985, are: professional/technical 13.3–15.8, 18%; managers/administrators 9.3–11.3, 21%; clerical 15.6–20.0, 29%. Conversely, farm workers are the smallest group and the only one declining, 2.8 to 1.9 (34%). Both blue-collar workers and service workers (except household) can expect continued moderate increases (Chart 9).

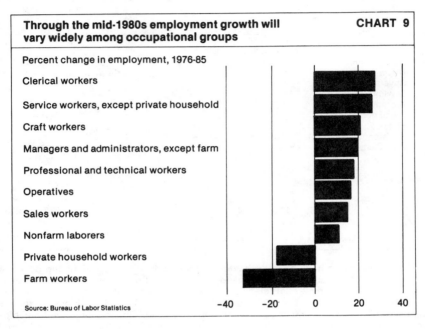

Through the mid-1980s employment growth will vary widely among occupational groups   CHART 9

Percent change in employment, 1976-85

Clerical workers

Service workers, except private household

Craft workers

Managers and administrators, except farm

Professional and technical workers

Operatives

Sales workers

Nonfarm laborers

Private household workers

Farm workers

Source: Bureau of Labor Statistics   −40   −20   0   20   40

Tomorrow's job opportunities look even better when you add, to the foregoing figures, those for replacements due to deaths, retirements, and transfers. Though exact data are not yet available, reasonable projections are that through 1985 replacements will make twice as many job opportunities as employment growth in almost every major occupation.

Another graphic omitted here (No. 10) is a bilateral chart of subdivided bars (growth/replacement), the two negative bars (declines) being for farm and private household workers.

The last section of the article uses three graphics to deal with education and employment. Nos. 11 and 12 are simple bar charts showing that the more education people have the less unemployment and the higher incomes they have. No. 13 shows (by single-line graph) that earnings of high school graduates were an increasing percentage of those for college graduates in the early seventies but have been decreasing since 1974.

Here are quick restatements of additional points the article makes:

—In our increasingly specialized society, the kind of education one gets is often as important as the amount.

—For deciding on both the kind and amount of education to get, a student needs (1) to make a careful self-analysis (see our p. 310), (2) to get specific information about types of education preferred in various occupations, and (3) to learn how to enter each appealing occupation (as explained in the *Occupation Outlook Handbook*).

Though the preceding explanations and illustrations give you a good look into graphics, we still think the following suggestions on the uses of different graphics may be helpful as a kind of summary/reminder. We'll also interweave two kinds not formerly illustrated.

1. A table is usually the starting point for quantified graphics of other kinds. We don't illustrate tables here because you've already seen many in use. If you want to see more, however, flip through our two longest illustrations of reports, beginning on pp. 511 and 573.

2. Use line graphs (perhaps marking the tops of columns in a bar chart) to represent trends according to time. Usually the perpendicular axis should represent volume of the subject treated and the base (or horizontal axis) should represent time. Two or more different kinds of lines can show relative quantities as well as the absolute quantities of several subjects at any given time.

3. Use segmented bars or pie charts (preferably moving clockwise from 12:00) to represent the proportions in the breakdown of a whole. Usually the color or shading of sections distinguishes the parts (which should not be confusingly numerous). They should be labeled with both the raw figures for precision and (usually the more important point) the ratio or percentage of the whole for easy comparison.

4. A kind of hybrid showing the partitioning characteristics of multi-line graphs, segmented-bar charts, and pies is the belt chart in Figure 14–1. Intended to give only an impressionistic (rather than precise) picture of six and a half decades, it gives a pretty good idea without any precise figures.

5. Use maps for geographcial distribution of almost anything; organization charts of rectangles arranged and connected to show lines of authority and communication; flow charts showing movement and stages in processing; blueprints giving precise sizes and relationships; and photographs picturing accurate size, texture, and color. All are useful graphic devices in their places, which are sometimes in engineering, architectural, and other professional/technical work instead of in business. In any case, you need to keep them simple enough for easy reading and concentrated on the point under discussion.

Time magazine in its April 9, 1979 issue (p. 20) made effective use of a map chart to supplement its story about the near catastrophe at the Three

FIGURE 14–1 Government employment as a percentage of total employment

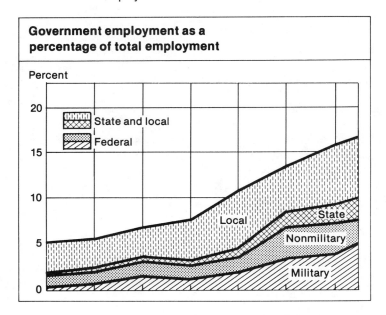

Government employment as a percentage of total employment

Mile Island nuclear power plant. On a pink map of the country it placed keyed symbols to show the locations of • 72 existing reactors, ▲ 94 others under construction, and △ 30 planned.

The map in Figure 14–2, using side-by-side piles of sales contracts as bar charts (with percentage figures) for the two years covered, is particularly effective for showing shifts in regional sales. One of the reasons is that the one chart involves multimedia—map, bar chart, and just a hint of pictograms.

6. Use symbolic pictograms (such as little people representing workers or bags of money representing profits) to add interest, especially for nontechnical presentations, when you have the time and money and are preparing a report in enough copies to justify the cost.

But *keep all the little characters the same size* (although each may represent any quantity) and vary the *number* of them to represent different total quantities (usually lines of them making bar charts). Otherwise, you mislead because the volume in the pictogram involves a third dimension (depth perspective) not shown in the pictogram. Of two cylindrical tanks representing oil production, for example, one actually twice as big as the other looks only slightly bigger because of the unseen third dimension. (If you remember from your geometry that the volume of a cylinder is $\pi r^2 h$, you'll see why.)

FIGURE 14–2   Percentage of Sales District, Gaylor Manufacturing Company

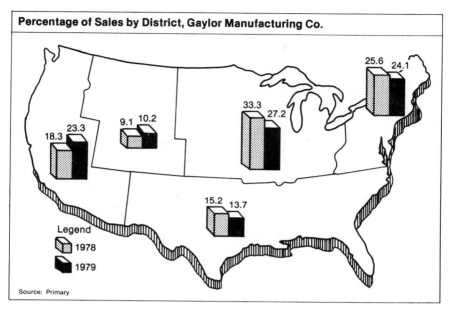

Percentage of Sales by District, Gaylor Manufacturing Co.

Legend
1978
1979

Source: Primary

As a weekly news magazine wanting to report current quantified data interestingly, *U.S. News & World Report* makes frequent use of pictograms, purely for their interest value, while the figures appear in other forms. For instance, in a thorough article on inflation (October 2, 1978, p. 33) it used eight pairs of bars to present (in black) the current costs of eight cost-of-living items and (in red) the costs five years later (assuming continuation of the rate of inflation). Along with the cost figures at the top of each bar was (above each pair) a clever little symbolic drawing: a hospital bed for a day in the hospital, a pack of cigarettes, an ivy-covered tower, an apron (maid service), and so on.

7. If you have to provide multiple copies of your report, consider whether your graphics are reproducible. What may be fine for offset printing may not work in some kinds of photocopy processes. Computer-generated graphics, increasingly common, often pose problems. A computer printout or a photograph of a visual display may be of such poor quality that you would lose important details in reproduction, necessitating expensive and time-consuming tracing or redrawing.

8. Graphics and other visual aids (usually flip charts or slides) for oral presentations pose problems peculiar to speaking situations, and we deal with these at the end of Chapter 17.

Documentation

Since a report is usually the basis for an executive decision which may be costly if it is wrong, business executives rightfully expect reports to answer at least two important questions: What are the facts? How do you know? In an analytical report, two more questions arise: What do you make of (conclude from) these facts? Then what do you recommend that I do?

The second question means that the report must provide evidence that the information is trustworthy. Usually you do that by explaining your sources and methods of research as a basis for judgment about the report's soundness. The only exceptions are in the reports of unquestionable authorities (whose word would be taken at face value) and in cases where the methods and sources are already known or the presentation of the facts clearly implies them.

In short reports usually you can best explain the sources and methods in incidental phrases along with the presentation of data, as in the following:

```
Four suppliers of long standing report him as prompt pay
and . . . .
Standard quantitative analysis reveals 17 percent
carbon . . . .
Analysis of the balance sheet reveals . . . .
```

Notice how the illustrative reports in Chapter 16 (the short ones) interweave the references to methodology of research and to published sources —right within the text of the report.

In the complete analytical report the introduction explains methods and mentions printed sources (which the bibliography, footnotes, and/or other citations in the text explain more specifically).

At least, any report writer except the recognized authority precludes what one reader expressed as "the distrust I have of those people who write as if they had a private line to God."

Since you often use some published materials in collecting data for major reports, citing those sources is an important part of assuring your reader about the soundness of the facts. By paraphrasing a recognized authority (or quoting directly when justified—rarely, as explained on p. 451), you add support for and impact to your statements. When you use another author's special ideas, facts, or wording, however, to avoid plagiarism you have a moral (and in some circumstances a legal) obligation to give credit where it is due. You do *not need to cite* your source for information (as distinct from the exact wording) that is "in the public domain"—information that is (1) common knowledge, (2) obvious, or (3) readily available in many sources of the kind (like dictionaries and encyclopedias). Otherwise, you cite your sources by one of the somewhat varied but established systems.

Unfortunately, *bibliography* forms are not standardized. For the past 50 years the trend in documentation forms has been toward simplicity and efficiency, especially in business, industry, and the sciences. This statement does *not*, however, mean less documentation, but more efficient forms. Some people in the humanities, on the other hand, have tended to hold on to the older forms, especially their punctuation. Others have adopted the library practice of capitalizing only the first word and proper nouns (specific names of people, products, and places) in titles. *So unless you are sure that both you and your reader(s) understand and prefer other generally accepted forms used in your field (in the main professional journals, for example), we recommend that you use the following content and form.*

Readers generally expect a bibliographical entry to give the author's name, the title (of both an article and the journal), and (for books) the edition (if not the first), the publisher and place of publication, and the volume (if more than one); the volume number (if on the magazine) and all page numbers for magazine articles; and the date of publication for anything (noting n.d. for "no date" when you can't find it).

Preferably the pieces of information are in that order. Some people omit the publisher of a book or put it in parentheses with the place and a colon preceding. The same people (usually in the humanities) use roman numerals for magazine volume numbers and follow immediately with the date in parentheses. In some specialized fields even the date or title may come first.

Usually the several entries in a bibliography appear in alphabetical order by author's name, which is inverted for the purpose. In some specialized fields, however, you will find other arrangements; and in extensive bibliographies (unusual in reports) you often find books and articles alphabetized separately, with headings for each group.

Unless you choose to follow the well-established form of your special field, we suggest that you be up to date and enter books as

```
Wilkinson, C. W., J. H. Menning, and C. R. Anderson (eds.),
Writing for Business, Third Edition, Richard D. Irwin, Inc.,
Homewood, Illinois, 1970.
```

In the humanities, however, most authors would enter this book as

```
. . . , Third edition.  Homewood, Ill.:  Richard D. Irwin,
Inc., 1970.
```

Even in this simple entry, you have three somewhat unusual items:

1. Three people worked on the book, but the name of only the first needs to be inverted for alphabetizing.
2. Since the "authors" were editors rather than writers of the book, you see *eds.* right after their names.
3. Because the book is not the first edition, the entry tells which it is. Some

writers would add, at the end, 369 pp., $9.95—two pieces of information usual in reviews of new books but not in bibliographies.

The recommended form for magazine articles is

```
Gallagher, William J., "Technical Writing:  In Defense of
Obscurity, "Management Review, 55:34-36, May, 1979.
```

Or (often in the humanities):

```
Arnold, C. K., "How to Summarize a Report," Supervisory
Management, VII (July, 1979), 15-17.
```

If you want to be more helpful to the reader, you may annotate your bibliography with brief notes indicating the content and your evaluation of the book or article:

```
Darlington, Terry, "Do a Report on It," Business, 94:74, 93,
May, 1978.
Good treatment of report functions and short, simple, direct
approach for report writing.  Especially good on five-point
plan for organizing.
```

You need to note two points here:

1. Titles of parts like magazine articles and book chapters are enclosed in quotes; but titles of whole publications are underscored (italics in printed copy), with the first word and all others except articles (*a, an, the*), prepositions, and conjunctions capitalized.
2. Listings of magazines do not include the publisher and place but do include the volume number (if available) and all page numbers, hyphenated for inclusive pages and separated by commas for jumps in paging.

If no author's or editor's name appears on a book or article, the entry usually appears in the alphabetical list by first word of the title (not counting *a, an,* and *the*). Sometimes, however, a writer chooses to alphabetize by publisher instead—pamphlets, booklets, reports, and the like put out by corporations and governmental agencies. Thus you will see entries like

```
"Are Your Memos on Target?" Supervisory Management, 9:39-40,
August, 1975.
Texaco, Inc., Annual Report of 1979.
U.S. Department of Agriculture Bulletin 1620, Characteristics
of New Varieties of Peaches, U.S. Government Printing
Office, 1974.
```

(Note, in the first illustration, that when a comma and a stronger mark—question mark or exclamation point—need to come at the same place, you simply omit the comma.)

At those points in the report text where you make use of printed sources, you also tell the reader about them by specific references or citations. One way of doing so is *footnoting*, which is decreasing in use (especially in business and technical writing) because footnotes heckle readers. A better method for most situations, now coming into wider and wider use, is to interweave the minimum essentials of a citation subordinately right into the text, like this:

```
Wilkinson says ("The History and Present Need of Reports,"
  The ABWA Bulletin, 19:14, April, 1979) that reports . . . .
```

For other illustrations, see pages 2, 471, and 667.

Still, footnote citations (indicated by raised numbers in the text and matching numbers before the notes) may be necessary in some cases to keep long, interwoven citations from making the reading difficult. Remember, however, that footnotes at the bottom of the page (or worse, grouped at the end) are more interruptive than parenthetical citations.

The first footnote or interwoven citation, plus whatever bibliographical information may appear in the text, is a complete reproduction of the bibliographical entry with two minor changes: The author's name is in the normal order (given name or initials first), and the page reference is the specific page or pages used for that particular part of the report. Accordingly, first footnote references to a magazine and a book would be as follows:

```
¹H. R. Jolliffe, "Semantics and Its Implications for Teachers
  of Business Communication," Journal of Business
  Communication, 1:17, March, 1979.
²J. H. Menning, C. W. Wilkinson, and Peter B. Clarke,
  Communicating through Letters and Reports, Sixth Edition,
  Richard D. Irwin, Inc., Homewood, Illinois, 1976, p. 469.
```

Later references to the same works can be shortened forms with the specific page number(s) and just enough information for the reader to identify the source. Usually the author's surname, the title, and the page(s) will do, whether interwoven in the text, put in footnotes, or divided between the two. Thus later references could be as shown below:

```
Jolliffe ("Semantics and Its Implications," p. 18) makes the
  point that . . . .
Menning, Wilkinson, and Clarke (Communicating . . . , p. 29)
  discuss letters in three broad categories: . . . .
```

The short-form citations of sources, enclosed in parentheses here, could be footnotes if the writer prefers.

The old practice of using Latin abbreviations (such as *op. cit., ibid.,* and *loc. cit.,* to mention only a few), which have long confused many people, is disappearing along with footnotes. Except in scholarly writing for other scholars, the practice is to use English words and a few standard abbreviations like *p.* for *page* and *pp.* for *pages*—preceding page numbers which do not follow volume numbers.

The newest and probably the best bibliographical citation system—coming into wider use, especially in science and industry, probably because of its efficiency—involves these steps:

1. Numbering the listings in the bibliography after you've arranged them in the usual way (alphabetically, as explained on p. 489).

2. Using these numbers and the specific page number(s), usually separated by colons and enclosed in parentheses, at the points in the report requiring documentation—usually just before the periods at the ends of sentences, like this (4:39).

3. Explaining the system at its first use, by footnote or parenthetical note something like "(4:39, meaning p. 39 of Item 4 in the Bibliography)."

(Look through the report beginning on p. 511 for illustration of this method of citing published sources.)

Letters, speeches, and interviews used as sources of information do not belong in a bibliography. The method for citing them is by footnoting or by interweaving in the text the information about the giver and the receiver of the information, the form, the date, and any other pertinent facts.

Although we've given the main points about documentation, several large books and many smaller ones, plus numerous pamphlets, deal extensively with this subject. As further illustration of bibliography forms, and as sources of more detailed information about them, footnotes, and other details of form, we list the major publications:

A Manual of Style (Twelfth Edition), University of Chicago Press, Chicago, 1969.

The MLA Style Sheet (Second Edition), Modern Language Association of America, Washington, D.C., 1970 (revised as *MLA Handbook*, 1977).

U.S. Government Printing Office Style Manual (Revised Edition), U.S. Government Printing Office, Washington, D.C., 1973.

Turabian, Kate L., *A Manual for Writers of Term Papers, Theses, and Dissertations* (Fourth Edition), University of Chicago Press, Chicago, 1973.

✿   ✿   ✿   ✿   ✿

Beyond that, the preparation of a report depends on the particular form to be used; and the form you choose should be the one best adapted to the situation, as explained along with the illustrations in Chapters 15 and 16. (The cases for reports of different kinds are all at the ends of those two chapters.)

chapter 15

Analysis and illustration of complete analytical reports

A BIRD'S-EYE VIEW OF REPORT FORMAT

IN PETTY DETAILS the makeup of complete analytical reports varies only a little less than the organizations sponsoring the reports. Hence we cannot tell you the details of any report form that will be acceptable universally or specifically to the particular organization for which you may work.

Yet in the larger aspects of report parts and their interrelations, agreement far exceeds disagreement. In this chapter we propose to explain and illustrate report makeup with emphasis on the generally acceptable major points. Since you will also want some guidance on details, however, we will suggest *a* good way to handle them; but, as we do, we ask you to remember three things:

1. What we present on details of form is *not the only way.*
2. Since we are talking here about complete analytical reports, which are long and are written, we refer to report *writers* and *readers*. (We'll explain shorter reports in Chapter 16 and oral reports in Chapter 17.)
3. We do not present the illustrations as perfect reports, and certainly not as wording to be followed slavishly or copied parrotlike. At best, they show acceptable content, form, and general style for their particular situations as starters to your thinking—not as solutions to all your problems.

Layout and pagination

Most complete analytical reports include three broad categories of several parts each. The parts marked with asterisks in the following list normally do not appear as separate parts except in long, formal reports; but the others are almost universal—and in the order listed.

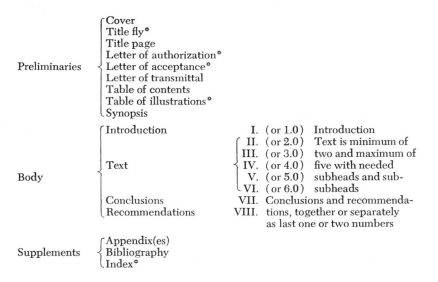

Preliminaries
- Cover
- Title fly*
- Title page
- Letter of authorization*
- Letter of acceptance*
- Letter of transmittal
- Table of contents
- Table of illustrations*
- Synopsis

Body
- Introduction
- Text
- Conclusions
- Recommendations

I. (or 1.0) Introduction
II. (or 2.0) Text is minimum of
III. (or 3.0) two and maximum of
IV. (or 4.0) five with needed
V. (or 5.0) subheads and sub-
VI. (or 6.0) subheads
VII. Conclusions and recommenda-
VIII. tions, together or separately as last one or two numbers

Supplements
- Appendix(es)
- Bibliography
- Index*

The following specifics will help in layout and pagination:

1. Generally each of the listed parts except text, conclusions, and recommendations begins a new page; otherwise, only the filling of one page calls for a new one. If used, the table of illustrations may go on the same page with the contents if space allows without crowding. Each appendix begins on a new page.

2. Counting the preliminary pages begins with the title fly, if used (and pages *after* the title page get lowercase roman numerals). Pages in the body and supplements take arabic numerals. The first page number of any part beginning a new page goes at the center bottom of the page; others appear (preferably) at least three spaces above the end of the first line. No page numbers need adornments such as parentheses, hyphens, periods, and underscores.

3. For bound reports, the "bite" of the binding requires typing with an extra wide margin so that the binding will not hide any writing and margins will appear equal when the report is open.

Optional and minor parts

Now, before we present the parts that require full discussion and illustration, let's clear out the no-problem parts and the optional parts marked with asterisks in the preceding list.

The *cover*, much like the cover of a book, is there to hold the report together and protect it. But unless it is transparent or has a cutout revealing the identifying title page, it needs to carry at least the title (perhaps in shortened form) and the author's name. (It may carry the rest of the title-page information too.)

As the name suggests, the *title fly* is a full page carrying only the title. Whatever its use in printed books, it is only excess paper in typewritten reports. If used, it counts as the first of the preliminary pages (lowercase roman numerals), although the page number does not need to appear on it.

When the person who has the problem to be solved and pays for the report makes the assignment by a *letter (or memo) of authorization*, a copy of it should appear in the report. This situation is most likely when the assignment is a big one, especially if it is a public affairs problem or the report writer is an outsider working on a consulting basis. By showing what the assigned job was, the letter enables any reader to judge the adequacy of the report. To make sure of getting a useful report, the writer of the authorization needs to state the problem precisely and make clear the purpose, scope, and limits on time, money, and the like. Asking specific questions and, if known, suggesting sources, methods, or approaches may help further, and also save money.

A *letter of acceptance*—rarely included—is the answer to a letter of authorization. Together they constitute the working agreement or contract.

A *table of illustrations* will help only if some of the tables and graphics might be useful to a reader independently of the discussion around them. If used, in table-of-contents form it lists separately the tables, charts, and figures in sequence by their identifying numbers and titles—and gives the pages on which they appear.

An *index* would serve little purpose in most reports both because they are not long enough to need one and because they are not used the way a reference book is. Ordinarily the table of contents adequately serves the purpose of helping a reader to find a certain point. If, however, you find that you must prepare an index, take some good advice from people who have tried indexing: (1) Hire a professional indexer to do the job or (2) study at least one of the several helpful books on the subject before you start. Indexes done by nonprofessionals are mostly rather poor, including those in most textbooks—because they are usually too scant and too full of errors.

STANDARD SHORT PRELIMINARIES

Title page

The title page is usually the first of the preliminary pages (counted as lowercase roman numbers down to the introduction), but the page number does not need to appear on it. Four other blocks of information usually do: the title itself, the name and title of the person who asked for the report, the name and title of the writer, and the place and date. In many instances the name of the organization where both writer and reader work is desirable information. When needed, a brief abstract, a list of people or departments to receive copies, and project or serial-number identifications may appear also.

Phrasing the title well is usually the main problem. (Unfortunately the writing of functional titles—as opposed to literary-style titles for stories, poetry, plays, and movies—is something schools do not generally teach.) First, a good report title, like any other title or heading in functional writing, should be *precise* in indicating clearly the content and scope to be covered. Frequently, however, first-attempt report titles are too broad, too narrow, or tangential—suggesting more or less than intended or a related rather than the real topic. A good report title narrows the topic and then zeroes in on the real problem. Secondarily, a good report title should be *interesting*—at least to the intended readers. (You cannot reasonably expect to interest everybody in most report topics.) As a third desirable quality, a good report title should be *concise*—have no wasted words like "A Report on . . . ," "A Study of . . . ," or "A Survey of. . . ."

An example will make clearer some frequent false steps and final solutions to the problem of writing *precise, interesting,* and *concise* report titles. A student proposed a report on "A Study of the Compensation of Executives." Discussion with the professor quickly led to omitting the first four words, and then changing to "Executive Compensation" for a further 33 percent reduction in words. That adequately solved the problem of *conciseness.*

Further discussion soon revealed, however, that the student never intended to write about all executives but only high-level ones in corporations. The problem of *precision* had come up—in the usual way, pointing to a need for *narrowing the topic* to the intended coverage. But that wasn't even the worst part of imprecision in this case. Despite the emphasis on *compensation,* the student wasn't even interested in the executives' basic salaries, having already seen evidence that up to $600,000 annually didn't keep executives from leaving jobs. The student revealed that the real topic of interest was evaluation of several new means some corporations were beginning to use to keep their top executives. Traditional means—high salaries, stock options, bonuses, and retirement programs (the things most people would envision from the word *compensation*)—were only tangential to the main topic.

The student felt pride in accomplishment with "New Methods Corporations Use to Retain High-Level Executives"—but almost gave up when the professor said it wouldn't do. The assigned report was to be an *analytical* report, and this title suggested a mere presentation of undigested facts.

Assuming assignment by Pow Chemical Company to study the problem and write a report on what the corporation might do to reduce executive turnover, the student (with only a little more help) arrived at a different title: "Pow's Possible Benefits from Applying Some New Means Used by Corporations to Retain High-Level Executives." That title narrowed the topic and then zeroed in on the real problem. It said *precisely* what the report was to be about (no more, no less) and implied an analytical rather than informational report. (You might note that it doesn't even—and doesn't need to—contain the key word of the original, *compensation.*) The first three words could not help *interesting* Pow officials, the intended readers. But is it *concise*—not short, or brief, at 16 words—but concise? Are all the words *possible, applying, some,* and *used by corporations* worth their space? What do you think?

Since an analytical report is about a specific problem of an individual or group, its title should indicate that specificness, often to the extent of naming the person or group as well as the problem. You can't answer such a general question as "Should Spot Radio Advertising Be Used?" The answer would be sometimes yes and sometimes no. For that reason, one student phrased a title as "Why the P. L. Lyon Company Should Discontinue Spot Radio Advertising."

That title, however, was a *final* title, written *after* the writer had done the research and made the analysis. Knowing what the decision was, and knowing that the key point would be readily acceptable, the reporter reasonably chose to tell the reader directly—as in an A–plan letter. To have phrased it that way *before* doing the research, however, would have been to act on preconception that could have prevented the writer from facing facts fairly.

With the title well done, you should have no more trouble with the title page. In looking at the accompanying illustration (p. 511), note how the writer grouped information into four parts and used balanced layout (each line centered) for good appearance.

Letter of transmittal

Following the title page—unless the report is an extensive and formal one, including such things as a copyright notice, title fly, letter of authorization, and letter of acceptance—page ii (counted, but not necessarily numbered) is a letter of transmittal. (In a formal public-affairs report with large numbers of indefinite readers, a typical preface often replaces the personalized letter of transmittal.)

Written after the report is completed, in regular letter form and in a style appropriate to the circumstances (Chapters 1 and 2), the letter of transmittal must do at least two things: transmit the report and refer to the authorization. In informal situations one sentence can do both: "Here's the report on fish poisoning you asked me to write when we were talking on May 10." Usually it needs to be a little more formal than that, but it needs no bromidic "As per your request, . . ." and rarely such formality as "In accordance with. . . ." Certainly it needs to subordinate the reference to the authorization to avoid a flat and insulting sound—seeming to tell about the request for the report as if the reader were too dumb or forgetful to remember. In the rare cases where no authorization happened, instead of the reference to it the writer tells enough background to arouse interest.

Despite the importance of conciseness and the possibility of doing in the first sentence all it *has* to do, a letter of transmittal will say more, if for no reason than to avoid a curt tone. Some additional things it might talk about (but not all in any one letter) are the appropriate ones of

—A highlight particularly significant in affecting the findings, or a reference to special sections likely to be particularly interesting to the reader.

—A summary of conclusions and recommendations (or even an interwoven synopsis as on p. 574) if the reader is likely to be sympathetic and unless a synopsis two or three pages later says the same thing. Even then, the letter can give very briefly the general decision but not supporting data (as on p. 512).

—Side issues or facts irrelevant to the report but supposedly interesting or valuable to the reader.

—Limitations of information, time, and/or money if they are true and not a part of the introduction, where they naturally belong—and provided that they do not sound like lazy excuses.

—Acknowledgments of unusual help others have given but you have not cited later as sources.

The letter may appropriately—almost always should—end with some expression indicating the writer's attitude toward the significance of the report and/or appreciation for having the opportunity to work on it. If you are in the business of making such studies, you surely appreciate business. If you're within the company, you certainly should appreciate the opportunity to demonstrate your ability and to learn more about the company. Your superior's giving you an important report assignment is a chance to make a good impression (and be marked for promotion). The value of that chance and a good report could easily suffer, however, if you do not express your appreciation for the chance. (See p. 512.)

Table of contents

The next part, usually page iii (with the number centered at the bottom, as always on a page with extra space at the top because of a part heading), is the table of contents (or simply contents). It sets out the major, if not all, headings of the report and their beginning page numbers. Thus it quickly shows the organization and serves as a handy guide for the reader, especially the busy reader who may want to check only some parts. In the absence of an index, it needs to be adequately detailed for the purpose.

To list in the table of contents the table itself and those parts that come before it would look a little odd; the reader would already have seen them. You therefore list only those divisions (with subdivisions down the scale as far as you think helpful) following the table. Remember, however, that the *preliminary parts down to the introduction are* not *parts of the outline and do not get outline symbols,* such as *I* and *A* (or 1.0 and 1.1) but only their names and page numbers (small roman numerals). If a separate synopsis comes immediately after the table of contents, for example, you list it flush left without an outline symbol, as the first thing on the list.

Then comes the real outline of the report—the headings and subheads. In most reports you may well give all of them, reproduced in exactly the same wording as elsewhere but not necessarily in the same type. Preferably you should put the outline symbols before them—in the decimal system or in capital roman numerals for the major divisions (including the introduction, conclusions, and recommendations) and capital letters for their subdivisions. (*Remember that roman numerals, like arabics, line up on the right.*) If any heading is too long for one line, break it at least seven spaces before the page-number column and indent the carry-over. After each heading is a leader line of *spaced* periods (with a space or two before and after) leading to the page-number column, as in the accompanying illustration (p. 513). For proper appearance (vertical alignment), make *all* those periods while your typewriter carriage is on either even or odd numbers on the scale.

Supplementary parts such as appendixes and the bibliography continue the arabic page numbers of the body copy, but they do not carry roman numerals to the left in the table of contents because they are not logical parts of the discussion being outlined.

The table of contents may be single- or double-spaced, or single-spaced within parts and double-spaced between, whichever makes the best appearance on the page; but double-space at least between the parts and major divisions.

Synopsis and/or abstract

Written after you complete the report proper, the synopsis is a condensed version of the whole report (preliminaries, introduction, presentation of facts and the interpretations of them, and conclusions and recommendations). It is the report in a nutshell—usually reduced somewhere between 10:1 and 20:1. In most cases you reduce the introduction even more and the conclusions and recommendations less because they deserve the main emphasis as the report's reason for being.

Since a synopsis stresses results, in terms of the psychology of communication you might feel that you should not use one in a report which needs to be strongly convincing because of the reader's likely resistance. In such a situation the condensed presentation of findings might not be adequate to do the necessary convincing before the reader sees the unwelcome or inadequately justified conclusions. (You would be using A–plan organization for a C–plan situation—as explained on pp. 78–82.) The increasing recognition of readers' benefits from having synopses in long reports and the way readers read such reports, however, override the psychological objection. Neither psychologically nor practically can you hold an impatient reader away from the conclusions long enough to read a long report anyway, the way you can on a short one or on a letter.

So—as in a report which may properly follow the deductive A–plan because the results are probably welcome to the reader—even in a long report which needs to convince, the synopsis serves several important purposes:

1. It saves time in many cases by giving all a busy reader wants.
2. Even for the reader who goes on through the whole report, the synopsis gives a bird's-eye view which helps in reading the rest more easily and more intelligently because already knowing the final results makes clearer how each fact or explanation fits.
3. Often the synopsis also serves as the basis for a condensed oral presentation to a group of important "readers" such as a board of directors.
4. Sometimes a number of readers who do not get the whole report but need to know the essence of it get what they need from reproduced and distributed copies of the synopsis.

Particularly for the first and last uses, many executives now insist that reports coming to their desks have *one-page* synopses up front—an increasing trend. You should therefore try to keep synopses down to one page, even if you have to single-space within paragraphs (but of course double-space between).

For an example of a good synopsis, read the detailed one below. It specifically and concisely synopsizes a report of six major divisions (besides the introduction and the conclusions and recommendations) running to 27 pages. Desirably, it focuses on a quick presentation of results (the conclusion and implied recommendation) in the first paragraph, while also making clear the purpose, the readers and authorizer, and the writers. Then it summarizes, in a paragraph for each, the six data-filled sections in the same order and proportionate space given the topics in the full report.

For readers not used to standard kinds of market-research data for choosing favorable locations, we give you the topics of those six sections (not the informative headings actually used, as suggested in Item 1, p. 472): Population and Buying Units; Buying Income; Retail Sales; Drugstore Sales; Overall Business Factors and Stability; and Business Activity.

Synopsis

Savannah people are likely to buy more at a Rexwall Drug Store than Charleston residents are, according to this market evaluation prepared for the Chairman of the Board, Rexwall, Inc., by Factseekers, Inc.

Though metropolitan Charleston merchants serve 11,000 more customers from the shopping area, Savannah retailers can expect some trade from almost twice as many out-of-town buyers (340,000 versus 184,000). Savannah's 1,000 more family units more than compensate for the fact that the Charleston family averages 3.62 people while the smaller Savannah family averages 3.4.

Savannah individuals average $85 more buying income, but the larger Charleston families average $35 more per family for a total of half a million more annual buying income. With less first-mortgage money to do it, 2,800 more people in Savannah have built homes in the past four years; but 17,000 more Charlestonians own automobiles.

The higher income of the individual Savannah buyer and the larger number of customers from around Savannah explain why $2.5 million more passed through the hands of Savannah retailers last year. Individually, Savannah residents spent $75 more; the small Savannah family, however, spent only $55 more.

Though five years ago Charleston druggists outsold those in Savannah by an average of $3,000, last year the 61 Savannah drugstore managers and owners collected about $5 million— $170,000 more than 62 Charleston druggists—for an average of $4,000 more per drugstore in Savannah.

Overall business factors also point to Savannah as the choice. Savannah's estimated business volume of $989 million is almost

```
twice that of Charleston.  Since a significant part of this
difference is attributable to the 10 million more tons of
cargo handled by the Savannah docks, Savannah consumers and
retailers will feel the pinch of recessions and strikes more
than Charlestonians.  The extra $36 million added by Charleston
manufacturing, however, is almost as uncertain in the stability
of that city as the effects of shipping are on the economy of
Savannah.  Charlestonians benefit from $35 million more of the
relatively stable wholesale business; but $32 million more
agricultural income from farms averaging $4,000 more in value
helps to bolster the Savannah economy.
Certainly Savannah's business activity has been consistently
better than Charleston's in the past four years.  Though the
trend continues up in both cities, construction has averaged
$12 million more annually in Savannah.  Bankers in Savannah
have consistently received about 10 percent more deposits than
their Charleston counterparts have—for $150 million more in
commercial accounts and $12 million more in savings.  In both
cities postmasters have collected about 8 percent more each
successive year, but Savannah citizens have steadily paid for
$200,000 more postage than Charlestonians have.
```

Since a synopsis derives exclusively from the report itself—which has adequate illustration and documentation—it needs neither graphics nor citations. But you do need to give the main supporting facts. Otherwise the synopsis becomes a nutshell with no meat. This is one reason we use the term *synopsis* rather than *abstract*.

Abstracts are of two kinds—topical, giving *only the points discussed* (shells without meat); and informative, giving the findings about each topic, with emphasis on conclusions and any recommendations made. A synopsis is like an *informative* abstract, emphasizing results, but is usually fuller and more helpful.

CONTENT AND FORM OF MAJOR PARTS

Introduction

The introduction to a complete analytical report serves primarily to answer the second of a report reader's two inevitable questions: How do you know? Rarely does it answer any part of the first question: What are the facts? If that question needs a brief and early answer (before the text gives all the facts), the synopsis does the job. Unless a synopsis or informative abstract is a part of the introduction, therefore—as in some forms of reports—the introduction is no place to put your data.

Since the introduction begins the *body* of the report—which also includes the text (the facts and analyses), conclusions, and recommendations if the reader wants them—the title of the whole report appears at the top of the page. Remember to set up that title exactly as on the title page, to reign as the superior over all other headings—in content as explained on page 496 and in form as explained on page 473. (Number the page 1, centered at the bottom as always on a page with extra space at the top because of a heading there.)

The first real problem in writing an introduction (often best done after the other parts) is selecting a heading for it. The stock term *Introduction,* which fits all but none well, is neither a precise nor an interesting preview of the contents. The illustrative report we're using, you'll notice (p. 515), does better. You can too after reading further below about the content of introductions. One of the best we've ever seen was "The WHY and HOW of This Report," but you don't need to use its wording. In fact you should not copy anybody's word patterns in a title or anywhere else, especially if they are unusual. You should look at illustrations for ideas and principles of communication—then express your thoughts in your own way. Regardless of what it says, the heading of the introduction, as the first major division of your outline (usually I or 1.0), should be in the same grammatical and type form you intend to use for all the other major-division headings. (See *parallel structure* p. 470, and *headings,* p. 472.)

In explaining how you know your forthcoming facts to be reliable, you need to state your *purpose, methods,* and *scope* so that the reader can judge whether the research would produce information that is sound and adequate for the purpose. Clear and explicit statement of the purpose is essential. No reader can judge a report without knowing what the writer set out to accomplish. Similarly, unless the research seems basically sound (in methodology and scope) for the purpose, the reader naturally discredits the whole report. The introduction, then, is an important part of the conviction in the report and therefore deserves careful attention from both writer and reader.

The section headed *Purpose* may take several paragraphs for full explanation, especially if it includes history or background of the problem; or it may be short. Long or short, it should contain some *one* sentence which is a pointed, concise statement of the problem you set out to solve. That sentence should come early, too. So, although any necessary background of history is the natural start, to avoid delay if it becomes very long you should state the key purpose sentence early and use the flashback method to follow quickly with clarifying background. As another alternative, you may relegate any very long background story to an appendix and refer the reader to it—especially if it is nonessential for most readers.

Methods and *scope* come under separate headings or (because they are often nearly inseparable) under a combined heading. Your reader does want to know, however, what you intended to cover (scope) and how you got and analyzed your information (method—that big question again, How do you know?). In a study involving a choice or evaluation, for example, the introduction needs to explain the *criteria* or *standards* used, as a part of method and scope or as a separate part. In fact, since the criteria in such a report should become the major subdivisions, explanation and justification of them should be an important duty of the introduction.

How thoroughly you need to explain your methods depends on two major points: (1) how new and questionable your methods and findings are and (2) your reputation as a researcher. On both bases nobody questions the audit report of a reputable auditing firm that says no more on methods than the following: ". . . in accordance with generally accepted auditing standards, and accordingly included such tests of the accounting records and such other auditing procedures as we considered necessary in the circumstances." Most report writers, however, cannot depend so completely on either such standardized procedures or their reputations to convince their readers that they used sound research methods.

A frequent question is how much methodology to put in the introduction and how much (if any) to relegate to an appendix or to interweave along with the presentation of findings. No simple answer fits all cases and relieves you of thinking. A general answer is that you explain your methods at the best place(s) to show that your facts have a solid basis in valid research. Your reader will want at least a general idea from the introduction. If specific details of research procedure, special materials and apparatus, or technique are too difficult for your reader(s) to remember and associate with the later resultant findings, you had better omit the specifics from the introduction and interweave them with the presentation of findings. (A specific question with its answers from a questionnaire is a good example.)

Like long and unnecessary background, certain details of methodology may sometimes go in an appendix, but only if (1) they would interrupt or unduly slow up the fast movement of the report proper and (2) most readers of the particular report would not want or need them. (Detailed explanations of unusual statistical procedures are good examples.)

Besides the standard parts (purpose, method, and scope), an introduction may take up one or more (rarely all) of several other possible topics. Some people think that an introduction should start by explaining the *authorization*—who asked for and who wrote the report—leading into or enveloping the purpose. Though the illustrated report (p. 515) does that, we don't think it is usually the best practice. The letter of transmittal will already have given that information. The first paragraph of a synopsis might have, also, because readers of widely distributed synopses would not have the duplicating letter of transmittal.

Unless the letter of transmittal has already done so, the introduction should forewarn the reader of any unavoidable *limitations* that make the report less than might be expected—limitations of time, money, or availability of data, for example. The explanation may be a part of method and scope if it is not so extensive as to need its own heading. But in no case should you use it as an excuse for your own shortcomings.

Sometimes a report uses technical words or certain terms applied in a sense unfamiliar to some likely readers. If so, you may explain them in the introduction or, preferably, in brief parenthetical statements immediately following the first use of each special term. If the list is extensive, the *glossary* may be an appendix.

The important point is for the introduction to answer the big question— How do you know?—*before* the reader asks it.

Then you are ready to present the assuredly reliable facts.

Before asking the reader to go on this mental journey, however, consider whether you can help by giving a final reminder of the route: a concise statement of your *basic plan.* Such a statement should not be long or detailed in its itemization of *all* your headings. It *does* need to remind the reader of the major steps in your organization and logic—usually naming, in order, the topics from II (or 2.0) to the conclusions in your table of contents.

Usually one effective sentence can chart the way through to the end, like this: "As bases for determining the more favorable market conditions, this report examines—in this order—population characteristics, buying power, retail sales and drugstore sales and the attendant competition, stability of the economy, and the current business outlook." If you compare this statement of plan to the separate synopsis presented earlier (p. 501), you will see that they both reflect the careful organization of the same report.

Text

Even the lazy writer who gets by with *Introduction* as the heading for that part cannot get by with *text* as a heading covering the report's biggest part, which presents the findings and analyses of them. The stock term, fitting all reports and therefore useful in talking about them, fits no one report well.

But more important, the text section of the report is fundamentally the report; so if you try to phrase a suitable title for the section, it will be the same as the title of the whole report. Then the basic elements of your report—the factors or criteria which serve as the basis for the final decision— become third-degree headings with seemingly too little significance.

That is the first of the two major problems confronting the writer in presenting the text: (1) showing the reader the organization carefully worked out as the third step in report preparation and (2) phrasing well the findings of the second step (collection of data) and the interpretations made in the fourth step. Satisfactory solutions to both are necessary if you are to give your reader the reliable information wanted.

Your main methods for showing the overall organization, the relations between parts, and the relation of each part to the whole are headings and subheads, topic sentences, and summary and anticipating statements. (You will find ample illustrations of all in the illustrative report on p. 511 ff.)

The headings and subheadings grow directly out of your attack on the problem, where you broke it down into its elements and further subdivided it by raising questions about each. Now that you are presenting the facts that provide the answers, you need only phrase these elements and questions into headings and subheads. Remember that good headings, like functional titles, are indicative, interesting, concise, and (in some cases preferably) informative to the extent of telling the most important findings about the respective parts. (Notice the heads in the report, pp. 516–33.)

Just as a well-phrased heading may tell the main point about the section over which it stands, a topic sentence can give the essence of a paragraph and clearly foreshadow what the paragraph says. The topic sentence puts the big point across fast, arouses the reader's interest in seeing the supporting details that follow, and makes reading easier because of the preview. Although the resulting deductive paragraph plan is not the only one possible, it is the most useful for most kinds of writing, including report writing.

Reversing the plan produces a paragraph which presents a series of facts and arguments leading to a summarizing and maybe a concluding sentence at the end.

Both plans may apply to larger sections as well as to paragraphs. In fact, both a paragraph's topic sentence and the first part of a larger section may reflect, summarize, or provide a transition from a preceding part, as well as give the essence and preview of what is to follow. And endings of both paragraphs and larger parts commonly summarize them, show the significance of the just-completed part to the whole problem at hand, and foreshadow what is to follow in the next section (as does the ending of the illustrated introduction on p. 516). Although the summaries may imply the advisability of a certain action, they should not go further and steal the thunder of the recommendation section by actually saying that the action should be taken.

Little more need be said about how to put the findings of fact and the interpretation into words. You have already learned in Chapter 14 to use commonly understood words, short and direct sentences and paragraphs, itemizations, summarizing and transitional phrases and sentences, headings and subheads, and graphic aids to words. You know, too, that you need to support your statements of questionable fact with explanations, additional specific and concrete details as evidence, citations of sources, and any meaningful statistics.

But remember that graphic presentations are not complete in themselves, that they only help words to present facts. They cannot interpret. The reader who wants an analytical report will consider your job only half done if you present a mass of undigested data and leave the interpreting undone. But if you put graphics and comments about them close together so that the reader can see both at once, each supplements the other.

References to the carefully chosen, most suitable graphics (about which you learned in Chapter 14) should be *subordinate* to the interpretation of the facts shown. The mere fact that the graph is there, or even the facts shown in the table or graph, are less important than the *significance* of those facts to the whole problem or the particular point being made at the time. So the emphasis should be on the interpretation. (Note the references to charts throughout the text of the illustrative report, p. 516 ff.)

Here's a flat example which is short only because it forces the reader to dig in its Figures 1 and 2 for the information:

> The greatest majority of the students interviewed showed their preference for buying at home in place of buying in the larger cities of Birmingham or Tuscaloosa. The overall percentage for the entire body of male students represented by the sample was 78. The freshmen showed an even greater tendency for home buying by their percentage of 84.
>
> Figure 1, below, gives a picture of the place of purchase of the entire group without regard to the nature of the group. Figure 2 divides the group according to the students' rank.

This rewrite is more informative, emphatic, and readable:

> When University of Alabama men are ready for a new suit, they buy at home 78 percent of the time. Although 4 out of 100 will buy in Tuscaloosa and 7 in Birmingham, as shown in Figure 1, these 11 atypical cases do not warrant extensive advertising.
>
> The Alabama man, although never weaned from hometown buying in the majority of cases, does slowly shift his clothes-buying sources from home to Birmingham to Tuscaloosa. The gain of only 13 out of every 100 purchasers over a four-year span, however (Figure 2), only confirms the suspicion that Bold Look advertising dollars in Tuscaloosa would be wasted.

Although basically an interpretation may point out trends, high and low points, and significant differences brought out by comparisons and analyses of facts and figures presented, you need not waste words by talking about "a comparison" or "an analysis of" or "a study of." If you state the significances, you imply the comparison, the analysis, or the study. And the comparisons become more quickly clear and significant if you put them in terms of percentages or ratios instead of, or in addition to, giving the raw figures. (See p. 467.)

To avoid monotony of both sentence pattern and length, especially in a series of similar comparisons, consider different types of sentence beginnings. Nearly always you can do better than use the expletives "It is . . ." and "There are . . . ," which waste words, delay the idea, and lead you to weak and awkward passive constructions. (See p. 42.)

And unless the logic of the situation clearly dictates otherwise, you'll do best to use the present tense throughout the text. When a reader reads it, your report analyzes, presents, takes up, examines, establishes, and finally concludes (all present tense). Of course, you'll have to use some past and future tenses; but in general, use them for matters of historical record and things not yet done. You have to assume that your most recent information is still applicable; hence, even though last year's sales figures are a histori-

cal record of what people bought, you are justified in saying, "People buy
... ," meaning that they did buy, they are buying, and they will buy. (See
p. 470.)

With the facts and analyses well organized, clearly presented, and
sharply summarized at the ends of sections, you have led the reader to your
statement of conclusions and (if wanted) recommendations.

Conclusions and recommendations

When you put your conclusions and recommendations into words, they
should not be surprising—and they won't be if you have done an adequate
job of the preceding part. There you should have presented all the evidence
and analysis necessary to support your conclusions. No new facts or analyses
should appear in the conclusions or recommendations.

Whether you separate conclusions and recommendations into two parts
makes little difference. Some people prefer separation because, they say, the
conclusions are strictly objective, logical results of what the report has said,
whereas the recommendations are the individual writer's personal suggestions of what to do about the problem. Whichever point of view and plan
you use, the important thing is to be as objective as possible in stating both
conclusions and recommendations.

As evidence of that objectivity in your conclusions, and as a means of
saving the reader the trouble of looking back into the text to see that you *do*
have the data, you may well lift basic figures or statements from the earlier
presentation and interweave them into the conclusion sentences. The writer
of the synopsis illustrated on page 501 knew that the reader could not possibly retain the 200 or more facts and figures given as evidence in 27 pages of
analysis. In reminding the reader of the significant evidence affecting the
decision in the conclusion, shown below, that writer wisely attached a specific figure to every fact. Note, too, the specific wording of that ending section—as well as the selectivity and brevity.

```
            VII.  THE PREFERRED CITY: SAVANNAH
Although a Charleston druggist enjoys the advantages of
     —a population with a half million dollars more buying
       income annually and families with $34 more to spend
     —11,000 additional potential customers
a Savannah drugstore would likely sell more because of these
advantages:
     —$170,000 additional drugstore sales and $4,000 greater
       sales per drugstore
     —$2.5 million more retail sales and $162 more per person
       spent in retail stores
     —1,000 more families and per capita income $87 higher
     —four-year trend increases of 8 to 10% in construction
       (12 million more), bank deposits ($150 million more),
       and postal receipts ($200,000 more).
```

Both conclusions and recommendations need to be as pointed and posi-tive as the facts and the writer's judgment will allow. (Usually itemization will help you to make them so and help the reader to see them as such.) If you toss the problem back to the reader with indefinite conclusions or al-ternative suggestions, you leave the feeling that the salary or fee paid you for doing the report has been wasted. Still, the reader retains the right of final decision; so even when asked for your recommendations, present them as definite suggestions but certainly not as commands. The example just cited—phrased specifically in terms of the objective of the report, to select the city which will likely be the more profitable scene of operations—avoids indecision on the one hand and its equally undesirable opposite, im-perative command.

STANDARD SUPPLEMENTS

Appendix

Although the report reproduced as an illustration (pp. 511–34) did not need an appendix, many reports do. The key to the decision is this: Use an appendix for material which the reader does not *need* to see to understand the text but which some readers may *want* to see to be sure your textual statements are clear and valid. Frequent uses are for survey question-naires too extensive for presentation in the introduction and not essential to the reader's understanding of the text; for extensive formulas and statistical calculations; for extensive history, or detailed experimental methodology too long for the introduction; and for large maps, diagrams, or tables of fig-ures that may be the basic data of the whole report but do not belong at any particular place in the text. Often the best way is to put a big table in the appendix and use appropriate figures from it as spot tables at key places in the text.

Bibliography

As we said before, on almost any big problem somebody has published something relevant. If that applies to your problem, finding and reading what others have written is almost certainly the quickest and easiest way to get at least some of the information you need. When you do that, you must tell what your sources are, not only to avoid the accusation of pla-giarism but to show that you didn't just dream up the facts and to get the backing of the other writer for what you say—and perhaps to provide your reader with places to get fuller information.

Your footnotes and/or internal citations in the text give the specific ref-erences (pp. 489–92). But at the end you list—in alphabetical order of authors' surnames, or titles if the sources are unsigned—books, magazines, and other printed sources (but not letters and oral communications, which you cite in the text or in footnotes). These include all such sources used for background information or for specific facts, ideas, or direct quotations.

For several reasons a writer may choose not to compile a bibliography—for instance if the report is fairly short and involves few published sources which are identified through internal citations. But this is the exception rather than the rule for acceptability. To illustrate, however, we refer you to the short analytical report on pages 573–87. Anybody could take the sources cited in the report and compile a bibliography.

For another illustration, we present the following bibliography from a 20-page report. After arranging the items alphabetically, this author also provided item numbers for concise, specific citations in the text (p. 492). The spacing is the preferred form of single within items (except when preparing copy for a printer) and double between them.

PUBLICATIONS CONSULTED

1. "Airlines Will Sacrifice Power to Obtain Lower Jet Noise Level," Aviation Week, 66:34, February 25, 1979.

2. "Boeing Sets Suppressor Flight Test," Aviation Week, 65:41, April 1, 1978.

3. "Portable Jet Engine Muffler Design," Aviation Week, 64:74–75, April 8, 1977.

4. Richards, E. G., Technical Aspects of Sound, Elsevier Publishing Co., New York, 1978.

5. Richards, E. G., "Research on Aerodynamic Noise from Jets and Related Problems," Royal Aeronautical Society Journal, 57:318–42, May, 1978.

6. "Silencing Jet Fleet Will Be Costly," Aviation Week, 64:47–48, May 27, 1977.

* * * * *

For the feel of report continuity, read straight through the following illustrative report (pp. 511–34). It illustrates adequate handling of the standard parts of a complete analytical report. Notice particularly its careful organization, phrasing of informative headings, and use of topic and summary statements needed at the beginnings and endings of sections in long reports.

Then, as further help before you prepare such a report, we suggest that you test this one against the checklist that follows it (pp. 535–41), as you will certainly want to check your own before final typing.

Although the checklist which follows the illustrative report is primarily for complete analytical reports, many of the items apply to all reports. For greatest usefulness the sections appear in the order of presentation in the final report. Remember, however, that this is only a checklist. If you need fuller explanation of a point, find it in the appropriate chapter or in Appendix B. (The index may help.)

WHY BIRMINGHAM IS A BETTER LOCATION THAN MEMPHIS

FOR F. LEE MASON TO BEGIN LAW PRACTICE

Prepared for

Mr. F. Lee Mason

by

Robert E. Norman

Director of Research

New York, NY 10017

November 27, 19xx

FACTSEEKERS INCORPORATED
1127 Main Street
New York, New York 10017

RESEARCH DEPARTMENT   November 27, 19xx

Mr. F. Lee Mason
3807 15th Avenue
Tuscaloosa, Alabama 35401

Dear Mr. Mason:

Here is the report you requested on September 6 evaluating
Birmingham and Memphis as possible locations for you to begin law
practice.

The report shows Birmingham is the better city for you because of
income, competitive, personal, and economic factors. As you requested,
I emphasized a specialty in tax law and the partnership form of
organization.

I am glad to have the opportunity to prepare this report for you and
will be happy to serve you again.

Sincerely yours,

FACTSEEKERS, INC.

Robert E. Norman
Director of Research

Contents

Synopsis

Birmingham is a better location than Memphis to begin law practice, according to this study prepared for F. Lee Mason by Factseekers, Inc.

Although Memphis has a higher ratio of residents to lawyers (1,218 to 1 versus 1,200 to 1), Birmingham has a higher ratio of residents to law establishments (3,068 to 1 versus 2,533 to 1) and fewer tax lawyers (2% versus 4%). Profits of the average partnership are 12.7% higher and total profits per establishment are 36% higher in Birmingham.

In Memphis the median age is four years lower, the land area is three times as large, the population is growing rather than declining, median school attendance is approximately one year more, and about 5.5% more of the population is in the $15,000 and above income level. Memphis's city government spends 4½ times as much as Birmingham's. Birmingham, however, has more large employers, better continuing education for lawyers, and better within-city transportation.

Birmingham has a bigger variety of better quality sports events, although Memphis does have hunting, fishing, and water sports equal to Birmingham's. UAB's medical school, Samford's law and pharmacy schools, and special programs at other schools provide better higher education in Birmingham. Health care in Birmingham has gained national recognition. The Memphis Arts Council and The Memphis Academy of Arts, on the other hand, support many programs that make cultural activities better in Memphis.

Unemployment is 0.5% lower, income of the average factory worker is 20% higher, retail sales are up 7% more, and factory workers' income is up 12.5% more in Birmingham. But Memphis's effective buying income is $4 billion as compared to Birmingham's $3.7 billion. Median household EBI in Memphis ($12,905) is growing 1.3% faster than in Birmingham, where the median is $11,958.

WHY BIRMINGHAM IS A BETTER LOCATION THAN

MEMPHIS FOR F. LEE MASON TO BEGIN LAW PRACTICE

I. Problems and Procedures of the Report

A. Purpose and methods

This report evaluates Birmingham, Alabama, and Memphis, Tennessee, to select the better city for F. Lee Mason to begin law practice. Its criteria are those agreed on in the contractual arrangement and reflected in Items II-V of the "Contents," p. iii.

Information presented here comes largely from *The U.S. Census of Business, The U.S. Census of Population, U.S. News & World Report,* and various publications of the Chamber of Commerce in each city. In some cases I developed the percentages I used from the raw data given in the publications.

B. Scope and limitations

Two of the most important criteria used in this evaluation are competition and income of existing law firms. Inspection of competition starts with how many and what kinds of lawyers now practice in each city but, as requested, considers more carefully the number of tax lawyers and partnerships. Income of the attorneys, a major factor in the decision, appears in terms of profit per establishment.

Secondary factors examined because of their important influence on law practice include characteristics of the population, city government spending, area employers, continuing education, and transportation.

Family life in each city gets careful attention because an attorney usually does not change cities and will want the best for his family and himself.

1

Second in importance only to income and competition, the general state of
the economy has an influence on the legal profession, although perhaps not as
great an influence as on some industries. No matter how large the demand for
legal services, clients may forego or delay seeking the services if they can't
afford them.

As requested, I made no attempt to compare the laws of Alabama and
Tennessee. Similarly I did not consider any kinds of taxes or housing. A
choice among the many types and prices of homes depends on individual
preference.

C. Basic plan

The bases for evaluating the two cities and arriving at the conclusions and
recommendations are, therefore, income and competition, their relevant
secondary factors, family life, and the economy.

II. Competition and Income More Favorable in Birmingham

Less competition and larger income are desirable factors of major
importance in choosing the better city.

A. Number, type, specialty of existing law firms favor Birmingham

1. Ratio of population to lawyers.—Memphis has a higher ratio of residents
to lawyers than Birmingham. Memphis and Birmingham have 632 and 616
lawyers, respectively (12:4-34, meaning pp. 4-34 of Item 12 of the Bibliography).
Memphis's population is 770,120 while Birmingham's is 739,274. Thus
Memphis has one attorney for every 1,218 residents and Birmingham's ratio
of residents to attorneys is 1,200 to 1, as shown in Table 1.

3

TABLE 1 Lawyers, Population, and Persons per Lawyer

	Birmingham	**Memphis**
Population	739,274	770,120
Lawyers	616	632
Persons per Lawyer	1,200	1,218

Source: **Census of Legal Services, 19xx, pp. 4-34.**

A new attorney in Memphis would have more prospective clients to attract than one in Birmingham. Also since Memphis has more people per lawyer, the number of persons not already associated with a lawyer should be larger there. But since the number of lawyers and the number of law establishments differ, the numbers and types of existing establishments warrant examination.

2. Ratio of population to law establishments.—Birmingham has a higher ratio of residents to law establishments (meaning "a single physical location at which business is conducted" not identical with "firm," which may consist of one or more establishments). The numbers of law establishments in Memphis and Birmingham are 304 and 241 respectively (1:4, 17). The ratio of residents to law establishments for Birmingham is therefore 3,068 to 1 and for Memphis 2,533 to 1.

Since people in Birmingham have fewer law offices per person to chose from, new attorneys will have a greater chance of attracting clients in Birmingham. Even though Memphis has the advantages in the ratio of population to lawyers, Birmingham's lead in the ratio of population to law establishments may be more significant. Prospective clients tend to choose between law establishments or firms rather than between lawyers within firms. Since most

4

firms are of the type with more than one lawyer (as shown below), the ratios on establishments seem most useful.

3. **Types of law establishments.**—Partnerships comprise a greater percentage of law establishments in Birmingham than in Memphis. Law establishments, as the Census Bureau classifies them, are sole practitioners, partnerships, professional service organizations, and other. An establishment owned by two or more persons, each of whom has a financial interest in the establishment, is a partnership. A professional service organization is an establishment founded under state professional association or corporation statutes. Other includes establishments whose legal form is unknown or not one of those above.

The numbers and percentages of various kinds of law establishments for both Birmingham and Memphis appear in Table 2.

TABLE 2 Law Establishments by Type

	Birmingham		Memphis	
	Number of Establishments	Percentage of Total	Number of Establishments	Percentage of Total
Total	241	100	304	100
Sole Practitioners	83	34	118	39
Partnerships	100	42	89	29
Professional Service Organizations	2	1	13	4
Other	56	23	84	28

Source: Census of Legal Services, 19xx, pp. 4–17.

Partnerships, with which we are primarily concerned, probably exist more frequently in Birmingham because they are the most advantageous form of

5

organization in terms of income (discussed later); but form of organization is most likely overshadowed. The speciality of the lawyer's practice probably has even more significance.

4. Specialty of law practice.—Birmingham has fewer tax lawyers and fewer in the combined specialties of tax and corporate law. Lawyers specializing in taxation comprise 2% of the total in Birmingham and 4% in Memphis, while corporate lawyers comprise 4% and 3%, respectively, as shown in Table 3. Thus Birmingham has 6% of the total in these two groups while 7% of all

TABLE 3 Number of Lawyers in Practice by Specialty

	Birmingham		Memphis	
	Number of Lawyers	Percentage of Total	Number of Lawyers	Percentage of Total
Total	616	100	632	100
Tax	13	2	27	4
Corporation	23	4	19	3
Banking and Commercial	12	2	30	5
Criminal	3	1	35	5
Domestic Relations	4	1	1	—
Insurance	18	3	19	1
Negligence	37	6	35	6
Patent, Trademark, Copyright	—	—	7	1
Real Estate	37	6	49	8
Wills, Estate Planning, Probate	19	3	15	2
Other	42	7	30	5
General	408	65	375	60

Source: Census of Legal Services, 19xx, pp. 4-34.

Memphis's lawyers are in these two groups. Although a new lawyer in Birmingham has less competition, comparison of incomes points up the real advantage.

B. Income of law firms larger in Birmingham

1. Gross receipts, profits, profits per establishment.— Total Birmingham law establishments have larger gross receipts, larger aggregate profits, and larger profits per establishment than those in Memphis. Also Birmingham

6

partnerships exceed Memphis partnerships in all these areas. Profits per establishment for all types of establishments are $56,618 and $41,586 in Birmingham and Memphis, respectively. Partnership profits per establishment in Birmingham are $121,120 and in Memphis $107,472, as shown in Table 4 (12:4-9, 4-17). Thus on the average partnerships make 12.7% more in Birmingham than Memphis and total profits per establishment are 36% higher

TABLE 4 Receipts and Profits by Type of Establishment

	Receipts ($1,000)		Profits ($1,000)		Profit Per Establishment	
	Birmingham	Memphis	Birmingham	Memphis	Birmingham	Memphis
Total	30,893	30,670	13,645	12,642	56,618	41,586
Sole Practitioners	4,029	5,373	593	1,904	7,144	16,135
Partnerships	24,270	17,403	12,112	9,565	121,120	107,472
Professional Service Organizations	na	2,911	na	(1,629)		125,308
Other	na	4,983	na	4,858		57,833

na — Not available

Source: Census of Legal Services, 19xx, pp. 4-9, 4-17.

in Birmingham, revealing one reason for Birmingham's higher income levels.

2. **Income levels.**—Birmingham lawyers have a higher median income and more Birmingham lawyers have income of $10,000 or more. Median incomes of lawyers in Birmingham and Memphis are $15,000+ and $14,901, respectively. In Birmingham 73% of the lawyers make $10,000 or more while 71% of Memphis's lawyers are in this category. Birmigham lawyers have a slight edge in the $15,000-and-above income level; but approximately 50% of the lawyers in both cities are in this group, as shown in Table 5 (10:2-663) (11:44-712).

7

TABLE 5 Income Levels of Lawyers and Judges

| | Birmingham | | Memphis | |
	Number	Percentage of Total	Number	Percentage of Total
Total	827	100	936	100
$1-$1,999 or less	36	4	42	4
2,000- 3,999	31	4	34	4
4,000- 4,999	11	1	31	3
5,000- 5,999	40	5	18	2
6,000- 6,999	24	3	36	4
7,000- 7,999	26	3	43	5
8,000- 9,999	54	7	66	7
10,000-14,999	189	23	202	22
15,000 or more	416	50	464	49

Source: **Characteristics of the Population, 19xx, Part 2, p. 663.**
Characteristics of the Population, Part 44, p. 712.

Even though income and competition, which favor Birmingham, are
probably most important in choosing the better city, other factors which
influence law practice (such as population characteristics, city government,
major employers, continuing education, and transportation) deserve
consideration.

III. **Factors Influencing Law Practice Yield No Clear Favorite**

A. **Population characteristics more favorable in Memphis**

1. **General characteristics.**—Memphis's population (770,120) is 4% larger
than Birmingham's (739,274), and it grew 25.3% during the past decade while
Birmingham's declined 11.7%. Memphis, with a land area
of 217.4 square miles, is about 3 times as large as Birmingham with 79.5
square miles. Memphis also has a smaller population per square mile (3,542)
as compared to Birmingham (9,299).

The growing population of Memphis is a favorable trend for law practice and
business in general. Also the larger land area should make office facilities
easier to find in Memphis and less expensive because the city is more diverse.
But the growing population may counter this desirable effect by creating
more demand for business facilities.

The median age in Memphis (26.2 years) is lower than in Birmingham (30.3
years). Approximately 50% of the population of both cities is between 18 and
65. Birmingham has a larger percentage of the population in the 18-and-over
group with 67.4% as compared to Memphis's 63.7% (9:630, 3:762). The lower

8

median age and the growing population of Memphis should mean Memphis will soon have a larger percentage of the population in the over 18 age group—the primary users of legal services.

2. Education.—Memphis's population is better educated than Birmingham's. Thus the people should be more willing to seek legal assistance in business organizations, wills, estate planning, and tax planning. The median years of school attended in Memphis is 12; in Birmingham, the median is 11.2. Memphis has a larger percentage of the population in the higher education categories. As shown in Table 6, 6.1% more of the population of Memphis has completed four years of high school or more and 2.5% more have completed four years of college or more (3:631,763). This higher education level is probably one reason for higher incomes in Memphis.

TABLE 6 Education of the Population

	Birmingham	Memphis
Median Years Attended School	11.2	12
Percentage of Population Having Completed:		
5 or less School Years	8.7%	7.3%
4 Years High School or more	44 %	50.1%
4 Years College or more	7.4%	9.9%

Source: County and City Data Book, 19xx, pp. 631, 763.

3. Income.—The median family income in Memphis ($8,646) is higher than in Birmingham ($7,735), and a greater percentage of the families of Memphis have incomes of $15,000 or more. In Memphis 16.5% make $15,000 or more while 11% make $15,000 or more in Birmingham, as shown in Table 7 (3:633,765). Thus Memphis's residents can pay more readily than Birmingham's for legal services, and they will most likely demand more legal assistance since they tend to be wealthier unless the tax bite removes their advantage.

9

TABLE 7 Income of the Population

Percentage of Families with Income	Birmingham	Memphis
$3,000 or less	15.5	12.9
3,000- 4,999	13.7	12.1
5,000- 6,999	14.7	13.4
7,000- 9,999	22.9	20.8
10,000-14,999	22.2	24.4
15,000-24,999	9.2	12.4
25,000 or more	1.8	4.1

Source: County and City Data Book, 19xx, pp. 633, 675.

B. City government expenditures larger in Memphis

The city government in Memphis spends approximately $183.4 million

yearly or 4½ times Birmingham's expenditure of $40.9 million. On a per capita

basis, Memphis spends $256 as opposed to $91 for Birmingham. Memphis

spends more total dollars in each category of spending than Birmingham,

even though Birmingham spends more as a percentage in some categories, as

shown in Table 8 (13:636,768). The larger expenditures of Memphis's city

government should make Memphis a better place to work, as well as live.

TABLE 8 City Government Expenditures (1970)

	Birmingham		Memphis	
	Total Spent (Millions)	Percentage of Total	Total Spent (Millions)	Percentage of Total
Percentage Spent For:				
Education	16.46	40	84.7	46.2
Highways	4.6	11.3	6.6	3.6
Public Welfare	0.02	0.05	0.6	0.3
Police and Fire	10.5	25.6	28.0	15.3
Sanitation	3.4	8.2	11.2	6.1
Total	40.9	100	183.4	100

Source: County and City Data Book, 19xx, p. 636; 19xx, p. 768.

C. Large employers more numerous in Birmingham

Birmingham has more large employers than Memphis. Firms with 1,000 and

over employees number 19 in Birmingham as opposed to 16 in Memphis. In

the 3,000-and-over employee category, Birmingham has ten firms and

Memphis has nine. The larger the firm the more likely it will require some type

of legal service.

Some of Birmingham's major employers in the public and private sectors are U.S. Steel, U.S. Pipe and Foundry, the University of Alabama in Birmingham, American Cast Iron Pipe, and Alabama Power. Some of the larger ones in Memphis are Firestone Tire, International Harvester, Sears, and the U.S. government (1, 6). All of these firms need varying degrees of legal aid, possibly even full-time counsel.

D. Continuing education better in Birmingham

Birmingham has better facilities for lawyers to continue their education. Cumberland School of Law, Alabama's largest law school, is in Birmingham; and the University of Alabama is a one-hour drive from Birmingham. Both of these schools have part-time programs for lawyers. Memphis, conversely, has no law school (2:4) (7:22).

E. Transportation more suitable in Birmingham

City transportation is more favorable in Birmingham, but out-of-city travel is more favorable to and from Memphis. The fact that Birmingham's interstate highways go through the heart of the business district makes transportation time to downtown from the residential areas shorter than in Memphis, where the completed interstate highways bypass the city. Also since three interstate highways meet in Birmingham, all sections of the city are near one of them.

Memphis, on the other hand, has the advantage in out-of-city travel. Five trunk and five regional air lines serve Memphis's new international airport with approximately 300 flights daily. Birmingham has four major airlines and three fixed-base private aviation companies. Both cities have the services of seven major railroads and two national bus lines. Memphis, the second largest inland port on the Mississippi River, gets service from six barge lines.

11

Birmingham does not now have port facilities but has plans to build a port nearby (7:16) (2:9).

These factors that influence law practice in a secondary manner give neither city an advantage. Population characteristics, city government expenditures, and transportation to other cities favor Memphis, while major employers, continuing education, and travel within the city are better in Birmingham. While neither city gains a clear advantage on these secondary factors, no choice should depend on strictly business factors, anyway, because family life is important.

IV. Family Life Better in Birmingham

The quality of family life depends on the friendliness of the climate, the type of recreational facilities, the quality of the arts and cultural activities, the educational opportunities, and the health-care facilities.

A. Climate more desirable in Birmingham

Birmingham's average annual temperature is 62° with an average summer temperature of 81.6° and an average winter temperature of 46.5°. With an average summer temperature of 80° and an average winter temperature of 43.8°, Memphis's average annual temperature is 61.5°.

Average annual rainfall is 53.05 and 49.78 inches, respectively, in Birmingham and Memphis. Average monthly rainfall in Birmingham is 4.4 inches and in Memphis it is 4.1 inches. The approximate dates of the last frost are March 2 in Birmingham and March 21 in Memphis. November 25 in Birmingham and November 6 in Memphis are the approximate first frost dates, as shown in Table 9 (4:4, 7:3), next page.

TABLE 9 Climate

	Birmingham	Memphis
Average Annual Temperature	62.0	61.5
Average Summer Temperature	81.6	80.0
Average Winter Temperature	46.5	43.8
Average Annual Rainfall	53.05"	49.78"
Average Monthly Rainfall	4.4"	4.1"
Approximate Last Frost Date	March 2	March 21
Approximate First Frost Date	November 25	November 6

Source: **Birmingham Magazine, February 19xx.**
Memphis Area Chamber of Commerce, 19xx.

B . **Recreation more plentiful in Birmingham**

Birmingham's spectator sports are on a bigger scale and more plentiful than

Memphis's. College football, one of Birmigham's biggest sports attractions,

draws more fans than other sports in Birmingham. The University of

Alabama and Auburn University play home games at Birmingham's Legion

Field. Memphis State University plays its home games at the Liberty Bowl

Stadium (home of the annual Liberty Bowl Classic). College basketball is

available in both cities. The University of Alabama and Auburn University

play some games at the Birmingham Civic Center. University of Alabama

home games are only one hour from Birmingham in Tuscaloosa. Memphis

State's home basketball games are in the Mid-South Coliseum. Samford

University also has home basketball games in Birmingham.

Birmingham's newest sport is hockey. The Birmingham Bulls of The World

Hockey Association play at the Civic Center. Memphis's professional sport is

golf. The PGA's Danny Thomas Memphis Classic is at one of ten private golf

courses in Memphis. Memphis also has ten public golf courses and 136

baseball fields. Golf is also a big attraction in Birmingham, partly due to the

friendly climate.

Automobile racing is a huge attraction at the Alabama International Motor

Speedway only 45 minutes from Birmingham. It is the world's longest

13

enclosed race track.

Tennis is a growing sport in Birmingham both for participants and
spectators. The $30,000 Birmingham International Tennis Tournament brings
in top-ranked players for a week each winter. The Racquet Place is a good
indoor tennis facility, and outdoor courts are plentiful throughout the city.
Ice skating is also becoming popular in Birmingham with the opening of a
new ice skating lodge.

Participative sports such as hunting, fishing, and water skiing are
plentiful in both cities. Near Memphis many enjoy hunting for duck, squirrel,
rabbit, quail, and dove. Memphis also holds the National Bird Dog
championships.

For sightseeing, Arlington Ante Bellum Home, The Botanical and
Japanese Gardens, The Jimmy Morgan Zoo, and the Vulcan are in
Birmingham. In Memphis, Mississippi River cruises, Overton Park Zoo and
Aquarium, Chucallssa Indian Village, and Brooks Memorial Art Gallery are
main attractions (7:24) (2:8) (4:2).

Since participatory recreation is relatively equal in both cities,
Birmingham's edge lies in spectator sports. A city with a good combination of
sports and cultural activities is difficult to find, though.

C. **The arts better in Memphis**

Offerings in the arts are slightly better in Memphis than in Birmingham, but
professional performers appear most in Birmingham. The Memphis Arts
Council, which is dedicated to the promotion and support of the arts as a
vital aspect of community life, enriches local cultural life. It funds many
groups and special events. Brooks Memorial Art Gallery displays an

14

outstanding permanent collection of paintings and schedules circulating
exhibitions of national interest. The Memphis Academy of Arts offers a
variety of services to the community, including free-lance work and
commissions by students and faculty.

The Memphis Opera Theatre presents operas with national and
international stars in leading roles. The Memphis Symphony Orchestra, The
Memphis Ballet Society, and The Beethoven Club present symphonies,
ballets, and classical recitals. Theatre Memphis, one of the oldest little theater
groups in the country, produces six plays each year. Memphis also enjoys
productions by many touring companies, including Broadway plays,
Metropolitan Opera, and concert artists (7:26).

In Birmingham three civic theatre groups, campus productions, a dinner
theater, and numerous road shows provide a variety of theater productions.
In one week Liberace, Pearl Bailey, Doc Severinsen, and Hal Holbrook played
in Birmingham.

Birmingham's 80-member professional symphony plays a seven-month
season. Birmingham Music Club, oldest in the South, schedules outstanding
artists. Birmingham has civic opera, string quartet, civic chorus, organ recital
series, connoisseur concerts, a special symphony series, and active college
music departments. Four dance companies and a creative dance organization
perform in Birmingham. Birmingham-Southern College offers the Southeast's
only ballet degree. The Museum of Art holds many famous works of art (4:3).

D. **Higher educational opportunities better in Birmingham, but
preparatory schools better in Memphis**

1. **Higher education**.—Birmingham's higher educational opportunities
allow a wider choice than Memphis's in field of study and type of institution.
Birmingham's largest university, the University of Alabama-Birmingham,
trains students in its nationally recognized medical school in the fields of

15

medicine, dentistry, optometry, nursing, and community and allied health resources. UAB also offers undergraduate degrees in liberal arts and business. The graduate school awards degrees in a wide range of fields, but most degrees are in science and medicine. Memphis State University has long been recognized as the regional center for higher education. The graduate and undergraduate schools at Memphis State offer a wide range of degrees. The Southern College of Optometry and the University of Tennessee Center for Health Sciences provide training for health careers in the Memphis area.

In Birmingham, Samford University, with schools of law, pharmacy, and nursing; Birmingham-Southern College, which offers the only major in dance in the Southeast; and the University of Montevallo, with its extensive program to train driver-education instructors and emergency-vehicle operators, offer programs in almost every field. The Memphis Academy of Arts, LeMoyne Owen College, and The Joint University Center round out Memphis's major institutions. Also both cities have several community and junior colleges (7:22) (2:4) (4:2).

The larger offerings of colleges with regionally and nationally recognized programs make higher education better in Birmingham; but secondary, elementary, and kindergarten schools are better in Memphis.

2. **Elementary and secondary education.**— Memphis has a better preparatory school system than Birmingham. The Memphis public school system ranks seventh largest in the nation. In metropolitan Memphis 197 schools employ 7,284 teachers and have an enrollment of 138,294. The ratio of pupils to teachers in Memphis is 19 to 1. Birmingham's 210 area schools have an enrollment of 128,890 and employ 5,394 teachers, resulting in a 24 to 1 pupil-teacher ratio, as shown in Table 10 (7:22), (5:1), next page.

16

TABLE 10 Number and Size of Elementary and Secondary
Schools, Metro Area

	Birmingham	Memphis
Number of Schools	210	197
Number of Students	128,890	138,294
Number of Teachers	5,394	7,284
Pupil-Teacher Ratio	24 to 1	19 to 1

Source: Memphis Area Chamber of Commerce, 19xx.
The League of Women Voters of Greater Birmingham, 19xx.

For the preschoolers, Memphis offers over 100 public and private
kindergarten and day-care centers. The majority of students who attend pre-
school in Birmingham go to private, usually church-based, programs. A few
public programs are operating, however (7:22) (5:1).

E. Health care more advanced in Birmingham

Medically speaking, the Birmingham area is one of the most advanced
communities in the nation. Nineteen hospitals with 5,044 beds serve Jefferson
and Shelby counties. The medical industry employs 14,000 workers in the
health services and allied fields. The University of Alabama Medical Center,
foremost in Birmingham, provides the training ground for many doctors,
dentists, and eye specialists; has cardiac-care facilities known worldwide; and
ranks in the top 5% percent in the nation in specialized burn care. Virtually
all the major hospitals have been renovated within the last ten years.
Birmingham is a major referral center in the Southeast, and patients come
from all over the world for open-heart surgery (2:5).

The Memphis health-care system, which has the Memphis Medical Center
at its heart, consists of 19 hospitals with over 6,600 beds and over 15,000
physicians. The Medical Center includes the nation's largest private hospital,
the tenth largest medical school, and specialty clinics of international
reputation. The completion of Memphis's construction program will provide
the area with a network of four peripheral health-care facilities (7:21).

17

Even though family life appears better in Birmingham, bad economic conditions would reverse these good factors or lessen their enjoyment.

V. Economic Trends Healthier in Birmingham

A. General economic conditions more favorable in Birmingham

Retail sales, as compared with one year ago, are up 10.9% in Birmingham and 4% in Memphis (3:C-3, C-75). Department store sales rose 3.2 percentage points more in Birmingham than Memphis, where they were up 7.5% as compared to one year ago, as shown in Table 11. Unemployment is 7.1% of

TABLE 11 General Economic Conditions

	Birmingham	Memphis
Unemployment	7.1%	7.6%
Income of Average Factory Worker	$12,284	$10,178
The following are compared with a year ago:		
Retail Sales	Up 10.9%	Up 4%
Department Store Sales	Up 10.7%	Up 7.5%
Nonfarm Employment	Down 1.3%	Down 1.0%
Factory Workers' Income	Up 15.7%	Up 3.2%
Construction Activity	Up 1.5%	Down 15.5%

Source: U.S. News & World Report, October 25, 19xx, pp. 85, 87.
Survey of Buying Power, July 26, 19xx, C-3, C-75.
Survey of Buying Power, July 21, 19xx, C-2, C-74.

the work force in Birmingham as compared with 7.6% in Memphis. Nonfarm employment is down in both Birmingham (1.3%) and Memphis (1%). Income of the average factory worker adjusted to an annual basis is $2,106 higher in Birmingham. Factory workers' income as compared to a year ago is up 15.7% and 3.2% in Birmingham and Memphis, respectively. While construction activity is up 1.5% over the last year in Birmingham, it is down 15.5% in Memphis (3:85, 87). Thus Birmingham's economy shows more favorable trends and is better than Memphis's in every category listed except nonfarm employment.

B. Effective buying income larger in Memphis

Total effective buying income, median household effective buying income, and the increase in median household effective buying income are larger in

Memphis. Effective buying income (EBI) is *Sales and Marketing Management's* measure of disposable personal income—wages, salaries, and other income minus federal, state, and local taxes and fines, fees, and penalties. Total EBI for Memphis and Birmingham are $4 billion and $3.7 billion, respectively. Median household EBI is up 11.5% since last year, to $12,905 in Memphis. Birmingham's median household EBI is $11,958, up 10.2% since last year (8:C-3, C-75) (9:6-2, C-74). Since EBI depends greatly on current economic conditions, the trends of the economy should probably be the primary consideration. So Birmingham has the better economy.

VI. Birmingham—the Preferred City for F. Lee Mason to Begin Law Practice

Since Birmingham enjoys the advantages of

- 535 more residents per law establishment

- a greater number of partnerships

- fewer tax attorneys in total and as a percentage of the total

- 12.7% higher partnership profits

- higher median income for attorneys

- better continuing education

- better transportation within the city

- more desirable climate

- more recreation opportunities

- better higher education and health care

- and more favorable economic trends

a new attorney interested in forming a partnership and specializing in tax law would likely do better there. Although Memphis does have the advantage in population characteristics such as income and education levels, city government expenditures, the arts, preparatory education and effective buying income, the factors in which Birmingham leads are more numerous

19

and more important in making the choice. So I recommend that Mr. Mason

begin his practice in Birmingham.

534

20

Bibliography

1. Birmingham Area Chamber of Commerce, *Major Employers in the Birmingham Area,* 19xx.

2. *Birmingham and You,* South O'Town Realty Co., Birmingham, Alabama, 19xx.

3. *County and City Data Book,* 19xx, U.S. Government Printing Office, Washington, D.C. 19xx.

4. "For Newcomers, and Perhaps You," *Birmingham Magazine,* February, 19xx.

5. The League of Women Voters of Greater Birmingham, *Know Your Schools,* The Birmingham Area Chamber of Commerce, Birmingham, Alabama, 19xx.

6. Memphis Area Chamber of Commerce Pamphlet 976M1000, *Memphis Major Employers,* Memphis Area Chamber of Commerce, 19xx.

7. *A Profile of Mid-America's Big New City—Memphis,* Memphis Area Chamber of Commerce, 19xx.

8. "1976 Survey of Buying Power," *Sales and Marketing Management,* July 26, 19xx.

9. "1975 Survey of Buying Power," *Sales and Marketing Management,* July 21, 19xx.

10. U.S. Bureau of The Census, *Census of the Population, 19xx, Vol. 1 Characteristics of the Population, Part 2,* U.S. Government Printing Office, Washington, D.C. 19xx.

11. U.S. Bureau of the Census, *Census of the Population, 19xx, Vol. 1 Characteristics of the Population, Part 44,* U.S. Government Printing Office, Washington, D.C. 19xx.

12. U.S. Bureau of the Census, *Census of Selected Service Industries, 19xx, Subject Series, Legal Services,* U.S. Government Printing Office, Washington, D.C. 19xx.

Checklist for Complete Analytical Reports

PRELIMINARY PARTS AND MECHANICS (PPM)

1. If you use a *cover*, be sure it carries at least the title and author's name (or is transparent, or has a cutout so that these items on the title page are visible). Make sure it has the appearance you want and is the right size for your report. See pp. 495.

2. The *title page* needs at least four items: (*a*) the title (phrased for precision, interest, and conciseness—pp. 496–98—and typed as explained on pp. 472–74), (*b*) the authorizer's name and title, (*c*) the author's name and title, and (*d*) the place and date (in that order and in center-balanced or other pleasant design—pp. 496 and 511). It may also have the organization's name, a brief abstract, a distribution list, and/or a project- or serial-number identification.

3. A *transmittal letter or memo*, in regular letter/memo form (Chapter 1):

   a. Starts by transmitting the report and, naturally and subordinately, referring to the topic and authorization (p. 498).

   b. May reveal briefly only the general decision or may synopsize the report (unless a separate synopsis comes later).

   c. Ends expressing appreciation (and perhaps willingness to help further). (See p. 498 for fuller explanation and other possible contents and pp. 512 and 574 for illustrations.)

4. The *table of contents* (or simply contents, p. 499) lists the later successive parts and body sections of the report, with beginning page numbers for all and (optional, but helpful) outline symbols before the body sections.

   a. A separate synopsis (if used, p. 500), as the next page following the contents table, is the first item listed (with no outline symbol, flush at the left margin, and with the first of your vertically aligned, spaced-period leader lines between items and the page number column). See p. 513.

   b. The greatest part of the table of contents shows the organization/outline of the body, as explained on p. 502 ff. and illustrated on p. 515 ff.

   (1) Whether you give outline symbols (preferable and helpful—in either decimal or roman form—p. 462) and all levels of heads and subheads (or just the first two or three) is your option (or assignment, or the organization's SOP—standard operating procedure).

   (2) In any case the wording (not the type form) of heads here and in the report must be identical.

Checklist for Complete Analytical Reports

(*continued*)

    (3)   Break too-long lines to leave at least seven spaces between them and the page-number column, indent the carry-over(s) and subdivisions, and make leaders of at least three spaced periods, with a space before and after.

    (4)   Double-space between at least the parts and major divisions, and systematically single-space elsewhere only to keep to one page.

    (5)   Remember that page numbers and roman outline-symbol numbers line up on the right.

  c. Supplementary parts (i.e., optional appendix and bibliography) do *not* have outline symbols but do carry on the arabic page numbering of the text.

5. A separate *synopsis* (SY) or *informative abstract*—the report in a nutshell, reduced between 10:1 and 20:1, but preferably to *one* page—is usually single-spaced with double spacing between paragraphs.

  a. Make the first paragraph stress the problem solution (or its main part) and subordinately reveal enough about the authorizer, purpose, and preparer for extra copies of the synopsis alone to be clear.

  b. Compactly and specifically present (in a paragraph for each major division, in order and preferably in proportion) your main supporting facts and figures, while subordinately interweaving any necessary background, method, and scope.

  c. Emphasize findings, not analysis—preferably in present tense. Rely on sequence and only short transitional words for coherence.

6. Give early, careful attention to the special *report mechanics* (RM) (layout and typing and, if needed, the generally applicable points of mechanics (GM)—see TM in Appendix B):

  a. Double space the body and make its bottom and side margins 1–1½″, top slightly less, plus extra space for the bite of any binding used.

  b. Start a new page only to (1) start a new part (the body is all one—see p. 494), (2) leave a bottom margin, or (3) allow for at least two lines of copy below a heading.

  c. Starting with the title fly, if used, count preliminary pages down through the synopsis and (beginning with the table of contents) number them in lowercase romans.

Checklist for Complete Analytical Reports

(*continued*)

   d. Give all later pages arabic numbers, *without decorations* (p. 494), a double space above the right ends of lines (except centered at the bottom on first pages of report parts).

   e. Vary placement, spacing above and below, and type form of headings to show different levels. Underline any not in solid capitals and double-space centered heads of more than one line. See pp. 472–74.

ORGANIZATION/OUTLINING (O)

1. Phrase your title to indicate the nature, purpose, and limits of your study and to provide a basis of classification (see p. 496 and Item 1, p. 461); then make the text's major divisional headings on that basis.

2. The basis may point to comparison, partition of a whole, factors to be considered, or (rarely) time periods or spatial areas, but not likely to cost-benefit or before-after analyses or source or method of getting the information. In making comparisons leading to a choice, use the criteria as the main divisions, the subjects as subheads, and anything about methods as interwoven material.

3. Use no heading for your whole text (p. 460) and no single subhead anywhere (Item 4, p. 463). The major divisions of your report (symbolized by 1.0, 2.0, 3.0 . . . or I, II, III . . .) are first the introduction, then the logical divisions of your topic (the text, usually in two to five parts), and your conclusions and recommendations (together or separate).

4. Phrase each heading to cover any and all of its subdivisions.

5. In phrasing, placing, and sequencing all division headings at all levels, make clear the relationship of each part to its whole and its function in your interpretation. Outline symbols may help.

6. Maintain parallelism of grammatical form among headings of the same class (p. 470), using synonyms where necessary to avoid monotony of wording.

7. Try to make your headings informative (not just topical) as well as precisely indicative of what they include (pp. 472 and 496).

8. Use just enough headings to help show your organization.

9. Use placement and type variations in headings (and maybe outline symbols) to show their status in the outline and relations to others (pp. 472–74).

Checklist for Complete Analytical Reports

(continued)

INTRODUCTION (I)

Clear presentation of the *purpose, method, scope,* and *basic plan* is the main duty of the introduction, to provide a basis for judging the report's soundness.

1. Put the exact report title at the top of the first page of the body.
2. Then, for this first major division, try to phrase a more meaningful title than the stock term "Introduction." See p. 503.
3. Though you may need several paragraphs to explain your *purpose* clearly enough, (*a*) be sure your purpose is compatible with your title and organizational plan and (*b*) provide one particular sentence that is a pointed, concise statement of your problem.
4. Give a short history of the problem only if needed as a lead-in to purpose (details, if helpful, can go in a later flashback—or maybe appendix).
5. Explain your *methods* of gathering data specifically enough to show thoroughness and be convincing; but significant details beyond a reader's ability to remember (like questions in a long questionnaire or settings and measurements in a laboratory experiment) can best come in later with the data.
6. As part of *scope,* clearly show any limits of coverage not made in the title; but justified (not excuse-making) limits of time or money are more appropriate in the letter of transmittal.
7. You might include a glossary for a large number of necessary unusual terms; for only a few, preferably explain each parenthetically the first time it comes up.
8. Try to cover the required elements of the introduction without breaking it into too many pieces (more than *purpose, method, scope,* and *plan*), especially if the parts are short.
9. In a "Basic Plan" section at the end of the introduction, brief the reader on the sequence of major topics coming.
10. Keep findings, conclusions, and recommendations out of the introduction. If you want to get them to the reader early, a synopsis or even the letter of transmittal is a better place.

STYLE (S)

1. Remember that a natural style is clearer, easier, and more interesting than impersonal style for both writer and reader (pp. 474–76.

Checklist for Complete Analytical Reports

(*continued*)

2. Enliven your style and increase readability by (*a*) using commonly understood words and short, direct sentences and paragraphs, (*b*) making people (not things) subjects and/or objects of many if not most sentences, (*c*) using mostly active voice, (*d*) eliminating "It is" and "There are" sentence beginnings, (*e*) using discrete (but not overlisted) itemizations for pointed, concise statements like conclusions and recommendations, (*f*) putting the emphasis where it belongs (see *Emp* and *Sub* in Appendix B), and (*g*) presenting quantities in easily read and remembered forms (ratios, fractions, rounded numbers, simplified percentages, rankings—see p. 467 and Fig in Appendix B). Remember that the relative status of something (percent, ratio, or rank-qualitative factors) is often more significant than the absolute value (quantitative).

3. To avoid seeming prejudiced, state plausible assumptions made, give immediate and specific evidence to support points, give all the same kind(s) of information about each compared subject, and avoid emotionally persuasive passages and disclaimers like "objective," "unbiased," "impersonal."

4. Use the universal present tense to indicate continuing existence for things and tendencies that existed in the past, exist now, and are likely to continue.

5. Don't use headings as antecedents of pronouns; your text should read coherently without the heads.

6. Make clear, by topic statement at the beginning of each big section, the topic and any subdivisions (in the order of later treatment). See p. 469.

7. At the end of a sizable section, sum it up with emphasis on its significance to the overall problem (and preferably with a transitional forward look to the next topic).

8. Interpret key points from graphics in relation to your objective, *emphasizing the message* and (by parenthetical, midsentence, or nonsubject mention) *subordinating the reference to the graphic and its location.*

9. By evidence, explanation, and logic lead the reader to foresee likely conclusions and recommendations coming; but (ordinarily) leave the explicit statetments of them until the end.

GRAPHICS (GR)

1. Use graphics whenever helpful; but omit useless ones (p. 477).

Checklist for Complete Analytical Reports

(*continued*)

2. Choose the best kind, form, and arrangement of graphic for the kind of data (pp. 485 ff. and Gr in Appendix B).

3. For reader convenience, place graphics near the discussion (small ones maybe on graph paper on the same page, larger ones on the next page).

4. Give graphics proper titles, numbers (charts and tables in separate consecutive series), labeled parts, and crediting of published ones as Source: (plus your regular footnote or other citation form).

5. Give reliable dates of graphic information (not always the date of publication), maybe in parentheses after the title.

6. Lead in with discussion of the point and proper introduction of the graphic (emphasizing what to see in it), tell *subordinately* where it is if not in sight (p. 539(8)), and (usually) follow with necessary key points of emphasis or interpretation.

7. For easy reading and close relationships, consider small spot tables closely associated with different points, though they may all come from one collective source table (appendix material) that buries key points.

DOCUMENTATION (DOC)

When you use others' material (except as explained in Item 1 below), you must give credit (to avoid plagiarism) and you want to cite the source as support for your point. The usual means for published material are a bibliography and specific citations in the text, source indications on graphics, and possibly footnotes.

1. Put in your bibliography an alphabetical listing of publications from which you used an author's special ideas, facts (including graphics), or quotations. See pp. 488–92 for explanations and forms. The word *special* means that the requirement does not apply to information that is (*a*) common knowledge, (*b*) obvious, or (*c*) widely available in many sources of the kind.

2. Make specific citations (at the points you used others' materials) in the simplest way. See pp. 491–92 for explanations, the report (pp. 511–34) for illustrations, and GR 4 above for citing sources of graphics. Remember that to promote continuity and ease of reading, interweaving citations into the text is preferable to footnotes.

3. Avoid repeating a citation (except for different page numbers) as long as you're drawing from the same source.

4. For convenience, number footnotes (if used) anew on each page.

Checklist for Complete Analytical Reports

(*concluded*)

5. Cite the basic circumstances in the text or a footnote where you use information from interviews, speeches, and letters (which do *not* belong in the bibliography); explain questionnaires, observations, and experiments as sources in the methods section of the Introduction (plus necessary specific questions, conditions, or procedures, along with the findings in the text—I 5 above.

6. Use no source citations for the synopsis, conclusions, or recommendations; they all derive from the text, where needed source citations must appear.

7. Though you have some choice of the documentation forms you use (pp. 488–92), unless restricted by assignment in school or on the job, be sure to use an established, clear, and consistent one and *get it exactly right*—in content, capitalization, sequence, and punctuation.

CONCLUSIONS AND RECOMMENDATIONS (C/R)

1. Introduce no new facts in the section; it derives from, maybe quickly recaps, and interprets information presented before.

2. Put conclusions and recommendations (together or separately—p. 508) in their order of importance.

3. State conclusions and recommendations pointedly (specifically and concisely, with key supporting facts and figures), as firmly as your information justifies (rarely involving "prove"), and (preferably) itemized.

4. Take a stand (including "My findings prove nothing," if necessary); being wishy-washy suggests inadequacy or incompetence.

5. Make sure your conclusions and recommendations derive from facts and explanations formerly presented; leave surprise endings to mystery writers.

6. You may conclude and suggest action but not command.

CASES FOR COMPLETE ANALYTICAL REPORTS

Whether you are going to use Cases 1 and 2 or not, you should read them for points that should apply to nearly any major report-writing project.

1. Subject to approval by your instructor, choose a topic for your report. Preferably it should be a real problem actually faced by a company, organization, or individual; if not, it should be a problem likely faced by

someone somewhere. It should be for one reader or a very limited group of specific readers. A term-theme topic or something like a textbook chapter will not do because it is not a report. If you can't quickly give the name or title of somebody other than a teacher who might ask for such a report, your topic is unsuitable. It should be an analytical report: the relevant facts plus interpretation and evaluation of the advantages and disadvantages (the pros and cons) of at least two alternatives and the eventual selection of one in your final conclusions and recommendations. In other words, it must be a problem which you help someone to solve. See the list in Case 3 for suggestions if you can't readily think of one—perhaps from your own work experience.

It should be a topic for which you can get information in the library *and* (not *or*) through either interviews, questionnaires, or your own observation or experimentation.

You should settle on a topic early in the term and should not change topics after midterm for any reason. The kind of problem we're talking about usually takes 10 to 20 pages for the text alone and requires most of the school term. You and your teacher will of course cover regular class work and the shorter assignments meanwhile.

As your instructor directs, be prepared to submit on one typed page

a. A tentative title (not *now* worded to show a preconception of the outcome, but clear, concise and catching). (See p. 496.)
b. A one-sentence statement of the purpose of the report. (See p. 503.)
c. An indication of who the readers are and your relationship (actual or assumed) to them. (See p. 439.)
d. Sources and/or methods of collecting data, including the titles of five items from your tentative bibliography. (See pp. 447 ff.)
e. Major divisions (with subdivisions, if you like) of the coverage or body of the report. (See pp. 460–64 and 493–94.)

Be prepared at any time to give your instructor a progress report in memo form, indicating what you have accomplished, what difficulties you've encountered, what remains to be done, and your plans for finishing. (See p. 563.)

At the time directed by your instructor, submit the report with title page, letter of transmittal, contents listing, synopsis, body (including introduction, facts and interpretations intermingled but in two to five major divisions, conclusions, and recommendations), bibliography, and appendix if necessary.

As further clarification and suggestion, here are some of the better topics chosen by students in one class:

Comparative evaluation of swimming pool (or goldfish pool) disinfectants under specific conditions.

Comparative evaluation of materials and procedures to reduce black-shank damage to tobacco plants (specific conditions).

Whether X Company should expand (or restrict, or diversify) its product line (or territory).

You'll find a long list of other possibilities in Case 3.

2.   One of the requests coming to your desk as director of Factseekers, Inc., New York 10032, is from the president of (name of firm supplied by your instructor). The company is a chain of retail (type of store supplied by your instructor) stores with outlets in most major cities. The chain is now contemplating opening a store in either one of two cities (names of two cities supplied by your instructor).

The letter to you as director, signed by the company president, reads:

Will you please submit in report form your analysis of retail sales possibilities for (specific goods) in (names of two cities)?

Before deciding where our next branch will be, we would like the opinion of a firm of your caliber.

Naturally we want to know the story on population, buying power, retail sales—with special emphasis on (specific goods)—competition, and current business. But please include other data which will be helpful to us in making our choice.

Your problem is only to determine which city would likely bring us the larger volume of sales. Please do not attempt to cover taxes, wage scales, real estate costs, or availability of sites, and maybe crime rates that might affect us. After your determination, we will require a shorter report on each of those topics.

Since we plan to have the store in operation within a year's time, will you please confirm that you can submit the report no later than (specific date as assigned), subject to the same rates as on previous studies?

From secondary library sources you can get all the necessary comparative data: *Statistical Abstract of the United States; County and City Data Book; Market Guide of Editor and Publisher;* Rand McNally's *Commercial Atlas and Marketing Guide; Sales Management Survey of Buying Power; Marketing/Communication's* studies like *Sales Planning Guide* and *Major American Markets;* and *Consumer Markets,* published by the Standard Rate and Data Service. The foregoing are some of your more useful sources. But they are not intended to be an exhaustive list. You will of course want to consult the censuses of population, business, and manufacturers for (respectively) breakdowns of populations, influence of wholesaling and retailing on the local economy, and the value added to the economy by manufacturing. In all cases you will want the latest reliable data; recency of information is important.

Your entire analysis should be focused on the answer to the question: Which of the two towns is a better market for selling more of the specific merchandise this store sells? Population is, of course, a factor—size as well as distribution and character. The retail market area always needs examining. Income figures are significant (a person with $4 is in a better position to buy than one with only $2). Retail sales indicate whether people are willing to spend their money (total retail sales, per capita retail sales, and retail sales figures in the particular line you're investigating—if you can find them). Sources of business strength are appropriate considerations (a manufacturing town suffers more than a distribution center during a recession; a community depending primarily upon farming for its sustenance weathers economic storms more readily than one heavily dependent upon shipbuilding, for instance). And the current business picture (as measured by construction, postal figures, employment, and bank deposits) is important for its diagnostic value.

The list of topics above is merely to help you start thinking about what to include; it is not intended to be inclusive, orderly, or arbitrary. For instance, no study of this kind would ever omit competitive factors.

This is assigned: Exclude any discussion of banking facilities, communications facilities (newspapers, radio stations, advertising agencies), and transportation facilities. These are adequate in both cities and so would not affect the decision. Furthermore, the people would have done enough reading themselves to know where the cities are—and the pertinent geographical and climate features.

Once you've made the final decision of what factors to include and—just as important—the order in which to lay them out, the analysis becomes a matter of simply comparing the two cities simultaneously to show which city is the better market—more people with more money to spend, and the apparent willingness to spend it, especially for this kind of merchandise.

Do not attempt to turn out a chamber of commerce root-for-the-home team piece of propaganda. Impersonally, impartially present the facts about the two cities and make your decision on the total evidence.

An analytical report is not just a compilation of tables and labels. Your report must present the facts in statistical display (graphics primarily, for readability). Without these, your report has no base and, in the reader's mind, no authenticity. But the most significant part of the report is your own expository (analytical) comment which explains the significance of the data you have gathered.

Of course, your grade will depend partly on physical appearance and mechanical correctness (freedom from errors in spelling, punctuation, and grammar). Counting most heavily, however, will be

1. Organization (the order of points for logic and emphasis).
2. Readability (stylistic factors).
3. Complete, authentic evidence and its reliability, analysis, and documentation.

3. Parts of this assignment probably are not suitable for a large class in a small community because too many students would be getting in too many business executives' hair. This danger can be less serious, however, if students work in teams, at least on the data-collecting part of report writing. Also, consider the listed topics, which are *not* report titles, just suggestions to start thinking about what could be an endless list of the same kind of thing.

For your choice of the following topics, assume that you can and will arrange amicably for access to, observation of, or experimentation with the obviously necessary facts (usually available only in a small local firm). Then write the kind of report (form, tone, and length) which the facts and the situation seem to require (or your instructor assigns). Assume that the appropriate person has asked you to do the report, and assume an appropriate position for yourself. In most cases you will likely be an employee; but in some, you might reasonably assume that you are a consultant on a fee basis. Each situation is to involve thorough study of existing conditions and application of well-established, up-to-date principles (learned from courses, articles, books, and/or people) leading to recommendations for wise decision about or betterment of the situation.

Approved vacation practices in a specific local firm.

Traffic-accident "hot spots" in a town or city (or, if too large, an appropriate area).

A campus bus service? Volume? Pay? Routes? Costs/income? Franchised/school operated?

Student costs of attending your school (low/medium/high). See p. 554, get the information, and be specific.

Causes for failure in college work (student/school viewpoint).

Justifiable improvements at a specific sorority/fraternity/dorm.

A new (or up-for-sale) riding stable in your town—prospects for success?

Student TV, magazine, or newspaper preferences/habits at your school.

Proper credit (less, same, more?) for this (or other) business communcation course.

Best buy in this year's (under 10—hp outboard motors, vacuum cleaners, . . .)?

English errors students make in (first business communication course).

Training needed for writing/speaking done by local business executives in first five years out of college.

Student reasons for choosing to attend your school.

Paralegals—should X Law School train them?

Paramedics—should X Medical School train them?

Needed improvements in X Company's employee motivation.

The absentee-worker problem at X.

Bugs in X's inventory control.

The letter writing done by a small local firm. (Only students who have studied letter writing should attempt this assignment.)

The public relations of a local firm (limited parts, if necessary).

The accounting procedures of a local firm (limited aspects, if necessary).

The advertising program and budget (not copy) of a small local firm.

The advertising copy (not program and budget) used by a local firm.

The physical layout (floor plan) of a local store (same problem a housewife works on when she moves the furniture around).

The hiring and firing and promoting criteria (or just one criterion) and procedures in X (business firm), related to personnel turnovers.

The financing arrangements of . . . .

The stock control procedures of . . . .

The fringe benefits (or just one) or salary scales of . . . .

The materials-handling procedures of . . . .

Pilferage losses and control in . . . .

A motion-time study of some local processing or manufacturing operation.

Any other problem of this type which you think of and can get facts on, and which your instructor approves.

Proposed equipment and procedures for fire prevention and/or fighting in a certain forest, building, or operation.

Should a given company devote some of its lands/efforts to producing . . . (a kind of production or service not now emphasized).

Solution to the problem of poor growth and fruiting/flowering of certain plants on a large lot (or crops on a specific field or farm).

Critical analysis (with suggestions) of the company publications of a comparatively small local firm.

Possible computer applications in a local library (or company).

Suggestions for improving appeal and income at a small fee-charging, publicly or privately operated park and lake.

Would a proposed campground (private, specific location) be a successful business venture?

Analysis of a local company's employee relations problems, with suggestions for improvement.

Would a specific large wood products company be wise to set up a sawmill and/or paper mill in a certain locality where it has some landholdings?

To have or not to have coffee breaks for a given company's employees.

What the people of a 10,000–100,000 community think of their public schools, with emphasis on suggested improvements.

Any of these problems can generate an oral report if your instructor so directs.

4. Track the performance of the stocks of several companies in a field (automobile, insurance, hospital, steel, whatever) over a period of time

agreed upon between you and your instructor, but preferably at least ten years. This will depend on your sources and the amount of time you have for research. Compare the stocks' performance against the Dow Jones Industrials Average, factoring in changes in dividend payments, stock splits, and the like. Pay particular attention to the volume of trades in the stocks versus the volume of trades of the Dow Jones Industrials or the market. Your object is to analyze the stocks and come to conclusions as to which are suitable for long-term investment (resistance to large swings in the market and a general trend upward) and which might be useful for short-term investment (abrupt movements up and down, correlation with the market).

Basic sources of data are the files of *The Wall Street Journal* and *Barron's* for stocks and Dow Jones Average and the indexes to financial periodicals for other information. Your library will undoubtedly yield a number of books dealing with stock investment and the stock market which will familiarize you with these topics. A number of firms advertise in *Barron's* offering charts of stocks' performances which often contain a good deal of other information and can save you a great deal of time. (A talk with a local stockbroker may also yield some of these.) On a proper request, many of these will send selected charts to students free or at small cost.

At your option (or that of your instructor) you may consider in your report such other factors as changes in the nation's economy, political changes, and environmental factors (energy, weather, and so on). The more elements you consider in your report, naturally, the longer and more complex it will be. If you deliver an oral report rather than a written one, your report will be shorter and, perhaps, simpler, but you will have to deal more carefully with visual aids.

5. Though the following case is about local golf-tournament facilities, a student may—with teacher approval—make the necessary adjustments and write a comparable report on local facilities for any other kind of athletic tournament, or about facilities for a business or professional meeting.

For the American Golf Association, you are to prepare a report on the golf courses in your area, an early step toward getting a regional pro-am tournament in your area. Your report will not overtly "sell" the AGA but should come up with an honest appraisal of the facilities available. You should consider courses within a 20- or 30-mile radius in your report, but restrict yourself to the number of courses you and your teacher agree you can reasonably inspect (probably two to four).

You will have to go to each golf course. Carefully look over the clubhouse, especially the restaurant or other food service facilities. How many people can they accommodate? At one time? Over a three-hour period? What about a bar? Room for desks and tables for registration, scorekeeping, and officials? A room that could be set up for a press room? Adequate parking spaces available? Area nearby adaptable for additional parking? Think of as many items to investigate and report on as you can. Try to imagine a tournament being staged at the course and what activities will take place and what will be needed for them at the clubhouse and clubhouse area.

Play the course if you can, but walk it in any case. Make a sketch of each hole showing tees, fairway, rough, bunkers (sand traps), tree and water hazards, and the greens. If you have watched coverage of golf tournaments on television, you will have an idea of the kind of simple maps of holes you should prepare. Get a scorecard for the course: This will give you the distances and pars, and usually a map of the course you can base yours on.

Through your own observation or interviews with golfers and course personnel, define the most difficult holes on the course. You should include sketches or maps of these in your report that are more detailed, perhaps, than those for less difficult holes.

Pay attention to the condition of the tees, greens, and fairways, especially the greens. If your library has some of the books on golf course design, they will give you a wealth of information and some excellent ideas of other things to look for.

Your personal research should result in a wealth of data from which you can describe the courses in your area. On the basis of your investigation, recommend which course should get the tournament, and which others would be suitable as back-up courses and practice courses.

6. Though the following case is on scouting a baseball team, teacher and student can agree to adapt it to any other kind of team.

Assume that you are a scout for any major-league baseball team and that your team faces any other team in an important game (or series). On the basis of a thorough analysis of the opposing team's and its individual players' past records, recommend specific tactics.

You may assume that you scouted the opposing team many times and recorded individual and team records in detail. Since you didn't really, get your data wherever you can—next-day newspaper accounts, special baseball books, or the most recent *World Almanac* (which has a surprising amount of detail on baseball).

Obviously, your report will be addressed to the manager. Would your players also read all of it or even the parts that most affect how they should play their positions?

This report requires considerable knowledge of the kind of game involved—in this case, baseball. (Incidentally, the idea for this assignment came from post-series newspaper accounts of just such a report prepared by the series winner and given credit by the manager for his team's winning.)

7. Inspect the equipment and/or furniture in a laboratory on your campus where at least some of it needs to be replaced. Write a report which evaluates the equipment and/or furniture and specifically justifies and recommends any replacements and/or additions. To whom should you address the report? What role are you playing—i.e., who do you assume you *are* to be writing the report? What other sources of information will you use to supplement inspection? Should you recommend specific brands, models, and prices of things to be bought? If so, you will need to get acquainted with catalogs and brochures on such things—or with the famous Sweet's File, the architect's bible, available in any architect's office or architectural library.

As a modification of the situation, write the report proposing and justifying just what equipment and/or furniture to buy for a new laboratory, a whole building, or some other new structure your school is now constructing.

8. The president of the small company where you work, Miriam Day, is the twin sister of Morton Day (Case 18, p. 596) and is facing the same kind of labor unrest. Hearing from Morton about how his new IRA plan has calmed his workers down, and having read an article that says a Keough plan is sometimes better, Miriam Day asks you to compare the two for possible use in the company. Take a small real company about which you can get information, assume that Day gives you a deadline (the due date your teacher assigns you), and write the complete analytical report your president wants.

9. Obtain a copy of the *Business Publications* edition of Standard Rate and Data Service. If your library does not have this monthly publication, see if you can get an out-of-date copy from a local advertising agency, or write to Standard Rate and Data Service, Inc., 5201 Old Orchard Road, Skokie, Illinois 60076, for the price on a single copy.

SRDS Business Publications lists just about every trade magazine or business publication in this country, and a good number of foreign ones. Each listing contains a wealth of information about the magazine, including advertising rates, mechanical requirements, editorial policy, circulation, and so forth. Also, many magazines place advertisements in the directory, with further information for potential advertisers.

Choose one of the larger categories, such as "Metalworking" or "Electronics" or "Chemicals." Choose a product common to the field you will work in (lathes for "Metalworking," for instance, testing instruments for "Electronics," or protective clothing for "Chemicals") and assume you work for the advertising agency serving that manufacturer.

Completely analyze the magazines in the category you are working in, on as many points as you can. The listings are comparable, so this is fairly easy. Determine which magazines are the leaders, which are second best, and which are specialized and not directly comparable to the more general magazines in the field. On the basis of your exhaustive analysis, recommend which eight magazines your client should advertise in, and why. Justify rejecting at least four others.

For an idea of what goes into a media report like this one, check for textbooks and other books and articles on media selection in your library. An interview with a local advertising agency executive or company advertising manager would be very helpful, as would be an interview with an appropriate professor or two.

By agreement, teacher and student can control the size of this project by limiting the number of publications to be reported on. To enlarge it, say for a group to handle, consider also using SRDS publications on radio and television stations and consumer publications, and preparing a full-scale media plan using a variety of media.

| # Preparing short reports

Letter reports
Memorandums
Justification reports
Progress reports
Credit reports
Annual reports
Short analytical reports

THE BEST FORM for a report depends on the situation—mainly who its recipient is (and the relation to the reporter), its purpose, and its length.
This chapter explains and illustrates various kinds of short reports written
in the most important forms. To save your time and our space, we use cross
references instead of repeating relevant parts of the two preceding chapters (for research methods and certain aspects of report organization,
forms, and style) and the following one (for oral reporting). Thus this
chapter concentrates on written short reports.

As with all reports, classification of short ones can be on various bases.
Form and content are the two most common. To avoid making up new
names for short reports, however, in this chapter we list and discuss them
by their common names, although this plan involves shifting and therefore
does not provide a strictly logical classification.

Because reports apparently named for their content have become pretty
well associated with certain forms, however, the seeming violation of logic
in classification is more apparent than real. The primary basis of classification here is therefore form (with the exceptions explained where they
apply). Yet our primary emphasis is not on learning the forms themselves
but on the uses of different forms and the information, organization, interpretation, and style in the reports.

*As you study these topics, please realize that we do not present the
illustrations as perfect reports, and certainly not as models for you to follow slavishly or copy parrotlike. At best, they show acceptable content,
form, and general style for their particular situations as starters to your
thinking on these points for your situation.*

Although we recognize that strictly informational, periodic reports are the most numerous kind, we do not devote our main attention to them because they are mostly printed forms to be filled in with figures and perhaps a little other writing. We therefore treat the commonly used forms which do raise real report-writing problems.

LETTER REPORTS

Many short reports of one to four pages are in regular business letter form. Usually they go between organizations rather than between departments of the same organization, where memorandum form is more likely.

Since the letter report is likely to be longer than the usual letter, however, and since it *is* a report, it may, while otherwise using the regular letter form explained in Chapter 1, take on the following special features of reports:

1. More than usually careful organization.
2. Objectivity (absence of emotional suasion, viewing both sides of the situation, enough interweaving or implying of methods and sources to assure soundness).
3. Use of appropriate subject lines, subheads, and itemizations where helpful.
4. Use of graphic devices where helpful and economical.

Depending on whether the message will likely meet with reader approval, disappointment, or resistance, the letter report should follow the A–, B–, or (rarely) C–plan, as explained on pp. 78–82 and illustrated thoroughly in Chapters 5, 7, and 8, respectively. More specifically, any of the organizational plans discussed on pp. 463(8) may apply to a letter report.

Although a letter report, like any other, needs to convince the reader that its facts are reliable, it rarely needs a separate section or even a separate paragraph explaining authorization, purpose, or methods and sources used in collecting data. Most likely the writer got the assignment because the boss knew that person had the information immediately available, was already a recognized expert on the subject, or knew just how to study the problem. For the simple problems appropriate to letter reports, the methods and sources are frequently so obvious as to need no explanation anyway.

If any explanations are necessary, usually the best way to give them is in incidental phrases interwoven right along with the information: "Inspection of . . . reveals . . ."; "Legal precedent in cases like . . . is clearly . . ."; "Microscopic examination shows . . ."; or ". . . , according to such authorities as. . . ."

Indeed, letter reports are like other reports except for the form which gives them their name, the limits of length and hence of topics for which they are suitable, and their usually more familiar style. A letter in impersonal style would be almost a joke. We do not think any kind of report should necessarily be in impersonal style, and even those people who do will almost certainly approve a natural style in letter reports.

Two common types of letter reports are those about job and credit applicants (personnel and credit reports), already discussed on pp. 111 and 112–13, respectively. You should study both the explanations and the illustrations there. Notice that both the illustrations use subject lines effectively. Note, too, that both begin immediately with important information because they face no problem of reader disappointment or resistance (A–plan).

Personnel and credit reports, however, do have the legal problem of avoiding libel suit by referring to the request for information, trying to be fair to both parties, and asking confidential use of the information. Notice how the two illustrations handle that problem.

These two kinds of reports should be informational, in that they should rely on facts and subordinate or entirely eliminate unsupported opinions —and certainly recommendations. But letter reports may be either informational or analytical. In some cases they are more nearly directives than reports, but directives are more likely to be in memo form.

Because the following message is somewhat bad news and the reader may be reluctant to take the suggested action, the report uses the more convincing inductive rather than the faster-moving deductive plan. You will note, too, that it uses no subject line. To do so would defeat the psychological purpose of the inductive plan of getting in the arguments before giving the conclusion. As you always should when you have a step-by-step procedure or a series of pointed, emphatic principles, qualities, conclusions, or recommendations to convey, this report uses itemization effectively at the end.

```
Dear Mr. Rogers:
In our audit of your company's books on January 16, we
discovered that for years the total net profit has been added
to surplus.  This procedure is usually correct.

For the past three years you have had a bond agreement,
however, which specifies that a sinking-fund reserve of
3 percent of the par value of the bonds must be set up
annually out of surplus.  That agreement is legally binding.
Moreover, state law requires you to set up the reserve in this
situation.  Only the remaining profit, of course, can be
added to surplus.

Laws of this type protect investors and brokers who desire a
true picture of the financial condition of companies.

The laws also give you protection.  Setting up a
separate reserve prevents the unlawful declaration of
```

dividends by directors. In other words, the proper
presentation of surplus figures is an aid to better
management.

We therefore recommend that you

1. Take immediate steps to set up the reserve.

2. Transfer to it now, from surplus, 3 percent of the par
   value of the bonds for each of the past three years.

3. Regularly each year for the duration of the bond
   agreement transfer the required amount from surplus to
   the reserve.

Both the shortness and the nature of the material made divisional headings unnecessary in the preceding illustration.

Conversely, both length and content make headings almost mandatory
for effective presentation in letter reports of two pages or more, as in the
following. It is a reply to a school superintendent's request that recent
graduates report on their college expenses for passing on to high-school
seniors. (You'll notice that the way of life pictured is not common on college campuses today, but that does not keep the report from showing the
helpfulness of carefully classifying information under suitable headings.)

Dear Mr. Loudenslager:

Please give John my congratulations on his good record in
school last semester. Apparently he will be ready for college
next year; so I hope the information you requested will help
him as well as your other seniors.

I've based the cost figures I'm giving on one semester here
for a male student. Although I have not kept detailed records,
my figures are more realistic than the somewhat outdated ones
in the catalog you have.

Being neither plush nor poor, I have spent according to the
Typical column, but I have classmates whose expenses more
nearly match both the Liberal and the Conservative figures.

Estimated Expenses Table

	Conservative	Typical	Liberal
Course fee	$000	$000	$000
Room and board	000	000	000
Books and supplies	00	00	00
Physical education	00	00	00
R.O.T.C.	00	00	00
Clothing	00	00	00
Laundry and dry cleaning	00	00	00
Transportation	00	00	000
Incidentals	00	00	000

FIXED EXPENSES

Course fees.—Although the regular course fee is $000, certain
courses and curricula like music, law, medicine, and veterinary

medicine do require extra fees. Insofar as I know, these extra
fees have not changed from the catalog you have.

Physical Education.—All students must take two years' credit
in gym. The $00 fee is for locker rental and wear and tear on
equipment.

R.O.T.C.—All able-bodied students may take two years' credit
in military science. When the equipment is returned after
completion of the course, the fee will be refunded.

VARIABLE EXPENSES

Living Expense

College residence halls.—Adequate dormitories are available
on the campus. Meals are served in the dining rooms seven
days a week. Room and board is $000 a semester. The resident
supplies linen, toweling, and pillow.

Fraternities.—Room and board in a fraternity may vary from a
low of $000 to a high of $000. The average is about $000.

Cooperatives.—A student who desires to may join a co-op, in
which a group may defray part of the cost of living by each
helping with the work. Room and board in a co-op usually runs
to about $000 a semester.

Individual rooms.—Rooms in approved homes cost about $00–$00
a semester, two students to a room. Food in local restaurants
costs about $000–$000.

Apartments.—Rent for an apartment will run from $00 for the
most modest to $000, depending upon closeness to school,
quality and comfort, and whether the student shares it or
occupies it alone. Utilities are usually extra and are not
included here.

Working for meals.—Students who want to do so can nearly
always find jobs working for their meals in dormitory dining
rooms or in local restaurants.

Clothing.—Some students who attend college buy nearly entirely
new wardrobes. Others may get along quite well for some time
with what they have. So clothing expense is highly variable,
as my figures in the table show. For most students, college
clothing costs should be only a little more than for high
school clothing.

Laundry and dry cleaning.—Facilities are available for a
student to do laundry in the dormitories. Several laundromats
are also convenient to the area. Dry-cleaning prices are the
same as at home.

Transportation

At school.—The majority of the activities are on the campus
or within walking distance. Bus fare to town is 30 cents a
round trip. Taxis are also available. The student who expects
to have a car will find that a jalopy is not the thing here
and that keeping a respectable car can hardly cost less than
$000 a semester. Depreciation alone could cost that much on
some cars without anything for insurance, upkeep, and gasoline.

To and from school.—Most students will find it inconvenient as
well as expensive to go home more than twice a semester. The
round-trip bus fare, the cheapest way, is $00.00.

Incidentals

Necessities.—Students need a small amount of money to spend while out with a group for coffee, cokes, shows, and the like. Also, there is the ever-present emergency of haircuts, shoestrings, razor blades, toothpaste, etc. Normally one may expect to spend $000 a semester on such things.

Dating.—Taking a girl out for an evening can cost a lot of money, or it can be fairly inexpensive. Some of the larger dances can cost up to $00 for the evening. The item is highly flexible.

If anyone in your senior class has any specific questions about this school, I'll try to answer as best I can. One thing you can safely tell all who are thinking about coming here: They had better learn to write correctly and to handle simple math or they will be in trouble.

Except for Item 1 (on form), the checklist for memos on page 560 applies equally to memo and letter reports.

MEMORANDUMS

Just as letter reports are more likely for communicating between organizations, memorandums are more appropriate within an organization. There they flow in quantity—especially with increasing use of word processing and photocopying equipment and the goals of speed, efficiency, and economy that have made unnecessary even the formerly used specially printed memo forms. (Still the efficiency of Speed Letters and the government's Two-way Memo—three sheets with interleaved carbons —retain a place for themselves.) The headings used in the illustrations of memorandums in this section show the main variations in form, and Item 1 of the checklist for memos (p. 560) gives further details.

Except for the differences in form and use, memorandums generally follow the instructions already given for letter reports. They are, however, inclined to (1) be ephemeral and hence less formal (often being handwritten without carbon), (2) make even greater use of itemization (almost characteristically), and (3) become directives going down the chain of command.

One of the most common and effective techniques is itemization. Numbering each paragraph almost forces a writer into careful organization, precise statement, and conciseness.

Two simple memos showing slightly different forms illustrate—one, to "All Occupants," is wholly typed and the other, to "Andrea," is handwritten on a printed form on light-blue stock (in layout, our favorite).

January 12, 197–

TO: All Occupants of Business Administration Building

FROM: R. F. Noonan, Building and Utilities Department

SUBJECT: Interruption of Electrical Service

The electricity will be off in your building on Tuesday, January 13, from 8 a.m. to 4 p.m.

UNIVERSITY OF FLORIDA

DATE *Jan. 20*

MEMO TO: *Andrea*

FROM: *CWW*

SUBJECT: *Work for today*

Since I have an appointment downtown during your working hours, please

1) record the grades of the attached papers in my grade book.

2) check the revised class lists against my rolls and return the lists to the Registrar with proper notations.

3) get the *Congressional Record*, vol. 88, Part 9, from the Library and copy Congressman Hill's comments on p. A-1486, and

4) make a table showing percentages, by class and major, of students on the E#255 lecture lists (both lists in one table).

We will provide temporary electric service for lights only in departmental offices.

All electricity will be off for approximately one-half hour from 8 to 8:30 a.m. and again from 4 to 4:30 p.m. for connection and removal of the temporary service.

Notice these details in the two memos: One is on an ephemeral topic to one reader; so efficiency pointed to a quick, handwritten memo. The other went to many people; so it was photocopied in sufficient number. Since some of its readers would not have known who "R. F. Noonan" was, he gave his official title. The other writer would have wasted time even with a full signature. The careful phrasing of subject lines in both indicates the contents concisely, and the underscoring makes them stand out. Itemization seemed helpful in one but would have served no purpose in the other, and the writers used it accordingly. Neither needs the kind of authenticating signature a bank requires on your check. Where that is necessary, the usual practice is for the writer to initial by the name in the "From" line.

The following memo shows a usual layout, typical A–plan, and a typical problem:

```
Date    :  2/10/80
To      :  Mr. J. G. DeWolfe
From    :  R. R. Fortune
Subject:  REDUCING ABSENTEEISM CAUSED BY RESPIRATORY DISEASES
```

1. <u>Conclusion.</u>—Our recent high rate of absenteeism seems to be a result of too low humidity. Absentees reported colds or other respiratory diseases as the causes in 73 percent of the cases.

2. <u>Humidity in relation to respiratory diseases.</u>—According to the U.S. Public Health Service, the higher the humidity in buildings the lower the rate of respiratory diseases. You can see this relationship in Figure 1 on the attached pages. The explanation is that a high humidity prevents excessive cooling from evaporation of skin moisture.

3. <u>Desirable humidity-temperature relationships.</u>—Although our 68 degrees is considered the best temperature, it isn't warm enough for most people unless the humidity is about 40. Ours is 20. As Figure 2 of the USPHS study shows, a humidity above 50 makes most people feel clammy and below 30 causes them to feel a dryness in their noses and throats.

4. <u>Recommended corrective steps.</u>—To reduce absenteeism, improve the health of our personnel, and enhance employee relations, I suggest the following:

   a. Raise the humidity to 40 by making a pan with the necessary evaporation surface for each radiator (to be concealed from view by the radiator covers).

   b. Assign the janitors the job of keeping water in the pans.

   c. Purchase one temperature-humidity guide for each office. Besides providing a constant check on room conditions, these meters will remind the employees that you have done something about their comfort and health.

      Prices range from $2 to $200. The cheapest ones are likely to be inaccurate; but the Wechsler at $8.50

```
carries the recommendation of Consumer Reports.  It
looks like a small clock with two red hands pointing
to temperature and humidity scales.  Hardware,
department, mail-order, and specialty stores carry it
in varied colors to fit the decor of any office.
```

JUSTIFICATION REPORTS

Another kind of short report often using memo form has its own special name. Of course, any analytical report could be called a justification report because it draws conclusions (and makes recommendations if wanted) and presents facts to justify them. But as used in report writing, the justification report is a special kind.

Almost invariably it is an initiating report in which the writer makes an original proposal, rather than a requested study, although it may well be the requested full write-up of a suggestion that you have dropped in a suggestion box.

It is deductive (A–plan) presentation that gives the recommendation immediately, followed by concise statements of the most important considerations and conclusions, before giving detailed explanations and supporting facts. Thus it *quickly* gives all a busy reader needs to know (*if the reader trusts the writer*). Probably this point is the main reason for the increasing popularity of the justification report among executives. But if the reader wants to read the whole explanation, the plan is still good. The reader can follow the details better by having already read the conclusions and recommendations.

You will provide good organization and coverage for your justification reports if you set up the five standard headings and do the following in this order:

1. State the purpose in one sentence. The first part, in phrase or dependent-clause structure, should mention a benefit. The second part should be the recommendation in an independent clause.
2. State the cost and saving (or advantages) in no more than two sentences. Don't delay the fast movement by explaining here.
3. In a third part called "Procedure" or "Method of Installation" or whatever is most appropriate, cover concisely such things as necessary space, personnel, training, special materials, time, restrictions (rules, regulations), and interruptions of work. Usually one to three sentences will do.
4. Itemize the conclusions, state them pointedly, and keep them to the minimum number that will cover all aspects. One of them has to be on cost and saving. They are not always all benefits; some may point the other way. One commonly overlooked is the goodwill of all people concerned.

Checklist for Memos

1. Form:
   a. Use a neatly arranged heading, including at least the company name (if needed for identification) and a dateline.
   b. Begin To, From, and Subject at the left; preferably, double-space between them; and use colons right after each or align all the colons with the one after Subject. In either case, align the beginnings of what you fill in after the colons.
   c. Use courtesy titles (Mr., Ms., Mrs., Miss) with the names of others (but not yours) if you would in talking with them; do not use official or professional titles unless some readers might not know them or you need to show authority.
   d. For emphasis, underscore or capitalize subject lines. End-of-line periods are unnecessary, even undesirable.
   e. Single-space within paragraphs and double-space between.
   f. Use itemizations, headings, tables, and graphics where helpful.
   g. For pages after the first, put at least the addressee's name, the date, and the page number on the first line and triple-space below it.
   h. Use no salutation, complimentary close, or typed name of writer at the end; sign only nonroutine memos requiring authentication, unless your organization's practice is otherwise.
   i. When used, file and other references may go under a flush-right date or to the right of the To-From-Subject block. (Copy distribution lists more commonly appear at the end instead.)

2. Organization and coverage:
   a. Bring in your main point (whether it is a request, conclusion, recommendation, or something else) in the first sentence unless your reader might resist; if so, lead up to it with whatever facts, reasons, or explanations are necessary to convince—especially any reader benefits you can point out.
   b. Be sure to make clear that your information is valid and pertinent by showing what the problem is and how you got your information to solve it (unless obvious); but see 3b.
   c. Effective dates (for directives)—and when necessary, other time limits, places, and people concerned—are important points.
   d. Consider whether you should mention alternatives to your recommendation.
   e. Should you explain more specifically how to carry out your proposal?
   f. Be sure you have covered all points your reader will need or want covered—especially all steps in your logic.
   g. Check your sequence for coherence, logic, and psychological effect (A–, B–, or C–plan).

Checklist for Memos
(*continued*)

3. Style:
   a. Make the subject line indicate the content accurately.
   b. Emphasize the important and avoid undue emphasis on the unimportant. What you found out and the likely effect are more important than how you found out or from whom; so for 2b, usually you should just imply or interweave in incidental phrases the necessary but unknown parts of purpose and method of the report. Usually the reader will already know the purpose; and if not, stating the facts will usually imply it and your method of getting information: "Sixty-two percent of your employees favor a company snack bar" indicates both the problem and the survey method.
   c. Be sure your terminology, sentence length and structure, and paragraph length and structure make for quick, clear, easy reading. Short words, sentences, and paragraphs usually help; itemizations and tabulations may help further.
   d. Display really significant data, conclusions, and recommendations by such means as increasing white space around them, decreasing line length, itemizing, and tabulating.
   e. For coherence (and often for conciseness), precede displayed items with an appropriate introductory statement.
   f. Don't develop a fever (with numerous strong adjectives and adverbs, for example); remain logical and objective.

4. Tone:
   a. Soften commands for acceptable tone; sharp imperatives rankle even in directives. "You will . . ." and "You must . . ." are too commanding for most situations. Four directives from which you can usually select one appropriate one are (in descending order of sharpness): "Please . . . ," "Will you . . . ," "I ask that you . . . ," and "I would appreciate your. . . ." "If you will . . ." is usually too weak.
   b. Phrase recommendations for acceptable tone (depending on the reader-writer relationship and the firmness of your conviction): "You must . . . ," "I recommend . . . ," "I suggest . . . ," "The only way . . . ," "The best solution is . . . ," and "Probably the wise decision is. . . ."
   c. Direct accusations (stated in independent clauses) are always objectionable.
   d. Positive is better than negative phrasing.
   e. Item 2a is an important factor in tone.
   f. Consider whether to write impersonally or (usually better) naturally ("Employees will receive their checks . . ." or "You will receive your checks . . .").

5. In a discussion section (sometimes called "Discussion of Conclusions" or "Explanation of Advantages"), give all the details supporting the statements already made—itemized to match the itemized conclusions. Interweave into your explanations enough of your methods to answer the reader's question: "How do you know?" This point applies particularly to your method of figuring cost and saving.

The following typical example illustrates both plan and technique:

HOW MECHANICAL PENCILS WOULD SAVE MONEY FOR MORGAN COMPANY

Purpose.—To save the Morgan Company more than $200 in pencil expense each year, I recommend that we purchase mechanical pencils instead of wooden ones for employee use.

Cost and Savings.—A year's supply of mechanical pencils and refills would cost about $457 as compared with more than $685 for wooden pencils—a yearly saving of well over $200.

Procedure.—A dependable automatic pencil manufacturer—Ray & Company, Rome, Georgia—would supply the yearly need of about 750 pencils with the Morgan name on them at the quantity-discounted price of 40 cents each. The stockroom clerk could distribute them.

Conclusions.—The Morgan Company would gain four benefits by using mechanical pencils.

1. We would save at least $225 a year.

2. The stockroom clerk would have fewer pencils to store and issue—750 compared with over 13,000.

3. Employees would be more careful about misplacing them.

4. Mechanical pencils stay sharp and thus provide uniform, neat writing without loss of time and patience at the pencil sharpener.

Discussion of Conclusions.—

1. During the past three years pencils have cost us about $1.80 a year per employee, as shown by the following calculations:

	19—	19—	19—	Average
Pencil costs	$ 765	$ 554	$ 731	$ 684
Employees	450	298	395	381
Cost per employee ...	1.70	1.86	1.85	1.80

Converting to mechanical pencils would require, for each employee, an estimated two pencils (at 40 cents each) and 40 cents worth of lead and eraser refills, for a total annual cost of $1.20 per employee.

Cost comparison shows a saving of $228.60 with mechanical pencils:

```
Cost of wooden pencils, 381 employees, @ $1.80 ..... $685.80
Cost of mechanical pencils, 381 employees, @ $1.20 .   457.60
     Saving ........................................ $228.60
```

2. In the past three years, the clerk in the stockroom has had to allot space for about 1,104 dozen, or 13,248, pencils and has also had to take the time (considerable in the aggregate) to distribute each one. Having only 762 pencils to store and issue would release space and time for other things.

3. Since mechanical pencils are more valuable and more conspicuous (especially with the Morgan name on them) than wooden ones, I believe employees would be more careful about carrying them home and not bringing them back. Those misplaced might be worth at least a part of their cost as advertising.

4. The mechanical pencil needs no sharpening and writes with the same neat uniformity throughout its use, instead of becoming progressively blunter and less neat. Moreover, mechanical pencils would avoid interruptions to thinking and work when employees take their wooden ones to the pencil sharpener (which often annoys by breaking the lead or needing to be emptied).

You might well notice several specifies about the preceding report. The writer who *initiated* this idea—usual for this kind of report—moves fast in presenting the basic idea and facts. The boss, if trusting the reporter, may approve after reading less than the first half; but simply reading further provides details if wanted. The clear, concise, and prominent (by underlining) but easily typed heads serve as guideposts to the reader. And the matched pair of itemizations helps the reader relate pointed conclusions with supporting facts and explanations. Deserved emphasis justifies the inevitable repetition of cost and saving—the reason you make such proposals, though neither has to be in dollars and cents. Perhaps most important of all, notice how the writer *concisely but subordinately interweaves* only enough methodology to answer the reader's question: "How do you know?" But the writer wasted no words about tracking down former pencil costs. The answer is obvious.

Although the form of justification reports is commonly memo, it may be letter or some other such as that illustrated. A title page like that of the complete analytical report may precede the form illustrated. If so, the title would be on both pages. In letter or memo form the title would serve as the subject line. Of course, the five division heads may be centered heads or sideheads above the text if you prefer. If you use memo form, Item 1 of the checklist for memos (p. 560) will apply. Then you can use Items 1–5 on page 559 as the subheads under Item 2 of that checklist and have a good checklist for justification reports.

PROGRESS REPORTS

As the name suggests, a progress report tells how you are getting along on a project. It may be a single, special report or one in a series of required periodic reports. (In a series the last one is the *completion* report.) As a periodic report, a progress report is usually strictly informational. A special progress report is likely to be analytical because of the special problem that called for it.

The general purpose of a progress report is to keep the top management informed so that it can act wisely. An owner may want to consider whether to continue as planned, change the plan or methods, or drop the project. A contractor may need to consider such questions as when to order certain materials, whether to increase the people and equipment assigned to a job, and whether to bid on another job.

Basic contents of a progress report are the answers to three questions:

1. Whether the project is on schedule.
2. If the project is not on schedule, why not?
3. What will be done next and what the plans and prospects are for completion on schedule.

Although neither those nor the following are necessarily the subdivision headings, a progress report may cover any or all of the purpose and nature of the project (usually the reader already knows), what has been done, present status, what is now being done, plans and outlook for the future, and unexpected developments. The last may be of major importance if the report is designed to get a decision on a problem that has arisen. In series, each progress report briefly summarizes former work reported but stresses developments since the preceding report. Progress reports on research projects may or may not include tentative findings and conclusions—depending on the writer's confidence in them and the immediate need for them.

No single plan is always best for a progress report. What is best depends upon the whole situation, especially the content, deserved relative emphasis of parts, and the attitudes and wishes of the reader.

Preferably all the progress reports in a series should follow the same plan. It may be topical by divisions of the subject (supervision, equipment, materials, and labor; or steps, phases, or divisions of the job); or it may be chronological (by days, weeks, or months; or past, present, and future). One simple plan calls for

1. The transitional elements of background and summary of work already done.
2. The body giving the details of recent progress.
3. The prophetic or future prospects, in relation to scheduled completion date.

A more specific but somewhat flexible plan is

1. Quick introduction (purpose and nature of the project, unless known; summary of work to date; status, including any significant results).

2. More detailed summary of earlier progress reported, if any.
3. New progress (work done, methods and personnel, obstacles and what you've done about them) in relation to schedule.
4. Realistic forecast (plans in relation to schedule, and recommendations or requests, if any).

More important than *what* plan, in most cases, is that you have *a* plan—a unifying thread to hang your beads on.

Like the plan, the form of progress reports may vary with the circumstances. Short ones usually are in memo or letter form, longer ones in some adaptation of complete report form.

Since the form, plan, and content of progress reports vary so much and we cannot well illustrate all the possibilities, we think we can help most by illustrating some common weaknesses in progress reports: (1) having nothing to say but trying to pretend that you do, (2) using pompous jargon to cover up, and (3) being nonspecific. The following humorous illustration[1] properly lampoons the main weaknesses.

STANDARD PROGRESS REPORT FOR THOSE WITH NO PROGRESS TO REPORT

During the report period which ends (fill in appropriate date) considerable progress has been made in the preliminary work directed toward the establishment of the initial activities. (Meaning: We are getting ready to start, but we haven't done anything yet.) The background information has been surveyed and the functional structure of the component parts of the cognizant organization has been clarified. (We looked at the assignment and decided that George should do it.)

Considerable difficulty has been encountered in the selection of optimum materials and experimental methods, but this problem is being attacked vigorously and we expect that the development phase will proceed at a satisfactory rate. (George is looking through the handbook.) In order to prevent unnecessary duplication of previous efforts in the same field, it was necessary to establish a survey team which has conducted a rather extensive tour through various facilities in the immediate vicinity of manufacture. (George and Harry had a nice time in New York last week.)

The Steering Committee held its regular meeting and considered rather important policy matters pertaining to the overall organizational levels of the line and staff responsibilities that devolve on the personnel associated with the specific assignments resulting from the broad functional specifications. (Untranslatable—sorry.) It is believed that the rate of progress will continue to accelerate as necessary personnel are recruited to fill vacant billets. (We'll get some work done as soon as we find someone who knows something.)

The following progress reporters did much better, as a writer usually does when having something to say to somebody for some purpose. Espe-

---

[1] So widely reprinted in the literature of report writing as to be in the public domain—like many jokes.

cially if all goes well, as in the first item, the report is easy to write. (All these writers used memo form; we'll begin with the subject line.)

SUBJECT: <u>Monthly Progress Report No. 2 on Orangeville Expressway</u>

<u>Present status</u>

1. Work on the 10.8-mile section of expressway running south to Brownville is on schedule. The final surface is 80 percent complete. We have had no delays during the past month and have regained the two days formerly lost and reported.

2. The 18.4-mile section of expressway running north to Malden remains approximately two weeks behind schedule. We have cleared the right of way to Malden, and the roadbed is completed along the first 8.6 miles north of Orangeville.

3. We completed the overpass for U.S. 1 on December 14, ahead of schedule by 18 days.

<u>Expected progress</u>

1. During January we expect to complete the southern link to Brownville except for the drainage preparation and the approaches. Work on them will most likely have to fit in between rains normally expected at this time of year in this area, especially in the valley of Hogtown Creek. Present progress and normal weather expectations suggest that this link will be ready for traffic just before the completion deadline of March 3.

2. During this month we will extend the roadbed along the north section to Malden. The first layer of tar will go on a 5-mile strip, beginning at Orangeville and extending north. Additional workers being hired should insure completion of this section before the deadline of June 24.

Sometimes progress reporters must explain their difficulties to defend themselves and to justify requests, as in the following:

SUBJECT: <u>Special Report on Interlocking Plant Installation</u>

Because of a shortage of track cable, I am asking your permission to advance cutover day to at least January 18. The installation is now about 88 percent complete, as shown by the broken line on the attached graph [omitted here to save space] comparing the predicted work schedule and the actual schedule.

If the track cable ordered December 1 arrives within the next few days as promised two weeks ago, and if we have good weather, the future work schedule should appear as the dotted projection line. This points to 100 percent completion on January 18.

Since progress reports often deal with technical work, you need not be surprised if you fail to understand some things in some of them. If you have trouble with the following, for example, remember that the technical writer did not write for you but for another technical person, who understood perfectly. (The situation accounts for the stiff, formal style.)

This report also illustrates a not unusual organization around topics rather than time, while the time sequence and relation to schedule are still clear.

SUBJECT: Progress on Prototype Power Supply for Collins
           (Job 280)

At the end of three weeks on the two-month schedule for developing a prototype power supply for Collins Radio, the project is two days ahead of the preliminary time estimate. The circuit has been designed and tested for dependability. It is now undergoing final inspection.

1. Results of circuit dependability test.—The test circuit operated within the desired limits of $\pm$ 2 percent of the desired voltages and currents. Measured by a thermocouple in the 3' $\times$ 3' $\times$ 3" base mounting plate of aluminum, the temperature readings (with attendant voltages) ran as follows:

Hour	Transmit Voltage @ 200 Ma.	Receive Voltage @ 110 Ma.	Bias Voltage @ 65 Ma.	Temperature (Degrees Centigrade)

[No use to waste space in this book on the recorded results.]

2. Printed circuit board.—The basic sketch work for the printed board is finished. The component placement and hookup connections were frozen yesterday. Now the enlarged negative is being drawn. It should be ready for the developer on January 13, five days ahead of the final acceptance date.

3. Chassis design.—The chassis drawings went to Alsfab on January 9. The prototype chassis, with finishes of black anodize on the base and gray enamel on the cover, will be ready on January 14. The dimensions are 6" $\times$ 4" $\times$ 3" or 2 inches smaller than the maximum Collins allowed.

4. Remaining work.—The printed board has to be etched and built. It will be tested in the small chassis, and the complete unit has to be tested for all conditions, including vibration, moisture, and temperature. Unless now-unseen troubles develop, the present rate of progress should continue, and the prototype should be ready for shipment by February 7.

CREDIT REPORTS

A typical credit report, illustrated as a letter report on page 112, illustrates those written by individual references about a credit applicant. But various trade associations, credit bureaus, and special credit-reporting agencies have to write so many credit reports that each develops special forms for convenience and the economy of standardization.

Because the purpose of a credit report is always the same and known to the reader, and because the methods and scope are always the same, the credit report omits the introduction. Because the credit report is an informational rather than analytical report, it also omits conclusions and recommendations. And because it is a short-form report, it omits other parts of a complete report—all except the text and perhaps a synopsis.

But because the credit report must protect the writer against libel suit, it includes the necessary legal defenses (in addition to assumed truth in the facts presented) by specifying confidential use for the purpose mentioned in the request for it. Because the four C's of credit—capital, character, capacity, conditions (see p. 135)—are the bases for credit decisions, the report invariably covers these topics (but not under these headings). The information includes anything which might have a significant bearing on the credit worth of the subject (individual or firm) and omits anything else.

The old report in Figure 16–1 is just one of the many kinds, but it illustrates most of the points. When you notice how the note in fine print at the bottom provides legal protection against libel suit, you will understand that Dun & Bradstreet (the granddaddy of credit-reporting agencies) had to get permission from Simpson to release this report for educational purposes—and why D&B sent an old report.

ANNUAL REPORTS

In accounting to their various publics for their management of funds entrusted to them, corporations and governmental units summarize each year's activities in their annual reports.[2]

In the middle of the 19th century, when annual reporting really started, stockholders were the only public considered. Since they were usually wealthy and educated—or advised by investment specialists—early annual reports were little more than financial statements in the formal accounting terms of the day. And the usual attitude of management was to tell as few people as possible as little as possible.

Today all that is changed. Stockholders have increased greatly (now estimated at about a tenth of the U.S. population, many of whom are not acquainted with accounting terminology). Labor has increased its power and become intensely interested in corporate affairs. The changed thinking of the times considers corporations essentially public institutions affecting the public welfare. Management has seen that its publics include stockholders, the financial community, employees, customers, government

---

[2] Although most annual reports are not short, they are largely factual reporting (informational) rather than the analytical studies of problems with conclusions and recommendations discussed in the preceding chapter. They are periodic reports and are something of a special type and form. Certainly they are the most voluminous of reports (many companies distributing more than a million copies annually), and the writings about them are probably the most numerous (we could easily give you a ten-page bibliography). Yet we do not think they deserve extensive treatment here in view of the purposes of this book. Still, you deserve some introduction to them, and it belongs in this chapter more appropriately than elsewhere.

FIGURE 16–1 Credit Report

$$\mathcal{D}un\ \&\ \mathcal{B}radstreet\ \mathcal{R}eport$$

RATING
CHANGE

SIC	NAME & ADDRESS		STARTED	RATING

52 51

SIMPSON HARDWARE CO   CD 26 FEB 2 19-- N
SIMPSON, WILLIAM J., OWNER   HARDWARE & PAINTS   1948   E 2 .
Formerly E 2½

495 N MAIN ST.
SPRINGFIELD OHIO

TRADE   DISC-PPT
SALES $89,446
WORTH $27,908
EMPLS   1 + 1 P.T.

SUMMARY   AN ESTABLISHED BUSINESS CONDUCTING A STEADY AND PROFITABLE VOLUME. FINANCIAL CONDITION IS WELL BALANCED.

TRADE

HC	OWE	P DUE	TERMS			SOLD
1551	356		2-10-30	Jan 19 19--	Disc	1948 to date
900	600		2-10		Disc	yrs
400			2-10-30		Disc	1950 to 11-1-6-
1600	300		30		Ppt	Active acct
733	112				Ppt	yrs

FINANCE

Statement Dec 31 19--

Cash on hand & bank	$ 4,604	Accts Pay	$ 3,064
Accts Rec	1,315	Accruals	621
Mdse	19,158		
Total Current	25,077	Total Current	3,685
Fixt & Equip	4,008		
Auto	2,113		
Ppd & Def	395	NET WORTH	27,908
Total Assets	31,593	Total	31,593

Net Sales January 1, 19-- to December 31, 19--, $89,446; gross profit $19,551; monthly rent $175; lease expires 19--. Fire insurance on fixtures $4,000; on merchandise $20,000.
Signed Jan 30, 19-- SIMPSON HARDWARE CO. by W.J. Simpson, Owner

-----O-----

When Simpson took over the business in 1948, sales were about $45,000 a year. By working long hours and advertising in the Suburban News he built up volume a little every year. Also there has been an increase in residential building on his side of town. Profits have increased as sales have expanded. Cash withdrawals from the business have been conservative. Merchandise turns satisfactorily and Simpson has been able to improve his financial condition a little each year. Carries good balances at his bank and has not borrowed since 195-.

OPERATION

Retails shelf hardware and tools (65%), S & W Paints (20%) and housewares, cutlery, garden implements, glass, lawn mowers, seeds and sporting equipment (15%). About 90% of sales is for cash; 30 day credit is extended to contractors and householders. Two clerks, one part-time, are employed. LOCATION: Rents a store 25 x 60 in a residential shopping area on the outskirts of town. Premises are well maintained.

HISTORY

Style was registered by Simpson July 17, 1948. Used for buying and advertising. Owner purchased this established business July 1, 1948 from Ralph T. Meyers. Capital was $18,000 of which $10,000 was a loan since repaid.

William J. Simpson, born 190-, is married, a native of Ohio. After graduating from Miami University in 1930, taught school until 1936. 1937-1945 employed by the Wilson Wholesale Hardware Co., Columbus, Ohio, latterly in the accounting department. 1946-48 was a salesman for Davis & Crocker, wholesale builders supplies, Springfield.
2-2 (201 49)

officials, and the general public. It has realized that many of these people are not educated in accounting and that many of them are interested in more than strictly financial data. They want to know about wages, fringe benefits to workers, products, research and development of new products, and overall policies—for example, company ecological policy.

Annual-report writers today, therefore, try to write so that everyone can understand, and they try to cover topics of interest to all publics. With the realization that people are inclined to distrust and take a dim view of things they don't know about, management has shifted to the attitude of telling as many people as possible as much as possible (limited only by security regulations and information that might hurt the competitive position of the company).

Indeed, today the annual report is a major part of the public relations programs of most corporations, a means by which they hope to tell their story to all their publics to justify their existence and their way of doing things. They know that any business firm exists, in the long run, only with the approval and patronage of a public whose goodwill it has. Most corporations therefore make their reports available to anybody who asks, and some go to considerable expense to make their reports appealing, readable, and informative.

Some have gone so far in telling their stories that the reports seem more like propaganda or advertising brochures than objective reports—and have sometimes thereby lost faith and face. But the usual annual report today is highly informative about the organization it represents. The facts presented are quite reliable. If you read annual reports knowing that they are likely slanted (by not telling everything rather than by misrepresentation), you will be adequately cautious—and well informed.

Usually today's annual reports contain a letter from the highest official as well as financial statements and the auditor's statement of opinion (sometimes called the "certificate"). Often the letter from the president or chairman of the board is only a short introduction to a review of outstanding influences, developments, and trends affecting company operations. Frequently it is both an introduction and a synopsis. And in some cases it is the entire report, running to 10, 12, or more pages.

Either way, most annual-report writers adapt all the devices already mentioned here—readable style, liberal use of meaningful headings, graphic illustrations—to make reading easy and interesting and the reports effective representatives for their organizations.

You can find a tremendous volume of material about annual reports in the library. And as we mentioned in the chapters on application letters, you can get examples by writing to almost any corporation. The annual report of a company is a source of information which anybody should read before investing in a company's stock or applying for a job with that firm.

SHORT ANALYTICAL REPORTS

As you have seen, some of the short reports in forms already discussed have been informational while others have been analytical. Yet the name "short analytical report" often has a special meaning in report-writing circles—a meaning indicating a certain form rather than any very definite limits of length. In that sense—the sense used in this section only—a short analytical report is like a complete analytical report which the writer has cut down by (1) omitting certain parts, (2) combining parts where possible, and (3) writing less in the remaining parts simply because their topics require no more. Even so, it is still likely to be longer (maybe up to ten pages) than what we generally mean by short report (usually five pages or less).

Since the parts of a short analytical report all have parallels in the complete analytical reports discussed in the preceding two chapters, we see no need to explain and illustrate them extensively here. For your study of short analytical reports, therefore, we ask you to keep in mind the following points as you reconsider the preceding two chapters.

1. The short analytical report usually omits all the preliminaries (p. 494) except the cover (possibly) and the title page, letter of transmittal, and (possibly) the synopsis.
2. It often also combines the letter of transmittal and synopsis, omits the table of contents and depends on headings throughout the report, omits the bibliography and provides the full references as footnotes or interwoven citations, and interweaves the essential parts of possible appendix material right into the text.
3. It may (but rarely does) also put the title-page information at the top of the first page and move right into the next part on that page; combine the essentials of authorization, transmittal, and synopsis as a summary right after the title-page information; and omit the introduction as a separate part and interweave its essentials into the text. It could thus have only three sections—the title-page information, the summary, and the text. This is about as far as it can go. Any report would have these elements, although they might be arranged differently and presented in different forms.

The following report (slightly revised for our purposes) is a good short analytical report. We know additional improvements we could make—and you may see some too—but notice particularly:

1. The exactness of the title, including the general answer (appropriate in the final title but not in a tentative one, where it would show preconceptions). The appropriate tentative title should change only the first word—to "Would."
2. The telescoping (omitting certain standard parts of longer reports like

those discussed in the preceding chapter and combining others). In this case you see the letter and synopsis combined, omission of the table of contents but provision of its information in a well-displayed system of heads and subheads, and replacement of the bibliography with published sources interwoven in the text.

3. The use of tables and charts where they help to highlight important quantities (the original contained others, omitted here because we do not think they were worth their space and costs in this book).

4. The smooth continuity and coherence of the whole report, helped by numerous beginning topic sentences and paragraphs and ending summary-transition sentences and paragraphs.

Because the short analytical reports discussed in this chapter are simply cut-down versions of the complete analytical reports discussed in the preceding chapter, you need no checklist for these. You can easily use the applicable parts of the checklist for complete analytical reports (pp. 535–41).

SHORT–REPORT CASES

1. Daniel Webb, District Manager, Phillips Petroleum, P.O. Box 17921 of a nearby large city, has asked you (a part-time attendant at the station) to write a letter report on whether University Gas Station should continue operating a full-service island. You have taken two surveys over a span of two days—100 self-service and 100 full-service customers. Self-service customers answered 31, 37, and 31 percent yes/no/indifferent on the question of liking to pump their own gas. Their indifferent answers were inconsequential on the other questions, where their yes answers were (on why use self-service) 68 percent to save money, 64 percent to save time, though gas odors bother 25 percent and 91 percent would like an attendant to check under the hood. Yes answers from full-service customers (on why use full service) were 20 percent to save time, 50 percent to get hood checked, 40 percent to avoid odor and mess. Indifferent answers (10 percent) came to only the time-saving question.

Besides questioning customers and observing operations, you also interviewed Jerry Gregory (another employee) and Harvey Brislan (manager of the station). According to Brislan (with whom both you and Jerry agree), the station can't run efficiently with just one employee, for it has too large a volume for both self-service and full-service islands though one attendant could handle both islands if both were self-service. Furthermore, all three of you agree, the station would probably sell more gas if both islands were self-service. When there's a large number of full-service customers, the self-service customers tend to be left out. What happens then is that potential customers are lost. People generally want fast ser-

HOW A CORRESPONDENCE-IMPROVEMENT PROGRAM

WOULD SAVE MONEY AND BUILD GOODWILL

FOR BURNS, INC.

Prepared for

Mr. C. D. James, President

By Patricia Jean Barksdale

Assistant, Research Department

January 28, 1980

Letterhead

January 28, 1980   RESEARCH DEPARTMENT

Mr. C. D. James, President
Burns, Inc.
2619 Powell Street
San Francisco, California 81001

Dear Mr. James:

Here is the report you requested on October 20 evaluating the possibilities for
improvement and, if needed, the best methods Burns could employ to
improve the quality of its correspondence.

The report shows that Burns could both save money and improve goodwill by
instituting a correspondence-improvement program.

To achieve the quality we want to maintain in our correspondence, Burns
should employ an instructor to conduct classes, issue a correspondence
manual, and hire a permanent supervisor to maintain quality correspondence.

In the month given me to prepare this report, I have learned some interesting
and useful facts which I believe will help you in establishing a
correspondence-improvement program. Please call on me if I can help further.

Sincerely yours,

(Ms.) Patricia Jean Barksdale
Assistant

HOW A CORRESPONDENCE-IMPROVEMENT PROGRAM

WOULD SAVE MONEY AND BUILD GOODWILL

FOR BURNS, INC.

Purposes, Methods, and Plan

Purposes

This report has two purposes:

1. to determine whether Burns needs to improve its correspondence and
(if so)

2. to propose and explain the actions needed.

Methods

Information to serve the first purpose comes from analyzing 1,000 outgoing letters and making a careful estimate of Burns correspondence costs. To stratify the sample, the office manager provided copies of letters from each department and from each dictator in proportion to their usual letter-output percentages.

Three methods provided the information for making the recommendations: a) a reading of the current literature on correspondence-improvement programs, b) a questionnaire survey of companies experienced with such programs, and c) interviews with two experienced correspondence consultants.

Basic plan

For clear explanation in logical sequence, the report considers: a) the costs of Burns letters, b) the quality of Burns correspondence, c) the effectiveness of correspondence-improvement plans, and d) the usual procedures and costs of the most effective plans. Analyses of the facts about these topics provide solid bases for the conclusions and recommendations.

1

The High Costs of Correspondence

The average cost of business letters today is $4.77 (according to the latest report of the Dartnell Corporation, which annually studies and reports such figures). On the basis of this figure, Burns spends more than a million dollars yearly on correspondence:

Average number of letters annually	212,500
Average letter cost	$4.77
Yearly correspondence expense	$1,013,625.00

The high total expenditures for correspondence seem to offer a vast area for possible savings, and analysis of outgoing Burns letters points to one quick and easy start.

Among the 1,000 letters studied, 8% were duplicates of the same message going to three or more persons. In many cases apparently a good form could do the job and save most of the waste. But let us figure on a surer, though more costly, way. Only a little training should teach Burns dictators to use the efficient secretaries and office equipment to save an estimated $75,000 annually.

Saving of 8% of annual costs ($1,013,625)	$81,090.00
Less (estimated) attributable training costs	1,000.00
Less (estimated) duplicating, stationery, and	5,100.00
stamping costs (at $0.30) on 17,000 letters	$74,990.00
(8% of 212,500)	

In addition to the ready dollar saving of $75,000 a year on correspondence, however, Burns also needs to consider the intangible yet highly significant goodwill and other effects of its correspondence.

3

Unfavorable Correspondence Conditions in Burns

The impression a company's letters make on the public can either win or lose business. As the respected business columnist Sylvia Porter recently said, "To get your money's worth, you must be sure every letter helps to improve public relations."

Burns letters are not the good Company representative they should be. Their tone, language, and formats all show shortcomings that provide areas for improvement.

Offensive expressions, other undesirable tone, and waste costly

Approximately two out of five letters leaving Burns offices are probably doing as much harm as good. Yet Burns need not feel that it is exceptional in this way. Professor C. R. Anderson reports that 40% of 1,000 photocopies he read in a firm where he was consulting represent letters that never should have gone out ("Correspondence Inefficiencies," *Journal of Business Communication*, 4:13-18, January, 1980). Still, the fact that other firms send out bad letters does not mean that Burns should.

Letters containing offensive expressions.—Of the letters that Burns sends to readers, 18% contain offensive expressions (Chart 1).

CHART 1
Percentage of Letters Containing Offensive Expressions
or Unanswered Questions

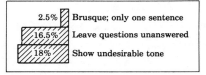

2.5%	Brusque; only one sentence
16.5%	Leave questions unanswered
18%	Show undesirable tone

So Burns is spending over \$180,000 a year to drive business away (0.18 × 212,500 × \$4.77). Accusing the reader ("You failed . . ." or "neglected . . ."), implying distrust or stupidity ("You say . . . ," "If so, . . . ," "Obviously . . ."), and the like certainly destroy rather than build goodwill.

A short, snappish answer often seems peevish and distasteful to readers, whether intended to be or not. Every one of the 2.5% of the sample letters that were just one sentence gave that impression of brusqueness form of offensive expression.

No company can afford such loss of goodwill and waste of money. Burns dictators definitely need instruction in letter courtesy.

Unnecessary duplication.—About one in six (16.5%) of Burns letters leave questions unanswered. Not only does having to write again annoy customers—unless they decide to drop the subject and go elsewhere with their business—but Burns dictators waste time in preparing letters to answer questions they should have answered in the first letter.

If they have to write again for each letter leaving unanswered questions, a waste of another \$167,248.12 a year results (212,500 × 0.165 × \$4.77). This problem apparently occurs because a dictator reads the incoming mail carelessly and dictates before planning to answer what the inquirer asked.

Language in Burns letters ineffective and hurtful

Many of the Company's letters are not creating the best public image because of wordiness, trite expressions, spelling errors, and poor sentence and paragraph structure.

CHART 2

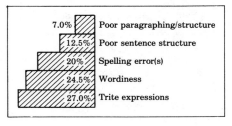

7.0%	Poor paragraphing/structure
12.5%	Poor sentence structure
20%	Spelling error(s)
24.5%	Wordiness
27.0%	Trite expressions

5

Though wordiness (in 24.5% of the letters) and the use of trite expressions (27%) are not the worst of English weaknesses, the fact that more than one out of four of Burns letters uses them means Burns letters often sound pompous and dull reader interest. Wordiness stems from deadwood phrasing, rather than good idea presentation, and indicates lack of careful thought or inability of the dictator. Wordiness and triteness, along with misspellings (in a fifth of the letters), reflect ignorance or lack of thought or care, none of which is good for public relations.

Worse, however, are the more serious instances of poor sentence and paragraph structure in 12.5% and 7% (respectively) of the letters. Paragraphs of 15 lines or more (in 7% of the letters) and sentences averaging 32 or more words (in 5%) do not exist in good letters where the current literature suggests an average of 16-20 words per sentence and less than eight lines per paragraph for good readability. Long paragraphs are uninviting and hard to read. Often these faults (particularly when reinforced by wordiness, triteness, and distracting misspellings) lead to difficult reading, failure to understand, or misunderstanding—if the letters get read at all.

The price is too high to waste on such ineffectiveness as an addition to the loss of respect and goodwill. Clearly Burns dictators need motivation and/or training to do better; and since the secretaries at least originate the misspellings (and perhaps some complimentary closings, though the dictators are finally responsible for both), apparently the secretaries need help too. Even the first impressions a reader gets of a letter from its greetings, format, and adieu deserve attention.

First impressions from letter formalities and formats unfavorable

Since Burns letters are often the only direct communication contact readers have with the organization, even the first impressions our letters make are important. The appearance and tone of the stationery, layout, and standard courtesy phrases create a picture of the firm. Faulty letters such as many going out from Burns reflect unfavorably on the Company, its dictators, and its secretaries. Since Burns stationery (paper and printed letterhead) would score well on any reasonable standard, the matters of concern are the phrasing of titles, salutations, and complimentary closings and the typing.

CHART 3

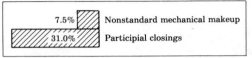

| 7.5% | Nonstandard mechanical makeup |
| 31.0% | Participial closings |

Participial closings.—The survey of Burns correspondence reveals that the largest percentages of improper phrasings are participial and other outmoded closings. Thirty-one percent of the letters end with outmoded expressions such as "Looking to your reply . . ." and "Until such time, I remain, etc." About one out of three letters dictated indicates to a customer a lack of up-to-dateness at Burns, Inc.

Nonstandard mechanical makeup.—Almost one in 12 (7.5%) of the letters contain variations in mechanical makeup. These variations often result from inconsistency on the part of various typists when the dictator does not specify the form of letter. Such variations are not necessarily errors, since all forms that are consistent are correct; but the outmoded or ultramodern form does characterize the writer and the company. Since the modern trend is toward simplicity, Burns could save much time and money by adopting a simple form that would suggest that Burns is neither out of date nor frivolously ultramodern.

7

Though the dictator is finally responsible, most secretaries have a
considerable (and often a free) hand in determining the appearance and the
courtesy formalities of letters they type. Since more than one out of three
Burns letters goes out with some degrading blemish in these areas,
apparently both the dictators and secretaries at Burns need some training or
study on letter appearance. A study of the topic in the leading textbook on
business communication (Wilkinson, Clarke, and Wilkinson, *Communicating
Through Letters and Reports*) would probably be sufficient. To show a united
front and to ease the job of a secretary who types for several dictators, Burns
might well adopt one form.

XXX

Wasteful duplication, poor tone and language, and blemishes on the
physical appearance show the unsatisfactory quality of Burns
correspondence. The unfavorable conditions are costing unnecessary
thousands of dollars yearly and are also causing a loss of goodwill and
business. Only 24%, less than one in four, of the letters Burns now
sends out are of top quality—clear, correct, complete, and considerate of the
reader's feelings.

Correspondence improvement offers Burns a vast area for savings in both
money and goodwill.

8

The Success of Correspondence-Improvement Programs

Results at companies using letter-improvement programs include improvements in letter quality, in attitudes of correspondents, and in customer relations.

The following excerpt from "Letter Training Program Pays Off," an unsigned feature on page 377 of the January, 1980, issue of *Printers' Week,* comments on the improvement received from correspondence instruction: "Bring in an instructor who has had experience in writing letters as well as in teaching. Conduct regular classes for several weeks. Require each member of the firm connected with letter writing—from the president to the typist— to attend. Then watch your letters improve!"

The same source lists the names of 57 companies which have carried out letter-improvement programs. The 55 replies to questionnaires sent to these companies indicate favorable results from their programs.

Improvement in letter quality considerable

The first and most important question asked was "What do you believe was the effect of your program on the quality of the company's letters?" Almost three-fourths (39 of the 55) say they have received considerable satisfaction with significant improvement in quality. Twenty-seven percent see no noticeable difference, and 2% note slight improvement.

Attitude of correspondents favorable

More than three-fourths of the firms (42 of the 55) report correspondents' favorable attitudes toward their programs. Only 4% report unfavorable reactions.

9

One typical comment is: "On the whole, both correspondents and typists appreciate the constructive criticism of the instructor. Nearly all are enthusiastic when they realize how important their letters are in building goodwill for the company."

Both correspondents' approval and improvement in letter quality indicate that the programs improve the companies' public relations.

Customer relations improved

To the inquiry "What do you believe was the effect of the program on your company's customer relations?" more than two-thirds report considerable improvement. Sixty-nine percent report considerable improvement, whereas 20% consider the improvement slight and 11% notice no apparent change.

A favorable comment states that "Since completion of our training program, we have received fewer complaints than ever before; and many customers have written letters of appreciation."

Improvement in letter quality, correspondents' favorable attitudes, and better customer relations show that other companies' correspondence-improvement programs are successful. The type of program which works best, however, is more difficult to determine.

The Costs and Methods Used by Other Companies with Successful Programs

Most companies which have successful correspondence-improvement programs use a correspondence manual, a permanent supervisor, and (to start) a special instructor.

Correspondence manuals effective

A correspondence manual for reference is an important part of a letter-improvement program. The usual manual contains both instructions and examples of approved styles for company letters to serve as a guide for dictators and transcribers.

Of the 55 companies questioned, only a little more than half (51%) said yes when asked "Do you have a correspondence manual?" Those companies which use a manual, however, readily realize its importance and benefits. Of those that report using one, 86% answered yes to "Do you believe it has helped to improve letter writing?"

Evidently the others (49%) do not realize the benefits that users receive from manuals. They serve both as guides to new employees and as reminders and handy references to established employees. In most cases a manual seems to be most beneficial to follow up and answer questions that arise after completion of the course of instruction.

In discussing the benefits of the correspondence manual, one respondent commented, typically, that "The correspondence manual issued at the close of our training period served to crystallize the information presented by the instructor. It is always available for quick reference."

A correspondence manual justifies itself in a letter-improvement program, however, only if its benefits outweigh its cost.

Cost of a manual about $500

In replies to the queston concerning the cost of correspondence manuals, $500 to $700 is the most frequent answer (43%). One-fourth of the firms (25%) paid $600 and over for their manuals, 2% less than $400, 1% spent $400 to $500.

The advantages of the savings in time and money which result from the use of a correspondence manual seem to justify the cost in the thinking of most firms. Evidently, then, a good correspondence-improvement program

11

will provide a manual.

The most successful programs, however, do not depend on a manual alone but also provide a correspondence supervisor.

Correspondence supervisors maintain effectiveness

The correspondence supervisor serves as an adviser to the employees concerning problems and as an inspector to make sure the letters maintain standards of quality. Without the supervisor, dictators and transcribers lapse into their old habits, according to companies which have tried to operate without a supervisor.

The survey reveals that 58% of the companies make use of a correspondence supervisor or someone else who assumes the duties under another title. But 42% do not have a correspondence supervisor.

A greater percentage (58%) of firms make use of a supervisor than make use of a manual (51%). And unanimously all 32 companies which have a supervisor agree that a competent one is effective in maintaining letter quality.

The following comment from one firm further illustrates the need for a correspondence supervisor:

> The letter-improvement classes we held five years ago made correspondents conscious of their responsibilities for several months. But since we had no supervisor to encourage consistent effort to make letters effective, correspondents became lax again. Our new program provides for a supervisor who will spot-check outgoing mail and hold regular classes for discussion of letter problems.

Evidently a supervisor helps to keep the letter quality up to par. The most effective letter-improvement program should make use of both a supervisor and a manual.

Still an additional element appears in the most successful programs.

All sources recommend instruction to start

All articles read, many comments made by interviewees and respondents to the questionnaire, and the advice of a professional letter-writing consultant point to the wisdom of an instructional program as a necessary start to a letter-improvement program.

Dr. J. H. Mensing of Del Monte, the interviewed professional consultant, says that in his varied experience few companies have been successful in greatly improving their correspondence without a definite program of instruction to start. Much of the job, he says, is getting employees to recognize the importance of good letters to their companies and themselves. Although inspiration and exhortation alone will not do much good, some motivating along with good instruction on how to improve usually does produce good results.

Dr. Mensing's statements are in line with specific comments heard or read elsewhere, and he offers a program based on 25 years of successful experience.

Dictators and transcribers would attend 10-week courses in separate groups. Five groups with 17 dictators each and two groups with 20 typists each would include all of the 85 Burns dictators and 40 transcribers while keeping the classes down to effective working groups. Dr. Mensing proposes to analyze letters dictated by each correspondent and to give individual suggestions on the paper (in person, when necessary). Under his professional direction, employees are practically assured of learning the much-needed fundamentals of good letter writing. His fee for each class is $1,000 or $6,000 for the whole instructional program.

13

By employing Dr. Mensing to conduct the proposed classes, Burns would be taking a step that everyone with successful experience in attempts at correspondence improvement seems to agree is essential.

The Recommended Program

The high cost of correspondence and the deficiencies in the quality of letters at Burns, Inc., definitely indicate that the company should institute an improvement program as soon as possible.

Published articles, the experiences of firms that have worked at improving their correspondence, and the advice of a professional consultant all suggest that the best plan is a three-pronged attack:

1. Employ a professional teacher to motivate and instruct employees as the first step.

2. Provide a correspondence manual for ready reference.

3. Appoint a permanent correspondence supervisor to keep up the motivation, help with special problems, and spot-check outgoing mail to catch and correct any developing laxness.

To solve the problem of poor letters at Burns, Inc., I therefore recommend that the company take these three steps in order as soon as practicable. Specifically, I recommend Dr. J. H. Mensing of Del Monte as the professional consultant and teacher to start the program.

With the recommended program in operation, at a cost of about $7,000 ($6,000 + $500 + overhead), both Professor Anderson's and my estimates suggest that Burns should expect to save at least 50 times that much a year by writing fewer but better letters and by avoiding duplication. The biggest improvement, however, would be the better company image Burns correspondence would put in the minds of its readers.

14

Bibliography

1. Anderson, C. R., "Correspondence Inefficiencies," *Journal of Business Communication,* 4:13-18 (October, 1971).

2. Howard, Henry, "Cutting Correspondence Expense," *U.S. Business,* May, 1971, pp. 29-31.

3. "Letter Training Program Pays Off," *Printers' Week,* January, 1971, p. 377.

vice, and those that are impatient will leave when the service they desire isn't readily available.

University Station's full-service charge is 5 cents a gallon above the self-service price, and its daily additional labor expense (for the additional attendant required for the full-service island) runs $40. A one-week check of the full-service pumps shows sales (Monday through Sunday) of 307, 368, 356, 446, 636, 693, and 480 gallons (an average of 469.43). About $5 a day is added to the profits through sales of oil and other things at the full-service island.

2. As Harvey Brislan (preceding case), assume that you had the foresight and initiative to see the situation as described and to write a *justification* report to Dan Webb (enhancing your standing with him and avoiding his asking somebody else to prepare the report). Do it now (as you should have months ago), assuming that you collected the information the part-time attendant did.

3. As a long-time concerned (and recently victimized) citizen, write a memo to the chief administrative officer (mayor?) or group (city council?) of your city about the increasing rate of uncleared crimes. (*Cleared* means that the suspected criminal has been arrested and charged.)

What you want to say comes out of four facts:

1. The following set of figures from a nationwide study made by a Chicago professor of sociology last month.
2. The fact that (incidentally) your back door was bashed in two weeks ago when you were out of town and your $500 TV set was taken (no arrest yet).
3. Your city taxes are going up nearly every year (11 percent last year).
4. The city Police Department got a 7 percent increase at the beginning of this year (mostly for police officers' pay increases, according to the local paper).

| | Cleared | | National Average |
Type of Crime	This Year	Last Year	Last Year
Murder	87.5%	100.0%	75%
Rape	51.5	20.0	51
Robbery	52.0	62.0	27
Assault	9.0	57.0	62
Burglary	12.9	9.0	16
Larceny	9.8	14.6	20
Motor Vehicle Theft	19.4	10.0	15
Total	12.5	17.8	21

Though you may feel indignant, write reasonably instead of emotionally, as Lincoln suggested by his quip that a drop of honey catches more flies than a gallon of vinegar.

4. As a new employee in the Advertising Department, International Airlines, 2300 North Street, N.W., Washington, DC 20037, write a memo with graphics to George Garn, head of advertising. International has been running 30-second TV ads at prime time (between 5:30 and 6:30 P.M.) during the popular news presentations on CBS, ABC, and NBC. Ads up to now have featured mainly businessmen rushing to catch a plane; but already 18 percent of business passengers are women. Your concern is that more women should be featured in the ads in view of their increasing role in employment and in airplane travel.

Women are increasing in the work force at a rate of almost 2 million every year. More than half the country's 84 million women, including a majority of mothers with school-age children, now work or seek jobs. The management-consulting firm of Sandler & Heidrick, Inc., says the number of women corporate officers in the 1,300 largest companies rose to 416 last year—a one-year increase of 28 percent. According to the U.S. Departments of Labor and Commerce 6 percent of the nation's working women are managers and administrators, 1 percent farm workers, 35 percent clerical workers, 7 percent sales workers, 6 percent schoolteachers, 21 percent service workers, 15 percent blue-collar workers, and 10 percent other professionals. Among the approximately 38 million women in non-farm jobs, 87.3 percent are white and 12.7 percent black. Marital status shows 19.0 percent single, 56.4 percent married, and 24.6 percent divorced, separated, or widowed. In addition, millions of other women work at home or in volunteer tasks each year. Mothers working at or seeking jobs represent 53 percent; 47 percent are not in the labor force.

Women also are going to professional schools in record numbers. The Labor Department says that they will comprise 18 percent of all professionals in seven years. About 10,000 are studying engineering—ten times as many as nine years ago. Total earnings of working women seven years ago were $127.4 billion; today they are $254.3 billion (up 100 percent). Working women earning $25,000 or more seven years ago numbered 25,000 and today 217,000 (up 768 percent). Life insurance coverage in force for women ran $200 billion seven years ago and today $380 billion (up 90 percent). Individual women holding American Express Cards six years ago numbered 0.7 million; today there are 1.9 million (up 171 percent).

5. Use the facts in the previous case. As director of personnel and training, write a memo with graphics to the sales/promotion department of your life insurance company, Providential, 720 West Wisconsin Avenue, Milwaukee, WI 53202. You feel that your company has overlooked the large market of women executives and suggest a direct marketing mail campaign. In your memo you might also suggest a time when you are free to meet with the sales/promotion department.

6.   Using the data in Case 4, p. 589, assume that you are working in the advertising department of American Express. You feel that your job is to get backing for a campaign promoting American Express cards to women. Before you begin work on the campaign (direct mail, ads in women's magazines, TV spots) you write a memo with graphs to Hugh Mayer, Vice President—Marketing.

7.   As a management trainee in the Iowa regional office of Nationwide Insurance Company, you have observed how crowded the working conditions are; so you have investigated possible solutions. Last year your office increased its policies in force by 12.1 percent from the year before in homeowners insurance and 29 percent in commercial fire policies; and you expect to do even better next year. With the growth of business, the demand for underwriters, claims representatives, and file clerks has increased; but the area partitioned off for the file section has not. File clerks find it hard to keep records in order without adequate room to do so.

The present building, built in 1954, has a foundation designed to support only one floor; therefore you cannot build upward. You do not have sufficient land to expand outwardly. Nationwide policy is to buy a minimum of 25 acres for new regional offices. Locating and developing this land, however, would not give immediate relief for the problem.

Your reading on the problem seems to suggest microfilm as the solution. You've found seven pertinent articles—four of which are specific success stories for microfilms: three in *The Office* (87:40–41, April, 1978, about a bank; 86:114–18, September, 1977, about Michigan Blue Cross; 86:44–45, September, 1977, about Flying Tiger Line) and one in *Infosystems* (24:80, December 1977, about Datsun). In another article ("Taking the Mystery Out of Microfilm," *The Office*, 87:69, January, 1978), Richard J. Connors says that microfilm can save over 90 percent of the space needed for paper files. Connors also says, "Microfilm virtually eliminates misfiles (1–5% in most paper systems); so files can be found quickly and accurately." Two other articles generally support Connors and add these points:

1.   Microfilm reduces record retrieval because thousands of files can be stored in a single file cabinet available at the touch of a button, resulting in a cost saving by reducing the work hours searching for a document ("Pro and Con on Micrographics and the Office," *Administrative Management*, 38:116, November, 1977).
2.   You can file 25 inches of paper on microfilm for what it usually costs (about $6) to file one inch of paper in a paper system. Also, microfilm images last longer than paper files ("Taming the Paperwork Explosion," *Management World*, 5:3, July, 1976).

Since your automobile section occupies the largest amount of space in the building, you estimate that by converting the approximately 500,000 auto policies to microfilm you can gain about 4,000 square feet of office for the file section—about what you seem to need for the next several years.

According to Bob Hall, your service superintendent, who carefully observed a similar microfilm conversion for the Missouri-Kansas office, you would need 50 persons to work in your conversion efforts (to minimize disruption of operations). He suggests that you hire college and high-school students. If you hire 14 employees to be trained as lead workers (as Hall suggests) and 36 students two weeks later, their combined pay will be $62,382.40 (14 × 58 days @ $3.07/hr. × 8 hrs. and 36 × 48 days at the same rate).

Using figures Hall gave you from the Missouri-Kansas conversion, you and the purchasing department figure (proportionate to the sizes of the jobs) that you will need to spend about (figures rounded) $147,000 for new microfilm files, cameras, readers, jackets, film, processing equipment, and miscellaneous equipment and supplies; $9,500 for rental of temporary (conversion-period) equipment; and the $62,500 for temporary employees, for a total of about $219,000. Not all of that, however, can be justly charged to the conversion. For $147,000 spent on new equipment, you will have left at least nine of its ten years of useful life (worth $132,000 and making the cost only $15,000 for the one full year of depreciation on its extra-heavy use during conversion). Furthermore, Loren Devore of corporation headquarters has agreed to allow you $70,000 for the used equipment you listed as salvage when/if you convert to microfilm; and the accounting department figures you will get $7,000 investment tax credit on the figured equipment purchases.

Since the benefits are clearly worth more than the remaining $10,000 cost, write a justification report to T. M. Covington, Deputy Regional Vice President, recommending the conversion.

8. You work directly with the vice president of marketing, Orville Smith, as a marketing trainee for the White Supermarket Company, your city. One of the jobs of trainees is to keep Smith informed about what the competition is doing in different areas of the city. You do this by "shopping" a grocery list at other stores. You are to obtain prices for the following items at three different grocery outlets and to prepare a memorandum report for Smith showing the prices for each item at each store and total cost of the list: fresh oranges, lettuce, cabbage, Cokes, dog food, tomato soup, vinegar, cooking oil, pork and beans, apple jelly, peanut butter, paper napkins, dish soap, canned green beans. Be sure that your comparison includes only comparable sizes, weights, or quantities. Use the same brands in each store wherever possible, otherwise those of apparently equal quality. Do not use any item that is on sale at one or more stores (your boss would get information on sale items from newspaper ads).

9.   As George P. Hayes, 1536 Hewitt Avenue, St. Paul, MN 55101, you have received this letter:

Would you please send me your analysis and recommendations on the following common stocks: Canadian Breweries, Inc., Merrill Island Mining Corporation, and McLean Industries. [Substitute any three as directed by your instructor.]

I am considering the addition of shares in any or all of these corporations to my stock portfolio. I've heard that you have recently finished some research into the evaluation of stocks as an investment and would like for you to apply the criteria you have developed to these issues.

Naturally, I'll be interested in learning something about the nature of the industry in which each of these companies operates; the size of each company and its scope of operations; net assets per common share of stock in each company and the dividend histories; and any operating details which might affect future price increases.

Please *do not limit* your discussion to my suggestions, Mr. Hayes, but do keep in mind that I like to move into and out of the market and that I am looking mainly for an increase in market price over the next 12 months rather than a long-range income from my investment.

Call it intuition (I've been pretty lucky on this basis before!)—but I feel I simply must have your report in my hands no later than a month from today (when I shall have a certificate of deposit of $10,000 maturing).

Mrs. P. M. Swartz, 90 Black Hawk Road, Big Stone City, SD 57216, obviously wants information and recommendations. What information is really significant? Submit the letter report.

10.   Assume that you have a scholarship from the Wadsworth Foundation based primarily on industry and seriousness of intent rather than high scholarship. Wadsworth does expect satisfactory work and above all diligent effort. As part of your responsibility to the foundation, you must write a report once a year on your progress during the past year. Using the facts of your own record, write in letter form a progress report to Faye Cunningham, Director of Scholarships.

11.   At this point you have completed the major part of your course and this text. Review your progress and write down your weaknesses and strengths and draw a conclusion as to your growth. Submit your discoveries and conclusions about your progress to your instructor.

12.   Assume that you are working on a class project that will require several weeks (say a major report such as discussed in Chapters 14 and 15) and that your teacher asks for a progress report to see how you are coming along (in reference to what you should have done by the specified date).

13. Write a memo to Norman Linebaker, Vice President for Sales, from Scott Phelps, Promotion Manager. Use as the subject new tractor exhibits. Your company is Paragon Promotions, general promoters of farm equipment to farmers. You are sending color prints of four mock-ups of exhibit designs done by your promotion section. If Linebaker approves the designs this week, you can have finished exhibits ready for use by the first of next month. Ask him to phone you by Monday with any suggestions. To help in making decisions, the following size and cost data may help: Design A, 6′ × 12′ × 9′ (two colors); Design B, 6′ × 9′ × 9′ (three colors); Design C, 6′ × 12′ × 9′ (four colors); Design D, 8′ × 12′ × 9′ (five colors). For most local shows and demonstrations of tractors to farmers either design A or B should be OK. Only for major regional or national shows will design C and D be helpful. Plans call for three major shows this year: Coleman, Texas, two months from now on 12–15; Macon, Illinois, in three months, 20–22; and Blue Mound, Iowa, four months from now. Scheduling of shows is spaced so that one of either Design C or D will be adequate along with enough A's and B's. Ask him to tell you his preference (C or D) unless there's a feeling that both should be used.

14. As safety engineer for the Carolina Power and Light Company (Raleigh, NC 27607), you get the job of writing a memo to all outdoor crew members recommending certain precautions when lightning threatens. Your boss, Louise Belden, director of safety, wants to see, approve, and distribute; but you are to write to the workers, not her. Lightning has killed seven workers this year on the job—one a week ago—and has injured others. Fortunately last month you received from the National Safety Council (of which you are a member) a report of a three-year study on self-protection from lightning. Since that report was for the general public, you'll have to select points from it, organize the points appropriate to your employers' working conditions, and write your memo, using these notes you have taken:

When possible, go indoors, but not in the shower or tub bath. Fireplaces as well as radiators, stoves, metal pipes, plumbing fixtures, and electrical appliances such as television sets, radios, lamps, and refrigerators should be avoided. If caught outdoors, avoid the highest object in an area, especially isolated trees (keep twice tree height away). For quick action when you sense warning signs (hair stands on end or skin tingles), crouch down immediately. Get away from hilltops, open spaces, wire fences, power lines, exposed sheds, and metal farm equipment, clotheslines, and rails. Drop metal fishing rods or golf clubs and seek refuge in a cave, ditch, or canyon, or under head-high clumps of trees in open forest glades. Get out of the water if swimming, and off small boats. A truck or car offers excellent protection (don't touch metal parts). People hit by lightning may be touched without danger—carry no electrical charge—(may appear dead but can often be revived by prompt mouth-to-mouth and cardiopulmonary resuscitation).

15.   As city manager in a sizeable city with an excellent three-year-old city hall, you want to write a justification report to the five city commissioners recommending two daily 20-minute breaks for employees and an arrangement for an employee snack bar in available space in the hall. Adapting the selected space will cost $1,700, according to a careful estimate made by the contractor who built city hall.

Though breaks have never been approved, your talks with the nine department heads and every tenth name on alphabetical lists of employees reveal that about 67 percent of the 200 employees take one or more anyway (15–40 minutes), conscientious workers resent the liberties taken by others (and many of the guilty feel guilty), and department heads have quit trying to prevent the unapproved breaks.

The city attorney tells you that your proposals are legal, within the power of the city commissioners to authorize. The proposed breaks are in line with allowed coffee-break time of at least half the business and industrial firms of the city and with the nation-wide practices of three fourths of such firms (as reported in a recent survey by the National Office Management Association, *Coffee Breaks in U.S. Business and Industry*, Philadelphia, 1979, p. 17). Three usual restrictions—which you would want to attach—are that no more than half the employees of a department may be out at any time, breaks longer than 20 minutes will result in deduction of an hour's pay (though with good cause and special permission of the immediate superior, an employee may occasionally combine two breaks for the day), and break time is not to compensate for tardiness or early departure.

The doctoral dissertation—*Efficiency and the Coffee Break*, Harvard Press, Boston, 1978, p. 268—of E. E. Jennings, now professor of personnel management at Harvard, reports that breaks up to 20 minutes increase office-worker efficiency 4 percent in the morning and 6 percent in the afternoon.

From three highly respected restaurant owners who would like the concession, the best offer you could get was from a local man: A five-year lease renewable by mutual agreement, he to pay the city $100 a month plus 2 percent of gross profit. The hall is three blocks from any presently existing restaurant.

16.   As an executive trainee in the Arcola, Mississippi, store of J. P. Taylor and Company, you were somewhat surprised to see that clerks in the piece-goods department used an ordinary yardstick attached to the counter to measure yard goods. They then labored at calculating the charges.

Wondering about the accuracy of the measurements and the calculations, one day you secretly asked customers leaving the store to let you check their purchases of ribbons, lace, elastic, eyelet trim, and dress and drapery materials. On the 50 purchases checked, you found an average of three inches in excess (though the individual discrepancies ranged from one half to eight inches), despite 17 cases of short measurement (none of which exceeded three inches). You also found four errors in the calculations—two for 10 cents and two for $1 in favor of the customer and one a customer had caught (and the clerk had corrected) because it was an overcharge of $1.

You want to suggest the purchase of a Measuregraph, a small cloth-measuring machine which is bolted unobtrusively and easily to the counter with four screws, and costs $90. It measures exactly and also calculates prices automatically, thus making easy and more accurate such calculations as 4⅜ yards at $2.67. The manufacturer guarantees the machine for one year, but information from the manufacturer's salesman and from users' testimonials indicates that it will probably last at least five years.

17. Speery and Cunningham, a consulting firm you work for, has been hired to investigate lowering the decibel count from 90 to 85 or lower for Rand Engineering Company, Cambridge, Mass., by the Occupational Safety and Health Administration. Decibels are units of measured noise, with zero representing the threshold of hearing and 130 the threshold of pain. Although the difference of only 5 decibels seems insignificant, the contrast in sounds between 85 and 90 decibels actually is enormous. Every 10-decibel increase in sound approximately doubles the amount of "perceived loudness." For example a medium jet engine has 160, air-raid siren 140, discotheque 120, bulldozer 110, steel-mill blast furnace 100, subway train 90, vacuum cleaner 70, auto traffic near freeway 60, private business office and average home 50, whisper 20.

Approximately 1,500 more Rand manufacturing workers would be saved from hearing impairment if the 85-decibel standard were adapted, rather than the 90-decibel average. (About 770,000 manufacturing workers in the United States would be similarly protected. Workers were not counted in other occupations, such as transportation and construction.) Cost to Rand (and other manufacturing firms) of complying with the 85-decibel average would be $21,497 for each worker saved from a hearing handicap. Cost for compliance with the 90-decibel level would be 13.5 billions—or $19,286 per employee whose hearing remains undamaged.

If Rand continues to operate as it has, probably 2,000 of the workers will incur job-related hearing handicaps by retirement age. Compliance with the 90-decibel standard should reduce this number to 500. Use of 85 decibels as the average noise level would result in only 150 employees with noticeable hearing loss. (A hearing handicap according to the government is a loss of 25 decibels in hearing ability—or the inability to understand quiet speech in a still room.)

Issuing ear muffs and ear plugs has not been satisfactory in other plants. A survey by Employers Insurance of Wausau of 1,148 plants which issued ear protectors to employees revealed that only 22.5 percent of the programs remained in effect longer than six months. Your company, too, found that most plants failed to issue ear protection to new employees and that the regular employees felt that they could not work comfortably with the protection coverings.

Other facets of the noise proposal would require regular tests of the hearing of workers subjected to loud noises, and of hearing-conservation measures to protect those found to have impaired hearing because of job noises.

18. The employees of your small, independent hardware company (Moore-Bradley), which has six branches in your state, have begun to ask about a retirement plan. As comptroller you have been asked by the president, Morton Day, to suggest a plan that will pacify employees but cost little or no money. Trained in finance and keeping up with the subject, you've decided to write a report to the president recommending that your company offer IRA to workers on an individual-option basis. IRA (or Individual Retirement Account), a special tax-deferred savings plan, provides a nest egg for workers who do not benefit from formal company pension plans. It became available under federal law and IRS (Internal Revenue Service) regulations January 1.

As comptroller you can set up the books so that you can help salt away 15 percent of an employee's income up to a maximum of $1,500 annually. The cash deposited in an IRA will be deducted from the worker's paychecks and will not be counted as income at income-tax time on the W–2 forms. And the income earned on IRA deposits (the best current interest rates you can get safely) is not currently reported for tax purposes. All taxes on the funds are deferred until they are withdrawn after workers retire, when they are usually in a much lower tax bracket. At that point, payments from an IRA can be enjoyed without loss of social security benefits, too.

The Frudential Insurance Company is one of the largest insurers entering the IRA field. It plans on 50,000 to 65,000 IRAs this year. Bay View Federal Savings and Loan in San Francisco opened payroll-deduction IRA plans with nine companies during the first 12 days of last month.

Use the following table to explain the tax advantages of an IRA. But remember that your boss (Day) is in hardware, not an income-tax specialist. Furthermore, if he approves, he (or you) will have to explain the plan so that the employees can understand. Better write it that way now.

Taxpayer in 25 percent bracket

Money Invested in	*IRA*	*Taxable Fund*	*Gain in Using IRA*
5 years	$ 8,456	$ 6,155	$ 2,301
10 years	19,771	13,824	5,947
15 years	34,914	23,382	11,532
20 years	55,178	35,293	19,885

Taxpayer in 50 percent bracket

Money Invested in	IRA	Taxable Fund	Gain in Using IRA
5 years	$ 8,456	$ 3,982	$ 4,474
10 years	19,771	8,598	11,173
15 years	34,914	13,949	20,965
20 years	55,178	20,153	35,025

19. Before you write your application letter and data sheet later in the course, but after reading Chapter 9, you are to think about the job and the company you would like to work for. To avoid loose thinking (and to help your teacher help you too), assume the role and fictitious name of a client adviser in a large employment agency and—

1. Get a job description from the *Directory of Opportunity*.
2. Select a company by reading annual reports, Moody's series, business periodicals, card catalog. CPA firms like Ernst and Ernst and investment companies like Merrill Lynch, Pierce, Fenner and Smith have helpful pamphlets.
3. Find out what the market is like today from *Occupational Outlook Handbook* (put out by the U.S. Bureau of Labor) and the *College Placement Annual*.

With this information write a letter report (addressed to yourself but turned in to your teacher) on the job (description), the company, and the market or outlook for you and the company. Make your references to the sources subordinate to the information.

20. Use a subject line and write to I. B. Stearns, President, from M. K. Stanley, Director of Finance, telling him that the total revenues this year went up to $201.6 million or an 8 percent gain over last year. Your overall tax bill went up to $50.4 million which represented 25 cents of each revenue dollar. Revenues from overseas sales went up 10 percent or $83.5 million while domestic revenues went up 7 percent to $118.1 million. Biggest factor was the high federal taxes. Local taxes increased rapidly too. Local taxes went up from $23.1 million five years ago to $38.6 million this year. This is an annual growth rate of 11 percent a year. Earnings per share of common stock increased 7 cents this fiscal year to $2.08. Income for common stock was $45.8 million. Stanley recommends that of this amount, $32.9 million to be paid out in dividends while $12.9 million be reinvested in the business. This will permit a common stock dividend of $1.40 per share.

21. As Martin Bellinger, personnel director of Four–N Company, write a memo report to R. H. Hamilton, Executive Officer, on the progress in the

equal employment opportunity program in your company, using today's date. Your study included male and female of Caucasians, blacks, Orientals, American Indians, and Spanish, for three years ago and now, during which time total employment grew 14 percent. You are reporting on just the blacks and whites because the other groups made up such a small percentage.

Percentage of male, female, and black employees in each job category for three years ago and now

Job Category	Male		Female		Black	
	3 Years Ago	Now	3 Years Ago	Now	3 Years Ago	Now
Officials and managers ...	99.0%	97.2%	1.0%	2.8%	0.3%	0.9%
Professionals	96.9	92.1	3.1	7.9	0.9	2.0
Technicians	88.1	85.7	11.9	14.3	2.4	4.1
Sales workers	99.7	96.0	0.3	4.0	2.2	3.5
Office and clerical	28.0	19.3	72.0	80.7	2.6	4.1
Craftsmen	98.6	97.2	1.4	2.8	3.2	3.6
Operatives	60.5	58.7	39.5	41.3	6.2	6.9
Laborers	78.1	70.3	21.9	29.7	10.9	12.0
Service workers	77.2	84.6	22.8	15.4	5.4	6.4
All categories	75.4	72.7	24.6	27.3	3.6	4.5

The key word here is *progress*. As a principle and an agreement with EEOC (Equal Employment Opportunity Commission), the 4–N Company is committed to evolutionary (but not revolutionary) employment practices that lead to a work force which reflects the statistical picture of the competent people in the population of the area.

22. Assume that you are Donald R. Samdahl, tool-room foreman, and you want to prepare a justification report for your boss Harvey Mappin, Operations Manager, Robinson Machine Company, New Brunswick, NJ 08901. For three years the Robinson Company has been sending tools for numbering to the Revere Electric Company, Patterson, New Jersey, for a cost of $477.50 annually, or 16 cents per tool. Robinson has more than 6,000 items in the tool room, and purchasing department records indicate that annual replacements and additions average 2,980 items. Also, there's added cost of bookkeeping and transportation. And you're getting tired of all the lip (or worse) you have to take from mechanics when they want a tool and it's gone to Patterson for numbering.

An electric pencil with necessary attachments costs $63.85 and is made by the Heinz Products Company. Instruction on its use will be given to the employees of Robinson in an hour's time with no interruption of tool-room operation. Your men spend most of their time on tool maintenance, except during the rush at the first of the shift, and they would have plenty of time to number new tools as they are received. Much of tool maintenance is performed as a time filler.

23.   Andrew Beck, owner of Beck Furniture Company (makers of furniture and built-ins, Austin, Texas), has the problem of high electric bills (jumped from an average $3,500 a month three years ago to $7,500 per month last year and estimated to be $10,000 per month this year). He priced standard modern electrical generating equipment but felt he couldn't afford the price: one half to three quarters of a million dollars. To help solve his problem he calls on you, a former electrical engineer for Texas Lone Star Company, Dallas, now doing private consulting, to advise him.

You discover that Beck has been burning wood sawdust for 20 years at the rate of ten tons a day. He even spent $125,000 last year for automatic disposal equipment, including air pollution control. Unbeknown to Beck, a cubic foot of sawdust has the same BTU (British Thermal Unit) value as a cubic foot of lignite coal. Thinking of the sawdust as fuel, when you looked for a steam boiler and electric generators you found that the Navy was decommissioning many of the old ships and for $300,000 you could purchase (from the famous old hospital ship *Hope*) the boiler, three 500-kilowatt steam generators, the coolers, the circulating system, and the switching system (and move them from Brownsville and set them up in Austin, in about six months). By using the generator setup from *Hope* and sawdust from the furniture manufacturing process, Beck can save money on electricity. In your judgment (based on inspection) all these pieces of equipment should last at least ten years. Justify the purchase of the equipment. Assume salvage of excess disposal equipment of $62,500 and five yearly payments on remaining loan at 10% on balance.

24.   As a sociologist-demographer consultant to *Ebony* magazine, you have the job of helping the editors and writers keep informed on the progress of the 24 million blacks the magazine strongly desires to appeal to by careful adaptation. To help *Ebony* serve in this changing society, you collected the following facts from the U.S. Census Bureau's four-year study, "Social and Economic Status of the Black Population," published last July. Basically the study compares significant figures four years ago (labeled "then") and now. Write a memo using these facts and explain the interesting and significant trends. Though the editors might see the effects these trends should have on the content and style in *Ebony*, you want to go as far as you can in pointing them out—as recommendations. (Interpret the given data but stress trends rather than the constantly changing raw figures, next page.)

25.   After a thorough study of sales and profits for Wiggle Piggle grocery chain, Lincoln, Nebraska, you, a management consultant, have the job

Median famliy income	Blacks	Whites	Blacks' Income as Percentage of Whites' Income
Then	$6,279	$10,236	61.3
Now	$7,808	13,356	58.5

Unemployment	Then	Now	Increase
Blacks	8.2%	9.9%	21%
Whites	4.5	5.0	11

Education	Then	Now
Proportion of blacks in college (age 18–24)	15%	18%
Proportion of blacks with 4 years of college (age 25–34)	6.1	8.1

Migration	Moving in	Moving out	Net Migration
West	172,000	49,000	+123,000
South	276,000	241,000	+ 35,000
Northeast	88,000	143,000	− 55,000
North central	96,000	199,000	−103,000

Black demography	Then	Now	Change
Suburbs	3,433,000	4,101,000	Up 19.5%
Central cities	12,909,000	13,777,000	Up 6.7
Small towns, rural areas	5,714,000	5,748,000	Up 0.6

of recommending to the board of directors technological innovations that might help increase the profits. Last year sales at minimarkets increased 22 percent, despite high prices; their pretax profits, as a percentage of sales, averaged 4.8 percent, as opposed to a bare 1.1 percent in supermarkets like Wiggle Piggle. Supermarkets depend on high volume, not high markups, for their profits. Some suggestions you've thought of or heard of include computerized warehouses, automated checkout systems, meat cutting by laser or electronic beam (to reduce waste and labor costs), solar energy to power frozen-food cases, and computer hookups with savings and loan associations. This last appeals to you, and you have the go-ahead sign from First Federal Savings and Loan and the Nebraska Supreme Court, which ruled that the stores would not be acting as savings and loan branches.

Customers are enthusiastic about the system because neither First Federal nor Wiggle Piggle levies a service charge on their transactions, according to the two stores where a pilot study was conducted. The managers of the two pilot stores found that this system attracted more customers to their stores, curtailed time-consuming check-cashing operations, and reduced bad-check losses. Banks want to put in the same type of system, but they cannot put terminals in locations more than 50 miles away from the bank's main or branch office according to a ruling by U.S. Comptroller of the Currency James Smith (ruling of last December).

A customer of the S and L can present a deposit or withdrawal slip and a coded identification card to a Wiggle Piggle employee, who punches the transaction onto a typewriter-size console tied into First Federal's main computer. Once the central computer approves a withdrawal transaction, funds are transferred from the customer's savings account to Wiggle Piggle's account and the Wiggle Piggle employee hands over the cash. A customer wishing to make a deposit writes a check payable to Wiggle Piggle; the computer credits the customer with the deposit and debits the grocery chain's account.

26. Moving across the United States is big business to your Bowe Chemical Company, since you pay for the moves of new employees and employees whom you transfer. There's no way to guarantee a perfect move; but from the Interstate Commerce Commission (ICC), which requires every moving company to hand it and each potential customer a copy of its performance report for the previous year, you have made a chart of 21 moving companies. From these figures select a company (identified by number—left-hand column) that would be the best carrier for moving your employees' household goods. Your short report in memo form goes from you, the treasurer, to the president, Donald Shellabarger, explaining your choice and your reasons.

		Shipment (percent)			
Moving Company	Under-estimated (percent)	Picked up Late	Delivered Late	With Damage Claim of $50 or More	Average Time to Settle Claim (days)
1	24%	5%	19%	23%	42
2	25	16	21	24	54
3	24	5	23	17	40
4	26	4	24	13	46
5	23	6	12	16	18
6	21	21	30	17	24
7	8	5	12	16	52
8	21	2	16	19	37
9	20	8	14	13	46
10	16	18	21	15	45
11	16	11	26	12	20
12	25	1	20	12	26
13	11	7	30	16	63
14	25	1	27	20	44
15	21	1	14	26	28
16	27	13	15	16	50
17	30	2	12	17	67
18	23	1	16	11	32
19	19	10	18	11	43
20	25	16	15	13	31
21	17	3	23	13	46
Average for all 21 carriers	21%	7%	19%	16%	41 days

27. As supervisor of refrigeration and air conditioning at the biggest hospital in your area, you have a crew of three service and repair mechanics and three mechanic's helpers. Because of the amount of work, the turnaround time (report, work-order, repair) on repair and nonroutine service jobs is sometimes a month; and your department has been taking a considerable amount of heat (flak) from everybody else. Although the hospital has grown from 250 to 350 beds over the past five years, your crew has remained the same. Furthermore, 60 percent of your equipment is ten or more years old; and, according to your experience and an article in the *Refrigeration and Air Conditioning Journal* last month (pp. 15–19), frequency and seriousness of repair on such equipment rise rapidly in the last 5 years of its 15-year normal-expectancy life. The article also says that regularity of maintenance affects the average life more than the amount of running does. Your replacement costs for the past four years seem to be in line with the article: (in round numbers) $17,500; $26,250; $35,000; $43,750.

You and all your crew feel that you need a fourth work team of a mechanic and a helper to take some of the pressure off your work force. You also all agree that the best mechanic you know you can get is one of your helpers; Aubrey Ilkerson (just over three years on the job; knows the equipment; has been servicing it under supervision, as the other helpers have, for two and one years). If you upgrade Ilkerson to mechanic, you will need to add two more helpers; so the added costs will be $20,800/yr. (increase of $4,160 for Ilkerson going from $4/hr. to $6/hr. for 52 weeks of 40 hrs. and two new helpers at $4/hr.).

You want to prepare a justification report to convince your boss (Eugene Scott, the plant manager) to authorize your plan. You want to have your program in effect by late spring, before the warm weather increases your work load. You are sure you can reduce the turnaround times on both service and repair—and thus increase patient and employee comfort (and, you hope, reduce the flak you and your crew swallowed last summer); but you also feel strongly (because of experience and the *Journal* article) that you can arrest if not reverse the steadily increasing replacement costs by more regular maintenance service, more prompt repair, and (in some cases) repairing instead of replacing.

28. For other memo cases, see GS 3, 24, and 26 beginning on page 300.

CASES FOR SHORT ANALYTICAL REPORTS

1. At Y University the students complained about the lack of parking spaces near their classes and the inadequate time (ten minutes) between classes for the distances from building to building. The campus police and faculty complained about rampant illegal parking, and everybody com-

plained about the dangers (from heavy and often erratic campus traffic) to students and faculty going on foot between buildings. To help with these problems, you and the other officers of the Student Government Association recommended that the university buy trams and that $5 of the $10 parking tag (required on student cars parked on the campus) be allocated to pay for the trams. The university went along and bought four trams for $161,000 last March—to be amortised over the expected life of 20 years.

Now that the trams have settled in on their first full year of operation and facts from experience are available, the university has asked for a report on the success of the project; and you, who started the thing (and are now working as assistant to the university business manager), are to write it. The pointed questions are whether the trams are serving their purposes, whether the system is financially sound, and how well students and faculty like it.

The trams cover four routes and are scheduled to go 375 miles a day for the 150 school days in the two-semester year (will not run during the smaller-enrollment summer sessions). Three trams run ten hours each per day (7:30–5:30) and one runs six hours (5:30–11:30) at night five days a week. During the month you checked carefully, you found that each tram-hour of operation costs $4.97 ($3 for the specially trained student driver, 77 cents for maintenance, and $1.20 for fuel and oil). Insurance for the four costs $3,000 a year. Despite the fact that 12,000 of the 16,000 students bought campus-parking tags for cars, the trams picked up 62,018 riders during the 20-operating-day month checked.

The student newspaper voluntarily ran (gratis) your motivational lead-in and questionnaire and set up deposit boxes at all building entrances. After stirring all together, you withdrew 200 student and 100 faculty responses, making a split sample of each. Closeness of split-sample results showed you had a valid sample. Significant percentages (student/faculty) are: easier parking 89/93; reduced class tardiness 78/73; saved time 97/89; improved safety 89/96. Only two major complaints came out: post more map-and-schedule cards and stick to them; in cold or rainy weather, require drivers to put up the curtains. The campus police department reports a 76 percent reduction in illegal parking.

2. The magazine you work for (*Living*, 215 Long Beach Boulevard, Long Beach, CA 90801) has been built around home decoration, house plans, gardening, entertaining, recipes for good eating, and homemaking. The senior editor, Gloria Kazimann, calls you in and asks you what you think about adding a section on leisure. As a marketing analyst you are to gather the facts and write a report on how people in the United States spend their time and money at leisure—not for publication in *Living* but to indicate whether a section on leisure might have enough appeal (and, if so, what kinds of articles and advertising might have the most appeal).

Government and industry data show that last year Americans' enthusiasm for entertainment, sports, travel, and self-improvement led to outlays of $180 billion—12.5 percent above the previous high the year before. Trend lines suggest equal activity this year. Statisticians estimate that leisure spending can be expected to double again in the ten years ahead. Foreign travel climbed an estimated 6 percent for a record outlay of $12.6 billion. Numbers of vacation trips within the country continued to soar, despite the rising cost of gas for cars. People made at least 210 million recreational visits to national parks, about double the number ten years ago. Sales of boats and other recreational vehicles boomed. At least 255 million spectators went to major sporting events during the year.

Today 98 percent of all U.S. households have TV, an estimated 13 million of them wired for cable-TV reception, at a billion dollars annually in fees. Over $12 billion went for stereo gear, radios, television sets, and other consumer electronic products. Still book sales were on the upswing too. Theme parks, like Disney World in Orlando, Florida, attracted more than 14 million visitors last year, up 7.8 percent. Disneyland (California) reports that nearly 11 million attended. Astroworld, a theme park in Texas, reports a 19.9 percent increase in admissions for last season. Four major amusement parks run by Six Flags, Inc., had a combined increase of 8 percent in attendance. At Mount Rushmore in South Dakota, attendance rose to 2.3 million; attendance gained by 8.6 percent at Stone Mountain Memorial Park, Georgia, and jumped 20 percent at Johnson Space Center near Houston, to top 1 million.

Thomas Burke of the Marriott Corporation, which operates restaurants in 38 states, says, "Americans are eating out in growing numbers. Seven years ago about 1 food dollar out of every 4 was spent eating away from home, but today it's 1 out of 3. Three years from now, at this rate, about 50 percent of the food dollar will be spent eating away from home." Moviegoers spent $1.3 billion for tickets in the first six months of last year, up 17 percent from the record level of the same period the previous year. Broadway theaters expect to break attendance records this season, with over 10 million patrons from June of last year to May of this year. So far ticket sales are up 12 percent. Opera for the first seven weeks of this season ran at 94 percent of capacity, a bit higher than last year, even though ticket prices increased by 13 percent and the season was extended to 30 weeks. Nationwide, a Harris Survey showed that 62 million Americans went to at least one live theater performance, 24 million attended a dance performance, and 78 million visited some kind of museum last year.

According to the U.S. Department of the Interior, 24 outdoor recreation activities attract millions (who take part five or more times a year): walking or jogging, 96.7 million; picnicking, 84.0; pool swimming, sunning, 83.5; bicycling, 66.1; fishing, 61.9; nature walking, 61.9; beach swimming, sunning 59.5; tennis, 40.9; boating 34.3; riding off-road vehicles 33.8; hiking or backpacking, 21.1; hunting, 24.5; developed-site camping, 21.0; sledding, 20.8; golfing, 18.9; ice skating, 15.7; primitive-site camping, 15.0; horse-back riding, 13.5; water-skiing, 13.1; canoeing or kayaking, 9.0; snow-mobiling, 7.8; sailing, 7.8; downhill skiing, 7.3; cross-country skiing, 2.0. In addition many millions garden, sightsee, visit parks, and take part in other leisuretime events.

3.   John Roberts, financier, wants a report showing the project's sound-ness before helping you open a sporting goods store in Main City, USA. Main City has a total population of 130,000 with a projection estimate two years from now of 134,000, according to the current Survey of Buying Power Data Service, p. 13 in *Sales and Marketing Management* Magazine, 633 Third Avenue, New York. The same page shows number of house-holds as 39,800, with a projection estimate two years from now of 43,900. Median percentage of population by age group is as follows: median age, 27.8; age 0–17, 27.3 percent; 18–24, 18.7; 25–34, 14.3; 35–49, 15.6; and 50 and over, 24.1. Total EBI is $633,208,000; the median household's EBI is $13,047,000. On the same page you find the percentages of households by EBI group: $8,000–$9,999 (7.1); $10,000–$14,999 (16.2); $15,000–$24,999 (26.9); $25,000 and over (16.9). In other words, a total of 60 percent of Main City's households earn above the moderate income of $10,000.

Retail sales (again page 13) measure the drawing power to local retail establishments; and per household retail sales measure the characteristic of spending, as shown in the table. Managers from five local sporting goods

	Last Year	This Year
Total retail sales	$429,533,000	$689,822,000
Per household retail sales	10,792	15,713

stores say they serve a wide variety of customers, but students are generally the primary buyers. All say that apparel generates the most revenue (jerseys, gym shorts, uniforms, warm-ups, hats, and footwear). All these five managers say that the general interest in sports is growing, and they predict expansion in the future.

The state university has 16,000 students. According to Intramural Sports Director Steve Martin, 5,632 or 32 percent of students and faculty partici-pated in university recreation programs last fall. Spring participation in-creases to 7,744 students and faculty, equaling a 44 percent rate. Football, basketball, volley ball, softball, and swimming are the main team sports. Individually oriented students who like to jog or play tennis are not in-cluded in the intramural figures. The university provides 20 tennis courts for open play to students and faculty. Racquet-ball courts, basketball courts, and the natatorium provide the main recreational facilities. Thomas

Field and Hinton Park provide areas for touch football and softball. The university's athletic teams include 400 students; intercollegiate sports include football, cross country, basketball, wrestling, swimming, golf, baseball, tennis, and track.

Tim Parker, director of the county Park and Recreation Department, supplied you with the figures in the table. Main City's recreation facilities

	Age	Participation (number)
Little League baseball	13–18	185
Little League football	9–14	425
Basketball league	16 and up	700
Bowling league	all ages	35
Volleyball teams	16 and up	330
Tennis teams	all ages	105
Softball teams	16 and up	8,400
Total equals 10,180 participants.		

include 17 public parks, 19 playgrounds, 21 softball fields, one baseball field, two swimming pools, and 18 tennis courts. The county school system has 12,952 students in grades kindergarten through 12. All students are required to take physical education. The usual team sports of football, cross-country, basketball, baseball, and track are provided, and many clubs or service organizations have teams.

The YMCA's main branch has a youth program which has 2,300 members (boys and girls, 6–17). Paul Morrow, youth director, reports a 35 percent increase across the board in sports. Participation has doubled in the last three years. Average yearly increase is 15–20 percent. Youth sports are as follows: fall soccer, 450; winter basketball, 500; spring soccer, 600; summer baseball, 600; summer basketball, 150; making a total of 2,300. The adult program at the YMCA reports a total membership of 600 men and women. The other YMCA, the Benjamin Barnes branch, reports a youth program of 255 and an adult program of 35.

Main City's temperate climate with an annual average temperature of 73.2 degrees and an annual average of 201 clear days makes it conducive to sports.

4.   Assume that Kermit Kilgore, owner of a successful restaurant on a well-traveled boulevard in Main City, USA (see preceding case for facts) asks you to do a report on whether the restaurant, The Blue Max, should expand its facility. The restaurant (20 sq. ft. per seat, 6,000 sq. ft.) has the capacity to seat 300. The lounge (15 sq. ft. per seat or 2,250 sq. ft.) seats 150. You have observed that on Thursday, Friday, and Saturday custom-

ers sometimes have to wait as much as 45 minutes to be served during the peak business hours from 6:30 to 9 P.M. People have been turned away from the lounge on Wednesday, Thursday, Friday, and Saturday nights. If The Blue Max could expand 2,000 square feet, then there would be capacity for 100 additional seats in the restaurant (20 sq. ft. per seat) or 133 seats in the lounge (15 sq. ft. per seat).

Land behind The Blue Max (150' × 240', 36,000 sq. ft.) is for sale at $75,000. The land required for the expansion of the building would be 50 by 40 feet (2,000 sq. ft.). About 25,000 square feet would be needed to provide 100 parking spaces and entry/exit lanes. A parking space that leaves enough clearance for the opening of car doors measures 18 by 9 feet, so 100 parking spaces would take 16,200 square feet. Adequate entry/exit lanes usually take about half as much area as the parking spaces in a lot. So the 36,000 square feet would be adequate for all uses, including some flower beds, shrubs, and small green lawn areas.

From a local contractor, Robert Blakeney, you learn that building cost will be approximately $50 per square foot, or $100,000 ($50 × 2,000 sq. ft.). In a talk with Ora Lee Hill, interior designer and decorator, you estimate that it will cost about $100,000 for furnishings and decorating the new area. Blakeney estimated that to pave the parking lot and do the landscaping and planting you'd have to figure on $10,000.

Present sales on Sunday have run $2,000 and nothing for the lounge. On successive week days the restaurant brought in $3,600 and the lounge $800; $4,500 and $1,200; $4,600 and $1,400; $4,900 and $1,900; $5,000 and $2,100; $5,000 and $1,900; making a week's total of $38,900.

Competition comes mainly from the dining rooms in seven motel/hotels and nine smaller but long-established restaurants. The 122 fast-food places, two truck stops, and three cafeterias draw largely from a different clientele. There's some competition from the food service at the four country clubs, whose clientele is also mostly different (in a different direction).

Despite this competition, Kilgore (from experience) and you (from observation of customers waiting during a typical week) estimate that The Blue Max could increase business in the restaurant at least 15 percent (or in the lounge by 10 percent) through the considered expansion. Other considerations (plus that speculation) help to determine whether to expand the restaurant or the lounge (if either): (1) kitchen facilities are already capable of handling the expansion, whereas behind-the-bar facilities are not; (2) despite twice as high profit margins in the lounge as in the restaurant, the increased restaurant receipts might produce more profit; and (3) since peak lounge business comes a little later in the evening than peak restaurant business, some excess lounge customers might be more likely to be seated in available space in the restaurant than the other way around.

5. Using the facts about Main City (Case 3), write a report to Harriet Chew, owner of the exclusive Oxford Galleries, in Central City (population 340,000), 60 miles from Main City. The only larger city near Main City is Central City, where there's a great variety of furniture stores. Chew would like to expand and thinks that a branch in Main City might be a good business move. Oxford Galleries carries only quality furniture like Heritage, Baker, Kittenger, Heywood-Wakefield, and Drexel. As an analyst for Fackseekers, 541 Spring Arcade, Los Angeles 90008, you find that Main City has 38 furniture stores, four outdoor furniture stores, and one firm that leases furniture. Of the 38 stores, only one, McCall's Interiors, has quality furniture. Your report will not go into specific store location.

6. Assume that you have chosen a career. Write a four- to eight-page report giving figures on such things as employment (supply and demand), salaries, qualifications, and professional opportunities for growth and advancement in the line of work you are planning to do. Before you write the report, do secondary research at the library and do primary research by having an interview with someone in the field of your interest. You are to quote from or paraphrase sections of that interview. You are to write this short analytical report to Frank Williams, long-time, 60-year-old friend of yours in a nearby city. Williams is willing to back you financially for a master's degree, but he wants this report showing a not-too-risky project before he hands out the cash. You have agreed to pay him back during the first five years you are employed.

7. When George Turnipseed's little seven-year-old bait shop (George's) burned 18 years ago, George expanded into a bigger building in downtown Traverse City, Michigan (49684), and expanded his line to all kinds of fishing and hunting equipment and supplies. He now asks you to give him a report on whether he should incorporate, and so gives you recent financial statements and tells you a lot of his history.

Turnipseed is 55 and the only member of the family or among the 17 employees interested in or capable of running the business. If he were out, a replacement as manager might not look after the best interests of the owner(s); dissolution would close off a stream of considerable income; and selling out would bring a considerable long-term capital gain (and tax) but would kill the goose that is laying golden eggs. If the business were incorporated and Turnipseed (as president) were out, the vice president would merely take over until the stockholders elected a new president.

Though George's has had to go outside the business for capital only once (during the move and big expansion), doing something like that in the foreseeable future might be difficult; bankers fear proprietors with only not-very-liquid inventory as collateral in periods of tight money, and interest rates can soar. A corporation could sell stock or issue bonds to raise money, probably quicker and cheaper. But starting the business cost only state and county license fees of $6 and $4, while incorporation would cost about $2,500 in legal and other paperwork charges and lots of time and headaches from winding red tape into desired curlicues—file application, issue stock, set up a management team (president, vice president, and secretary required by law) and learn the corporate game, including how to play the house organ.

Corporate form makes easier the transfer of ownership rights. Stocks or bonds sell, trade, or pass along as an inheritance just as readily as cash. As a corporation, George's (not just George Turnipseed) would be liable for all the business debts and no personal property could be taken as payment. Should George's go bankrupt, owners would have lost only the money invested in the stock, no personal assets. Probably the biggest point in considering incorporation for George's is the income-tax question, because IRS treats proprietorships as individuals and quite differently from corporations. The present corporate tax rate is 22 percent on the first $25,000 of taxable income and 46 percent above that. The personal rate reaches 22 percent at $15,000 and progressively climbs upward. Furthermore, Subchapter S allows corporations the choice of the rates, saving money for those earning less than $15,000.

George's (as a corporation, but not as a proprietorship/individual) could deduct the $4.75 a week paid on each of 17 employees for Blue Cross/Blue Shield group medical and group term life insurance and the depreciation on the minnow truck ($550 a year, five-year straight line) and minnow tanks ($2333, 15-year SLD). By making himself president of the corporation at $22,000 salary, his wife vice president at $8,000, and his married daughter secretary at $6,000 (her present job and pay), George could also deduct the salaries, along with the former $1,203,000 operating expenses, from gross income of $1,250,000. If he also took 51 percent of the stock himself and 49 percent for his wife, they would each get about $1,000 in dividends, and a $100 tax exclusion (assuming a 50 percent payout of corporate earnings). Thus the corporation could take advantage of Subchapter S and pay essentially no tax. Mr. and Mrs. Turnipseed (filing jointly) would pay tax on their salaries and dividends ($30,000 plus about $2,000) minus personal exemptions and $200 dividend exclusions—a tax of about $7,000—instead of paying taxes on $47,000 minus personal exemptions—a tax of about $13,000.

8. Assume that your boss, Clinton Grimes, is just back from Europe where he was most impressed with the Hypermarket—a combination discount store, supermarket, and warehouse under a single roof. Typically it sells both food and nonfood items at 10–15 percent below normal retail prices and stacks merchandise as high as ten feet. *Cost:* $11 million; *foot-*

age: food and general merchandise, 250,000 sq. ft., supermarket, 42,000 sq. ft., general merchandise, 103,000 sq. ft.; *parking:* 3,000 cars; *number of checkouts:* 49 up front, 11 department registers; *opening stock at retail:* $5 million; *estimated annual income:* $35 million. Also assume that Grimes is the owner of a large shopping-mall chain and that you are his operations manager. Grimes called his management team together to discuss the idea of establishing a Hypermarket in the United States, but there was some dissension—Americans would not react favorably to a store with 250,000 square feet. Since there are no Hypermarkets in the United States, there are no facts. Your assignment is to write up a questionnaire and/or interview shoppers and see if there is acceptance of the Hypermarket idea. Then write a report to Clinton Grimes based on your findings.

9. The biggest chain grocery in your locality is having quite a problem nationally with various forms of larceny—$8 million of losses last year through customer shoplifting, employee theft, and so on. The management therefore issued a memo directing the manager of each store to study the situation and institute needed changes. (If you need another memo situation, here's one.) The local manager, under whom you work, tossed the directive memo (and thus the ball) to you. You are to confer for any information already known, to study the layout and procedures by on-the-spot observation and questioning, and to propose the things to be done to reduce losses. The job may or may not include a memo or other set of directions to all store employees on just what to do when they know or suspect that larceny or pilferage is going on. This could be a separate memo assignment, requiring a good knowledge of the law and/or law enforcement procedures—perhaps a talk with some police officers.

10. The owners of the Spell-Dees Nursery, Beaumont, Texas (Tom Spell and David Dees), have asked you, the office manager, to submit a report analyzing demand over the past few years. You've gone through the sales records of the past four years to see what sells the best as a guide to what to plant the most of, what to reduce, and maybe even what to discontinue. Classifications are hard to set up; for instance, there's no way to tell what kinds of roses are in most frequent demand—but at average sales of $2, it's a safe bet that not many prize rosebushes are sold. But you've worked out the classifications, the number of bushes sold for the last four years, and the average sales price of each variety. Your records show that you average about 5 percent replacements; that is, about 5 out of every 100 plants sold have to be replaced under the terms of your replacement policy: replacement at one-half price if the plant dies within the first year. Your profit margin is about 50 percent.

Study the figures for what they imply in the way of increasing or decreasing demand for particular types and for the relative profitability of the various items. Then make recommendations about next year's stock.

Gross sales of shrubbery by the Spell-Dees Nursery in the last four years

	Four Years Ago	Three Years Ago	Two Years Ago	Last Year	Average Sales Price
Abelia	2,896	2,980	4,422	4,460	$ 2.25
Ashfodi Juniper	136	144	202	235	3.00
Azalea	2,940	3,672	6,440	8,756	6.00
Berkman Arborvitae	146	105	137	165	3.50
Boxwood	126	262	344	423	18.00
Camellias	2,888	3,070	4,175	5,480	12.00
Cherry Laurel	174	198	234	256	9.00
Dogwood	81	76	143	166	4.00
Gardenia	1,178	1,239	1,897	1,976	9.00
Ilex Bullata	602	875	1,092	1,160	4.50
Ilex Burfordi	247	288	370	406	6.00
Ilex Rotundifolia	1,786	1,930	2,706	2,816	3.00
Irish Juniper	176	189	259	278	3.00
Ligustrum	2,982	2,646	4,562	4,250	4.50
Nandina	3,364	3,544	3,782	3,802	3.00
Pfitzer Juniper	2,078	2,108	2,986	3,208	2.50
Photinia Glabra	472	381	277	199	2.00
Roses	7,271	7,492	8,792	9,879	2.00
Sargent Barberry	601	507	488	462	3.00
Spirea	192	160	107	126	2.50
Spirea Thunbergia	148	164	92	86	3.00
Yellow Jasmine	296	243	203	194	4.00
Total	30,780	32,270	43,710	48,783	

Submit the report to the owners in attractive, readable form. Use a title page as a cover, a letter of transmittal which is also a synopsis, and the analysis.

11. Doris Fields, director in charge of the placement bureau at the University of Oklahoma, Norman 73069, decided to find out what personnel managers prefer in letters of application from college graduates. So she asked you, the director of the research bureau, if you would help. After joint consultation with the head of the department of business communications, the head of the vocational guidance department, and the head of statistics, you prepared and sent the following questionnaire to 500 personnel managers in Colorado, Indiana, Illinois, Ohio, Michigan, and Pennsylvania. The replies of the 324 who returned the questionnaire are tabulated below. From this material prepare a short analytical report for Fields which will help when she talks to applicants. Copies will also be available in school libraries. Submit the report to Fields with cover, title page, letter of transmittal (which is also an epitome), table of contents, the analysis, and conclusions and recommendations.

1. Which of the following do you prefer from an applicant?
   - 9   Application letter only
   - 86   Application letter and résumé
   - 106 Application letter with placement office credentials sent separately
   - 123 Application letter and résumé with placement office credentials separately
2. Which of the following is more important to you in evaluating an applicant:
   - 55   Application letter
   - 37   Résumé
   - 232 Both equal in importance
3. *a.* Do you object to a duplicated letter of application?
      - 234 Yes   90 No
   b. When considering several applicants for a job, do you eliminate those who send you a duplicated letter of application?
      - 221 Yes   103 No
4. *a.* Do you object to a commercially printed data sheet?
      - 48 Yes   276 No
   b. When considering several applicants for a job, do you eliminate those who send you either of the following:

Mimeographed data sheet	222 Yes	102 No
Commercially printed data sheet	17 Yes	307 No

5. Which of the following do you prefer?
   - 123 Applicant's letter addressed to you by name, followed by your title
   - 85   Applicant's letter addressed to "Personnel Manager"
   - 116 No preference
6. What is your reaction to the following kinds of enclosures with the application?

   Return-addressed postal card
   - 29 Favorable   207 Unfavorable   88 Neutral

   Return-addressed stamped envelope
   - 64 Favorable   71 Unfavorable   189 Neutral
7. *a.* What is your reaction to an applicant's sending you a follow-up letter within a month after the original application?
      - 252 Good   10 Annoying   62 Neutral
   b. If your answer to the above question is "Good," why do you favor a follow-up? (More than one reason allowed.)
      - 73   Shows persistence
      - 178 Indicates interest
      - 220 Lets me know still available
8. In selecting inexperienced employees, which of the following backgrounds do you prefer? Please rank on a 1–2–3–4 basis (highest rank = 1).
   a. Applicant who participated in many extracurricular activities and maintained passing grades
      - (1) 37, (2) 74, (3) 114, (4) 99
   b. Applicant who participated in several extracurricular activities and maintained above-average grades
      - (1) 102, (2) 124, (3) 79, (4) 19

c. Applicant who worked to help pay school expenses and maintained above-average grades
   (1) 164, (2) 106, (3) 36, (4) 18

d. Applicant who participated in no extracurricular activities and maintained honor grades
   (1) 93, (2) 93, (3) 106, (4) 82

9. On many résumés or application letters the applicant lists several specific references—usually under a caption labeled "References."

   a. When do you check these references?
      187 Before the interview
      120 After the interview
       17 Do not check

   b. Do you want this list of references included on the application?
      210 Yes   66 No   48 Immaterial

   c. If your answer to the above question is yes:
      (1) How many references do you prefer? Please encircle your choice.
          (1) 0, (2) 16, (3) 193, (4) 72, (5) 43
      (2) What types of references do you prefer? (Check as many as you desire.)
          314 Previous employers
           37 High-school teachers
           25 Dean of the college
          282 College teachers of related courses
          193 Former supervisors
           14 Other (banker? doctor? minister? family or fraternity friend?)

10. Many college students have worked. Do you want to know about these jobs
    —whether related or not?   304 Yes   20 No
    —part-time while attending school 298 Yes   26 No
    —full-time during summers   306 Yes   18 No

PART FOUR

Oral business communication

chapter 17 | # Oral business communication

["Really, now you ask me," said Alice, very much
confused, "I don't think—"
"Then you shouldn't talk," said the Hatter.]

THROUGHOUT OUR DISCUSSION of letters, memos, and written reports, we have constantly reminded you of the important part oral communications play in business, industry, government, and other sectors of our society. Indeed, repeated studies of executives and managers show that they spend more of their communication time in speaking than in writing.

To manage well, then, you must be effective in both written and oral communication. Whatever the form, a skilled communicator has the advantage in being better able to get subordinates to follow instructions, to get useful information and ideas from others, and to report information to superiors.

For three reasons, in this book we have chosen to give you a thorough treatment of the main kinds of written business communication first and now to help you apply the important principles in effective oral communication:

1. Communication shortcomings that employers complain about in their employees nearly always concern the inability to *write* well.
2. Written work is the better medium for teaching and learning not only the basic language skills of conciseness, correctness, and precision but also for learning to apply the important principles of organization and psychology for effectiveness in business communication.
3. The transfer of learning from written to oral application is much easier and more effective than going the other way.

Training and practice in writing, however, are not substitutes for training and practice in speaking. Ideally, education for a would-be business executive would contain, in addition to business writing courses, a course or two in business speaking taught by a teacher who knew both speech and the principles of business communication using a textbook written by a similarly qualified author. Since no such ideal situation exists, our selective treatment here provides the best treatment available by concentrating on *business* speaking and *the application of effective business communication principles* presented in the earlier parts of this book.

Since both written and oral business communication use the same language and should use the same principles of organization and psychology, what you have learned so far in this book will apply to oral messages. Therefore we will not repeat (but only remind you by cross-referenced page numbers) as we help you transfer the principles and give you additional pointers applicable to the main kinds of oral communication you are likely to need in business—oral reports, interviews, conferences, and dictation. First, however, you need to consider some basics of effective speaking applicable in all kinds of business communication.

BASIC PREPARATION FOR EFFECTIVE SPEAKING

Getting rid of bad habits

To begin with, you have been talking (largely just conversing) longer than you've been writing—and (unless you're very unusual) you probably have some poor speech habits which can hurt you in various ways if you don't correct them:

1. Carelessness in validity and precision of statement, economy of wording, or grammatical propriety are all harmful to business communication. *Solution:* Practice giving them care in your speech as in your writing; improvement in each will reinforce the other.
2. Slovenly or incorrect pronunciation and enunciation may cause misunderstanding (or *not* understanding) and (when you write) misspellings which strike most people as unsightly warts on your competence. *Solution:* Notice how well-educated speakers place accents, assign sound qualities to vowels, and say distinctly all the syllables in key words. If in doubt, check the dictionary—and follow what you find.
3. Inattention to the principles of good organization in sentences, paragraphs, and longer statements that often causes wordiness, incoherence, and even confusion. *Solution:* Carry over into your speaking the principles of organization you have learned in becoming a good writer. Since you talk much more frequently than you write, you will both write *and* speak more clearly, concisely, and effectively if you constantly try to speak that way.

Recognizing similarities to and differences from writing

Certainly, successful speeches have central themes, adequate and reliable facts, coherent and compact organization, clarity and vividness of phrasing, and other stylistic considerations characteristic of good writing as explained in Chapter 2 and throughout this book.

Though written and oral business communications have many similarities, their major differences deserve attention too. All of them will at times influence what you say (or *should* say) and how you say it.

Written	*Oral*
A reader can (if desired) reread unclear or difficult passages.	Except in dyadic (two-person) or small-group situations, a listener must understand the first time or not at all.
A reader's immediate reaction is unknown—no direct feedback exists.	Immediate listener reaction is known—direct feedback does exist, even in groups.
The reader sets the pace.	The speaker sets the pace.
Attention span is usually longer in reading than in listening.	An audience's attention span is limited (though usually increasing with maturity).
A reader has few physical restrictions (may move about).	An audience usually is subject to physical restrictions (must remain seated).
A written record exists (permanent).	No record exists (ephemeral) unless recorded.

Written	*Oral*
Information retrieval is relatively easy.	Information retrieval from a recorded speech is more difficult.
A writer must spell, punctuate, and paragraph.	A speaker must enunciate clearly and pronounce, inflect, and pause appropriately.
Readers are quick to catch even small errors.	An audience is usually not so critical.
A writer may not know all who will read (pass-along readership).	A speaker usually knows and can see who the audience is.

Preparing the speech, the setting, and yourself

Of course your major job in connection with making a speech is preparing what you will say and how you will say it. Both the what and the how, however, depend so much on other factors (like the purpose, topic, methodology, audience, length, and circumstances) that we shall discuss them with specific adaptation to the main kinds of business speaking as we take them up later.

Preparing the physical setting may be wholly, partly, or not at all your responsibility, though usually you will have some say about at least any audiovisual aids needed. Whether you initiate the whole thing or accept an invitation to talk, you need to know from the start at least the date, time, place, and kind and size of audience.

Also helpful is knowledge about whether your presentation is a one-shot, one-speaker affair or one on a panel or in a series. If other speakers are in the picture, certainly you need to know the general topic, theme, and purpose as well as who the others are, their parts or angles or slants, and who precedes and follows you.

Whether you are primarily responsible or not, you will be wise to check in advance on the seating (adequate capacity?), stage settings, temperature controls, lighting, audiovisual facilities, amplifying system (if wanted), and even whether the doors will be open in time for you to set up.

Sometimes you can have a curtain hung on one wall (preferably the one facing the speaker) to kill echoes if the walls and ceiling are hard surfaced. Remember, however, that an audience that fills a room will do much to absorb echoes; so simply spreading out your audience's seating might be sufficient.

If you are using projection equipment or an amplifying system, who will control them? Try them out in advance—you don't want any surprises when you are speaking.

Preparing yourself for making a speech involves your voice, physical appearance, and mental attitude. Ideally, you should follow the Greek motto: moderation in all things. Look neat, clean, and properly combed and clothed for the occasion and your audience. Avoid the appearance of a truck driver just ending a long haul or a manikin modeling the flashiest new clothes.

If you want to improve your speaking voice, here are some simple exercises you can start with. Though they are good for long-range improvement, they can help some after only several minutes a day for a few days. First, get access to a tape recorder. As you probably know, your voice doesn't sound the same to others as it does to you.

1.   Proper breathing, essential to good speaking, begins with the diaphragm. Using it properly will give your voice a more pleasant tone, fuller range, and better projection without straining. To practice, put your hand on your stomach and take a deep breath. Your stomach and hand should move forward. Then exhale by pulling your diaphragm in to force the air out. After a little practice, say and record a few sentences.

2.   If your speech seems muffled or indistinct, you may need to practice placing your tongue properly. To practice, relax your tongue and place it low in your mouth behind and just touching your lower front teeth. Then say and record the vowels (a, e, i, o, u) in all their forms, long and short. Repeat until your vowel sounds are clearly distinguishable.

3.   Since the lips play a major part in forming the sounds of our language, they have to work hard. If yours don't, you'll find yourself mumbling, your vowels will be poorly differentiated, and some of your consonants will be indistinguishable. To strengthen your lips, with your lips apart smile as widely as you can; then quickly purse your lips as if you were going to whistle. Repeat the exercise till you can enunciate distinctly.

4.   If your voice is nasal and sounds harsh to you, you may have a lazy uvula. To loosen it up, open your mouth wide and say "Ahhhhhh." Now say it again, but this time bring the sound into your nasal passages. Alternate saying "Ahhhhhh" normally and nasally and feel your uvula open and close. Now that you know what it feels like when open, you can practice keeping it that way when you speak.

To get yourself in the right frame of mind to give a speech successfully, you may have to remind yourself of how well you are prepared, that you *can* do it—in short, psych yourself up. Your body language—posture, gait, nuances of expression, how you hold your limbs, and so on—will signal to your audience how you really feel. And since these signals are almost impossible to control consciously, we think you will do better to remove the causes of adverse body language. So think positively.

Having prepared well, let the mental attitude you reflect by eye, posture, and gait be that of neither a whipped dog nor a bantam rooster. Instead, calmly reflect confidence and competence. You *are* prepared, you know; perhaps you've practiced your speech before a mirror and timed yourself until any earlier feelings of insecurity are gone. You know more about the subject than the audience does or you wouldn't be speaking in the first place. Those people are there to hear what you have to say, not to hurt you; so you have no reason for "stage fright." You're going to give them what they came for—and make them glad they came.

If the game plan calls for you to walk in and take over, do just that—at the scheduled time and place, confidently but not arrogantly.

Getting into speaking position favorably

If, however, you are to wait in front of your audience for an introduction, sit comfortably relaxed. You prepared both your speech and your clothing before coming in, you know; so let them alone now or you will create a bad impression that you came unprepared.

After the introduction, walk erectly and confidently to your speaking position (notes at the ready), thank the introducer, and move right into your subject. The more poise, confidence, and efficiency you show in these short maneuvers—based on knowing your subject and having your notes ready instead of having to fumble for them—the greater audience respect and support you will get.

We have no firm, invariable advice about whether you should sit or stand, except possibly to sit for small groups (under ten) and stand for large ones. In general, if in doubt, stand. And if you can arrange it, do not use a lectern or podium. A lectern is a crutch for many speakers. They hang on to it desperately, use it as a barrier between them and the audience, and generally hope it will hide their nervousness. It never does. A lectern is useful only for holding your notes and, if needed, a light. Beware, by the way, of lecterns with microphones on them. Your voice will bounce off the surface of the lectern as well as go directly into the mike, sometimes causing a distracting echo.

When the time comes to begin actually speaking, you should be feeling calm and confident, but not arrogant.

GIVING THE SPEECH

Good speaking is, of course, a combination of many elements—the thought content, the style (mainly word choice, sentence patterns, and the organization and transitions), the voice in all its manifold variations, gestures, all forms of facial expressions and other body language, and the metacommunications (the *milieu*, as the French say, meaning the total of surrounding circumstances).

Fortunately, in preparing your speech, the physical setting, and yourself, you will have taken care of the first two and the last one. You could wisely give some prior attention to the others, too, but you can't firm them up completely beforehand—even by writing out the speech with fully "orchestrated" markings for voice variations, gestures, and other body language. You would, at best, look and sound like a ventriloquist's puppet.

Like an accomplished conductor rehearsing an orchestra, you need to have practiced with your orchestra of words, voice, gestures, and so on, so that in your speech you can (without a "musical score") call upon the various instruments to come into play at the right times and for the best effect. Here are a few specific suggestions.

Your voice

Your voice is the major instrument in your orchestra and must be well tuned and played. What voice should you use for speeches or oral reports? Try to speak naturally and easily. Your normal, natural voice is the best. If you try to change your voice without thorough practice first, you'll sound strained and unnatural and distract your audience's attention from what you are saying.

Never, never (if you can avoid it) read a speech! No one without a great deal of training reads a speech well enough to keep an audience awake. What reads well on paper is usually awful when read aloud. Instead, use notes, listing *only* the points you want to cover (perhaps with subheads) and any appropriate quotations too long to memorize easily. You'll be much more natural and far more interesting to listen to. If you are forced to read a speech (say for a speaker who couldn't come) overemphasize changes in the tone and pitch of your voice. Also exaggerate your gestures and expressions. In short, overact a little since you want to break away from "reading aloud" to "talking" what you are reading.

When speaking to an audience, especially a large one, you must project your voice. But projection does not mean shouting. If you shout you may be heard but not understood. Your volume should be sufficient for your farthest listener to hear you without straining but should allow you some volume left over to use for emphasis. If you cannot easily make yourself heard without straining, use a public address system.

In a speech situation you will have to use more variation in the pitch of your voice than for normal conversation. What may be acceptable variation of pitch in a conversation will sound like a monotone in a speech. Be on guard, however, against the tendency to raise the pitch too much and become strident or screechy as you project your voice.

Oral reporting and formal speaking require more than normal attention to pronunciation and enunciation, too—no slurring and certainly no "asides." Speak slowly, and distinctly pronounce all the parts of words, especially the ends, leaving no uncertainty about what you said.

Posture and movements

When speaking, your posture should be erect, alert, confident, relaxed, and *natural*. Your shoulders should be down and loose, not hunched and tense-looking. Keep your stomach in and up—you'll look better and you'll be able to speak better. And keep your backside in; don't slouch. Your feet should be a comfortable distance apart with your weight concentrated on the balls of your feet. Bend your knees slightly; don't lock them back. Locking your knees leads to strain and quivering and may cut off circulation.

Let your hands hang naturally at your sides and don't move them unless you are going to turn a page in your notes or gesture for emphasis. Never put your hands in your pockets or clasp them in front of or behind you. That will cause you to slouch or lean forward. Standing comfortably erect may feel awkward at first, but look at yourself in a mirror. Don't you look more authoritative, commanding, and assured?

Just as you walked calmly and deliberately to a place in front of your audience, move calmly and deliberately around the stage while talking. You should use walking around for emphasis sparingly, however; like all emphatic devices, it loses its effect from overuse. Generally, the more audiovisual aids you use in giving a talk the fewer movements you should make. The important thing is to direct your audience's attention to what you want. Moving around can sometimes retrieve an audience's attention, but too much distracts from what you're saying.

Keep gestures restrained and natural unless the situation requires some overacting. When you do gesture, be aware of what you're doing. Gestures are strong reinforcements to language, but the meanings of many of them are not definite. As rough rules, the more formal the occasion, the more restricted your gestures should be; and the larger your audience, the more exaggerated so that people far away from you can see them clearly.

When you describe something, hold your hands up and apart to show the size. Use your hands to help show spatial relationships, motion, and direction. You can reinforce abstract points by holding up an index finger or pounding a fist into your hand. You can emphasize something by pointing at your audience, making a punching motion, and the like. If you are making a number of points, for emphasis (and for clear transition) hold up the appropriate number of fingers as you tick off each point. You will be wise, however, to try out your gestures before a mirror before you try them out on an audience.

Keep your facial expressions under control, using them only to reinforce what you are saying. Be animated: frown, look sad, outraged, puzzled, whatever you need. You should give the impression of being warm, alert, bright, assured, animated, confident, but not arrogant. And don't forget to smile; an audience responds most favorably to a happy, confident smile. The only way to tell what reaction you are getting is to look your audience in the eye. So make eye contact with members of your audience on a random basis, moving from side to side within but not around or over the heads of your audience—and certainly not on the far wall or your notes (except for momentary glances).

Your language

In speaking as in writing, you must adapt your language to your audience. Before speaking, decide on the level of formality you want to use. But be aware that most untrained speakers use far too formal and ornate language in an effort to overcome a deficiency (usually imaginary) in position or authority. High rhetoric has long been out of style; so keep your language natural. You will get immediate feedback from your audience if your level of formality is inappropriate, and you can quickly adjust (another good reason for speaking from notes instead of a complete text).

Restrict your use of jargon. An occasional use is desirable to indicate that you are "with" the audience; but too much is hard to understand, even when your audience knows the meanings. Also avoid emotionally charged words. They are generally too highly exaggerated for a business situation, and your audience will recognize them for what they are . . . and mistrust you.

Nobody is perfect, and in front of an audience you may make a slip. Don't panic. If you handle the situation right, your audience can remain unaware of your problem; and if it does show, you'll have sympathy. If you make a grammatical error or mispronounce a word, ignore it and keep right on talking. You will thus force your audience to forget your slip quickly and concentrate on what you are saying. If you repeat the word or phrase later, you can do it correctly.

If you forget what comes next in your speech, keep looking thoughtfully at your audience or move about the stage contemplatively until you gather your thoughts. Audiences are not as critical as you may think. In the general run of business speaking they do not expect a professional presentation unless listening to a professional speaker. Your audience will, however, expect you to know your subject, be prepared to talk intelligently about it, and come to a conclusion—requirements you should easily meet when the time comes.

If possible, keep a talk to no more than five or six major points—more are hard to assimilate. Make the transitions clear by any or all means (p. 469) as you shift from one point to another. To give your audience time to digest a major point, you may want to follow it with some lighter material to change pace for the moment.

Special attention tactics

At the beginning of your talk, get your audience's attention immediately. Don't begin uselessly with an egotistic expression like "I'm pleased to be here" or a plea for sympathy like "I'm not used to speaking; so I hope you'll overlook my weaknesses." The best beginning for a speech is the subject—or conclusion if you think your audience will be in favor of what you are going to say. If not, you may want to begin with your arguments before coming to the conclusion. Some specific ways of beginning a speech, roughly in order of effectiveness, are:

1. A rhetorical question.
2. An illustration that leads logically into your subject.
3. A fact or opinion that sets up the first point you want to make.
4. An apropos quotation (such as the one at the beginning of this chapter).
5. A humorous anecdote (which sometimes makes seriousness hard to achieve later).

People's attention spans are short, rarely more than 15 or 20 minutes unless stimulated. You will know when you are losing your audience by the glassy eyes. Here are some preventatives and remedies for an inattentive audience:

1. Slow down your delivery of hard-to-understand material and speed it up for more easily comprehended matter.
2. Provide clear transitions between subjects and show how they *relate* to each other (see pp. 469–70). One of the best ways to lose an audience is to shift topics unannounced. You will befuddle and anesthetize with what seems to be nonsense because it does not relate to the topic you *were* talking about.
3. Eliminate distractions. Curtain off windows that have attractive views, make sure there is no movement behind or to either side of you, ...
4. Use language your audience readily understands. When in doubt, tend toward the simple.
5. Be animated, energetic. Don't stand like a statue, but gesture, vary your facial expressions, move around some.
6. Talk directly to individuals, changing from one to another, from side to side, and from front to back of the audience (as with eye contact).
7. Use visual aids: slides, chalkboard, an object you hold up. . . .

You can regain an audience's wandering attention by:

1. Changing the volume of your voice, keeping in mind that a low voice is better than a shout.

2. Making a change in the level of formality if it fits naturally with what you are saying and you can logically use it for effect.
3. Using attention-getting devices:
    a. Direct a question to a member of the audience you point to (and await the answer).
    b. Make a quick joke or comment that has the "slow burn" effect (and stand smiling, watching as the fire spreads in the audience).
    c. Mimic somebody or something the audience knows (maybe even yourself, the way you've been droning on).
    d. Make a grossly exaggerated gesture or change of pace or volume (kick a chair, s-p-e-l-l s-o-m-e-t-h-i-n-g o-u-t, YELL!), turn to a visual aid (which can serve other purposes than arousing a drowsy audience), say something pertinent but stupid, then pause, looking hard at your notes, throw them in the wastepaper basket, glower at them, turn back to the audience, correct the stupidity, and go on with your speech.

Audiovisual aids

Four questions determine whether you will want to use audiovisual aids:

1. Does the *occasion* justify preparing and using audiovisual aids? For instance, if you are going to sit down with one person and informally deliver your report, would slides or a flip chart be appropriate?

2. Will the benefits justify the *costs* in time and money? Does your budget have enough in it to pay for preparing audiovisual aids?

3. Do you have sufficient *time* before giving your report or speech to prepare audiovisual aids? To prepare slides, for example, you must arrange for a photography session, get a photographer, line up the subjects or objects to be photographed or have someone prepare charts or graphs, conduct the photography session, develop the slides, sort them to pick the best, and arrange them for projection.

4. Are the necessary *facilities* available where you will speak? Projector? Screen? Projector stand? Power source? Public address system? Chalkboard?

Use audiovisual aids only to help your listener or audience better understand what you are saying, never simply because you have them available or just for dramatic effect (except as waker-uppers or unless the occasion calls for some entertainment along with the information). Audiovisual aids play the same part in oral reports that graphics do in written ones: they help make quantitative data clear and quickly and easily comprehensible.

Some common audiovisual aids are: slide projector, overhead (transparency) projector, motion picture projector, opaque projector, videotape player, flip chart, chalkboard, felt board, actual object, model of an object, poster (large drawing, picture, etc.).

The two basic rules for visual aids are (1) they must be clearly visible to all members of your audience, and (2) they must be quickly comprehensible to all members of your audience. The second rule gives the most trouble.

Generally, when a visual aid fails to do its job, the fault is due to either or both (1) too much information, or (2) information presented too small or too densely to be seen. Common examples are charts with too many lines on them or charts whose lines are too fine or light to be seen, and illustrations (such as photographs or detailed drawings) that even when projected are too small to show what the speaker intends.

We recommend that when preparing visual aids you constantly keep in mind that presenting information is wasted effort unless the audience can readily comprehend it. You can find more detailed information on this subject in the many books on giving talks using audiovisual aids, and especially in the fine publications of Eastman Kodak.

When you use a visual, explain it, don't read it, to your audience. *Never* read anything to people that they can see and read themselves. To do so is insulting, implying that they cannot read. Avoid the hackneyed "As this slide shows . . ." introduction to a visual aid. Simply project the next slide or expose the next chart, and keep on the subject of your speech by launching directly into *explaining* it: "The rise in snow tire sales over. . . ."

Be careful not to block the view of a visual aid from any members of your audience. If, for instance, you want to point to something on a chart or a projected image, use a pointer and keep well to the side of the screen or chart. Talk to your audience, *not* to the visual aid you're using. You can control your audience by breaking eye contact to look at a visual aid only when you want your audience to look at it, and reinforce this by pointing to the visual aid. Stop pointing and regain eye contact with your audience when you want to redirect attention to you.

Ending the speech

Some people have as much trouble ending a speech or oral report as they do a letter. As with a letter, the time to quit talking is when you have finished saying what you planned to say. Avoid the natural temptation to close your speech with any expression of hope that you have done well or a hesitant declaration that you think you have finished. When you are done, gather up your notes and sit down.

If a question-and-answer session is to follow, then you may have to announce that you have finished: "That concludes my report. I'll be glad to answer any questions." Here are five ways to end a talk that unmistakably signal to your audience that the end is coming:

1. Summarize the points you covered.
2. Challenge your audience to meet the objectives outlined in your talk.

3. Appeal to your audience to do what you want.
4. Wrap up the major point you want to make with an apt illustration, anecdote, or quotation.
5. State your intention to do whatever you advocated.

ORAL REPORTS

We begin with oral reports in our application of the preceding principles for effective speaking because

1. Oral reports vary more and make use of more of the basic guidelines than interviews, conferences, and dictation do.
2. Early in your career, your first contact with upper management may very well be an oral report. Though you may give oral reports infrequently, such reports can be tremendously important to you and your organization.
3. Learning how to give oral reports well can give you self-confidence and poise that will help you in the other forms of oral business communication and hence in both your working and private life.

Oral reports serve the same mission as written reports: they help the receiver make a decision by providing needed facts and/or ideas. They also answer the same questions as written reports (Is something feasible? Should some action be taken? What's the best way?) and share the same characteristics (they are management tools; they are assigned jobs; they are delivered to superiors; they are directed to a specific and usually limited audience; they give more than normal attention to organization; they make use of devices for clear communication; they are expected to be accurate, reliable and objective; and they follow the form, content, and length best suited to their particular function).

An oral report may be as informal as a conversation between two people or as formal as a full-scale presentation to a large audience, complete with audiovisual aids. Where in this range a particular oral report will be depends (as with written reports) on the occasion, the kind and amount of information transmitted, the relationship between reporter and listeners, and so on. In general, oral reports tend to be shorter than written reports simply because detailed information is hard to communicate orally and because listeners have shorter attention spans than readers.

You go through exactly the same steps in preparing an oral report that you do in preparing a written one. You plan your attack (p. 445), get the facts or evidence you need (p. 447), organize your material for coherent presentation (p. 460), analyze it for interpretation and solution to the problem (p. 464), and then present it clearly and concisely in appropriate style (p. 468).

If you have not already read Chapters 13–16 (especially 14), which deal primarily with written (and incidentally with oral) reports, we urge you to do so now. Virtually all of what we say there applies to oral reports —and we will point out the differences.

Planning the attack in preparing an oral report involves essentially the same six procedures as for a written one (p. 445 ff.), though a few differences do arise.

1.   In the second procedure, considering conditions that influence the report, the *size* of the receiving group and the *occasion* will have a bigger influence. Size of readership makes little difference in planning a written report except that increased size is likely to increase disparity of age, experience, and knowledge of and interest in the subject. Readers have the choice of reading or not reading. (Even so-called "required reading" sometimes is not read, as any experienced teacher knows.) But in a large audience, some members may be there against their wills; so retaining their attention may be a special burden for the speaker.

2.   An even bigger difference is that in oral reporting you communicate through many more means than the content, style, and appearance of a written report. Your physical appearance and body language (including eye contact, facial expressions, gestures, stance) and your voice (quality, pitch, enunciation, pronunciation, pace and pauses, . . .) are all tools. Even the usually desirable use of audiovisual aids is a greater problem for the oral reporter (especially in large groups) than their counterparts (graphics) are for a report writer.

3.   Usually a report reader provides the physical surroundings (the milieu or whole set of circumstances for the activity). However, that burden—sometimes a considerable one—falls on the oral reporter and deserves planning time.

Only in the data-collecting step do other differences between written and oral report preparation *seem* to exist—but they are mirages not there when you look carefully. Let us explain.

Our ten-page explanation of "Collecting the Facts" (p. 447 ff.) is in a college/university textbook where part of the purpose is to teach students to research substantial business problems for several months and prepare thorough reports of 20 or more pages. We know that most business reports are not that long. Yet we give this in-depth instruction, as well as instruction on preparing the more common shorter reports, for several reasons:

1.   Doing a thorough job on a sizable report-writing problem is the best way for students to learn to prepare reports (big topic or small, long or short, written or oral).

2.   Those who have seen the wide range of information sources (bibliographic and other) will help improve the vision of many myopic business people who look only at company-generated data.

3.   When the big report problem does come up—as it does from time to time (maybe 10 or even 20 times as long), particularly in industry and

government studies—former students so trained will sail through while those who have not been through the rough waters are likely to flounder. (But when long reports do come up, you can bet they will not be oral.) A good reporter adapts the data-collecting procedures to the problem, regardless of whether the presentation of the report is to be written or oral.

In other words, to make a good oral report, you need to (1) learn how to prepare the particular kind of report by studying Chapters 13–16 and what we've said on the present topic, "Oral Reports," and (2) present the report as explained above in this chapter.

Speech and Oral Report Checklist

1. **Before the talk:**
   - *a.* Was the speaker's overall appearance attractive and suitable for the occasion?
   - *b.* Did the speaker walk in front of the audience quietly and confidently?
   - *c.* Was posture acceptable?
   - *d.* If the speaker carried notes, were they inconspicuous?

2. **During the talk:**
   - *a.* Was the speaker's voice natural and expressive (not montonous and dull)?
   - *b.* Did the speaker project voice properly for everyone's clear hearing?
   - *c.* Did the speaker announce the title of the speech or report?
   - *d.* Did the speaker pronounce and enunciate clearly and correctly?
   - *e.* Was the level of language and use of jargon appropriate?
   - *f.* Did the speaker maintain erect posture?
   - *g.* Did the speaker make effective use of gestures?
   - *h.* Did the speaker maintain eye contact with the audience?
   - *i.* Did the speaker keep the audience's attention?
   - *j.* Was the speaker aware of audience reaction?
   - *k.* Did the speech or report follow a clear and appropriate plan?
   - *l.* Was the talk connected by effective transitions?
   - *m.* Did the speaker make proper use of any audiovisual aids?
   - *n.* Did the speaker do anything distracting?

3. **After the talk:**
   - *a.* Did the speaker come to a logical conclusion(s)?
   - *b.* Did the speaker summarize the points covered?
   - *c.* Did the speaker adequately signal the end of the talk?
   - *d.* Did the speaker exit confidently and gracefully?

A listener sees and/or hears only your presentation of your speech or oral report and can judge it, therefore, only by what you say. We structure our checklist for speeches and oral reports from the audience's point of view, then, to help you keep your listener(s) foremost in your mind as you prepare to talk.

INTERVIEWS

Nature, importance, kinds

In turning to interviews, we take up another widely used and important tool in business and industry. Like many tools, however, interviews can be very productive or very damaging.

Four traits characterize most good interviews:

1. They are not the group communications we have been discussing but are dyadic (on a one-to-one basis).
2. They are not like a purposeless conversation but have a specific purpose and concentrate on a specific subject.
3. They are not (at least not usually) interrogations but are with the willing consent of both parties and have none of the accusatory atmosphere of an interrogation.
4. In interviews, as in good conversations—instead of monologs or long-winded pontifications—half the job of each participant is listening.

Because of that last point, therefore, we recommend that you turn now to Appendix A (pp. 668–72) and see if what we say there can't help you become a better interviewer or interviewee by becoming a better listener.

The common types of interviews in business and industry are:

1. Personnel interviews
    a. Employee screening and hiring.
    b. Orientation, instruction, training of employees new to a job.
    c. Review of employee progress.
    d. Discussion of employee grievances, firings, resignations, and problems.
2. Research—making plans, determining what has been done/discovered, possible uses, next steps, and so on.
3. Exploratory—determining the existence, cause(s), and cure(s) of a problem with an employee or activity.
4. Opinion sampling—pages 454–59.

Whatever type of interview you engage in, the basic structure and purposeful nature of interviews allow three general plans for conducting one:

1. *Directed.* A directed interview is completely planned from start to finish. Often the interviewer will have a checklist of questions to follow, especially when an interviewer is not thoroughly trained and when

doing opinion sampling. In personnel work, organizations use directed interviews when different interviewers screen different applicants for the same job or jobs. Directed interviews minimize the effects of any interviewer bias on the results and interpretations.

2. *Nondirected.* In a nondirected interview the person being interviewed can set or at least influence the subjects covered and the directions of flow in the interview. As a way of eliciting information, the interviewer plays a much more reactive role than in a directed interview. The nondirected approach is useful in grievance, counseling, and exit (resignation or termination) interviews and forms the basis of psychoanalysis.

3. *Stress.* Conducting a stress interview involves intentionally putting the interviewee in a hostile situation, under artificial stress, to see the reaction. We think that such an interview has little justification unless such stress is an essential part of a job. You may establish the interviewee's irritation or anger threshold but lose a potentially good employee, who will likely feel contempt for your questionable practices.

But because we want you to recognize if someone subjects you to a stress interview, here are the six usual devices for conducting one: The interviewer will (1) criticize or ridicule your appearance at the start, (2) take and maintain a threatening, unfriendly tone, (3) deliberately interrupt you repeatedly as you are about to make a point, (4) criticize or ridicule any opinion you express, (5) ask you very personal (perhaps insulting) questions, and (6) purposefully allow long silences to develop and try to force you to end them.

The commonest kind of interview in business and industry is the directed personnel interview. Here is a guide that will help you conduct successful interviews (after which we'll give you a similar guide for being interviewed). To be specific, for both parts, interviewer and interviewee, we'll assume a job-application interview.

The employer (interviewer)

Preparing for the interview. Have available all the information you will need about the job: rank, salary, duties, location, hours. . . . Before you call in an applicant, set the stage: clear your desk, check your own appearance, alert your secretary to intercept any phone calls or visitors, close the blinds to avoid silhouetting yourself, and review the applicant's application or résumé.

Beginning the interview. To relax the applicant, be friendly and welcoming as you shake hands and offer a seat. Sitting on facing chairs or on a couch rather than behind your desk removes a physical barrier and reduces the "formal office" atmosphere. Taking another minute or two to "review" the applicant's résumé gives the applicant a chance to settle down and look around.

The first question you ask is critical since it sets the tone. Remember that you need to hire someone; so be in a positive frame of mind and treat every applicant as a potential employee. A common opening is "Tell me about yourself," but the question is so general that most applicants don't know where to start and the interview begins on a nerve-shaking basis. A better way is to begin with a shared interest—a hobby or personal or business experience. Then proceed to your first question.

To get the applicant to open up, begin with questions that the applicant should be able to answer positively. Examples are whether the applicant satisfies the job's educational requirements, whether the applicant is physically able to perform the job, or whether the working hours are acceptable.

At the beginning avoid falling into the trap of giving more information about the job than just enough to get the applicant answering you easily and naturally. Once you start giving a "sales pitch" on the job and your company, getting the interview back on the track with the applicant giving *you* information will be very hard.

Getting information. Once the applicant has begun to open up, you can go about your task of learning whether you have a desirable prospect. Try not to ask questions answerable yes or no, which tell you little. Instead, ask questions calling for comment. For instance, rather than asking "Do you like purchasing?" ask "What activities do you like best about being a purchasing agent?" Try to make each question (or its answer) lead logically into the next.

In asking questions about former jobs, try to avoid chronological order. Whatever answers you get, be sure not to show any disapproval or disbelief, even if you feel that way. Keep the applicant talking openly while you listen and watch carefully for symptoms of uneasiness, casual remarks, or "lapses of memory."

When a period of silence develops, you can wait for the applicant to end it by saying something—often very revealing information—if you don't allow the silence to last too long and undo all your efforts to create a natural and relaxed atmosphere.

You'll need to take some notes—which are more accurate than memory and more encouraging to the applicant than just listening. But don't be scribbling away all the time or whenever the applicant is saying something personally unfavorable or discussing a negative topic. Even so, be sure to cover your notes so the applicant cannot see what you are writing —or better, use the item number only of a preplanned checklist and jot down by each number your coded evaluation on the point.

Giving information. Once you have heard all the information you need, you should have a pretty good idea whether the applicant is worthwhile. If not, terminate the interview as graciously as you can.

We recommend that you never turn down an applicant face to face. If you do, it will generate the natural question, "Why?" If you trap yourself into explaining, you may be in for an argument and possibly anger or tears. Reject the applicant later in a carefully worded, considerate B–plan letter (pp. 79 and 204).

If, however, you have a good prospect, now is the time to sell your organization and persuade the applicant to join it. You can describe your organization's structure, what it does, and what the opportunities are for advancement (without firm promises!). You can tell more about the job: duties, promotion possibilities. . . . You may want to describe how you choose new employees, what criteria your organization uses in its selections. If necessary to persuade the applicant to sign on, you can go into fringe benefits (hospitalization, pension plan, profit-sharing, vacation policy, and the like). Otherwise leave discussion of fringe benefits until after the applicant has agreed to come to work for you.

Ending the interview. The thing to avoid is an awkward, indefinite, and disorganized ending, especially if because of an interruption from outside (phone, visitor, . . .) that makes you look disorganized. You can maintain your image of competence if you follow a planned sequence of events to wind up the interview. A good first step is to ask if the applicant has any questions about the job, your organization, or the interview. Next, summarize what the two of you have discussed. The applicant's acceptance of or comment on the summary tells you how clear things are and signals that you are bringing the interview to a close. Both you and the applicant should be agreed on what actions each is to take following the interview.

The applicant (interviewee)

Preparing for the interview. As a job applicant, you have only one objective in an interview: to convince the interviewer you can successfully do the job and become a desirable part of the organization. Since most employment interviewers have pretty definite ideas about the kinds of people they want to hire and the kinds they don't, preparing for the interview may well start with study of things that might hurt your chances or even disqualify you. Professor Frank S. Endicott, long-time director of placement at Northwestern University, has given us the following list (in order of frequency) from his survey of 153 companies:

WHY SOME EMPLOYMENT INTERVIEWEES AREN'T HIRED

1. Poor personal appearance.
2. Overbearing, conceited, or know-it-all attitude.
3. Inability to express self clearly (poor voice, diction, grammar).
4. Lack of planning for career (no purpose and goals).
5. Lack of interest and enthusiasm (passive, indifferent, or lazy).
6. Lack of confidence and poise.

7. Overemphasis on money, best dollar offer.
8. Poor scholastic record, just got by; marked dislike for school work.
9. Unwilling to start at the bottom, expects too much too soon.
10. Makes excuses, hedges.
11. Lack of maturity and decisiveness.
12. Lack of courtesy (ill mannered, tactless).
13. Condemnation of past employers.
14. Fails to look interviewer in the eye.
15. Loafs during vacations.
16. Friction with parents.
17. Sloppy application.
18. Merely shopping around.
19. Lack of knowledge of specialty.
20. No interest in company or in industry, or never heard of company.
21. Emphasis on whom one knows (not what).
22. Unwillingness to go where sent.
23. Cynical or radical attitudes.
24. Intolerant (strong prejudices).
25. Narrow interests.
26. Spends much time with movies, TV.
27. No interest in community activities.
28. Inability to take criticism.
29. Late to interview without good reason.
30. Asks no questions about the job.

To achieve your objective of getting the interviewer's favorable evaluation, you need to know three things so that you can make a good appearance and sell your qualifications.

1. You must know exactly what you want to do (see p. 308 ff.). To enter an interview (presuming you get one) and tell the interviewer you aren't sure what you want to do is a sure sign of immaturity. You are mistaken if you think because you say you want to work in a specific job that an organization will not then consider you for anything else. Remember that the organization called you in because it thinks you can fill a need. In reality, it will consider you for all the openings it has at the time.

Suppose that, between the time an organization invites you for an interview and the time you come in for it, the sales department announces it has a critical need for a representative. Human nature being what it is, the organization will look at *everyone* who comes in, regardless of specialty, as a potential sales representative. So you see, indicating exactly what you want to do often opens up opportunities that would have been closed had you made some weak, general statement about your career desires.

2. You need to know about the organization and the field it operates in before you can undergo an intelligent interview. You should already have done most of the research before sending in your résumé. When the organization invites you for an interview, you need to know much more

about how the organization is structured, its problems, needs, activities, plans for the future, and the like. Most of this you can get from annual reports, brokerage house reports, *Standard and Poor's* and *Moody's* manuals, and articles in periodicals (check the periodical indexes in your library). You want to build up a stockpile of facts about the organization that you can interweave into your presentation during the interview, showing the interviewer that you are interested in the organization and its activities and that you have prepared yourself for the job and the interview.

3. You must know specifically what you can do for the organization. If the interview results from your reply to an advertised job opening, you will know. But even if you come in as a result of a prospecting application, the organization will tell you before the interview what job it is considering you for.

You will therefore want to arm yourself with as much information as you can about the job in question. What are the usual duties of someone doing that job? What is the customary salary range? What career paths does the job generally lead to? You can get the answers to these questions by consulting government publications describing various jobs, talking to people who work in such jobs, and talking with professors who teach in that area.

All of this is the necessary background information you should have for the interview. But your primary objective in the interview will be to describe yourself and your qualifications so as to convince the interviewer you are the logical choice to fill the job.

First prepare a list of the points about yourself you want to cover in the interview: applicable training, important prior job experience, personal traits, and so on. Now commit these to memory. They are the absolutely essential items you must discuss with the interviewer.

Next write down and then memorize two or three success stories. These should do with problems you met and solved, recognized successes, earned promotions, and the like. These may come from earlier jobs or from your education experience. Have them ready to use at appropriate times in the interview.

Third, project what questions the interviewer might ask. At this point you need to do some important thinking. Tough questions should not appear to you as threats designed to trip you up and cost you the job. (The interviewer may be applying some mild stress, but bear in mind that questions reflect the organization's need to learn enough about you to make an intelligent evaluation.) Look at questions as opportunities, even invitations, for you to sell yourself. Here are 25 questions that interviewers commonly ask and that many applicants have trouble handling. Go over them and work up answers that sell you (such as our suggested answers to the first few to get you started). If you have ready answers to these questions, an interviewer is not likely to unsettle you.

1. Tell me all about yourself. (Two suggested answers, depending on the atmosphere of the interview, are: "Surely. Would you like me to start with my last job, my education, my. . . ?" or "On my last job I had an experience which I think shows that. . . ." Such a general question is a direct invitation for you to sell yourself; so start with your strongest point.)

2. How would you describe your personality? (This may sound like a "no win" question, but it is really an excellent opportunity for you. Since you will be hired for your strengths, not your weaknesses, don't admit to any weaknesses. Don't make the mistake of admitting to a small weakness just to appear human. Say something like "I believe I am ambitious, tolerant, patient, sympathetic—all qualities you would want in a . . . ," and continue selling yourself.)

3. What are your long-term/short-term career goals? (You have to have some, and they should be realistic in view of your age and present progress.)

4. Have you established any new goals recently? (A trick question, since your answer is subject to the interpretation the interviewer places on it. Not having established any goals recently can mean either you are immature for not revising your plans or unimaginative and stodgy for the same reason! You will have to answer in light of the interviewer and how the interview is progressing.)

5. What are your plans for graduate study? (The key here is to indicate a willingness to study further while clearly understanding that the job and the organization come first: "Though I expect to devote most of my time and energies to (the job), I hope I will have occasion to continue my studies.")

6. How do other people describe you? (Again, admit no weaknesses.)

7. What are your strongest/weakest personal qualities? (About the only "weakness" you can safely admit to is an impatience with people who repeatedly fail to do their job.)

8. Why do you think you will/will not be successful in. . . ?

9. What have been your most satisfying/disappointing work/school experiences?

10. Describe one or more situations in which your work was criticized.

11. What do you do in your spare time?

12. Why do you want to work for us? (Answering will be easy if you did your research beforehand.)

13. Why should we hire you? (*This* is what you came to the interview to tell! So tell it.)

14. What can you do for us now? (The job in question, of course. Describe those things about you that will indicate that you can perform the job right away and with a minimum of training.)

15. How long will you stay with us?

16. Give some examples that support your stated interest in the job/organization/area of work.

17. Do you prefer staff or line work? Why?

18. What do you look for in a job?

19. What about this job interests you most/least? Why?

20. Why did you quit your present/previous job?

21. What supervisory or leadership positions have you held? (If you are a new graduate, don't apologize for not having been a manager in business—no one would expect you to have been one. Point proudly to whatever leadership

functions you performed while in school, since they are a good indication you will achieve similar positions in the world of work.)

22. Would you prefer on-the-job training or a formal training program? Why?
23. Why did you choose your major?
24. Why are your grades so low?
25. What geographic location do you prefer? Why? (Unwillingness to move is among the major reasons otherwise qualified applicants do not get jobs with big companies.)

Armed with a knowledge of the organization and what it does, a memorized list of your strongest selling points, and ready answers to questions like those above, you are mentally well prepared for the interview. Only the physical preparation, packaging the "product," remains.

The cliché that the best physical preparation for an interview is a good night's sleep is still absolutely true. If you are well rested, you will perform at the top of your abilities, as you want to do.

You must make a good appearance. As with most situations, how you look will be the basis for the first impression; and an interviewer's unfavorable first impression will set up an obstacle you will spend most of the interview trying to overcome. The image you want to present is therefore of someone the interviewer can easily visualize successfully working for the organization.

Dress formally enough to *suit the occasion*. While for some jobs a sport coat and slacks or a sweater and skirt may be suitable, a suit is more likely to present the image you want. Bear in mind that dark, subdued colors are more "sincere" and "serious." Coordinate your accessories to your clothing. Brown shoes do not match a blue suit, nor does a red patent leather belt match a green skirt suit. A well-tailored suit is a good investment for both men and women. Cheap clothes look cheap and make you look cheap too.

Good grooming is, of course, a must. You should be clean and clean-smelling. Shine your shoes, trim your nails, have your hair cut and/or styled, shave, and go easy on the after-shave or perfume. Strive for a clean, well-groomed, *natural* appearance.

Before the interview. When you go to an interview, carry an attaché case. It will give you a businesslike air and let you carry extra résumés, paper, paper clips, and anything else you find necessary.

Arrive for an interview five to ten minutes before the scheduled time, no earlier and no later. If you arrive too early you will appear overanxious. Besides, the longer you have to sit and wait, the more nervous you may become, leading you to make mistakes. Never, of course, arrive late for an interview. If the interviewer keeps you waiting more than 25 minutes, ask for another appointment and leave. Keeping you waiting may be a stress tactic, but in any case you will lose nothing by leaving after rescheduling the interview.

You may be asked to fill out an application form while waiting for the interview (but only for a low-level job). Before filling out the form, ask if you can take it with you, fill it out later, and mail it in, explaining that you will have plenty of time to give all the information wanted. This tactic can keep you from having to scribble away in the waiting room, making you appear "clerical."

When you fill out the form, do so legibly and in ink. Leave no empty spaces, writing "not applicable," "to be discussed in interview," or "see attached résumé" when you do not want to give information on the form. Do not fill out the part of the form asking for your history of jobs. People apparently design such forms to make it impossible for you to present your work experience favorably. Instead, attach your résumé to the form and refer to it.

The organization may very well interview you at lunch or invite you to lunch in the course of your visit. If so, *do not drink*, even if invited to do so and if your host does. Explain that you want to keep your head clear for this most important time. No one will criticize you for that.

Now that you are mentally and physically prepared for the interview, go in there and *sell your qualifications*.

Beginning the interview. Your guiding principle during an interview is that time is limited (most interviews do not go beyond 30 minutes) and you have to develop your sales presentation on yourself. Your job in the interview, then, is to make the points you need to make that you decided on earlier. Thus you will want to exert some control over the directions the interview takes.

Your job will be easier if you can adjust the usual superior-to-subordinate relationship of interviews to a more equal footing between you and the interviewer. You can begin to do this as soon as you enter the interviewer's office if you strive to present a confident, self-assured image—but not a cocky or arrogant one. Whether you are a man or a woman, shake hands *firmly*. You needn't crush bones, but holding out a hand as limp as a dead fish makes a poor impression. After you are seated, do not smoke. Even if the interviewer lights up and invites you to, refrain. Nobody looks good when smoking. And of course you will not chew gum.

If the interviewer follows the usual practice of beginning with small talk to put you at ease, swing the conversation onto your strong points as quickly as you can. If, for instance, the interviewer comments on your hobby of playing golf, you can remark that the game has certainly taught you patience and how to deal with frustration, and this has stood you in good stead in. . . .

That puts the interview on the track you want—dealing with you as a potentially good employee. If the interviewer submits you to a stress interview (and such tactics may be unintentional), your behavior is to remain calm, patient, reasonable, and gracious. *Never get angry!* Simply keep steering the interview back on track until the interviewer realizes you will not succumb to stress tactics.

During the interview. To understand your attitudes and motivations, the interviewer may commence a depth interview—probing with broad, open-ended questions to get you to reveal your feelings and attitudes. Generally these will be "Why" and "How" questions. "How did you get the promotion to assistant sales manager?" "How do you feel about Sanders after working for him for three years?" "Why was that experience so important to you?" If you have prepared yourself as we recommended above, such questions should not trip you up. Just keep thinking of every question as an opportunity for you to talk about yourself and your strong qualifications.

Keep your voice moderate, clear, and expressive as you talk to the interviewer. Equally important, maintain eye contact all the way through. You don't want to get into a staring contest, but to fail to look the interviewer in the eye, especially when discussing something less than favorable to you, will unavoidably make an impression of dishonesty and/or weakness. If you have trouble looking into the interviewer's eyes, concentrate on the bridge of the nose, or look at the space directly between the eyes.

When the interviewer asks you a question that does not let you lead into a discussion of one of your strong qualifications, answer as briefly and positively as you can. Remember that you won't have much time to present your sales pitch; so minimize time spent on (for you) nonproductive questions and answers. When you make a point, stop. Try not to ramble on, especially just to fill a silence.

Try not to brag or boast; doing so never makes a good impression. You should be able to talk positively, assuredly, and self-confidently about your successes, especially if you have prepared your answers ahead of time. Keep the interview on your good points, resisting any interviewer efforts to get you to talk about your weak ones. A reply something like this will usually do the job: "Yes, I might have handled that differently, and now I would; but the important things I accomplished then were. . . ." When confronted with a wrong interpretation on the part of the interviewer, or an untrue assertion, don't deny it; that appears argumentative and defensive. Instead, respectfully and positively correct the interviewer. Finally, never say anything bad about a past employer. You will only make yourself look bad and warn the interviewer that in the future you may "bad-mouth" this organization too.

Constantly during the interview you will be gauging the feedback you get from the interviewer: expressions, remarks, gestures, body language. . . . You will quickly know when things are not going well, and you can take steps to improve the tone of the interview. Above all, however, you must listen. If the interviewer ever thinks you are not listening, you may very well find the situation deteriorated beyond saving. That is why, earlier in this chapter, we suggested you study what we say about listening in Appendix A (pp. 668–72).

Talking about salary. Because salary discussion is so important in the hiring process, we give it special attention in this section.

Ideally, as an applicant you want to avoid any talk of money until after the organization has offered you a job, or at least until after you have completed your sales pitch on yourself. In any case, the longer you can postpone it, the more information you will have about the organization and the job, and the better you will be able to negotiate.

You want the organization to state the first salary figure. The organization naturally will want you to be the first to quote an amount. This situation often results in a "You go first—No, you go first" routine that would be amusing if so much were not at stake.

If the interviewer asks you about your present or last salary, dodge as gracefully as possible to avoid giving it. If you cannot get out of it, give the total compensation figure, including all fringe benefits, such as vacation, medical plan, retirement or pension plan, profit sharing, and the rest.

If the interviewer brings up the question of salary too soon in the interview by asking what salary you want, reply that you think the salary basis should be what you can contribute to the organization and resume selling yourself. If the interviewer presses you, be indefinite: "The customary for this job." "Your usual range for such work." "In the thirties." If you have done your homework, you should know about what the job should pay before you go in for the interview. If you are forced to quote a dollar amount, and you think the top salary for the job is, say, about $22,000, overlap it on both sides and say, "$19,000 to $25,000." This, you hope, will begin the negotiations at the top end of the scale. If you have no real idea what the job should pay, as a last resort quote a figure 20 percent above your last salary.

Remember that salaries are almost always negotiable. The first figure you hear from the organization should be your base for negotiating. If you state the first figure, the organization surely will see that as the base for negotiations.

The better you have sold yourself, the stronger your bargaining position will be. Negotiate your salary based on, in order of preference, your real worth to the organization, your need for the top of the salary range, offers from other organizations, your interest in furthering your career, and your needs. We do not believe many people have ceased being considered for a job because they asked for more money than the organization first offered. If the organization is unwilling to negotiate, the answer will be "No, that is as much as we will pay," and you can then accept or refuse the offer.

Ending the interview. When you sense the interview is approaching its close, you want to accomplish four things, in this order: (1) summarize your strongest qualifications for the job in a final statement, (2) express your enthusiasm for working for the organization, (3) thank the interviewer for an interesting interview, and (4) make sure both of you agree on what the next step will be.

After you have said goodbye, leave. Don't remain in the reception room or elsewhere around the offices, for you will appear to be indecisive or at a loss what to do next.

After the interview. As soon as possible after leaving the organization's offices, write down the names of the people you met and any other information you learned. Don't trust this to memory—it is vital that you have everything correct and the names spelled right. Also note what strengths and weaknesses about yourself came out in the interview, what went well, and what didn't. This can help you in future interviews and will aid you in writing the thank-you letter.

You must, the day after the interview or as soon thereafter as practicable, write a thank-you letter to the person who interviewed you. We have given you recommendations on how to handle this kind of message (Chapter 10, p. 363). Unless you go back for further interviews, this is your last chance to sell the organization on hiring you; so don't overlook briefly touching on your strong points.

CONFERENCES

With conferences we go from speech situations and the dyadic (one-to-one) communication situations of interviews to group communication. We did not take up conferences after speeches and oral reports because we want to emphasize that conferences are oral communication situations *between* people, not speeches *at* them. The free interchange of ideas that ideally characterizes conferences is absent in speech/report situations and the tensional seeking and giving of information in interviews.

Conferences are popular in virtually all kinds of organizations because they provide an environment for two-way communication and immediate response from both management and lower level people.

Whether conferences are impromptu meetings or formally scheduled and conducted discussions, they share three attributes:

1.　Three or more people. If less than three attend, it is a conversation or an interview.
2.　A leader. Without a planned or natural leader, a conference will degenerate into a "bull session" or an argument.
3.　A specific objective. Without a specific objective, a conference will be only an unstructured, time-wasting discussion group.

Business conferences usually fall into one of three categories. The first is information-giving upward, usually a report to superiors. The second is information-giving downward, which gives directions, instruction, or information to subordinates. The third is information-seeking, in which management looks for information or advice.

Any conference is a team effort and when run properly will avoid the faults of conferences that have given them a bad name in some organizations. Too many conferences are time-killers and lead only to further conferences. Others, because of ego trips or bad planning, take more time than their objectives or results justify. In the end, poorly planned conferences waste an organization's time, personnel, and money. Therefore we think proper planning is essential to successful conferences.

Planning the conference

When planning a conference, ask yourself (1) whether a need exists to justify one and (2) whether a conference is the best way to handle the situation.

If you are convinced that a conference is justified and is the best approach, your next questions are (3) how to define its objective and (4) whether the objective is attainable. If you cannot define a conference's objective, you can hardly expect others to contribute to meeting it.

Next, consider (5) what topics the conference should cover (the agenda), (6) in what order, (7) whether one conference will be sufficient to cover all of them, and (8) what kind of conference to hold (information-giving, information-seeking, brainstorming . . .).

If you have fixed the conference's objective, agenda, and type, you are ready for the next step, (9) picking the participants. Ideally you should never invite people to participate in a conference just to keep them informed or because they might be hurt or insulted if not invited. The participants in a conference should be only those directly concerned with the problem or situation under discussion. Like most ideals, this one is hard to achieve; but the more directly each participant is involved the more successful your conference is likely to be.

Next you must take up what is probably the most important question about any conference: (10) who is to lead it. Just as a good leader can stimulate participants to achieve the objectives, a poor leader can make a conference futile. We discuss the characteristics of effective conference leadership in the next section, but basically the best leader is one who talks little but stimulates others to talk. The leader should not necessarily be the highest ranking participant—who might inhibit free interaction among the other participants.

Now nearly ready, you still have two related groups of questions to answer: (11) who is going to take notes or make and distribute a record of the conference. (Don't make the mistake of the man who handed a pad of paper and a pencil to a woman at a conference with instructions to take notes, only to have her caustically inform him that she was the treasurer of the corporation!) If you plan to tape-record the conference, will the presence of the microphone inhibit anyone? Remember, too, that tape recordings must be transcribed, a lengthy and therefore costly process.

As the final step in planning, you will need to (12) consider the location, the physical setup, and interruption-control measures. Usually you will want a conference room or an office large enough to hold all the participants. In any case you will first have to reserve the room for the time you will need it. Be sure of enough chairs. And if the meeting is large, you may want to set out name cards telling everyone where to sit.

While you are arranging for the conference room, decide if you should furnish pads of paper and pencils at each seat, whether to set out ashtrays (no ashtrays serve as a useful deterrent to smoking in a closed room), and if carafes and glasses are present, remind yourself to have them filled. Now is the time to arrange for audiovisual equipment. Finally, if the conference will be long enough to justify a break, do you want to have coffee or other refreshments available?

Controlling the temperature in a meeting room is often a problem since you must compensate for the heat generated by bodies (and a lot of bodies in a room will generate a lot of heat). An overheated room makes people drowsy, while one that is too cold keeps people thinking about their discomfort instead of the conference. A good compromise, if you can arrange it, is 68° F or about 2 to 4 degrees below the normal comfort range.

Because messages and telephone calls are common disruptions to conferences and often serve only to boost the egos of the persons receiving them, ideally you should forbid any interruptions except in cases of extreme emergency. However, you will probably not be able to do more than unplug the telephone and ask everyone's secretary not to interrupt the conference unless really necessary.

For informal meetings you may simply call the participants on the phone to tell them about it. For bigger or more formal conferences, send each a memo. In either case, inform people early enough so that they will have sufficient notice to schedule time for the conference.

The more you tell participants before the conference starts, the better they will be able to prepare for it, and the more likely they will contribute successfully. To that end, announce the objective of the conference and list the agenda. This information will help participants to gather materials they will need and also serve for the leader to refer to during the conference to keep the discussion on course. Cover also the essentials of the date of the conference, the time it will begin and the projected time it will end (to help participants plan their other activities), and exactly where the conference will meet. You may, if addressing subordinates, include an admonition to be on time and, if appropriate, things you want them to review beforehand. So everyone will know who is coming, you might well include in your memo a list of all the participants.

Leading the conference

We said above and we repeat here, a successful conference depends on effective leadership. Without direction, most meetings quickly degenerate into argument at the worst and into wasted time, indecision, or inaction at the best. Though resorting to the more esoteric rules of parliamentary procedure is usually unnecessary, a leader does need to know enough to keep the conference running smoothly by giving everyone an equal chance to contribute.

To begin with, the leader must respect the participants in the conference. Whether superiors or subordinates, if the leader indicates a lack of esteem for them they will react angrily and turn from contributors to obstructionists. A wise conference leader, then, will never threaten, embarrass, ridicule, or insult anyone.

A conference that yields useful results comes from maximum contribution by the participants. To encourage participants, the leader should try not to dominate the conference. That is one good reason for the leader to sit with the participants, not to stand looking down at them. Anything that tends to separate or elevate the leader is counterproductive. This fact is why a U-shaped table is a poor arrangement. An oval or rectangular table is much better; but the wise leader will sit in the middle of one of the longer sides, not at an end.

Everyone in a conference should feel free to contribute; that open intercommunication is what makes a meeting into a conference. A protracted monolog or dialog that excludes others discourages them from getting into the discussion. In fact, the leader who allows such a monolog or dialog to develop implies approval of it.

Basically, then, leading an effective conference is a matter of successfully dealing with people. Here are some of the more common problem types and situations you may run into and some suggestions for handling them as a conference leader:

The nonparticipant. Unless you think it will overly embarrass the person, try directing a question to the nonparticipant to break through the shell and bring out a contribution to the conference.

The violent argument. When two or more participants get into an argument, allow one side to finish stating its case, then give the other side equal time. Do not allow interruptions; your goal is to help each side clearly understand the other side's position.

The private conference on the side. Ask the people involved to share their conference with the rest of the group. If this doesn't work, ask them nicely to hold their own conference later so that you can get this one back to its task.

Leader of the revolution. If a participant tries to take over your leadership job, a useful technique is to place the revolutionist on your immediate right or left where your eyes won't meet. If this person tries to interrupt other participants, you can effectively squelch such interruptions by a hand motion or whispering a request to be quiet until recognized.

The timid soul. Place a shy or introverted participant directly opposite you, thus allowing responses to you rather than to the entire group.

The uninvited guest. The best remedy for people who join your conference without being asked is to tell them to leave. If an uninvited guest is your superior, however, you may be able to do little about it except try to prevent undue interruptions.

The late arrival. Regardless of your precautions, someone will usually come late. You can minimize the disruption by making sure that the empty chair is nearest the door. (Unless you're a very close friend and on bantering terms, snide remarks before the group are—as doctors say—contraindicated.)

The chronic arguer. If one of those people who disagree with everything gets going, don't make the mistake of reacting directly yourself. You will split the conference into two sides, yours and the arguer's, effectively destroying your all-important neutrality. Instead, get the other participants to react to the arguer, using your position as a leader to keep the conference progressing by making the arguer the "devil's advocate."

The contemplative ones. When participants go into glassy-eyed reveries, direct questions specifically to them. If you get no reaction, just sit there a few moments until the silence does get through.

The tongue-tied participant. When someone can't seem to get to the point or is unable to make a point, tactfully state the point back as best you understand, preferably in the form of a question, "You think the cost of the new pump is too high, right?" If you get agreement, you have helped over a rough spot.

The surprise package. If a participant brings up a point outside the scope or agenda of your conference (usually in an attempt to impress a superior or embarrass a competitor), interrupt and firmly get your conference back on the agenda (promising to discuss the point after the conference is over, if willing).

Ending the conference

Before you dismiss the participants, summarize what the conference accomplished so that everyone understands the conclusion(s) or agreement(s) reached.

Afterwards, you may want to distribute a summary or the minutes of the conference to the participants and others who should be informed. Put these in outline form, stripped of all the frills (it's no time to editorialize). Distributing the minutes serves to: (1) create a written record of what the conference accomplished; (2) assure that all the participants agree with the result(s) of the conference (for you will hear if anyone doesn't!), and (3) clarify the participants' assignments, if any.

Participating in a conference

Your progress in an organization may depend heavily on how you show up in conferences. They may be the best means you have to bring yourself to upper management's (your bosses') favorable attention.

As a start, do your homework: be prepared to discuss *all* the items on the agenda, especially the interesting and important ones. A little study of the background of a major problem (causes, losses, past attempts to solve, reasons for failure, proposals for solution) can make you look good in the eyes of everybody—some of whom may not have done their homework so well. Take some time to consider carefully any ideas you may have before presenting them to a group.

As a good participant, you will want to both speak and listen; but above all, listen well. In fact, a useful and common technique is to wait until most of the others have said something before speaking yourself since you will then have more information to work from.

Even if everyone at the conference seems to be employing the technique, you can still turn it to your advantage by waiting until the silence just begins to become embarrassing and then relieving it (and the conference leader) by starting the discussion. The best entering wedge is a question rather than a statement of opinion, since a statement may unintentionally put you into opposition to other participants as they react to you. Beginning with a question is more likely to force them to make statements, which can then be to your advantage.

DICTATION

Dictation, the fourth and last of our major oral business communication forms, is easy to learn. Without some study and practice, however, you probably will not make the most effective use of this common office procedure. So what we say here is to help you be more efficient and effective in dictation. Whether you dictate directly or through a telephone and/or dictation equipment to your secretary or a typist in a stenographic pool makes few significant differences (which we shall point out).

First, however, we want to make two big points:

1. To your secretary you may dictate; to your customer, never.
2. Efficiency in dictating bad business messages is no virtue. You must know *how* to write effective letters, memos, and reports before you can dictate them (and the preceding chapters in this book will teach you).

Getting ready to dictate

Besides learning how to compose good business messages before you start dictating, you have some other preparations to make. Don't put yourself in the position of having to stop dictating (especially if directly to a secretary) to get something you should have had at hand to begin with. Get together all the information you will need: letters you need to answer, invoices you have to write about, files on matters you want to cover. . . .

Plan what you are going to say and how you will say it in each letter, memo, or other piece you are going to dictate. Make notes to yourself (perhaps right on the papers you are going to talk about), work up outlines . . . in other words, organize first. (An increasing practice that saves time for everybody involved stems from making notes on papers to be answered. Often by expanding the note a little you can really give all the answer you need to, especially in internal communications. All your secretary has to do is make a photocopy to file and return the original as an answer.) But never make the juvenile mistake of writing out your dictation in longhand and then reading it to a secretary or dictation machine!

If you are going to use a dictation machine, know what its capabilities and limitations are. Learn where all the controls are and what they do. Spend some time practicing with the machine, at home if necessary, so that when you begin to dictate you will feel relaxed and comfortable. You might well play back some of your dictation so you will know how you sound.

Dictating

Whether you dictate direct or use a telephone and/or dictation machine, dictation is dyadic communication; it involves two people, you and a secretary or typist. Regardless of the setup for your dictation, remember that a live human being will be on the other end whether you can see the person or not.

If you work with a secretary, you and your secretary must respect each other and know each other well enough to work calmly and efficiently together. You can help your secretary by setting aside a period for dictation at about the same time each day. Making it routine will help your secretary more efficiently plan a day's activities. Dictating in the morning is the best since your secretary will have the remainder of the day to transcribe the dictation, rather than waiting until the next day when shorthand notes may have "cooled off."

Minimize interruptions while you're dictating. Cut off your phone and close the door if you need to. To further conserve your secretary's time, minimize your use of rough drafts. Rough drafts double or triple the time spent on a piece of writing. If, however, you have access to word processing equipment, you can often have as many rough drafts as you desire, making changes all along the way—especially useful when preparing long, involved reports.

The time to give a secretary or typist instructions is *before* you begin to dictate a message, not after you have finished. Nothing enrages a secretary more than to type a three-page message only to find at the end that you wanted a letter instead of a memo! So here's a list of things you may want to give instructions about before beginning to dictate:

1. Identify yourself if you are dictating to a machine in a word processing center or stenographic pool or in any other situation where the transcriber might not know who you are.
2. Give any special instructions, such as rush job, air mail, certified mail, and the like.
3. Specify the form of message you want: letter, memo, draft, whatever.
4. Specify the stationery: letterhead, memorandum form. . . .
5. Specify the number of carbons or photocopies.
6. Specify the names and addresses of those your message is to go to. (An efficient system in answering correspondence is to number the incoming messages with matching numbers on the dictation, letting the transcriber get the names and addresses from the messages you answer.)
7. Fully describe any enclosures.

Much of the success of your dictation will depend on how well the transcriber hears and understands you. To begin with, talk directly toward your secretary or the microphone—not to a window or to the top of your desk.

Talk naturally. If you're acquainted with the person you're writing to, try to visualize the face. Even if you are not personally acquainted, a careful look at a letter you're answering will often enable you to visualize the face behind it. Your dictation will just naturally sound more empathetic if you do. But remember that you're dictating a written message. Using natural speech patterns will help to signal pauses for punctuation, clauses, sentences, and so on. Natural speech will also help you avoid dictating in a monotone; it's deadly to listen to and can cause your transcriber's mind to wander, resulting in mistakes.

Enunciate clearly to the point of exaggeration (it won't sound exaggerated to the transcriber). Spell out words that sound alike, such as "accept" and "except," and the names of people, places, and products unless the spelling is obvious or you are sure the transcriber knows. Spell out any unusual words and especially jargon or technical terms. Taking a few seconds to spell out something is far easier than making your secretary or typist question you about it or try to guess what you meant.

Your secretary can take your dictation easier, too, if you remain seated and resist the temptation to pace around your office, smoke, or chew gum. Some people dictate too fast and some dictate at almost a snail's pace. You can make it easier for your transcriber if you vary your speed, slowing down for difficult parts. And try not to be nervous about dictating. It's contagious.

While you should try not to dictate what the typist doesn't need (because dictating simple spelling and punctuation, for example, would imply ignorance), too much is better than not enough. If you know who will transcribe your dictation, you will know, for instance, how much punctuation to dictate. If you are unsure, play it safe and dictate any punctuation that is complex or doubtful. Do not assume that whoever types your messages will take care of spelling, punctuation, grammar, diction, and syntax for you; you will seldom have such a paragon working for you, especially early in your career.

Don't include jokes and extraneous comments when dictating. They often leave the transcriber wondering whether they belong in your message—and slow down the transcription process.

Most authorities say you should dictate paragraph breaks, and we agree. Paragraphing is an integral part of the writing process, and as an author (even of a memo) you should bear the responsibility for it. Signal a paragraph break by saying "Paragraph" or "New paragraph."

When you want to capitalize a word, such as "Computer," say "Capital computer" or "Cap computer." If you want something typed all in capital letters, say "All capitals" or "All caps."

If you dictate a quotation, indicate the quotation marks by dictating "Quote" and "Unquote." You know the names of all the punctuation marks, and we have already advised you to dictate punctuation when the proper punctuation is not obvious. Two marks that often present problems to transcribers are the question mark (?) and exclamation point (!). To avoid uncertainty, we recommend that you always dictate these two. (Incidentally, a useful abbreviation for "Exclamation point" is "Bang.")

While dictation direct to a secretary is still in wide use, most people recognize that dictation equipment is more efficient and economical because (1) interruptions don't waste time while a secretary waits for the dictator to resume dictating after looking up something or answering the telephone, (2) recorded dictation doesn't "cool off" as shorthand notes may overnight or over a weekend, (3) a secretary can do other things in time otherwise spent taking dictation, and (4) most people dictate faster to a machine than to a person.

If you use dictation equipment, make regular use of the indicator so your transcriber will know the approximate length of your messages. A practiced transcriber who is familiar with your dictation style will know roughly how much typed copy a given spread between your indicator marks will make and can turn out a centered, balanced letter on the first try.

When you make a mistake, correct it immediately. Otherwise you may mislead your transcriber or forget to make the correction. Announce that you are going to make a correction by saying "Correction," use the correction indicator to further alert your transcriber, identify what you are correcting, and dictate the corrected matter.

You can also help your transcriber by announcing the end of a message with "End of letter," "End of memo," or whatever is appropriate, as well as marking it on a machine indicator.

After dictating

First of all, turn off your machine when you are finished. You don't want to unintentionally record anything embarrassing or confidential.

When you get back your transcribed message, *read everything carefully before you sign it*. Remember, as dictator you, not the typist, are responsible for any errors.

When you must correct a typing error, be diplomatic and considerate: even the best of secretaries (or word processing machines) have off days now and then. Try to make it a learning experience for both you and the typist. Don't unnecessarily mark up a letter or memo so that it requires retyping. Use a pencil *lightly* so that the typist can erase your marks and white-out the errors without having to retype the whole page.

And—in the same vein of being a diplomatic and considerate (and wise) employer—when your secretary or typist does good work, give the deserved compliment. A compliment or a thank you may not replace a salary raise, but it does wonders for morale.

CASES FOR ORAL COMMUNICATION

1. For any of the cases for long or short written reports, prepare instead an oral report, following your instructor's directions regarding length, visual aids, and so on.

2. After receiving your graded analytical report (or before if time makes it necessary), assume that (*a*) your class is the board of directors which will make a decision on your recommendations, (*b*) you will have 10–15 minutes to make your report to them orally, (*c*) you will use at least one visual aid, and (*d*) the board will be judging you as an employee as well as on your report.

3. Read a current article on some aspect of business communication and write (as your instructor directs) a review or condensation of the article. In two or three minutes, tell your class about the review or condensed version of the article, using your jottings as speech notes, *not* a script.

4. Review the checklist in Chapter 9 (p. 343) and prepare a well-organized written list of incomplete-sentence jottings about yourself for a stranger who is to introduce you as an expert on a topic you are to speak about (this may be you in the future, but be realistic). At random, and with only a few minutes for preparation, have a classmate introduce you using your notes.

5. As an alternative, assume the person who was to introduce you in the above case could not come. Using your notes, introduce yourself.

6. Individually or in groups, as your instructor directs, visit a bank, a savings and loan association, and a credit union. Give an oral report on which is the best source of a loan of several hundred dollars to tide you over for a few months.

7. Individually or in groups, as directed, visit one each of a jewelry, clothing, hardware, and drug store. Report on the differences and reasons for one of the following:
   a. Main points in their credit policies.
   b. Their furnishings and fixtures.
   c. Other areas as your instructor specifies.

8. When you are a half to three quarters finished with your analytical report, give an oral progress report to your classmates. Is your project on schedule? Why or why not? What will you do next? What obstacles have you encountered and how have you handled them? Will you finish on time?

9. With one student playing the role of interviewer and the other playing that of applicant, conduct an employment interview before the class. For realism this should be for the job the "applicant" hopes to get upon graduation.

10. In a conference made up of a suitable number of students, consider any problem of national, local, or school scope, coming up with realistic solutions if possible. The student chosen as leader should be responsible for as much organizing of the conference as is appropriate. Participants may be as cooperative or obstructive as the instructor directs.

11. Treat any of the following letter or memo cases as an oral report case: Chapter 5 (replies with no sales possibility), Cases 3 and 4, pp. 156–57.

12. For other cases, see GS 2, 8, 11, and 17 (persuasive to a group), 23 (conference), and 34 (introducing yourself to a group) beginning on p. 300.

Appendixes

appendix A | The communication
process and
semantic principles

THE COMMUNICATION PROCESS

WHETHER YOU ARE writing or talking, reading or listening, you are doing one half (sending or receiving) of the two-way process of communication.

Essential to this process are symbols—usually words. (We are not concerned here with smoke signals, smiles, gestures, winks, and other forms of nonverbal communication—though they are all parts of the whole communication story.) When you have an idea to convey to somebody else, you cannot just hand over the idea; you necessarily use symbols of some kind. In oral communication, these are sounds; written, they become words, figures, charts, and other marks on paper. The first step in communication, then, is the message sender's formulating ideas into symbols.

These sounds or written symbols do not communicate, however, until they go through some channel from the sender to the receiver.

Then, to complete the communication process, the receiver has to interpret these symbols back into an idea in essentially the same way the sender had to formulate the idea into symbols.

This simple-sounding three-step process of symbolizing, transmitting, and interpreting nevertheless involves many possibilities for breakdown of communication. If the person with the idea or concept has not learned to talk or is mute, or the would-be receiver is deaf, for example, they obviously cannot communicate orally. If the sender does not know how to write, or the receiver to read, they cannot use written symbols. Similarly, we leave to the Postal Service, telephone, telegraph, radio, TV, and satellite communications the manifold problems of transmitting symbols from sender to receiver with a minimum of interference (called "noise" by communications specialists).

But if the person with an idea has not learned the English language (a system of symbols) well enough for the expression of ideas according to the system, or if the receiver cannot interpret according to the system, they cannot communicate effectively—and they are our problem.

These two steps of formulating concepts into meaningful, standard symbols (frequently referred to as encoding) and interpreting the symbols (decoding) are the two major points of communication breakdown. Although many of the causes of communication breakdown involve decoding, we are concerned primarily with encoding.

SOME BASIC SEMANTIC PRINCIPLES[1]

Fundamental to communication is this general principle: *The symbols used must stand for essentially the same thing in the minds of the sender and the receiver.*

Just as our money is a medium of exchange for goods and services, our language has developed as a medium of exchange for ideas. Although the unit values of both may change with time and circumstances, at a given time and in a given set of circumstances the values of both are pretty well set. You therefore cannot pay a bill for 35 cents by offering a quarter, and you cannot convey the idea of localism by offering the word *colloquialism.* Good diction—choice of the proper word to represent the sender's idea—is thus a minimum essential in oral or written communication.

The fact that the sender's chosen words must also be in the receiver's vocabulary complicates the diction problem. You can't use perfectly good Greek to communicate to a person who knows only English. You can't use the highly technical language of medicine, law, engineering, insurance, or accounting to communicate with people who don't know the terms. They're all Greek to the nonspecialist. If you want to communicate, then, you must *estimate your receiver's vocabulary and adapt your own accordingly.* In general, you are justified in using unusual words or the special language of any field only if you're sure all your receivers know the terms or you explain them as you go along.

---

[1] The bibliography of semantics is extensive, and the books vary greatly in difficulty. If you want to read further on the subject, we suggest that you see the following books in the order listed: David K. Berlo, *The Process of Communication: An Introduction,* Holt, Rhinehart & Winston, Inc., New York, 1960; William V. Haney, *Communication: Patterns and Incidents,* Richard D. Irwin, Inc., Homewood, Ill., 1960, and *Communication and Organizational Behavior,* 1967; Bess Sondel, *The Humanity of Words: A Primer of Semantics,* World Publishing Co., Cleveland, 1958; Stuart Chase, *Power of Words,* Harcourt, Brace, New York, 1954; Stephen Ullman, *Semantics: An Introduction to the Science of Meaning,* Barnes & Noble, Inc., New York, 1962; Irving J. Lee, *Handling Barriers in Communication,* International Society for General Semantics, 1968; S. I. Hayakawa, *Language in Thought and Action* (4th Edition), Harcourt, Brace, New York, 1978; John L. Austin, *How to Do Things with Words,* Harvard University Press, Cambridge, 1962; Alfred Korzybski, *Science and Sanity,* Institute of General Semantics, Lakeville, Conn., 1948; Ragnar Rommetviet, *Words, Meanings, and Messages,* Academic Press, New York, 1968; Noam Chomsky, *Studies on Semantics in Generative Grammar,* Mouton, The Hague, 1972.

Even words which properly name a broad group of things for both sender and receiver, however, may still not reproduce in the mind of the receiver the sender's specific concept. If you write *machine* while thinking *typewriter*, your reader is likely to miss your intent by envisioning a calculator, a mimeograph, or some other machine. To communicate well, then, a sender must *use words specific enough* for the necessary precision.

Even then, words alone are far from the whole of this system of symbols we call the English language; *the way they're put together, punctuated, and even spelled can make a vast difference*. A bear does not have a bare skin. To a reader who follows the English system of placing modifiers as close as possible to the things they modify, "Only three men passed the first screening" does not mean the same as "Three men passed the first screening only." To the reader who knows anything about the punctuation of essential and nonessential clauses, "The prices which are higher than those last year for the same items are simply too high" does not mean the same as "The prices, which are higher than those last year for the same items, are simply too high." To get the right idea, the reader has to assume that the writer didn't know how to handle participles when writing "Having hung by the heels in the 30-degree temperature overnight, we found the venison made an excellent breakfast." That writer tried to pass a lead nickel in our medium of exchange, the English language. Remember the fundamental principle: *The symbols used must stand for essentially the same thing in the minds of the sender and the receiver*.

Here are eight specific principles as subheads of the general principle.

1. *A statement is never the whole story.* Even in reporting the simplest event, you omit some details which another reporter might well have told. Usually you report only on the macroscopic level, omitting additional details that microscopic or submicroscopic examinations would reveal.

But you also omit much of the macroscopic. Even if you think you cover the standard *who, where, when, why, what*, and *how*, another reporter could easily add more details and more specifics on each of them. By way of illustration, consider how infrequently you see, in other reports, certain details that are standard in police reports of traffic accidents: mental and physical condition of the driver(s), weather conditions, condition of the car(s) and roadway, etc.

Whether you are sending or receiving the facts and arguments in a court case, you do not have the whole story. Even the witness who takes an oath to tell the truth, the whole truth, and nothing but the truth, never does; additional questions could always bring out more. Even an application letter of ten pages does not tell the whole life story of the applicant.

This concept of inevitable incompleteness—often called "abstracting" and defined as calling attention to some details while neglecting others— is basic in the thinking of semanticists. The International Society for General Semantics has therefore titled its journal *ETC.*, thus stressing Korzybski's suggestion that writers use the abbreviation as a reminder and warning that their statements are incomplete.

The importance of the incompleteness concept stems from the dangers of ignoring it—the "allness" fallacy. If you consider only parts of a whole and judge the whole, you're in danger of the logical fallacy of hasty generalization and unsound conclusions like those of the six blind men who each described an elephant after feeling only one part. If you forget that you do not have all the facts, you are in danger of closing your mind to other facts and points of view. You may think your way is the only way. You thus act on the basis of preconception and may become unteachable, intolerant, dogmatic, and arrogant.

Recognizing that you never have the whole story, on the other hand, helps to keep you open-minded, tolerant, and humble. That's one of the values of travel and of a broad education: to open the mind and replace the provincialism of the person who knows only a small area. The Italians have a proverb which makes the point: *Assai sa chi sa che non sa*, freely translated as "He knows a lot who knows that he doesn't know."

2. *Perception involves both the perceived and the perceiver.* Since you are never telling or considering the whole story, you are *selecting*, from all things that might be or have been said, *those which seem to you important*. What you say about a thing or how you react to it, then, often depends as much on you as on what the thing really is.

Both your judgment of what is important to select and your conclusions based on selected facts depend on the kind of person you are. And you are what you are (different from anybody else) because of different inherited traits and different experiences. Your special interests, values, tastes, and attitudes will naturally cause what you say about a thing or how you react to a statement to differ from what anybody else would say or do. In effect, you are a special filter. Another filter (person) with different characteristics would filter out different things. Hence neither of you can be strictly objective.

When we claim to be objective, we are deluding ourselves—and others if they believe us. And when we expect others to be objective or to see things exactly as we do, we are simply being unrealistic. Constant recognition of this point will help to keep you reasonably tolerant of people who disagree a bit.

A famous French movie aptly illustrates the point that a person's background influences decisions—sometimes more than the factual evidence. The movie gives a life history (selected, of course) of each juror in an important trial and shows how the different backgrounds produced different votes in the jury room, even though all jurors had heard and seen exactly the same evidence.

Thorough recognition of the point—that in terms of background and point of view the other person may be just as nearly right as you are—can go a long way toward preventing disagreements by making you cautious about using *is* dogmatically. When you use *is* to connect a noun and adjective ("Harry Smith is honest"), you are saying that the quality of honesty belongs to or exists in Smith.

This predicate-adjective construction, using what some semanticists call the "*is* of predication," actually misrepresents reality and often seems dogmatic because the receiver either knows different facts about Smith or defines honesty differently. If you remember that what you know about Smith (not *all* the facts) *and* what honesty means to you (probably somewhat different from what it means to the other person) influence your thinking about Smith, you are more likely to say, less dogmatically, "Harry Smith seems to me . . ."—and to avoid an argument or even a fight.

Two subpoints about the perceiver and the perceived deserve special attention.

a. By the psychological principle of projection, we are inclined to attribute to others our own characteristics and feelings. People who pay their bills are inclined to assume that others will too. The reverse is also true. A credit manager—and anybody else who wants to avoid being duped—needs to realize that views of things depend heavily on the kind of person involved and that others may have different views. The wise credit manager will use the statistician's rather than the psychologist's meaning of *projection:* Get information about a credit applicant's past reputation for paying bills, project the trend line, and decide to approve or disapprove the application according to where the projection points.

b. Psychologists also tell us that we are inclined to resist the unpleasant. Facts and ideas that go contrary to our preconceptions, wishful thinking, and other selfish interests are among the unpleasant things we must face because they provoke us to change our comfortable old ways. A semantically sound person will therefore try to avoid the comfortable but antisemantic idea in "Don't confuse me with facts; my mind's made up."

3. Statements or actions based on whims, feelings, imaginings, preconceptions, customs, traditions, and platitudes are questionable. Although you never get all the relevant facts, and although you can never be strictly objective in evaluating those you do get, you should get what facts you can and evaluate them as objectively as you can. You need not give up and use the excuse "all or nothing." Ignoring observable facts will almost certainly lead you into conflict with reality. And when you go too far "out of touch with reality," as the psychiatrists say, you base action on emotion instead of reason, and you go to the bughouse.

A reasonable approach to problem solving involves two beginning questions: (*a*) What are the facts? (*b*) How do you know? Because of the importance of instantaneous response in some simple situations, we have certain reflex mechanisms (for blinking the eyes, sneezing, etc.) that do not involve thinking. But you are courting real trouble if you make reflex responses to complex situations. Fortunately, as situations become more complex, the allowable time for decision becomes greater, and reactions become voluntary. A reasonable person will use some of that time to collect and consider at least some of the significant facts—as some semanticists say, will look at the territory before drawing a map; will be extensionally instead of intensionally oriented; will look outside the skin for some facts instead of relying wholly on internal feelings and cogitations. To do otherwise is to act on prejudices, preconceptions, and whims.

While considering the collected data, you need to ask, "How do you know that this information is reliable?" Many platitudes, prejudices, customs, and the like stem from assumptions that simply do not line up with reality. Even "well-established" teachings of science changed after the discovery of new evidence by such researchers as Harvey, Pasteur, and Reed. The atom that could not be split, according to "authoritative" books not many years ago, has been split. More recently, discoveries in outer space are bringing into question many of the "established" principles meteorologists and astrophysicists have followed for years.

If scientists—who generally pride themselves on being careful in collecting data and in drawing conclusions, and who usually have good equipment—can be so wrong and so dogmatic as they have been on some of these things, should we all not learn the lesson of humility and caution? Should we not all be careful about the adequacy and the reliability of what appears to be information, and about the validity of our conclusions?

Surely we should all see the dangers of accepting information from old books. And the disagreements among "authorities" in almost every field should warn us to question "authoritative" statements or at least to check them as best we can against our own experience. Even then, reasonable humility would seem to warn that we rarely "prove" anything well enough to justify saying such and such *is true*.

Incidentally, our best modern scientists have just about learned their lessons. They now admit that they usually deal with probabilities rather than certainties.

If the careful research methods and conclusion making of scientists still lead to questionable results and probable truths, what of the statements of people who do not bother to get the facts at all and, without thinking or checking, act on the bases of prejudices, preconceptions, whims, etc.? A semanticist would at least warn you to take what they say with a few grains of semantic salt.

4. *Facts, inferences, and value judgments are not the same thing.* If you have ever heard a court trial, you have probably heard a judge order some testimony stricken from the record because the witness was stating opinions or conclusions (inferences) rather than things seen, heard, felt, etc. (sense data). The fact that our legal procedures do not allow inferences as evidence (except inferences by experts in the field) reflects soci-

ety's faith in sense data and its lack of faith in inferences unless made by people specially qualified to make them. Most of us would do well to be more skeptical of the mouthings of people who have not bothered to get the facts—and especially of nonexperts talking on professional topics.

You see why if you consider the nature of sense data, inferences, and value judgments. Sense data usually approach certainty, inferences vary all the way from near certainty to slight probability (usually depending mainly on how many verifiable facts form the basis for them), and value judgments are nearly always debatable.

For example, you see a good friend in a men's store on December 20. She tells you that she wants to buy a tie for her husband Joe and asks your help in selecting a pretty one. After she disapproves three ties you suggest and then you disapprove three she is considering, you leave her to make her own choice because you see that the two of you don't agree on what is a nice tie (value judgments). On December 27 you see Joe wearing a tie that seems to be new and looks like one of the three Jane suggested and you disapproved. More courteously than sincerely, you say, "That is a pretty tie Jane bought you." (Note the dogmatic *is*, discussed in Item 2 above.) Joe says that he hates to be so disagreeable, but he thinks it's ugly and Jane didn't buy it. You see that your value judgment matches Joe's better than Jane's; and when Joe tells you that a friend gave him the tie, you see that you took a calculated risk with your inference—and lost. (Note that to make this decision, you have to assume that Joe is reporting facts.)

Not even the courts rule out inferences completely, however. Judges make them, and jurors' votes are pure inferences. As a matter of practicality, we make and act on inferences all the time. We have to. We cannot always know with the near certainty of sense data; many times we have to act on inferences and thus take calculated risks. Even *calculated* risks, however, have *some* data base and are safer than wild guesses or hunches.

The danger in inferences is not in acting on them but in acting on them *as if* they were completely reliable. By recognizing the risks we take when acting on inferences, or even on hunches, we can reduce the danger considerably because otherwise unexpected turns of events will not surprise us.

To avoid deluding ourselves and others with whom we communicate, then, we will do well to remind ourselves and forewarn others of the *bases* on which our statements rest. A statement, like a ladder, is no more secure than its foundation. *Our readers and listeners have a right to know about the foundations if they are going to risk their necks on our ladders.*

Still, we need not make ourselves as ridiculous as the skeptical farmer who, when asked to observe that black sheep in the pasture, remarked, "At least it is black on this side." He did seem a bit ridiculous, but he was semantically no sucker.

5. *No two things are exactly alike.* Even things so much alike that they appear identical to the naked eye always reveal differences under close inspection. To be absolutely precise in naming things would require a different word or other symbol for each. Obviously, such precision is impractical—and unnecessary for most purposes.

General words, naming whole groups of things similar in one or more aspects that concern us, help us in classifications. Thus we can save words and time by talking about, or otherwise treating, somewhat similar things collectively instead of individually. If what we say or do with the group applies equally well to all members of the group, we operate efficiently.

Trouble arises quickly, however, when we group things on the basis of a few similarities and then act as if all things in the group were identical in all ways. Such a situation exists when colleges try to treat all freshmen alike because all are first-year students, ignoring the great variety of interests and abilities in the individuals.

Some ugly results of ignoring differences and stressing similarities are faulty categorizing (or labeling or pigeonholing) and faulty analogy making. Thus we get the unsound, unyielding, and prejudicial stereotyping so often seen in fiction. Not all cowboys, politicians, professors, business people, delinquent credit customers, Russians, or blacks are alike—although they may have some similarities that justify the grouping *for a particular purpose.*

As a communicator, you can do several things to help solve the problem. For one thing, you can *use symbols (usually words) that are specific enough for your purposes.* When you do mean your statement to apply equally to a number of somewhat similar things (perhaps all new customers), be efficient and use the group name instead of handling each separately; but surely you should not lump together for similar handling as "delinquent accounts" the good customer who got behind because of a temporary misfortune and the marginal risk who tried to skip by moving and leaving no address. And if what you say applies only to typewriters, don't say machines. If it applies only to portables, don't say typewriters. If it applies only to Royal portables, don't just say portables.

Accepting the premise of uniqueness, and recognizing the fallacy of identity, some semanticists recommend using the "which index." To distinguish which individual they are referring to in a group name, they suggest using subscript numbers after the name, $typewriter_1$ being different from $typewriter_2$. Carried to extremes, this system is as impractical as the limitless vocabulary necessary to give each individual thing a name; but used in moderation, it can help. In either case a little use of it will remind you of an important point: If significant differences exist in the group named, make clear which members of the group you are talking about. "Businessmen who do such and such things are unethical" is quite different from "Businessmen are unethical."

For another thing, you can *consider significant differences along with similarities.* Analogies, similes, and other metaphors pointing to the similarities between two things help greatly in explanations. Indeed, they become almost necessary, because teaching and learning involve explanation of the unknown in terms of the known. Dictionaries explain words in terms of other words presumably known to the dictionary user. You often hear and read explanations in terms of a football game, which you presumably understand. Because you know English verbs generally go like *stay, stayed, stayed,* you can usually form the past tense and the past participle of a verb you have just learned. But if the new verb is *think,* the analogy misleads you.

That misleading analogy points to three warnings to heed to make analogies helpful rather than harmful.

a. Since no two things are exactly alike, no analogy can be complete. Although *stay* and *think* are both English verbs, they belong to different classes. Although we speak of synonyms, they are alike only in some ways and are not always interchangeable.

b. Because two or more things always have some differences even when they are largely similar, *an analogy never proves anything.* The truth may slip through one of the holes that make the difference between the two "analogous" things. Stock-market and weather forecasters are often wrong because they have failed to consider significant differences in generally similar background conditions.

c. In using analogies, you must be sure your reader understands the supposedly known side of your analogy. Otherwise, you are in the position of one explaining a Russian word in Chinese terms to a person who knows neither language.

6. *Some either-or, black-white classifications are legitimate, but most are not.* The question is *whether your two-part classifications are mutually exclusive.* A person is either married or not; no one can be both married and not married at the same time. But you cannot say with equal validity that the same person is tall, intelligent, honest, and the like. Where do you draw the line between intelligent and not intelligent, honest and not honest?

You are being true to reality when you use either-or, black-white, *two-valued logic for mutually exclusive things*—things that cannot both exist at the same time. But most things are continua, with gradations, shadings, or degrees between the extremes. For them you need a "how-much index." Applying black-white logic to them ignores the gray. It is similar to the false dilemma in logic. And like the false dilemma, it comes mostly from the unthinking, the intolerant, and the dishonest among us. The results are delusions of self and others, intolerance, and hard feelings if not fights.

As a communicator, you can do several things to avoid the undesirable consequences of two-valued thinking. First, you must recognize the difference between legitimate (mutually exclusive) two-pole classifications and continua. Then you can use the readily available facilities of English to show the proper gradations in continua. English contains not only somewhat similar nouns of varying degrees of specificity and strength but a large supply of adjectives and adverbs with similar variations. Moreover, the adjectives and adverbs have three standard degrees of comparison like *good, better, best* and *speedily, more speedily,* and *most speedily.* If you still feel the need for better indication of the degree of grayness in a continuum, you can always *add* specific details, as in "Quickly (3.2 seconds) the operator turned the heavy (5-ton) crane around and. . . ."

7. *Things change significantly with time.* Nature works as a dynamic process. As part of nature, Joe Smith today is not exactly the same as Joe Smith yesterday, much less ten years ago. Significant aspects of a present situation may not have existed in the past and may not continue in the future. To be true to reality, you need to *consider the date* in connection with statements sent or received. Some semanticists refer to this principle as the necessity for the "when index." Ignoring it produces what some call the "frozen evaluation."

Most universities recognize the point (consider the date) in readmitting students, after specified lengths of time, after dropping them for poor scholarship or infraction of rules. On the other hand, we have many instances of "frozen evaluations." Most homes would run more smoothly if parents would recognize that their teenagers are no longer babies. Ex-convicts could readjust to normal living much more easily if their neighbors would at least give them a chance to show whether they have changed, instead of pinning permanent labels on them. Many blue laws on statute books should be rescinded.

To unfreeze some of our thinking, we may as well get used to reinterpretations of the Constitution—and to changed usages and new dictionaries of English. Our language is not static. Fighting new English textbooks and new dictionaries (which do not make but merely record current usage) is more futile than fighting city hall; its fighting the whole country. Surely a credit manager should know that the facts which force refusal of requested credit may change in a few months—and should hold open the possibility of reconsidering them.

8. *Words are not identical to the objects they represent;* they are just symbols of concepts that exist only in the mind. They do not have meanings themselves but only the power to represent or evoke meanings in our minds.

Concrete objects react on our various senses to give us our concepts of those things. We then use words to represent those concepts. Only the physical objects are real; our concepts and the symbols (words) to represent them are the first and second levels of abstraction in the "ladder of abstraction" or "structural differential" which semanticists talk about.

In this scheme, clearly the names we give are not the things themselves —even names that have referents (concrete, tangible objects to which they refer). If you question this statement, try eating the word *pie* the next time you get hungry for something sweet. Or since a word is to its referent as a map is to its territory, just take a walk on your map the next time you want to take a trip. As Korzybski repeatedly explains, our words merely represent the world of events and things outside our skins but are never the real things. Ogden and Richards (*The Meaning of Meaning*) present the symbolic nature of language as a triangle, the three points representing referent, thought, and symbol.

This semantic principle of the symbolic nature of language points to these suggestions for better communication:

a. Insofar as possible, use words with real physical objects or actions as referents, and make them specific enough to call to the receiver's mind the particular referent. If your receiver has seen or touched the kind of thing you are talking about, the concepts you want to convey about it are clearer than if you talk in generalities or talk about abstractions (concepts like loyalty and honesty that do not exist in the physical world but only in the mind). Even when your word has a referent, avoid equating the word with the physical object (for which it is only a symbol) or with some facet of it: "Russia *is* the Berlin Wall" or "Communism *is*. . . ."

b. Although you cannot avoid the use of some abstract words (which have no referents in the physical world), try to keep them to a minimum. Then consider the context in which they are used. If you have described several actions taken and then you commend the person for *integrity*, the context makes clear what you mean by the otherwise abstract word *integrity*. That's the way abstract words are used best: as summarizing words.

c. Especially in reading and listening, try to look behind the words and envision the things and ideas the words represent. You can remember the thought much easier than all the exact words used to represent it. And in taking notes or answering questions about what you've heard or read, present the concepts in your own words except for key words and phrases. If you concentrate on words, you'll likely learn the words and repeat them parrotlike without understanding the thought they were intended to convey. Instead, concentrate on "What does the message sender mean by those words?"

LISTENING AND READING

Speaking and writing are forms of the initiating or encoding phase of communication. Listening and reading are forms of the receiving or decoding phase. Considerable skill in each is vital for a literate individual in today's civilization.

Most training in schools is devoted to writing, reading, and—to a lesser extent—speaking. Yet from the time we start to learn, we spend at least as much communicating time in listening as we do on all the other three. As we advance and become more proficient in and dependent on reading, many of us, unless we consciously strive to do otherwise, steadily deteriorate in listening efficiency.

But how much easier we can make our learning and living if we develop and maintain skill in listening (to TV, radio, lectures, sermons, interviews, conferences, directives, conversations, etc.), which accounts for about three times as much of our communication time as reading does!

The task of listening[2]

Neither good reading nor good listening is easy. Both require training, either supervised or self-disciplined. Of the two activities, listening is the more demanding and the more difficult for most of us. The written word is always there for the reader to go back to. The spoken word, once uttered, is gone unless stored in the hearer's mind (a job that most of us do not perform well). The reader can proceed at a self-chosen speed; the listener must adapt to the pace of the speaker.

Learning to be a good reader does not make you a good listener, either, any more than learning to be a good listener makes you a good reader. Several differences in the two communicating processes help to explain why. Not only are the styles different (greater variety in sentence length and style, much more use of phrases, more personal references, more informality, more repetitions, and more adaptations in the oral), but the role of the nonverbal is even more significant. A speaker's gestures, facial expressions, pitch of voice, inflections, rhythm and speed, and pronunciation constantly affect the final message to listeners. The reader uses eyes alone. The listener uses eyes and ears.

We talk much more slowly than our minds can comprehend what we hear. Since our minds operate so much faster than our mouths, when someone else is talking we tend to put our excess mental capacity to work thinking about what we are going to say when our turn comes to speak; and we cease to concentrate on what the other person is saying. This natural human tendency is one we must *learn* to overcome—even though it takes work.

Learning to listen well is the single biggest thing you can do to improve your own personal relations. When you really listen to someone, you take a big step toward avoiding conflict by *understanding* that person. Further, when you listen well, you help others to work out their problems (listening is, after all, the basis of counseling and psychiatry). Good listening will

---

[2] See Ralph G. Nichols and Leonard A. Stevens, *Are You Listening?* McGraw-Hill Book Co., Inc., New York, 1957, 235 pp.; Ralph G. Nichols and Thomas R. Lewis, *Speaking and Listening*, William C. Brown Co., Dubuque, 1965, 357 pp. Both these publications contain extensive bibliographies.

lead others to communicate full information to you instead of skipping some things because you are evidently not listening, and fuller information will help you to be more successful in your chosen activity. Finally, as you demonstrate good listening, you will lead others to improve their listening practices, resulting in an overall improvement in communication.

Although in everyday living you will listen and learn in interviews, lectures, conferences, and conversation, the following suggestions apply primarily in listening to speeches and lectures.

Identify the subject and plan. Most speakers will deliver planned talks organized in the traditional pattern of introduction, thesis, body, and conclusion.

Many excellent speakers will tell a story, or quote from some well-known authority or publication, or say something startling first to secure your favorable attention. Such a beginning may be appropriate, even germane, but rarely is it of the essence. Many excellent lecturers dispense with the irrelevant beginning and start immediately with genuine subject matter, and wisely so.

The essential point for concentration is when the speaker announces the subject, why it is pertinent, and the plan of presentation. If you are not tuned in for this thesis statement, you are going to have difficulty following the rest.

Stay tuned in. The body of the speech (the longest part) includes the several points that support the speaker's fundamental proposition or thesis. The evidence may be statistics, testimony, stories, and/or explanation and logical analysis, to name some forms.

Major points and the evidence supporting them may come in *deductive* order (usual if the purpose is only to inform). This is, stated very simply, generalization followed by supporting detail. If the purpose is to persuade, an *inductive* order (generalization after evidence) will be better—and more likely if the speaker is a good one.

Obviously, this is the part on which you should exercise your powers of concentration and your critical faculties. *The questions of completeness, validity, appropriateness, and recency are significant here.*

You will find this part easier to follow (and more interesting) if, when possible, you check the speaker's announced plan of presentation against delivery and *stay on the alert for transitions*—those statements signaling a change of point. The points or principles (the *ideas*) the speaker establishes fill in the blueprint of the plan and establish the final structure. The *facts* supporting the principles are subheads.

If the speaker announces no plan, try to anticipate what is coming. If your guess proves to be right, you'll feel pleasure—and probably reveal it in feedback to the speaker. And if you're wrong? Never mind, you'll have concentrated better and benefited from the mental exercise of comparison and contrast.

Good speakers (and good writers) build up their points or principles step by step so that the conclusion suggests itself before it arrives. In an informative speech the conclusion is often very short. It may be no more than a quick recap of the main points and a brief statement of how the subject or speech is significant to the audience. The conclusion of the persuasive speech may be a little longer. The persuasive speaker may not reveal a stand until the end. In addition to establishing the real objective, some speakers may use strong argument. Question. Challenge. But reserve judgment until you've had the time to sift and revaluate—to review and rebuild.

When you're the trapped victim of a speaker who indulges in harangue, cajoling, or bombast (especially if backed only by scant, prejudiced, one-sided, or unsound "facts" or logic), tune out; you're entitled to stop listening.

Be sensible; control your note-taking. The temptation to apply pencil or pen to paper and start to record a speaker's words *verbatim* is one that is too great for many listeners to overcome—unfortunately. This kind of note-taking causes the listener to lose many of the significant ideas, to become confused, and eventually to become frustrated and give up on note-taking—and usually on listening also.

Most speakers and lecturers agree that good listeners take good notes. They also agree that those who take good notes *listen a lot and write a little.* Possibly the best piece of advice we can give you is to keep your notes brief and clear during listening (complete thoughts for major points; just words and short phrases for supporting details). You can expand and review later.

Rarely does an introduction merit recording. Even the thesis is better not written down when first stated—although you certainly want to have it clearly in mind when the speaker launches into the supporting main points and evidence. (Write it down after you've heard enough to state it precisely.) Even the brief outline or plan (if the speaker gives you one) is better recorded point by point as you go along rather than at the time the speaker first announces it. As a good listener, you strive to understand each main point your speaker makes. If you're too preoccupied with catching errors or taking notes, you won't get the message. Withhold your judgments and decisions until after you have reviewed the main ideas and thesis.

The careful distinction between fact and idea leads a listener to one system of note-taking that is economical and efficient. Divide your paper into two columns, one for principles and one for facts. You'll have difficulty determining which is which sometimes. But the effort will help you to concentrate and will provide enough useful reminders for later review. You'll have more entries in your facts column than in your principles column. If you have to slight the recording of one, slight the facts; concentrate on the principles.

The sooner you can review your notes after the speech, the better. Of course, as you listened, you should have mentally questioned for completeness, adequacy and appropriateness, authenticity, recency, and omission of data. An even more fruitful time to do this is shortly after the talk in a review of notes, supplementing and rebuilding, questioning, searching for negative evidence, and finally arriving at an evaluation.

Avoid the main stumbling blocks to good listening. Without the wish and the will to, you won't profit from anyone's suggestions. Our pointing out some common failings, however, may help you to improve.

To begin with, accept the fact that listening is hard work demanding patience and an open mind—a considerate, even charitable, mind. Most of us much prefer to consider our own individual interests and air what is on our own minds. The temptation to tune out and escape to reverie or daydreaming is ever with us.

Sometimes we are prone to pretend attention when our minds are not receiving any ideas being transmitted. No speaker with much experience gets fooled by the head nodder, the glassy-eyed starer, the marbleized "thinker." Such audience characters are only fooling themselves. They are no more interested in listening than the foot tapper, the pen flipper, the book slammer, etc. If you fall in one of these classes, wake up—and learn.

Another stumbling block is undue attention to the speaker's appearance, voice, or speech characteristics. A word is only a symbol, not reality; a speaker's appearance is only an outward shell, not an indicator of mind; speech is only the vehicle, not the idea. Although we all like to be personable people and do respond almost automatically more to good-looking people than to those who are not, don't shut yourself off from learning because of a person's physiognomy, size, dress, or voice characteristics. The mind may have a lot to contribute.

All too often we are guilty of abruptly rejecting or dismissing a speaker and subject because we consider them dull or difficult. Remember that the "dull" speaker is probably doing just what the assignment was—to give you facts and ideas—and refusing to insult your intelligence, or take pay under false pretenses, by entertaining you instead. Be selfish: Take for yourself what is meaningful and useful. Very few "uninteresting" speeches are devoid of something useful.

As for rejecting the difficult discourse, remember that this can become a pattern of progressive mental deterioration. The more you do it, the flabbier and more superficial your mind becomes. The only suggestions we can make are continually renewed determination to "hear the speaker out" and a planned effort to tackle uninteresting as well as difficult material.

Another stumbling block is the tendency of listeners to let physical surroundings distract them. Airplanes, buses, trains, thunder, and other outside noises are sometimes loud, and rarely can the listener do anything about them. But they are noises that most of us easily ignore when we want to (during a favorite TV program, for instance).

Many times, however, you can control physical circumstances. Windows and doors close as well as open. Heating mechanisms turn off as well as on. If you as an individual can't control the distraction, enlist the aid of the speaker. Even if neither can do anything and can't move to a more favorable place, at least you will be alert to the fact that both will have to exert extra effort to concentrate on effective sending and receiving of the message.

A reminder of something already said will summarize the key point: In your listening, concentrate on principles, not detailed facts presented in support of principles. Emphasis on facts makes you lose principles, which are the most significant parts of speeches; emphasis on principles makes you not only get the principles or ideas but also helps you remember many of the facts that support them.

Efficient reading

Much of what we've said about listening also applies to reading. We shall therefore discuss this form of the receiving phase of communication in much less detail.

If you are reading only for pleasure, you can relax and be almost passive as you proceed at whatever pace you please. If you are not satisfied with your reading pace, you may want to enroll for one of the reading-improvement courses offered by many schools and counseling services or clinics. The aim of these courses is to increase the reader's rate and comprehension. If no such work or counseling is available to you, you may want to read some of the excellent books on the subject.[3]

If you are reading for information and instruction (as opposed to pleasure or entertainment), you can profit even more from such courses and books. The following brief suggestions give you only the main points of some of these books.

When you read an informative publication (book, section, chapter, or article):

---

[3] We suggest that you start with these books in this order (some of them have bibliographies to direct you further): Mortimer J. Adler, *How to Read a Book*, Simon and Schuster, Inc., New York, 1940; A. L. Raygor and D. M. Wark, *Systems for Study*, McGraw-Hill Book Co., New York, 1970; G. A. Gladstein, *Individualized Study*, Rand McNally, Chicago, 1967; William W. Farquhar et al., *Learning to Study*, Ronald Press Co., New York, 1960; Luella Cole, *Students' Guide to Efficient Study*, Holt, Rhinehart & Winston, Inc., New York, 1960; Walter Pauk, *How to Study in College*, Houghton Mifflin Co., Boston, 1962; Francis P. Robinson, *Effective Study*, Harper & Bros., New York, 1970; George D. Spache and Paul C. Berg, *The Art of Efficient Reading*, Macmillan Co., New York, 1966; Horace Judson, *The Techniques of Reading*, Harcourt, Brace, New York, 1963; Paul D. Leedy, *Read with Speed and Precision*, McGraw-Hill Book Co., Inc., New York, 1963, and *A Key to Better Reading*, 1968; Paul C. Berg, et al., *Skimming and Scanning*, Educational Developmental Laboratories, Huntington, N.Y., 1962; A. L. Raygor and G. B. Schick, *Reading at Efficient Rates*, McGraw-Hill Book Co., New York, 1970.

1. Understand the scope and limitations of the subject as evidenced in the title and often in a subtitle, the preface, and introductory comments.
2. Determine as closely as you can the primary purpose, which may be only implied. Phrase it in your own words.
3. Take advantage of mechanical aids (indentions, paragraphing, outline symbols, change of type, etc.) and transitions as you read through the first time *rapidly*. Don't ponder over phrases or even whole sentences; don't look up definitions. *Read through and read fast!*
4. When you've finished, try to recall as much as you can. Check the theme or central idea you have formulated against the author's expression of it either in the ending or in the beginning.
5. Reread the material paragraph by paragraph. (The first rapid reading will decrease your reading time at this stage, and much that was foggy the first time will be clear.) If you own the material (but not in library materials, please!), underscore key words and topic sentences, often at the beginning or end.

Then you can take further steps:

1. If you are reasonably certain of the meaning of a word from the context, you are probably safe in not looking it up. Otherwise, look it up and pencil the appropriate definition in the margin.

2. When the article or chapter is fairly short and not formally organized, you're probably better off simply to write a short précis.

3. When the article or chapter is formally organized, you may want to write a formal outline. Such outlining is another step in remembering and is vital if you need to submit an oral or a written report.

These suggestions apply if you want or need to do more than record and possibly transmit what some author wrote. If you want or need to evaluate (as for a review), you will have to answer such questions as the following:

1. About the author:
   Who? Position or status? Authority? Biased?
2. About the treatment:
   a. Are generalizations supported by evidence? Ample? Secondary or primary? Based on sound research?
   b. Is coverage of major points adequate? Significant omissions?
   c. What is the announced or apparent intended audience? Is treatment adapted to this audience?

You can add to this list. Certainly it is not intended to be exhaustive.

And remember, no speaker or writer is infallible. A printed statement often means nothing more than that the statement is in print.

appendix B | **Concise writer's handbook**

THIS ALPHABETICAL LIST of short, easy-to-remember **symbols** will save a teacher's time in marking papers and will help students wanting brief explanations of errors frequently found in business writing.

The **symbols** (the bold-faced part of each entry) are easy to remember because they are nearly all abbreviations of already familiar grading or proofreading terms. Even the few abstract, unalphabetized ones at the end are mostly standard proofreader's marks.

The list includes everything teachers and students of business writing are likely to need for correcting the English in their papers. Although it is much more concise than the usual English handbook, it omits only those points college students already know or don't need to know. We based our selection of the included items on a combined 85 years of experience in observing the good and the unacceptable in the writing of students in 23 colleges and universities.

The explanations of points of grammar and usage are based solidly on the studies of linguists—the true authorities.

A, an Use *a* as the indefinite article if the following word begins with a consonant sound (including the now pronounced *h* in *hotel* and *historical*—and combined consonant and vowel sounds, as in *European, usage, unit,* and *eulogy*); use *an* if the next word begins with a vowel sound, including words beginning with silent *h* (*hour, honor, honest*).

Ab Before using an abbreviation, make sure it is appropriate, understood, and correct in form (including capitalization, spacing, and punctuation). Ordinarily, you should not abbreviate dates and states (except that the Postal Service has a complete system of state abbreviations for envelope addresses—adapting to electronic mail sorting). Mr., Mrs., Dr., A.M., P.M., c.o.d., f.o.b., and e.o.m. most commonly appear as abbreviations. Also, abbreviation is preferable for many specialized terms in almost every professional field of work or study. Check your dictionary or specialty handbook if in doubt about an abbreviation.

Accuracy Get facts, names, addresses, and statements right. If your statement may be misinterpreted, restate it so that it is clear.

Accusations. See p. 65.

Adapt to your reader's interests, reading ability, and experience. A message that seems to be written for somebody else, or for nobody in particular, is less effective than one which seems to fit the reader. See p. 85.

Agreement of subjects with their verbs and of pronouns with their antecedents is essential to clear, inconspicuous communication. Don't be confused by other words that come between two that are supposed to agree.

1. Notice that the first sentence about agreement is an illustration of the first point: *agreement* (singular) is the subject of the verb *is;* but between them is a prepositional phrase with four plurals. As other illustrations, consider

    Selection of topics *depends* on the reader's knowledge and interests.

    Lee also tells how important the arrangement of the records offices *is.*

    Part, series, type, and other words usually followed by plural phrases are frequently pitfalls to the unwary writer:

    The greatest part of their investments *is* in real estate.

    A series of bank loans *has* enabled the firm to stay in business.

2. *Any, anyone, each, every, everyone, everybody, either,* and *neither* all point to singular verbs (and pronouns)—except that in an either-or situation, with one noun singular and one plural, verbs and pronouns agree with the closer noun.

    Any of the women in the group *is* willing to give some of *her* time to helping the group when asked.

    Either board members or the president *has* power to act on the point.

    Neither the mayor nor the council members *are* allowed to use city-owned automobiles in transacting *their* own business.

3. Two separate singular subjects combined by *and* require a plural verb or pronoun; but when combined by *besides, either-or, together with,* or *as well as,* they take a singular:

    Mr. Weeks and his secretary *do* the work in the central office.

    Considerable knowledge, as well as care, *is* necessary in good writing.

    But note:

    The honorary president and leader of this group *is* Mr. Anderson (one person, two titles).

4. Be sure your pronouns agree in number and gender with their antecedents (words they stand for).

    The company plans to move *its* main operations closer to *its* major source of raw materials.

    The benefits students get from studying the practical psychology, writing skills, and ways of business in good courses like letter writing and report writing will help *them* throughout life.

5. Relative clauses beginning with the pronouns *who, that,* or *which* require verbs agreeing with the antecedents:

    The manager is one of those *persons who* expect unquestioning loyalty.

    The *actions* in the life of any animal which *interest* a biologist are those concerned with food, shelter, protection from enemies, and procreation.

6. Plural-sounding collective subjects take singular verbs and pronouns when the action is that of the group but plural verbs when the action is that of two or more individuals in the group:

    The board *is* having a long meeting.

    The board *have* been arguing and disagreeing on that point for months.

    Twenty-five dollars *is* a reasonable price in view of. . . .

    The faculty *are* allowed almost complete freedom in the conduct of *their* classes while the administration *plays its* part by providing the facilities, general policy, and record keeping. (The collective faculty acting as individuals, the administration acting as a group.)

7. Beware of letting the complement tempt you to make the verb agree with it instead of the subject:

    Our main difficulty *was* errors in billing.

    The biggest cost item *is* employees' salaries and wages.

(In most such situations, however, rewriting would be better, to avoid equating a subject with a predicate noun of different number.)

8. Certain words deserve careful attention because their form is an uncertain or misleading indication of their number:

   a. The meaning of the whole context determines the number of *any, all, more, most, some,* and *none.*

   b. *Acoustics, economics, genetics, linguistics, mathematics, news, physics,* and *semantics* are all singular despite their look and sound; *deer* and *fish* are both singular and plural; and *mice,* like *men,* is a plural word despite the singular smell.

9. Beware of words whose forms are in transition, like *data.* The original forms, from Latin, were singular, *datum,* and plural, *data.* In modern usage, *datum* is disappearing and *data* is coming into use as both the singular and plural form.

   All the data are in.

   All the data is in (the more commonly seen modern usage).

Ambiguous—more than one possible meaning and hence not clear. Usually you can clear up the temporary confusion by (1) correcting a faulty pronoun reference (see **Ref**) or (2) rewording to straighten out a modifier so that it can modify only what you intend (see **Mod**).

He took over the management of the business from his father when he was 55. (When his father reached 55, Carl took over management of the business.)

We agreed when we signed the papers that you would pay $100. (When we signed the papers, we agreed that you would pay $100 *or* We agreed that you would pay $100 when we signed the papers.)

And is a strong coordinating conjunction—one of the most useful and most troublesome of words.

1. It should connect (in the sense of addition) only things of similar quality and grammatical form. Used otherwise, it produces faulty coordination between an independent and a dependent clause, misparallelism, or sentence disunity. See **Sub, Para,** and **Unit.**

   The plans call for a new four-story building, and which will cost $4.5 million. (Omit *and;* it can't connect an independent clause to a dependent one.) See **Coh.**

   In this course you learn the ways of the business world, the principles of practical psychology, and to write better. (The infinitive *to write* is not parallel with the nouns *ways* and *principles*. Make them all the same form before connecting them by *and*.) See **Para.**

We feel sure that the saw will serve you well, and we appreciate your order. (The two ideas are not closely enough related to appear in the same sentence—probably not even in the same paragraph.) See **Unit.**

2. *And* is properly the most-used connective, but don't overuse it to connect a series of independent clauses into a long, stringy sentence. If the clauses deserve equal emphasis, you can make separate sentences. If not, subordinate the weaker ones. See **Sub.**

The consultant first talked with the executives about their letter-writing problems *and* then took a sample of 1,000 carbon copies *and* classified them into two groups *and* 45 percent of them were for situations that could just as well have been handled by forms. (After talking with the executives about their letter-writing problems, the consultant classified a sample of 1,000 carbon copies from the files. Forty-five percent of them were for situations that could just as well. . . .)

3. *And* may properly begin a sentence, but only if you want to emphasize it.

4. *And* is not proper before *etc.;* the *et* in *et cetera* means *and*.

5. Except in formal writing *and/or* is acceptable to mean either or both of two mentioned possibilities.

Ap The appearance of a letter, as of a person, should be pleasant but unobtrusive and should suggest that the writer is competent, accurate, neat, and alert. It requires a good grade of paper, proper spacing, typing with a reasonably fresh ribbon, and clean type without messy erasures or glaring errors. Check Chapter 1.

Apostrophes (usually considered with punctuation, although they belong with spelling) should appear in:

1. Possessives (except *its* and the personal pronouns): before *s* in singulars (*man's*); after the *s* in plurals if the *s* or *z* sound is there to make the word plural (*ladies'* but *women's*).

2. Contractions: to mark the omission of a letter (*isn't, doesn't, it's* —meaning "it is," quite different from the possessive *its*).

3. Plurals of symbols: figures (illegible *8's*), letters of the alphabet (one *o* and two *m's*), and words written about as words (too

many *and's* and *but's*), though some authorities now restrict this use to avoiding confusion.

Appropriateness to the situation is an important test of good English. Is your statement too slangy, colloquial, or formal for the occasion? See **Adapt** and p. 49 for a discussion of levels of usage.

Assign Follow the facts and directions in the assignment. Although you should fill in with necessary details of your own invention, you are not to go contrary to the facts or the spirit of the assigned case, and you are to make only reasonable assumptions. See p. xii.

BB Browbeating the reader is redundant and insulting.
Clark plans to use two approaches to attack the fast-food market. These approaches are: (1) capture the shopper who wants a more convenient way to prepare and eat meals at home and (2) lure the lunch-time shoppers into the store. (Put the colon after *market* and omit *These approaches are.*) See also **P10**.

Capitalization is pretty well standardized (except that newspapers set their own practices and hence are not guides for other writing).

1. Capitalize the names of specific things, including the titles of people, but not general words. For instance, you capitalize the name of any specific college, university, or department; but you write:

    A university education may well cost $12,000, regardless of the department in which one studies.

    L. W. Wilson, president of the University of. . . .

    When President Wilson came. . . .

    You capitalize any specific course, room, lake, river, building, etc., but not the general words. So you might write:

    I am taking Economics 215.

    I am majoring in engineering.

    Now I must go to a history class in the Liberal Arts Building, after stopping to see a professor in Room 115.

    Next summer I may fish mostly in Portage Lake and some in the Ausable River, although I prefer river to lake fishing.

    Of course, you capitalize *English, French, German*—all the languages, because they derive from the names of countries.

2. In titles of books and articles capitalize (though library materials don't) the first word and all others except articles (*a, an, the*), prepositions (like *of, to, in, on, for*), and conjunctions (like *and, but, or, nor, although*)—unless you use solid capitals.

3. Capitalize the seasons (spring, summer) only when you personify them (rare except in poetry).

4. Capitalize sections of the country (the South, the East Coast) but not directions (east, west).

5. Capitalize people's titles (*Mr., Mrs., Ms., Miss, Dr., Colonel, Professor, Judge, Governor, President*) and terms of family relations (*Uncle Jim*) when used before names but only to show unusual respect when used in place of or after names:

   Yes, Son, ...
   The Senator then went. . . .
   After Mother had seen. . . .

6. Capitalize the first word after a colon only if it starts a complete sentence. (In an itemized listing, you may capitalize the first word of items even though they are incomplete sentences.)

Cardinal numbers (*one, two, three; 6, 7, 9*) are preferable to ordinals (*first, second, third; 1st, 2d, 3d, 4th*, or *2nd, 3rd*) in dates except in very formal invitations and legal documents, or when you separate the day from the month. Since the simple ordinal forms may be either adjectives or adverbs, they need no -*ly* endings, ever.

On October 7 . . . ; sometime in November—probably about the 7th.

Case in modern English is a problem only with personal pronouns. (It is no problem with English nouns. One form serves for all cases of nouns except the possessive, and the only problem there is remembering correct use of the apostrophe.) For pronouns:

1. Use the nominative case (*I, we, he, she, they, who*) for the subject of a verb (other than an infinitive) and for the complement of a linking verb (any form of *to be* except the infinitive with a subject).

2. Use the objective case (*me, us, him, her, them, whom*) as the object of a verb or preposition and as the subject or object of an infinitive (except *to be* without a subject). In informal speaking and writing, however, *who* is acceptable as the object of a preposition unless it immediately follows the preposition, especially if it is in the usual subject position:

   Who was the letter addressed to?

3. Use the possessive case to show possession and to serve as the subject of a gerund (a verb form ending in *ing* and used as a noun):

   His accusing me of dishonesty . . . .
   My thinking that a . . . .

4. The case of an appositive (an immediately following, and usually parenthetical, explanation like *this*) is that of the thing explained.

5. Watch case particularly after *than* and *as* and in compounds with a name and a personal pronoun:

He is better informed on the subject than I (*am informed* implied).

I am a more cautious man than he (*is* understood).

He is not so cautious as I (*am* understood).

Virginia and she went . . . (subject).

I am to pick up Virginia and her . . . (object of verb).

He told the story to Virginia and her (object of preposition).

Choppy, jerky, short sentences are slow and awkward. Usually the trouble is (1) incoherence (the sentences don't follow each other naturally—see **Coh**); (2) poor control of emphasis (all the ideas in independent clauses, although of different importance—see **Sub**); or (3) lack of variety (all the sentences of the same pattern, usually all beginning with the subject or nearly the same length—see **Var**). Try combining several of the sentences, subordinating the less important ideas, and stressing the important ones in the independent clauses (see **SOS 3**).

Cl Immediate clearness is a fundamental of good writing. Make sure your reader can get your meaning quickly and easily. Usually a statement that is not immediately clear requires more exact wording, fuller explanation, or recasting of a faulty, ambiguous, or involved construction.

Coherence means clearly showing your reader *the relationships between ideas*. It comes best from a logical sequence with major emphasis on the important ideas, with less on the related but less important ones, and with any necessary conjunctions to indicate what relationships exist. Incoherence comes from mixing unrelated ideas together in the same sentence or paragraph, but particularly from linking unrelated ideas or ideas of different importance by *and*.

1. Plan ahead—get your ideas in logical sequence *before* you write. You can group seemingly unrelated ideas with a topic sentence such as "Three factors deserve special consideration." Such a sentence will clearly show that the three following sentences or paragraphs are related.

2. Give your ideas proper emphasis (see **Emp** and **Sub**). Important ideas should be in independent clauses or separate sentences. Two closely related and equally important ideas can be

together in a compound sentence. Put a less important idea in a dependent clause attached to an independent clause, making a complex sentence.

3. Carefully choose transitional words or phrases if you need them to smooth the natural sequence of ideas (see **Tr**). Consider the following as examples:

And . . . moreover, besides, in addition, also, furthermore.

But . . . however, nevertheless, yet, still, although, while.

Either-or . . . neither-nor, else, whether.

Therefore . . . consequently, hence, as a result, accordingly, so, ergo, thus. (Check for *true* cause-effect relation.)

Because . . . since, as, for, the reason is.

Then . . . after that, afterward, later, subsequently.

Meanwhile . . . during, simultaneously, concurrently, while.

Before . . . preceding, previously, prior to.

If . . . provided, assuming, in case, unless.

4. In papers longer than a page or two—and even more so in similar oral presentations—you probably will need even more than the three preceding means of showing the relationships of ideas and thus keeping the reader on the track. (See "Headings and Subheads," pp. 472–74.)

Conciseness (which is not necessarily brevity) depends on leaving out the irrelevant, leaving unsaid what you can adequately imply (see **Imp**), and cutting out deadwood. See p. 35 ff. for explanation and illustration of techniques.

Connotations—the overtones or related meanings of words—are often as important as the denotations, or dictionary meanings. Be sure that the words you use are appropriate in connotations as well as in denotations. Consider, for example, the connotations in the following: *cheap, inexpensive, economical; secondhand, used, previously owned; complaint department, customer service department; basement store, thrift store, budget floor.*

Copying from the assignment or from other people produces writing that doesn't sound like you. Put your ideas in your own words. You won't learn much about writing by copying other people or the phrasing of illustrations in the text. Read them for ideas, approaches, and psychology; then express your ideas in your own phrasing.

Cpr Comparisons require special attention to these points:

1. Things compared must be comparable. Usually the trouble is omission of necessary phrases like *that of, that on, other,* or *else.*

The markup on Schick shavers is higher than *that on* Remingtons. (You can't omit *that on* or you'll be comparing the height of a Remington—measured in inches—with the markup on Schicks—a percentage.)

Frank Mosteller sells more Fuller brushes than any *other* salesperson. (Without *other,* the statement is illogical if Frank is a salesperson; he can't sell more than he himself sells.)

2. Incomplete comparisons mean nothing; complete them.

You get more miles per dollar with XXX. (More than with what?)

This material has a higher percentage of wool. (Higher than what?)

3. Be sure to use the correct form of comparison words. Comparisons involving two things usually call for adding -*er* (the comparative) to the simple form (*cold, slow*). Those involving more than two usually require the -*est* (or superlative) form (*coldest, slowest, fastest*).

For words of three syllables or more—and for many with two and some with only one—the better form is *more* plus the simple form (for the comparative) or *most* plus the simple form (for the superlative): *more frequently, most hopeful.* Some words can go either way: *oftener* or *more often; oftenest* or *most often.*

4. Watch these idioms: Complete the *as much as* phrase and use *to* after *compare* when pointing out similarities only, *with* when pointing out any differences:

Price increases may be worth as much *as,* if not more than, the dividends on a common stock purchase.

Comparison of X *to* Y shows that they involve the same principles.

Comparison of sales letters with application letters shows that they have minor differences.

5. Some words (*unique, empty, final,* for example) are logical absolutes and hence cannot take comparative or superlative forms.

CS Comma splice—a serious error. Except when they are in series or are short and parallel, two or more independent clauses require separation by a period, a comma and a coordinating conjunction, or a semicolon (which may or may not require a following transition like *that is* or one of the conjunctive adverbs). See **SOS2** and **P2.**

CSP Select a central selling point (in a sales letter) and give it the major emphasis by position and full development. Scattering your shots over too many points leaves the major ones weak. See **Emp** and **Dev.**

Date Date all letters and reports (except possibly ephemera). Any papers worthy of going into files need dates. Write dates in the standard form (*November 2, 1980*) unless you have good reason to do otherwise. Your most likely good reasons could be: (1) You are in the armed services, where the form *2 November 1980* is standard; or (2) you're writing a formal notice, where you use words with no figures, or (3) you're writing an informal note and may well use the form *11/2/80*. Modern business writing usually does not abbreviate months and does not use the ordinal forms. See **Card.**

DC Dramatized copy would be more effective here. See pp. 117, 122(4).

Deadwood phrases add nothing to the meaning but take writing and reading time. See **Conc** and the list of frequent deadwood expressions on p. 38.

Develop your point more thoroughly with more explanation, definition, specific details, classifications, comparisons, or examples to make it clearer, more interesting, more convincing, or more emphatic. See **Spec.**

Diction Use a more suitable word. The big test, of course, is whether the word, including its connotations, conveys your thought accurately. Consider whether your words are easy for your reader to understand; whether they give a sharp, vivid picture by being natural and fresh instead of pompous, jargonistic, or trite; whether they give a specific, concrete meaning instead of a fuzzy or dull concept because they are general or abstract; and whether they are appropriately informal, formal, standard, technical, or nontechnical—according to the topic and reader.

Watch especially the following often-confused pairs: *accept, except; adapt, adopt; affect, effect; almost, most; amount, number; already, all ready; altogether, all together; beside, besides; between, among; capital, capitol; fewer, less; formerly, formally; imply, infer; it's, its; loose, lose; marital, martial; maybe, may be; moral, morale; oral, verbal; personal, personnel; principal, principle; sometime, some time; with regards to, in regard to; your, you're;* and *too, to, two.*

Directness saves words, speeds up reading, and makes your ideas clearer. Don't waste words by beginning too far back in the background of the subject, by stating what the reader already knows, or by expressing what will be clearly implied if you begin with the key thought. Write direct, active-voice sentences beginning with the important word as the subject. The expletives "It is . . ." and "There are . . ." are indirect, passive, and wordy (see **Exp**).

Documentation, or telling your sources, is necessary when you use the ideas of others—to avoid plagiarism and to convince your reader by showing that you have the backing of cited authorities for what you say. See pp. 488 ff. for discussion and illustrations. Also see reports checklist (p. 540).

Emphasis, divided among your ideas according to their relative importance, is basic to good communication.

1. When you state important ideas, give them deserved emphasis by one or more of the following methods: putting them in the emphatic beginning or ending position of your letter or paragraph, putting them in independent clauses, developing them thoroughly (including intentional repetition), phrasing them in active voice, and perhaps underscoring them or writing them in solid capitals (or a different color). See p. 34 for fuller explanation.

2. When you have negative, unimportant, already known, or other ideas that don't deserve emphasis, avoid overemphasizing them. Some useful methods are putting them in unemphatic middle positions, putting them in dependent clauses or phrases, and giving them brief mention or just implying them. Particularly objectionable is overemphasis on things the reader obviously knows and on things that are (or can be) adequately implied. The first insults the reader's intelligence, and both waste words:

    Spring is just around the corner. You'll be needing. . . . (With spring just around the corner, you'll. . . .)

    On October 3 you asked me to write a report on. . . . I have finished it and am. . . . (Here is the report requested in your letter of October 3. . . .)

    I have your letter of April 20 in which you ask for quotations on X. I am glad to give you our prices. Our present prices on X are. . . . (Just omit the first two sentences. They're implied in the third.)

3. Transitional words like *and, but,* and *however* usually do not deserve the emphasis they would get at the beginning of a sentence; and prepositions usually do not deserve end-of-sentence emphasis. Indeed, this point of emphasis is the only legitimate reason for objection to such words in these positions.

Enclosures   See pp. 19, 35, 120, 122(5), 282(5).

Etc., An abbreviation of Latin *et cetera*, meaning *and so forth*, is appropriate only when the reader can easily fill out the incomplete list (as in "Please take even-numbered seats 2, 4, 6, etc."). Otherwise, it can mean only "Reader, you guess what else I mean to include," and this does not communicate. Because *etc.* is an abbreviation, it takes a period; but because it is anglicized, it need not be italicized (or underscored in typed copy). In no case should you write "and etc."; *et* means *and*.

Expletives (*it is, there are*) nearly always make your writing unnecessarily wordy, weak, and passive. They often improperly dodge writer responsibility for statements, and they always slow up the reader's getting to significant information.

Expletives usually result from a misguided attempt to write an impersonal style. If you write them in first drafts, revising to remove them will make better sentences at least nine times out of ten. In general, then, you should avoid them, although sometimes they may help to soften a command or avoid presumptuousness in a recommendation, or ease reader acceptance of bad news.

It was thought that you would prefer. . . . (I thought you would. . . .)

There are four important factors involved. These are: . . . . (The four important factors are. . . .)

It will be necessary to have your. . . . ("You must send . . ." might be too commanding.)

Figures are better than words (except at the beginning of a sentence) for serial, telephone, page, chapter, chart, catalog, and street numbers; for money, dimensions, and dates and time (except in formal announcements); for all quantities when several are close together (but not adjoining) in a sentence or paragraph; and for other isolated quantities requiring more than two words. (As an acceptable replacement for the two-word rule, your teacher may authorize usual newspaper practice: Use figures if the quantity is above ten.)

1. If a quantity comes at the first of a sentence, write it in words or recast the sentence.

2. When a sentence involves two different series of quantities, use figures for one and words for the other to avoid confusion; if more than two, use a table.

   On the qualifying exam, ten percent of the applicants scored 90–100, thirty percent 80–89, ...

   Please make six 2″ × 3″ and three 5″ × 7″ black-and-white prints.

3. The old longhand practice of stating quantities twice—in fig-

ures followed parenthetically by words—is unnecessary and undesirable in type or print, although it still sometimes appears in legal documents, and always in checks, for double certainty and security.

4. Except in dates, street numbers, and serial numbers, use a comma between groups of three digits, counting from the right.

5. Except in tables involving some cents, periods and zeros after money quantities are wasted typing and reading.

6. Two-word quantities between 20 and 100 require the hyphen (*twenty-six*).

7. Cardinal numbers (*1, 2, 3, 4,* etc.) are preferable to ordinals (*1st, 2d, 3d, 4th*) in dates except when the day is separated from the month. See **Card** and **Date**.

8. Since ordinals are either adjectives or adverbs, an *-ly* ending is never necessary or desirable.

Flattery, especially if obvious, is more likely to hurt than help. See p. 60.

Fragments (phrases or subordinate clauses posing as sentences) are serious errors (because they show ignorance of sentence structure) except when perfectly clear and intentional—as they usually are when professional writers use them for special effects. But they are like dynamite in the hands of the unskilled. Beware! Attach them to the independent clauses to which they belong (see **P3**) or change their wording to make them the complete, independent sentences they pretend to be.

> The latter being the better way. (This is a phrase fragment which should be attached by comma to the preceding sentence. Or you could simply change *being* to *is.*)

> One job in revising any paper is checking for and correcting any fragments. Which is easy to do. (The second "sentence" is a dependent clause and hence a fragment unless attached—by a comma—to the preceding.)

Gobbledygook is big-wordy, roundabout, long-winded, or stuffed-shirt language. Characteristically it shows two or more of those traits and comes in long sentences and paragraphs. Avoid it like poison; it works against both clarity and ease of reading.

Graphic devices of various kinds can often supplement words to make the information clearer, easier, or more interesting. Use them where they will help, but only if they will. See pp. 477 and 539.

Gw Goodwill, a basic requirement of a business letter, is lacking or poorly handled here. See Chapter 3.

Idiomatic usage—the natural, customary, accepted way of saying certain things—is correct that way simply because that is the way we say it, although it may defy grammatical analysis and rules. Idioms are so numerous and varied that full explanation would be tedious here. Usually, however, an error in idiom is use of the wrong preposition. Consider *possibility of, possible to, necessity of, need for,* and *ability to.* See **Prep.**

Imply rather than express the idea, to save words or avoid overemphasis. See **Emp** and pp. 33–37.

Italic print, indicated by underscoring in typewritten and handwritten copy, can emphasize occasional words, or mark the title of a book or journal, or mark a word, letter, or figure used as an illustration or typographical unit (instead of for its meaning). It is also the way to indicate an unanglicized foreign-language expression used in English context.

> Italics are *not* the *preferable* way to mark titles of *parts,* such as the title of an article in a journal or a chapter in a book. Quotation marks are preferable for that purpose.
>
> Chapter 2, "The Second Test of a Good Letter," stresses clear, natural style and general linguistic *savoir faire.*
>
> *Convenience* and *questionnaire* are often misspelled.
>
> Use of fewer *I*'s and more *you*'s would improve many letters.

Item Itemize complex series and lists (like this) to (1) emphasize the points, (2) avoid complex punctuation, (3) force yourself to state your points more precisely and concisely, and (4) grab your reader's attention.

Jargon is fuzzy or inappropriate writing attributable to pompousness, circumlocution, deadwood, abstractness, big words, technical terms (written to nontechnical readers), or hackneyed expressions. It is the opposite of simple, natural, clear writing. Avoid it.

Juxtapose (put side by side) facts and ideas that the reader needs to consider together. For instance, wholesale and retail prices need to appear together (with the difference and percentage of markup figured) if they are to mean as much as they should to the retailer being asked to stock the product.

K Awkwardness in expression calls attention to itself, and it may confuse the reader. Reconstruct your sentence or change word order for a more natural flow.

> A so-called split infinitive (putting a modifier between *to* and a verb) is usually undesirable only because it is usually awkward.

K/S   Known to the reader. Omit or **Sub**ordinate.

lc   **L**ower case needed here, instead of capital. See **Cap.**

Logic   Avoid statements which will not stand the test of logic or for which the logic is not readily clear. Perhaps you need to supply a missing step in the logic. Maybe you need to state your idea more precisely. Or maybe you need to complete a comparison to make it logical. (If the last, see **Cpr** for fuller explanation.)

Mechanics   See **TM.**

Modifiers should come in the sentence where they fit most naturally and make the meaning clearest. To avoid awkwardness and write clearly, you have to make sure that each modifier relates clearly to the thing it is supposed to modify. As a general rule, the two should be as close together as natural sentence construction will allow.

1.   Participles (usually phrases including a verb form ending in -*ing* or -*ed*, and usually at the beginning of a sentence) require careful attention lest you relate them to the wrong word (or nothing at all).

Smelling of liquor, I arrested the driver. (The officer did not intend to say that he himself had been drinking.)

After soaking in sulphuric acid over night, I set the specimen up to dry. (The scientist didn't really soak.)

Infinitives can be "misrelated modifiers" the same way:

To enjoy the longest, most dependable service, the motor must be tuned up about every 100 hours of operation. (The motor cannot enjoy dependable service.)

In order to assist you in collecting for damages, it will be necessary to fill out a company blank. (The two infinitives dangle because they do not relate to any proper doers of the actions indicated.)

But absolute phrases (a noun plus a participle) and participles, gerunds, and infinitives naming an accepted truth rather than the action of any person or thing do not need to relate to any subject:

The sun having set, the fish began to bite.

All things considered, Steve is the better man.

Counting all costs, the little X is not an inexpensive car.

To judge from results, that was an effective method.

2.   *Only, almost,* and *nearly* are tricky words. Watch where you put them. Consider the varied meanings from placing *only* at different spots in "I can approve payment of a $30 adjustment."

Monotonous   See **Var.**

Mood   The usual indicative and imperative moods (for normal statements and commands) give almost nobody trouble. But be careful with the subjective or conditional mood for verbs after commands and wishes, and for uncertainties or conditions contrary to fact (especially in formal writing). See **SW.**

Natural writing avoids triteness, awkwardness, and pomposity. Clichés, trite and hackneyed expressions, and jargon suggest that a writer is not thinking about the subject and the reader; awkwardness suggests carelessness; and big words and pomposity suggest that the writer is trying to make an impression. Think through what you want to say and put it simply, smoothly, and naturally. Although you cannot write exactly as you talk, you should try to write with the same freedom, ease, simplicity, and smoothness. See p. 40.

Negative in letter writing means anything unpleasant to your reader. Since you want the reader's goodwill, you should avoid the negative when you can and subordinate it when you can't avoid it. Insofar as possible, stress the positive by telling what you have done, can do, will do, or want done instead of their negative opposites. See p. 88; and for methods of subordinating, see p. 34, **Emp,** and **Sub.**

Objectivity   Use of emotional or feverish words (especially if extensive) suggests a prejudiced rather than an objective view of the situation and therefore causes the reader to lose faith in the writer—especially a report writer. See pp. 465 and 474.

Obvious statements—when they are unnecessary as bases for other statements—at least waste words; and when they appear in independent clauses, they show poor control of emphasis and may insult the reader's intelligence. When you need to state an obvious fact as the basis for something else, put it in a dependent clause and use the independent clause for the new idea. (See **Emp** and **Sub.**)

New York is America's biggest city. Therefore. . . . (Since New York is America's biggest city, ...)

Punctuation which follows the conventions of written English is a *helpful device for both reader and writer in communicating clearly, quickly, and easily.* But when it goes contrary to the understood conventions, it does not help and may even confuse.

You should not try to use even good punctuation, however, as a crutch for bad writing. Heavy punctuation cannot make a bad sentence into a good one; the need for it suggests revising the sentence rather than trying to punctuate the involved statement. The best style is so direct and simple that it requires little punctuation except periods at the ends of sentences. Still, you cannot write much without need for some internal punctuation. Here are the conventions most commonly violated:

P1   Use a comma between two independent clauses connected by *and,* *but, or,* or *nor* if no other commas are in the sentence; but be sure you are connecting two clauses rather than a compound subject, verb, or object.

You may buy the regular Whiz mixer at $18.75, but I think you would find the Super Whiz much more satisfactory (two clauses).

We make two grades of Whiz mixers and sell both at prices lower than those of our competitors' products (compound verb; one subject).

Be sure, too, that you don't use obtrusive commas before the first or after the last item in a series or between a subject and its verb, a verb and its object, or a noun and its adjective. Also, you do not usually need a comma after a transitional word (*and, but, however, therefore*), but using one emphasizes the word.

P2   The semicolon is a pivotal mark; avoid using it between expressions unless they are of equal grammatical structure (usually two independent clauses or two items in a complex series). Use a semicolon between two independent clauses unless connected by *and, but, or,* or *nor;* and even then, use a semicolon if the sentence already has a comma in it (as in this one). Typical weaker connectives requiring the semicolon between two independent clauses are *therefore, so, moreover, hence, still, accordingly, nevertheless, furthermore, consequently,* and *however.* When these words are simple connectors not between two independent clauses, however (as right here), they are set them off by a pair of commas unless they fit so smoothly into the sentence that they require no marks.

Jets made airline maintenance men relearn their jobs; the jet manual is twice as thick as the old one for prop planes (no connective).

The preceding sentence could be two, of course; but because the ideas are closely related, it is better as one. (Commas elsewhere in this sentence require a semicolon before even a strong conjunction.)

Good letter writing requires proper punctuation; therefore you must know how to use the semicolon (weak connective).

The proper style for letters is simpler and less involved than for most other writing, however, and therefore does not require very complex punctuation procedures. (*However* is a simple transition, *not used* between two clauses here and *not* close-knit into the phrasing the way *therefore* is; so it needs commas while *therefore* goes unmarked. Note, too, that the weak connective *so* requires the semicolon because it connects two clauses.)

P3 Use a comma after all first-of-sentence dependent clauses, long phrases, or other phrases containing any form of a verb. But when these forms or appositives or transitional words appear elsewhere in a sentence, use commas only with nonrestrictive (nonessential) ones. Nonrestrictive statements add descriptive detail about an already identified word and are not necessary to the logic or grammatical completeness of the sentence; restrictive ones define, limit, or identify and are necessary to convey the intended meaning or complete the sentence. If, on reading aloud, you naturally pause and inflect your voice, the statement is nonrestrictive and requires the comma(s).

Because the dependent clause comes at the beginning, we have to use a comma in this sentence.

We do not need a comma in a complex sentence if the dependent part comes at the end or in the middle and restricts the meaning the way this one does.

Having illustrated the two points about dependent clauses at the beginning and restrictive clauses elsewhere in the sentence, we now use this sentence to illustrate the use of a comma after a long phrase at the first of a sentence. (Because it includes a verb form, it would require a comma even if it were short, like "Having illustrated the point, we now leave the topic.")

The three points already illustrated, which are certainly important, are no more important than the point about using commas to set off nonrestrictive clauses anywhere, which this sentence illustrates. (In fact, it illustrates twice: Both the *which* clauses could be omitted; they are nonrestrictive because they merely give added information unnecessary to either the meaning or the grammar of the basic sentence.)

Sometimes you need a comma to prevent misreading—especially after a gerund, participle, or infinitive:

In the office, files had been emptied all over the floor.

By shooting, the man attracted the attention of the rescue party.

Thinking that, he was unwilling to listen to reason.

Seeing the foreman's unwillingness to help, the men gave up.

P4 Be sure to put in both commas—or dashes or parentheses—around a parenthetical expression in the middle of a structure. Direct addresses ("Yes, Mr. Thomas, you may . . .") and appositives (restatements like this one that follow immediately to explain a term) are typical examples. But, like clauses, some appositives are restrictive or so closely related that they require no punctuation, while others are nonrestrictive or so loosely related that they do.

His starting point that good punctuation is a matter of following the conventions has not had enough attention.

His second point, the importance of writing letters so smoothly and naturally that they require little internal punctuation, would preclude most punctuation problems.

General Motors opened a new plant in Akron, Ohio, in November, 1979, to produce certain auto parts.

P5 Use commas to separate coordinate adjectives. As two tests for coordinacy, see if you can put *and* between the adjectives or invert their order without producing awkwardness. If so, they are coordinate and require a comma.

Proper punctuation can help greatly in writing a clear, easy-to-read style.

Fairly heavy white paper is best for letterheads.

P6 The comma is the usual punctuation between items in a series (preferably including one before the *and* with the last item, because it is sometimes necessary for clearness and is always correct). But if any item except the last has a comma within it, use semicolons at all points between items. (Suggestion: If only one of a series requires an internal comma, consider putting it last and using commas between the items.)

Make your writing clear, quick, and easy to read.

Use commas between independent clauses connected by *and, but, or,* or *nor;* semicolons between independent clauses with other connectives or no connecting words; commas for dependent clauses and verbal or long phrases at the beginnings of sentences, for nonrestrictive ones elsewhere, and for simple series; and semicolons for complex series like the one in this sentence.

P7 Dashes, commas, and parentheses are all acceptable in pairs around parenthetical expressions that interrupt the main part of the sentence. The choice depends on the desired emphasis and on the other punctuation. Two dashes (called "bridge dashes") emphasize most, commas less, and parentheses least of all.

If the parenthetical part contains internal parentheses, dashes must surround it; if it contains commas, then dashes or parentheses must surround it. (Of course, only a pair of parentheses can surround a whole sentence which gives explanations, relatively unimportant additional detail, or side information not germane to the trend of the discussion, as this sentence does. In that case the period comes inside the closing parenthesis, although it comes outside otherwise.)

A single dash—made on the typewriter by two hyphens without spacing before, between, or after—may mark an abrupt change in the trend of a sentence or precede an added statement summarizing, contrasting, or explaining the first part. In this second function, it is the "pickup dash."

Your main weaknesses in writing—misspelling, faulty punctuation, and incoherence—deserve attention before you write letters.

Errors in spelling, punctuation, or coherence—these all mar an otherwise good letter.

A letter writer must avoid the common errors in writing— misspelling, bad punctuation, and incoherence. (Of course, the colon could replace the dash here; but ordinarily it should not unless the preceding statement is a formal introduction, usually indicated by the word *following*, or unless it is an introduction to an itemized list.)

P8 Hyphenate two or more words (unless the first ends in *-ly*) used to make a compound adjective modifying a following noun.

Fast-selling product, wrinkle-resistant material, long-wearing soles, never-to-be-forgotten experience

Note that the point usually does not apply when the adjectives follow the noun.

The material is highly wrinkle resistant and long wearing.

Certainly it does not apply when the adjectives modify the noun separately. See **P5**.

These slacks are made of a hard, durable material.

The compound-adjective principle does apply, however, to double compounds made with one element in common, where the "suspension hyphen" follows the first: three- and five-pound cans; only light- and middle-weight boxers.

The hyphen also marks the break in a word at the end of a line. See **Syl**.

Other less-frequent uses of the hyphen include (1) spelling of fractions as modifiers (*three-fourths* majority) and two-word quantities between 20 and 100, and (2) prefixing words or syllables to names (*post-Hitler* Germany), to other words beginning with the same vowel as the end of the prefix (*re-entry, pre-established*), or to any word that might otherwise be confusing (*re-collect*, not *recollect; re-cover*, not *recover*).

P9   Quotation marks are primarily for short, exact quotations (not paraphrasings) of other people's words and for titles of *parts* of publications, such as magazine and newspaper stories or book chapters. (The titles of journals and books should be italicized—underlined in typed copy—or written in solid capitals. See **Ital** and **Cap.**) If a quotation is more than two or three lines long, you should indent it from each side, single-space it, and omit quotation marks.

When closing quotation marks and other marks seem to come at the same place, the standard *American* practice is as follows: Place commas or periods *inside* the closing quotes; place semicolons or colons *outside;* and place question or exclamation marks inside or outside depending on whether they are part of the quotation.

P10   The colon is either an anticipating or a separating mark. As an anticipator, it appears after introductory lead-ins to explanations or quotations, especially if the lead-in includes such formalizing terms as the word *following* or if the explanation is lengthy or itemized.

> The X Company's ink was even redder: its third-quarter loss of. . . .

> Three main benefits deserve your attention: . . . (Enumeration follows. Notice that you do not need—indeed should not use —a browbeating, word-wasting expression like "these benefits are" before or after the colon!)

> On the use of the colon, Perrin says: . . . . (Long quotation follows.)

Because the colon is also a separating mark, however—used to separate hours from minutes and volume numbers from pages, for example—it should not serve as an anticipating mark when the lead-in phrasing fits well as an integral part of a short, informal statement. Some people call this misuse the "obtrusive colon."

> The three main advantages are (colon would be obtrusive here) speed, economy, and convenience.

> Perrin reports that (no colon; not even a comma) "*Will* has practically replaced *shall* in. . . ."

Almost invariably words like *namely, that is, for example*, and *as follows* are wasted (and browbeating) when used with a colon. The introductory phrasing and the colon adequately anticipate without these words.

We have several reasons for changing: namely the . . . (Omit *namely.*)

We had several reasons for changing. These reasons are: . . . . (This is worse. Omit *These reasons are;* put the colon after *changing.*)

Although practice varies, usually you should capitalize the first word after a colon only if it begins a complete sentence; but if itemizations follow, you may capitalize even though each item depends on the introductory statement for completeness.

The same idea applies to the end punctuation of items following a colon. If the items make complete sentences, put a period after each; but if all are to be considered one sentence, use comma or semicolon at the end of each (except the last, of course) as in other series—or you may use no end punctuation.

P11 Underlining in typed or handwritten copy specifies italic type when printed. Its main uses are to mark titles of books and journals, to emphasize, and to indicate unanglicized words. In copy not to be printed, underlining should go with any heading not written in solid capitals. Otherwise, the heading, which is really a title for the copy over which it stands, does not stand out sufficiently. (A printer would make it stand out by using big or boldface type.)

Type underlining is preferably continuous, rather than broken by individual words, because it is easier both to type and to read that way.

P12 Besides its well-known use at the end of a question, the question mark in parentheses immediately following a statement or spelling indicates that the writer is uncertain and unable to determine. Obviously, it should not be an excuse for laziness; but if you have only heard a difficult name, for example, and have to write to that person, you'd better use the mark than unconcernedly misspell the name.

A question mark should not appear after indirect questions and is unnecessary after commands softened by question form, but some writers feel that it further softens commands.

We need to know what your decision is. (This is an indirect question.)

Will you please ask the secretary in your office to change my mailing address. (This is a softened command, with or without the question mark.)

P13 Ellipsis (three *spaced* periods) means that something has been left out, and you *must* use this mark when giving an incomplete quotation. Note that if an omission comes at the end of a sentence, you need to add the appropriate end-of-sentence punctuation, usually a fourth dot for the period. Ellipses are also coming into wide use, especially in business, as an additional way to mark parenthetical expressions (see **P7**); but this practice has not yet achieved total acceptance.

"We the people of the United States . . . do ordain and establish this Constitution. . . ."

This rotary dump hopper car . . . like our open-top hopper car . . . comes in a wide range of sizes.

Paragraphs in letters and reports are the same as in other writing—unified and coherent developments of topics—except that they tend to be more compressed and shorter for easier readability. (The symbol ¶ may replace **Par** to indicate an impropriety on paragraphing.)

1. Keep your paragraphs reasonably short. Long ones are discouragingly hard to read. Especially the first and last paragraphs of letters and memos should be short (rarely more than three or four lines). Elsewhere, if a paragraph runs to more than about eight lines, you should consider breaking it up for easier readability. Certainly you should ignore any idea that a paragraph has to be more than one sentence.

2. But develop your paragraphs adequately to clarify and support your points—by explanation, detail, facts and figures, or illustrations and examples.

3. Make each paragraph unified and coherent by taking out elements irrelevant to the topic, by organizing carefully, and by showing the interrelationship of the ideas. Consider beginning with a topic sentence and/or ending with a summary. See **Unit** and pp. 45 and 681 (**Coh**) for further tips.

4. (**Coh**) Show the relation of the paragraph to the preceding (by following logical sequence, carrying over key ideas, and/or using transitional words) and to the purpose of the whole paper or section (by pointing out the significance and/or by using transitional words or sentences).

    Paragraph unity also includes. . . . (*Also* means some of the explanation has preceded.)

    Carrying over key words and using transitional words are both means of providing unity between paragraphs as well as within them. (As *well as* means we've discussed unity *in* paragraphs and now will discuss it *between* them.)

5. **Par** with **No** before it means "No new paragraph needed here because you are still on the same topic and within reasonable paragraph length."

Parallelism means using the same kind of grammatical structure for ideas that you use coordinately, as in pairs, series (including lists), comparisons, and outlines. These structures state or imply relationships usually indicated by *and*, *but*, or *or* and hence should relate only full sentences to full sentences, nouns to nouns, verbs to verbs, active voice to active voice, plural to plural—indeed *any* grammatical form only to the same grammatical form in the related part. Watch for parallelism with *not only . . . but also, as well as, larger, less expensive*, and the like. (See p. 463, Item 5, for parallelism in outlines.)

One of the duties of the airline cabin attendant is to offer customers magazines, pillows, and hang their coats (two plural nouns and a verb improperly connected by the coordinating conjunction *and*).

The No-Skid knee guard is long wearing, washable, and stays in position (two adjectives connected by *and* to a verb).

John Coleman is 39, married, and a native (two adjectives and a noun).

If we fair each side of the arc, we produce a more practical airfoil section and an increase in performance is attained. (Active voice related to passive. Rewrite the last part as "increase performance.")

The next step is baking or catalyzation. (Use "baking or catalyzing.")

Swimming is better exercise than to walk (a gerund compared with an infinitive).

Parallelism in pairs, series, and comparisons is largely a question of logic; you can add together and compare only like things. See **Log.**

Passive voice (in which the subject receives rather than does the action indicated by the verb) is usually wordy, awkward, and weak. Most of your sentences should therefore use the active voice. It makes important words (usually persons or products in letters) the subjects and objects of your verbs, as they should be.

Writers often use passive constructions in a misguided effort to avoid *I* and *we* as the subject. If you feel that you must avoid them to prevent monotony of sentence pattern, you should see p. 42 instead of resorting to the passive. If you feel that you must avoid them to increase objectivity, you are working under a false impression; you can be just as biased without them. But you can avoid the first person and the passive at the same time, as explained in the first illustration below.

Still, you may find appropriate use for passives to convey unwelcome information, to meet a thesis director's or company executive's unsound requirement that you write impersonally, to avoid a direct accusation, to put emphasis on something other than the doer of the action, or to weaken an otherwise rankling command or recommendation.

Your Long-Flight skis were shipped this morning by our mailing department. (Can be made active and impersonal, as "Two Long-Flight skis are on their way; they left the mailing department this morning.")

The subject has been considered from the following viewpoints: . . . . (The requirement of impersonal style may justify the passive here.)

The mower apparently has not been oiled adequately (avoids accusing the user).

Careful attention should be given to . . . (weakens a possibly rankling command).

It is recommended that. . . . (Though this weakens and avoids egotism in a recommendation, surely you can find a better way. This deserves criticism for both a **Passive** and an **Expletive**.)

PD Psychological description (interpreting facts and physical features of a product in terms of reader benefits) is the real heart of selling. Unless your reader readily makes the interpretation, pure physical description is ineffective in selling. So when you name a physical feature of a product you're selling, show the reader what it means in terms of benefits. (See p. 117 and pp. 265–66).

The Bostonian Sporty shoe has Neolite soles and triple-stitched welt construction. (Better with **PD**: The Neolite soles and triple-stitched welt construction cause the Bostonian Sporty to last long and keep your feet dry.)

Personalized messages written for and adapted to specific readers are more effective than mass broadcasts. What seems to be for everybody has less interest to anybody. Even form letters should be worded to give the feeling that the message is directed to each reader. Expressions such as "Those of you who . . ." and "If you are one who . . ." give just the opposite impression. (See p. 86.)

Plan your letter more appropriately for the circumstances as an A–, B–, or C–plan. (See p. 78.)

Pompous   Try to express the thought simply, not to impress the reader.

Pr   Follow more generally acceptable business practice.

PR   Personal references (names of people or pronouns referring to them) not only help to keep the reader in the picture and produce you-attitude (**YA**); they help to avoid the passive (**Pas**), to make your writing specific and concrete instead of general and abstract (**Spec**), and to make your writing easier and more interesting to read. Naming or referring to persons—Flesch suggests at least 6 percent of your words—is an important element in readability.

Prepositions indicate relationships within a sentence.

1. Be sure to use the right one for your construction. Some words require certain prepositions; others vary prepositions for different meanings. See **Id**.

    Ability *to;* agree *to, with,* or *in;* compare *to* (for similarities only) or *with* (for likeness and differences); different *from.*

2. When you use two words that require different prepositions, use both:

    Because of your interest *in* and aptitude *for.* . . .

3. Don't use many of the .45-caliber group prepositions (*according to, in regard to, by means of, in connection with, on the part of*) for squirrel-size ideas or your prepositions will "bulk too large," as Perrin says.

PV Insofar as possible, keep the same point of view in a sentence, a paragraph, or a whole letter. Make only logically necessary shifts, and let your reader know by providing the necessary transitional words. Watch carefully for shifts in time, location, and those whose eyes you seem to be looking through. For effective you-attitude, look through the reader's eyes whenever possible. See **YA**.

R Bring your reader into the picture early—and don't forget later. The reader is the most important person involved with your letter. See **Per, PR, PV,** and **YA**.

Redundancy includes not only useless repetition but wasting words saying things that are obvious or clearly implied. Avoid it.

Ref The references of your pronouns must be immediately certain and clear to your reader—not ambiguous, too far away, or merely implied. Except for the few indefinite pronouns (*one, everybody, anybody,* and *it* referring to the weather), a pronoun confuses or distracts a reader unless it refers clearly to a preceding noun and agrees with it in number and gender. *Each, every, any,* and their combinations *anybody* and *everybody* are considered singulars requiring singular verbs and pronouns; but see **Agr** for further explanation of agreement.

1. Often the trouble with a pronoun reference is that the antecedent is just too far away. Ordinarily a pronoun tends to "grab

onto" the closest preceding noun as its antecedent. So construct (or reconstruct) your sentences with that tendency in mind— lest you mislead your reader. Repeat the antecedent or change the word order so that the reader knows immediately what the antecedent is.

2. Guard particularly against *this, that, which, it,* and *they* making vague reference to ideas of whole preceding clauses instead of clear, one-word antecedents.

Dayton adopted the plan in 1914 and has kept it ever since, which is a good example of the success of the council-manager form of government. (What does *which* refer to?) After reading a book about television engineering, the young man wanted to be one of them. (One of what? The antecedent is only implied.)

3. Don't use the same pronoun with different meanings in the same sentence:

The directions say that it is up to the owner to change the filter whenever it needs it.

Repetition of words or ideas seems wordy and monotonous unless it serves a justified purpose. Restatement of important ideas deserving emphasis, however, is often desirable; but even then, the restatement usually should be in somewhat different words to avoid monotony.

Resale material—reassuring a customer that a choice of goods and/or firm was a good one—not only shows your service attitude (**SA**); it helps keep incomplete orders and delayed shipments on the books, rebuilds reader confidence in adjustment situations, and serves as a basic idea in collections. Look it up in the Index and read about it in connection with the particular type of letter involved.

SA Service attitude—showing a genuine desire to give the kinds and quality of goods and services wanted, favorable prices, and various conveniences, plus unselfish reassurance of appreciation for business—can go a long way toward overcoming a reader's feeling that you are indifferent. Your basic techniques are to interweave into your letters some sales promotion material (**SPM**) and resale talk (**Res**). See p. 71.

SC Show more success consciousness (self-confidence). See page 90.

Selfish interest (yours) is something both reader and writer assume, but it does not help your cause and therefore is best not mentioned. For more interest and persuasion, show what's in the situation for *the reader*. See **YA** and p. 82.

Shifting of tense (time), voice (active-passive), mood (indicative, imperative, subjunctive), or person (first, second, third) should come only when the logic of the situation dictates it; otherwise it leads to incoherence and loses or confuses readers. See **PV**.

Simplify Needlessly big words or involved sentences are hard to read.

Sincerity is essential if you are to be believed. Don't pretend or overstate your case. See p. 68.

Slow movement is desirable only in a B–plan letter where you must reason calmly with the reader to justify the unpleasant point you are preparing to present; otherwise, it is objectionable.

1. Don't use too many words before getting to an important point. Starting too far back in the background, giving too many details, or saying things that should be implied are the most frequent faults.

2. Don't use too many short, choppy sentences and thus slow up a message that should move fast.

SOS Errors in sentence organization and structure are sometimes serious enough to justify the distress signal.

1. Don't present a phrase or dependent clause as a sentence. Usually correction requires only attaching the dependent element to the preceding or following sentence (on which it depends). See **Frag**.

   In answer to your request concerning what the company is like, what has been accomplished, and the future prospects. Here is the information I have been able to acquire. (Replace the period with a comma.)

2. Don't use a comma—or no punctuation at all—between two independent clauses unless a strong conjunction (*and, but, or,* or *nor*) is there. The error is not basically one of punctuation (as discussed in **P1** and **P2**) but the more serious failure to recognize what a sentence is. You need a period if the two statements are not so closely related that they ought to be in the same sentence, or a semicolon if they are.

   The credit business is big business some people estimate that it is as much as 86 percent of American business (period needed before *some*).

   Running two sentences together without punctuation is about the worst error a writer can make, however it is little worse than using a comma where a semicolon is required, as in this sentence. See **P2**.

3. Don't put words together in unnatural, confusing relationships that the reader has to ponder to get the intended meaning. (See **K** and **Mod.**)

> Just because you want to sell I don't want right now to buy. (The fact that you want to sell doesn't mean I want to buy.)

4. Don't put ideas together with connectives that falsely represent their relationship. See **Coh** and **Unit.**

Spelling errors rarely confuse or mislead, but they nearly always have an equally unfavorable effect—they cause bad spellers to lose face and their readers' faith. So here are the most important tips on spelling and a list of words frequently misspelled in business writing. Study both—carefully.

1. *Ie* or *ei:* When pronounced like *ee*, write *ie* except after *c*, as in *achieve, believe; receive, deceive, perceive*. The exceptions are *either, neither, leisure, seize*, and *weird*. When pronounced otherwise, write *ei* (as in *freight, height, forfeit*) except in *die, lie, pie, tie, vie*, and *science*.

2. Double a final single consonant preceded by a single vowel (*a, e, i, o, u*) in an accented syllable when you add a suffix (*-ing, -ed, -er*) beginning with a vowel (*plan, planning; shop, shopping*). Note that if the word already ends in two consonants, or one preceded by two vowels, you do not double the last consonant (*holding, helping; daubing, seeded*). Note, too, that you usually do not double the consonant unless in an accented syllable (*refer, referred, references*). Two new exceptions, *benefitted* and *travelled*, can now go either way.

3. Drop a final, unpronounced *e* preceded by a consonant when you add a suffix beginning with a vowel (*hope, hoping; owe, owing*); but retain the *e* after *c* or *g* unless the suffix begins with one of the front vowels, *i* or *e* (*noticeable, changeable, changing, reduced*).

4. Change final *y* to *i* and add *es* for the plural if a consonant precedes the *y* (*ally, allies; tally, tallies*); otherwise, just add *s* (*valley, valleys*).

5. Add *'s* for the possessive of all singulars and of plurals which do not end in *s* (*man's, men's, lady's*); add only apostrophe for *s*-ending plurals (*ladies', Davises', students'*).

6. Hyphenate fractions used as modifiers (*nine-tenths* depleted) and double-word quantities between 20 and 100 (*twenty-one, thirty-two, forty-four, ninety-eight*).

7. Get somebody to pronounce for you while you try to spell the following words commonly misspelled in business. Then study those you miss (along with others which give you trouble, from whatever source) until you are sure of them.

a lot	faze	principal
accidentally	forty	principle
accommodate	government	privilege
accurate	grammar	probably
achievement	guarantee	proceed
acquaintance	height	procedure
acquire	imagine	prominent
affect (to influence)	immediately	psychology
among	incidentally	pursue
analyze	interest	quantity
apparent	interpret	questionnaire
appropriate	it's (its)	realize
argument	laboratory	receive
attorneys	led	recommend
beginning	lose (loose)	referring
believe	maintenance	renowned
category	moral (morale)	repetition
choose (chose)	mortgage	sense
comparative	necessary	separate
conscientious	noticeable	stationary
conscious	occasionally	stationery
consensus	occurrence	succeed
consistent	offered	surprise
convenience	omitted	than (then)
decision	original	their (there)
definitely	paid	thorough
description	passed (past)	transferred
disastrous	perform	tries
effect (result)	permissible	too (to, two)
efficiency	personal	undoubtedly
embarrass	personnel	unnecessary
environment	possession	until
equipped	practical	using (useful)
exaggerate	precede	varies
excellence	preferred	whether (weather)
existence	preference	writing (written)
experience	prejudiced	
explanation	prepare	

Specific wording, like a sharp photograph, helps the reader get a clear idea; general words give only a hazy view.

1. If you are inclined to use the general word for a class of things, consider the advantages of giving the specific kind in that class

(machine—mower; office equipment—files, desks, chairs, and typewriters; employees—salesclerks, janitors, secretaries, and others).

2. Another kind of specificness is giving supporting details, illustrations, examples, and full explanations for general statements made. If you use generalities to gain conciseness in topic and summarizing statements, be sure to provide necessary supporting explanations or further details; otherwise, your unsupported statements may not be accepted, even if understood. See **Dev.**

3. Still another important kind of specificness is giving the evidences of abstract qualities you may use. If you are inclined to say that something is a bargain, an outstanding offer, of the highest quality, revolutionary, best, ideal, or economical, give the concrete evidences for these qualities instead of the abstract words. In an application letter, if you want to convey the idea that you are intelligent, industrious, honest, dependable, and sociable, give the evidence and let the reader draw the conclusions. You will sound too cocky if you apply these words to yourself, and your reader will not believe them anyway, unless you give the supporting concrete facts.

SPM Sales promotion material (when appropriate and unselfish) not only shows a service attitude (see **SA**) and produces some additional sales; it helps to take the sting out of early collection letters and provides a pleasant ending for essentially bad-news letters, provided that the situation is not too seriously negative. See p. 74.

Style See Chapter 2 and (especially for reports) pp. 468–72 and 538.

Subordinate Don't overstress negative ideas, facts the reader knows, or insignificant points. If you must say them, put them in the middle of the paragraph or letter, devote little space to them, and/or put them in dependent clauses or phrases. Since dependent clauses are particularly useful in subordinating, here are some of the main beginning words that make clauses dependent: *after, although, as, because, before, if, since, though, till, unless, until, when, where, while.*

SW Shall-will; should-would. General usage differs so much from formal usage of *shall* and *will* that formal practice now sounds old-fashioned and stiff in most letters and reports. In general usage (which is appropriate for business writing), *will* has almost completely replaced *shall.* Formal usage calls for *shall* with the first person and *will* with other persons to indicate the simple future, and for the reverse to indicate firm promise or determination.

More important for business writers is the distinction between the simple futures and their conditional forms, *should* and *would*. Using the simple future sometimes seems presumptuous.

I will appreciate your giving me your answer by November 20 so that. . . . (*Would*, in place of *will*, would remove the presumption that the reader will answer, by using the conditional mood and saying, in effect, "*If* you will answer . . . I will appreciate it.")

Syl Divide words at the ends of lines only at syllable breaks, and then only if each part has at least two letters and is pronounceable. If in doubt about where to divide a word, check the dictionary.

TM Typing mechanics If you are an untrained typist, these tips may help:

1. Standard within-line spacings are (*a*) five for paragraph indention; (*b*) two after a colon or end-of-sentence punctuation (including an enclosing end parenthesis); (*c*) one after all other punctuation except as explained below; (*d*) none after an opening parenthesis or before or after a hyphen.

2. Abbreviations pose a spacing problem: some (like our governmental alphabet soup—HEW, IRS, SEC, CAB, for example) are solid; others (even with the same meaning) go various ways. Learn the main ones; look up the others in your dictionary.

3. Dashes (not at all the same as hyphens—see **P7** and **P8**—are preferably two hyphens with no spacing.

4. For quotations of more than four lines, space above and below, indent from each side, single-space, and use no quotation marks.

T-t-t A tea-table turn is an abrupt shift from the pleasant to the unpleasant. Typically, the statement is sweet for a few sentences. Then the next begins, "However, ..." The situation is quite like that of Mrs. Jones and friends already at a table when Mrs. Smith arrives a little late and Mrs. Jones says, "Isn't that a beautiful new dress Mrs. Smith has; but . . ." and everybody has the sinking feeling, "Poor Mrs. Smith!"

Tabulate or itemize when you have lots of figures to present or a series of distinct points to make. Itemization will make you think more sharply and state your ideas more precisely and concisely. Thus you produce clearer, quicker reading and more emphasis. Furthermore, **item**ization grabs readers' or hearers' attention.

Telegraphic style (omitting subjects, connective words, and articles, as in telegrams and newspaper headlines) is not acceptable practice in letters, memos, and reports.

Ten Watch the tense (time indicated by your verbs) for appropriateness in the individual verb and logic in the sequence of verbs. Do not shift tenses unless the logic of the situation requires.

Normally you use the present, past, or future according to the time of the action you are reporting. A special use of the present tenses deserves careful attention, however, for some situations: You use the present (called the "universal present") for statements that were true in the past, are true now, and will be true later. We say the sun *sets* in the west (universal present) even though it may have set hours earlier. Any statement you might make about what a book *says* fits the conditions. If you now read a book written even in 1620, it still *says*. . . . Similarly in reporting on your research findings (which presumably are still true), you use the universal present tense. To do otherwise would imply doubt about the present validity of your results. (See pp. 470 and 507).

The law of supply and demand *means* . . .

The 1972 edition *says* . . .

The tense of the key verb in an independent clause governs a sentence. So the tenses of other verbs or verbals indicate time relative to the time of the main verb:

I will do it as soon as I am able (a future and relative present).

I had hoped that I would be able to go (a past perfect and relative future).

Tone Watch out for a tone of distrust, indifference, undue humility, flattery, condescension, preachiness, bragging, anger, accusation, sarcasm, curtness, effusiveness, or exaggeration. See pp. 60 ff.

Since salutations and complimentary closes are the first and last indications of your feelings about the formality of your relationship to your reader, be sure they represent those feelings accurately. See p. 16.

Transitions between sentences in a paragraph, between paragraphs, and between sections in longer presentations must show their relationships. Your best method is use of a thread of logic that will hold your thoughts together like beads on a string. When the logical thread does not make the relationship clear, however, you need to do so by repeating a key word or idea from the preceding or by using a connecting word or phrase that shows the relationship. See **Coh, Unit,** and p. 469.

Trite expressions (a form of **Jar**gon) are usually overused and hence worn-out figures of speech that dull your writing. The remedy is to state your idea simply in natural, normal English or to use an original figure of speech.

Unity (of sentences, paragraphs, or whole pieces of writing) requires that you show how each statement fits in or belongs (is not irrelevant). Applied to a sentence or paragraph, **Unit** means that the statement seems irrelevant or that the several ideas are not closely enough related to be in the one sentence or paragraph. When applied to a whole letter or report, it means that the content seems so varied as to lack a central theme and should be put in two or more separate papers. Often, however, the writer sees relationships that justify putting things together as they are, and the fault is in not showing the reader the relationships—an error of coherence (see **Coh**).

> Please put your answers in ink and have your signature witnessed by two people. One of our envelopes is enclosed for your convenience. (The envelope is not a convenience in doing what is requested in the first sentence. The two unrelated ideas should not be in the same paragraph. Adding "in returning your answers" would help.)

Usage refers to the appropriateness of the language to the situation. A passage or expression marked with the symbol may be too formal and stiff, literary, flashy, or highbrow; or too slangy, familiar, crude, or lowbrow. The normal, natural English of educated people conducting their everyday affairs is neither formal nor illiterate but informal and natural. That's what you should use for most letters, memos, and reports.

Be on guard against the following illiterate forms (mostly the result of bad pronunciation): "He is prejudice" (*prejudiced*), "He is bias" (*biased*), "usta" or "use to" (*used to*), "had of" (*had*), "would of" (*would have*), "most all" (*almost all*), "a savings of" (*a saving of*).

Variety (of diction and of sentence pattern, type, and length) is necessary to avoid monotony, which puts readers to sleep. Achieving variety should be a part of the revision process, however, and should not distract your thoughts from saying what you want to say in writing a first draft.

In your revision, see that you haven't begun too many successive sentences the same way (especially not with *I* or *we*). If you have repeated yourself, cut out the repetition unless you need it for emphasis; and then change the wording if the two statements of the same idea are close together.

The usual English sentence pattern is subject-verb-complement; in revision, vary the pattern to avoid a dull sameness. (Page 42 lists various kinds of sentence beginnings.)

Good style also requires variety in sentence type. Some of your sentences should be simple (one independent clause); some should be compound (two independent clauses stating two closely related ideas of nearly equal importance); and some should be complex (at least one independent clause and one or more dependent, all expressing related ideas but of unequal importance). Especially to be avoided are too many successive simple sentences for ideas not deserving equal emphasis or too many compound sentences connected by *and.* (See **Sub.**)

Although most of your sentences should be relatively short (averaging 17–20 words for easy readability), you will produce a monotonous choppiness if all your sentences are in that range. See **Sim** and **Chop,** and revise accordingly.

Wordy See pp. 35 ff.

YA You-attitude. The you-attitude is certainly one of the three most important points about letter writing. People do things for their own benefit, not yours. If you want to persuade them to act, you have to show them the advantages to themselves. Both your reader and you know that you're interested in yourself. To deny that would be insincere and disbelieved. But you need not put your selfish interests in the letter; the fact that you want something is no reason for the reader to act. The benefits going the other way are. Write about *them.* See **Self** and p. 82.

To show readers what is in the situation for them, you have to visualize their ways of life and show how your proposal fits in. See **Adapt.**

Although using more *you*'s than *I*'s or *we*'s may help, it is no assurance that your letter has you-attitude.

X Obvious error. Proofread carefully and correct such errors.

∾ Invert the order or sequence of words or ideas.

⌒ Close up the unnecessary space.

¶ New paragraph needed. See **Par.**

Additional space needed here.

𝓰 or **𝄕** Delete (take out); unnecessary.

✛ Move in the direction pointed.

Index

*This book has been set in 10 and 9 point Cale-
donia, leaded 2 points. Part numbers are 14
point Helvetica italic and part titles are 24
point (small) Helvetica. Chapter numbers are
12 point Helvetica italic and chapter titles are
18 point Helvetica. The size of the type page
is 27 by 45½ picas.*